THE ADMINISTRATIVE
REGULATORY PROCESS

The Administrative Regulatory Process

Florence Heffron
University of Idaho

with

Neil McFeeley
University of Idaho

Longman
New York & London

THE ADMINISTRATIVE REGULATORY PROCESS

Longman Inc., 1560 Broadway, New York, N.Y. 10036
Associated companies, branches, and representatives
throughout the world.

Developmental Editor: Irving E. Rockwood
Editorial and Design Supervisor: Frances A. Althaus
Production Supervisor: Ferne Y. Kawahara
Manufacturing Supervisor: Marion Hess

Library of Congress Cataloging in Publication Data

Heffron, Florence A.
  The administrative regulatory process.

  Includes index.
  1. Administrative law—United States.
2. Administrative procedure—United States. I. McFeeley,
Neil. II. Title.
KF5402.H43   1983   342.73'06   82-20828
ISBN 0-582-28189-X

Manufactured in the United States of America

Printing: 9 8 7 6 5 4 3 2 1   Year: 91 90 89 88 87 86 85 84 83

Short Table of Contents

Preface   xiii

1 Scope and Impact of Administrative Regulation   1

PART I THE CONSTITUTIONAL, LEGAL AND POLITICAL FRAMEWORK OF ADMINISTRATIVE POWER

2 Constitutional Principles and Administrative Power   30
3 The Federal Constitution: Meaningful Restrictions on Administrative
   Regulation   52
4 Statutory Restrictions on the Administrative Process   85
5 The Environment of Regulation: Formal Controls and Informal Pressures
   on the Regulatory Process   116
6 Regulatory Theory   147

PART II BASIC ADMINISTRATIVE PROCESSES

7 Collecting the Facts: Administrative Investigatory Procedures   171
8 Informal Actions   199
9 Rules and Rule Making   226
10 Adjudicatory Procedures   256

PART III JUDICIAL CONTROLS

11 Judicial Review   293
12 Obtaining Monetary Redress from Government   318

PART IV REGULATION: CONSEQUENCES AND REFORMS

13 The Consequences of Regulation   347
14 Regulatory Reform   372

Appendix I: Administrative Procedure Act   401
Appendix II: Model State Administrative Procedure Act (1981)   427
List of Acronyms   464
Table of Cases   467
Index   475

Contents

Preface   xiii

1   Scope and Impact of Administrative Regulation   1

   Origin and Evolution of Administrative Regulation   1
      Creation of Administrative Regulatory Power
      Development of Administrative Adjudicatory Power
   Current Scope of Administrative Regulation   6
   Varieties and Types of Agencies Exercising Regulatory Power   8
   Administrative Regulation in Action   11
      The Food and Drug Administration Tries to Ban Saccharin
   An Overview of the Regulatory Process   16
   Scope and Coverage of the Book   21

PART I

THE CONSTITUTIONAL, LEGAL, AND POLITICAL FRAMEWORK
OF ADMINISTRATIVE POWER

2   Constitutional Principles and Administrative Power   30
   Delegation of Powers   31
      Delegation of Power at the State Level
   Separation of Powers   40
      Separation of Powers at the State Level
   Rule of Law Versus Administrative Discretion   43
      Administrative Discretion at the State Level
      Reconciling the Irreconcilable?
   Conclusion   48

3   The Federal Constitution: Meaningful Restrictions on Administrative Regulation   52

   Due Process   52
   Equal Protection   55
   Core Constitutional Rights   63
   Explicit Constitutional Rights   64
      First Amendment
      Second Amendment
      Third Amendment
      Fourth Amendment
      Fifth Amendment
      Sixth Amendment
      Seventh Amendment

Eighth Amendment
Ninth Amendment
Tenth Amendment
Implicit Constitutional Rights   72
  Privacy Rights
  Travel Rights
  Residency Rights
  Employment Rights
  Rights of Mental Patients
Constitutional Theory vs. Administrative Reality—Aliens in America:
  When Is a Person Not a Person?   77
Constitutional Rights, the Courts, and Administrative Regulation   80

4   Statutory Restrictions on the Administrative Process   85

The Federal Administrative Procedure Act (APA)   85
State Administrative Procedure Acts   96
Authorizing Statutes   99
  The Mandate to Regulate
  The Powers to Regulate
  Required Procedures
  Reviewability of Administrative Action
  Authorizing Statutes: The Specifics of Regulation
Legal Rights   104
Appropriations Statutes   108
Administrative Regulation in a Federal System   110

**5   The Environment of Regulation: Formal Controls and
Informal Pressures on the Regulatory Process**   116

Congress   118
  Formal Powers
  Informal Powers and Pressures
The Presidency   124
  Formal Controls
  Informal Pressures
The Courts   129
The Administrative Hierarchy   130
Agency Overlaps   132
State and Local Governments   135
The Press and the Public   137
Clientele Groups   138
The Rise and Impact of Public Interest Groups   141
Conclusion   142

6   Regulatory Theory   147

Theories of Regulatory Origin   147
  Economic Regulation: Origins
  Social Regulation: Origins

Theories of Regulatory Behavior 151
   The Life Cycle Theory
   Subgovernment/Regulatory Capture Theories
   Theories of Individual Regulators' Behavior
Systems Approach to Regulatory Analysis 158
   General Systems Theories
Conclusion 164
   Summary
   Difficulties of Theory Construction
   Need for Eclecticism

PART II
BASIC ADMINISTRATIVE PROCESSES

7 **Collecting the Facts: Administrative Investigatory Procedures**   171

   The Functions of Administrative Investigations 171
   Major Types of Investigatory Activities 173
      Records, Reports, Red Tape
      Physical Inspections
      Legislative-Type Hearings
      Body Searches: Physical Inspections of Individuals
      Subpoenas
      The Administrative Investigation
   Judicial Attitudes Toward Administrative Investigations 183
      The Period of Restrictiveness: 1880-1940
      Period of Permissiveness: 1941-1965
      The Contemporary Period: Redefining the Fourth Amendment:
      1966–Present
   Administrative Investigations: Conclusion 195

8 **Informal Actions**   199

   Informal Action: The Lifeblood of the Administrative Process 201
   Informal Actions 202
      Summary Action
      Publicity
      Advice and Advisory Opinions
      Policy Statements
      Negotiated Settlements
      Applications
      Friendly Persuasion
   Informal Administrative Actions in the Administrative Process 215
   Informal Action: Disadvantages and Problems 216
   Recommendations for Improving and Controlling Informal Actions:
      A Critique 221

9 **Rules and Rule Making**   226

   Definitional Problems: A Rule Is a Rule Is a Rule Unless It's an Order or a
   Ruling or . . . 226

Rule Making vs. Adjudication
Rule Making vs. Informal Action
The Major Varieties of Administrative Rules   231
Procedural Rules
Interpretive Rules
Substantive Rules
Rule-making Procedures   235
Formal Rule Making
Informal Rule Making
The Practical Mechanics of the Rule-Making Process   238
Bias in Rule Making
Hybrid Rule-Making Procedures   247
Presidential Modifications of Rule-Making Procedures   250
Federal Rule-Making Procedures: Changes and Reforms   252

10   Adjudicatory Procedures   256

The Opportunity to be Heard: When Required   257
Statutory Requirements
Constitutional Requirements for a Hearing
Adjudication versus Rule Making
Timing of the Hearing   266
What Kind of Hearing?   268
Notice
Right to Counsel
Public Intervenors
Prehearing Conference
The Presiding Officer
Evidence
The Initial Decision
Court-Mandated Hearing Procedures
Institutional Decisions   280
Final Orders   282
Conclusion   285

PART III
JUDICIAL CONTROLS

11   Judicial Review   293

Judicial Review: Availability   293
Unreviewability   294
Legislative Preclusion
Action Committed to Agency Discretion
Action Unsuited for Review
Sovereign Immunity
Standing   299
Primary Jurisdiction, Exhaustion, Ripeness   306
Scope of Review   309

Adjudicatory Decisions: The Substantial Evidence Test
Scope of Review: Rule Making
Scope of Review: Informal Action
Judicial Review as a Check on Administrative Power   313

12   Obtaining Monetary Redress from Government   318

Obtaining Redress: Federal Law for Federal Actions   319
   Government Liability
   Officer Liability
Obtaining Redress from State and Local Governments   331
   State Law
   Federal Law
   State Governments
The King Can Do No Right: Consequences of Expanded Governmental
Liability   339

PART IV
REGULATION: CONSEQUENCES AND REFORMS

13   The Consequences of Regulation   347

Regulation I: Economic Regulation   349
Regulation II: Social Regulation   354
Regulation III: Subsidiary Regulation   358
General Consequences of Regulation   361
   Economic Impact
   Political Consequences of Regulation

14   Regulatory Reform   372

Substantive Reform Proposals   372
   Regulation I
   Regulation II
   Regulation III
Procedural Reforms: Changing Patterns of Political Control   387
Internal Agency Reforms: Procedures and Personnel   393
The Prospects for Regulatory Reform   396

Appendix I: Administrative Procedure Act   401

Appendix II: Model State Administrative Procedure Act (1981)   427

List of Acronyms   464

Table of Cases   467

Index   475

Preface

Administrative law and regulation have become increasingly salient in both practical and academic public administration. This book is addressed to both of their concerns and attempts to provide an overview of the political and legal aspects of the regulatory process, the controversies surrounding it and the major reform proposals that have been suggested to improve it. The text is designed primarily for use in public administration courses in administrative law. Although it provides extensive coverage of traditional administrative law concerns of rule making, adjudication, procedural due process and judicial review, the book also includes coverage of informal administrative actions and political controls over regulation and regulators. Case studies of recent administrative actions are used throughout the book to illustrate the complexity and relevance of the contemporary regulatory process.

I would like to thank William Gormley, University of Wisconsin–Madison; Victor Rosenblum, Northwestern University School of Law; Stephen Chitwood, Georgetown University; Dennis Dresang, University of Wisconsin–Madison; and William McLauchlan, Purdue University, for their helpful suggestions in reviewing the manuscript. To Linda Phipps, who patiently and expertly typed and retyped countless revisions of the book, I owe special thanks. I would also like to thank Julie Pontasch and Mary Koefod for their assistance in typing. I am particularly indebted to Marianne Jones, who provided invaluable and extensive research, editing and all-around assistance in the completion of the final draft. Finally, I am very grateful to the editors at Longman, whose patience was not only a virtue but also nearly endless.

Florence Heffron

THE ADMINISTRATIVE
REGULATORY PROCESS

Chapter 1

Scope and Impact of Administrative Regulation

ORIGIN AND EVOLUTION OF ADMINISTRATIVE REGULATION

On July 31, 1789, the first Congress of the United States authorized the President to appoint an administrative official to "estimate the duties payable on imports."[1] Thus began a phenomenon that has become one of the most important aspects of contemporary American government: the delegation of rulemaking power to administrative agencies. Since that first authorization, Congress has repeatedly given these agencies the power to promulgate rules and regulations that have the same impact as the laws of Congress. This delegation of power has continued throughout American history, sometimes slowly and at other times, as during the New Deal, the post-World War II period, and the 1960s and 1970s, in spurts of blinding rapidity. Today at least 58 agencies at the federal level have some form of rule-making authority and issue about 7,000 rules and policy statements annually.[2]

The power to formulate rules is only one aspect of administrative regulatory power. The full scope of that power includes the authority to interpret laws and regulations, to enforce rules and regulations, to try cases involving violations of those rules, to hold hearings both of an investigatory and adjudicatory nature, and to impose sanctions on violators. The essence of administrative regulatory power is that, traditional concepts of separation of powers notwithstanding, it combines in a single agency legislative, executive, and judicial power.

The expansion of administrative power was a direct result of the general expansion of the power and responsibilities of government in American society. The development of an industrialized, urbanized, and interdependent society has required a more active role for government as protector of individual rights, mediator of disputes, provider of largesse, and stabilizer of the economy. The expansion of regulatory power has paralleled the growth of industrialization in this country, and the social and human costs of that industrialization have been one of the major precipitating factors for government intervention in the economy. No one theory can adequately explain the creation of the various and diverse agencies and types of governmental regulation. Unquestionably, some economic regulatory actions were initiated at the direct request and with full support of major segments of the industry involved. Federal meat inspection, radio broadcasting, and airline regulation are cases in point.[3] For other agencies, the impetus for creation was more complex. Political reform groups, consumers, and those adversely affected by the status quo exerted pressure for regulation which was either overtly or covertly supported by the potential regulatee: The Federal Trade Commission and the Federal Reserve Board exemplify this situation.[4] The recognition of widespread social and economic inequality and the need and desire to alleviate this pervasive inequality also served as a major impetus to the expansion of governmental involvement. Rarely, however, did government, on its own initiative, undertake these responsibilities. Far more frequently it was pressured into action by the demands of interest groups, by the industry to be regulated, by the media, by the existence of crisis situations that threatened the basic stability or survival of the country, or by some combination of all of the above.[5]

Creation of Administrative Regulatory Power

A brief look at the circumstances surrounding the initiation of six different regulatory actions demonstrates the interrelationship of social and economic problems and government intervention. The six—regulation of railroads, the creation of the Federal Trade Commission, the establishment of the Securities and Exchange Commission, the passage of the Occupational Safety and Health Act of 1970, the passage of the National Environmental Policy Act of 1969, and the addition of the Title IX Amendments of the Education Amendments Act in 1972—run the gamut both of time and type of regulatory activity.

By the late 1800s, the railroads, having been fostered and promoted through extensive government subsidies, had become the central form of long-distance transportation in the United States. Their growing importance and profitability, however, had also been accompanied by a variety of questionable business practices and abuses which had proven particularly harmful to midwestern farmers and smaller businessmen.

> The evils of highly speculative railroad building, irresponsible financial
> manipulation, destructive competitive warfare, fluctuating and discriminatory rate
> adjustments, and overreaching exercise of monopoly power brought their inevitable
> reactions.[6]

Unable to contend with these practices themselves, the farmers through organizations such as the Grange first sought relief at the state level. Finding themselves stymied by a Supreme Court which ruled state action an impermissible interference with interstate commerce, the farmers turned to Congress for help. The support of railroads desiring to control excessive price competition on long-haul routes contributed to Congress's willingness to create in 1887 the Interstate Commerce Commission (ICC), the first of the independent regulatory commissions. The ICC was to ensure that rates were "just and reasonable" and to prevent discriminatory rates and practices by the railroads.

Whether or not the ICC fulfilled the expectations of its creators, it served as a model when disgruntled consumers and businesses sought protection from monopolistic business practices in the early 1900s. Although Congress had first attempted to curb the power and growth of monopolies in 1890 with the passage of the Sherman Antitrust Act, the attempt had proven to be highly unsuccessful. Dependent upon criminal trials and court injunctions, and frowned upon by the Supreme Court, the Sherman Act had neither prevented the formation of new monopolies nor broken up existing ones. Pushed by demands from the newly formed Progressive Party and the rumblings of socialism from the left, in 1912 the two major political parties, Democratic and Republican, endorsed the concept of creation of a new regulatory agency to curb unfair methods of competition. When major business groups added their support, the establishment of the Federal Trade Commission (FTC) became inevitable. In 1914, Congress passed the Federal Trade Commission Act and empowered the newly created FTC to issue cease and desist orders, to conduct investigations, and to define and prevent unfair methods of competition.

The stock market crash of 1929 and its widespread catastrophic effect on individuals and the economy paved the way for federal regulation of the securities market. The 1920s had been marked by an acceleration in abuses in the sale of securities accompanied by fantastic profits made from the gullibility of smaller buyers. Speculation and fraudulent practices abounded. Once again state attempts at regulation, in the form of "blue sky" laws requiring full disclosure of the nature of the securities and the company offering them, proved ineffective when directed at companies engaging in interstate commerce. Although Congress had been aware of the problems in the securities market since the 1913 investigation by the Pujo Committee, it took financial disaster to propel it into action. Congress's initial response was the enactment of the Securities Act of 1933 which required full disclosure of a company's financial condition when it offered securities of over $100,000 for public sale in interstate commerce. Originally, these statements were required to be filed with the FTC, but with the decision to extend regulation to the stock exchanges Congress turned full authority over to the newly created Securities and Exchange Commission (SEC).

By 1970, if one were inclined to take Department of Labor statistics at all seriously, indications were that workers in the United States ought to be warned: "Caution: Work may be hazardous to your health." In that year the Labor Department's Bureau of Labor Statistics estimated that each year more than 14,500 Americans were killed on the job, more than 2.2 million suffered disabling injuries, and nearly 390,000 were afflicted with occupational diseases such as bisinosis and asbestosis, with a consequent loss of $1.5 billion in wages and $8 billion in gross national product.[7] Prodded by loud and insistent demands from organized labor, particularly the Oil, Chemical and Atomic Workers Union,[8] public interest health groups, and the publicity surrounding a 1968 mine blast in Farmington, West Virginia, that killed 78 miners, both President Lyndon Johnson and his successor, President Nixon, endorsed passage of legislation by Congress to protect the health and safety of American workers. Congress finally responded by passing the Occupational Health and Safety Act of 1970 which required the Secretary of Labor to promulgate national occupational health standards and established as national policy that workers were entitled to "a workplace free from recognized hazards that had caused or were likely to cause death or serious physical harm to employees."[9] Actual enforcement responsibility for the law was turned over to the Occupational Safety and Health Administration (OSHA) which was created in 1971.

On January 28, 1969, near Santa Barbara, California, an offshore oil drilling platform blew out and released 235,000 gallons of crude oil which gradually oozed onto the beaches at Santa Barbara, destroying marine life and rendering vast numbers of waterfowl helpless or maimed. For concerned environmental groups and millions of previously unconcerned Americans, Santa Barbara was the Armageddon in the war against pollution. Throughout the latter half of the 1960s, old line conservation groups such as the Audubon Society and the Sierra Club and newly formed organizations such as the Environmental Defense Fund had been warning that the continuous and systematic destruction of America's air, water, wildlife, and natural resources could not continue without serious consequences to the health and quality of life of all people. The Santa Barbara oil spill dramatized their concerns and in the face of extensive public support and interest group pressure, Congress reacted by expanding the responsibility of the federal government for protecting the natural environment. In December 1969, it passed the National Environmental Policy Act which required federal agencies to accompany all proposed actions which might have an impact on the environment with an Environmental Impact Statement which was to be reviewed by the newly created Council on Environmental Quality. In 1970, Congress passed the Clean Air Act Amendments which unequivocally established the authority and responsibility of the federal government for establishing, achieving, and maintaining acceptable air quality throughout the United States. The Environmental Protection Agency (EPA), created by a presidential reorganization plan, was assigned primary responsibility for enforcement of the Amendments. In 1972, EPA was given responsibility for improving the quality of the nation's waterways. As additional environmental hazards were identified (toxic waste disposal, extensive use of dangerous pesticides, for example) the responsibility of EPA was legislatively expanded to include regulation of those hazards.

The environmentalists were far from being the only groups that were restive and unhappy with the status quo of the 1960s. Historically an oppressed majority, women were also becoming more vocal about the varieties of laws and circumstances that had trapped them into second-class citizenship. As the other disadvantaged groups had done before them, women's groups turned to government to redress their grievances. Just as government had responded to the other groups, it slowly began to respond to the demands of women's groups. In 1963, the Equal Pay Act was passed. In 1964, discrimination in employment based on sex was added to the list of types of illegal discrimination specified in Title VII of the Civil Rights Act. By 1972, measurable progress for women's rights was negligible and demands for action intensified. One of the responses that Congress made in that year was Title IX of the Education Act Amendments. Title IX prohibited discrimination based on sex in all programs and activities in all educational institutions which receive federal money, from preschools to postgraduate schools and everything in between. To implement the law the Department of Health, Education and Welfare was instructed to draw up and promulgate regulations covering the full gamut of school practices from admissions to housing and employment to sports programs for the 16,000 public school systems and 2,700 colleges and universities that would be affected by the law.

Government regulation has expanded, as these examples indicate, because conditions have required that expansion or because the public, industry, or interest groups have demanded it. Every expansion of government regulation in reality means an expansion of administrative power and activity. Once Congress and the President have agreed to the assumption of new responsibility, practical necessity mandates that an administrative agency be empowered to give life, meaning, and effectiveness to these new policies. While Congress can define the general goals that it wishes to see accomplished and can check to determine if those goals are being accomplished, singly and collectively, it is incapable of handling the masses of detail or applying general principles to the vast and changing varieties of institutions and circumstances that enforcement of these laws requires. For example, while Congress can prohibit sex discrimination in federally-funded education programs, if it had to specify every practice that constituted sex discrimination in every educational institution and program, such discrimination might be abolished sometime, but in the interim the myriad of other legislative responsibilities would have to be ignored and the legislative process would become hopelessly mired in endless detail. Consequently, Congress has increasingly pursued the pragmatic course: It determines general goals and directions and delegates to administrative agencies the responsibility of specifically interpreting and applying its policies by formulating the ever-present "rules and regulations."

Development of Administrative Adjudicatory Power

The origin and development of administrative adjudicatory power, the ability to hear and decide individual cases arising under the jurisdiction of the agency, have similar roots and causes. Logic and pragmatism indicate that once an agency has formulated rules and regulations, it should enforce them. In order to enforce them, the agency must investigate to see if they are being obeyed. If it determines that an individual is violating the rules, in the first instance at least, it only makes sense for the agency to hold a hearing, receive and weigh the evidence, determine if a violation has occurred, and punish violators. Which is not to say that courts could not do this. However, consider the burden that would be imposed on the courts with only cases involving the Title IX regulations and then multiply that times the hundreds of cases involving rules and regulations of all other federal agencies. The impact of dealing with all these cases on the courts would be similar to the impact on Congress in trying to work out all the applications of its statutes: a hopeless situation for an already overburdened judicial system.

If necessity is the first reason for administrative adjudication, judicial imcompetence and administrative expertise are the second. Many areas of regulation involve a high degree of technical expertise and specialization to deal adequately with the issues that arise in contested cases. When the Federal Communications Commission or the Nuclear Regulatory Commission must resolve issues that arise in a specific case, they must draw on engineering, accounting, scientific, and technical information which their staff and experience amply provide. Similarly, other administrative agencies, even though they may deal with less technical subjects, have decided advantages over courts as far as resolving cases arising under their regulations is concerned: familiarity, continuity, and specialization. The need for systematic and uniform regulation also supports the need for agency determination of cases that arise under agency rules and regulations. Finally, the slowness, complexity, and expense of the judicial process provide additional grounds for permitting administrative agencies to adjudicate their own cases. The result of all this has been that the federal courts, up to and including the Supreme Court, have gradually acquiesced and occasionally insisted upon the administrative exercise of judicial power. Accepting and recognizing their limitations, and like Congress wishing to preserve their time and effort for broader or more relevant exercises of their power, the courts have become increasingly reluctant to involve themselves in the substance of administrative action.

CURRENT SCOPE OF ADMINISTRATIVE REGULATION

The United States has become a regulatory state: a society in which almost every activity engaged in by organizations or individuals is subject to administrative regulation and control. The extent of this regulatory power and the benefits as well as the costs that it imposes can be partially indicated by the following list of responsibilities and powers of administrative agencies:

1. The rates that consumers pay for telephone service and electricity are determined by administrative agencies, as are the interest rates that savings and loan institutions may pay depositors.
2. Administrative agencies protect individuals from racial, sexual, and age discrimination in the major aspects of their lives: employment, education, and housing.
3. Administrative agencies determine who does and does not get radio and television licenses.
4. Administrative agencies ensure that the food we eat is pure, wholesome, and free from harmful additives and that the drugs that we purchase are both safe and effective.
5. The right to join a labor union and to be protected from unfair labor practices is safeguarded by administrative regulatory power.
6. Administrative agencies are responsible for ensuring the safety of our workplaces, our methods of transportation, and the countless products that we purchase as consumers—from toys to clothing to automobiles.
7. Administrative agencies are responsible for protecting us against monopolies, false advertising, air and water pollution, incompetent physicians, nurses, subminimum wages and working conditions, unfair and misleading credit transactions, and fraud in securities purchases.
8. Administrative agencies determine who is eligible for welfare, Food Stamps, veterans benefits, Medicaid, Medicare, and Social Security.
9. Administrative agencies determine how much of our income we get to keep and whether a person may be admitted to or remain in this country.

The list could go on almost endlessly. No attempt has been undertaken to make it all-inclusive. The point is that every day, every American's life is directly and continuously affected by administrative action or inaction. Whether the result of all this administrative power is beneficial or harmful will be considered later. For now, a recognition of the scope and importance of that power is all that is relevant.

It is equally relevant to recognize that in reality the legislative and judicial output of administrative agencies has long since outstripped in both volume and scope the legislative and judicial output of Congress and the courts. For example, the *Code of Federal Regulations*, which is the codification of administrative regulations currently occupies over a dozen feet of library space, each inch of that composed of 700 double column pages in minuscule print.[10] By comparison the *United States Code*, Congress's laws, requires only three and a half feet of library space. The *Federal Register*, which is the annual compendium of federal regulations, was 61,261 pages long in 1979. Similarly, the adjudicative output of administrative agencies far exceeds that of the courts. For example, in 1963, the United States district courts disposed of a total of 11,000 criminal and civil cases. In that same year, administrative agencies disposed of 81,469 adjudicated cases.[11] In 1976, the 625 administrative law judges of the Social Security Administration settled 180,000 cases; the 505 judges of the entire federal judicial system handled 129,683 civil and criminal cases.[12]

It would be completely misleading to leave the impression that all of this administrative regulatory power is concentrated at the federal level. Both state and local levels of government also have vested extensive regulatory power and responsibility in their administrative agencies. State agencies, among other things, license physicians, barbers, lawyers, architects, cosmeticians, liquor dealers, and funeral directors, as well as regulate commerce within their boundaries and provide the regulatory framework for all levels of public educational institutions. Localities are charged with the responsibility of enforcing building codes, fire, health, and safety regulations and standards.

For most people in this country the vast majority of the direct contacts that they have with government are likely to be with administrative agencies. For many individuals their perceptions of government generally will be influenced by the nature and tone of these contacts. For all the beneficial purposes intended by administrative regulation, it must be understood that administrative power has been exercised arbitrarily, capriciously, and unconstitutionally by countless administrators and administrative agencies. Such actions have ranged from the compulsory sterilization of welfare recipients as a condition of eligibility for Aid to Families with Dependent Children (AFDC) payments, to the physical abuse of mental patients, prisoners, and students, to the multitudinous and sometimes shocking seizures of property by agents of the Internal Revenue Service, to federal narcotics agents playing gangbusters in the homes of innocent and uninvolved people.

The extent of criticism of administrative regulation has increased in volume and intensity in recent years. Currently, both friend and foe of regulation find little satisfaction in the results of the regulatory process. Supporters of the substance of regulation charge that countless agencies have failed to accomplish the legislative goals that were assigned to them. Administrative timidity, laxness, and senility are commonly identified as the major faults of the agencies and their personnel. The economic regulatory agencies are attacked for having long since come under the domination of the industries that they are supposedly regulating, with the result that protection of the public interest becomes synonymous with granting the regulatees whatever they demand. Prices and rates are allowed to increase, quality of service and products to deteriorate, competition to disappear, unfair trade practices to flourish as consumers, workers, and the environment are left unprotected and vulnerable.

Opponents of substantive regulation are equally fervent in their attacks on the administrative process. They allege that the administrators have needlessly intruded themselves and their rules into the most intimate and private aspects of the lives of individuals with a consequent narrowing of freedom and violation of basic constitutional rights. Businesses, educational institutions, and the President charge that the proliferation of regulations needlessly increases the costs of doing business and that the regulators operate in blithe indifference to the inflationary impact of the requirements that they are imposing. Small businesses charge that they are unfairly singled out for enforcement procedures and that the cost of compliance with endless nitpicking rules is driving them out of business. "There is mounting evidence that excessive regulation is hamstringing our economy, handcuffing our business enterprises and robbing the consumer through increased inflation brought on by the costs of complying with regulation," charged Republican Representative John B. Anderson.[13]

Congress complains that it has lost control and that agencies routinely ignore congressional intent and wishes. Everybody complains that the rules themselves are masterpieces of legislatic, bureaucratic gobbledygook that no one except a lawyer can possibly understand. Administrative procedures are attacked for their slowness, complexity, and expense.

All of these criticisms will be dealt with to a greater extent in a later chapter, but for now two points need to be emphasized concerning the future of administrative regulation. First, the conditions that originally mandated the creation of most administrative regulatory agencies are still very much with us. Administrative power has been and is the necessary and unavoidable counterbalance to the vast power that corporations and industry in this country have developed over the lives, health, safety, and happiness of Americans. Second, despite the barrage of criticism of regulation, the American public remains basically supportive of it. A series of polls taken by Louis Harris between 1974 and 1978 asked: "In the future do you think there should be more government regulation of business, less government regulation or the same amount?" Sixty-two percent favored either more regulation or the same amount as at present.[14] Although reforms in the substance and conduct of regulation could and probably should be made, administrative regulation is a necessary component of life in an industrialized, interdependent economy and society.

VARIETIES AND TYPES OF AGENCIES EXERCISING REGULATORY POWER

The exercise of regulatory power is not restricted to any one particular type or form of administrative agency. At the federal level, agencies within cabinet departments, independent agencies, and independent regulatory commissions all have similar and far-reaching regulatory powers. The determining factor as to whether an agency has regulatory power is not its administrative form or location, but rather the decision by Congress that the activities falling within the agency's scope require that the agency have rule-making and adjudicatory power to accomplish its mission. Although historically Congress did display a preference for independent regulatory commissions to regulate specific sectors of the economy, as the scope of national responsibility expanded every type of agency in existence at the federal level came to be vested with regulatory power.

The independent regulatory commissions (IRC's) have tended to receive the lion's share of attention and criticism in considerations of government regulation of business. The commission form was first utilized at the state level and its successful use there encouraged Congress to try it at the national level when it first attempted to regulate the railroads in 1887. The basic characteristics of federal independent regulatory commissions are that they are multiheaded, bipartisan in composition, not located within any other agency or department, and not directly in the President's chain of command. In theory at least, these commissions are supposed to be capable of providing nonpartisan flexibility, continuity, and expertise in the regulatory process. Invariably given longer terms than the President, and protected from dismissal by him, commissioners are supposed to use their lengthy tenure to maximize their expertise and independence. Although the Interstate Commerce Commission, the first of the federal IRC's, has never exactly lived up to these theoretical aspirations, Congress has never disavowed the commission form as a regulatory device, and has continued to utilize it sporadically when creating new regulatory agencies.

Other independent regulatory commissions are the Civil Aeronautics Board, the Federal Trade Commission, the Securities and Exchange Commission, the Federal Maritime Commission, the National Labor Relations Board, the Board of Governors of the Federal Reserve System, the Federal Communications Commission, the Nuclear Regulatory Commission, the Consumer Product Safety Commission, and the Equal Employment Opportunity Commission. Taken together, these commissions have sweeping responsibilities for regulation of specific industries and for protecting consumers and workers. Usually regarded as the most "advanced" of regulatory agencies in terms of their procedures, the commissions are also considered by critics to be the most susceptible to capture by regulated interests since their independence leaves them unprotected by other political agencies or actors.

Equally important as regulators are agencies located within cabinet departments. Every cabinet department has some type of regulatory power and the number of agencies within these departments which actually exercise this power is nearly impossible to pin down. Some of the most visible and well known of these cabinet agencies are

- *The Food and Drug Administration* within the Department of Health and Human Services, which has responsibility for ensuring the purity and safety of food, drugs, and cosmetics;
- *The Internal Revenue Service* within the Department of Treasury, which attempts to ensure the inevitability of taxes for most Americans;
- *The Immigration and Naturalization Service* within the Department of Justice, which has almost plenary power over entry, residence, and exit by aliens in this country;

- *The Occupational Safety and Health Administration* within the Department of Labor, charged with ensuring that all workplaces are free from hazards which might negatively affect the health and safety of workers; and
- *The Forest Service* within the Department of Agriculture and the *Park Service*, Department of Interior, both with responsibilities for protecting natural resources and the public's recreational interests.

The scope, type, and impact of the regulatory power of these agencies is identical to that of the commissions, as are the procedures that they must follow. The major distinctions between the two types of agencies are their administrative form and location within the executive branch. The cabinet agencies are located within departments whose secretaries are chosen by and directly subject to the President. Further, they are headed by a single administrator rather than by a board or commission.

The independent agencies share certain features in common with both cabinet agencies and IRC's. They are not located within a cabinet department, but they have a single appointed administrative head and they are subject to presidential control and direction. Two of the most well known and powerful of the independent agencies are the Environmental Protection Agency and the Veterans' Administration, which both have extensive regulatory functions and duties.

Still another type of agency which has been given regulatory power is the government corporation. Somewhat similar to their private counterparts, government corporations' primary function is to run a "businesstype" enterprise whether that be a railroad (AMTRAK), an insurance company (Federal Deposit Insurance Corporation), an electric power generating facility (Tennessee Valley Authority), or a postal service (the United States Postal Service). Like IRC's, they are multiheaded (the governmental equivalent of a board of directors), but unlike commissioners, corporation board members may be dismissed by the President.

Finally, even agencies located within the Executive Office of the President (EOP) have been vested with regulatory powers. Although the Executive Office primarily consists of staff agencies whose functions are to advise and assist the President in carrying out his responsibilities as chief executive, on rare occasions EOP agencies have been assigned regulatory functions. One of the most recent examples was the selection of the Office of the Emergency Preparedness to administer the wage-price freeze imposed by the Nixon administration in 1971.[15]

A logical question that might arise at this point is, what differentiates the regulatory power of these different types of agencies and why are different types chosen? If politics were logical, the administrative process would probably work a lot better than it does, but unfortunately that is not the case. There are no systematic differences in either regulatory power or procedures among the various types of agencies, nor is there a uniform, logical reason for selecting one type of agency over another. There are, instead, multitudinous political reasons for vesting regulatory power in one type of agency at one particular time and in a completely different type at another time.

Independent regulatory commissions are lasting monuments to legislative distrust and dislike of the chief executive. During periods of legislative-executive conflict Congress frequently used them as a method to expand national power without directly expanding presidential power (the creation of the Consumer Product Safety Commission in 1972). Just as frequently, however, Congress has created such commissions during periods of legislative-executive harmony and cooperation (the Securities and Exchange Commission).

Single-headed independent agencies may be created to maximize their visibility and emphasize congressional concern over a specific problem (EPA) or in response to demands from a powerful clientele group which insists that promotion and protection of their interest cannot be guaranteed by an agency buried in the bowels of a cabinet department (Veterans' Administration). Agencies may be located in cabinet departments because such location seems to provide protection from hostile or corrupt influences (the Forest Service, Department of Agriculture), or because the agency's mission is directly related to that of the department (Social Security Administration, DHHS). A government corporation may be created because its function is primarily "business-like" (TVA) or because another type of organization has failed and the function must still be carried out (AMTRAK, the Postal Service). A particular form of organization is utilized for regulatory purposes not because of any underlying theoretical or logical framework, but because of the variety of political forces and factors that were dominant at the time of the agency's creation.

The diversity of forms of regulatory agencies at the state level resembles that at the federal level and in some states surpasses it. There are departments, boards, commissions, and independent agencies; some have been created by statute and some by state constitutions, and all regulate in profusion in every state. The heads of these agencies may be appointed by the governor, elected by the citizens, or designated by the regulatees, as is the case with many of the professional self-regulatory agencies such as medical examining boards. At the county and city level the situation is duplicated. Every type of agency known to administrative theory exercises regulatory power, and when new types are created, they undoubtedly will also be given such power.

At the federal level one other specific administrative agency merits recognition at this point: the Administrative Conference of the United States (ACUS) which was created by Congress in 1964. The Conference is composed of from 75 to 91 members representing each agency and department having regulatory responsibility, as well as outside experts on administrative law and procedure. The Conference is headed by a chairperson appointed by the President and confirmed by the Senate and a 10-member council also appointed by the President. Since its creation it has been responsible for recommending and securing significant legislative and administrative improvements in the regulatory process. Two examples are the encouragement of public participation and intervention and adjudicatory procedures and the 1976 amendment to the Federal Administrative Procedure Act waiving sovereign immunity in all nonmonetary actions brought against federal government agencies.

ADMINISTRATIVE REGULATION IN ACTION

Far too many students, to the extent that they think about administrative regulation at all, tend to view it as a boring, incomprehensible process that is far removed from their everyday lives. That this is not the case should be amply illustrated by the following example of the regulatory process in action.

The Food and Drug Administration Tries to Ban Saccharin

Some observers have noted that Americans are obsessed with the desire to be thin, as long as that thinness can be gained without exercising or controlling the amount of food consumed. The annals of American regulatory history are replete with examples of the seemingly endless gullibility of the overweight and their willingness to purchase any product offered, no matter how absurd or occasionally dangerous it may be, if promised thinness and fitness with no effort. Private enterprise has not been hesitant in supplying the gullible with such products. In the 1950s, there was the Relaxcisor, a marvelous device that promised to make a user slim, fit, and perfectly proportioned without lifting a finger. These marvelous results were accomplished by attaching rubber pads to pertinent parts of one's anatomy and then zapping electrical current through them. Unfortunately, if the effectiveness of the Relaxcisor was questionable, its safety was not. Finally convinced by constantly mounting research evidence that it was dangerous and could trigger heart attacks, kidney malfunctions, and epileptic attacks, the Food and Drug Administration (FDA) ordered it off the market in 1970.

By then the Relaxcisor had been surpassed as a weight control fad by artificially sweetened products. The weight conscious could consume soda pop, cookies, cakes, canned fruit, KoolAid, gelatin, candy, and countless other food products, all sweetened with cyclamates, and all low calorie, and still reach the promised land of thinness. And consume they did. The diet food and drink industry became a billion-dollar industry and was rapidly growing when it ran afoul of the Delaney Amendment and the Food and Drug Administration.

The Delaney Amendment is one of the most controversial laws currently in existence at the federal level. It was added to the Food, Drug and Cosmetic Act in 1958 at the insistence of Representative James Delaney (Democrat, New York). It specifies that

> no additive shall be deemed safe . . . if it is found, after tests which are appropriate
> for the evaluation of the safety of food additives, to induce cancer in man or animal.

The FDA, of course, is required to ensure that all food additives are safe and to ban those that are not. Usually there is considerable room for agency discretion as to whether an additive should be banned or not since "safety" is a relative term and subject to interpretation. The Delaney Amendment, however, seemingly leaves little room for such discretion: if a substance has been proven to induce cancer in man or animal, it is not safe and the FDA must ban it.

One additional point of great relevance to the FDA and its regulation of additives is that there were already hundreds of these additives being used prior to 1958 when Congress finally required manufacturers to prove the safety of an additive before putting it in food. Since manufacturers were not required to test those additives and since the FDA had neither staff nor time to do so, the GRAS (generally recognized as safe) list was developed. Additives in long use were automatically put on it and could be used in food. The presence of an additive on the GRAS list did not mean that it was safe; it meant that nobody had proved that it was not. Both cyclamates and saccharin were on the GRAS list.

The first disturbing research results concerning cyclamates had reached the FDA as early as 1954 when a study by the Food Nutrition Board of the National Academy of Sciences (NAS) reported that test results indicated a highly suspicious frequency of lung, kidney, and skin cancers among laboratory animals tested with cyclamates. Sporadically, until 1968, NAS continued to report research results that raised questions concerning cyclamates' safety. In 1968, FDA chemists tested cyclamates on chicken embryos and reported a direct correlation between cyclamates and birth defects, deformities, and chromosome damage. Convinced by mounting research evidence, the FDA proposed to ban cyclamates as an additive.

The reaction to the proposed ban ranged from approval to outright dismay. The most disbelieving and dismayed were the major producers of diet soft drinks and the consumers of those beverages. Demands for a congressional investigation or for presidential intervention and accusations that the FDA was un-American reverberated throughout Washington and the country. The FDA persisted and cyclamates were banned as a food additive in October 1969. The controversy surrounding that decision has not yet been settled. There were, however, three factors present at that time which made the decision to ban cyclamates more feasible than the current controversy surrounding the saccharin ban: First, there was the ready availability of saccharin as a cheap and effective substitute; second, the sugar industry, more powerful and well organized than at present, rallied to the cause; and third, the general attitude toward government regulation, both in Congress and among the public, was far more supportive and favorable than at present.

Cyclamates are banned. Long live saccharin. Food producers quickly switched to the use of saccharin and soon it was found in the same vast number of products as cyclamates had been: sugarless gum, toothpaste, lip balm, mouthwash, soda pop, cookies, cake mixes, and countless other food products. As later research was to indicate, one of the age groups that is the heaviest consumers of saccharin is children under the age of ten. It is estimated that one-third of the children in this age group consume saccharin and their consumption of it has increased by 160 percent since 1972. Furthermore, the highest percentage of saccharin users by sex is males under the age of 10.[16] Saccharin, as anyone's grandmother will tell you, has been around and used for a long time. Doubts about its safety, which grandmother may not tell you, have been around nearly as long.

In 1903, a group of volunteers for the Department of Agriculture, called the "poison squad," tested for five years by direct consumption a variety of chemical food additives. Research procedures were somewhat less refined then than currently, but that chemical feast convinced the poison squad that saccharin should be banned. The politics of the regulatory process have changed less than research procedures, and when President Theodore Roosevelt, who used saccharin constantly, pointed out that "anyone who thinks saccharin is injurious to health is an idiot," the proposed ban did not go into effect.[17] In 1912, a ban on saccharin was imposed, but it was lifted during World War I.

By the early 1970s, research interest in saccharin was revived and the FDA began receiving research reports from independent scientific studies that raised questions about saccharin's safety. In 1971, tests by the Wisconsin Alumni Research Foundation indicated that 7 out of 15 male rats fed saccharin as 5 percent of their diets for two years developed bladder tumors.[18] The FDA's initial response was to remove saccharin from the GRAS list and to require that all products containing saccharin carry a warning label cautioning that the product should only be used by those who must restrict their intake of sugar.

On the basis of a 1973 FDA study which indicated that saccharin could cause cancer in rats the FDA requested the National Academy of Sciences' National Research Council to review the evidence. In 1974, the Academy reported back that it could not conclusively state that saccharin caused cancer in laboratory tests on rats and raised the possibility that the carcinogenic agent might be OTS (orthotoluene sulfonamide), an impurity found in saccharin. The groundwork for the controversial Canadian research study was laid.[19]

FDA scientists received and began studying the Canadian report in early 1977. That study began in 1974 and ran for two and one-half years. It indicated that of 200 animals fed OTS-free saccharin, 21 developed bladder tumors; none of the animals fed OTS developed such tumors. The study further indicated that second generation rats whose mothers had been exposed to saccharin during pregnancy showed a similar high rate of cancer. The Canadian study was the third two-generation study to produce evidence that saccharin is carcinogenic in rats.[20] Despite considerable debate and misgivings over the results, methods, and conclusions of the study, a panel of FDA scientists recommended that saccharin be removed from the GRAS list and banned as a food additive. On March 9, 1977, acting FDA commissioner Sherwin Gardner announced that the FDA proposed to ban saccharin as a food additive, effective in mid-July 1977. The proposed ban would have eliminated the use of saccharin in foods, beverages, and cosmetics likely to be ingested and in drugs where it was used only to improve taste. It would have permitted continued marketing of saccharin as a single-ingredient drug available without prescription, provided that manufacturers proved it was medically effective in controlling diabetes or obesity.[21]

The FDA announcement of the proposed ban immediately generated a storm of resentment and resistance which made the reactions to the cyclamate ban appear mild in comparison. The diet soda and food industry created the Calorie Control Council to act as the spearhead of a concerted lobbying effort to forestall the ban. The CCC ran two-page advertisements in major U.S. newspapers urging concerned readers to write their congressmen. Members of Congress were flooded with constituent mail and phone calls protesting the ban. The first official congressional response took the form of "routine" oversight hearings by the Health Subcommittee of the House Committee on Foreign and Interstate Commerce.

The issues raised at those hearings were the ones that were to dominate the continuing debate over the FDA ban, and in a broader sense are recurrent themes in many conflicts involving government regulation. The first major issue concerned the validity of the scientific evidence on which the ban was to be based and particularly the experimental methods used to test saccharin. To nonscientists, a category into which the overwhelming majority of congresspersons fall, the contention raised by industry groups that "a human being would have to drink 500 cans of diet pop a day to consume the equivalent of what those unfortunate Canadian rats did," had at least superficial validity. FDA scientists and other researchers defended the method but the procedure was clearly baffling to many members of the public, the press, and Congress in particular.

The second issue involved the lack of agreement among scientists and health professionals on the interpretation of the data, even if it were valid. FDA scientist Dr. Richard Bates contended that if the Canadian data were applied to humans, the "'maximum level of risk' to humans in developing bladder cancer would be four cases [of cancer] per 1000 population if 10 cans of diet soda a day were drunk over a lifetime and four cases[22] [of cancer] per 10,000 population if only one can a day were drunk." Other scientists were equally adamant that banning saccharin would cause greater damage to the public health since diabetics would turn to sugar with far more certain damage to their lives and health.

The final issue was public resentment at one more unnecessary violation of freedom and individual rights. "Millions of Americans . . . think we have violated their freedom of choice. They think this time we've gone too far, and frankly, I am not so sure they are wrong," Representative Claude Pepper (Democrat, Florida) informed the subcommittee.[23] Although no formal action was taken by Congress at that time, the Senate Committee on Human Resources requested the Office of Technology Assessment (OTA), a congressional staff agency, to review the scientific evidence on which the FDA was basing the ban.

Undeterred, the FDA held public hearings, as required by the Federal Administrative Procedure Act, on May 18 and 19, 1977. The hearings, as is frequently the case, turned up little new evidence but permitted a thorough airing of the issues. The report from OTA was equally inconclusive. The OTA panel of scientists agreed that saccharin was a potential carcinogen but disagreed as to how serious a risk was involved in its continued use.[24] Public opposition, however, had not abated and congressional intervention appeared increasingly likely. Various bills were introduced in the Senate to postpone the ban. Further complicating the situation were new Canadian government research reports received by the FDA which reconfirmed the earlier findings. On the basis of those reports, the FDA strengthened the proposed ban to bar all sales of saccharin. Because of the change in the substance of the regulation, FDA commissioner Donald Kennedy announced that the FDA would extend the period for public comment until August 31, and postpone the final decision until October 1977.

However, Congress intervened and the FDA did not impose the ban. On November 4, 1977, Congress passed legislation which delayed the ban for eighteen months and required that during the interim, new studies be performed by the National Academy of Sciences on both saccharin, specifically, and food additives in general. The FDA and the National Cancer Institute were also instructed to study the actual human impact of saccharin use. The only consolation that public health interest groups received from the legislation was a requirement that during the moratorium, all products containing saccharin carry a warning label and all retail stores selling such products post clearly visible and readable warning signs.

In November 1978, the NAS released its first report on saccharin and more or less affirmed the previous research findings. It agreed that saccharin was a weak carcinogen and that it promoted the development of cancer initiated by other substances. The NAS report also pointed out that there was no scientific evidence for the claimed medical benefits of saccharin for diabetics or the obese. Beyond that, however, the NAS would not go. It made no recommendations for FDA action and concluded that "the ultimate judgment must be made through the socio-political process."[25]

If the administrative process is frequently slow, the political or, more aptly, the legislative process can be even more so. The moratorium expired on May 23, 1979; Congress was still trying to decide if the moratorium should be extended, if the Delaney Amendment should be repealed, or if the entire catalog of federal food regulation law should be revised. The FDA chose the path of least congressional resistance. Although technically in violation of the law, the FDA put a hold on the saccharin action until Congress could decide its preference. In early 1980, three new scientific studies on saccharin were released. Despite claims by the diet food industry, the studies failed to give saccharin a clean bill of health, and were able to ascertain only that while overall there seemed to be a lack of significant relationship between saccharin consumption and urinary tract cancer, for some groups of the population—children, young women, and pregnant women—danger was more pronounced. Finally, in June 1980, Congress voted to extend the moratorium until June 30, 1981. In July 1981, Congress extended the moratorium for two more years.

The attempt by the FDA to ban saccharin illustrates many of the major aspects of the contemporary regulatory process and the circumstances in which regulatory agencies must operate. Although Congress creates the agencies and passes the legislation which they must enforce, agencies cannot always rely on congressional support in enforcing the legislation if the rules they promulgate antagonize powerful interest groups or run counter to public opinion. Second, many regulatory decisions involve complex technical and scientific questions on which there may be little or no agreement among the experts. In such a case, the agency must make decisions on less than totally complete evidence, based on its expert assessment of that evidence. Third, many regulatory decisions involve more than one administrative agency, and although in the saccharin ban the agencies were in basic agreement, just as frequently disagreements occur and jurisdictional battles result. Additionally, the saccharin ban indicates that the much-criticized slowness of the regulatory process results from two major causes: first, procedural requirements such as notice, required hearings, and weighing the evidence; and second, political reality—opposition and resistance that delay regulatory action. Finally, regardless of the ultimate decision made on saccharin, the case clearly indicates the impact that regulatory action or inaction can have on the lives and health of individuals and on the business community.

AN OVERVIEW OF THE REGULATORY PROCESS

The FDA case illustrates some of the problems of formulating regulations, but rule making is only one aspect of the regulatory process. As Figure 1.1 indicates, the total administrative regulatory process consists of ten basic steps, from authorizing legisla-

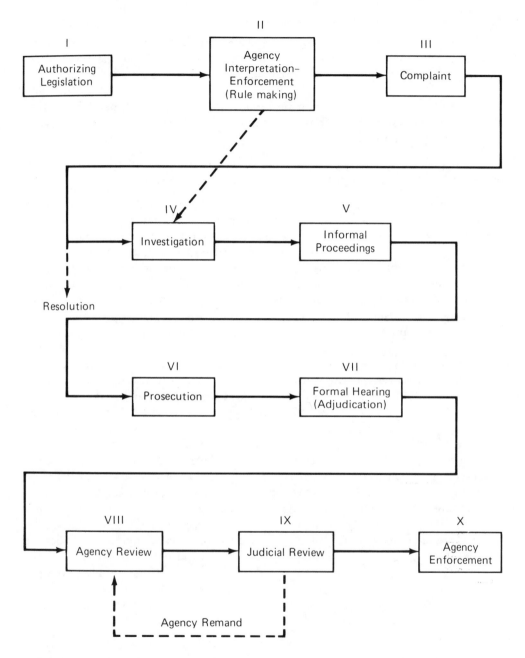

FIGURE 1.1   The Administrative Regulatory Process: An Overview

tion through active enforcement action against an individual or business. Most regulatory actions do *not* go through all ten steps; in some instances rules are promulgated and either obeyed by those at whom they are directed or not actively enforced by the agency. Also, in some instances administrative adjudication is based on legislative requirements, not on administrative rules. The majority of cases where an investigation is undertaken are terminated by informal proceedings, but in some of the most important regulatory actions in terms of social and economic impact, all ten steps will be involved.

To illustrate what occurs at each step an examination of enforcement of the Title IX amendments barring sexual discrimination in educational institutions in a hypothetical case will be used:

Step I: The authorizing legislation requiring HEW to enforce the ban against sexual discrimination in education programs was passed by Congress in 1972.

Step II: Agency interpretation: formal rule making. Although Title IX may have banned sexual discrimination in all educational programs, the law was typically vague as to what specific practices constituted discrimination and what full compliance with the law required. Such determination had to be made by HEW and formal regulations issued specifying what was required of educational institutions in every aspect of their programs and operations. This required HEW to determine which schools were and were not covered by the law and then to issue rules covering admissions policies, classes and curriculum, housing, financial aid, athletic programs, and employment practices.

Following required procedures and encouraging maximum participation and consultation in the rule-making process, HEW required three years to formulate the initial set of regulations interpreting Title IX. The final regulations were announced on July 21, 1975. HEW was immediately bombarded with requests for clarification and revisions, particularly with regard to the requirements for equal funding for men's and women's athletics. In December 1978, HEW Secretary Joseph Califano issued his "interpretation": although colleges must equally fund men's and women's athletics on a per capita basis, football was exempted from the requirement. That interpretation satisfied no one and Califano's successor, Patricia Harris, issued a new interpretation in December 1979: except for scholarships, colleges do not have to spend the same amount for each female athelete as for each male. Although considerably more restrictive in applicability, the new rules still posed difficult problems for many schools and failed to satisfy college administrators, feminist sports groups, and the NCAA, the major men's sports governing body which predicted the destruction of intercollegiate athletics. Since the rule-making process will be covered in depth later, it is sufficient to note at this point that the regulations were the result of a long, complex, conflict-ridden process and, typically, satisfied almost no one at all. One of the most controversial rules required equal athletic opportunity for members of both sexes and specified the criteria that would be used to determine if a school were complying.

Step III: Complaint. At this point, the remainder of this example will be hypothetical. Coed College provides lavish financial support for all types of men's athletics but women's sports fare rather badly. The women's tennis team, for example, has not been provided with new equipment for 15 years and must regularly solicit donations to pay its travel expenses. Convinced that this satisfies neither the letter nor the spirit of HEW regulations, members of the team write to the regional office of HEW. Their complaint is referred to the Office of Civil Rights (OCR).

Step IV: Investigation. What and how soon anything happens to a complaint received by OCR depends on many factors. There is no guarantee anything will happen, since the decision not to act is within agency power. If hundreds of complaints have been received, it is quite likely that the agency will be backlogged and have insufficient personnel to investigate all the complaints it has received. It is equally likely that even if it does decide to investigate, six months and frequently more will elapse before it has time to respond. But assume that the complaint reaches the regional OCR at a fortuitous time and it decides to investigate. Investigatory procedures are numerous and varied but in this instance might include sending out a team of investigators who will examine financial records, observe actual procedures and programs, question college administrators, students, faculty, and the complainants, hold informal public meetings, and attempt to verify if the complaint has merit. Such an investigation can become lengthy and it may be months before an initial recommendation is made.

Step V: Informal proceedings. If the investigators determine the complaint is without merit, the case will be closed, but again assume that they decide that the complaint is justified: Coed College does not provide equal athletic opportunity for women. The investigators will report their findings to OCR and OCR will attempt to arrive at a negotiated (informal) settlement with the college. OCR negotiators, college administrators, and complainants will meet and confer and OCR will attempt to get administrators to remedy inequities in a way that is satisfactory to all parties. Frequently, the outcome of all these informal negotiations will be a "consent agreement" by which the affected party agrees to cease certain practices and/or to undertake remedial actions. Although termed informal, such an agreement once signed is legally binding and violations may result in the imposition of penalties. The advantages of such a settlement are obvious: It saves everyone involved time, effort, and money, and results in the remedying of a legal wrong.

Step VI: Prosecution. Coed College, however, is not persuaded. Its administrators are convinced that the law is unjust, the regulations unreasonable, the complainants troublemakers, and the college blameless, fair, and equitable. An informal settlement is not to be had and both the OCR investigators and the complainants are equally convinced that the college administrators are wrong on all counts. The investigators recommend formal action to their superiors. Once again the workload and adequacy of staffing of the agency will determine what and how soon further action occurs.

In this instance, however, the decision is made to proceed against Coed College. The administrative equivalent of a prosecuting attorney is chosen, a notice of opportunity to be heard is issued to the college administrators, and an adjudicatory hearing is scheduled. The agency investigators proceed to collect evidence, a prehearing conference is held, a final informal settlement offer is made, and Coed College rejects it.

Step VII: Formal hearing. An administrative law judge, an attorney employed by the agency but who acts in a quasi-judicial capacity, is chosen and assigned to preside at the hearing which is the administrative equivalent of a trial and proceeds along the same lines. The one major difference is that there is *never* a jury in an administrative hearing. Subpoenas are issued requiring witnesses to appear and documents to be produced; examination and cross-examination of witnesses occur; a full record is maintained and lawyers are everywhere. The judge hears all the evidence, rules on all objections, and in general controls the course of the hearing. Time once more becomes a relevant consideration since some adjudicatory hearings can drag on for months or even years. Ultimately, however, all of the witnesses will have been heard, all of the evidence presented, and the hearing concluded.

At this point, the focus shifts entirely to the administrative law judge since he/she must make the decision based on "substantial evidence" in the record. He/she will weigh all the evidence, consider both the facts and the law, including agency regulations, and will issue a reasoned opinion, including all conclusions of law and fact and any "order." In this particular case, although Coed College lawyers did their best, the judge decides that the facts support the complaint that the college does not provide equal athletic opportunities for women students. He/she orders Coed College, over a five-year period, to equalize financial aid opportunities for women and men athletes. The penalty for failure to obey the order is termination of all federal educational monies to Coed College. The order is served on college administrators.

Step VIII: Agency review. To put it mildly, Coed College is not well pleased with the decision. On the other hand, the complainants are not very enthused about it either since they view it as a halfway, drawn-out method that will leave women's sports still substantially less funded than men's programs. The college, citing procedural errors and wrongful interpretation of law and regulations, decides to appeal the decision. The appeal works it way up through the administrative hierarchy of HEW until it eventually ends up on the desk of Secretary of Education.* The process that he follows in arriving at a final decision remains cloaked in nearly the same mystery as surrounds the process by which the Supreme Court arrives at decisions, but ultimately he concurs with the administrative law judge and the final order, bearing his signature, is issued to Coed College.

Step IX: Judicial review. Coed College is no more impressed with the Secretary's final decision than it was with the administrative law judge's. Again alleging violations of due process and federal law, the college's lawyers challenge the agency's decision in federal court. Normally, if upon review the court finds procedural errors or error in interpretation or application of law, it will "remand" (send back) the case to the agency for a new hearing. Whatever the decision of the federal district court, however, there is still the possibility of appealing that decision to the U.S. Court of Appeals and ultimately to the United States Supreme Court. In reality most appeals do not go to the Supreme Court, but for those that do the time lag involved is considerable, as it is to be measured in years rather than months. In our example, Coed College loses again and finally has nowhere else to go with its appeals, unless, of course, it can convince Congress to change the law.

Step X: Enforcement. At last the administrative decision has the full force of law. Coed College may refuse to comply with the order only if it wishes to accept the

---

* To add chaos to confusion, in the midst of this process, the Department of Health, Education and Welfare was reorganized out of existence, and a new Department of Education was created with responsibility for interpreting Title IX.

penalty of losing federal funds. Assuming that it does not, it will comply, no matter how reluctantly, and the Department of Education will monitor, as closely as it has time and personnel, that compliance. That will, in this instance, mark the end of the administrative regulatory process, and should result in more equity for women's sports at Coed College.

SCOPE AND COVERAGE OF THE BOOK

The preceding example illustrates the broad scope of the administrative process and some of the complexities of that process that cause it to be so lengthy and time-consuming. It also illustrates the great impact that administrative regulation has on our economy, individual liberties, health and safety, and in many instances on the entire society. In addition, it points out the interrelation of politics and law in the regulatory process. Every step in the process is circumscribed by required legal procedures and forms and by political realities.

This book will be concerned with all of these facets of administrative regulation. It will explore "administrative law" which in the past has been primarily concerned with defining the power and procedures of administrative agencies. This emphasis on proper legal procedure has been based on the deeply ingrained, if somewhat naive, American belief that as long as proper procedure is followed, justice automatically results. In a political system that is dominated by lawyers it should not be too surprising to discover that proper procedure is considered to be *legal* procedure. Many textbooks on the administrative process cover the required legal procedures exhaustively, often to the extent of ignoring other equally relevant aspects of the administrative process. Since a full understanding of the process requires a broader-based approach, this text will synthesize, as administrators and affected parties must, these legal requirements with the political realities and policy consequences of the regulatory process. It will emphasize the impact of that process on individuals, the political and economic system, and the society as a whole, and will also cover the substance, social-economic impact of regulation, and the political environment which shapes, controls, and guides the regulatory process.

The first chapter sought to place the administrative regulatory process in its historical and organizational context and give some illustrations of the operation of that process. Part I will cover the constitutional basis of administrative power and the major constitutional and legal restrictions on the scope and exercise of that power. It will explore the political environment of regulation and examine the impact of that environment on the regulatory process.

With the legal and political framework established and defined, Part II will explore in detail the basic steps of the administrative process, their impact on individuals and groups, and how these steps are affected by legal and political requirements.

Part III will deal with a major source of control over the administrative process: the judicial checks that are available to safeguard against the arbitrary use of administrative power. Each of these separate types will be explained and evaluated in terms of their effectiveness and limitations.

Part IV will be concerned with measuring and critically evaluating the consequences of major types of regulation on individuals, businesses, and the economy. Once this evaluation has been completed an overview of the major categories of suggested reforms for the regulatory process will be presented.

This book, then, will be concerned with the entire administrative regulatory process and the environment in which it operates. Since this process is such a significant and controversial one, this book will attempt to supply the necessary information for individuals to evaluate that process and its results. Since all Americans are affected by that process, some as administrators and all as citizens, it is essential to understand it.

NOTES

1. Kenneth Davis, *Administrative Law: Cases-Texts-Problems*, 6th ed, (St. Paul: West Publishing Co., 1977), p. 6.

2. Douglas Castle, "In Defense of the Public Service," *Public Administration Times*, May 1, 1980, p. 3.

3. See Gabriel Kolko, *The Triumph of Conservatism* (New York: Free Press, 1963); Walter Emery, *Broadcasting and Government* (East Lansing: Michigan State University Press, 1961); Richard Caves, *Air Transport and Its Regulators* (Cambridge: Harvard University Press, 1962).

4. See Arthur Link, *Wilson and The Progressive Era* (New York: Harper and Bros., 1954).

5. For a more detailed discussion of theories of creation of regulatory agencies see Barry Mitnick, *The Political Economy of Regulation: Creating, Designing and Removing Regulatory Forms* (New York: Columbia University Press, 1980), and James Q. Wilson, *The Politics of Regulation* (New York: Basic Books, 1980).

6. I. L. Sharfman, *The Interstate Commerce Commission*, vol. 1 (New York: Commonwealth Fund, 1931), p. 14.

7. "Partisan Battle Faces Job Safety Bills in Congress," *Congressional Quarterly*, November 13, 1970, p. 2790.

8. Eugene Bardach and Robert A. Kagan, *Going by the Book: The Problem of Regulatory Unreasonableness* (Philadelphia: Temple University Press, 1982), p. 16.

9. "Congress Approves Comprehensive Job Safety Bill," *Congressional Quarterly*, December 25, 1970, p. 3053.

10. Davis, *Administrative Law*, p. 3.

11. Kenneth Davis, *Administrative Law Text*, 3rd ed. (St. Paul: West Publishing Co., 1972), p. 3.

12. Jerry L. Mashaw, Charles Goetz, Frank Goodman, Warren Schwartz, Paul Verkuil, and Milton Carrow, *Social Security Hearings and Appeals* (Lexington, Massachusetts: Lexington Books, 1978), p. xi.

13. Larry Light, "Increasing Attention Focused on Regulatory Reform Plans," *Congressional Quarterly*, March 31, 1979, p. 560.

14. Clark Bell, "A Case for Federal Regulations," *Spokesman-Review* (Spokane, Washington), February 4, 1979, p. H4.

15. Robert Kagan, *Regulatory Justice* (New York: Russell Sage Foundation, 1978), p. 24.

16. R. Jeffrey Smith, "NAS Saccharin Report Sweetens FDA Position, But Not by Much," *Science*, November 24, 1978, p. 852.

17. Elizabeth Wehr, "Congress Plans Major Review of Food Laws," *Congressional Quarterly*, February 10, 1979, p. 233.

18. "Saccharin: Where Do We Go from Here?" *FDA Consumer*, April 1978, p. 18.
19. *FDA Consumer*, p. 18.
20. Smith, "NAS Saccharin Report Sweetens FDA Position, But Not by Much," p. 852.
21. *FDA Consumer*, p. 16.
22. Mark Link, "Proposed Saccharin Ban Causes Controversy," *Congressional Quarterly*, March 26, 1977, p. 540.
23. Link, "Proposed Saccharin Ban Causes Controversy," p. 541.
24. "Saccharin Ban Delay?" *Congressional Quarterly*, June 11, 1977, p. 1164.
25. Wehr, "Congress Plans Major Review of Food Laws," p. 234.

PART I

The Constitutional, Legal, and Political Framework of Administrative Power

Although administrative regulatory power is far-reaching in scope and impact, that power is neither the self-creation of power-mad bureaucratic monstrosities nor unlimited. Every exercise of such power is and must be based on some grant of authority from Congress or the state legislature. In turn, this must be capable of being traced to some power delegated to the legislature by the relevant constitution or retained by it under common law. Both the substance and procedures of administrative agencies are limited by authorizing statutes, Administrative Procedure Acts, and the Constitution. Finally, as the saccharin case indicates, political conditions, public opinion, and interest groups also play an important role in determining and limiting the reach of administrative power. The primary concern of Part I is with this legal and political environment within which administrative regulation is conducted.

The oldest source of governmental regulatory power predates the Constitution by centuries. Under British common law, government was traditionally recognized as having the power to regulate "public utilities": any business "affected with a public interest." This common law concept became an accepted principle of American legal tradition, although its exact meaning and extent was unclear. Originally, it included all those businesses operating under authority of a public grant of privileges, licenses, or franchises, particularly if given monopoly status: public inns and conveyances, and certain occupations. As states began to expand their regulatory activities, they began to include more and more businesses in the public utilities category. Finally, in 1877 the Supreme Court determined that a business was affected with a public interest "when used in a manner to make it of public consequence, and [it] affects the community at large. When, therefore, one devotes his property to a use in which the public has an interest, he, in effect, grants to the public an interest in that use, and must submit to be controlled by the public for the common good."[1] Although seemingly clear, this definition provided little specific guidance as to which businesses are affected with a public interest and hence subject to regulation. The definition gradually broadened to include grain elevators, insurance agents, loan institutions, packers and stockyards, securities dealers, private contract carriers, milk producers and retailers, and countless other businesses. Once it was determined that a business was affected with a public interest it was subject to government regulation, which included the power to regulate the rates charged, quality and quantity of service provided, and conditions of production.

Another major basis of governmental regulatory power which predates the Constitution is the police power: the inherent power of government to legislate to protect the health, safety, morals, or welfare of its people. The police power has served as the basis for laws requiring compulsory vaccination of individuals, local zoning ordinances, regulation of alcoholic beverages, compulsory sterilization of the mentally retarded, licensing of pharmacists, physicians, and various other professions, and regulation of wages and working conditions in industry.

The public utilities concept and the police power have been predominantly used as bases for the exercise of regulatory power at the state and local government level. Congress, when it has expanded the reach of federal regulatory power, has preferred to rely on one or more of the 18 powers delegated to it in Article I, Section 8 of the Constitution. Even a casual reading (and students of administrative law should read them carefully) of the first 17 of those powers suggests the possible breadth of federal regulatory power. When the eighteenth power, "To make all laws which shall be necessary and proper for carrying into execution the foregoing powers, and all other powers vested by this Constitution in the government of the United States or in any department or officer thereof," is added, the constitutional framework of the substance and methods of regulation emerges as broad and permissive. The creation of administrative agencies vested with authority to make rules and adjudicate cases is both necessary and proper in order to carry out the specific powers found not only in Article I but throughout the Constitution.

Three of the powers granted to Congress have been particularly important in expanding regulatory power: the commerce power, the power to tax and spend to promote the general welfare, and the various specified powers relating to providing for national defense. Their combined impact has provided the federal government with ample constitutional authority for a vast variety of regulatory activities.

Congress is specifically granted power to "regulate commerce with foreign nations; among the several states and with the Indian tribes" (Article I, Section 8, Clause 3). The Supreme Court has frequently been called upon to define the key concepts in the commerce clause—"commerce," "regulate," and "interstate"—and has gradually expanded their meaning to permit congressional regulation of almost all business activity carried on in the United States. *Gibbons v. Ogden*[2] provided the basic judicial definitions on which later cases were based:

> Commerce, undoubtedly, is traffic, but it is something more,—it is intercourse
> . . . between nations and parts of nations in all its branches. . . . The subject to

which the power is next applied is commerce "among the several states." The word "among" means intermingled with . . . . [It] cannot stop at the boundary line of each state, but may be introduced into the interim.

If Congress has the power to regulate it, that power may be exercised whenever the subject exists. . . . What is this power?

It is the power to regulate; that is to prescribe the rule by which commerce is to be governed. This power, like all others vested in Congress, is complete in itself, may be exercised to its utmost extent, and acknowledges no limitations other than are prescribed in the Constitution.

Defined in this manner the commerce clause unquestionably authorizes federal regulation of railroads, motor carriers, airlines, telephone, telegraph, and countless other business transactions directly in interstate commerce. Whether such activities as manufacturing and all the assorted circumstances surrounding it such as working conditions, labor relations, wages and salaries were included in the commerce power was not clear, and, initially, the Supreme Court was not inclined to permit their regulation. Economic reality and the flood of New Deal regulatory legislation persuaded the Court to change its mind. In upholding the constitutionality of the Fair Labor Standards Act of 1938 which provided comprehensive regulation of working conditions including minimum wages and maximum hours and required employers to keep records of wages and hours, the Court affirmed that the power to regulate commerce extended to "production for commerce, even if the production itself was entirely intra-state."[3] Just how far intrastate that power could reach was clearly exemplified in the Court's decision in *Wickard v. Filburn*.[4] To stabilize production and prices in agriculture, Congress authorized the establishment of production quotas for wheat. Filburn had been allotted a quota of 11.1 acres; he produced 23 acres of wheat, none of which was intended for sale. Nevertheless the Court held that his production directly affected interstate commerce and consequently he was liable for statutory penalties.

Whether a business may be regulated by Congress now depends on whether that business affects or is affected by interstate commerce, and as *Gibbons v. Ogden* stated, the scope of that regulation is unlimited except for other specific limitations in the Constitution. Since today there are very few, if any, businesses that do not in some way "affect" interstate commerce, even if that effect is no more than purchasing materials that have traveled in interstate commerce, the reach of commerce regulatory power extends to almost all commercial establishments in the country.

The disbursement of billions of dollars of federal money annually to the elderly, the indigent, the ill, the disabled, the unemployed, and countless other groups of Americans constitutes one of the major areas of federal regulation. As politicians in Washington are fond of saying, "there's no such thing as a free lunch," and one way that beneficiaries of government largesse pay is by being subjected to voluminous regulations covering a wide spectrum of their personal lives and activities. It is more than coincidental that the Social Security Administration which disburses over $130 billion a year in benefits is also the largest adjudicative system in the Western world.[5]

Legally, if Congress has the power to provide these benefits, it has the power to limit eligibility and determine under what circumstances largesse shall be provided, subject, as with the commerce power, to other specific limitations in the Constitution.

Congress unquestionably now has such power as long as the purpose of the expenditure is "to promote the general welfare." From the Supreme Court's perspective, this is not to be interpreted as including only objects which fall within the delegated powers of Congress but may be used to promote a broad national public welfare.[6] Although the Court wavers on exactly how much government regulation and intrusion is permissible when it provides benefits, it has consistently maintained the power of general regulation in benefit programs. In upholding mandatory home visits of AFDC recipients, the Court pointed out:

2. The agency, with tax funds provided from federal as well as state sources, is fulfilling a public trust. The State . . . has appropriate and paramount interest and concern in seeing and assuring that the intended and proper objects of that tax-produced assistance are the ones who benefit from the aid it dispenses. . . .

3. One who dispenses purely private charity naturally has an interest in and expects to know his charitable funds are utilized and put to work. The public, when it is the provider, rightly expects the same.[7]

If expenditures have formed a basis for several regulatory agencies, taxing, the other half of the power, has provided the basis for one of the most powerful, and some would argue most arbitrary, regulatory agencies at the federal level: the Internal Revenue Service (IRS), Department of the Treasury. One of the distinguishing characteristics of IRS as a regulatory agency is the inclusiveness of its jurisdiction; while individuals can avoid the regulatory power of most agencies by not engaging in activities subject to their regulation or by not accepting benefits, theoretically, if an individual has any source of income whatever he is subject to IRS jurisdiction to the extent that taxes are unavoidable, and so to IRS and its volumes of regulations.

The Constitution grants Congress and the President numerous specific powers to provide for national defense and security. The exercise of certain of these powers involves obvious regulation, as young men will no doubt notice when they go to register with the newly reactivated selective service system. Iranian students who were compelled to check in with immigration officials pursuant to an executive order issued by President Carter were also experiencing the scope of regulatory power that protecting national security provides. The internment of Japanese-American citizens, seizure and operation of industries during World War II, loyalty oaths, security checks, and countless other regulatory actions have been based on the national defense powers. Any regulation based on national security grounds is almost unchallengeable from a constitutional perspective.

Less obvious than these examples are the plethora of regulations that have been promulgated in connection with grants and contracts to provide goods and services to the Defense Department (DOD). In one year DOD let 10.4 million contracts for a total value of $46 billion.[8] Just like recipients of government benefits, contractors also have to accept regulation as part of the package in dealing with government, and the regulations come not only from the contracting agency but also from the Office of Federal Contract Compliance, the Merit System Protection Board, the Office of Management and Budget, and the General Accounting Office (GAO). The extent of these regulations is well illustrated by HEW, which as contractor equaled the Defense

Department. For its 330 programs which involved contracts, HEW had issued over 12,000 pages of regulations.[9]

Other specific provisions in the Constitution have provided the base for various other regulatory agencies, for example, the power to establish a uniform rule of naturalization is the basis for the existence of the Immigration and Naturalization Service. However, the three most important bases of regulatory authority are the ones just discussed. Singly and in combination they provide full constitutional authority for the vast bulk of governmental regulatory activities. The Constitution neither forbids nor discourages regulatory activity; it fully authorizes such activity as a legitimate method of achieving specified ends and carrying out the delegated and inherent powers of government.

Having established the constitutional basis of regulatory power, the next step is to examine the major constitutional, legal, and political limits on that power and its exercise. General constitutional principles, such as nondelegation of powers, separation of powers, and rule of law, are frequently invoked as prohibitions against or at least as severe restrictions on the permissible extent of administrative regulatory power. Chapter 2 examines the role that these principles have played in setting limits on administrative power. Chapter 3 discusses some specific constitutional provisions which constitute active and viable restraints on administrative action. In chapter 4 the major statutory restrictions on administrative procedure will be covered. Finally, chapter 5 examines the constraints imposed on the agencies by their political environments.

NOTES

1. *Munn v. Illinois*, 94 US 113 (1877), p. 126.
2. *Gibbons v. Ogden*, 9 Wheaton 1 (1824).
3. *United States v. Darby*, 312 US 100 (1941).
4. *Wickard v. Filburn*, 317 US 111 (1942).
5. Jerry L. Mashaw, Charles Goetz, Frank Goodman, Warren Schwartz, Paul Verkuil, and Milton Carrow, *Social Security Hearings and Appeals* (Lexington, Mass.: D. C. Heath, 1978), p. xi.
6. *United States v. Butler*, 297 US 1 (1936); *Steward Machine Co. v. Davis*, 301 US 548 (1937).
7. *Wyman v. James*, 400 US 309 (1971), p. 318.
8. Ira Sharkansky, *Wither the State?* (Chatham, N.J.: Chatham House Publishers, 1979), p. 111.
9. Ibid., p. 119.

Chapter 2

Constitutional Principles and Administrative Power

The Constitution provides not only the legitimate basis for the exercise of regulatory powers; it also is one of the major sources of limitations on those powers. These limitations fall into two major classifications: underlying, if unspecified, principles which permeate the entire Constitution and specific provisions which clearly delineate the boundaries of permissible governmental action. This chapter will be concerned with the role that basic constitutional principles have played in structuring and limiting administrative power. Even though the substance of regulation may be authorized by the Constitution, a major line of argument directed against the exercise of that power by administrative agencies has been that it violates underlying constitutional concepts. While all but the most unrelenting of laissez-faire theorists would concede that Congress may, based on the commerce power, decide that the railroads should be restricted to charging "just and reasonable rates," whether Congress may authorize the Interstate Commerce Commission to determine and define precisely what a just and reasonable rate is, investigate to ensure that railroads are in fact following its guidelines, try and fine violators of those guidelines, and force some but not all railroads to roll back rates is considerably more controversial. Opponents of regulation have argued that to grant such powers to the ICC or any other administrative agency violates three basic principles of the Constitution: the nondelegability of delegated powers, separation of powers, and the rule of law.

At least superficially, the opponents have a good case. Regulation does involve the delegation of legislative, judicial, and executive powers to administrative agencies; it does combine these powers in a single agency; and the agencies have tremendous discretion as to whether, how, and against whom to enforce the law. Until the late 1930s, the majority of cases in the area of administrative law were primarily concerned with challenges to the legitimacy of the administrative process based on one of these three principles. Gradually the courts found various ways to reconcile constitutional theory with administrative reality. The reconciliation was neither easy nor simple. How it was accomplished and the extent to which these principles currently limit administrative regulation will be explored in the following sections.

DELEGATION OF POWERS

One of the most frequently raised constitutional objections to administrative regulatory power has been the doctrine of nondelegability of powers which holds that power delegated to one branch may not be redelegated to another. Although the prohibition against delegation of powers is often associated with separation of powers,[1] nondelegation is distinct from and possibly more fundamental than separation of powers,[2] since provisions against nondelegation could exist in any governmental structure.

One of the most commonly cited sources of the rule of nondelegation is the common law maxim *delegata potestas non potest delegari*: power that has been delegated originally may not be redelegated. In the private law of agency if an individual authorizes another to act as his or her agent, that individual would not want the agent to delegate that power to still another. When this is translated to the public sector it implies that since the people through the vesting clauses in Articles I, II, III of the Constitution delegated the legislative power to Congress, executive power to the presidency, and judicial power to the courts, none of these institutions may redelegate its power to any other institution. The Supreme Court agreed in 1831: "The general rule of law is, that a delegated authority cannot be delegated."[3]

Various other sources for the idea of nondelegation have been suggested. Robert Cushman argues that nondelegation is grounded in the ideal of due process of law; nondelegation prevents denial of due process resulting from unrestrained discretion.[4] Sotirios A. Barber argues that the rule of nondelegation can be found in the idea of constitutional supremacy: that delegations which are really abdications of power by Congress or the courts violate the constitutional agreement between the people and their government.[5] This formulation by Barber allows a wide scope of delegation as long as the ultimate legislative or judicial authority accepts accountability and responsibility for the actions.

Whatever its source, the concept of nondelegation of power has received a great deal of attention in administrative law. Many cases have been brought to the Supreme Court alleging that regulatory actions violate the rule of nondelegation. As noted earlier, the first Congress passed laws which delegated rule-making authority to the executive, and the Supreme Court found ways to uphold these and later laws conferring legislative and judicial authority on executive agencies. Yet the maxim against delegation remained strong. In 1892, Justice Harlan of the Supreme Court asserted, "That Congress cannot delegate legislative power . . . is a principle universally recognized as vital to the integrity and maintenance of the system of government ordained by the Constitution."[6] This inflexible statement against any delegation was inaccurate in 1892, and with the expansion of administrative regulatory power in the twentieth century, is even more inaccurate today. Faced with a theory–necessity conflict the Court has almost always permitted delegation of both adjudicatory and rule-making power. Most of the cases alleging that regulation constitutes a violation of delegation of powers that have reached the Supreme Court have dealt with the rule-making authority of agencies. The Court has consistently upheld such delegation as long as it could be justified on the basis of one of six theories: named contingency, filling in the details, delegation with meaningful, meaningless, or no standards, and finally, delegation in contravention of legislative standards.

(A) **Named Contingency:** "The earliest and logically the most restrictive form of delegation permitted by the federal courts was the power to declare the facts on which the operation or suspension of congressional policy was contingent."[7] This "named contingency" method of permitting administrative agencies to exercise delegated powers originated in the 1813 case of *The Brig Aurora v. United States*,[8] and was reiterated in the case of *Field v. Clark*,[9] the only two cases in the nineteenth century involving delegation that reached the Supreme Court. The *Aurora* case involved the attempt by the United States to remain neutral in the Napoleonic Wars between England and France while protecting American ships and sailors from seizure by both belligerents. The Non-Intercourse Act of 1809 specified that an embargo was to be placed on British and/or French commerce after the President determined and proclaimed that one or both failed to respect American neutrality. The *Aurora* tried to run the embargo, was captured, and its cargo condemned. The owner challenged the sentence on the grounds that the presidential proclamation had been authorized by an unconstitutional delegation of legislative power to the President. The Supreme Court disagreed and upheld the government. The opinion recognized that Congress had provided that if a specified set of facts—a "named contingency"—which Congress had identified occurred, then the law passed by Congress would go into effect. This retained the legislative power within the Congress. In *Field v. Clark*, the Court relied on *The Brig Aurora* to uphold Congress's authorization to the President to suspend favorable tariff rates for other nations when the President determined that the specific nation was imposing unequal duties on American agricultural products. Again the Court held that the President had no legislative power but only the power to ascertain the existence of a particular fact and issue a proclamation to that effect: "Legislative power was exercised when Congress declared that the suspension should take effect upon a named contingency."[10]

Although named contingency is in many respects the most restrictive type of delegation, in recent years Congress has tended to limit its use, to impose strict reporting requirements on actions taken by the executive pursuant to such delegations, and to subject those actions to legislative veto. For example, historically Congress had permitted almost unrestricted power to the President to determine and proclaim the existence of national emergencies. Once the President had determined the existence of an emergency and issued a proclamation, some 470 statutes permitted him to exercise broad and sweeping powers to regulate the economy, ration consumer goods, impose censorship, and control transportation and communications facilities. Finally, in 1976 Congress restricted this sweeping delegation of powers. The National Emergencies Act of 1976 terminated all existing states of emergency, abolished most emergency statutes, and provided that although the President could proclaim a national emergency, Congress could terminate it by concurrent resolution. All rules and regulations issued during the emergency must be reported to Congress. Similarly, the 1979 Export Administration Act, used by President Carter to embargo shipments of grain to the Soviet Union, specifies that the President may impose embargoes for "national security reasons" on goods "that make significant contributions to the enemy's military capability and would prove detrimental to U.S. security." Embargoes imposed for "foreign policy reasons" are to be determined after weighing six specified criteria, and if agricultural products are involved, the embargo is subject to congressional veto.[11] To the displeasure of some members of Congress, the grain embargo was imposed for "national security" rather than "foreign policy" reasons and was not subject to veto.

(B) "Filling in the details": Chief Justice John Marshall first described and upheld the power to "fill up the details" of statutes in an 1825 case involving delegation to federal courts.[12] Marshall argued that Congress, in dealing with subjects of less significance, may make general provisions and give power "to those who are to act under such general provisions to fill up the details." The theory was first applied to the administrative regulatory process in 1911 in *United States v. Grimaud*.[13] Congress had authorized the Secretary of Agriculture to protect the national forests by making rules and regulations governing the use of the forests. Violation of the rules was a crime. Grimaud was indicted for grazing sheep without the permit required by the regulations promulgated by the Secretary. He argued that Congress had unconstitutionally delegated its power to make laws and define crimes to an administrative official. The Court disagreed and upheld the delegation on the grounds that violation of the regulations "is made a crime, not by the Secretary, but by Congress." The administrator did not write the laws but was merely "filling in the details." This "subordinate legislation" was obviously necessary to apply the general congressional statutes to specific cases and thereby implement the congressional mandate.

(C) Meaningful Standards: As Congressional delegations increased in number and in scope beyond "named contingencies" or the "power to fill in details," the Supreme Court developed a third approach to the rule of nondelegability. This approach, which first appeared in the 1903 case of *Butterfield v. Stranahan*,[14] was to allow delegations as long as they were accompanied by meaningful standards:[11] "[D]elegation is permitted where the legislature sets 'standards' to delimit the scope of agency discretion."[15] Butterfield dealt with a 1897 act which authorized the Secretary of Treasury to set minimum purity and quality standards for imported tea. The Court upheld this delegation on the grounds that the Secretary was not legislating but only carrying out the expressed congressional purpose of excluding the lowest grades of tea:

> This, in effect, was the fixing of a primary standard, and devolved upon the Secretary . . . the mere duty to effectuate the legislative policy declared in the statute . . . [I]t does not, in any real sense, invest administrative officials with the power of legislation. Congress legislated on the subject as far as was reasonably practicable, and from the necessities of the case was compelled to leave to executive officials the duty of bringing about the result pointed out by the statute.[16]

This "standards" approach was reaffirmed in 1928 in *J. W. Hampton Jr. & Co. v. United States*,[17] which involved the delegation to the President of the power to adjust tariff rates to equalize production costs. Chief Justice (ex-President) Taft upheld the delegation: "If Congress shall lay down by legislative act an intelligible principle to which the [executive agency] . . . is directed to conform, such legislative delegation is not a forbidden delegation of legislative power." Since the "intelligible principle" or meaningful standard was present in the congressional policy of cost equalization, the executive could be delegated the power to effectuate the policy by the flexible tariff. This doctrine of "delegation with standards" is the accepted modern approach: "Congress, of course, does delegate powers to agencies, setting standards to guide their determination."[18]

(D) Meaningless Standards: In many instances the standards Congress has provided have been imprecise and provided little specific guidance to administrators. For example, the Interstate Commerce Commission is authorized to fix "just and reasonable" rates; the Securities and Exchange Commission is authorized to maintain a "fair and orderly market" and apply "just and equitable principles of trade"; and the Federal Communications Commission is to issue broadcast licenses in "the public interest, convenience or necessity." When the Supreme Court has had to review these vague general standards it has, with only two exceptions, held them to provide sufficient guidance. The Court sustained the Emergency Price Control Act of 1942 which delegated to the Price Administrator (of the Office of Price Administration, an executive agency) the power to establish maximum prices that were "generally fair and equitable" in his judgment. The Court held that Congress had sufficiently "laid down standards to guide the administrative determination.[19] In *Lichter v. United States*, the Court found "excessive profits" to be a sufficient standard[20] and in *Tagg Brothers & Moorhead v. United States*, it found "just and reasonable" to be adequate.[21]

In 1932, in *New York Central Securities Corporation v. United States*,[22] which dealt with the delegation to the Interstate Commerce Commission of the power to authorize railroad consolidation if it "will be in the public interest," the Court held this standard was adequate since it was based on years of ICC experience with regulation of the railroad industry. The Court again upheld that the public interest standard in regulation of the communications industry in *National Broadcasting Co. v. United States* "as concrete as the complicated factors for judgment in such a field of delegated authority permit."[23] The Court recognized in both instances the reality that Congress could give only very general direction to administrative agencies in new or complex regulatory fields.

In 1975, in response to the Arab oil embargo, President Gerald Ford placed a fee on imported oil. This dollar-per-barrel fee was designed to promote conservation and reduce dependence on foreign sources; its "chief purpose however, was to pressure Congress into passing Ford's energy bill."[24] In response to a challenge to the constitutionality of the "fee," Ford argued that the power had been delegated by the Trade Expansion Act, which authorized the President to "take such action, and for such time, as he deems necessary to adjust the imports of [the] article . . . so that . . . imports will not threaten to impair the national security." The Supreme Court in *FEA v. Algonquin Sng. Inc.*[25] upheld the President's action as authorized by the Act and its legislative history and concluded that however vague the standards, they "are clearly sufficient to meet any delegation doctrine attack."

(E) No Standards: Occasionally Congress provides no standards at all for the administrative regulatory agencies to follow, and the Supreme Court has upheld even this type of delegation of power. Congress authorized the Federal Home Loan Bank Board to promulgate regulations for the liquidation of mismanaged federal savings and loan associations but the authorizing statute contained no standard to guide the administrative power. In *Fahey v. Mallonee*,[26] the Court held that since banks had long been subject to federal regulations and no new crimes were created or regulated, standards were not an absolute necessity for the regulatory authority. In 1953, the Court upheld a regulation by the ICC which set new rules for the trucking business. The Court held that a provision in the authorizing statute which delegated the power to "administer, execute, and enforce all provisions of this part, to make all necessary orders in connection therewith, and to prescribe rules, regulations, and procedure for such administration" was adequate authorization for the agency.[27] *Arizona v. California*[28] sustained "the most sweeping possible delegation of power to the Secretary of Interior to apportion waters of the Colorado River."[29] The Court held that it was permissible for Congress to authorize the Secretary to formulate and supervise a plan for water use with no guidance but his expertise.

(F) Delegation in Contravention of Standards: Finally, on at least one occasion the Court not only permitted but required an agency to ignore legislative standards and make a decision based on its own expertise. The case involved an application of Mackay Radio and Telegraph Co. to provide international radiotelegraph service in competition with RCA. The Federal Communications Commission granted the permission on the basis of a provision in the Federal Communications Act of 1934 which stated that "all laws of the United States relating to unlawful restraints and monopolies . . . are hereby declared to be applicable to . . . interstate and foreign radio communications." RCA sued, arguing that the FCC should use its own expertise to make the decision. The Court held that the FCC should not depend entirely on its interpretation of national policy but make its own evaluation of the needs of the industry and the society. For the Commission to depend only on the congressional standard would be an abdication of "one of the primary duties imposed on it by Congress." The Commission was instructed to base its decision on "its own judgment in this matter, educated by experience, and supported by consonant findings," not on "an imagined national policy."[30]

Although the overwhelming majority of Supreme Court cases have upheld delegation, in two cases involving the New Deal the Supreme Court did strike down statutes on the grounds that they involved impermissible delegations of legislative power to the executive. Both cases were decided in 1935 and both dealt with President Franklin Roosevelt's attempts to improve the economy during the Depression through the National Recovery Administration (NRA), a New Deal agency created by the National Industrial Recovery Act of 1933. In the first case, *Panama Refining Co. v. Ryan*,[31] Congress had delegated to the President the power to prohibit the interstate shipment of "hot oil" produced in excess of state quotas. Although section 9(c) of the Act which authorized presidential action provided no standards at all; § 1 of the Act provided a list of standards including promoting "the general welfare by aiding cooperative action among industrial groups," facilitating management-labor unity, erasing unfair competitive practices, stimulating consumption, rehabilitating industry, and conserving natural resources. The government had not even taken the delegation challenge seriously; the then Solicitor General, Jackson, reported that "the government's brief of 227 pages and 200 more of appendix devoted only 13 pages to the subject."[32] The Supreme Court, however, ruled that the lack of standards in §9(c) and the failure of §1 to specify which standards to apply were an unconstitutional delegation of legislative power: "The Congress left the matter to the President without standard or rule, to be dealt with as he pleased."

The second case, the "sick chicken" case, *A. L. A. Schechter Poultry Corp. v. United States*,[33] concerned the promulgation of certain codes for the live poultry industry based on a congressional authorization to develop and enforce codes of fair competition for all industries. The Supreme Court, in a unanimous opinion, struck down the code-making authority of the NIRA as an unconstitutional delegation of legislative authority. The Court held that there were no standards in the Act and that it gave the President "unfettered discretion to make whatever laws he thinks may be needed." Congress had failed to perform its "essential legislative function" of establishing the "standards of legal obligations," and such a "sweeping delegation of legislative power" was unconstitutional. Even Justice Cardozo agreed that this "is delegation running riot" since the only standard was "fair competition."

Although *Panama Refining* and *Schecter* are not considered authoritative precedents, they have never been formally overruled and the nondelegability doctrine continues to be raised in cases challenging administrative regulatory authority. The federal courts, when reviewing these challenges, almost invariably attempt to determine if standards are provided.[34] Judges have long been aware that failure to provide standards limits the judicial reviewability of an administrative action, since they have no way of determining if an agency is adhering to legislative intent. Equally important, Congress has also come to realize that sweeping delegation undermines its powers and magnifies that of the executive. Eventually, Congress may discover that the legislative veto is likely to be less effective in controlling administrators than provision of meaningful standards in the authorizing legislation.

In at least one recent case the Supreme Court also strongly implied that some congressional powers, specifically the taxing power, may be nondelegable. In *National Cable Television Association v. U.S.*[35] the Court carefully weighed whether the charges imposed by the FCC, pursuant to Congressional authorization, were "fees" or "taxes," and decided they were fees since "it would be such a sharp break with our traditions to conclude that Congress had bestowed on a federal agency the taxing power."[36]

The distinction between imposing a fee and levying a tax may seem negligible but both Congress and the courts are capable of making that distinction and apparently agree that the taxing power should not be vested in the President. The Trade Expansion Act of 1962 authorized the President to impose quotas or fees on imports to adjust the supply of any commodity if the national security was threatened. In March 1980, the President announced that he was imposing an oil import fee of $4.62 per barrel of crude oil. The price increase was to be applied only to gasoline and would have resulted in a 10 cent/gallon increase in prices. The action was objectionable on several grounds and was immediately challenged in district court and Congress. One of the challenges was that it was an unconstitutional executive imposition of a tax which would bring in $10 billion in revenue in one year. The district court sidestepped that issue but disallowed the fee on the grounds that Congress had not delegated the President authority to pass-through the fee to only gasoline products.[37] Members of Congress met the question head-on: What the President had done was impose a tax and that was an impermissible overstepping of constitutional boundaries. In the first override of a Democratic presidential veto since 1952, Congress repealed the fee.

One other recent Supreme Court decision also indicated that at least one member of the current Court believed that there are limits on legislative delegation. In a concurring opinion in *Industrial Union Department, AFL-CIO v. American Petroleum Institute and Marshall v. American Petroleum Institute*,[38] Justice Rehnquist argued that Congress had improperly delegated to OSHA the power to determine whether to protect worker health and safety at all costs or to weigh the economic costs of such protection in industrial health regulations. From one perspective at least, Rehnquist's point is valid. The Occupational Safety and Health Act is purposefully vague. It authorizes the Secretary of Labor to set standards which most adequately assure, "to the extent 'feasible,' . . . that no employee shall suffer material impairment of health," from exposure to hazardous substances in the workplace.[39] Despite the repeated use of "feasible" and "feasibility" in the statute, nowhere is a definition provided nor are economic costs of the regulation mentioned. Congressional proponents and opponents of OSHA were decidedly reluctant about being charged with putting a price tag on human life. Amendments to the Act which would have required consideration of the costs of regulations were defeated in both houses.[40] Daniel Krivit, counsel for the House Subcommittee on Labor, which handled the OSH Act, explained that "the Act left it open and Congress did not face up to the issue of costs; although most of us believed costs would be a factor taken into account."[41] Wishing to avoid a sensitive and controversial issue, Congress left it to the discretion of the administering agency whether and how to weigh costs of health protection for workers. It was this that Rehnquist most strenuously resented:

> If we are ever to reshoulder the burden of ensuring that Congress itself makes the critical policy decisions, this is surely the case in which to do it. It is difficult to imagine a more obvious example of Congress simply avoiding a choice which was both fundamental for purposes of the statute and yet politically so divisive that the necessary decision or compromise was difficult, if not impossible to hammer out in the legislative forge.

Which is, of course, usually the major reason that Congress provides such broad and sweeping delegations to administrative agencies.

A third area in which nondelegation may still have applicability is in cases involving restrictions on individual personal rights. For example, delegation of unrestricted discretion in deciding whether to grant passports or parade permits has been held unacceptable. The unrestrained power to refuse to issue parade permits infringes on First Amendment rights and such a law "without narrow, objective, and definite standards to guide the licensing authority, is unconstitutional."[42] The authority of the Secretary of State to deny passport applications impinges on the "right to travel," a personal liberty protected under due process. The Court held that if "that 'liberty' is to be regulated, it must be pursuant to the lawmaking functions of the Congress . . . And if that power is delegated, the standards must be adequate to pass scrutiny by the accepted tests."[43] Over the objections of the minority, the Supreme Court majority again pursued this line of logic in 1976 in striking down a Civil Service Commission rule barring aliens from federal employment:[44]

> In other words, agencies still may not now be delegated uncontrolled discretion or granted unlimited power. What apparently has happened is that the delegation doctrine is now cloaked in the language of due process and measured by the procedural safeguards surrounding the agency's exercise of power. Agency performance rather than the legislative delegation is becoming the critical standard.[45]

As long as Congress retains the ultimate authority to rescind the authorizing legislation delegating the rule-making function and does not completely abdicate the field, the courts have upheld the delegation.[46]

The courts have been equally permissive in allowing the delegation of adjudicatory powers to administrative agencies. As early as 1810 the Supreme Court upheld the delegation of such power on the basis of the "quasi" concept.[47] As long as judicial review of agency action is available and the standard for illegal activity is reasonably specific, federal courts have sustained the delegation of adjudicatory power.[48] Further, they have permitted agencies to adjudicate cases involving both "public rights," rights created by Congress to protect the public in general, and private rights, those of one individual against infringement by another.[49] Pragmatism and judicial self-protection have played a large role in permitting this type of delegation, as was clear in a 1977 opinion upholding the power of OSHA to impose fines on violators:

> When Congress creates new statutory "public rights," it may assign their adjudication to an administrative agency . . . Congress is not required to choke the already crowded federal courts with new types of litigation.[50]

A related area which has concerned both courts and Presidents has been subdelegation: the transfer of power delegated by Congress to agency heads to subordinate agency officials. Statutes generally authorize "the Secretary," "the commission," or "the administrator" to issue rules, decide cases, and exercise other powers. In reality, of course, these top officials rarely have time to be actively involved in all the rules and decisions formulated by the agency. Both officially and unofficially a great deal of subdelegation occurs. The Supreme Court's original attitude was that subdelegation was impermissible; if presidential approval was required by statute, then the President must personally make the decision.[51] Similarly, the court refused to permit the Wage-Hour Administrator to delegate the power to issue a subpoena to regional directors.[52] Neither decision has been officially overruled by the Supreme Court. Congress settled the issue concerning presidential subdelegations by the passage of the Presidential Subdelegation Act of 1950 which permits the President to subdelegate his powers to any official appointed with the advice and consent of the Senate.[53] The lower federal courts have settled the issue for other types of subdelegation, without Supreme Court objection, so that subdelegation is allowed.

Presidents have been ambivalent about the issue of subdelegation. For the most part, they have recognized its necessity but have usually preferred that Congress delegate authority directly to them since this increases their flexibility and power over subordinates.[54] On the other hand, recent Presidents, responding to increasing criticism of government regulation, have viewed the tendency of department and agency heads to subdelegate rule-making authority to the point of abdication, with less favor. In March 1978, President Carter issued an executive order requiring, among other things, that agency heads must personally review all proposed regulations.[55] Reality quickly triumphed and in response to protests from agency heads, that portion of the executive order was rescinded with considerably less fanfare than had accompanied its imposition.

Delegation of Power at the State Level

The situation at the state level has to a certain degree paralleled that at the federal level. State legislatures, faced with the same complex problems as Congress, responded by delegating legislative and judicial powers to state regulatory agencies. State courts, however, were considerably less willing than federal courts to accept such delegation, and initially invalidated a large number of such delegations. Early cases asserted that legislative and judicial powers could not be delegated to administrative agencies[56]

Gradually, state courts were compelled to accept delegation as a practical necessity. Just as at the federal level, state courts developed certain "legal fictions" to justify these delegations. The most commonly utilized of those fictions was the quasi-powers concept and the requirement of legislative standards. In defining quasi-powers, state courts used certain "true tests" to "distinguish between the 'truly' legislative or judicial powers, which could not be delegated, and those merely 'administrative' powers which could be entrusted to agencies."[57] Those merely "administrative" powers came to encompass the whole range of legislative and judicial authority. In addition, state courts have insisted on "standards" to guide regulatory agencies in their exercise of delegated power. Cooper notes that some state laws have been struck down because they delegate authority to administrative agencies with no standards to guide the regulation of substantial personal or property rights. Similar to the federal courts, the state courts have accepted minimal, vague, or meaningless standards such as "the public interest" and "just and reasonable." Of course, the delegation of power from states to local governments has been upheld virtually without exception or, indeed, litigation.

Recently, some state courts have moved in the direction of deemphasizing the ritual demand for standards and have become more concerned with ensuring that the legislature provide procedural safeguards to protect individuals against arbitrary and capricious administrative action.[58] State legislatures have also attempted to improve their own control over how broadly delegated powers are exercised through the extensive use of legislative preview and review of administrative rules. Despite this, a strong case can be made for more stringent state court review of sweeping delegation. Unlike Congress, the majority of state legislatures are part-time and only partially professionalized institutions. They have neither the time nor in most cases the capability of continuous oversight to determine how well administrative agencies adhere to legislative intent. Consequently, the safeguard of judicial scrutiny is especially important to protect against arbitrary use of administrative discretion and to ensure that administrative actions follow proper procedures.

SEPARATION OF POWERS

As has been indicated, administrative regulatory agencies have been vested with all three categories of governmental power: rule making (legislative), adjudication of specific cases (judicial), and enforcement (executive). Since separation of powers occupies a position in American political mythology as unassailable as the doctrine of nondelegability of power, such combination of functions in the agencies has also been repeatedly challenged as unconstitutional.

The Framers of the Constitution definitely agreed with the concept of separation of powers. As James Madison explained it in *The Federalist Papers*: "The accumulation of all powers, legislative, executive, and judiciary, in the same hands, whether of one, a few, or many, and whether hereditary, self-appointed, or elective, may justly be pronounced the very definition of tyranny."[59] However, as was true with nondelegation, the Constitution does not explicitly deal with the meaning or necessity of separation of powers. The concept is implied by the grants of power in Articles I, II, and III. Article I begins, "All legislative powers herein granted shall be vested in a Congress of the United States . . ." Article II states, "The executive power shall be vested in a president . . .," while the third Article states, "The judicial power of the United States shall be vested in one supreme court, and in such inferior courts . . ." Theoretically, one might conclude that the Constitution demands a rigid division of power: *all* legislative powers in Congress, *all* executive powers in the presidency, and *all* judicial powers in the courts. In reality this is not the case. As Madison remarked in Federalist #47 referring to the theoretical progenitor of the necessity of separation of powers, Montesquieu: he "did not mean that those departments ought to have no *partial* agency in, or no *control* over the acts of each other. His meaning, as his own words impart . . . can amount to no more than this, that where the *whole* power of one department is exercised by the same hands which possess the *whole* power of another department, the fundamental principles of a free constitution, are subverted."[60] Instead, the Constitution provides for a mixture and blending of powers among the branches. The President, for example, possesses a veto over legislation and also exercises judicial power in granting reprieves and pardons and nominating judges. Congress must consent to executive treaties and appointments, sets up agencies, and has the power to establish the lower federal courts and regulate appellate jurisdiction of the Supreme Court. The judiciary may declare either executive or legislative actions unconstitutional, interprets laws, and reviews administrative agency cases. From the very beginning, the United States has not had a rigid separation of powers but rather "separate institutions sharing powers."[61]

The blending of power in administrative agencies can be traced back to the passage of three laws in the first session of the first Congress.[62] One initiated benefits to veterans and provided that disabled veterans should be paid pensions "under such regulations as the President of the United States may direct," thus granting rule-making power to the executive branch. The other two statutes dealt with the administration of customs duties and vested adjudicatory powers in the hands of port collectors who were authorized to decide the amount of duties payable.[63] The administrative regulatory process unquestionably combines executive, legislative, and judicial functions within one agency.[64]

Despite this, a challenge to administrative power today as a violation of separation of powers would be highly unlikely to be upheld in the federal courts. The courts have long since recognized and accepted the necessity of the mixing of functions in the agencies if government is to operate effectively or to survive at all. Although the courts have not formally abandoned the ideal of separation of powers, they have not found it to be a real limit on the administrative regulatory process and have developed two general methods of allowing the agency to exercise all three functions: the use of the "quasi" concept and the "shared powers" principle.

Rather than describing the agencies' powers as legislative or judicial, the Court has characterized them as "quasi-legislative" or "quasi-judicial."[65] The concept goes back at least to 1810 and to Chief Justice John Marshall. When the 1789 statutes which vested adjudicatory authority in port customs collectors were challenged as a violation of separation of powers Chief Justice Marshall upheld their constitutionality since the port collector was "only" a "quasi-judge."[66] Various later cases also upheld the exercise by agencies of rule-making or adjudicatory powers on the basis of the "quasi" concept.[67] The Court reemphasized this understanding in the 1935 case of *Humphrey's Executor v. United States*,[68] in upholding congressional restriction of presidential power to remove commissioners of the FTC except for cause. The Court noted that the Commission was not primarily an executive agency but "was predominantly quasi-judicial and quasi-legislative."

This legal fiction has not always pleased critics of the administrative process or Supreme Court Justices, as is evident in this dissenting opinion filed by Justice Jackson:

> They [administrative bodies] have become a veritable fourth branch of the Government, which has deranged our three-branch legal theories much as the concept of a fourth dimension unsettles our three-dimensional thinking. Courts have differed in assigning a place to these seemingly necessary bodies in our constitutional system. Administrative agencies have been called quasi-legislative, quasi-executive or quasi-judicial, as the occasion required, in order to validate their functions within the separation-of-powers scheme of the Constitution. The mere retreat to the qualifying 'quasi' is implicit with confession that all recognized classifications have broken down, and 'quasi' is a smooth cover which we draw over our confusion as we might use a counterpane to conceal a disordered bed.[69]

The distinction between "quasi" and the real thing that the federal courts have ascertained may not be apparent to the subjects of regulatory enforcement. As Bernard Schwartz notes, when a trucker is convicted of violating an ICC rule on safety precautions in transporting explosives, he may have violated only a *"quasi-law,"* but "we may be certain they do not incarcerate him in a *quasi*-cell."[70] Similarly when a person is committed to a mental institution, there is little "quasi" about the straitjacket, and an illegal alien detained and preemptorily trucked to the Mexican border by INS is unlikely to grasp the fine distinction between quasi-arrest and police arrest. Similarly, were the Federal Trade Commission and the Federal Communications Commission to succeed in their attempt to promulgate regulations to limit or eliminate advertising on children's television, the network revenue lost as a result of these quasi-laws would not be measured in quasi-dollars.

The second legal doctrine developed to reconcile the conflict between administrative necessity and constitutional theory is the concept of shared powers. Several Supreme Court justices have recognized that American government in both theory and practice is one of separate institutions sharing power. This is based on the constitutional mixing of legislative, judicial, and executive functions in the system of checks and balances, historical practice, and the necessity for regulatory agencies to possess elements of all three functions. Justice Jackson noted in 1952: "In designing the structure of our Government and dividing and allocating the sovereign power among the three coequal branches, the Framers of the Constitution sought to provide a comprehensive system, but the separate powers were not intended to operate with absolute independence."[71] The Supreme Court in 1977 rejected ex-President Nixon's constitutional claim in his attempt to regain control over his presidential papers as resting upon the "archaic view of the separation of powers as requiring three airtight departments of government."[72] The Court, using this idea of sharing of powers, has upheld the exercise of legislative and judicial powers by administrative regulatory agencies as long as some higher authority remained as a check on that power.

Recently, the theory of separation of powers has been used to challenge the legitimacy of the increasing use of legislative vetoes over federal regulations. From the perspective of the executive branch, separation of powers requires that the actual administration of policy be exclusively an executive function and that rule making is an essential part of this policy implementation. The legislative veto injects the Congress into the details of administration and consequently "infringes on the Executive's constitutional duty to faithfully execute the law."[73] Somewhat ironically, the executive's other major constitutional objection to such vetoes invokes the theory of shared powers:

> They also authorize congressional action that has the effect of legislation while denying the President the opportunity to exercise his veto. Legislative vetoes thereby circumvent the President's role in the legislative process.[74]

The continuing debate over these vetoes illustrates both the complexity of the administrative process and the rhetorical and legal viability of the separation of powers doctrine.

Separation of Powers at the State Level

The status of separation of powers as a limit on state and local administrative agencies is similar to its federal status, even though many state constitutions explicitly require a strict separation of powers. For example, Maryland's constitution states:

> That the Legislative, Executive and Judicial power of Government ought to be forever separate and distinct from each other; and no person exercising the functions of one of said Departments shall assume or discharge the duties of any other.

And the Constitution of Massachusetts provides:

> In the government of this Commonwealth, the legislative department shall never exercise the executive and judicial powers, or either of them: The executive shall never exercise the legislative and judicial powers, or either of them: The judicial

shall never exercise the legislative and executive powers, or either of them: to the end it may be a government of laws and not of men.

These requirements of a rigid separation of powers have led state courts to resist the uncontrolled exercise of all powers by state and local regulatory agencies, particularly if there is a concentration of power so great as to threaten the independence of other departments of government or if there is unreviewable finality of administrative decision in rule making or adjudication.[75] For example, a 1962 Illinois case held the exercise of judicial power by tax agency invalid because courts were excluded from any review.[76]

For the most part, however, state courts have recognized and accepted the need for combined powers in regulatory agencies. As far back as 1895 a California court upheld the exercise of legislative power by an administrative official,[77] and more recently a Connecticut court upheld the authority of a dental commission to investigate, prosecute, and adjudicate charges against dentists charged with unprofessional conduct.[78] The state judiciaries' recognition of the necessity of a combination of powers within state regulatory agencies developed in a manner similar to that at the federal level. Most state courts recognize that in order to function effectively administrative agencies must exercise legislative and adjudicative powers. As long as there remain safeguards against abuse, the courts have upheld the combination of powers in administrative agencies.

Separation of powers remains relevant in discussions of American government because it continues to serve one primary purpose: to prevent all powers from being concentrated in one institution or one person. The administrative regulatory process does not subvert this concept of separation of powers. "The very fact that administrative agencies today are permitted to perform all the functions of government indicates that the courts have seen no constitutional objection to such a combination of legislative, judicial, and executive power in the hands of one branch, provided basic controls exist through congressional and judicial surveillance."[79]

RULE OF LAW VERSUS ADMINISTRATIVE DISCRETION

One final general constitutional principle which has continuing relevance for administrative action is the concept of "rule of law." Although nowhere explicitly defined in the document, the Constitution and the American legal system are founded on the rule of law, the belief that government should be one of "laws and not of men." This is evident in the whole idea of a *written* Constitution, a document containing the fundamental rules of governance which limits the arbitrary exercise of power by an individual or any institution. As Fredrick A. Hayek stated, the principle of rule of law "means that government in all its action is bound by rules fixed and announced beforehand—rules which make it possible to foresee with fair certainty how the authority will use its coercive powers in given circumstances and to plan one's individual affairs on the basis of this knowledge."[80] The expectation is that those announced and written laws will be uniformly interpreted, uniformly applied, and uniformly enforced. All persons should be treated equally and administrators should be strictly limited in performing the functions assigned to them by the legislature.

Unfortunately, this theoretical ideal again directly conflicts with administrative reality and the necessity for administrative discretion: allowing administrators to decide if, when, how, and against whom the laws and rules will be enforced. This administrative discretion is magnified when the legislature provides no or vague, meaningless standards which permit and require that administrators themselves must determine the substance and applicability of the laws. Choice is the essence of discretion and discretion is the essence of administration.[81]

Frequently overburdened, understaffed, and underfunded, administrators must make choices as to how to allocate their resources. For example, the Federal Trade Commission in 1978 had 1,662 employees, a budget of $58 million, and responsibility for enforcing a wide conglomeration of statutes across the entire spectrum of the American economy. In the single area of policing deceptive advertising, the FTC receives over 13,000 complaints a year. Obviously, not all 13,000 can be rigorously investigated; of those that are, not all can be taken through the formal adjudicatory process. Instead the FTC picks and chooses which complaints to investigate, and after investigation decides on the nature of enforcement action to be taken. Almost invariably that action will be informal with the initial complainant being omitted from the settlement negotiations. The business will be given the choice of accepting the informal settlement or facing a long, costly formal procedure.

In 1976, in response to nationwide consumer complaints, the FTC launched a secret probe against one of the largest debt collection firms in the United States, National Accounting Systems. In other words, it chose one company out of many possible "targets" to be investigated. As a result of the investigation, the FTC presented National Accounting Systems with two choices: (a) sign a consent agreement, by which the company would admit no wrongdoing but nevertheless would agree not to repeat the behavior under penalty of fines and formal action, or (b) proceed through a full FTC adjudicatory hearing and be liable to the full penalties of the law.

The extent of FTC discretion in this case was not limited to selecting which firm to move against and what type of settlement to offer. Even more important was its choice of deciding that the behavior engaged in was illegal and that it had jurisdiction over that behavior. Since Congress did not specifically provide the FTC with such authority until October 1977, both of those decisions were subject to debate, if not legal challenge. Although the FTC asserted authority under the Truth in Lending Act, it had issued no regulations on debt collection practices nor did that Act mention such practices. Further, when NAS signed the consent agreement, the FTC announced that the terms of that agreement would be applicable to the entire industry, again exercising discretion to bypass the rule-making process.

Discretion, then, is the leeway an administrator has, because of the imprecise nature of authorizing statutes or regulations, to make individual decisions on interpretation, application, and/or enforcement of the law. Discretion is not only necessary, but is beneficial in a society that believes in the concept of "individualized justice." Without discretion laws could not deal equitably with the unique facts and circumstances presented by specific cases: It could not treat unequals unequally. Should a small business operating on an extremely narrow financial margin and without any recorded accidents affecting worker safety be treated the same as a major, high-profit industry, such as the chemical industry with an extensive track record of both industrial accidents and industrially induced health problems for workers? The ability to provide differential responses to these situations requires that the legislature permit administrators and courts considerable discretion in implementing the law. Discretion is a major source of creativity and innovation in government and law since it allows administrators to experiment in a relatively inexpensive fashion to achieve improvements in implementation of public policy

Congress has recognized the reality of discretion both in the general language of delegating statutes ("fair and reasonable," "public convenience and interest," etc.) and in the Administrative Procedure and Federal Tort Claims Acts. The APA, §701(a), specifically exempts actions "committed to agency discretion" from judicial review, and the Federal Tort Claims Act exempts claims arising from performance of discretionary functions.

Discretion is not an unmixed blessing. The same discretion that permits the FTC to protect harassed debtors also permits inspectors of the Bureau of Mines to allow safety violations to continue with the result that the United States has one of the highest mining industry accident and fatality rates in the world. Discretion means that some laws will go unenforced: Some of the guilty will escape unscathed, and others will, through informal settlement, avoid the full penalties that the law provides. Some, however, will not escape, and the law will have been nonuniformly interpreted, enforced, and applied.

Until recently, federal courts had little to say concerning administrative discretion, particularly selective enforcement or nonenforcement. Congress had statutorily foreclosed review of most discretionary actions and even where not foreclosed the courts had shown little enthusiasm for such cases. In 1962, the Supreme Court held that the decision of a prosecutor to prosecute one individual but not others allegedly guilty of the same behavior was constitutional:[82] "The conscious exercise of some selectivity in enforcement is not in itself a federal constitutional violation."[83] Unless the selective enforcement decision was based on some invidious, discriminatory classification such as race or religion the Court found it permissible. One of the lower federal courts stated the need and permissibility even more clearly in affirming the discretionary power of the Attorney General:

> To say that the United States Attorney must literally treat every offense and offender alike is to delegate to him an impossible task; of course this concept would negate discretion. . . . It is not the function of the judiciary to review the exercise of executive discretion whether it be that of the President himself or those to whom he has delegated certain of his powers. . . . The Constitution places on the Executive the duty to see that the laws are faithfully executed and the responsibility must reside with that power.[84]

In the early 1970s, some court decisions indicated an increasing interest in reviewing discretionary actions. The statutory justification for doing so was §706(2)(A) of the APA which is somewhat inconsistent with §701(a): §706 permits the courts to set aside an action found to be "arbitrary, capricious, or an abuse of discretion." In *Dunlop v. Bachowski* (1975),[85] the Supreme Court held that the decision of the Secretary of Labor on whether to bring action to set aside the results of a union election following complaint by a union member was reviewable, and the Secretary must provide a statement of reasons for his decision so that the reviewing court could determine whether it was arbitrary or capricious. Lower federal courts also required the Secretary of Agriculture to supply reasons for his refusal to suspend registration to DDT under the Federal Insecticide, Fungicide and Rodenticide Act.[86] The impact of these cases appears to have been limited, however, and for the most part federal administrative decisions not to take action are unchallengeable.

Administrative Discretion at the State Level

This situation is duplicated at the state and local level and may involve even more serious deviations from rule of law. The bulk of actual policy enforcement in this country is done or not done at those levels. As Davis points out, the police—"all 420,000 of them"—are administrators and the discretionary powers they possess are enormous.[87] In reality, it is the individual police officer and police departments that determine the actual scope and content of criminal behavior in our society, and, again, it is the decision to enforce or not enforce that is crucial and unreviewable. The same is true for noncriminal policy implementation: The day-to-day actions of line administrators in individual situations ultimately determine what policy is. The spiraling impact of discretion at federal, state, county, and individual employee levels on welfare or employment administration, for example, raises the question as to whether these programs are in any meaningful sense national programs.

For state programs primarily, the problems may be even more serious. State legislatures are more likely than Congress to delegate powers in a casual fashion with no description or record of legislative intent to guide administrators. In some states, at least, procedural requirements for even nondiscretionary agency actions are inadequate or lacking.[88] For the state courts the problem "has been to discover a method of reconciling the practical necessity of granting broad measures of discretionary power to administrative agencies with the inexorable imperative, demanded by the Rule of Law, that adjudicated cases be decided on the basis of general principles and standards known to the parties and applicable to all cases."[89]

Even though they have recognized the need for discretionary authority, state courts have intervened when they considered the rule of law to be endangered:

> In cases of demonstrated need, they have interposed their authority to insist on minimal guarantees of the right of individuals to be notified and to be heard before an administrative order is entered against them. They have insisted on certain requirements of fair procedure. They have accorded a measure of judicial review—somewhat broader, on the whole, than that commonly available in the federal courts—to set aside administrative action which violates constitutional or statutory provisions, which is without evidentiary support, or which is arbitrary or capricious.[90]

Reconciling the Irreconcilable?

Obviously there is tremendous tension between the ideal of rule of law and administrative discretion. Similarly, the ideal of individualized justice is in conflict with rule of law. No matter how skillfully and carefully drafted laws may be, they can never take full account of the myriad and unpredictable circumstances in which they will be applied. To ensure flexibility and fair treatment of different individuals in different circumstances administrative discretion is essential, and when legislators will not or cannot establish clear guidelines and priorities administrative discretion is inevitable. What quite justifiably alarms many critics is that there may be too much uncontrolled and unreviewable discretion committed to administrative agencies, and these critics have sought ways to alleviate the tension between the ideal and the reality.

There are three major approaches to controlling administrative discretion: judicial, legislative, and administrative. Discretionary actions could be made subject to strict judicial scrutiny and courts assigned the task of ensuring that equal justice under the law is rigorously followed by administrative agencies. Although this alternative has merit, it also has serious and negative implications which are most obvious in the area of selective enforcement. If the courts were given the power to compel the FTC, for example, to enforce all of the statutes under its jurisdiction against all offenders, the FTC would be compelled to admit that it lacks the resources to do so. The Court would then be faced with some rather unappealing alternatives: order the FTC to do so under penalty of contempt of court citation, order the FTC not to enforce anything against anybody (equal justice), or order Congress to provide the FTC with the necessary resources. The first alternative could result in imprisoning the entire staff of the FTC, which would accomplish nothing; the second alternative would penalize consumers and fair competitors and businesses and reward the largest and worst of the offenders; and the third alternative assigns to the courts a function that is so political and basic to government that it would warp and destroy the entire concept of representative and constitutional government.

A more constitutional, but perhaps just as impractical, solution is for the legislatures to limit discretion by providing administrators with clearer, more specific legislative standards, including priorities for enforcement in situations of scarce resources. This, after all, is one of the basic functions of an elected legislature and the problem with implementing this alternative is neither legal nor constitutional but rather political and pragmatic. One of the major reasons statutes are so vague, resources so limited, and priorities so unclear is that legislators, state and federal, have sought to alleviate the political consequences of making controversial choices by stating their decisions in broad language which alienates as few individuals and groups as possible, leaving the tough and unpleasant chore of specifically applying these decisions to administrators. After all, legislators are elected; administrators, for the most part, are not. Legislators prefer to take the credit for passing laws that please many and displease as few as possible, and vagueness helps satisfy this preference. Administrators have discretion and in many cases job security so they can handle the tough choices with fewer negative repercussions. Unfortunately, legislators, and Congress in particular, are equally reluctant to establish priorities, for this again involves making choices that are sure to displease some groups. The legislative veto partially accomplishes this desire for greater legislative control but at considerable cost to the ideal of rule of law. Administrative regulations are of low public and political visibility and they do exemplify administrative discretion at its peak. The veto allows legislators to take the credit for passing laws that have broad and/or vocal support and to nullify enforcement of those laws if any powerful interest objects. The result is not particularly compatible with the quest to ensure equitable and enthusiastic enforcement of the law against all offenders great and small.

The third alternative is to require the administrators to limit their own discretion by requiring them to establish their own priorities and standards. This solution is appealing but not particularly realistic either. Administrators may not be elected but they are highly political. Their professional survival depends not on votes from the electorate but on votes from the legislature on authorizing and appropriating statutes. Political rhetoric to the contrary, they are just as responsive to negative pressure as the legislators. For the dedicated administrator, vagueness is the single aspect of the entire system that permits the greatest accomplishments in pursuance of the agency mission and helps ensure personal survival. While many police chiefs may believe that enforcement of laws dealing with victimless crimes—gambling, prostitution, minor drug offenses—is an unwise use of departmental resources and may unofficially not rigorously enforce such laws, only a police chief who no longer values his job would officially promulgate regulations requiring patrolmen to ignore violations of such laws to concentrate on other crimes. As in life in general, some things in administration are better left unsaid. To spell out enforcement priorities is to encourage violation of those laws and rules that receive the lowest priorities; uncertainty is the administrator's greatest advantage and the violator's greatest disadvantage.

This of course does little to resolve the conflict between rule of law and administrative discretion, but the conflict in reality may be considerably less severe than critics have suggested. The grossest violations of uniform treatment are subject to legal challenge as violations of equal protection of the law; the courts do have and exercise scrutiny over these. The most politically offensive of such violations may be contested in the city council, legislature, or Congress. Finally, what so frequently is ignored is that administrators are not really any worse or any better than the population at large, and although empirical studies to support this are lacking, it is a safe guess to assume they have erred as many times to protect individuals as they have erred to protect or favor powerful interests. To view administrators as somehow different or more evil than Congressmen, judges, lawyers, or businessmen is to ignore a basic fact: In the words of a comic-strip character, "we have met the bureaucrats and they is us." If they err, and they do, they do so no more than politicians, judges, or college professors. If this is not satisfactory, then perhaps readers should consider that whoever told you life is supposed to be fair, lied.

CONCLUSION

Separation of power, nondelegability, and rule of law are fundamental constitutional concepts in the United States. They have not been, as we have seen, particularly relevant in restricting the growth or operation of the administrative regulatory process. Although they have been continually raised as objections to the power and procedures of administrative agencies, nonetheless Congress, state legislatures, and the courts have found ways of reconciling the realities of administration with constitutional theory. The result has been that these three concepts have not seriously restricted the growth of the regulatory process. They do, however, constitute boundaries, albeit at times imperceptible ones, on administrative practices.

Other aspects of the Constitution, specific provisions, have played a more meaningful role in restricting administrative power and behavior. The next chapter considers these more specific constitutional restrictions.

NOTES

1. See, e.g., Robert D. Cushman, *The Independent Regulatory Commissions* (New York: Oxford University Press, 1941), p. 427.

2. Sotirios A. Barber, *The Constitution and the Delegation of Congressional Power* (Chicago: The University of Chicago Press, 1975), p. 24. This volume is an excellent analysis of the doctrine of nondelegation. Much of the following discussion of the origin of the doctrine is derived from Barber.

3. *Shankland v. Washington*, 5 Pet. 390, 395 (U.S. 1931).

4. Robert F. Cushman, "The Constitutional Status of the Independent Regulatory Commissions," *Cornell Law Quarterly*, 24 (1938), 32.

5. Barber, *The Constitution and the Delegation of Congressional Power*, especially chapter 2.

6. *Field v. Clark*, 143 US 649, 692 (1892).

7. Barber, *The Constitution and the Delegation of Congressional Power*, p. 53.

8. 7 Cranch 382 (1813).

9. 143 US 649 (1892).

10. 143 US 649, 693.

11. Bob Livernash, "Congress Votes Four-Year Extension of Government Authority to Curb Exports," *Congressional Quarterly*, October 6, 1979 (vol. 37), p. 2220.

12. *Wayman v. Southard*, 10 Wheat. 1 (1925).

13. 220 US 506 (1911).

14. 192 US 470 (1903).

15. Glen O. Robinson and Ernest Gellhorn, *The Administrative Process* (St. Paul, Minn.: West Publishing Co., 1974), p. 39.

16. 192 US 470, 496 (1903).

17. 276 US 394 (1928).

18. *National Cable Television Assn. v. United States*, 415 US 336, 342 (1974).

19. *Yakus v. United States*, 321 US 414, 423 (1944).

20. 334 US 742, 746 (1948).

21. 280 US 420, 431 (1930).

22. 287 US 12, 16 (1932).

23. 319 US 190, 216 (1943).

24. Louis Fisher, *The Constitution between Friends* (New York: St. Martin's Press, 1978), p. 25.

25. 427 US 548, 559 (1976).

26. 332 US 245 (1947).

27. *American Trucking Association v. United States*, 344 US 298 (1953).

28. 373 US 546 (1963).

29. Robinson and Gellhorn, *The Administrative Process*, p. 103.

30. *FCC v. RCA Communications Inc.*, 346 US 86 (1953).

31. 293 US 388 (1935).

32. Robert H. Jackson, *The Struggle for Judicial Supremacy* (New York: Vintage Books, 1941), p. 92.

33. 295 US 495 (1935).

34. Glen O. Robinson and Ernest Gellhorn, *The Administrative Process*, 2d ed. (St. Paul, Minn.: West Publishing Co., 1979), p. 72.

35. 415 US 336 (1974).

36. James O. Freedman, *Crisis and Legitimacy: The Administrative Process and American Government* (Cambridge: Cambridge University Press, 1978), pp. 80–82.

37. Dale Tate, "President's Oil Import Fee Assailed in Congress and Court," *Congressional Quarterly*, May 17, 1980, p. 1307.

38. 445 US 607 (1980).

39. Section 6(6)5 of the OSH Act.

40. John Mendeloff, *Regulating Safety* (Cambridge: MIT Press, 1979), p. 22.

41. Quoted in Mendeloff, *Regulating Safety*, p. 21.

42. *Shuttlesworth v. Birmingham*, 394 US 147, 151 (1969).

43. *Kent v. Dulles*, 357 US 116, 129 (1958).

44. *Hampton v. Mow Sun Wong*, 426 US 88, (1976).

45. Robinson and Gellhorn, *The Administrative Process*, 1st ed., p. 105.

46. For a detailed discussion of this idea, see Barber, *The Constitution and the Delegation of Congressional Power*. He argues that "Congress may delegate to any agency . . . as long as its delegations are pursuant to choice among salient alternatives. Congress violates the rule of nondelegation when it deliberately evades its responsibility for choice no matter how it may delegate or to whom" (p. 49).

47. *Scott v. Negro Ben*, 6 Cranch 3 (1810).

48. *Sunshine Anthracite Coal Co. v. Adkins*, 310 US 381 (1940); *RFC v. Bankers Trust Co.*, 318 US 163 (1943).

49. Bernard Schwartz, *Administrative Law* (Boston: Little, Brown, 1976), pp. 60–63.

50. *Atlas Roofing Co. v. OSH Review Committee*, 430 US 442 (1976), at 455.

51. See Kenneth Davis, *Administrative Law and Government*, 2d ed. (St. Paul: West Publishing Co., 1975), p. 51.

52. *Cudahy Packing Co. v. Holland*, 315 US 357 (1942).

53. Davis, *Administrative Law and Government*, p. 51.

54. Richard Pious, *The American Presidency* (New York: Basic Books, 1979), p. 216.

55. Reprinted in *Congressional Quarterly*, April 15, 1978, p. 935.

56. For example, *Dowling v. Lancashire Ins. Co.*, 92 Wis. 63, 68, 65 N.W. 738, 31 I.R.A. 112 (1896): "That no part of the legislative power can be delegated by the legislature to any other department of the government, executive or judicial, is a fundamental principle in constitutional law, essential to the integrity and maintenance of the system of government established by the Constitution." See also *Whitten v. California State Bd. of Optometry*, 8 Cal. 2d 444, 65 p. 2d 1296, 115 A.L.R. 1 (1937); *Reid v. Smith*, 375 Ill. 147, 30 N.E. 2d 908, 132 A.L.R. 1286 (1940); e.g., *In re Opinion of the Justices*, 87 N.H. 492, 179 Atl. 344, 110 A.L.R. 819 (1935).

57. Frank E. Cooper, *State Administrative Law*, vol. 1 (Indianapolis: Bobbs-Merrill, 1965), p. 48. See his discussion of the tests and standards in chapter 3.

58. Kenneth Davis, *Administrative Law: Cases-Texts-Problems*, 6th ed. (St. Paul: West Publishing Co., 1977), p. 47.

59. *The Federalist Papers* (New York: Mentor Books, 1961), 47, p. 301.

60. Ibid., p. 302.

61. Richard E. Neustadt, *Presidential Power: The Politics of Leadership from FDR to Carter* (New York: Wiley, 1980), p. 26.

62. 1 Stat. 29 (1789); 1 Stat. 55 (1789); 1 Stat. 95 (1789).

63. Schwartz, *Administrative Law*, pp. 16–17.

64. For a good discussion of this mixture of functions, see Peter Woll, *American Bureaucracy* (New York: Norton, 1977), especially chapter 1.

65. *FTC v. Ruberoid Co.*, 343 US 470, 487 (1952), dissenting opinion.

66. *Scott v. Negro Ben*, 6 Cranch 3, 7 (U.S. 1910).

67. *The Brig Aurora*, 7 Cranch 382 (U.S. 1813), and *Butterworth v. Hoe*, 112 U.S. 50, 56 (1884), which recognized the exercise of "quasi-judicial functions."

68. 295 U.S. 602.

69. *FTC v. Ruberoid Co.*, 343 U.S. 470, 487 (1952), Jackson dissenting.

70. Schwartz, *Administrative Law*, p. 32.

71. *Youngstown Sheet & Tube Co. v. Sawyer*, 343 U.S. 579, 635 (1952), concurring opinion.

72. *Nixon v. Administrator of General Services*, 433 U.S. 425, 433 (1976).

73. Message to Congress, President Jimmy Carter, reprinted in *Congressional Quarterly*, June 24, 1978, p. 1624.

74. Ibid.

75. Cooper, *State Administrative Law*, vol. 1, p. 21.

76. *People ex rel. Isaacs v. Johnson*, 26 Ill. 2d 268, 186 N.E. 2d 346 (1962), cited in Cooper, *State Administrative Law*.

77. *In re Flaherty*, 105 Cal. 558 (1895).

78. *Ramanou v. Dental Commission*, 142 Conn. 44, Ill A. 2d q (1955), discussed in Cooper, *State Administrative Laws*, p. 25.

79. Woll, *American Bureaucracy*, p. 19.

80. Fredrick Hayek, *The Road to Serfdom* (Chicago: University of Chicago Press, 1944), p. 72.

81. Kenneth C. Davis, *Administrative Law Text* (St. Paul, Minn.: West Publishing Co., 1959), p. 25; see also his *Discretionary Justice: A Preliminary Inquiry* (Urbana: University of Illinois Press, 1971), and Jeffrey L. Jowell, *Law and Bureaucracy: Administrative Discretion and the Limits of Legal Action* (New York: Dunellen Publishing Co., 1975).

82. Edwin Tucker, *Administrative Law: Regulation and Enterprise and Individual Liberties* (St. Paul: West Publishing Co., 1975), p. 64.

83. *Oyler v. Boles*, 368 US 448, 456 (1962).

84. *Newman v. U.S.*, 382 F2d 479, 1967, quoted in Tucker, p. 64.

85. 421 US 560 (1975).

86. *Environmental Defense Fund v. Ruckelhaus*, 439 F2d 584 (D.C. Cr. 1971).

87. Davis, *Cases-Texts-Problems*, p. 496.

88. Cooper, *State Administrative Law*, p. 43.

89. Ibid., p 42.

90. Ibid., p. 44.

Chapter 3

The Federal Constitution: Meaningful Restrictions on Administrative Regulation

Although general constitutional principles have served as the grounds for recurring challenges to administrative regulatory power, they have been far less significant as limits on the administrative process than specific provisions of the Bill of Rights. As was indicated earlier, the Constitution was originally directed at the actions of legislators, judges, and chief executives and the extent of its applicability to administrative actions was unclear. As administrative agencies grew in number and significance, constitutional limits were gradually interpreted and made applicable to them. Today the Constitution serves as a major source of restrictions on administrative regulation and is an important aspect of the environment in which regulation at all levels of government is carried out.

In this chapter, three specific categories of constitutional restrictions will be considered: due process of law, equal protection, and "core constitutional rights." The realities and weaknesses of these restrictions will then be examined in terms of their application to the treatment and status of aliens within the United States.

DUE PROCESS

One of the most important constitutional limits on administrators at all levels of government is the requirement that they must follow "due process of law." The Fifth Amendment which restricts the federal government states that "No person shall . . . be deprived of life, liberty or property, without due process of law." The states are similarly bound by the Fourteenth Amendment: "nor shall any State deprive any person of life, liberty, or property without due process of law." Although the origins of due process go far back into English jurisprudence to the Magna Carta's "law of the land" in 1215, no precise definition has yet emerged from either legislative pronouncements or Supreme Court opinions, and its meaning is modified on an almost monthly basis.

Due process originated as a means to protect the accuracy of the fact-finding process in trials and gradually expanded to become a procedural protection of personal liberty against arbitrary government action.[1] Currently, there are two kinds of due process: procedural and substantive. Procedural due process deals with "how" the government acts: the procedures and methods by which it deprives a person of life, liberty or property. The content of the law is not of concern to procedural due process. Procedural review by the courts is limited in scope and is concerned only with ensuring that "fundamental fairness" and the essentials of justice have been followed by the government in its enforcement of a law.[2] Substantive due process, however, is concerned with the substance of a law: the "what" of governmental action. The impact of substantive due process is to withdraw "certain subjects from the full reach of governmental power regardless of the procedures used."[3] Under substantive review courts are concerned that the law itself or the government's action is reasonable and compatible with the Constitution. The concept that a court "employs to control the substance of legislation under the due process clause is that certain types of law go beyond any proper sphere of government activity."[4] This is a highly controversial role for a court to take since it substitutes judicial determination of public policy for both legislative and administrative judgment. From 1880 to 1937, the Court applied substantive due process primarily to protect the economic "liberty" of business enterprises by defining the term "person" in the Fifth and Fourteenth Amendments to include not only citizens and individuals but also corporations.[5] Since 1937, the·Court has shifted the emphasis to protection of individuals' "civil liberties" from governmental intrusion.

Although the great majority of administrative actions do result in depriving persons of life, liberty, and especially property, due process in administrative regulation has been primarily concerned with the procedural aspects of agency action. Courts will normally carefully scrutinize procedures followed by the agency and if they determine that proper procedures have been followed, will uphold the action. What constitutes proper procedures fluctuates constantly as the courts modify their interpretation of required due process on a case-by-case basis. For example, in 1975 the Supreme Court held that due process required that students be given "some kind of notice and afforded some kind of hearing" before public school administrators could suspend them for ten days.[6] But in 1976 the same court ruled that due process did not require an opportunity to be heard prior to administering corporal punishment to a student.[7] Thus even the most conscientious administrators find the concept of due process a troublesome one, especially since it is one of the most common grounds that courts use to strike down administrative action. Since there is no set definition of due process, administrators must rely on two major sources for guidance: legislative pronouncements and judicial interpretations.

The major legislative attempts to define the requirements for procedural due process for administrative actions are the Federal Administrative Procedure Act and state administrative procedure acts. These acts, designed to protect the rights of persons against arbitrary administrative action by regularizing procedures, will be discussed in greater detail in following chapters. The acts are general in scope; they specify procedures that almost all agencies in the executive branch must follow in their formal regulatory processes. In addition, Congress and the state legislatures also impose specific procedural requirements for certain agencies in the authorizing legislation that creates the agency and establishes the scope and nature of its responsibilities and powers.

As mentioned earlier, the courts consider due process as requiring "fundamental fairness" in administrative action and have interpreted this to require minimal standards of fairness which must be followed by administrators. These basic required standards include:[8]

1. *Notice*: "The fundamental principle of notice is that a man has a right to be alerted to activity that affects his interests."[9] All rules and regulations must be published openly in advance of their promulgation. All interested persons must be informed either personally or by publication of proposed actions that may result in an adverse effect upon them.

2. *Opportunity to be heard*: When an administrative action will result in the abridgement of a legal or constitutional right, the affected party must be granted a hearing before his/her rights are finally determined and must be permitted to appear personally and submit evidence. This evidence may be less "legalistic" than in judicial proceedings and "hearsay" and written evidence may be presented. As part of this process, fundamental fairness requires a reasonable opportunity to know the claims of competing parties, the right to counter these claims, and a decision based on substantial evidence in the record compiled at the hearing.

3. *The right to an impartial forum*: "Notice and the opportunity to present one's case will be meaningless if the decision or action which follows is made in a forum which is closed or prejudiced against consideration of the interest asserted."[10] This concept is at the heart of "due process"; administrative justice assumes that individuals' rights will be determined in a fair, impartial adjudicatory procedure. Due process also prohibits "ex parte" communications in these proceedings. This bars the deciding official from having any off-the-record contacts with interested parties before a decision has been handed down. In addition, the deciding official must be insulated from bias in other ways; that official must be free of conflicts of interest in the specific case and must be independent of political pressures through separation of the adjudicatory function from the other administrative functions.

These are only the minimal standards of due process and the concept is still evolving. Unfortunately for students and administrators, the courts are likely to continue to modify the requirements of due process as they must apply it to constantly changing situations, circumstances, and actions. Despite the uncertainty regarding its meaning, due process has a great impact on regulatory procedures. Administrators recognize that courts very carefully review the procedures they use and therefore carefully attempt to follow proper procedure. This has led to an emphasis (some would argue an overemphasis) on procedure in the regulatory process and to a "legalization" of administrative action. Having long since determined that courts tend to feel that only judicial-like procedures constitute "due" process, administrators have attempted to ensure that most of the trappings and symbols of the judicial process are present in the regulatory process. They have also tended to defer to lawyers' expertise in establishing their rules and procedures.[11] Since the primary concern of most courts in this area has been procedural due process, the "substance" of the action has frequently taken a back seat to the methods by which the action proceeds.

That concern has resulted in a situation where proceedings in a particular matter may drag on for months and sometimes years. (For example, the determination of the percentage of peanuts needed in peanut butter took the FDA nine and a half years.) Records of such cases occupy hundreds of pages as groups, individuals, and corporations take advantage of their due process right to be heard and present evidence. Much of the public criticism of "bureaucratic red tape" arises from the great care administrators take to follow proper procedures to the letter to protect their decisions from legal challenges. This has created one of the continuing dilemmas in the regulatory process: an apparent choice between either giving up certain procedural safeguards or accepting red tape, delays, and emphasis on the how rather than on the what. An unanswered and perhaps unanswerable question is whether this overlegalization, which has resulted from the application of due process to administrative regulation, is necessary to protect individual rights. Critics of overlegalization argue that certain rights may be more endangered than protected by the delays occasioned by the legalistic concept of due process. The dilemma is typified in the following question: Would we trade a "hasty"decision to terminate welfare payments to an improverished family for an "expeditious" decision of regulating an industry dumping wastes into a river? The dilemma may not be as irresolvable as it appears, if methods for protecting due process without overlegalization of the administrative process can be developed. Since the administrative regulatory process was not designed to replicate the judicial process, it may well be that there are more feasible forms of due process than judicial process. Some of these alternative forms will be examined later.

EQUAL PROTECTION

One of the strongest protections for individual liberties today is the constitutional requirement that all persons be accorded equal protection of the law. The ideal of "equality" has always been a basic component of American political beliefs even though that ideal has sometimes had to compete with the ideal of "liberty."[12] A logical derivative of the more general and unwritten concept of rule of law, equality under the law was made an explicit command by the equal protection clause of the Fourteenth Amendment which specifies "[N] or shall any State . . . deny to any person within its jurisdiction the equal protection of the laws."

As the discussion of due process indicated, the Fourteenth Amendment is applicable against the states. No other equal protection clause appears in the Constitution and it might seem that federal administrative agencies would not be bound by the concept of equal protection. However, the Supreme Court has held that, in most instances, the due process clause of the Fifth Amendment forbids the federal government from denying any person the equal protection of its laws.

The case which established that interpretation was *Bolling v. Sharpe*,[13] a companion case to *Brown v. Board of Education*.[14] Brown decided that state-required segregation of students in public schools on the basis of race violated the equal protection clause. *Bolling v. Sharpe* dealt with racial segregation in the public schools in the District of Columbia, which was a federal, not state, classification. The Court invalidated the federal practice on the basis that such racial segregation violated the due process clause of the Fifth Amendment since it deprived black students of liberty by impermissible methods. "[D]iscrimination may be so unjustifiable as to be violative of due process,"[15] and in view of the decision the same day in *Brown*, the Court recognized that racial discrimination by the federal government was unjustifiable. The Supreme Court has said that the same equal protection standards apply to both state and federal governmental actions: "Equal protection analysis in the Fifth Amendment area is the same as that under the Fourteenth Amendment."[16] However, some recent cases seem to indicate that "the Court will subject federal laws which burden aliens as a class to a more lenient standard of review because of unique federal interests in this area."[17] For the most part, however, the equal protection guarantee is generally identically applicable to both state and federal administrative actions.

"Review under both equal protection guarantees is always substantive in nature."[18] That is, unlike the due process guarantee, equal protection is not concerned with the procedures that administrators use but only with the results. The basic requirement of equal protection is that government must apply the law equally to all persons, treating similarly situated individuals in a similar manner. If the government, or one of its agencies, singles out (classifies) any identifiable group and subjects that group to different treatment from that accorded the rest of the population, it may be violating equal protection.

Almost every administrative action does single out groups for different treatment. Welfare recipients are treated differently from nonrecipients; the elderly are treated differently in social security administration; public employees are treated differently in labor relations; the wealthy are treated differently in income tax decisions by the Internal Revenue Service. The list of groups—including prisoners, Indians, and aliens—that are singled out for special treatment and the list of administrative actions—including business regulations, occupational licensing, and social welfare requirements which treat groups differently—is endless. The courts have held that for such classifications to be constitutional they must meet certain standards. Generally, the classification must be rational in the sense that the "singling out" of a class must be related to a legitimate administrative purpose: There must be a reasonable relationship between means (the classification) and ends (the purpose as defined by statute). If the classification results in the restriction of core constitutional rights of the groups singled out, the Court will require that the government demonstrate a compelling governmental interest as justification. Even if the government can demonstrate such an interest, however, the Court may still void the action if a "less drastic remedy," a method of accomplishing the government's purpose without violating the group's rights, is available.

The current meaning of equal protection has evolved mainly through court interpretation. Originally, the concept was used to protect the rights of blacks in the post-Civil War Period. During the laissez-faire era, which lasted from the 1880s until 1937, the Supreme Court utilized the clause to examine and sometimes to strike down economic classifications if they attempted to regulate business, since the "persons" in the equal protection clause also included corporations. However, in 1937 the Court changed with the New Deal and abandoned this type of active economic review, sustaining all economic classifications as long as they were related to a legitimate legislative end. The Court also began to scrutinize more carefully legislative and administrative classifications which affected individual liberties in order to determine if they passed muster under equal protection.

Currently, the courts apply four major criteria to determine if a classification is permissible and nonarbitrary:

1. *Clear basis*: There must be a clear basis for the classification. That is, there must be a readily understandable demarcation of those individuals included in or excluded from the specified group. Examples of this clear basis might include: aliens—based on noncitizenship; elderly—based on age; welfare—based on need; and income tax classes—based on income levels.

2. *Similar treatment*: Equal protection demands that persons in similar situations, with similar characteristics, be treated similarly. When administrative regulations classify individuals for different burdens or benefits, all "similar" individuals must receive those same burdens or benefits. Otherwise, the classification would be "underinclusive." One exception to this rule is if the basis for classification is numerical. For example, some regulations such as those of the Occupational Safety and Health Administration (OSHA) or Equal Employment Opportunity Commission (EEOC) affect business firms with "ten or more" employees yet do not apply to a firm with nine workers. Although the situation of these two businesses might appear to be identical, the Supreme Court has held that these regulations do not violate equal protection since the basis is a "numerical" one. Similarly, an individual who earns one dollar more a year than another individual may well be placed in a different income tax bracket and be treated in a somewhat different manner by the Internal Revenue Service.

3. *Different treatment*: A corollary to the similar treatment for similarly situated individuals rule is the requirement that persons in different situations should not be treated as if they were the same.[19] Treating "dissimilar" individuals in the same manner may also be grounds for concluding that an administrative classification is "arbitrary." This "overinclusiveness" of a classification may violate equal protection since it burdens some persons who are not similarly situated. Both of these situations, "overinclusiveness" and "underinclusiveness," constitute an arbitrary departure from rational classification. Before the courts can determine this, they must first determine if the purpose of the classification serves to advance some legitimate administrative purpose. "The courts must reach and determine the question whether the classifications drawn in a statute are reasonable in light of its purpose."[20] Consequently, courts use different standards of scrutiny for different types of statutes.

4. *Remedial legislation*: Not *every* somewhat arbitrary classification violates equal protection. If that classification is a component of "remedial" legislation, the courts have been less prone to invalidate it. In other words, government may

attempt at a particular time to alleviate only some problems; it is under no obligation to remedy *all* evils or problems at once. For example, opticians may be subjected to strict regulation as part of a legislative desire to protect consumers, while sellers of ready-to-wear glasses may be exempt from the regulations.[21] "Evils in the same field may be of different dimensions and proportions requiring different remedies. Or so the legislature might think. . . . Or the reform may take one step at a time, addressing itself to the phase of the problem which seems most acute to the legislative mind."[22] The Supreme Court has summed up this more lenient standard for remedial legislation in this way: "The State [is] not bound to deal alike with all . . . classes, or to strike at all evils at the same time or in the same way."[23] The government is therefore not obligated in this remedial area to provide the same to all persons, even though they may be similarly situated.

Courts judge the validity of administrative classification on the basis of whether they advance some legitimate governmental purpose. In most instances the standard of review is whether the classification was rationally related to the accomplishment of some legitimate purpose. This "minimum rationality" standard applies to cases involving most economic or social welfare legislation. The court, under this first general standard of review, will only require that the administrator or a legislature show that a rational relationship exists between the basis of classification (age, income, etc.) and the accomplishment of a legitimate governmental function (promotion of the general welfare, the regulation of interstate commerce, etc.). This is obviously a fairly easy relationship to demonstrate and the individual challenging the classification bears the burden of proving the classification invalid. The courts presume that such a governmental action is permissible. "It is enough that the State's action be rationally based and free from invidious discrimination."[24]

Classifications which involve "suspect" classes or which result in the abridgement of certain "fundamental" rights will be subject to "strict scrutiny" by the courts. This second standard of review is, in Professor Gunther's phrase, "strict" in theory and usually "fatal" in fact.[25] That is, courts are very suspicious of any classification infringing on fundamental rights or involving a suspect group, and the administrator bears the burden of proving that the challenged classification does not violate equal protection. In this type of classification, the administrator must show that the classification and the burden on rights is necessary to promote a *compelling* or overriding governmental interest (such as protection of the lives or property of that group or of society or preservation of the national security), "one whose value is so great that it justifies the limitation of fundamental constitutional rights."[26] The courts will *not* accept as a compelling interest the desire of an agency to "save money" or other "administrative convenience." Once a classification of this type is challenged, the courts will not defer to the decision of other branches of government but will play an active, independent role in determining whether the government has met the burden of proving the necessary relationship between the classification and a compelling interest. The justification for this judicial role was suggested by Justice Stone a number of years ago:

legislation which restricts those *political processes* which can ordinarily be expected to bring about repeal of undesirable legislation, [may] be subjected to more exacting judicial scrutiny under the general prohibitions of the Fourteenth Amendment than are most other types of legislation. [Citing cases involving restrictions of voting, speech, assembly] . . . [And] similar considerations [may] enter into the review of statutes directed at particular religious, . . . or national, . . . or racial minorities. [P]rejudice against discrete and insular minorities may be a special condition, which tends seriously to curtail the operation of those *political processes* ordinarily to be relied upon to protect minorities, and which may call for a correspondingly more searching judicial inquiry.[27]

There are two circumstances which will result in this strict scrutiny review. The first is if the classification results in burdens on the exercise of core constitutional or legal rights—the "fundamental" rights as defined by the Supreme Court. These will be dealt with in other portions of this text, but briefly they include constitutional rights explicitly listed in the Constitution, "implicit" constitutional rights as defined by the Court, and legal rights as defined by the legislature. Professor Tribe describes four instances in which the Court has upheld a classification which resulted in the abridgement of core constitutional rights:

Marston v. Lewis, [410 U.S. 679 (1973)] and *Burns v. Fortson*, [410 U.S. 686 (1973)] are perhaps the purest examples in the equal protection area. The per curiam decisions in those cases accepted the states' judgments that a 50-day durational voter residency requirement was "necessary" to promote the states' "important interest in accurate voter lists." [410 U.S. at 681.] See also *Buckley v. Valeo*, [424 U.S. 1, 25 (1976)] (strictly scrutinizing but upholding federal ceiling on contributions to political campaigns); *Roe v. Wade* [410 U.S. 113, 155, 163–64 (1973)] (strictly scrutinizing but upholding state bans of post-viability abortion).[28]

The second circumstance that calls for strict judicial scrutiny is when the classification, regardless of what right is concerned, involves some "suspect" grouping or, in Justice Stone's phrase, some "discrete and insular" minority. Such classifications are by their very nature constitutionally questionable and any use must be justified by the government as necessary to accomplish a compelling interest. Very few such suspect classifications have been upheld by the Supreme Court under strict review. For example, the only explicit racial discrimination upheld under strict scrutiny was that of Americans of Japanese descent during World War II in *Korematsu v. United States*,[29] the case in which the phrase "suspect" classification originated. The classifications which have been held to be suspect by the Supreme Court are those based on: (a) racial membership, (b) national origin, (c) religion, and (d) alienage.

Although the Supreme Court generally utilizes the two standards of review mentioned, there appears to be a third type of review midway between the others. This middle-ground standard allows the courts to exercise a review stricter than the "rational relationship" test when the classification does not deal with fundamental rights or suspect classes. It appears generally in cases dealing with "gender" and "illegitimacy" classifications and might be called the "important state interest/substantial relationship" standard. It was best expressed in an opinion dealing with a sex-based distinction in drinking ages: "To withstand constitutional challenge, . . . classifications by gender must serve important governmental objectives and be substantially related to the achievement of those objectives."[30] (This standard had earlier been suggested by several legal commentators, especially Professor Gunther.[31])

Currently, one of the most perplexing equal protection issues for many public and private agencies is whether "reverse discrimination," remedial action to assist groups previously discriminated against, is permissible. State universities, private industries, and various federal, state, and local agencies have adopted programs to increase the educational and economic opportunities available to women and minority groups. In many cases, these programs were developed to avoid adverse action by the Justice Department or other federal agencies under two sections of the Civil Rights Act of 1964: Title VI and Title VII. Title VI provided that any recipients of federal funds who discriminated against minorities in any aspect of their operations could have their funds terminated; Title VII made discrimination in private employment illegal. In 1972, Title VII was extended to state and local government employment practices. One of the most common responses of institutions has been to establish numerical goals for admission, hiring, and promotion for these groups.

In 1978, the Supreme Court decided *Regents of the University of California v. Alan Bakke.*[32] The *Bakke* case dealt with the special admission program of the University of California at Davis Medical School which set aside 16 of the 100 places in the entering class for members of minority groups. Bakke, a white male who had been denied admission to the medical school, argued that this was a racial quota which violated the Equal Protection Clause and Title VI of the Civil Rights Act of 1964 and brought an action for relief in state court. The Supreme Court accepted the case on certiorari and in June 1978, Mr. Justice Powell announced the complex judgment of a narrowly divided Court. Powell's vote was the swing vote for two distinct coalitions in three holdings.

The first holding of Powell and the quartet of Burger, Stewart, Rehnquist, and Stevens was that the Davis special admissions program with its quotas was invalid under the Fourteenth Amendment:

> The fatal flaw in [Davis's] preferential program is its disregard of individual
> rights as guaranteed by the Fourteenth Amendment. . . . [W]hen a state's
> distribution of benefits or impositions of burdens hinges on the color of a
> person's skin or ancestry, that individual is entitled to a demonstration that the
> challenged classification is necessary to promote a substantial state interest. [The
> Davis Medical School] has failed to carry this burden.

The second holding was that although the Davis program was invalid, the consideration of an applicant's race in admission decisions was not always barred. The second coalition of Powell, Brennan, White, Marshall, and Blackmun held that Title VI of the 1964 Civil Rights Act proscribed only "those racial classifications that would violate the Equal Protection Clause." The special admissions program at Davis did make a racial distinction; racial and ethnic distinctions "of any sort are inherently suspect and thus call for the most exacting judicial examination." As the Court had held before in a number of cases, "in order to justify the use of a suspect classification, a state must show that its purpose or interest is both constitutional and substantial, and that its use of the classification is 'necessary . . . to the accomplishment' of its purpose or the safeguarding of its interest." The Davis Medical School argued that its special admissions programs served four such purposes:

1. reducing the historic deficit of traditionally disfavored minorities in medical schools and the medical profession,
2. countering the effects of societal discrimination,
3. increasing the number of physicians who will practice in communities currently underserved, and
4. obtaining the educational benefits that flow from an ethnically diverse student body.

Powell's opinion found that the first three of the purported goals were not substantial enough to support the use of a suspect classification. The first reason was "facially invalid"; preferring members of a group "for no reason other than race" is "discrimination for its own sake." The second purpose, although legitimate, was not justified since Davis had no history of racial discrimination which might justify a classification which aids the disadvantaged at the "expense of other innocent individuals." Finally, the Medical School did not demonstrate the necessity of a racial classification in order to accomplish the third goal. The fourth purpose, the attainment of a diverse student body, was held to be a "constitutionally permissible goal." The "state has a substantial interest that legitimately may be served by a properly devised admissions program involving the competitive consideration of race and ethnic origin." However, as noted in the first holding, Powell held that this particular program was not "properly devised" since it was a simple quota; the "fatal flaw" in this preferential program is "its disregard of individual rights." In other words, the state could have used a "less drastic remedy" to accomplish its purposes. The third major holding of the "majority" of Justice Powell and the Burger, Stewart, Rhenquist, and Stevens coalition was that Alan Bakke should be admitted to the medical school. Since Davis could not carry the burden of proving that, but for the existence of the special admissions program, Bakke still would not have been admitted, and since the program was held unlawful, Bakke was entitled to be admitted.

The *Bakke* decision did little to clarify the permissibility of quotas, numerical standards, and minority set-aside programs, but it did guarantee that a plethora of cases involving such programs would be brought to the Court. The next major decision involving such programs was handed down in a case brought by a white worker involving a challenge to an affirmative action plan collectively bargained by a union and an employer. *United Steelworkers of America v. Brian F. Weber*[33] involved the question whether Title VII of the Civil Rights Act of 1964 as amended [42 USC § 2000e] prohibited private employers from granting racial preferences in employment practices. The Court, in a 5–2 opinion (Justices Powell and Stevens took no part in the decision), held that it did not and that the voluntary "quota" was permissible.

For many years blacks were systematically excluded from craft unions. In light of this fact and perhaps in fear of a possible discrimination suit by black workers or intervention by the EEOC, Kaiser Aluminum and Chemical Corporation and the United Steelworkers of America in 1974 entered into a collective bargaining agreement which contained an affirmative action plan designed to reduce racial imbalances in Kaiser's then almost exclusively white craft work force. The plan set hiring goals and established on-the-job training programs to teach craft skills to unskilled workers. Fifty percent of the openings in the training programs were reserved for blacks. Traditionally, the major determinant of admission to such programs had been seniority. In the first year of the agreement, the in-plant training program in Kaiser's Gramercy, Louisiana, plant accepted at least one black who had less seniority than several white applicants. One of those whites who was rejected, Brian F. Weber, brought a class action suit alleging that this racial preference violated §703(a) and (d) of Title VII of the Civil Rights Act, which prohibited employers and unions from discriminating against individuals on the basis of race, sex, religion, or national origin in either employment decisions or training programs. Both the district court and a divided Court of Appeals agreed with Weber and held that such employment practices giving racial preferences violated Title VII.

Justice William Brennan, writing for the Supreme Court, reversed the lower courts' holdings. His opinion emphasized the narrowness of the issue which the Court considered: "The only question before us is the narrow statutory issue of whether Title VII forbids private employers and unions from voluntarily agreeing upon bona fide affirmative action plans that accord racial preferences in the manner and for the purpose provided in the Kaiser–USWA plan."

The Court argued that a literal reading of §703(a) and (d) and *McDonald v. Santa Fe Trail Transportation Co.*,[34] which had held that Title VII protects whites as well as blacks from certain forms of discrimination, was misplaced in this case. Rather, the "spirit of the law" was essential, and the prohibition against racial discrimination in § 703(a) and (d) must be "read against the background of the legislative history of Title VII and the historical circumstances from which the Act arose." The Court examined those sources and concluded that the primary concern of the Act was to remedy the "plight of the Negro in our economy" and that Congress did not "intend wholly to prohibit private and voluntary affirmative action efforts as one method of solving this problem."

Justice Brennan's opinion buttressed this conclusion by examining §703(j) of Title VII. Opponents of Title VII wished the bill to read that nothing in the Act would "require *or permit* any employer . . . to grant preferential treatment." However, the majority refused to add "permit," implying that:

> Congress chose not to forbid all voluntary race-conscious affirmative action. . . . We therefore hold that Title VII's prohibition in § 703(a) and (d) against racial discrimination does not condemn all private, voluntary, race-conscious affirmative action plans.

The majority did not go further than it had to. It upheld the specific Kaiser plan as falling on the permissible side of the line of demarcation. It did, however, hint at the essential components of a permissible plan:

> The purposes of the plan mirror those of the statute. Both were designed to break down old patterns of racial segregation and hierarchy. Both were structured to "open employment opportunities for Negroes in occupations which have been

traditionally closed to them." At the same time the plan does not unnecessarily trammel the interests of white employees. The plan does not require the discharge of white workers and their replacement with new black hirees. . . . Nor does the plan create an absolute bar to the advancement of white employees; half of those trained in the program will be white. Moreover, the plan is a temporary measure; it is not intended to maintain racial balance, but simply to eliminate a manifest racial imbalance.

These elements—traditional patterns of discrimination, no discharge of innocent third parties, no absolute bar to advancement by whites, and temporariness—may be keys to the Courts' acceptance of a voluntary affirmative action plan to increase black employment opportunity.

In 1980, in *Fullilove v. Klutznick*,[35] the Court again upheld government action which provided preferential treatment for minorities. That case concerned the Public Works Employment Act of 1977 which required that 10 percent of all federal funds for local public works projects be allocated to minority contractors. Although the Court upheld the minority program by a 6–3 margin, the divisions that had characterized earlier decisions persisted. The Chief Justice wrote the Court's opinion; he was joined by Justices White and Powell. Powell filed a separate concurring opinion, as did Justice Marshall, joined by Brennan and Blackmun. The decision held that both the objectives of the set-aside to ensure that federal funds would not be used to perpetuate the effects of past discrimination and the means, the use of racial and ethnic classifications, were constitutionally permissible.

The division of the Court in these cases reflects society's uncertainty on equal protection and the questions of affirmative action and racial classifications. The Court has left the meaning and applicability of equal protection nearly as cloudy and as uncertain as the meaning of due process. These decisions add one more ambiguity to the already confusing environment of administrative regulation. The majority of the justices argued that remedial racial classifications may be allowed, especially if there has been racial discrimination practiced in the past. Administrators may be able to take race into consideration in their decision making, and indeed "quotas" may be permitted if there is proven racial discrimination. Affirmative action may be valid to achieve certain compelling governmental interests.

CORE CONSTITUTIONAL RIGHTS

In addition to the restrictions on administrative action provided by due process and equal protection guarantees, several other rights are protected by the Constitution. These essential right, are considered to be "core rights," and they may be abridged by the government only under exceptional circumstances and only in accordance with due process and equal protection requirements. These core constitutional rights are found both explicitly and implicitly in the Constitution; that is, they either (a) are specifically mentioned in the document (especially the Bill of Rights) or (b) may be reasonably implied from the explicit guarantees as necessary concomitants of explicit rights.

EXPLICIT CONSTITUTIONAL RIGHTS

The Bill of Rights, the first ten amendments to the Constitution, was proposed by the First Congress and ratified in 1791. These amendments were demanded by the American people because of their fear of a too-strong centralized government which could deprive them of their personal liberties. The Bill of Rights provides specific written protection for basic rights and continues to limit and restrict the powers and activities of the national government.

Since Amendment I stated, "Congress shall make no law," state governments were not originally bound by the restrictions in the Bill of Rights. As Chief Justice John Marshall noted in 1833, it was "universally understood" that those amendments applied only against the national government.[36] As time passed people also began to be concerned with the actions of the states and local governments. Through the use of the due process clause of the Fourteenth Amendment almost all of the guarantees found in the first ten amendments have been interpreted by the Supreme Court to apply to the states. The few substantive guarantees which have not been held to be applicable are the Second (right to bear arms), Third (quartering of soldiers), Tenth (reserved powers) Amendments, and the requirements in the Fifth and Seventh Amendments, respectively for indictment for serious crimes by a grand jury and for trial by jury in all civil cases involving more than $20.[37] The Court has held that the other Bill of Rights guarantees are a necessary part of "fundamental fairness" and the "universal sense of justice" demanded by the Fourteenth Amendment requirements for due process.[38] This concept of selective application to the states of Bill of Rights protections by the Court is referred to as the process of "incorporation." The applicability of the Bill of Rights to administrative action has been achieved through a process of incorporation similar to that used with state and local governments. The major distinction is that several of the provisions that are applicable to state action do not apply or are less strictly applied to the administrative process. Since federal law and federal court decisions make administrators at all levels personally liable for actions that violate individuals' constitutional rights, administrators must be aware of the content, scope, and applicability of core constitutional rights to their on-the-job behavior.

First Amendment

The First Amendment states that "Congress shall make no law respecting an establishment of religion, or prohibiting the free exercise thereof; or abridging the freedom of speech, or of the press; or the right of the people peaceably to assemble, and to petition the Government for a redress of grievances." The rights specified have been considered so fundamental that they were the first to be incorporated by the Supreme Court,[39] and all First Amendment guarantees are applicable against the states and administrators.

The two aspects of religious freedom protected by the First Amendment, the establishment clause and the free exercise clause, are occasionally incompatible. The problem is that there is a narrow line between prohibiting any establishment and at the same time allowing free exercise. For example, would denying permission for religious services to be held in state university buildings deny students the right to exercise their religion? Would allowing such services constitute an establishment of religion? The dilemma inherent in the phrasing of the First Amendment was summarized by Chief Justice Burger:

> [T]he Court has struggled to find a neutral course between the two Religion Clauses . . . either of which, if expanded to a logical extreme, would tend to clash with the other. . . . The course of constitutional neutrality cannot be an absolutely straight line; rigidity could well defeat the basic purpose of these provisions, which is to insure that no religion be sponsored or favored, none commanded and none inhibited.[40]

In answering the preceding question in 1981, in *Widmar v. Vincent*,[41] the Supreme Court held that if university officials allowed general use of their facilities to student groups, they could not deny access to student groups simply because those groups wished to discuss religion. To do so would be violative of the students' right to both free exercise and free speech. At the same time, however, the Court left intact a lower court ruling which had upheld a ban on the use of public *high school* buildings for student prayer meetings. The distinction seemed to be that the Court viewed university students as "young adults," capable of understanding that the university's free access policy was "one of neutrality toward religion." High school students evidently lack such discernment.

The Establishment Clause forbids government from taking any action "respecting" an establishment of religion. This is a prohibition not only on government favoritism toward a particular religion but also a ban on government sponsorship of any religion. The Supreme Court utilizes a three-part test for challenges under the clause: in order to withstand challenge the government action (a) must have a secular *purpose*, (b) must have a primary *effect* which neither advances nor inhibits religion, and (c) must not foster an excessive *government entanglement* with religion.[42] Finally, the action must also not create political divisiveness along religious lines.[43]

The second religion clause protects the belief and practice of religion from governmental abridgement. Although belief might be absolutely protected, certain religious practices will not be permitted if they violate nondiscriminatory legitimate governmental interests. For example, polygamy and refusal to pay taxes because of religious belief are not protected. However, government must make some accommodation to religious practices and administrators must be careful not to abridge the free exercise of religion unless it is required to carry out a legitimate program. The Court usually balances the burden on the exercise of religion against the state interest.[44] It upheld the compulsory vaccination of an individual who argued that this violated his religious beliefs on the grounds the state had a legitimate government interest in protecting public health.[45] Several state courts have upheld the requirement for vaccination of children before they were admitted to school.[46] The complexity of the situation that confronts administrators is indicated by the situation of state unemployment compensation administrators who had to determine if they could deny benefits to a Seventh Day Adventist who, because of her religious beliefs, refused to accept positions which required her to work on Saturday. Since federal law and regulations specify that only persons who are unemployed through no fault of their own are eligible for benefit payments, the state administrators ruled that the Seventh Day Adventist was ineligible.

The Supreme Court disagreed and ruled that to deny her unemployment benefits would interfere with her exercise of religious beliefs and the state interest was not significant enough to override that burden. The benefits had to be paid.[47] Similarly, in *Thomas v. Review Board of The Indiana Employment Security Division*,[48] the Supreme Court ruled that the state could not deny unemployment compensation benefits to a Jehovah's Witness who quit his job rather than be transferred to a position which required him to participate in the manufacture of armaments, which he claimed was forbidden by his religion:

> Where the state conditions receipt of an important benefit upon conduct
> proscribed by a religious faith, or where it denies such a benefit because of
> conduct mandated by religious belief, thereby putting substantial pressure on an
> adherent to modify his behavior and to violate his beliefs, a burden on religion
> exists.

In this case, the state had shown no countervailing interest sufficient to justify the infringement of Thomas's First Amendment freedom.

The next clause in the First Amendment prohibits government from abridging freedom of speech or press or generally freedom of "expression." These rights are at the basis of a democratic political system. Although they are not absolutely protected in practice, any government action which does abridge them will be carefully scrutinized by the courts to ensure that due process has been observed and that the abridgement is necessary to serve some compelling government interest. For example, Selective Service Boards were prohibited from reclassifying individuals so that they would be drafted as a "penalty" for engaging in antiwar speeches and protests. The Court considered this to have a definite "chilling" effect on free speech with no countervailing state interest.[49] The Court has upheld the federal Hatch Act and similar state restrictions which forbid civil service employees from engaging in partisan political speeches and activities because that restriction is necessary to the accomplishment of the compelling public interest of having a neutral, competent public service.[50]

Administrative censorship of speech through the mail is unconstitutional; in 1965, the Supreme Court struck down an act which gave the Postmaster General the power to censor mailings from communist countries and in 1971 extended that decision to "void laws authorizing postal authorities to make administrative determinations of obscenity, exclude it from the mails, and cut off all mail to persons sending it."[51] On the other hand, the Court has upheld the right of customs officials to seize obscene materials as long as strict due process requirements are followed.[52]

The courts have allowed the government to place more restrictions on the public air waves than on the traditional printed press since this air space is public property and there are only a limited number of radio and television channels which the government, the Federal Communications Commission, must allocate in the public interest. For example, radio and television stations may be required by the FCC's fairness doctrine to grant "equal time" to opposing viewpoints,[53] while no equivalent requirement may be applied to newspapers' editorials.[54] Stations may also be "censored" of programs that contain "dirty words" even though they could not be proven obscene.[55]

Similarly, the courts have allowed more restrictions of the motion picture industry than of the print media. The government has a very difficult time when it attempts to exercise prior restraint over print media, but may require all motion pictures to be licensed before being shown, if proper procedures are established.[56] In contrast, the executive branch was unable to prevent the publication of the "Pentagon Papers," a "classified" history of the U.S. involvement in the Vietnam War, because such prior restraint was felt to bear a heavy presumption of unconstitutionality and the government was unable to establish the necessity of the restraint to protect a compelling public interest such as national security.[57] A majority of the justices did recognize that government could restrain publication if a compelling public interest were endangered. This was the issue in the case involving the publication of information about making an H-bomb by the *Progressive* magazine. It might also be noted that the Burger Court has held that administrators need not give members of the press special access to information. For example, newspaper reporters are not guaranteed a special right to interview prisoners.[58]

Related to freedom of speech and press as part of freedom of expression are the prohibitions against abridging the rights of assembly and petition. Again, administrative action may not abridge these freedoms without coming under the close scrutiny of the courts. The Amendment protects the peaceful assembly of people in public places for lawful purposes, which implies a right of "association" as well. Therefore, an individual cannot be punished or deprived of public employment for mere membership in certain organizations.[59] In 1976, the Supreme Court invalidated political patronage dismissals as a violation of rights of association as well as an impermissible infringement on free speech.[60] Assemblies may be regulated so that public order may be preserved as long as such regulations are fairly administered and precisely drawn.[61] The right to petition includes the freedom to combine and lobby the legislative, executive, or judicial branches without, for example, violating antitrust laws.[62] However, the right to petition does not forbid the appropriate application of antitrust statutes.[63] The right of individuals to petition federal administrative agencies for the issuance of rules is explicitly guaranteed in Section 553 of the Federal Administrative Procedure Act (APA).

Second Amendment

The Second Amendment states that "A well regulated Militia, being necessary to the security of a free State, the right of people to keep and bear Arms, shall not be infringed." Its purpose is to prevent Congress from disarming the state militias. It provides no constitutional right for a private citizen to retain weapons. Congress could [and has used] several delegated powers—taxation, interstate commerce, postal, and so on—to regulate private ownership of firearms and their sale and transportation in interstate commerce. As long as the regulations do not interfere with the right of a state to maintain a militia they have been upheld by the courts.[64] The Second Amendment has not been "incorporated" by the Court to restrict state action. Therefore it is likely that any state or local government regulations of firearms are permissible under the federal constitution. However, many state constitutions do have clauses explicitly restricting any regulation of firearms.

Third Amendment

The Third Amendment bars the quartering of soldiers and is generally irrelevant to administrative regulation.

Fourth Amendment

The Fourth Amendment states that "The right of people to be secure in their persons, houses, papers, and effects, against unreasonable searches and seizures, shall not be violated, and no Warrants shall issue but upon probable cause, supported by Oath or affirmation, and particularly describing the place to be searched, and the persons or things to be seized." Generally, the prohibition against unreasonable searches and seizures means that, in criminal cases, a search is allowed only after the government obtains a warrant supported by probable cause. However, "reasonable" searches are allowed and the exceptions to the warrant requirement in criminal cases are expanding under the Burger Court. Prior to the middle 1960s, administrative searches, such as routine health, safety, and fire inspections, had to be "reasonable" but did not require warrants if they were carried out under legislative authorization. In 1967, however, the Supreme Court held that routine building inspections did involve intrusion on privacy, and if consent was not granted, inspectors must secure a warrant.[65] Such warrants do not require a showing of probable cause, and general "area" warrants may be issued upon the request of the administrative agency. Later cases applied this holding to federal industrial safety inspections by OSHA.[66] Although administrators opposed the warrant requirement and argued that it would hinder their ability to protect public health and safety, the flexible guidelines required by the Court have resulted in little, if any, harmful effects on enforcement processes.

Fifth Amendment

This amendment contains a number of provisions which protect criminal defendants but which do not currently apply to administrative actions. The requirement for grand jury indictments applies only to criminal procedures, as do the prohibitions against "double jeopardy" and "self-incrimination." The Fifth Amendment also contains the federal due process clause which has already been discussed. Finally, the Amendment declares that "nor shall private property be taken for public use, without just compensation," and this clause does apply to all governmental action. It limits the government's power of eminent domain, the power to take private property for public use, and was the first provision of the Bill of Rights to be incorporated within the Fourteenth Amendment and applied to the states.[67] The courts have recognized that property rights are important but that government may take such property in the public interest if the owner is fairly paid. Compensation does not need to be made prior to the seizure but adequate means must "be provided for a reasonably just and prompt ascertainment and payment."[68] Even when physical "taking" does not occur, as, for example, when airplanes take off at such low levels that private land close to public airports is not suitable for other use, government must compensate the owners of that land.[69]

Sixth Amendment

"In all criminal prosecutions, the accused shall enjoy the right to a speedy and public trial, by an impartial jury of the State and district wherein the crime shall have been committed, which district shall have been previously ascertained by law, and to be informed of the nature and cause of the accusation; to be confronted with the witnesses against him; to have compulsory process for obtaining witnesses in his favor, and to have the Assistance of Counsel for his defense."

The Sixth Amendment begins, "In all criminal prosecutions . . ." and deals with criminal procedures. Obviously these are not directly applicable to administrative proceedings, but several aspects are considered a part of "due process" and have been interpreted as requirements in the administrative process. The first clause requires a "speedy" trial and administrative hearings are somewhat related. Usually, hearings must be conducted "at the first instance"; as soon as the agency can get to the case on its docket. As liberal with administrative agencies as they are with judicial actions, the courts have permitted delays of five to ten years in scheduling cases as long as the agency can prove that it had no earlier available time to hear the case.

The second clause requires a "public" trial. Again, although trials apply only to criminal proceedings, in administrative hearings a written record must be maintained by the agency and that record must be available for public inspection and court review if the case is appealed. The next section deals with "impartial jury." Juries are not used in administrative proceedings, but impartiality on the part of the deciding official is mandated by the Federal Administrative Procedure Act. For example, in order to insure impartiality, the administrative law judge must be separated from the political and policy-making portions of the agency, and insulated from any types of pressure that would prevent a fair, unbiased decision. The next requirement of the Sixth Amendment is that trials must be held in the district in which the crime was committed. This requirement is reflected in several provisions of administrative law. For example, the APA requires that in scheduling administrative hearings "due regard shall be had for the convenience and necessity of the parties." Even more explicitly, cases brought under the Freedom of Information Act, which is an amendment to the APA, may be filed in the district court in Washington, D.C., or the district court closest to the principal place of residence or business of the complainant.

The next section of the Sixth Amendment requires that government inform the defendant of the nature and cause of the accusation. The requirements in administrative actions are the same; when the Federal Trade Commission decides to move against a firm which it believes is engaging in false advertising it must serve formal notice specifying the precise sections of the United States Code which are being violated and which actions of the company constitute the violation. When Geritol claimed that its product cured "tired blood," it was duly and formally notified by the FTC that the specific advertisements which put forth that claim were a cause for action by the FTC under various federal statutes.

The next section of the Sixth Amendment requires that accused individuals have a right to be confronted with the witnesses against them. To some extent this is also applicable in administrative proceedings. All persons facing administrative action must be allowed to confront the adverse evidence, although not necessarily the *persons* presenting such evidence, so that a "defense" may be prepared. The "compulsory process" clause also applies to administrative hearings. The Federal Administrative Procedure Act specifies that subpoenas shall be issued to a party on request. Finally, the Sixth Amendment specifies that defendants have the right to the "Assistance of Counsel." The Supreme Court has ruled that in criminal proceedings this means not only that a defendant has the right to be represented by an attorney if he could afford one, but that government must provide a lawyer if the defendant is indigent.[70] In administrative proceedings the APA requires that an individual who is compelled to appear and testify is entitled to be accompanied by an attorney, but there is no uniform equipment for agencies to provide counsel for a person who cannot afford one, although some federal agencies do provide for appointment of counsel to impoverished parties.

Seventh Amendment

The Seventh Amendment deals with jury trials in common law suits. Some have argued that any administrative action which seeks to impose monetary penalties (since, unlike the Sixth Amendment, the Seventh does not deal with criminal cases) must be accompanied by a trial by jury. However, the courts have refused to uphold this argument and, consequently, this amendment is irrelevant as a restraint on administrative action.

Eighth Amendment

This amendment states that "excessive bail shall not be required, nor excessive fines imposed, nor cruel and unusual punishment inflicted." The bail requirement does not apply to administrative actions since only one federal administrative agency, the Immigration and Naturalization Service, has the authority to detain individuals. The prohibition against excessive fines does apply to administrative proceedings. Of course, "excessive" is not absolute and is generally defined through reference to the agency's authorizing statute. If the legislature has specified what penalties may be imposed, the agency generally has the discretionary authority to decide, within those specified boundaries, what fines are appropriate. Few (if any) federal courts have been faced with challenges to administrative action based on this provision against excessive fines.

The last clause of the Eighth Amendment has become increasingly significant for administrative regulation. A number of administrative activities have come under this prohibition as the courts have held that certain types of administrative penalties or procedures may constitute cruel and unusual punishment as proscribed by the Eighth Amendment. In the last few years the courts have utilized this clause to require prison administrators to improve the conditions of their facilities to meet court established standards: "prisoners are entitled to be free of conditions which constitute cruel and unusual punishment." Such conditions include severe overcrowding (prison is "so crowded that inmates have to sleep on mattresses spread on floors in hallways and next to urinals"), extremely unsanitary conditions ("roaches in all stages of development" and an area "housing well over 200 men [with] one functioning toilet"), lack of protection from bodily harm ("inmates are repeatedly victimized by those who are stronger and more aggressive; . . . most prisoners carry some form of homemade or contraband weapon"), and failure to advance any valid function of correctional system. Courts recognize that

> prisons are not to be operated as hotels or country clubs. However, this does not mean that responsible state officials . . . can be allowed to operate prison facilities that are barbaric and inhumane. . . . Prisoners retain all rights enjoyed by free citizens except those necessarily lost as an incident of confinement.[71]

The Supreme Court held that failure to provide for medical needs of prisoners could also constitute cruel and unusual punishment.[72] In addition, the "cruel and unusual" clause has been utilized by the courts to protect mental patients. Administrators of mental institutions may be restrained from certain procedures because they may result in "cruel and unusual" punishment. Psychosurgery, various types of behavioral modification programs, and electroshock therapy are reviewed with suspicion by the courts when used on long-term or "problem" mental patients.

Finally, the courts have considered whether corporal punishment in public school constitutes cruel and unusual punishment. The Supreme Court held that the clause does not apply "to the paddling of children as a means of maintaining discipline in public schools."[73] The Court held that the Eighth Amendment was designed for the criminal context and that the proscription against cruel and unusual punishment is unnecessary in the public schools because their "openness" and "supervision by the community" afford significant safeguards against the kind of abuses from which the Eighth Amendment protects the prisoners."[74]

Ninth Amendment

"The enumeration in the Constitution, of certain rights, shall not be construed to deny or disparage others retained by the people." The Ninth Amendment clearly implies that there may be rights that are unenumerated or unmentioned in the Constitution but which nevertheless cannot be denied to individuals. The basis of the amendment is the concept that people retain "natural" rights even if those rights have not been specifically protected by written laws. The "Bill of Rights presumes the existence of a substantial body of rights not specifically enumerated but easily perceived in the broad concept of liberty and so numerous and so obvious as to preclude listing them."[75]

Only in the twentieth century did the Supreme Court begin to utilize the Ninth Amendment to protect previously unrecognized rights. Until 1965, no law had been "declared unconstitutional because of a disparagement of any of these unenumerated rights, nor had there been any suggestion that this amendment limited the powers of the states."[76] Then in *Griswold v. Connecticut*, the Court ruled that the right of privacy was one of those unenumerated rights that could not be denied by either state or federal action. The Ninth Amendment thus serves as a source and basis for certain implicit but fundamental rights which administrators are bound to respect.

Tenth Amendment

This Amendment deals with the "reserved powers" and states that powers not delegated to the national government by the Constitution are reserved to the states or the people.

These amendments constitute the explicit constitutional rights which protect individuals against the actions of federal and/or state administrative officials and which constitute one of the most important and enduring restrictions on administrative regulatory actions.

IMPLICIT CONSTITUTIONAL RIGHTS

As the Ninth Amendment indicates, those rights explicitly guaranteed in the Constitution are not the only rights that may not be infringed by administrative actions. Just as important are "implicit" constitutional rights, most of which have been "discovered" and declared by the courts. These implicit rights are ones that courts have decided are necessary outgrowths of the explicit rights or are so fundamental that they can reasonably be implied from the Constitution as a whole. Since these rights have been primarily defined by courts, they are subject to changing interpretations. The courts, especially the Supreme Court, may expand, contract, or modify those rights to meet changing circumstances. The most important of these rights are explained below.

Privacy Rights

The Supreme Court has held that certain areas of personal choice exist which government cannot invade unless it has a most compelling reason. Although no exact definition of this right of privacy has been formulated, at a minimum it includes aspects of marital choice, procreation, contraception, and child rearing, areas of deepest personal intimacy and frequently of great controversy. The Court has indicated that the right of privacy embraces both an "individual interest in avoiding disclosure of personal matters" and an "interest in independence in making certain kinds of important decisions."[77] In the most general terms the right of privacy extends to a wide variety of individual activities ranging from "autonomy with respect to the intimate aspects of identity"[78] to the preservation of "those attributes of an individual which are irreducible in his selfhood."[79] Although a few cases in the 1920s[80] recognized the right of privacy in decision making regarding family matters, the modern concept of privacy as an implicit constitutional right may be traced to *Skinner v. Oklahoma*.[81] That 1942 case, although never mentioning a "right to privacy," held a statute providing for the sterilization of persons convicted for the third time of felonies involving "moral turpitude" as a violation of equal protection. The Court noted the inequities of the Act—embezzlement was not a crime involving moral turpitude while larceny was—and held that the classification, involving the fundamental right of procreation, could not withstand strict judicial scrutiny. The Court explicitly established the right to privacy in 1965 in *Griswold v. Connecticut*.[82] Justice Douglas's opinion for the Court recognized the existence of a "zone of privacy created by several fundamental constitutional guarantees" and a "right of privacy older than the Bill of Rights." He attempted to establish a basis for this right in the First, Third, Fourth, Fifth, and Ninth Amendments which "have penumbras, formed by emanations from those guarantees that help give them life and substance." Those penumbras merge to create this "fundamenal personal right" of privacy. The other members of the majority argued that the right of privacy existed as a facet of liberty dealt with in the Ninth Amendment and protected by the due process clause against violation by either state or federal government actions. In a 1972 case, the Court extended this right of privacy by declaring invalid a law restricting the availability of contraceptives to married persons. Justice Brennan wrote for the majority and stated that if "the right of privacy means anything, it is the right of the *individual*, married or single, to be free from unwanted governmental intrusions into matters so fundamentally affecting a person as the decision whether to bear or beget a child."[83]

This right of bodily privacy in matters relating to procreation was further expanded in the abortion decision. Justice Harry Blackmun wrote the opinion of the Court which overturned a Texas law proscribing abortions. His decision held that that law violated the due process clause of the Fourteenth Amendment since there was no compelling state interest in a total ban on abortions which would justify the broad infringement of a woman's right of bodily privacy. "This right of privacy, whether it be founded in the Fourteenth Amendment's concept of personal liberty . . . [or] in the Ninth Amendment's reservation of rights to the people, is broad enough to encompass a woman's decision whether or not to terminate her pregnancy."[84] However, the state could limit that right when it could show an overriding state interest in the fetus or the health of the mother (as in the third trimester of pregnancy); a partial restriction on abortions under those circumstances was held to be allowable even if it restricted the exercise of the fundamental right of privacy since it was justified by a compelling state interest. The Court has made several subsequent decisions on the issue of abortion; it has held invalid requirements for approval of abortions by a committee of hospital staff members, by the husband, and by the parents of a minor as well as a ban on the saline amniocentesis method since none of these were shown to be reasonably related to any state interest compelling enough to justify the restriction on privacy.[85] However, the Court has upheld the right of a state to define fetal viability and has held that neither state nor federal governments were required to fund abortions.[86]

In other cases on the right of privacy, the Court has held that a federal law which prohibits "private schools from excluding qualified children solely because they are Black" violates neither "parental rights" nor the "right of privacy."[87] It affirmed a lower court's ruling which upheld Virginia's enforcement of a sodomy law against private, consensual homosexual acts of adult males.[88] It held that neither regulations specifying the length of a policeman's hair nor police disclosure of a person's shoplifting arrest (although the individual was not convicted) impermissibly violated rights of privacy.[89] But the Court also declared unconstitutional a zoning ordinance which restricted occupancy and defined the family. The Court held this to be an unjustified intrusion into personal choices involving family arrangements.[90]

All of these cases indicate the Court's view that several aspects of personal life (especially marriage, reproduction, and child rearing) are protected from governmental intrusion by the right of privacy. Any such intrusion by administrators must be justified as necessary for the accomplishment of some compelling state interest. In the absence of such a compelling interest any administrative action which violates the bodily or mental privacy of an individual will be disallowed by the courts and the administrator who committed the violation may be sued for monetary damages by the affected party.

Travel Rights

The Supreme Court has held that individuals have an implicit right to travel within the United States and abroad which is protected from federal and state intrusion. As a core constitutional right, the right to travel may not be easily abridged, but like all constitutional rights it is not absolute and may in some cases be restricted. That is particularly true with respect to the power of the federal government to restrict international travel.

The requirement that American citizens wishing to travel abroad must apply for and be granted a passport from the State Department was first imposed in the early part of the twentieth century. Prior to 1958, it was assumed that a passport was a privilege and Congress had granted almost unlimited discretionary power to the State Department to grant or deny a passport, with no procedural protections provided to applicants. In 1958, however, the Supreme Court overturned the State Department's denial of passports to individuals because of their communist background.[91] Dictum in the opinion stated that "The right to travel is part of the 'liberty' of which the citizen cannot be deprived without due process of law under the Fifth Amendment."[92] In 1964, in *Aptheker v. Secretary of State*,[93] the Supreme Court reaffirmed this right to travel when it held a congressional statute which forbade the issuance of passports to members of the Communist Party unconstitutional as a too drastic means of achieving a legitimate purpose: The law "too broadly and indiscriminately restricts the right to travel and thereby abridges the liberty guaranteed [against Congress] by the Fifth Amendment." In 1965, the Court did uphold a federal restriction on travel abroad. Congress prohibited travel to Cuba unless specifically authorized by the Secretary of State. In *Zemel v. Rusk*,[94] the Secretary had refused such permission. The Court reiterated that a right to travel existed but held that the fact that a "liberty cannot be inhibited without due process of law does not mean it can under no circumstances be inhibited."[95] The government restriction was justified in this by the "weightiest considerations of national security."

The concept of a right of interstate travel predates the Constitution. "The Articles of Confederation explicitly recognized the right of the people of each state to 'have free ingress and egress to and from any other State.' "[96] That explicit recognition was excluded from the Constitution but early Court cases indicated some rights existed, and following the Civil War the Court made that concept clearer. *Crandall v. Nevada* invalidated a state tax on every person leaving the State by railroad as an unconstitutional violation of the inherent right to travel, and *The Slaughter-House Cases*[97] recognized that right as a privilege of national citizenship. In 1941, the Supreme Court, invalidating a California law which imposed penalties for bringing an indigent into the state, reaffirmed the right of interstate travel as based upon the Commerce Clause.[98] Twenty-five years later the Court held that Congress could protect by legislation the "constitutional right to travel from one State to another."[99] Finally, in the landmark case of *Shapiro v. Thompson*,[100] the Court upheld the implicit constitutional right of travel and also created a new implicit right for Americans: the right to reside wherever one chooses. Neither laws nor administrative actions may restrict those rights unless a compelling state interest exists. No such interests had been proven by two states or the District of Columbia which had imposed one year residency requirement before individuals could be eligible for welfare payments. Therefore the Court struck those statutes down. The Court also stated that the "argument that the waiting period serves as an administratively efficient rule of thumb . . . will not withstand scrutiny."

Any administrative regulation that limits the right to travel must serve a significant purpose in order to withstand judicial scrutiny. This applies to international, interstate, and probably intrastate travel as well:

> The Supreme Court in *Memorial Hospital v. Maricopa County* left open the question whether to "draw a constitutional distinction between interstate and intrastate travel," but lower courts have uniformly treated intrastate travel as entitled to no less protection than travel across state lines. The Court of Appeals for the Second Circuit, in one of the major opinions on the subject, concluded that "the use of the term 'interstate travel' in *Shapiro* was nothing more than a reflection of the state-wide enactment involved in that case." The Second Circuit reasoned that it "would be meaningless to describe that right to travel between states as a fundamental precept of personal liberty and not to acknowledge a correlative constitutional right to travel within a state."[101]

Residency Rights

The right to reside wherever one chooses in the United States is closely related to the right to travel and is also now considered to be a fundamental right. *Shapiro v. Thompson*, as noted above, invalidated a residency requirement for welfare benefits. *Doe v. Bolton* invalidated a residency requirement of a Georgia abortion law[102] and *Memorial Hospital v. Maricopa County* struck down a one-year Arizona residency requirement for receipt of free medical care.[103] The Court found that a one-year state residence requirement coupled with a three-month county residence requirement for voting violated equal protection since it unnecessarily burdened a constitutionally protected activity.[104]

Not all residency restrictions are impermissible. The Court upheld requirements for voting registration as necessary to serve compelling state interests in preventing fraud;[105] it has upheld a one-year residency requirement for filing for divorce as justified by the state's interest in such an important decree;[106] and it has allowed localities to require their employees to reside within the community. In 1976, the Court determined that the distinction between public employee as citizen and as employee was clear and that there were compelling reasons which justified legislation requiring governmental employees to live within the jurisdiction which employed them.[107]

Employment Rights

In 1946, in the Full Employment Act, and again in 1978 in the Humphrey-Hawkins Act, Congress declared that it was national policy to ensure that every American capable and desirous of working should have that opportunity. These policy statements did not create a right to employment, and currently, as the unemployment rate indicates, no such right exists for Americans. In employment matters, however, constitutional rights are relevant in two areas: for public employees who have been explicitly granted tenure in their jobs, and for all persons in their attempts to find gainful employment. Once a public employee has been granted tenure in a position, that position becomes a "property right" of the individual and as is true with any property right, it may not be abridged without "due process of law." This means a tenured civil servant may not be dismissed without cause and without being provided an opportunity to be heard.[108] As is true with most property rights, the establishment of tenure in employment positions is one that is created and regulated by state law or ordinance of the governmental jurisdiction concerned. At the federal level Congress has provided tenure for the vast majority of civil servants. The result has been that once a civil servant completes a probationary period, the government can dismiss that civil servant only by following clearly specified administrative procedures.

In 1976, the Supreme Court decided the right of persons to seek, although not necessarily obtain, gainful employment was an essential part of the "liberty" guaranteed by the Fifth and Fourteenth Amendments. In *Hampton v. Mow Sun Wong*, the Court stated that "ineligibility for employment in a major sector of the economy . . . [was] of sufficient significance to be characterized as a deprivation of interest in liberty."[109] The case involved a Civil Service Commission regulation which barred aliens from employment in the federal competitive civil service. The Court found that the regulation was neither authorized by Congress nor justified by a compelling national interest. Consequently, since it resulted in the abridgement of an implicit constitutional right, the regulation was held invalid. The Court also quoted a 1915 case: "It requires no argument to show that the right to work for a living in the common occupations of the community is of the very essence of the personal freedom and opportunity that it was the purpose of the [Fourteenth] Amendment to secure."[110]

Rights of Mental Patients

As has been indicated, the federal courts are constantly expanding and modifying implicit rights. A classic and relevant example concerns the treatment of persons confined in state and federal mental institutions. Until very recently it was assumed that once a person had been committed to such an institution, he/she was more or less at the mercy of hospital administrators. Mental patients could be compelled to work at the most menial jobs, subjected to whatever kind of treatment—psychosurgery, electroshock therapy, medication—that administrators felt medically justified, or in many cases, confined for decades with no treatment at all.

In 1972, the federal district court in Alabama ruled that persons involuntarily committed to a state mental institution "have a constitutional right to receive such individual treatment as will give each of them a realistic opportunity to be cured."[111] That decision had a definite impact on the number and treatment of the institutionalized mentally ill in Alabama, but since it was only a district court decision its applicability outside of Alabama was limited. It was not until 1975 that a case involving the rights of the institutionalized mentally ill was decided by the Supreme Court. Kenneth Donaldson had been committed to Florida State Hospital by his father in 1955 with a diagnosis of paranoid schizophrenia. For fifteen years he remained in that facility, receiving little or no medical treatment. Throughout that time he constantly badgered hospital officials to release him. Finally, in 1971, with the assistance of the American

Civil Liberties Union (ACLU) he took his case to court alleging that he had been maliciously and intentionally deprived of his right to liberty, and under 42 U.S.C.A. §1983 filed a damage suit against the hospital administrator and state mental health officials. Section 1983 specifies that every person acting "under color of any statute, ordinance, regulation, custom or usage" of any state who deprives anyone of "rights, privileges or immunities" secured by the federal constitution or laws may be sued by the injured party for monetary damages. The federal district court agreed that involuntarily committed mental patients have a constitutional right to treatment and awarded Donaldson $38,500 in damages. On appeal the Fifth Circuit Court of Appeals upheld the judgment.[112]

The Supreme Court, in more cautious language, reaffirmed the constitutional basis of the right to treatment: "a state cannot constitutionally confine without more a non-dangerous individual."[113] That somewhat vague passage has been interpreted to mean "without treatment" and the case marked the beginning of a new era of constitutional restrictions on mental hospital administrative personnel and on the whole area of mental health policy. The implications were clear: commitment without treatment was con-stitutionally impermissible and administrators could be held personally liable for mon-etary damages under such circumstances. To avoid this, alternative policies would have to be developed, and one of these alternatives was deinstitutionalization. Thus the dis-covery of a new implicit constitutional right not only imposed restrictions on the administrative process but also resulted in the creation of a new policy approach.

The existence of implicit and explicit constitutional rights constitutes one of the most significant restrictions on the exercise of administrative regulatory power. In all their actions, administrators must follow due process and must avoid unjustifiable, unauthorized violations of both explicit and implicit constitutional rights, and when singling out any identifiable group for differential treatment must be sure that there is a legitimate and acceptable basis for so doing. The penalties for failing to satisfy any of these requirements are to have the action declared invalid by the courts and to run the risk of being held monetarily responsible for denying a person his/her constitutional rights.

CONSTITUTIONAL THEORY VS. ADMINISTRATIVE REALITY—ALIENS IN AMERICA: WHEN IS A PERSON NOT A PERSON?

In light of the above, it is logical to assume that an administrative action that results in the involuntary confinement of an individual for three years with no charges being filed and no opportunity for a hearing provided is constitutionally impermissible. Unfortunately, logic will not necessarily prevail if the individual is an alien seeking entry into the United States and if the administrative agency involved is the United States Immigration and Naturalization Service (INS).[114] Although the United States may be overwhelmingly a nation of immigrants, historically aliens (noncitizens) have been subjected to various types of discriminatory actions that would not have been permissible if applied to citizens. Although "persons" are entitled to due process and equal protection under the Fifth and Fourteenth Amendments, aliens have never been entitled to quite the same kind of due process and equal protection as citizens and corporations. Further, probably no agency at the federal level has been granted and exercises more discretionary power over its clientele than INS. Technically, Congress has granted this power to the Attorney General, but he is authorized to and has sub-delegated his powers to subordinates: employees of the INS.

INS has jurisdiction over almost every aspect of the lives of aliens: from determining whether they may enter this country, under what circumstances and for how long they may reside here, to determining if they have violated the conditions of their visas and ultimately deciding if they shall be deported. All of this is done pursuant to authority provided by the Immigration and Naturalization Act.[115]

One of the most interesting aspects of that law is the number of provisions that include the phrase "the Attorney General may, in his discretion," and then proceed to grant sweeping powers over aliens. For example, "in his discretion" the Attorney General (INS) may grant or not grant a visa, issue reentry permits to aliens who have left the country, adjust the status of aliens, and grant permanent residence status to aliens.[116] This discretion has translated into an ability on the part of INS to develop and use procedures in many of its dealings with aliens that bear little resemblance to the procedural niceties that are usually associated with "due process of law." Especially in matters relating to entry into the United States, the courts have imposed little restriction on either Congress or administrators. "Whatever the procedure authorized by Congress is, it is due process as far as an alien denied entry is concerned."[117] Since Congress has not specified any procedural requirements, in this instance no process is due process. Somewhat similarly, the treatment accorded illegal aliens who are apprehended by INS is also not circumscribed by strict procedural protections. Once apprehended an "illegal" who cannot demonstrate proof of official permission to enter the country is subject to "summary deportation" which in many cases consists of a hasty determination of status by an INS immigration inspector and an equally hasty one-way trip back to the country of origin.

Once legally admitted to the country, an alien does gain some legal status and some procedural protections in his/her dealings with INS. The Federal Administrative Procedure Act does apply to INS proceedings,[118] but it must be reiterated and understood that everything done is an *administrative* and not a criminal matter and the procedural protections provided are less stringent than is true in criminal processes.

If the courts took a long time to decide that at least certain aspects of due process were applicable to some matters concerning aliens, they have moved no more rapidly in applying the full scope of equal protection to the treatment of aliens.

The federal and state governments have and continue to discriminate against aliens in a variety of matters. In the past, states have been permitted, by both the courts and Congress, to bar aliens from practicing law and medicine, from operating bars, dance halls, or poolrooms, from owning land, from purchasing hunting and fishing licenses, and from holding public jobs. Until very recently, the federal courts, in reviewing those restrictions, usually found that these discriminatory actions were justified as necessary for carrying out some legitimate governmental purpose. For its part the federal government in the past barred aliens from government employment, limited their eligibility for social security payments and other forms of government benefits, but compelled them to serve in the military.

Only gradually and only partially has the Supreme Court erased the distinctions between citizens and aliens. As far as discriminatory treatment at the state level is concerned, the Court has held that barring aliens from law practice, civil engineering practice, and government jobs is impermissible[119] but has permitted states to bar them from becoming state policemen, teachers,[120] and peace officers, a category that includes correctional and probation officers, welfare fraud investigators, and persons responsible for enforcing food and drug laws.[121]

The ambivalence of the Supreme Court about the full applicability of equal protection to the treatment of aliens is perhaps most clearly illustrated in two cases where decisions were handed down by the Court on the same day in 1976: *Hampton v. Mow Sun Wong* and *Mathews v. Diaz*. In one case the Court ruled in favor of aliens and in the other it ruled against them, and both opinions were written by the same justice, John Paul Stevens. Both cases also involved administrative regulations rather than explicit statutory commands imposed by Congress.

In the *Mow Sun Wong* case, as previously indicated, the Court held that a regulation of the Civil Service Commission (now the Office of Personnel Management) first promulgated in 1883 which barred aliens from all federal jobs was an unconstitutional deprivation of the core constitutional right to seek gainful employment. The Civil Service Commission's fatal error had been a lack of a compelling interest which would have justified the discriminatory rule.

The Civil Service Commission offered several reasons for the rule: It provided a bargaining advantage for the United States in treaty negotiations; it encouraged aliens to become citizens; it was necessary to ensure the undivided loyalty of persons in sensitive positions; and the sweeping ban on aliens in all federal positions was administratively more convenient than deciding on a position-by-position basis which jobs were sensitive and which were not. Although these may seem to be laudable ends, the first two are clearly not the responsibility of the Civil Service Commission. The Court accepted the third as a legitimate compelling interest but one that could have been accomplished by a less drastic remedy.[122] The Court did note in passing that the President or Congress could, in the national interest, have imposed the citizenship requirement. Administrative convenience, rather like the need to save taxpayers' money, did not impress the Court as being a compelling national interest.

On the other hand the Department of Health, Education and Welfare's regulations which specified that only aliens who had been admitted to the United States for permanent residence and had lived in this country for five years were eligible for supplemental benefits under Medicare passed constitutional muster. Although HEW had unquestionably singled out an identifiable group and subjected that group to differential and adverse treatment, the Court decided that neither equal protection nor due process was offended.[123] The distinction, from Stevens's perspective, was that in *Hampton* a constitutional right was infringed, while in *Mathews* what was involved was the distribution of government benefits, or as Stevens put it, "the bounty that a conscientious sovereign makes available to its own citizens and some of its guests."[124] While Medicare benefits may be viewed from that perspective, from another perspective, which will be examined in the next chapter, they are also federal legal rights and had HEW promulgated rules which denied those benefits to blacks or men or persons of Irish ancestry, the suspicion is very strong that such a denial would be held to violate equal protection.

As this section should have made clear, aliens are different, and the nature of their difference will frequently permit administrators and legislators to treat them in ways that would not be allowable if applied to other groups of persons. Just how differently was illustrated by the treatment of Iranian students following the takeover of the American embassy in Tehran. On November 10, 1979, six days after the takeover, the President directed the Attorney General to examine the credentials of all Iranian students in this country to determine if they were in compliance with immigration rules. What followed was a thirty-day round-up of the students, which to district court judge Joyce Green was a clear violation of equal protection:

> The effect of the regulation . . . is to establish two classes of immigrant students . . . The need to express American anger at Iranian action is hardly sufficiently compelling to justify subjecting only Iranian students to a discriminatory, 30 day round up that violates the fundamental principles of American fairness.[125]

The Court of Appeals disagreed and upheld the procedure as consistent with the President's authority under the Constitution to carry out American foreign policy.

CONSTITUTIONAL RIGHTS, THE COURTS, AND ADMINISTRATIVE REGULATION

A vast number of administrative regulations directly affect and restrict the rights of individuals and businesses. The vast majority of these regulations if challenged would be upheld by the courts; the vast majority, however, will not be subject to such challenges. Both regulators and regulatees are well aware that as long as the infringement of constitutional rights is justified as necessary to accomplish some legitimate purpose and as long as the regulators have carefully followed prescribed procedures in their actions a court challenge is pointless. It is the existence of uncertainty about whether a particular action will be overturned by the courts, about the precise meaning of individual rights, and about whether the courts will accept a case for review which forms the real check on administrative power and compels administrators to be constantly wary about procedure and the substance of their actions. The knowledge that they may be held personally liable for monetary damages if they wrongfully abridge a person's constitutional rights also contributes to the effectiveness of these limitations.

The Constitution is a major and vital part of the legal framework of administrative regulation. Equally important are the laws that have been passed by Congress and the state legislatures which specifically interpret and apply constitutional provisions to administrative action. The next chapter will examine some of the major federal and state statutes which control the substance and procedure of administrative regulation.

NOTES

1. Peter Woll, *Administrative Law: The Informal Process* (Berkeley: University of California Press, 1963), p. 22.

2. John E. Nowak, Ronald D. Rotunda, and J. Nelson Young, *Constitutional Law* (St. Paul, Minn.: West Publishing Co., 1978), p. 381.

3. J. W. Peltason, *Understanding the Constitution* (Hinsdale, Ill.: Pryden Press, 1973), p. 136.

4. Nowak, *Constitutional Law*, p. 382.

5. *Santa Clara County v. Southern Pacific Railroad*, 118 U.S. 394 (1886).

6. *Goss v. Lopez*, 419 U.S. 565 (1975).

7. *Ingraham v. Wright*, 430 U.S. 651 (1977).

8. Some of the ideas and terms for this section arise from Emmette S. Redford's *Democracy in the Administrative State* (New York: Oxford University Press, 1969), chapter 6.

9. Redford, *Democracy in the Administrative State*, p. 136.

10. Redford, *Democracy in the Administrative State*, p. 142.

11. See, for example, Peter Woll, *American Bureaucracy* (New York: W. W. Norton & Co., 1977), chapter 3.

12. George H. Sabine, "The Two Democratic Traditions," *The Philosophical Review*, vol. 61, October 1952.

13. 347 U.S. 497 (1954).

14. 347 U.S. 483 (1954).

15. 347 U.S. 499 (1954).

16. *Buckley v. Valeo*, 424 U.S. 1, 93 (1976).

17. Nowak, *Constitutional Law*, p. 383, n. 5.

18. Nowak, *Constitutional Law*, p. 383. This section is derived largely from Gerald Gunther. "Forward: In Search of Evolving Doctrine on a Changing Court: A Model for a Newer Equal Protection," 86 *Harvard Law Review* 1 (1972); Nowak, p. 514; Peltason, *Understanding the Constitution*, p. 159; Joseph Tussman and Jacob Ten Broek, "The Equal Protection of the Laws," 37 *California Law Review* 341 (1949); and Lawrence H. Tribe, *American Constitutional Law* (Mineola, N.Y.: Foundation Press, 1978), chapter 16.

19. Tussman and Ten Broek, "The Equal Protection of the Laws."

20. *McLaughlin v. Florida*, 379 U.S. 184, 191 (1964).

21. *Williamson v. Lee Optical*, 348 U.S. 483 (1955).

22. 343 U.S. 483, 489 (1955).

23. *Semler v. Dental Examiners*, 294 U.S. 608 (1935).

24. *Dandridge v. Williams*, 397 U.S. 471 (1970).

25. Gunther, "A Model for a Newer Equal Protection," p. 8.

26. Nowak, *Constitutional Law*, p. 524.

27. *United States v. Carolene Products Co.*, 304 U.S. 144 (1938).

28. Tribe, *American Constitutional Law*, p. 1000, n. 3.

29. 323 U.S. 214 (1944).

30. *Craig v. Boren*, 429 U.S. 190 (1976).

31. Gunther, "A Model for a Newer Equal Protection."

32. 438 U.S. 265 (1978).

33. 61 LEd 2d 480 (1979).

34. 427 U.S. 273 (1976).

35. 448 U.S 448 (1980).

36. *Barron v. Baltimore*, 32 U.S. 243.

37. Peltason, *Understanding the Constitution*, p. 108.

38. See, e.g., *Palko v. Connecticut*, 302 U.S. 319 (1937).

39. See, e.g., *Gitlow v. New York*, 268 U.S. 652 (1925)—speech—and *Cantwell v. Connecticut*, 310 U.S. 296 (1940)—free exercise of religion.

40. *Walz v. Tax Commission*, 397 U.S. 664 (1970).

41. 450 U.S. 909 (1981).

42. *Lemon v. Kurtzman*, 403 U.S. 602 (1971).

43. *Meek v. Pittinger*, 421 U.S. 349 (1975).

44. *Wisconsin v. Yoder*, 406 U.S. 205 (1972).

45. *Jacobson v. Massachusetts*, 197 U.S. 11 (1905).

46. See, e.g., *Wright v. DeWill School District*, 385 S.W. 2d 644 (1965), and *McCartney v. Austin*, 293 N.Y.S. 2d 188 (N.Y. Sup Ct. 1968).

47. *Sherbert v. Verner*, 374 U.S. 398 (1963).

48. 450 U.S. 961 (1981).

49. See Larry L. Wade, "Selective Service and Draft Protestors: A 'One Man' Policy Decision," in James E. Anderson, *Cases in Public Policy-Making* (New York: Praeger, 1976).

50. *Civil Service Commission v. National Association of Letter Carriers*, 413 U.S. 548 (1973), and *Broadrick v. Oklahoma*, 413 U.S. 601 (1973).

51. Peltason, *Understanding the Constitution*, p. 117, citing *Lamont v. Postmaster General*, 381 U.S. 301 (1965)—"The first act of Congress ever to be held in conflict with the First Amendment"—and *Blount v. Rizzi*, 400 U.S. 410 (1971).

52. *United States v. Thirty-Seven Photographs*, 402 U.S. 363 (1971).

53. *Red Lion Broadcasting Co. v. Federal Communications Commission*, 395 U.S. 397 (1969).

54. *Miami Herald Publishing Co. v. Tornillo*, 418 U.S. 241 (1974).

55. *F.C.C. v. Pacifica Foundation*, 438 U.S. 726 (1978), which was the case involving a radio broadcast of a record which included George Carlin's "seven dirty words."

56. *Times Film Corp. v. Chicago*, 365 U.S. 43 (1961), and *Freedman v. Maryland*, 380 U.S. 51 (1965).

57. *New York Times Company v. United States*, 403 U.S. 71 (1971).

58. *Pell v. Procunier*, 417 U.S. 817 (1974), and *Saxbe v. Washington Post Co.*, 417 U.S. 843 (1974).

59. Nowak, *Constitutional Law*, citing *Keyishian v. Board of Regents*, 385 U.S. 589 (1967), and *United States v. Robel*, 389 U.S. 258 (1967).

60. *Elrod v. Burns*, 427 U.S. 347 (1976).

61. *Adderly v. Florida*, 385 U.S. 39 (1966), and *Shuttlesworth v. Birmingham*, 394 U.S. 147 (1969).

62. *Thomas v. Collins*, 323 U.S. 516 (1945), and *California Motor Transport v. Trucking Unlimited*, 404 U.S. 508 (1972).

63. *California Motor Transport*, 404 U.S. 508 (1972).

64. Peltason, *Understanding the Constitution*, p. 122. See also Tribe, *American Constitutional Law*, p. 226.

65. *Camara v. Municipal Court* and *See v. City of Seattle*, 387 U.S. 541 (1967).

66. *Marshall v. Barlow's Inc.*, 436 U.S. 307 (1978).

67. Peltason, *Understanding the Constitution*, p. 137, citing *Chicago, Milwaukee & St. Paul Ry. v. Minnesota*, 134 U.S. 418 (1890).

68. *Crozier v. Fried Krupp Aktiengesellschaft*, 224 U.S. 290, 306 (1912).

69. *Griggs v. Allegheny County*, 369 U.S. 841 (1962).

70. *Gideon v. Wainwright*, 372 U.S. 335 (1963), and *Argersinger v. Hamlin*, 407 U.S. 25 (1972).

71. All of the quotations are from *James v. Wallace*, 406 F. Supp. 318, USDC (1976) Middle District of Alabama, Memorandum Opinion of Johnson, Chief Judge.

72. *Estelle v. Gamble*, 429 U.S. 97 (1976).

73. *Ingraham v. Wright*, 430 U.S. 651 (1977).

74. 430 U.S. 651 (1977).

75. Joseph Story, 3 *Commentaries on the Constitution of the United States*, 1883, p. 715–16, cited in Tribe, p. 570.

76. Peltason, *Understanding the Constitution*, p. 146.

77. *Whalen v. Roe*, 97 SCT 869, 872 (1977). This section draws on Tribe, *American Constitutional Law*, chapter 15; Nowak, *Constitutional Law*, pp. 623ff; and William B. Lockhart, Yale Kamisar, and Jesse H. Choper, *The American Constitution*, 4th ed. (St. Paul, Minn.: West Publishing Co., 1975), pp. 1102ff.

78. Gerety, "Redefining Privacy," 12 *Harvard Civil Rights–Civil Liberties Review* 233 (1977), cited in Tribe, p. 887.

79. Paul Freund, 52d ALI Annual Meeting, 42 (1975), cited in Tribe, p. 889.

80. *Meyer v. Nebraska*, 262 U.S. 390 (1923), protecting right to teach German in grade school, and *Pierce v. Society of Sisters*, 268 U.S. 510 (1925), protecting right to send children to parochial schools.

81. 316 U.S. 535 (1942).

82. *Griswold v. Connecticut*, 381, U.S. 479 (1965).

83. *Eisenstadt v. Baird*, 405 U.S. 438 (1972).

84. *Roe v. Wade*, 419 U.S. 113, 153 (1973).

85. *Doe v. Bolton*, 410 U.S. 179 (1973) and *Planned Parenthood v. Danforth*, 428 U.S. 52 (1976).

86. *Planned Parenthood v. Danforth* and *Maher v. Roe*, 432 U.S. 464 (1977).

87. *Runyon v. McCrary*, 427 U.S. 160 (1976).

88. *Doe v. Commonwealth's Attorney*, 425 U.S. 901 (1976).

89. *Kelley v. Johnson*, 425 U.S. 238 (1976), and *Paul v. Davis*, 424 U.S. 693 (1976).

90. *Moore v. East Cleveland*, 431 U.S. 961 (1977).

91. *Kent v. Dulles*, 357 U.S. 116 (1958).

92. 357 U.S. at 128.

93. 378 U.S 500, 505 (1964).

94. 381 U.S. 1 (1965).

95. 381 U.S. 1 at 14.

96. Nowak, *Constitutional Law*, p. 668, contains a good discussion concerning the right to interstate travel.

97. *Crandall v. Nevada*, U.S. 35 (1867), and *The Slaughter-House Cases*, 83 U.S. 36 (1873).

98. *Edwards v. California*, 314 U.S. 160 (1941).

99. *United States v. Guest*, 383 U.S. 745 (1966).

100. 394 U.S. 618, 634 (1969).

101. Tribe, *American Constitutional Law*, p. 954 (footnotes omitted).

102. 410 U.S. 179 (1973).

103. 415 U.S. 250 (1974).

104. *Dunn v. Blumstein*, 405 U.S. 331 (1972).

105. See, e.g., *Marston v. Lewis*, 410 U.S. 679 (1973), which upheld 50-day requirements for voting in state and local elections although it noted that the requirement approached "the

outer constitutional limits in this area," and *Rosario v. Rockefeller*, 410 U.S. 752 (1973), which upheld residential requirements for voting in a primary.

106. *Sosna v. Lowa*, 419 U.S. 393 (1975).

107. *McCarthy v. Philadelphia Civil Service Commission*, 424 U.S. 645 (1976).

108. *Perry v. Sinderman*, 408 U.S. 593 (1972).

109. 426 U.S. 88, 102 (1976).

110. 426 U.S. 88, 102, quoting *Traux v. Raich*, 239 U.S. 33, 41 (1915).

111. *Wyatt v. Stickney*, 344 F. Supp. 783 (1972).

112. *O'Connor v. Donaldson*, 493 F2d 509 (1975).

113. *O'Connor v. Donaldson*, 422 U.S. 563 (1975).

114. *Shaughnessy v. United States ex rel Mezei*, 345 U.S. 206 (1953).

115. 8 U.S.C.A. 1201.

116. Kenneth Davis, *Administrative Law and Government*, 2d ed. (St. Paul, Minn.: West Publishing Co., 1975), pp. 236–40.

117. *Shaughnessy v. Mezei.*

118. *Wong Yang Sung v. McGrath*, 339 U.S. 33 (1950).

119. In re *Griffiths*, 413 U.S. 717 (1973); *Sugarman v. Dougall*, 413 U.S. 634 (1973); *Examining Board v. de Ortero*, 426 U.S. 572 (1975).

120. *Foley V. Connelie*, 435 U.S. 291 (1978).

121. *Cabell v. Chavez-Salido,*—U.S.—(1982).

122. *Hampton v. Mow Sun Wong*, 426 U.S. 88 (1976).

123. *Mathews v. Diaz*, 426 U.S. 67 (1976).

124. *Mathews v. Diaz*, 426 U.S. 67 (1976).

125. *New York Times*, December 12, 1979, p. A19.

Chapter 4

Statutory Restrictions on the Administrative Process

The legal environment of administrative agencies is multifaceted, consisting not only of general constitutional principles, specific limitations, and court interpretations, but also of a variety of statutes and executive orders specifying what agencies may and should do and how and when they should do it. The statutory environment of administrative agencies consists of three major parts: authorizing statutes which create the agencies and assign their jurisdiction and powers, appropriations statutes which provide them the financial resources to carry out their responsibilities, and the Administrative Procedure Act which establishes the general procedures that agencies must follow in rule-making, adjudication, and allowing public access to agency information. Combined, this statutory environment structures the nature, procedures, inputs, and, to a considerable degree, the outputs of regulatory agencies. The complexity of this legal environment is frequently compounded when the three sources impose conflicting demands on an agency: when, for example, Congress orders an agency to implement a program within a specified time but provides inadequate resources and no waiver from strict procedural requirements.

This chapter will be primarily concerned with examining the role that authorizing statutes, particularly those that create legal rights or entitlements, and the Administrative Procedure Act play in shaping the regulatory process. Since many federal programs are actually implemented by state and local governments, state administrative procedure acts and the impact of federalism on administrative actions will also be considered.

THE FEDERAL ADMINISTRATIVE PROCEDURE ACT (APA)

The Administrative Procedure Act establishes minimal procedural standards for all federal agencies which fall within its scope: "each authority of the Government of the United States, whether or not it is within or subject to review by another agency."[1] The agencies excepted from APA coverage are Congress, the Courts, the governments of the territories and the District of Columbia, military commissions, military authority exercised in time of war, court-martials, and agencies composed of representatives of the parties to the disputes determined by them. It does not supersede stricter procedural requirements imposed on agencies by their enabling legislation, but if the enabling legislation is silent as far as procedures are concerned the APA is applicable.

Although recently Congress has frequently provided specific procedures for specific agencies, in the initial phases of the development of administrative regulatory power it rarely did. Since the APA was not passed until 1946, following the proliferation of administrative agencies during the New Deal and World War II, the need for procedural guidance was obvious. The Administrative Procedure Act as finally passed was largely an outcome of the struggle among Congress, President Franklin Roosevelt, and the American Bar Association (ABA) to establish supremacy over the administrative process. The ABA was not particularly enthralled with the expansion of administrative power during the 1930s. Although motives are difficult to pinpoint, the ABA's campaign against regulatory agencies seemed to be based on two factors: the ABA's realization that its members were in danger of losing much of their traditional practice to the administrative process and a conservative rejection of the substance as well as the procedure of administrative action.[2] The ABA launched a full scale assault against the administrative process as it then operated. The ABA's first preference for revising the regulatory process was stated in a 1934 report:

1. Abolition of existing regulatory commissions.
2. Removal of adjudicatory functions from agencies.
3. Creation of a federal administrative court.
4. Judicial review of all administrative decisions.[3]

Most of the ABA's recommendations were incorporated in the Walter-Logan bill which was subsequently passed by Congress in 1940, but was vetoed by the President.

In the interim, Roosevelt had appointed his own committees to study and make recommendations for improving the administrative process. The first of these was the President's Commission on Administrative Management (the Brownlow Commission). It had concentrated its fire on the independent regulatory commissions, terming them "a headless fourth branch, a haphazard deposit of irresponsible agencies and uncoordinated activity. . . . [They] create a confusing and difficult situation . . . and enjoy power without responsibility."[4] Roosevelt, however, was less concerned about their independence than either the Commission or his successors in the presidency. In the first place, the majority of the commissions had been created during his administration and he had been able to control appointments to them. In the second place, he just did not accept that they were or could be independent from presidential control. He once remarked, "Congress cannot set up the ICC as a separate agency and not in any way related to the President. Therefore, the ICC, I think, would be on the wise side if, when asked for an opinion on a matter of policy, [it] would consult the President."[5] At any rate, he opposed legislation that would have abolished the commissions. In 1939, FDR encouraged the appointment of a committee by the Attorney General to study the administrative process. The Attorney General's Committee issued its final report in 1941, and the recommendations therein formed the basis for the Administrative Procedure Act.

Currently, the sections of the APA which deal with required agency procedures are found at 5 U.S.C. §551–559. The general content of those sections is summarized in Figure 4.1. Even a superficial examination of the Act indicates the extent to which it reflected the concerns of the Bar Association. Five of the nine sections deal with adjudicatory procedures and impose on agencies strict standards for the conduct of hearings, particularly in terms of separating hearing examiners (now administrative law judges) from investigatory and prosecutorial staff, requiring that parties be allowed to be represented by counsel, and in general imposing judicial procedural standards on the agencies. Critics have alleged that the APA was a lawyers' "Full Employment Act" and that it ignored the fact that agencies are not neutral arbiters, as the courts supposedly are, but are supposed to be interested parties acting as proponents of the public interest.[7] Ironically, the ABA and its members may have lost more than they gained. Certainly they did not get their desired administrative court, nor did they get unlimited judicial review of all administrative actions. More importantly, although the APA deals extensively with adjudicatory processes, it ignores completely informal administrative actions. Since these constitute the bulk of administrative actions (somewhere between 80 and 90 percent) the omission is significant.

Passage of the APA apparently satisfied Congress's needs to reform the administrative process. Twenty years elapsed before any amendments were made to the Act and only four major changes have been made to it since passage: the Freedom of Information Act of 1966 and 1974 Amendments; the Privacy Act of 1974; the Government in the Sunshine Act of 1976; and a 1976 Amendment added to the judicial

---

FIGURE 4.1 The Federal Administrative Procedure Act[6]

§551: Definitions

§552: Public Access to Agency Information

§553: Procedures To Be Followed in Informal Rule Making

§554: Adjudicatory Procedures:
When required; notice; prehearing conference procedures; presiding officers—separation of functions, ban on *ex parte* contacts

§555: Right to counsel in adjudicatory issuance and enforcement of subpoenas; required agency response to denials of petitions and applications

§556: Conduct of Hearings:
Presiding officers—powers, procedures for disqualifications; admissibility of evidence; right to cross-examination; requirements for record

§557: Adjudicatory Decision:
Initial decision; agency review; right of parties to submit proposed findings and recommendations for decision; final decisions

§558: Procedures for Imposing Sanctions; Requirement for Adjudicatory Procedures in Federal Licensing Determinations

§559: Effect of APA on Existing Statutes; Effect of Subsequent Statutes on APA

CHAPTER 7: Judicial Review: Reviewability of Actions; Scope of Review

---

review chapter waiving sovereign immunity in all nonmonetary cases brought against the government. The sections of the APA relating to rule making, adjudication, and judicial review will be covered in the chapters dealing with those subjects. At this point only the provisions, impact, and evaluation of the Freedom of Information, Privacy, and Government in the Sunshine Acts will be covered in detail.

The original APA had specified that "all public records were open for inspection unless for good cause they were held to be confidential." Bureaucratic organizations tend to prefer secrecy to openness, and by the mid-1950s an amazing number of administrative agencies had found good cause to refuse to allow public and in many instances congressional inspection of their records: The Department of Agriculture refused to identify cattle companies which held grazing permits; the Civil Service Commission would reveal the salaries of federal employees only to reporters it deemed "responsible"; the Department of Defense would not disclose which PX's on which military bases sold liquor by the bottle. A "paper curtain" had descended around the administrative process and an attitude of "it's none of your damned business" had spread throughout the bureaucracy.[8]

The 1954 elections had returned a Democratic House of Representatives to deal with a Republican administration, and tension over congressional access to executive branch information increased. The Freedom of Information Act was conceived, but as is not uncommon with legislation at the federal level, it had a lengthy—12-year—gestation period. Although it might be assumed that this length of time would ensure that the final product would be a model of precise and enforceable legislation, unfortunately the assumption is erroneous. The original FOIA was the outcome of a compromise between President Lyndon Johnson and the Democratic leadership in Congress and the result was a poorly drafted and vague piece of legislation whose requirements were subject to considerable interpretation (or misinterpretation). Persuaded by members of the executive branch that openness was not a good idea, Johnson was somewhat less than enthusiastic about the proposed legislation. In a meeting with House Speaker John McCormack and Majority Leader Carl Albert, Johnson graphically expressed his views on freedom of information and the bill's chief sponsor, Congressman John Moss of California: "I thought he was one of our boys, but the Justice Department tells me his goddamn bill will screw the Johnson Administration."[9]

To secure the enactment of any freedom of information legislation at that time required the deletion of most of the provisions objected to by the Johnson Administration. What remained and passed Congress was an Act filled with ambiguous provisions and requirements. In an attempt to clarify these provisions for executive agencies, the Attorney General issued a memorandum offering a line-by-line interpretation of legislative intent. At best, figuring out legislative intent for a two-house, 535-member institution is a difficult proposition, and it was even more so for the FOIA. The bill had been passed in different form by the two houses and the final measure was the result of a conference committee which kept no record and had been closed to any kind of publicity. The Attorney General decided and the federal courts agreed, that legislative intent could best be ascertained through the House committee report on the legislation. Coincidentally, that report was more favorable to executive withholding of information than the Senate report had been.

By 1974, the list of grievances against the original FOIA or at least its implementation was lengthy. Excessive delay in responses, exorbitant fees, failure to protect confidential information, the tendency of agencies to classify information into one or the other of the exempt categories, and inadequate judicial remedies were only a few of the problems individuals attempting to use FOIA had encountered. Watergate and Richard Nixon's extensive use of executive privilege further antagonized an already hostile Congress and provided the impetus for a change in the law. The 1974 amendments to the FOIA, which passed over President Ford's veto, attempted to clarify the ambiguities and solve some of the problems of the original law. The current FOIA (section 552 of the APA) provides that:

1. Agencies must publish in the Federal Register descriptions of central and field organization, rules of procedure, substantive rules, and statements of general policy.
2. Agencies must also publish rules and fees for freedom of information requests and indexes of most documents and records in their possession.
3. Agencies must make available for public inspection and copying final opinions, policy statements, and staff manuals.
4. Agencies must make documents and records available to any person requesting them as long as the information requested is reasonably clearly identified and does not fall under one of the exempt categories.
5. Agencies must respond to initial requests within 10 working days of their receipt and to appeals of denials within 30 days.
6. Any person who has been denied requested information and who has exhausted administrative remedies may file a complaint in the district court in the district where he resides or where the records are kept or in the District of Columbia.
7. The district courts are to give such cases precedence on their dockets and are empowered to direct the agency to produce the documents, to examine the documents in camera, and to determine if they have been properly withheld.
8. If the court determines that the documents were improperly withheld it shall order their release and may assess attorney fees and litigation costs against the government. Courts are also authorized to determine if an employee acted arbitrarily and capriciously in withholding the information. Such a finding is to be transmitted to the Merit System Protection Board which determines if disciplinary action is warranted.
9. Agencies are required to file annual reports with Congress on FOI activities.
10. The following categories of information are exempt from disclosure:
    a. Information properly classified for national security reasons.
    b. Internal personnel rules and practices.
    c. Trade secrets; privileged or confidential financial information.
    d. Inter- or intra-agency memos.
    e. Personnel and medical files.
    f. Reports compiled by or for agencies regulating financial institutions.
    g. Geological and geophysical information.

    h. Information exempt by other statutes.
    i Investigatory records compiled for law enforcement purposes that, only to the extent that disclosure would reveal confidential sources, deprive a person of a fair trial, constitute an unwarranted invasion of privacy, or interfere in various ways with investigation and enforcement.

    Assessments of the impact and implementation of the FOIA vary considerably. Some executive agencies are decidedly unenthusiastic about it and feel that it has overburdened their personnel and negatively affected their ability to function. The FBI and CIA complain, perhaps with good reason, the most vehemently about the evils of disclosure. The FBI has been inundated with requests under both the Privacy Act and FOIA. By the summer of 1977 it had a backlog of 15,548 requests for information. To comply with the Acts, the agency launched Project Onslaught: 300 FBI agents were brought in from the field to handle information requests. By 1978, the FBI estimated it was spending $4.5 million annually on information requests and claimed that it was encountering difficulties in investigations: People were becoming reluctant to disclose personal or confidential information that might be subject to disclosure.
    Stansfield Turner, Director of the CIA, was even more critical of open files. The FOIA, it should be noted, is available for use by any person, which means foreign nationals have the same access to information as American citizens. To the CIA this raises the possibility that one FOIA request may be equivalent to three KGB agents. Further, as Turner has noted, the CIA does get a lot of bizarre requests. It gets persistent demands from "King Edward the Ninth" of Allentown, Pennsylvania, for his files; it received a letter from a high school civics teacher warning that he was requiring all his students to make an FOIA request so they could see how the system works. Of equal irritation is the problem that when requests are denied and court challenges are made they are almost invariably filed in the complainant's district requiring CIA attorneys to pack their documents and travel. Turner's attitude towards the FOIA has not been improved by requests filed by "people like Philip Agee [an ex-CIA employee who has written several books very critical of the agency] who has vowed to destroy the Central Intelligence Agency."[10]
    Other executive agencies have been less hostile but not a great deal more supportive of FOIA. Compliance with the act appears to be good: For example in 1977, HEW received 42,197 requests and over 97 percent of them were granted;[11] EPA received 4,113 requests and denied 168 or 4.1 percent.[12] The relatively high levels of compliance with FOIA during the Carter Administration were at least partially explainable by guidelines issued by the Justice Department stating that it would defend agencies which refused to release information only if the agency could show that the release would cause "demonstrable harm."[13] The total cost of compliance with FOIA is unknown but for 1977, 39 agencies indicated costs of approximately $26 million.[14] The Congressional Research Service estimates the total annual costs of compliance to be approximately $50 million per year.[15]
    The FOIA also has had some unintended impacts. The principal users of the Act have turned out to be neither journalists nor the public but corporations and corporate attorneys. Over 80 percent of the requests made come from these two sources who

have discovered that FOIA is a less expensive, quicker, and less dangerous method of getting information on competitors than industrial espionage. For example, at one point Xerox requested the files on IBM's licensing agreements from the FTC. To ensure that they do not inadvertently disclose confidential information of this sort, some agencies have established special procedures. The Securities and Exchange Commission informed firms it regulates to mark information that should be considered confidential; IRS has made a similar suggestion to firms, and some agencies have suggested to corporate attorneys that they phone rather than write.[16] FOIA has also fostered the development of a new industry which obtains government information and then sells it to clients.

Prior to 1981, the amended FOIA had made much of the vast amount of information contained in government files accessible, although delays in responding to requests still occurred and in some cases the fees charged were rather large. Nevertheless, it had opened government to public scrutiny and encouraged other states and other countries to follow suit. Currently, over 36 states and Sweden have adopted Freedom of Information statutes and Australia, Great Britain, and Canada are considering adopting similar legislation.[17] As was indicated above, however, many federal agencies had only grudgingly complied with the law and consistently complained about the burdens the Act imposed on them. With the advent of the Reagan Administration, the complaints began to receive a far more sympathetic response from the White House than they had during the Carter Administration. On May 4, 1981, the Justice Department rescinded the Carter guidelines and announced that agencies were free to determine their own information release policies and could count on Justice Department support if court challenges to those policies were made. In October 1981, the Administration submitted its proposals for amending the FOIA to the Senate. Generally, the amendments would expand the exemption for law enforcement investigatory records to include all law enforcement records, expand the exemption for business trade secrets to include "other commercially valuable information," allow agencies to increase fees charged for information, and increase the allowable response time to requests up to one year depending on the nature of the information requested.[18]

The same congressional hostility and distrust of the executive branch that led to the FOIA amendments in 1974 also contributed to the addition of the Privacy Act amendments to the APA that same year. By 1974, members of Congress, civil liberties groups, the media, and many individuals had become concerned over the vast amount of information on individuals that was contained in government agency files. The extent of this government-maintained information was delineated in a report of the Senate Judiciary Subcommittee on Constitutional Rights. The report estimated that there were 858 federal data banks, 741 of which were computerized, containing 1,245,699,494 records.[19] Information included in these files ranged all the way from the income of individuals to, in some cases, their political beliefs and religious practices.

The depth and intensity, not to mention the triviality, of the information maintained in some of these files is indicated by this description of the contents of an Army Intelligence file that an individual obtained after passage of the Privacy Act:

> It said I owed 50 cents to my high school for not returning my locker key . . . It said I dated two or three times per week, but that I was never intimate with my

dates . . . It also said I was financially irresponsible because I [owed] $5 for a jaywalking ticket to the city of Seattle.[20]

That individual agencies maintained these files was disturbing enough; that through interconnection of computerized record banks government could put together a detailed profile of almost every individual in the country was horrifying, and if privately maintained data systems—bank and credit card records—were plugged in to such a system, a curious bureaucrat could, at the push of a button, discover what an individual had for lunch on December 12, 1979. The possibility that this information might be used for improper purposes had been confirmed by the Nixon Administration's attempt to use IRS records against political opponents and by a White House order giving the Department of Agriculture permission to examine farmers' tax records. Although that order was rescinded, disclosures that military and other unauthorized agencies were maintaining surveillance on civilian political activities increased suspicion of government information-gathering activities.

If executive agencies had been reluctant to comply with FOIA, some were openly hostile toward congressional interest in protecting the privacy of individual records. Senator Sam Ervin described the response of agencies to his subcommittee's inquiry into the data banks:

> Finding out about these [data] systems has been difficult, time consuming and a frustrating experience. The subcommittee met evasion, delay, inadequate and cavalier responses, . . . and all too often a laziness born of a resentment that anyone should be inquiring about their activities.[21]

Ironically, the FOIA compounded the possibility of the invasion of privacy of individuals by permitting access to these data banks. Although it authorized agencies to withhold such information, the FOIA did not specifically prohibit the release of individually identifiable records at the request of a curious person. The Privacy Act is aimed at preventing such disclosure and the result is that it and the FOIA have distinct and very different goals. While FOIA seeks openness and accessibility to government files, the Privacy Act seeks confidentiality. It has four primary goals: to restrict agencies from gathering unnecessary information on individuals, to ensure the accuracy of that information, to provide individuals with access to information maintained on them, and to prevent unwarranted disclosure of that information. Further, unlike FOIA, the Privacy Act is applicable to and utilizable by only citizens and aliens admitted to permanent residency.

The Privacy Act (§552a of the APA) specifically prohibits any agency from disclosing individual records to any other person or agency without permission of the individual involved unless (inevitably) it is

1. To officers of the agency who have a need for the record in performance of their duties,
2. To the Census Bureau,
3. To the National Archives,
4. To Congress,
5. To the General Accounting Office,

6. To an agency for criminal or civil law enforcement,
7. Pursuant to a court order,
8. To an individual for statistical research and the record is not individually identifiable,
9. To a person showing compelling circumstances affecting the health or safety of the individual.

Even privacy is a relative thing, and the Privacy Act in no way prevents government officials from using individual records or record systems for official purposes. It did not bar the Secretary of HEW from using government personnel records to track down government employees who had defaulted on government loans or from using Social Security records to find fathers who were delinquent in their child support payments and whose families were receiving AFDC payments (exemption 6 above). The protection is obviously far from absolute and extends primarily to completely unauthorized "fishing expeditions" by private persons or public agencies.

The next major section of the Privacy Act guarantees individuals a right of access to all records maintained on them. Every individual has a right to review and make a copy of such records. If, in reviewing such records, the individual discovers inaccuracies, then correction may be requested. Given the vast resources of government when it comes to collecting information, it might seem unavoidable that it would get accurate information. Unfortunately, this is not necessarily true. In the past and undeniably in the present, one of the ways that government agencies collect information on individuals is by talking to other individuals. Particularly in routine background checks on individuals who have applied for government jobs or who are in jobs that require security clearances, standard operating procedure is for investigators to interview neighbors, colleagues, ex-teachers, and acquaintances. The questions, Privacy Act notwithstanding, remain personal and subjective: Has/does this person use drugs, drink excessively? Does this person date? Does this person have normal sexual preferences? Is there anything unusual about this person's social life? It is impossible to ascertain how frequently personally damaging and inaccurate information is gathered through such techniques.

At least now, under the Privacy Act, an individual has an opportunity to review his/her files and if inaccuracies are discovered to request correction. The agency is required to respond to such a request within 10 days and either make the correction or explain the reasons for not doing so. The individual then has the right to appeal the refusal and request agency review. The agency has 30 days to respond to the appeal and if it still refuses to make the correction, it must inform the individual of his/her right to judicial review and must include a notation in the file as to which portion of the record is disputed. If judicial review is sought, the court may order the record amended, assess attorneys fees and litigation costs, and if it determines the agency willfully violated the act, award civil damages of no less than $1,000. Criminal penalties are also provided for wrongful disclosure of protected information.

The Act also attempts to restrict the amount and type of information that agencies may collect and the procedures used to collect it. Only such information as "is relevant and necessary" to accomplish the agencies' purposes is to be maintained. In collecting information that may adversely affect an individual's rights, benefits, and privileges under federal programs, every attempt should be made to collect the information directly from the individual involved. Agencies are forbidden from maintaining any record concerning how an individual exercises First Amendment rights unless expressly authorized to do so.

The degree to which the Privacy Act has actually accomplished its intended goals is debatable. One problem in its implementation has been the tendency of some agencies to encourage individuals to sign waivers of their rights guaranteed by the Act. Particularly in connection with employment background checks, it is frequently suggested to the applicant that signing the waiver may be helpful to his/her employment prospects since references which are guaranteed confidentiality are likely to be given more credibility than those which are subject to disclosure. Another problem confronting individuals who wish to use the Act is determining which agencies have records on them. The best source at this point is the annual compilation of Privacy Act notices published by the *Federal Register*. There are now several volumes of these compilations and they are poorly indexed,[22] which makes it difficult for the individual to ascertain all of the possible record systems that contain personal information. Further, like the FOIA, the Privacy Act contains several exemptions for record systems and records that are not subject to disclosure.

The annual reports filed with Congress give a partial indication of the impact of the Privacy Act. One of the most interesting aspects of the report is their revelation as to the number of record systems still maintained. Table 4.1 summarizes this data for 1976–78.[23]

To this point the Veterans' Administration has received more Privacy Act requests for information than any other federal agency, although it has not complained as vocally about the Act as the CIA and FBI have. Annual administrative costs for compliance with the Privacy Act have averaged $35–40 million.[24]

From the administrative agencies' perspective, the most serious problem in complying with the Privacy Act's requirements is not the time and expense but the potential conflict that may arise from requests for information made under the FOIA. The Privacy Act is aimed at preventing disclosure of individual informatiion to third parties; the FOIA, on the other hand, allows nondisclosure only if it would constitute a "clearly unwarranted invasion of personal privacy." Occasionally, an administrator may be confronted with a dilemma: "refuse to disclose information and risk a suit under the Freedom of Information Act by the individual denied access or disclose the

TABLE 4.1. Federal Record Systems

Number of	1976	1977	1978
Agencies	97	92	96
Filing Systems*	6,753	6,424	5,881
Records**	3.85	4.02	3.65

* In Thousands
** In Billions

information and risk a suit under the Privacy Act."[25] The combined impact of the two acts has been to spawn a vast amount of litigation[26] seeking clarification of the exempt categories and "reverse FOIA" cases brought primarily by corporations seeking to prevent disclosure of information that they had been compelled to supply government agencies.

Supreme Court decisions have not resolved the conflict. In *Chrysler Corporation v. Brown*[27] the Court held that nothing in FOIA prohibits disclosure:

> the FOIA by itself protects the subcommittee interest in confidentiality only to the
> extent that this interest is enforced by the agency collecting the information.
> Enlarged access to governmental information undoubtedly acts against the privacy
> concerns of nongovernmental entities and as a matter of policy some balancing
> and accommodation may well be desirable. We simply hold here that Congress
> did not design the FOIA exemptions to be mandatory bars to disclosure.

The Court did concede that there might be other statutes, in this instance the Trade Secrets Act, which barred disclosure. From the perspective of industries which are compelled to supply vast amounts of information to government agencies, this can hardly be construed as reassuring, if they are concerned about the confidentiality of that information.

This tension between disclosure, openness, and confidentiality is further reflected in the Government in the Sunshine Act (§552b of the APA). Passed in 1976, the Sunshine Act applies to all multiheaded boards, agencies, and commissions and requires that all meetings must be held in public unless by majority vote the members determine that to do so would not be in the public interest or would result in disclosure of information in one or more specified categories which closely parallel the exemptions in the FOIA. If the meeting is closed the agency must specify in writing the reasons for the closure and maintain a public record of the meeting which will be available for later inspection. Any person may challenge the closing of a meeting in district court and the burden is on the agency to prove rightful action.

The actual impact of the Sunshine Act on agency proceedings is unclear. A General Accounting Office report indicated that for 47 agencies covered by the statute for the period of March 1977–March 1978, 36 percent of their meetings were completely closed, 26 percent were partially closed, and 38 percent were open. A study conducted of 13 agencies in 1978 indicated that from the agencies' perspective, the Sunshine Act had not increased public participation in agency processes and had adversely affected the ability of agency members to discuss agency business informally. The major benefits that responding agencies perceived were reassurance of the public, improved preparation for meetings, and increased sensitivity about what types of information can be made public.[28]

An unresolved ambiguity in the Sunshine Act is whether and to what extent it prohibits ex parte communications, unofficial off-the-record contacts, in rulemaking procedures. The conference report on the legislation included a section barring ex parte communications on any pending agency business.[29] At least one Court of Appeals decision with certiorari denied by the Supreme Court combined the Sunshine Act with an executive order to hold that it did:

> Information gathered ex parte from the public which becomes relevant to a rulemaking will have to be disclosed at some time . . . Once a notice of proposed rulemaking has been issued, however, any agency official or employee who is or may reasonably be expected to be involved in the decisional process of the rulemaking proceeding, should refuse to discuss matters relating to the disposition . . . with any interested private party.[30]

If this proves to be a correct interpretation, this section of the Act could have a sweeping impact on agency rulemaking procedures.

For federal administrative agencies, the Administrative Procedure Act is the primary source of procedures that they must follow in rule-making, adjudication, and managing the information that they maintain in their files. Although considerably more specific than constitutional provisions requiring due process, the Act still deals only generally with required procedures and sets only minimum standards for action. Despite its generality it has unquestionably shaped and molded the administrative regulatory process into the form in which it currently operates. The recent wave of anti-regulatory sentiment in the country has resulted in considerable interest both within and outside of Congress in revising the Act and modifying its procedural guidelines. The major procedural revisions that have been suggested will be discussed in chapter 14.

STATE ADMINISTRATIVE PROCEDURE ACTS

Although states have been involved in regulatory activities, in some cases for longer than the federal government has, they have lagged behind the federal government in adopting administrative procedure acts. In 1937, the American Bar Association's Section on Judicial Administration created the committee on Administrative Agencies and Tribunals to deal with state level agencies. Proposed legislation was referred to the national Conference of Commissioners on Uniform State Law, which after study, revision, and further consultation with the ABA finally approved the Model State Administrative Procedure Act in 1946. In 1961, a Revised model State Administrative Procedure Act was published. By 1969, it had been adopted by only five states.

By 1974, 19 states had adopted a comprehensive APA based on the model act,[31] and another 24 had less comprehensive statutes dealing with regulatory procedures.[32] A word of caution is in order: Making valid generalizations concerning administrative law at the state and local levels is difficult since the exact content of that law differs from state to state. Even among the states which have adopted the model APA, considerable variations in required procedures exist, since each state has modified the Act to fit the individual needs and differences of that state. What is required or permitted in New York may not be in Texas and vice versa, and an individual interested in or affected by state administrative actions should check the laws and court interpretations of that particular state.

Since the model APA has formed the basis for many states' legal requirements on their administrative processes, and is likely to influence other states in the future, a basic understanding of its major provisions, particularly as it compares to the federal

APA, is important. Overall, the similarities between the two outweigh the differences: The definitions in the two are basically the same, as are the rule making and adjudicatory proceedings. There are some differences in terminology; for example, at the state level adjudicatory proceedings are called contested cases, and the federal law defines more terms. The model law and most state statutes limit its applicability to state agencies only and exclude municipalities and counties.

One of the major distinctions between the two acts is the absence of a Privacy Act, FOIA, and Government in the Sunshine requirement in the model state act. Several states have enacted their own versions of one or more of these provisions, although not usually as part of their administrative procedure act. Many states, for example, have separate open meeting laws that are more demanding than the federal counterpart. Florida's law, for example, applies to state, county, and local agencies and requires that all meetings must be open to the public. Four states, California, Florida, Minnesota, and Wisconsin, have even made this applicable to collective bargaining negotiations with public employees.[33]

Notice, publication, and filing requirements also differ considerably at the two levels. At the federal level the requirement for providing public notice of proposed action and final rule adoption is satisfied by publication in the *Federal Register.* Although this method has been criticized for inadequately publicizing federal action, it does provide an accessible, centralized, and known, if tedious, source that interested individuals may consult. Although the Model Act provides for publication of a monthly bulletin equivalent to the *Federal Register*, most states have not adopted this provision. Currently, only 12 states publish some form of a state register.[34] The expense and probable limited public circulation of such registers have encouraged the states to seek other methods. The most common procedure is to publish notices of proposed rules in the newspapers. The model state law provides that this should be "some newspaper having general circulation throughout the state," a provision which evidently has been copied in several states. This has created confusion and some problems for administrative agencies in states such as Idaho, which have no general statewide paper. Although agencies in these states attempt to satisfy the requirement by publishing notice in several papers in various regions of the state, they have no guarantee that this satisfies the requirement. Also, unlike federal law, state law specifies that the required notice must be published at least 20 days in advance of the intended action.

The model Act requires that the Secretary of State compile, index, and publish rules and that each agency make all rules, policy statements, and final orders, decisions, and opinions available for public inspection. Actual state procedures vary. Thirty-five states have administrative codes available for purchase,[35] but public response has been underwhelming. New York State sold only 58 copies of its original compilation and less than 100 copies of the annual supplements.[36] Although 42 states do provide for filing regulations with some central state agency, this ranges from the Secretary of State's office to the state Law Library.

Public participation in rulemaking procedures is strongly encouraged by the model Act. Unlike the federal APA it requires a public hearing if requested by 25 or more persons. In Idaho, at least, this has turned out to be a costly and sometimes frustrating provision. The state Department of Health and Welfare estimates that it spends at least

$25,000 annually scheduling such hearings. Most frequently the request comes from affected interest groups such as the Nursing Home Association and not infrequently no one attends the hearing The result is lost money and inevitable delay in the rule-making process. The model Act also permits interested persons to petition an agency requesting adoption of a rule and the agency must respond in writing to such a request within 30 days of receipt.

The financial problems that these mandatory participation provisions create for some state agencies are indicative of the more general problems that developing uniform procedures based on federal practice can cause. The mandated procedures in both the federal and model APA are "legalistic" and to follow them requires that an agency have constant access to legal advice. This may be no particular problem at the federal level or in some of the larger states where adequate personnel and resources are provided to secure that advice. In smaller states where the legislature fails to provide these resources, adoption of the model APA without modifications can create serious problems for administrative agencies. Lacking their own legal staff, the agencies must then rely on advice from the state's attorney general who may have no special expertise in administrative law and at any rate has many other responsibilities.

This problem is further illustrated by the difficulties some states confront in finding sufficient and acceptable hearing officers to preside over contested cases. While the volume of such cases handled by federal agencies justifies their being given special administrative law judges, for many state agencies contested cases may be so infrequent that it would be impracticable and financially impossible to hire full-time hearing examiners or administrative judges. States have taken various approaches to solving this problem. California has created an Office of Administrative Procedure with a separate unit of hearing officers who may be utilized by most state agencies as the need arises. Although certainly an acceptable method, this does involve the loss of some specialization and expertise. New York State's Civil Service Commission maintains a register of eligibles that agencies may use to select examiners.[37] Smaller states, such as Idaho, generally adopt an ad hoc approach to the whole problem. The choice of a hearing officer is up to each agency and usually an agency will hire an outside person on a per diem basis (pay ranges from $20 to $40 a day). Most agencies do not feel that a hearing officer need be an attorney and it is fairly common for them to hire someone who is not.

One other aspect of many state administrative procedure acts that differs from both the federal and model Act is the provision for some form of legislative referral and review of administrative regulations. By 1979, over 30 states had provided for some form of legislative review of administrative rules and regulations. The procedures used ranged from review by a Legislative Council to review by standing or joint committees with opportunity for the legislature as a whole to modify, amend, or repeal any and all administrative rules within specified periods of time, ranging from thirty to sixty days at the beginning of a legislative session. The wisdom and constitutionality of these legislative vetoes is as much questioned at the state level as it is at the federal level. In Michigan, for example, the Attorney General ruled that legislative review was an unconstitutional violation of judicial power. The legislature, however, ignored his opinion and in 1963, Michigan adopted a constitutional amendment authorizing a joint committee to suspend regulations issued after adjournment of the legislative session and requiring the legislature to act on the suspension one month after reconvening.[38]

Some states have gone even further by requiring legislative preview of administrative rules. Idaho requires that agencies notify a germane joint legislative committee of proposed rules 10 days in advance of the public notice, and hold the record of any public rulemaking hearing open for 10 days for any additional legislative comments.[39] The impact of these procedures varies, but at a minimum they do increase the amount of time required for rule-making procedures and like the provisions for mandatory hearings may increase the power of organized groups in the regulatory process. These are especially serious problems at the state level for two reasons: Frequently, state agencies which are administering federal programs are required to comply with new or amended federal rules immediately, and delays caused by state statutes can result in threats of termination of federal funds and legal actions taken by adversely affected parties. Second, in many states, organized public interest groups may be nonexistent or so poorly organized and funded that they are unable to counter the claims presented by industry representatives.

Overall, state administrative procedure acts serve as the primary source of procedures that state agencies must follow in rule-making and contested cases. Like their federal counterpart, they are an attempt to specify what due process requires of administrative agencies. For state administrators whose programs are wholly or partially funded by the federal government, these state laws are only the starting point for proper procedures. They are also bound by all the procedural requirements imposed on them by federal law and federal agency regulations. The complexity of the legal environment of these state agencies is staggering and frequently conflict ridden. State legislatures do not always like the conditions federal agencies impose on use of funds; federal agencies seldom like the resistance that the states have to their requirements. The state administrator is caught in the middle. The consequences of ignoring federal regulations can be serious, since not only does he who has the gold make the rules, but he may also take back the gold if one does not follow the rules. On the other hand, to ignore state legislative wishes is equally serious in terms of political and legal repercussions. Occasionally, it may seem to state administrators that the legal environment in which they must operate is a procedural quagmire in which the unwary administrator can become hopelessly mired. The full complexity of that environment will be examined later, but at this point one further question can be raised (and left unanswered): If all of this is bewildering and complex to state administrators who are at least familiar with the complexity and are educated and trained to deal with it, how must it appear to a Food Stamp or AFDC recipient who is less educated, may be familiar with English only as a second language, and yet depends on the system for physical survival?

AUTHORIZING STATUTES

Authorizing statutes are the primary source of both regulatory power and the agencies that exercise it. They provide the mandate for regulation, determine the structure and type of agency that will administer it, specify the nature and scope of power the agency will have, define procedures that must be followed, and determine the reviewability of agency action by courts, Congress, and the President. They may be extremely specific or extremely vague on any or all of these points, and most administrative agencies operate under several statutes which assign to them various powers and responsibilities. An administrative action which is not based on or exceeds statutory authorization will be struck down by the courts as an *ultra vires* action. Finally, authorizing statutes structure the political environment within which agencies operate and play a major role in determining the ultimate success or failure of regulatory attempts.

The Mandate to Regulate

The instructions and authority to regulate that Congress provides agencies range from extreme and detailed specificity to extreme and unstructured vagueness. The Delaney Amendment requiring the FDA to ban carcinogenic agents as food additives is an example of specificity of mandate, as is the Federal Coal Mine and Safety Act of 1969 which, in attempting to reduce the amount of respirable dust in coal mines, specified the quantitative measure of acceptable dust concentration. At the other extreme, the FTC's authorization to "prevent unfair methods of competition," the Federal Maritime Commissions's authority to set aside rate agreements that "it finds to be unjustly discriminatory or unfair, . . . or to operate to the detriment of the Commerce," are so vague as to be meaningless without further definition. Occasionally, Congress manages to surpass even this vagueness by providing no standards and committing the decision to "the discretion of the administrator."[40]

The impact of the vagueness or specificity of the statutory mandate on regulatory outcomes is a subject of considerable controversy. From one perspective, it has been argued that the vaguer the mandate, the more discretion the administrative agency has. The more discretion the agency has, the more subject it is to regulatee pressure and ultimately regulatee capture. The end result is either nonregulation or regulation that favors the regulated interests and assumes that their interest and the public interest are synonymous.[41] Conversely, according to this theory, specific mandates afford agencies little flexibility in interpreting and enforcing the law and thereby make them immune or at least more resistant to regulatee pressure. The resulting regulations more clearly approximate "the public interest" than the wishes and desires of those who are regulated.

Although this theory appears to have some validity in explaining the outcomes of some regulatory agencies—the Interstate Commerce Commission and railroads, the Civil Aeronautics Board and the airlines prior to 1976, the Federal Trade Commission prior to the mid-1970s—it by no means completely explains regulatory outcomes. In the first place, some regulatory agencies with very specific mandates have not successfully accomplished their assigned missions. Despite the specificity of the 1969 Coal Mine Health and Safety Act, a General Accounting Office investigation in 1973 revealed that the law had not been complied with, that the Bureau of Mines had failed to conduct required health inspections and had been negligent in its enforcement of the law.[42] Second, some agencies with vague mandates have nevertheless managed to pursue their regulatory goals with considerable zeal. Although the FTC in the initial periods of its existence did seem unable to function effectively and define its vague mandate in an operable fashion, in the mid- and late-1970s, with no more specific mandate, it launched some of the most aggressive proconsumer regulatory programs in American history. Similarly, the CAB, operating under unchanged statutory guidelines, undertook in 1976 concerted effort to deregulate the airlines and inject competition into an industry that had little experience with or desire for it. The same vagueness that permits an agency to tilt toward a regulatee, also permits it to tilt toward consumer, environmental, or the public interest if it so chooses or if other aspects of its total circumstances change to permit it to do so.

Another important aspect of the authorizing mandate is the number and compatibility of the goals that it establishes for the agency. As was pointed out, most agencies have several statutes that authorize them to exercise power. The Federal Trade Commission has responsibility for implementing the Federal Trade Commission Act, the Clayton Act, the Webb-Pomerene Act, the Robinson-Patman Act, the Wheeler Act, the Trademark Act, the Wool and Fur Products Labeling Act, the Fair Packaging and Labeling Act of 1966, and the Truth in Lending and Fair Credit Reporting Act, among others. Even agencies that have fewer statutes to enforce are likely to discover that they have been assigned multiple goals and will have to establish their own priorities for accomplishment of these goals. On some occasions the goals will be compatible, but more than likely they will be conflicting and the agency will have to select which goals to optimize.

One of the most common examples of conflicting goals assigned regulatory agencies is the requirement that an agency both regulate and promote an industry. The legislation never assigns relative weights to these goals and the agency is placed in the position of determining which goal to pursue. Similarly, agencies that administer entitlement programs which confer legal rights increasingly find themselves instructed to take vigorous and immediate action to reduce fraud and abuse in their programs, while at the same time ensuring that all eligible persons receive benefits. Such conflicting mandates can lead to various regulatory results. In some cases, as with vague mandates, the agency in exercising its discretion tilts towards those goals favored by the regulatees. In other cases, the agency remains ambivalent, sometimes pursuing one goal and at other times pursuing different ones with the result that no one is satisfied with its performance and it is accused of inconsistency and ineffectiveness. At times a form of administrative paralysis sets in. Unable to decide which goal to pursue, the agency pursues none and nothing is accomplished.

The Powers to Regulate

As important as the nature of the regulatory mandate is the actual power that authorizing statutes confer on agencies to carry out their mandates. The ability to promulgate legislative or formal rules which have the full impact of law is certainly an important power, yet many regulatory agencies are not provided with it. For example, not until 1974 and the Federal Trade Commission Improvement Act was the FTC unarguably given this power by Congress. In the absence of statutory authorization to promulgate such rules, an agency must rely on interpretive rules and policy statements which are not always accorded the same legal enforceability as legislative rules. The lack of explicit rule-making power may also encourage an agency to rely on the less consistent case-by-case approach to regulation.

The history of coal mine safety regulation in this country provides a clear example of how failing to provide an agency with meaningful power to carry out its mandate can undermine its efficacy. Congress first went on record in favor of mine safety in 1910; the initial statute, however, permitted safety inspections only with the consent and foreknowledge of the mine owner and even then the inspection was conducted by state, not federal, officials. Between 1910 and 1941, when the U.S. Bureau of Mines was authorized to make periodic inspections of coal mines, 12,000 coal miners were killed in mine explosions. However, the only enforcement power granted the Bureau of Mines by the 1941 law was to publicize safety violations. Not until 1952 was the Bureau finally given real enforcement power and then Congress erred in the direction of overkill: Unsafe mines could be ordered closed—but the only other enforcement power remained publicity. Reluctant to invoke that extreme sanction against the wishes of both mine labor and management, the Bureau of Mines remained essentially powerless and mine safety violations and accidents continued. Not until 1969 were intermediate forms of enforcement authority finally provided, although they, too, as previously indicated, proved ineffective.[43]

The extent and nature of investigatory powers provided an agency also affect its ability to regulate. Authorizing statutes specify whether the agency may inspect physical premises, records, and books, require records to be kept, issue subpoenas, investigate on its own initiative or only in response to complaints. Failure to provide adequate investigatory powers can cripple an agency. For example, following the Three Mile Island nuclear reactor accident, a special commission was appointed to investigate the disaster. Originally, the commission had the power neither to issue subpoenas nor to hear testimony under oath. Without these powers, commission members rapidly became frustrated with the futility of their task, and a month after its creation its chairman presented Congress with an ultimatum:

> It is unconceivable to me that we would not have this power . . . If the powers are not given for an extended period, I would expect the commission will have to resign because we won't be able to do our work.[44]

Congress gave the commission its desired powers and no one resigned.

The type and variety of sanctions that an agency may impose for illegal behavior range from publicity, issuing cease and desist orders, requiring corrective action, imposing fines, seizure of property, terminating federal funds to seeking criminal prosecution in the court system. Again, the authorizing statutes are the source of which of these sanctions an agency possesses. In marked contrast to the weak and ineffective sanctions provided the Bureau of Mines, the Internal Revenue Service has been given power to impose fines and to seize the assets of persons found to be delinquent in their federal taxes. The normal range of sanctions possessed by an agency falls between these two extremes, but the sanctions agencies can impose clearly affect their ability to regulate.

Required Procedures

Although the APA sets general procedures for agencies, many authorizing statutes require an agency to follow specific procedures beyond those found in the APA. The Federal Trade Commission Improvement Act of 1974 requires the FTC to follow rule-making procedures that are considerably more stringent than those found in the APA. The required notice is more extensive, a hearing is required, as is a mandatory public comment period, and the final rule must be accompanied by a statement of basis and purpose which includes an assessment of the economic impact of the rule.[45] Some agencies are required by their authorizing statutes to follow adjudicatory procedures when promulgating rules: the Food and Drug Administration in establishing food standards and the FTC in implementing the Fair Packaging and Labeling Act of 1966, for example. Other authorizing statutes not only encourage agencies to allow public intervenors in agency proceedings but also authorize the agency to provide compensation for public interest participation: the FTC Improvement Act, the Consumer Product Safety Commission Organic Act, and the Toxic Substance Control Act of 1976 administered by EPA.

When and if an agency must provide an individual with an adjudicatory hearing is not determined by the Administrative Procedure Act, although that act has several sections concerning procedures to be followed in such hearings; instead, §554 of the APA specifies that it is applicable "in every case of adjudication required by statute." In other words, when and if an agency must provide an opportunity to be heard depends on the authorizing statute, or in some cases where the authorizing statute is silent, on the nature of the impact of the action.

Specific requirements concerning adjudicatory proceedings are also found in many authorizing statutes. The Veterans' Administration, currently the dispenser of $21 billion a year in veterans' benefits, has a statutorily mandated internal appeals procedure, but the statute also specifies that a veteran may not be represented in these proceedings by a lawyer who charges more than $10 for the service. Similarly, although normally the burden of proof in an enforcement proceeding is on the agency, in cases involving false and misleading advertising, the FTC has statutory authority to shift the burden and require the advertiser to prove the truth of the claim.

Whether a federal agency actually implements its own programs or these programs are implemented by state and local agencies under the supervision of the agency is also determined by the authorizing statute. The Occupational Safety and Health Act permitted states to enforce the health and safety standards if they could prove that their programs were "at least as effective as" the federal program. Currently, 23 states operate their own programs under OSHA. Although this may, in some instances, be a more effective and efficient way of implementing a regulatory program, it makes it difficult to ensure uniformity of regulation and adds several more procedural layers to the regulatory process.

Reviewability of Administrative Action

Whether, and at what point, in the administrative process an action is subject to judicial, legislative, or presidential review may be specified in enabling legislation. In some instances that legislation may completely foreclose judicial review. For certain veterans' benefit programs, decisions of the administrator are final and "no other official or any court of the United States shall have power or jurisdiction to review any such decisions."[46] The pragmatic consequence of this provision is twofold: it gives the VA considerable discretion in interpreting the law and it guarantees veterans' groups, the American Legion and the Veterans of Foreign Wars especially, an essential role as the advocates of veterans in VA determinations.[47]

Increasingly, Congress is subjecting administrative rules to legislative review prior to implementation. Currently, at least 167 laws have provisions for congressional veto. The imposition of this requirement on specfic agencies clearly affects their rulemaking processes. At the very least it lengthens that process since in most instances the rules do not become effective until the time permitted for congressional veto has lapsed. At the very worst this procedure puts the agency at the center of the war between the President and Congress and leaves those who must enforce and/or obey the laws in a position of considerable uncertainty. This is clearly exemplified by the current status of regulations promulgated by the Department of Education to implement the 1978 Elementary and Secondary Education Act.

In April 1980, the Department of Education transmitted to Congress four sets of regulations concerning programs for arts in education, state educational improvement, law-related education, and the Education Appeals Board. Under the General Education Provisions Act such rules are subject to veto by a concurrent resolution of Congress. Contending that the regulations contradicted or exceeded legislative intent, Congress vetoed them. On June 5, 1980, at the request of the President, the Attorney General notified the Secretary of Education that the veto was unconstitutional. The Secretary of Education then instructed department officials to treat the disapproved regulations "as final and effective rules." Almost certainly the question as to the constitutionality of the veto will be taken to the courts.[48]

Authorizing Statutes: The Specifics of Regulation

To understand a specific administrative agency, then—its goals, purposes, procedures, and powers—it is essential to understand the specific statutes under which that agency functions. The authorizing legislation that creates the agency and assigns it responsibility and power also frequently requires it to follow detailed and specific procedures beyond those imposed by the Constitution, courts, and general procedural legislation. The nature of the mandate provided an agency structures its political environment, in large part determines the methods and procedures that it must use in implementing programs, and specifies the criteria by which the success or failure of a regulatory program should be judged.

LEGAL RIGHTS

In chapter 3 we discussed federal constitutional rights. An equally important category of individual rights with particular relevance to both federal and state administrative action is rights created and conferred on individuals by statute. As the scope of government has widened, government has bestowed more and more benefits on its citizens and sometimes noncitizen residents. Each program bestowing such benefits has been accompanied with an expansion of rules, regulations, and restrictions on the recipients. The list of such federal programs is lengthy. It includes Social Security, veterans' benefits, Medicare, Medicaid, Food Stamps, unemployment compensation, federal employee retirement benefits, loan guarantees, subsidies to countless industries, grants, contracts, and licenses of various kinds. At the state level, this list can be replicated and expanded: occupational licenses, drivers' licenses, liquor licenses, and educational opportunities.

Originally, it was assumed that these beneficences were gratuities or gifts that a generous government bestowed on some or all of its citizens. It also assumed that "what government giveth, government could taketh away" and could impose, as a condition of receiving such largesse, whatever terms it deemed suitable. These benefits were termed "privileges," and as far as courts and frequently Congress were concerned, when an agency was administering privileges, even no process was due process. Given the scope of these programs and the number of persons directly affected by them, the lack of procedural safeguards and the amount of administrative power they conferred over the lives of individuals became of great concern to courts and critics of the administrative process.[49] Even so the courts were reluctant to change their perspective on these beneficiary programs. As late as 1960, the Supreme Court persisted in viewing Social Security payments as privileges that Congress could withdraw, modify, or restrict and could impose any conditions on their receipt it deemed fit.[50]

The recipient was a supplicant who could be and frequently was subjected to heavy-handed, humiliating administrative treatment. If a woman wanted AFDC payments to feed her children, then she had to submit to midnight or dawn searches by welfare administrators seeking to discover the presence of a male in her home so that those payments could be terminated. Charity, gratuities, privileges—whatever they were called—these government benefits were dispensed with one motto overall: "If you're going to feed at the public trough, don't complain about the swill."

Gradually, however, both Congress and the courts began to change their perspective on these programs. The change began in the courts as early as 1931. While not attacking the privilege doctrine head-on, the courts began to apply the rule of unconstitutional conditions: Government could not require recipients of a privilege to submit to conditions that would otherwise be unconstitutional.[51] In other words, welfare recipients, for example, could not be required to surrender their right to freedom of speech or religion as a condition of receiving AFDC payments. This line of reasoning was later expanded to prohibit government from acting arbitrarily against a person and to permit potential and actual beneficiaries of privileges to challenge in the courts administrative actions that they alleged were arbitrary.[52]

While this was a marked change from allowing unfettered administrative discretion in dispensing benefits, it still left recipients in a disadvantageous position. The Supreme Court vastly improved that position in 1970 in its decision in *Goldberg v. Kelly*.[53] AFDC, one of the largest federal welfare programs, has always been viewed with ambivalence and occasionally distaste by politicians and the public. A need-based program, AFDC is unlike Social Security where recipients have made direct contributions into a special trust fund and are allowed to receive benefits regardless of economic status. To receive AFDC, persons must prove they are indigent; once that has been established they are entitled to "charity," as many perceive AFDC payments. Social stigma and discriminatory treatment have characterized the AFDC program since its creation and have left its beneficiaries in an unenviable public and legal position. It is doubtful that *Goldberg v. Kelly* changed the public status or acceptability of AFDC recipients. It unquestionably changed their legal status in regard to administrative agencies:

> Such benefits are a matter of statutory entitlement for persons qualified to receive
> them . . . they are more like "property" than a gratuity . . . Public assistance,
> then, is not mere charity, but a means to "promote the general welfare and secure
> the Blessings of Liberty to ourselves and our Posterity." The same governmental
> interests which counsel the provision of welfare, counsel as well its uninterrupted
> provision to those eligible to receive it.

Slowly but surely the courts have included a large number of governmental largesse programs under the legal rights umbrella. Currently—in addition to AFDC—Social Security, disability benefits, Food Stamps, veterans' benefits, unemployment compensation, Medicare, and Medicaid are among the programs that are classified as entitlement programs. In general, once it is established that the law creating the benefit program confers an entitlement to the benefits for all eligible persons, such persons have a legal right—a property interest—to those benefits. Consequently, such benefits—property—may not be denied or terminated without due process of law. Usually this means that individuals must be afforded an opportunity for a hearing of some sort at some point, if they are to be deprived of such benefits.[54]

Some other types of government benefits that were once classified as privileges have also been given the status of property rights. Government employment, if tenure has been *explicitly* conferred, may not be denied without due process.[55] However, the Supreme Court has made it very clear that the guarantee to the employment must be unambiguously spelled out in either law or administrative regulation. In upholding the refusal of Wisconsin State University to renew the contract of a nontenured faculty member without specifying reasons, the Supreme Court specified the circumstances that were necessary to establish a property right:

> To have a property interest in a benefit, a person clearly must have more than an
> abstract need or desire for it. He must have more than a unilateral expectation of
> it. He must instead have a legitimate claim of entitlement to it.[56]

In *Bishop v. Wood*, a police officer who had been terminated without a hearing contended that a city ordinance which provided that after six months an employee became a "permanent employee" who could be dismissed only for failure to perform work up to the standard of his classification implicitly granted tenure to all permanent employees. The Supreme Court disagreed: "an enforceable expectation of continued public employment . . . can exist only if the employer, by statute or contract, has actually granted some form of guarantee."[57]

Occupational licenses, drivers' licenses, and even liquor licenses, primarily conferred at the state level, have also been given the status of rights that may not be denied without due process, although the exact amount and type of due process required differs considerably from case to case.[58] Although there is no federal right to education,[59] if a state law or constitution establishes such a right, then it too becomes a property interest which educational administrators may not deny without due process.[60]

The Supreme Court's attitude towards its own expansion of the rights doctrine remains ambivalent. Just one year after *Goldberg v. Kelly*, without in any way modifying that decision, the Court, or at least Justice Blackmun, indicated that it had not completely accepted the view that AFDC was a right. In *Wyman v. James*, a case involving the power of welfare agencies to conduct home visits, Blackmun pointed out:

> One who dispenses purely private charity naturally has an interest in and expects to know how his charitable funds are utilized and put to work. The public, when it is the provider, rightly expects the same.[61]

Beyond this ambivalence, both Congress and the Court have become increasingly aware of the financial implications of making benefit programs entitlements. Under this type of program, once an individual has established that he/she meets eligibility standards, he/she has a right to and must receive the benefits. The Food Stamp program is a prime example of an entitlement program that became a financial nightmare. Established in 1964, the program received a $375 million authorization for the first three years and was switched to an open-ended authorization in 1970. No one knows quite why—poor policy analysis, unanticipated economic downturns, or fraud and abuse— but the program rapidly expanded beyond anyone's anticipation. By 1975, 19.6 million people were receiving food stamps and the cost of the program was over $5 billion annually. Federal and state administrators contended they were powerless when it came to controlling costs. No eligible person could be denied benefits, and apparently there were a lot more eligible persons than anyone had estimated. The mushrooming expenditure problem has been replicated in most of the entitlement programs, until currently they consume 59.1 percent of the federal budget and cost $340 billion in fiscal 1980.[62]

No one seems quite sure how or if these programs can be limited. Administrators certainly have no control over them; Congress may or may not be able to limit them, but despite some grumbling Congress has never failed to provide full funding. Only once has the Supreme Court grappled with the problem and indicated that this might be an area where the doctrine of political questions was relevant. The state of Maryland realized by the late 1960s that its contributions to the AFDC program were becoming uncontrollable and were straining the financial capabilities of the state. The amount that an AFDC recipient was entitled to was calculated by a formula based on number of children and circumstances under which the family lived, but the state specified a maximum amount that a family could receive, regardless of number of children. Although the state stipulated a variety of reasons for this maximum benefit, controlling overall costs was obviously the most important reason. In examining the permissibility of the state action, the Supreme Court upheld it as a reasonable classification and asserted that "the Fourteenth Amendment gives the federal courts no power to impose upon the states their views of what constitutes wise economic or social policy."[63]

Seemingly, then, these entitlements can be legally limited as long as the restrictions are reasonable and equitable. Politically, they may be more invulnerable. Some of them enjoy uncontestable public support; others are supported by vocal and active interest groups, and others, although less popular, have become so essential to the physical survival of recipients that Congress hesitates to limit them. Food Stamps is one of the most criticized programs at the federal level but Congress reneged on its attempt to limit expenditures in the program in 1980. When program costs exceeded the spending ceiling Congress had established for 1979, Congress passed an emergency appropriation to avoid a cut in benefits.

The administrative consequences of this gradual inclusion of government benefit programs as legal rights have been to compel administrators to provide various types of procedural protections to beneficiaries, to further legalize the administrative process, and to subject administrators of those programs at all levels to personal suits for damages under §1983. The burden has been placed on administrators to know what programs and benefits are federally protected rights and to take care not to abridge or deny those rights arbitrarily. The most common response has been to provide some form of adjudicatory hearing before or at least after an action is taken. Whether this actually results in meaningful protection for beneficiaries, what additional costs, both monetary and nonmonetary, it has imposed on the administrative process, and the degree to which it has enhanced employment opportunities for attorneys remain undetermined.[64]

APPROPRIATIONS STATUTES

Although authorizing statutes may vest agencies with seemingly impressive powers and responsibilities, unless Congress also provides the agency with monetary resources to carry out those powers, the likely result will be symbolism rather than substance. Although authorizing statutes do set recommended funding levels for programs, they do not provide the actual funds; those in almost all instances are provided by separate appropriations statutes, and frequently the gap between authorized and appropriated funds is substantial. For example, PL 94–142, the Education for All Handicapped Children Act, guaranteed a "free appropriate public education for handicapped children." Appropriated funding for the program in FY's 1979, 1980, 1981, and 1982 fell well below authorized levels, leaving the federal implementing agency, the Bureau of Education for the Handicapped, and state and local education agencies in the undesirable position of being legally committed to accomplish a goal beyond their financial capabilities.[65] Further complicating the financial status of programs is the tendency of authorization statutes to provide for multiyear funding levels while appropriations are made on a year-to-year basis subject to prevailing political trends.

The appropriations process is entirely separate from the authorizing process and has become subordinate to the budget process. The committees, the motivations of key actors, the norms governing that process are substantially different from those governing the authorizing process. Particularly with the arrival of Reaganomics, many regulatory agencies have seen their appropriations slashed while their responsibilities have remained constant and in some instances increased. EPA's operating budget for FY

1982 was cut 17 percent from FY 1981 funding levels at a time when its caseload had doubled and it had been assigned responsibility for the implementation of new laws to regulate toxic chemicals and wastes.[66] Regulatory policy may be substantially modified or even nullified without any change in the authorizing statutes if Congress fails to provide money for policy implementation.

Determining the aggregate amount of funds available for policy implementation is not the only way that appropriation statutes affect and control regulatory agency behavior. Depending on congressional mood those statutes may also be either very general or very specific concerning when, how, and on what activities or objects the funds provided may be spent. Particularly in recent years, opponents of regulation have used the appropriations process as a means of imposing specific limits on regulatory actions. Unable to get substantive change in legislation cleared by authorizing committees which tend to be supportive of the regulatory programs that they have created and oversee, the opponents have increasingly resorted to using riders on appropriations measures which limit the activities on which appropriated funds may be spent. OSHA, IRS, the Department of Health and Human Services, and the Justice Department have had riders attached to their appropriations bills prohibiting them from spending any money to carry out certain legislatively authorized activities. In 1981, the House, although not the Senate, approved amendments to appropriations for the Departments of Labor and Health and Human Services which prohibited the issuance of any rules containing hiring, promotion, or admissions quotas based on race, creed, color, or sex. In addition to provisions included in the appropriations bills, the Appropriations Committees may also include language in their reports instructing the agencies on how to spend funds. The Food and Drug Administration was instructed in 1979 and 1980 not to promulgate regulations prohibiting the addition of antibiotics to animal feed. The FDA unwillingly complied with the instructions.[67] Although such riders have been consistently criticized by congressional leaders for bypassing regular legislative channels they constitute an increasingly important set of restrictions on the regulatory process.

Funding cutbacks affect not only agencies' abilities to accomplish substantive results but also their ability to comply with mandated procedures. Under the Civil Service Reform Act of 1978, any federal employee fired from his/her job was granted the right to appeal the dismissal to the Merit System Protection Board and to have a hearing before the Board. The appeal must be filed within 20 days and normally the hearing granted within 70 days. Subsequent to their firing by the President for going out on strike in August 1981, 10,886 air traffic controllers filed such appeals. By March 1982, no hearings on those appeals had been held primarily because the Merit System Protection Board's budget had been cut by 16.6 percent and it had no money to conduct the hearings. The Seattle regional director of MSPB conceded that "the appeals hearing is a statutory right," but also pointed out "we are bound by law to stay within our budget."[68] Ultimately in this instance and quite likely in many other similar situations, the courts will have to resolve the question of whether financial limitations can restrict due process requirements on administrative agencies.

The statutory environment of federal regulatory agencies is complex, complicated, and frequently replete with contradictions. Compliance with substantive and procedural statutory commands depends on provision of necessary monetary resources. If those resources are not provided, are insufficient, or are accompanied with statutory language that nullifies authorizing legislation, actual regulatory outcomes are unpredictable and evaluating the agency's performance is difficult, if not impossible. Regardless of its complexity, however, the statutory environment has a determinative impact on all aspects of an agency's behavior.

ADMINISTRATIVE REGULATION IN A FEDERAL SYSTEM

Frequently when criticisms are made of "big government" and its intrusive regulation of individual and corporate behavior, the main thrust of those criticisms is aimed at the federal government. What critics and supporters of government tend to overlook is the vast expanse of regulatory activity carried on by state and local governments, and equally important, the number and scope of federally funded and mandated programs that are actually implemented by these governments. Medicaid, Food Stamps, AFDC, and Unemployment Compensation are only a few of the federal benefit programs administered by state and/or local governments. Each of those benefit programs has been accompanied by an increase in federal regulatory authority over the administering units. From 1960 to 1978, the total number of federal mandates imposed on state and local governments as conditions of federal aid increased from four to 1,034. Similarly from 1965 to 1980, fifty federal laws were passed that superseded state laws.[69] Many of the programs established by these laws allowed state enforcement within established federal guidelines. Environmental quality regulation, industrial safety, and inspection of meatpacking and food processing establishments are examples of "pure" regulatory programs required by the federal government but commonly enforced by the lower levels. The result is a highly complicated and fragmented system of regulatory administration operating in an extremely complex legal environment.

As Figure 4.2 indicates, for any given administrative program, legal limitations and requirements stem from various and multitudinous sources. These sources constitute a hierarchy with each level superseding any provision of those at lower levels which conflict with it. How these various sources interact to determine the precise content of administrative law for a specific regulatory action can best be explained through a specific example: tracing the right to privacy from the Constitution through state agency regulations safeguarding the confidentiality of public assistance records.

As pointed out in chapter 3, the right of privacy is an implicit constitutional right which developed through Supreme Court interpretation of the Fourth, Fifth, and Ninth Amendments. As interpreted by the Court, this right to be left alone included an interest in preventing the disclosure of personal information. By 1974, Congress recognized that one of the greatest potential threats to individual privacy was the possibility of improper use of the vast volume of information maintained on individual Americans in the files of government agencies. Congress's response was to pass the Privacy Act Amendments to the APA discussed above.

Of all the federal cabinet departments then in existence, the Department of Health, Education and Welfare maintained the most files on the largest number of individuals.

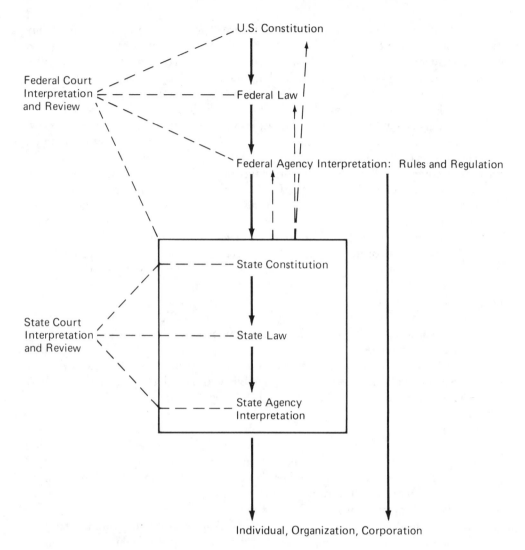

FIGURE 4.2   Administrative Regulation in a Federal System

Within that Department, the Social Security Administration's files tended to be the most encompassing in sheer numbers of individuals included. As far as administrative simplicity was concerned in implementing the Privacy Act, however, at least these were federally maintained files. But many of HEW's programs were implemented at the state and local level and the necessary records on individuals were also compiled and maintained at those levels. A preliminary question was whether these records were covered by the Privacy Act and the answer was by no means apparent from a superficial reading of the Act.

The key definitions in determining applicability in the Act were "maintain" and "system of records." "Maintain" was defined to include "maintaining, collecting, using or disseminating" records, and "system of records" was defined as a "group of any records under the control of any agency from which information is retrieved by name, number or identifying symbol of an individual." Considerable differences in interpretations of these terms exist among federal agencies. The Department of Labor which oversees implementation of the Unemployment Compensation Program has not interpreted the Privacy Act as being applicable to individual records in this program since they are maintained at the state level. HEW, however, adopted a more expansive view, and decided that the Act did apply to its programs that were administered by the states.

The full text of regulations promulgated by HEW to safeguard information for financial assistance and social service programs may be found in *45 Code of Federal Regulations*, Chapter II, Part 205. Section 50 of those regulations provides that pursuant to a state statute imposing legal sanctions, the state plan (detailed application for federal funds) must provide that use or disclosure of information covering applicants for these programs will be limited to public officials who require such information in connection with their official duties and these duties must be directly connected with the administration of HEW programs. This section illustrates two important aspects of federal regulations: They are commands—no rules, no money; and they may command not only the state administrative agency but the state legislature as well. Further, they may supersede provisions of state constitutions which conflict with them.

The regulations proceed to prohibit one specific practice that some state and county welfare agencies had adopted. A routine practice in some localities had been to publish lists of names of applicants and recipients in newspapers, based on the theory that the embarrassment and humiliation of having it publicly known that a person was a welfare recipient would discourage applicants. The HEW regulations left no ambiguity on this practice: It is impermissible.

Responsibility for enforcement and compliance then shifted to the state legislatures and state agencies. In Idaho, the legislature acquiesced and passed a law making it a misdemeanor punishable by a fine and jail sentence to fail to protect the privacy of public assistance records.[70] The state Department of Health and Welfare, pursuant to the Idaho Administrative Procedure Act, then promulgated its own regulations to guide its employees in maintaining the privacy of individual records.

The full complexity of the legal environment of administrative action is well illustrated by a further section of the Code of Federal Regulations dealing with determinations of eligibility for public assistance programs. Part 206 of this chapter requires that standards and methods used by the states must respect the rights of individuals under

1. The Federal Constitution
2. The Social Security Act
3. Title VI of the Civil Rights Act of 1964
4. All other relevant provisions of federal and state law

At the bottom of this hierarchy of procedural protections are individual administrators and the individuals or corporations over whom power is exercised and on whom benefits are conferred. For the knowledgeable, these procedural and substantive restrictions are a potent source of protection. For state and local administrators, the system frequently appears to be one of incomprehensible complexity and confusion. Frequently caught between conflicting commands from the federal government and the state legislature, subject to federal suit by dissatisfied clients, their frustration is understandable. Unfortunately, it is also irremediable. The American federal system is one of the most complicated political systems in the world, and the legal framework of its administrative process mirrors and magnifies these complications.

NOTES

1. 5 U.S.C.A. 551.
2. Frederick Blachly in George Wareen, ed., *The Federal Administrative Procedure Act and the Administrative Agencies* (New York: NYU School of Law Press, 1947), p. 30.
3. Robert Benjamin, "A Lawyer's View of Administrative Procedure," *Law and Contemporary Problems*, 26 (1961), 179.
4. Quoted in Fredrick Blachly and Miriam Oatman, *Federal Regulatory Action and Control* (Washington, D.C.: Brookings Institute, 1940), p. 144.
5. Quoted in Marver Bernstein, *Regulating Business by Independent Commission* (Princeton, N.J.: Princeton University Press, 1955), p. 63.
6. See Appendix I for the full text of the APA.
7. Blachly, in Warren, *The Federal Administrative Procedure Act and the Administrative Agencies*, p. 43.
8. Samuel Archibald, "The Freedom of Information Act Revisited," *Public Administrative Review*, 39 (July/Aug 1979), 313.
9. Quoted in Archibald, p. 313.
10. Stansfield Turner, "Whose Freedom of Information?" *Spokesman Review* (Spokane, Washington), October 30, 1979, p. 7.
11. Russell Roberts, "Faithful Execution of the FOI Act," *Public Administrative Review*, 39 (July/Aug 1979), 321.
12. L. G. Sherick, *How to Use the Freedom of Information Act* (New York: Anco Publishing Co., 1978), p. 71.
13. Laura Weiss, "Security Police Work Cited by Critics Seeking to Limit the Freedom of Information Act," *Congressional Quarterly*, July 11, 1981, p. 1243.
14. Harold C. Relyea, Letter to the Editor, *Public Administrative Review*, 40 (May/June 1980), 300.
15. Weiss, "Security" Policy Work Cited by Critics Seeking to Limit the Freedom of Information Act," p. 1244.
16. "Opening Federal Files," *Newsweek*, June 18, 1978, p. 86.
17. Harold Relyea, "The Freedom of Information Act a Decade Later," *Public Administrative Review*, 39 (July/Aug. 1979), 310.
18. Laura Weiss, "Questions Posed Concerning Reagan Proposal to Restrict Freedom of Information Act," *Congressional Quarterly*, October 24, 1981, pp. 2077–79.
19. "Privacy: Congress Expected to Vote Controls," *Congressional Quarterly*, September 28, 1974, p. 2612.
20. Sherick, *How to Use the Freedom of Information Act*, p. 53.
21. "Privacy," *Congressional Quarterly*, p. 2611.
22. Sherick, *How to Use the Freedom of Information Act*, p. 57.

23. From *Second, Third*, and *Fourth Annual Reports of the President*, "Federal Personal Data Systems Subject to the Privacy Act of 1974" (Washington, D.C.: Government Printing Office, 1977, 1978, 1979).

24. Ibid.

25. David M. O'Brien, "Freedom of Information, Privacy, and Information Control," *Public Administrative Review*, 39 (July/Aug. 1979), 326.

26. Glen O. Robinson, Ernest Gellhorn, and Harold Bruff, *The Administrative Process*, 2d ed. (St. Paul, Minn.: West Publishing Co., 1980), pp. 504ff.

27. 441 U.S. 281 (1978).

28. Thomas Tucker, "Sunshine—The Dubious New God," *Administrative Law Review*, 32 (Summer 1980) 552.

29. "Government in the Sunshine Act Cleared," *Congressional Quarterly*, September 4, 1976, p. 2425.

30. *Home Box Office Inc. v. FCC*, 567 F2d 9 (1977); cert. denied, 438 U.S. 829 (1977).

31. "Symposium on State Administrative Law," *Administrative Law Review*, 28 (Spring 1978) 148.

32. Walter Gellhorn and Clark Byse, *Administrative Law: Cases and Comments*, 6th ed. (Mineola, N.Y.: Foundation Press, 1974), p. 1160.

33. Benjamin Aaron, Joseph Grodin, and Joseph Stein, *Public Sector Bargaining* (Washington. D.C. Bureau of National Affairs, 1979), p. 214.

34. Gellhorn and Byse, *Administrative Law*, p. 88.

35. "Symposium on State Administrative Law," *Administrative Law Review*, p. 148.

36. Aaron, Grodin, and Stein, *Public Sector Bargaining*, p. 214.

37. Gellhorn and Byse, *Administrative Law*, p. 1044.

38. Boyd Wright, *Legislative Review of Administrative Rulemaking in North Dakota* (Grand Forks, N. D. Bureau of Governmental Affairs, University of North Dakota, 1976), p. 15.

39. *56 Idaho Code 22*.

40. See discussion on Immigration and Naturalization Service in chapter 3.

41. See Bernstein, *Regulating Business by Independent Commission*, pp. 263–67, and Theodore Lowi, *The End of Liberalism* (New York: W. W. Norton, 1969).

42. Duane Lockard, *The Perverted Priorities of American Politics*, 2d ed. (New York: MacMillan, 1976), pp. 11–15.

43. Lockard, *The Perverted Priorities of American Politics*, p. 11.

44. Commission Chairman John Kemeny, quoted in "Angry N-Probers Cancel Hearings," *Spokesman Review* (Spokane, Washington), May 18, 1979, p. 3.

45. Robinson, Gellhorn, and Bruff, *The Administrative Process*, 1980, p. 550.

46. 38 U.S.C.A. 211.

47. Bill Keller, "Clinks in the Iron Triangle," *Congressional Quarterly Weekly Report*, June 14, 1980, p. 1627.

48. *Congressional Quarterly*, June 7, 1980, p. 1580, and June 21, 1980, p. 1732.

49. See Charles Reich, "The New Property," 73 *Yale Law Journal* (1964), 733–86.

50. *Flemming v. Nestor*, 363 U.S. 603 (1960).

51. Bernard Schwartz, *Administrative Law* (Boston: Little, Brown, 1976), p. 223.

52. Schwartz, p. 224.

53. 397 U.S. 254 (1970).

54. See chapter 6.

55. *Arnett v. Kennedy*, 416 U.S. 134 (1977).

56. *Board of Regents v. Roth*, 408 U.S. 576 (1976).

57. *Bishop v. Wood*, 426 U.S. 341 (1976).

58. See *Schware v. Board of Bar Examiners*, 353 U.S. 232 (1957); *Bell v. Burson*, 402 U.S. 535, 540 (1971); *Misurelli v. Racine*, 346F Supp. 43, 47 (1972).

59. *San Antonio Independent School District v. Rodriguez*, 411 U.S. 1 (1973).

60. *Goss v. Lopez*, 419 U.S. 565 (1975).

61. *Wyman v. James*, 400 U.S. 309 (1971).

62. Harrison Donnelly, "Uncontrollable U.S. Spending Limits Hill Power of the Purse," *Congressional Quarterly*, January 19, 1980, p. 117.

63. *Dandridge v. Williams*, 397 U.S. 471(1970).

64. H. Friendly, "Some Kind of Hearing," 123 *University of Pennsylvania Law Review* (1975), 1267, 1279–1304.

65. Ervin L. Levine and Elizabeth Wexler, *PL 94–142: An Act of Congress* (New York: MacMillan, 1981), pp. 188–89.

66. Harrison Donnelly, "Fiscal '82 Supplemental Awaits House Action," *Congressional Quarterly*, April 17, 1982, p. 268.

67. Alan Murray, "House Funding Bill Riders Become Potent Policy Force," *Congressional Quarterly*, November 1, 1980, p. 3255.

68. "Controllers Lose Right to Budget Cuts," Spokane (Wash.) *Spokesman-Review*, March 21, 1982, p. 3.

69. David B. Walker, *Toward a Functioning Federalism* (Cambridge: Winthrop, 1981), p. 193.

Chapter 5

The Environment of Regulation: Formal Controls and Informal Pressures on the Regulatory Process

Regulatory agencies exist in a complex environment and are subject to a variety of formal controls and informal pressures emanating from Congress, the executive branch, the courts, and numerous extragovernmental actors. The constitutional-legal framework is one component of that environment; it establishes the broad parameters within which regulatory action occurs, determining whether an agency has the power and resources to take a contemplated action and if so, what procedures must be followed in taking it. What it does not determine or explain is why the agency has decided to act or not act, the specific content and nature of the action undertaken, or the timing of the action. Anyone who has recently traveled on a commercial airline may have noted the sign prominently posted at the boarding area informing passengers that overbooking occasionally occurs and that any passenger holding a confirmed reservation who is bumped from a flight is entitled to monetary compensation and a guaranteed seat on the next scheduled flight. Depending on the airline, the sign may or may not indicate that the reason for this policy is a regulation promulgated by the Civil Aeronautics Board (CAB). By studying the CAB's legal environment one could determine if it had the authority to make such a rule and the basic procedures that it had to follow in promulgating and enforcing it. No amount of examination or study of the legal environment would explain why the CAB waited so long to regulate overbooking, why it finally decided to do so, and why its ultimate response to the problem took the form that it did. Similarly, an exhaustive analysis of the FDA's legal environment would have failed to predict the outcome of its attempt to ban saccharin as a food additive. In both instances only an understanding of the total environment in which the specific action occurred would provide the insights necessary to comprehend the totality of those regulatory actions.

For each regulatory action a unique set of actors and interests conditions the ultimate agency response to the perceived regulatory problem. The CAB's active concern

116

with airline overbooking began in 1972. Ralph Nader had a speaking engagement in Hartford, Connecticut, on the evening of April 28, 1972; he held a confirmed reservation on an Allegheny Airlines flight from Washington, D.C., to Hartford. Unfortunately for Allegheny Airlines, that particular flight was overbooked and Nader was denied boarding. Although Allegheny offered him a seat on the next flight out or a refund on his ticket, he declined the offer and instead filed suit in federal district court for monetary damages. The district court agreed that Allegheny had engaged in unfair and deceptive practices in violation of the Federal Aviation Act of 1958 and awarded Nader both punitive and compensatory damages. On appeal, the Court of Appeals remanded the case to district court with an order to stay further action pending CAB determination of whether Allegheny had violated the law. Nader appealed to the Supreme Court and in June 1978, the Court ruled in his favor.[1]

In the four-year interim, the CAB had become actively concerned with airline overbooking. In 1973, it initiated the Emergency Reservations Practices Investigation, and in 1976 included airline overbooking as one of its top ten priorities for the year. The initial outcome of the investigation was a set of regulations proposed by an administrative law judge recommending that the Board establish a contingent no-show control program. Based on the results of the investigation, the administrative law judge had accepted the contention of the airlines that the primary reason for overbooking was passengers who made reservations but failed to show up for the flights. The airlines contended that they were compelled by economic necessity to overbook to compensate for losses attributable to no-shows. The solution to the problem as the administrative law judge perceived it was to penalize no-shows. The CAB, however, rejected this solution and in April 1976, issued its first notice of proposed rules concerning overbooking.[2]

Because of the complexity of the problem and the high level of interest in possible solutions, the CAB allowed over one and a half years of public comment on its proposed rules. During that time comments were submitted by consumer groups, airlines, travel agents, and hundreds of individual passengers. The original proposed rules were modified in response to the comments and in December 1977, new rules were again proposed and further public comment permitted. Finally in September 1978, the final regulations were issued. They neither prohibited overbooking nor did they allow penalties for no-shows. Although airlines were required to post signs informing passengers of the possibility of being bumped from a flight and their right to monetary compensation if this occurred, they did not specify passenger priorities or what procedures airlines must use in determining which passengers should get bumped on an overbooked flight. Each airline was left free to formulate its own policies and priorities. The rules did require the airlines to seek volunteers to surrender seats on overbooked flights and to offer monetary compensation ranging from a minimum of $75 up to twice the fare paid. The regulations attempted to accommodate as many of the competing views that were presented by interested groups and individuals as possible, with the result that they completely satisfied no one. Most participants did agree that they were an improvement over the situation that had existed prior to their promulgation.

The FDA saccharin ban discussed in chapter 1 had a very different outcome. In that case extensive informal pressure resulted in the exercise of formal powers by Congress forestalling the proposed regulation. Both cases illustrate the role that the political environment plays in shaping specific regulatory outcomes.

Eighty years ago the dominant belief in the discipline of public administration was that there was a strict separation between politics and administration. Politics was the process through which policy was made and included all of those activities and actors that influenced policy decisions. Administrative agencies merely executed and implemented policies determined by the "political" branches of government and were uninvolved in and unaffected by politics.[3] This belief has long since been abandoned and replaced by the realization that politics permeates the administrative process and that the agencies themselves are major actors in all phases of the process.

The general political environment of the regulatory process consists of those institutions, groups, and individuals who provide input into a regulatory agency's decision-making processes. The most important of these are

1. Congress: as a collectivity, as individual members who are interested in a particular action or agency, and, at a minimum, the four committees that are directly concerned with any particular agency—the House and Senate authorizing and appropriating committees
2. The President and members of the Executive Office of the President
3. Cabinet secretaries and administrative officials above the agency in the administrative hierarchy
4. The courts
5. Other agencies with overlapping or conflicting functions
6. State and local governments which actually implement a policy or are directly affected by it
7. The media
8. The public
9. The clientele or target groups
10. Other affected interest groups

This is not to suggest that for any specific action all of these participants will actually be involved, but rather that they constitute potential inputs into the regulatory process and their existence shapes and limits the nature and scope of regulatory action. Congress, the President, the executive hierarchy, and the courts exercise a variety of formal controls over the regulatory agencies. They also provide informal input into the regulatory process which in specific cases may be more important in determining outcomes than formal controls.

CONGRESS

Formal Powers

The Constitution vests Congress with an impressive array of powers over the administrative process. As was discussed in the preceding chapter, Congress is the primary source of regulatory power: Through authorizing statutes, it creates agencies, provides them with their mandate to regulate, the powers to achieve that mandate, and the specific procedures to be followed in carrying out those powers. What Congress creates it may also eliminate, and powers granted may be subsequently modified, restricted or rescinded. Other statutes establish generally applicable procedures to be followed in contracting, purchasing, fiscal and personnel management, and through the Administrative Procedure Act in rule making, adjudication, and enforcement and the permissibility and scope of judicial review of agency actions. The annual budgetary-appropriations process constitutes a continuing method of formal control and review of agency behavior. Finally, Congress also has the formal power of legislative oversight, the increasingly utilized legislative veto, and in the case of the Senate, confirmation of nominees to head many of the regulatory agencies.

Legislative oversight involves "congressional review of the actions of the federal departments, agencies, and commissions and of the programs and policies they administer."[4] The Legislative Reorganization Act of 1946 assigned to each of the standing committees the responsibility to "exercise continuous watchfulness of the execution by the administrative agencies concerned of any laws, the subject matter of which is within the jurisdiction of such committees." Although such continuous watchfulness is nonexistent given the press of other legislative duties and responsibilities of the committees, certain circumstances are likely to result in committee surveillance of an agency's behavior. Divided partisan control of Congress and the presidency, particularly if accompanied by policy disagreements between the two, frequently results in increased committee interest and involvement in how agencies are enforcing, or not enforcing, the laws Congress has assigned to them.[5] As the level of conflict between Congress and the President increases in a specific policy area, so does the level of congressional scrutiny of agencies involved in that policy area. The number, length, and intensity of committee hearings are likely to increase and agency administrators are frequently caught in the middle of the conflict over proper policy enforcement. Similarly, constant complaints either from individual constituents or from powerful interest groups concerning agency enforcement of the laws may also stimulate increased committee oversight. Similarly, allegations of corruption or publicized scandals will also result in congressional oversight. Finally, oversight may also be initiated to protect an agency from a hostile President, press, interest group, or budget or appropriations cuts.

In addition to committee oversight, the existence of the General Accounting Office (GAO) as an arm of Congress empowered to perform financial audits and performance/program evaluations of executive agencies serves as a continuing check on agency performance. The GAO is headed by the Comptroller General, who is appointed by the President with the advice and consent of the Senate for a 15-year term and is removable only by joint resolution of Congress. The GAO is required by statute to assist committee chairmen on request and may also undertake evaluations or audits at its own initiative. Although limited in both personnel and resources, the GAO has greatly enhanced congressional oversight capabilities.

The expiration of authorizing legislation and the consequent need either to reauthorize or to let a program die can involve the entire Congress in the exercise of oversight of the past performance of the relevant agency. The expiration of the Clean Air Act in 1982 and the intense conflict within both houses of Congress over its reauthorization has been accompanied by intense scrutiny of the EPA's enforcement procedures, the goals of the Clean Air Act, and the feasibility and desirability of accomplishing those goals. Similar conflict and congressional oversight also accompanied the attempt to renew the Voting Rights Act of 1965 in the same session of Congress.

The use of the Senate's power to confirm or deny presidential nominations to administrative positions has served at best as a sporadic control of regulation. Most confirmation hearings are pro forma events and most nominees are confirmed with little senatorial attention to either the nominee or the agency concerned. Occasionally, however, Senate scrutiny of a nominee may be extremely thorough and, even more rarely, a nominee may be rejected. The reasons for increased Senate scrutiny of presidential nominees to regulatory agencies are precisely the same as those that result in increased committee oversight: divided partisan control, interest group complaints, desire to protect an agency or program, or allegations of corruption either on the part of the nominee or within the agency. Increased senatorial scrutiny does not necessarily result in rejection of nominees; if a nominee generates too much interest or hostility within the Senate, the more likely result will be presidential withdrawal of the nomination prior to formal Senate action. President Reagan, for example, was compelled to withdraw William Bell's nomination as chairman of EEOC when it encountered servere criticism in the Senate because of Bell's lack of managerial experience and general unfamiliarity with equal opportunity laws. He was also pressured into withdrawing his nomination of F. Keith Adkinson when it became apparent the Senate Commerce and Transportation Committee would not confirm it.[6] Only rarely does the Senate actually reject a nominee: For example, from 1887 to 1968, the Senate rejected only 2 of 136 nominations to the Interstate Commerce Commission, and other regulatory agency nominations have been treated similarly.[7] As is true with most other types of power, the effectiveness of the Senate's confirmation power is not adequately measured by the number of times it has been exercised in a negative fashion. Its existence, the President's and the nominees' awareness of its existence, constitute a real if immeasurable control over who serve as regulators and how they conduct themselves during their tenure on the agency.

The legislative veto involves Congress in the direct administration of laws and allows it to prevent enforcement actions with which it disagrees without repealing the authorizing statute. With a legislative veto, Congress authorizes an agency or the President to take certain actions but provides that it must be notified of any proposed actions. The proposed action may then be vetoed within a specified time period by concurrent resolution, simple resolution (one house), or in some instances by committee vote. First used in the Reorganization Act of 1939, legislative veto provisions have proliferated in recent years and proposals for subjecting all administrative rules and regulations to such vetoes have received extensive support in both the House and Senate. The political and institutional controversy surrounding the use of legislative vetoes is discussed in chapter 14. However one evaluates these vetoes, they unquestionably expand the formal powers of Congress over the regulatory process.

Informal Powers and Pressures

Congress has a rather formidable array of formal powers over regulatory agencies, but as an institution it has an equally formidable array of responsibilities and interests. What this translates into is that most of the time Congress allows most administrative agencies great flexibility and pays little attention to their activities. Involved in the creation of the agencies, Congress is normally a permissive parent, tolerating most agency activities and inactivity with little concern. But even at the height of its tolerance and indifference, Congress exists as an omnipresent factor in the environment of a regulatory agency, and provides informal inputs, exercising control by "raised eyebrow," and communicating in various ways the sense of Congress about a particular agency and its activities.

Although an agency's authorizing statutes may empower it to engage in a broad range of vigorous regulatory activities, the agency may be well aware of the unwritten and informal limits imposed on its activities by the dominant sentiment in Congress as to how and against whom its powers should be exercised. One of the first rules of political survival that an agency learns is that doing nothing is a lot less likely to cause concern in Congress than doing something. For the most part, by doing nothing an agency, at least in the past, has been able to avoid antagonizing any powerful interest groups. Congress, an elective and highly political institution, operates on the "squeaky wheel" theory. Hearing no vociferous complaints about an agency, it is likely to ignore it. Conversely, any positive regulatory activity will directly affect someone: an individual, a group, a corporation. If those directly affected by the proposed activity perceive it negatively, they will react by complaining loudly to the media and to members of Congress. If the complaints are not counterbalanced by supporters of the regulatory activity, or if those supporters lack political power equal to that of the complainers, Congress will become interested in the proposed action. The first indication of that interest is frequently speeches made on the floor of Congress by individual members criticizing the agency and its actions. These are likely to be accompanied by press releases and media appearances denouncing the agency. If these activities are limited to a handful of congresspersons, particularly those who chronically berate government regulation, the agency may continue to pursue its proposed course of action. If, however, the opposition to the activity appears to be widespread and highly visible in Congress, an agency may be well advised to reconsider its activities. The FDA's response to street sales of DMSO is a clear example of the sensitivity of administrators to perceived congressional hostility. DMSO is believed by many to be an effective treatment for arthritis and other human ills; the FDA does not share this belief and DMSO has not been approved for human use. By mid-1980, retail sales of DMSO as a solvent degreaser were booming, and the FDA was not convinced that people were paying $23 for a half-pint of DMSO for degreasing purposes. Nevertheless, the FDA has been decidedly reluctant to crack down on DMSO sales. Bill Schwemer, an FDA official, explained the reasons for the reluctance:

> There are folks on the [Capitol] Hill, in industry, in the media and elsewhere that really believe wholeheartedly in "let the buyer beware." There have been a lot of signals to the FDA to be careful about what you can tell the public it cannot buy.[8]

From a normative perspective, the propriety of this kind of congressional control of administrative action is debatable. The argument can be made that if the agency's action is a lawful attempt to enforce a statute, it should pursue this enforcement activity without regard for informal responses emanating from Congress. From this perspective the agency should assume that the law is the law, and until that law is formally changed by act of Congress it must be enforced. This is the course that the FDA pursued in the saccharin ban case discussed in chapter 1, and is the course that the FTC followed in deciding to investigate and regulate the funeral home business. The other side of the theoretical argument is that agencies should be responsive to informal pressures from Congress because Congress is directly representative of the people and constitutionally well within bounds when it informally communicates its displeasure with an administrative agency. If the agency accepts this informal communication and backs off from a proposed action, then congressional control has been asserted and, in effect, Congress has controlled "by raised eyebrow."

Practically, the problems confronting an agency in this type of situation are as complex as the normative arguments. The FDA, for example, has suffered little permanent political damage because of its actions in the saccharin case. Although it compelled Congress to take formal legislative action to prevent saccharin from being banned, the FDA has not been subjected to any real diminution of its power, personnel, or funding. The FTC, however, has not been quite as fortunate. By failing to respond to a continuous stream of informal communications from Congress about vigorous consumer protection activities that have angered large segments of the American business community, the FTC finally found itself on May 1, 1980, flat out of money and compelled to suspend operations temporarily. As a matter of fact, the FTC has not had regular appropriations funding since 1976 because of congressional displeasure with its activism.[9] Without question the FTC could have avoided this formal sanction had it responded to the continuous flow of informal expressions of congressional displeasure during the preceding five years. The lessons to be learned from the FTC's experience are clear. Any agency which disregards the wishes of Congress, even if these wishes are not formally expressed, does so only at its own peril, and the pains and the penalties of such disregard are likely to include formal actions that decrease the agency's funding, personnel, and resources. Ironically, agencies are in the same position in regard to informal congressional actions as regulatees are in regard to informal agency action. In both cases, informal opinions and advice are not binding but failure to accept them may definitely result in negative, formal action. Just as the use of these informal procedures strengthens and improves the agency's formal powers, so does their use by Congress strengthen its formal controls.

Individual members of Congress and congressional committees and subcommittees also play an important role in the day-to-day existence of many agencies. Every member of Congress or his/her staff engages in individual casework for constituents. In the majority of instances this involves little more than staff members contacting an administrative agency at the request of a constituent whose veterans' benefits have been denied or whose social security check has been lost or delayed in an attempt to secure remedial action. But there is another category of communication between individual members of Congress and regulatory agencies that is not quite so benign, and the Federal Communications Commission (FCC) is an excellent example of how this second category can raise serious questions about the impartiality and public interest orientation of a regulatory agency.

To understand the total nature of the FCC and every other administrative agency's relationship with Congress, it is first necessary to understand the actual operations of Congress. To cope with its diversified and far-reaching responsibilities, Congress has been compelled to develop methods that increase its collective competence and expertise. The predominant methods it has developed to accomplish this are professionalization and specialization. Professionalization has been achieved by the increase in the average tenure of members of Congress and by the bureaucratization of Congress—the hiring of professional staff members for individuals, committees, and Congress itself. Specialization has been accomplished by the creation of the committee system, and by the 1970s with the devolution of actual power to the subcommittee level in both houses. Committee and subcommittee membership is continuous and remarkably stable, and during their service on these committees, members of Congress become experts on the substantive policy areas and agencies with which they deal. Other members of Congress routinely defer to the judgment of these experts and the result is that policy on an issue-by-issue basis is actually determined by a very few members of Congress. For the administrative agencies this means that for the most part the only members of Congress who are aware of their existence are those members who are on the relevant authorizing and appropriations subcommittees. When those subcommittees informally suggest or request an agency to do something, action is usually forthcoming.

By the early 1970s, various public interest groups including the National Parent-Teachers Association and Action for Children's Television were complaining about the excessive amounts of sex and violence on television. These complaints were transmitted to members of Congress and in 1974, the House Appropriations subcommittee ordered the FCC to submit to it a report on what the Commission was doing concerning this problem. Exactly what the subcommittee expected the FCC to do without violating the First Amendment and the Federal Communications Act ban on censorship was unclear and FCC Chairman Richard Wiley doubted that any formal action would be permissible. Nevertheless, wisdom dictated some kind of a response to the subcommittee's request. Consequently, Wiley initiated negotiations with television network executives to persuade them to do willingly what he suspected the FCC could not do legally. His persuasion, however, was backed by threat: "The bottom line . . . remained . . . do something to curb 'offensive' material or we, the FCC, will be forced to take action."[10] The networks did something; they agreed to amend the NAB Television Code and establish "family hour" the first hour of the evening prime time and banned "offensive" material from programs shown at that time. In response to informal instructions from Congress, the FCC used informal methods to accomplish the requested task.

The FCC is certainly not the only agency subjected to informal pressure from Congress, nor are these examples the only types of such pressure that occur. The propriety of such pressures may be arguable from some perspectives, but Congress collectively and singly tends to view them as part of the game. The dominant attitude in Congress was well expressed by the late Senator Dirkson of Illinois in 1960: "Ever since 1933, since I came here as a freshman Congressman, I have been calling every agency in government in the interest of my constituents." [He then gave an example of a CAB case pending and noticed for hearing to determine which of two airlines, one of which was Illinois-based, would be awarded a new route.] "I call up and inquire and I say a kind word about my constituents in Illinois. . . . I have called up—'communicated.' I wasn't authorized to do so. . . . I didn't call up the other side and tell them I was going to do it. . . . I went way beyond the trial examiner, I didn't even bother with him, he is just an intermediary. I went where the decision is to be made. The commissioner I talked to would have a vote. If it is a five man commission and I get three votes for my constituent, everything is hunkydory."[11]

THE PRESIDENCY

Formal Controls

The executive power shall be vested in a President. . . . [H]e shall take care that the laws be faithfully executed. ARTICLE II, SECTIONS 1 AND 3

Although the Constitution clearly designates the President as chief executive, it grants him few of the specific powers necessary to fulfill that responsibility and requires that he share most of his powers over administrative agencies with Congress. In some areas of administration Congress has granted the President statutory authority to control agency behavior; in other areas it has specifically restricted presidential ability to control the agencies. Consequently, although the President has an impressive assortment of formal powers over regulatory activity, he can seldom, if ever, completely control that activity, particularly in the presence of congressional opposition to the nature and direction of the control he attempts to assert. The insufficiency of formal powers has frequently resulted in Presidents resorting to informal pressures to secure desired regulatory results. The combination of formal powers and informal pressure guarantees the President a dominant role in the regulatory process, *if* he chooses to become involved. As the visibility and level of criticism of regulation has intensified so has presidential concern with regulatory activity, and recent Presidents have increasingly chosen to become involved in regulatory issues.

Control over the allocation of monetary resources is a fundamental power of chief executives. As we have already seen, Congress has the final word on the amount and allocation of monetary resources provided regulatory agencies. The President and his Office of Management and Budget (OMB) have the first word, however, and that has proven to be a potent tool in controlling agencies. The Budget and Accounting Act of 1921 first granted the President the power to assemble and prepare an executive budget to be submitted to Congress. This allows the President to establish spending priorities and to adjust agency budget requests to fit those priorities. Although Congress may and does change requested funding levels, normally it does so only incrementally. As the Reagan administration has amply illustrated, the President's budget preparation power structures the debate and forces Congress to react to the President's proposals. When he recommends severe cuts in an agency's funding level, as President Reagan has done with the Environmental Protection Agency, congressional supporters of the agency may be able to secure a restoration of some of the funds cut but will probably be unable to secure full restoration. Similarly, if a President wishes to enhance an agency's powers and enforcement capabilities he may request a substantial increase in appropriations; Congress will once again be compelled to make a decision based on the President's request. Once money is appropriated, the President is obligated to spend it unless he can secure congressional approval for recession of those funds.

Besides preparing the executive budget, the Office of Management and Budget assists the President in various other ways in his attempts to control the administrative process. Proposals for new legislation or modifications in existing law emanating from executive agencies must be submitted to OMB for approval. This legislative clearance function was first instituted in 1921 and has been increasingly important in ensuring that agency requests are in conformance with presidential preferences.[12] At the opposite end of the legislative process, OMB also recommends whether a bill passed by Congress should be signed or vetoed. In exercising the management part of its responsibilities, OMB recommends changes in agency management procedures and helps implement changes in those procedures that have been authorized by the President.

Presidents have long recognized that management procedures are an essential tool in controlling substantive administrative outputs. Recent Presidents have experimented with a variety of such procedures and techniques to enhance their control over the administrative process. Lyndon Johnson was particularly intrigued with Planning-Programming-Budgeting System (PPBS) which was first used by the Department of Defense and then by executive order in 1965 implemented in all federal agencies. An extremely complex and analytical type of budgeting, PPBS was intended to enhance presidential control over the executive branch. Richard Nixon discarded PPBS in favor of Management by Objectives (MBO) which similarly was intended to increase presidential control and OMB monitoring of agency performance. Jimmy Carter's major procedural innovation was Zero Base Budgeting which promised not only to enhance presidential control but also to help him reduce government expenditures. ZBB was discontinued by the Reagan administration which has chosen to place its faith in cost-benefit analysis to accomplish the same results. In each instance the practicalities of implementing the new techniques fell to the agencies with the guidance and assistance of OMB. Although none of these techniques has been uniformly successful in accomplishing the desired goals, they do illustrate the continuing quest of Presidents for methods to establish dominance over the executive agencies.

Executive orders, such as those used to mandate the use of PPBS and ZBB, are written commands issued by the President and published in the *Federal Register*. In addition to requiring agencies to adopt new procedures and management techniques, executive orders may be used by the President to establish implementation guidelines for substantive policy, particularly in areas where Congress has delegated broad authority, or to interpret constitutional requirements. Equal employment opportunity policy in the federal government was initially mandated by executive order, as was the recognition of federal employee labor unions and bargaining rights.

Congress has also granted the President limited power to reorganize executive agencies. The most recent reorganization statute allows the President to submit reorganization plans to Congress. Such plans may be vetoed by one house within 60 days of their submission; if neither house acts in that time period the plan becomes effective. Specifically excluded from presidential reorganization power were proposals to create or abolish agencies or functions and any proposals relating to independent regulatory commissions.[13] Within those relatively strict constraints he may transfer, merge, restructure, or consolidate regulatory agencies to make them more amenable to his preferences.

One of the most important executive powers in private organizations is control of the personnel function: the power to hire, fire, promote, reward, and punish subordinates. The Constitution specifically grants the President only the power to hire (appoint) and even that is shared with the Senate and more broadly for "inferior offices" with Congress as a whole. As was noted previously, the Senate normally allows the President considerable freedom in appointing high-ranking executive officials. The Reagan administration has clearly demonstrated how the appointment power may be used to change the general regulatory approach and attitude of an agency. The selection of Ann Gorsuch to head the EPA has resulted in a definite modification in that agency's approach to regulation. Similarly, the designation of James Miller III to replace Michael Pertschuk as chairman of the Federal Trade Commission has considerably cooled that agency's ardor for regulatory activism. The creation by Congress of the civil service system with its protection of permanent employees from dismissal for political reasons has restricted presidential ability to control lower-level employee behavior. Statutes which grant officials fixed terms usually exceeding that of the President in length and barring removal of officials except for cause are standard characteristics of the regulatory commissions. Such restrictions have been upheld by the Supreme Court and have further limited presidential control of the agencies.[14]

Finally, Congress has granted the President, through the Justice Department, control over several aspects of agency litigation and enforcement. The first of these controls is the "appeal clearance" power. Agencies wishing to appeal an unfavorable judicial decision must get approval from the Solicitor General's Office in the Department of Justice. Prior to 1977, only the Solicitor General could represent agencies in litigation. As of 1977, Congress permitted the legal staff of each agency to defend agency interests in court. Second, the Justice Department has the power to interpret the meaning of statutes for the executive agencies. These interpretations are binding on the agencies unless overturned by the courts or by Congress. An example of this power is the Attorney General's manual interpreting the provisions of the Administrative Procedure Act. The final power of the Department of Justice is enforcement, since only the Attorney General may initiate criminal prosecutions of violators of regulations.

The limits on the President's formal powers over regulatory agencies severely restrict his ability to control regulatory outcomes. The most severe limitation is the extent to which his powers are shared with Congress, and Congress has been perennially, if intermittently, jealous of its powers. It has frequently joined with agencies to oppose presidential initiatives. It has restricted his personnel powers, limited his reorganization authority, maintained final authority over financial matters, and established procedures that minimize presidential opportunities for interference in the regulatory process. Judicial review has also limited presidential power over the administrative process. Bureaucratic inertia and independence have also limited the efficacy of formal controls. The combined impact of these limitations has been to convince Presidents that if they really wish to change regulatory behavior they must combine formal powers with informal pressure and/or secure congressional cooperation.

Informal Pressures

Presidents and members of the Executive Office of the President (EOP) have been just as likely to resort to informal pressure to persuade agencies to regulate or not to regulate as have members of Congress. Presidents and their advisors, too, however, have far-reaching and diverse responsibilities and insufficient time to deal thoroughly with all of them. The result, as far as intervention in the regulatory process is concerned, is that such intervention is likely to be sporadic and inconsistent and frequently unsuccessful. Informal pressures take several forms: creating and communicating the general climate or attitude toward regulation, communication of sentiment concerning a specific regulatory action, and direct intervention in a regulatory procedure.

Our last four Presidents, Nixon, Ford, Carter, and Reagan, attempted to send a message to government regulators that in general they felt there was too much government regulation of private activity which had resulted in overloading businesses, schools, state and local governments with unnecessary paperwork and stultifying private initiative. Their campaign speeches, their press conferences, their addresses to Congress and the nation were filled with references to the evils of big government, the inefficiencies created by government regulation, and the need to correct these problems through deregulation, reorganization, cost-benefit analysis, and sunset legislation. Overall, the general climate they attempted to create was one that was at best unsupportive of regulation and at worst hostile towards it. To a certain degree they may have succeeded in dampening the enthusiasm of some agencies for aggressive new regulatory actions and this general attitude may well have encouraged agencies like the CAB, FCC, and the ICC to undertake significant deregulatory efforts on their own initiative.

Normally, however, Presidents have found it extremely difficult to change general regulatory approaches. The major barriers they have encountered have been time constraints, their own unwillingness to antagonize powerful groups, failure to develop and push specific alternatives, and the transitory nature of presidential administrations. Most Presidents have found it impossible to devote continuous attention to administrative problems. At any given time there are likely to be hundreds of issues and groups competing for the President's attention. Some of these issues, like foreign policy crises, must be responded to immediately; other issues have more public visibility and political salience than administrative regulation. The likely result is that the President concentrates on these issues and regulatory agencies resort to business as usual at least until the next election campaign. Regulatory agencies have supporters, regardless of how severely criticized they may be: OSHA may be despised by business but labor fought for its creation and would like to see it continued; truckers, or at least some of them, strongly support ICC regulation; women's and civil rights groups back equal opportunity regulation; and environmentalists and the majority of the public support clean air regulations. For a President, particularly one who desires reelection, the implications are clear: attempt to dismantle an agency or interfere in its operation only at the peril of antagonizing some powerful group. Further, generalizations about regulation are not likely to result in any significant changes unless they are backed up by specific proposals for change and usually Presidents do not have clearly defined policies for the multitude of regulatory arenas.[15] Finally, from the agencies' perspective all presidential administrations have something of a "here today, gone tomorrow" aspect. Agency personnel, relevant members of Congress, the statutes, and the concerned interest groups were in existence long before any particular President came into the White House and they will remain in existence long after he has vacated its premises. The combined impact of these factors makes it extremely difficult for a President to change general regulatory approaches and policies.

Presidential attempts to intervene in specific regulatory decisions have been constant, frequently successful, and occasionally improper or illegal. Lyndon Johnson frequently spoke of his commitment to equal rights for blacks, particularly in the area of education. Under Title VI of the Civil Rights Act of 1964, which Johnson regarded as one of his major legislative accomplishments, the Department of Health, Education and Welfare was authorized to terminate federal funds to any institution which practiced racial discrimination. The Office of Civil Rights within HEW was charged with primary responsibility and enforcement. Both OCR and the Commissioner of Education, Francis Keppel, approached their task with considerable vigor, if not much political widsom. In late 1965, the Office of Education ordered that new funds to the Chicago school system be deferred. Mayor Richard Daley immediately and directly appealed the decision to LBJ. The results were immediate and impressive: The funds were restored, the investigation of the Chicago school system was terminated, and the Commissioner of Education was replaced.[16] Johnson's interference with OCR was mild in comparison to that of Richard Nixon. Less dependent on black political support than LBJ, Nixon was from the beginning of his administration unenthusiastic about civil rights enforcement. In July 1969, his position was made perfectly clear when new guidelines were announced by the Attorney General and the Secretary of HEW. The major point of the guidelines was that the deadlines for school desegregation would be "both relaxed and, hopefully, enforced," and termination of federal funds would be deemphasized as an enforcement technique.[17] By February 1970, intervention and lack of support by the White House had become so persistent, that the director of OCR, Leon Panetta, resigned, protesting "the tendency of this administration to buy and sell everything, including its stand on civil rights, for political profit."[18]

Independent regulatory commissions have been no more immune to presidential pressure than cabinet agencies. John Kennedy, who was displeased, as all Presidents tend to be, with the quality of news coverage of his administration, tried to get Newton Minow, chairman of the FCC, to pressure the electronic news media for more favorable coverage.[19] Minow declined. The Truman Administration covertly intervened in SEC rulemaking proceedings which sought to abolish floor trading on stock exchanges. After direct contact from the White House, the SEC voted to reverse its decision to adopt the regulations.[20] The Eisenhower Administration's, and particularly presidential assistant Sherman Adams's, attempts to intervene in both SEC and FTC proceedings were well publicized, disastrous, and ultimately unsuccessful. And no President has been able to resist the temptation to get the Federal Reserve Board to adopt monetary and credits policies that are in alignment with those of the administration. Their lack of success has led every President from John Kennedy to Jimmy Carter to suggest that the term of the chairman of the Fed be made concurrent with that of the President.

One of the most unusual and successful interventions by the Executive Office of the President in independent regulatory commission policy making occurred in 1971. The Federal Communications Commission in regulating cable television had pursued a hesitant, inconsistent approach that was basically aimed at protecting network broadcasting and their local affiliates. That approach satisfied no one and by 1970, cable television associations, the networks, program producers, members of Congress, and the White House were pressuring the FCC to adopt a more comprehensive regulatory approach to cable regulation. Finally on August 5, 1971, the FCC issued a Letter of Intent to promulgate new regulations. The rules that were finally adopted, however, were drawn up not by the FCC, but were the outcome of a White House conference called by Clay Whitehead, director of the Office of Telecommunication Policy, a unit of the Executive Office of the President. Whitehead invited broadcasting, cable, and program production industry representatives to participate in negotiations held in his office. The Administrative Procedure Act notwithstanding, the result of those negotiations was a consensus agreement which was ultimately accepted by the FCC and promulgated as its 1972 rules on cable television.[21]

THE COURTS

Courts are an omnipresent aspect of the regulatory environment, but they are usually regarded as playing a formal, retrospective role primarily concerned with procedural aspects of the regulatory process. The formal aspects of judicial review will be discussed in chapter 11. At this point it should be noted that frequently, judicial review, even if limited to procedural questions, allows the courts to play the highly political roles of shaping the substance of regulatory outputs or compelling a reluctant regulatory agency to exercise its powers in new substantive areas. Even in cases where the overt issue is procedural, courts have been able to shape substantive outcomes to suit their predilections. The Supreme Court in the late 1800s and early 1900s unquestionably used its power to nullify economic regulatory actions that conflicted with its conservative philosophy and played a major role in relegating the FTC to a minor and ineffective role in policing the economy.[22] During the 1970s the lower federal courts tended to use procedural arguments to compel environmental regulators to reach the "proper" decision. Whether the *Vermont Yankee* decision of the Supreme Court which indicated its displeasure with lower court intrusion into substantive policy questions will actually limit such judicial activism is questionable.[23]

The courts have also, directly and indirectly, forced agencies to act when they have preferred to remain dormant. Unquestionably, the lower court decisions in the Nader–Allegheny Airlines case pushed the CAB into investigating the regulating overbooking practices. The first and most far-reaching Supreme Court decision specifically ordering a federal agency to expand its regulatory jurisdiction was *Phillips Petroleum v. Wisconsin* in 1954.[24] The Natural Gas Act of 1938 had given the Federal Power Commission (FPC) jurisdiction over the transportation and sale of natural gas in interstate commerce and over companies engaged in such transportation and sales. Nevertheless, the FPC, relying on another section of the Act, had resolutely insisted that it did not have authority to regulate the prices charged by independent producers of natural gas. Since these independents accounted for over 90 percent of the gas sold in interstate commerce, the FPC's inactivity had a significant impact on overall natural gas prices charged to consumers. Consuming states, including Wisconsin, had tried (without success) since the end of World War II to persuade the Commission to act. Finally they resorted to the courts and in *Phillips*, the Supreme Court held that the FPC had wrongly interpreted the 1938 Act and had the power and an obligation to regulate the prices charged by independents. The FPC proceeded without enthusiasm to carry out the court mandate. By 1959, it still had not decided which of a number of possible rate determination methods it would or should use, and once again found itself challenged in the Supreme Court for its failure to regulate. In *Atlantic Refining Co. v. Public Service Commission of New York*,[25] the Supreme Court emphasized that the FPC's jurisdiction was not discretionary. It had a positive obligation to determine just and reasonable rates for natural gas.[26] Ultimately, the FPC did regulate natural gas prices, although critics charged that it did so neither wisely nor well. Had it not been for court pressure, however, the FPC would not have done so at all.

Courts also have acted as a last-resort enforcement agency in certain areas where administrative agencies have failed or refused to act. The most visible and controversial of these areas has been school desegregation. As pointed out earlier, the Office of Civil Rights (DHEW–DHHS) had responsibility and authority to enforce Title VI of the Civil Rights Act of 1964 as it applied to institutions receiving funds administered by that department. At least initially and at least in the South OCR–HEW did attempt to enforce the law. By January 1968, it had terminated funds to 156 school districts in the South.[27] But with the change in political control of the presidency and the north-ward shift in school desegregation efforts, HEW lost its support and its enforcement momentum. Politically, it was one thing to terminate federal aid to a school district in Mississippi and quite another thing to attempt to terminate it to Mayor Daley's Chicago or to Boston or to New York or to San Francisco. The result was a shift from HEW administrative enforcement to litigation and court-ordered desegregation and, in some instances, court-ordered busing. The courts have shown great reluctance to be placed in this kind of situation, preferring the agencies to enforce their own regulations, and normally, under the doctrine of primary jurisdiction, they will insist that if the agency has enforcement power, it should use it. As the above example indicates, this is not always true.

THE ADMINISTRATIVE HIERARCHY

With the exception of the independent agencies, all regulatory agencies are located within a cabinet department and are subject to the control of administrative superiors who are political appointees. The proper role of these administrative superiors in specific regulatory decisions is once again unclear; their actual role varies tremendously depending on the saliency of the regulatory action at issue. The Food and Drug Administration, located now within the Department of Health and Human Services, is headed by a Commissioner who is nominally subordinate to the Secretary of the department and the Under Secretary. One of FDA's most controversial functions is the certification of new prescription drugs as safe and effective, which might at first glance appear to be purely a technical and scientific determination remote from political considerations. Sometimes this is true; other times it is not. Two specific cases illustrate clearly the role that "politics" and intervention by political superiors of an agency can play in regulatory decisions.

In the early sixties, thalidomide was widely marketed in Europe as the safest and most effective tranquilizer available. Its potential as a money-maker for American pharmaceutical corporations appeared unlimited—if only they could get FDA approval to sell it. Fortunately for Americans and in spite of strong pressure by political officials in HEW, that approval was never forthcoming. On September 12, 1960, the FDA received a new drug application from Merrell Company for thalidomide; on March 8, 1962, the application was withdrawn and thalidomide was never marketed in the United States. Although some malformed babies were born in the U.S. as a result of their mothers' use of the drug, we were spared the major problems that confronted Germany, Britain, and Canada where over 5,000 deformed births occurred as the result of thalidomide.

The new drug application for thalidomide had been referred to Dr. Frances Kelsey, a medical doctor in FDA. As is normal in such cases, the FDA does not itself test the drug but evaluates the required supporting documentation submitted by the manufacturer. Although Merrell's documentation indicated that its research and testing of the drug had revealed no dangerous side effects, Dr. Kelsey was not satisfied. She requested further information from Merrell. On the basis of that information plus articles that appeared in British and European medical journals, Dr. Kelsey became convinced that thalidomide was anything but safe. Merrell, however, was insistent that it receive permission to market the drug. During the time that the application was being reviewed, officials made over 50 direct contacts with FDA and HEW officials. Despite considerable pressure from both the FDA Commissioner and the Under Secretary of HEW, Dr. Kelsey resisted. When it finally appeared that the FDA Commissioner might accede to the pressure and issue the license, Dr. Kelsey released the story, including new data received from German researchers, to the *Washington Post*. The resulting media and public uproar was sufficient to dissuade political officials from any further intervention in the case and finally in March 1962, Merrell withdrew its application.[28] As proof that virtue does not always go unrewarded in the federal bureaucracy, Dr. Kelsey received a presidential award for distinguished federal service.[29]

A similar situation occurred in 1969 when the FDA Commissioner ordered Panalba, a combination drug of antibiotics, removed from the market because evidence indicated it was both ineffective and hazardous. Upjohn Pharmaceuticals, the manufacturer of Panalba, was not pleased with the FDA and requested a hearing. FDA officials refused the request and Upjohn persuaded the Congressman from Kalamazoo, Michigan, where company headquarters were located, to arrange a meeting with the Secretary and Under Secretary of HEW. These officials then tried to pressure the FDA commissioner to rescind the order. What preserved FDA autonomy in this instance was counterbalancing political pressure: support from the House Subcommittee chairman and members with jurisdiction over the FDA. Following hearings and considerable unfavorable publicity, the Secretary of HEW withdrew his opposition and the FDA decision was enforced.[30]

A final case which illustrates not only the role of hierarchical intervention in regulatory decisions but also interactions among various administrative agencies is the Battery Additive Case.[31] The victim or villain of this case, depending on one's perspective, was Jess M. Ritchie who had invented an additive which he purported was capable of prolonging the life of batteries. Mr. Ritchie ultimately found himself in conflict with three federal agencies: the Bureau of Standards, in the Department of Commerce; the Federal Trade Commission; and the U.S. Post Office. His basic problem was that when he proceeded to market his additive, battery manufacturers complained to the FTC that Ritchie's claims constituted false and misleading advertising. Ritchie obviously disagreed and tried to get the Bureau of Standards, which has responsibility for testing new substances for which patent applications have been filed, to endorse his product. The Bureau had been highly suspicious of battery additives for some time and after testing Ritchie's additive found it to be ineffective. The FTC, under pressure from the manufacturers, asked the Bureau to run additional tests. The Senate Subcommittee on Small Business, after urging from Ritchie, also joined the fray and demanded more tests. The Bureau tested and the results were the same—the additive was useless.

The FTC indicated that formal action was forthcoming; the Post Office acted. An order to prosecute Ritchie for using the mails to defraud was entered. Ritchie was nothing if not persistent. He got MIT to test his additive. MIT tests indicated it was effective. Ritchie and other small businessmen bombarded the Secretary of Commerce, Sinclair Weeks, with mail protesting the general and specific arbitrary treatment of small businessmen. A businessman in a Rupublican administration, Weeks was definitely sympathetic to Ritchie's plight. He persuaded the Postmaster General to rescind the fraud order, and then he fired the Director of the Bureau of Standards, Dr. Allen Astin.

The case might have ended at that point and politics would have clearly triumphed over technical and regulatory expertise and impartiality. However, Weeks had obviously underestimated the power of scientists and press coverage. He was inundated with protests from scientific organizations, consumer groups, and congressmen and the whole case was criticized in the press. It did not help that 400 scientists employed by the Bureau announced that they were planning to resign in protest. Weeks's response was to appoint a special committee of distinguished scientists to review the case. The committee advised Weeks to rescind the firing order. After three days of contemplation, presumably on what further problems ignoring the advice of his own committee would cause, Weeks announced that Astin would remain on a "temporary" basis. That was in 1954; 12 years later he was still there.

AGENCY OVERLAPS

As the battery additives case illustrates, many regulatory decisions and areas involve more than one agency. Civil rights legislation is enforced by the Civil Rights Division of the Department of Justice, the Equal Employment Opportunity Commission, the

Office of Civil Rights, Department of Education, the Office of Federal Contract Compliance, the Department of Housing and Urban Development, and various other agencies. Antitrust policy is enforced by the Antitrust Division, Department of Justice, the Federal Trade Commission, and each individual regulatory commission that has jurisdiction over a specific industry. Consumer protection responsibilities are scattered among so many federal agencies that a comprehensive listing would be difficult, if not impossible, since every regulatory commission and cabinet department has some responsibility for some aspect of consumer protection. In reality, few if any regulatory policy areas are committed to the exclusive jurisdiction of a single agency.

The reasons for this overlapping and duplication of regulatory functions are political and administrative. Pluralism in the legislative process results in pluralistic administrative structures. Just as interest groups battle to have legislation enacted, so do they battle over the administrative location of enforcement responsibilities for that legislation. Since the development of regulatory policy is sequential and usually spread out over decades, interest groups struggle to insure that each succeeding legislative addition to the policy is placed in a "compatible" agency. Sometimes the strategy is to divide and conquer, to ensure that responsibility is so diversified among competing agencies that little positive regulation will result. At other times the strategy is to divide and conquer to ensure that regulation is not entrusted to a likely but hostile agency. The Packers and Stockyards Act of 1919 is an example of the former; the 1970 amendments to the Federal Insecticide, Fungicide and Rodenticide Act (FIFRA), an example of the latter.

The meat-packing industry in this country has long been politically organized, powerful, and oligopolistic. It convincingly flexed its political muscle early in the twentieth century when it secured passage of a federal meat inspection law in 1906.[32] That legislation vastly improved the competitive position of American meat packers in international trade and resulted in standards that small meat packers could not economically satisfy. The result was a further concentration of power in the Big Five meat packers. In 1918, the fledgling FTC undertook an investigation of the meat-packing industry. The result of the investigation was a report to Congress that was sharply critical of the industry and that recommended curtailment of the monopoly in the industry through government ownership of the stockyards. Industry reaction was immediate and virulent: The FTC was denounced as a "hindrance to business" and pressure was put on Congress for legislative intervention. Congressional response was also immediate. The Packers and Stockyards Act of 1919 permanently removed the meat-packing industry from FTC jurisdiction and instead placed it under the far more sympathetic and responsive Department of Agriculture's newly created Packers and Stockyard Administration.[33] Thus a small portion of responsibility for maintaining competition in the economy was removed from the FTC and lodged in another agency, and this fragmentation has been repeated countless times since 1919.

FIFRA was orginally assigned to the Department of Agriculture for implementation. The law specified that before a pesticide could be marketed it must be registered by the USDA and that in order to secure registration the manufacturer had to prove its safety. Pesticides are widely used in this country and potentially affect the life and health of humans, domestic animals, fish, and wildlife. Because of the impact and the complexity of determining the long-range effects of pesticides, two cabinet departments, Interior and HEW, sought an agreement with Agriculture to review all pesticides submitted for registration. By 1969, environmental groups, members of Congress, and other government agencies were becoming increasingly critical of USDA's administration of the program. Between 1965 and 1969, USDA had registered 45,000 pesticides for use despite HEW objections to over 1,600 applications. So routinely were registrations granted that USDA had not even bothered to formulate procedural rules for handling them. In 1970, Congress responded to pressure; FIFRA was transferred to the Environmental Protection Agency for enforcement.[34] If this appears to have eliminated agency duplication in this policy area, appearances are deceiving. The single largest use of pesticides is agricultural production and the Department of Agriculture has remained involved in pesticide decisions. Its attorneys regularly appear in defense of pesticides at registration hearings before EPA. Its representatives have been particularly active in the 1980 reauthorization of FIFRA. USDA's power this time is impressive: The reauthorization bills are being handled not by the committees that handle general environmental legislation but by the House and Senate Agriculture Committees and they are far from pleased with EPA's handling of FIFRA.[35] Further, although EPA is responsible for registration of pesticides, both USDA and the FDA are responsible for inspecting meat, poultry, and produce to insure that no dangerous pesticide residues appear in any of these substances marketed for consumption. And what constitutes a dangerous residue is determined by the FDA based on research supplied by the National Institute of Environmental Health Sciences and the National Cancer Institute (Department of Health and Human Services).

The consequences of agency overlap and duplication for regulatory policy vary. At a minimum they create confusion and definitely put the unorganized, unrepresented, and uninformed at a decided disadvantage. They also create the inevitable disillusionment that occurs when an individual is subjected to the "bureaucratic runaround" of being shuffled from one agency to another trying to locate which has responsibility in that particular instance. Second, such overlap can cause excessive delays and inaction in the regulatory process particularly when combined with legal procedures. Nothing better exemplifies this than the El Paso Natural Gas Case which was bounced among the Federal Power Commission, the Justice Department, and the federal courts from 1959 until 1973. El Paso Natural Gas Company wanted to take over Pacific Northwest Pipeline Corporation. The FPC approved the merger; the Antitrust Division of the Justice Department contended it was a violation of the Clayton Act. Five times, each involving slightly different issues, the El Paso Case went to the Supreme Court; each time the FPC opposed the Justice Department. In the 14-year interval from the initiation of the merger and FPC approval to the final court order requiring El Paso to divest itself of Pacific Northwest, El Paso not only played the two administrative agencies off against each other but also spent over $1 million in lobbying efforts to persuade Congress to intervene and legitimize the takeover.[36] This diffusion of power can also create chaos in regulatory policy and foster inevitable irresponsibility, as each agency can claim that a specific action or inaction was not entirely its fault.

On the other hand, overlapping can serve beneficial ends. It broadens the channels for access to government decision makers and permits individuals and groups who are unsuccessful with one agency to seek a more responsive forum. It permits those who are convinced that Benzene is an imminent threat to public health to take their case to EPA, to OSHA, and to the Consumer Product Safety Commission seeking restrictions on its use, and, ironically, to prevail in all three agencies, only to lose in the Supreme Court. Overlapping enabled women from Alsea, Oregon, who complained that Forest Service (USDA) spraying of forests with 2, 4, 5-T (Agent Orange) was causing miscarriages, to take their complaints successfully to EPA when the Forest Service failed to respond. Further, because each agency is likely to have a different approach to problems and different types of expertise, when agencies with overlapping responsibilities do cooperate the outcome is likely to be a better, more informed decision. The Veterans' Administration, for example, ultimately will have to decide if Vietnam veterans who were exposed to Agent Orange spraying in Vietnam are entitled to compensation for illness that they attribute to that exposure. The validity of that decision will be considerably improved by studies, inputs, and actions being undertaken by EPA, National Institute of Environmental Health Sciences, the National Academy of Sciences, and the Department of Defense.

STATE AND LOCAL GOVERNMENTS

As was pointed out in chapter 4, American government regulation occurs in a federal system and many federal programs are actually implemented by state and local governments. For affected federal agencies, this means that these units of governments are active and occasionally hostile actors in their regulatory environments. Their recalcitrance can make the job of federal regulators unpleasant and difficult; their cooperation can facilitate an otherwise impossible task. The range of actors at lower levels of governments is vast. There are 50 state governments—each with a governor, a legislature, and thousands·of administrative employees; 3,043 county governments, 18,862 municipalities, 16,822 townships, 15,174 school districts, and 25,962 special districts.[37] Collectively and individually, they frequently resent and resist regulatory attempts by federal agencies.

At the state level, elective officials are likely to be the most resistant to federal agency regulations. In the words of the ex-governor of Iowa, Harold Hughes, "The chief executive and the legislature are likely to share the same attitude toward the federal government: that it is an alien and essentially hostile force."[38] They resent federal agency commands that they must legislate or lose federal money; the state legislature of Idaho fought the Department of HEW and its successor for seven years on the requirement to pass certificate-of-need legislation for health facilities in the state. HEW officials blustered, cajoled, and threatened and each year the battle and the political rhetoric escalated. God, motherhood, and the flag were invoked by the State legislature; Congress, the Constitution, the Supreme Court, and federal funds were invoked by HEW. Federal funds finally prevailed and the legislature acquiesced. Caught in the middle of this imbroglio were state administrative officials, and their attitude was interesting and possibly typical of state administrators. Individually and privately, they thought certificate-of-need legislation was an excellent idea; they believed that actual termination of funds was unlikely but unquestionably disastrous if it occurred. Publicly, they said little more than "those are the federal regs and you know those damned feds."[39] This illustrates a point that is frequently overlooked in considerations of the role of federal regulations in state politics: Many state and local administrators view these regulations as a potent resource in their dealings with the state legislature and political executives. State administrators are likely to share the same professional training and orientations that characterize federal administrators. Although political considerations at lower levels of government may prevent these administrators from aggressively pushing for actions that they deem necessary and beneficial, federal regulations offer them an unassailable reason for doing so. Equal opportunity, school desegregation, or restrictions on duplicative and expensive health care services may well have been desired by many professional state administrators; to pressure the legislatures for their enactment could have been professional suicide unless the reason for doing so was "federal red tape." For example, Bullock and Rodgers found that some school superintendents in Georgia informally advised federal officials that they would like to desegregate and would appreciate a federal court suit being brought to compel the action and thus protect them from local political opposition.[40]

In reality, the threatened termination of federal funds is considerably less impressive than it is in theory. Like the Bureau of Mines and its closure of mines, the sanction is too drastic and, as the Chicago–Mayor Daley–HEW example illustrates, too politically dangerous for most federal agencies to take. State legislatures and governors are not easily intimidated. Frequently the federal agencies make rules and the states ignore or interpret them to their advantage, depending on political circumstances in Congress and the presidency.

At the local level the types of potential government participants are similar to the state level. They include elective, appointive, and permanent executives and legislative bodies—councils, commissions, and school boards. Increasingly an intermediate level, regional councils of governments (COG's), is directly involved in implementation and review of federal programs. Like their counterparts at the state level, their attitudes toward federal regulations and federal regulators range from resentment and resistance to covert and overt support.

An outstanding but not unusual example of state and local involvement in, and some critics would allege perversion of, a federal program was the initial implementation of Title I of the Elementary and Secondary Education Act of 1965.[41] State and local education administrators, many of whom are members of National Education Association (NEA), one of the most powerful pressure groups at the federal level, had been actively supportive of the provision of federal aid to education since the end of World War II. The one qualifier to their general support was that such aid should not be accompanied by federal control and federal regulation. As usual, they got the money but they got the regulations as well. Title I was targeted federal aid; it was intended to be used to equalize educational opportunity for children from poverty-level families and funds were to be distributed on the basis of number of such children in school systems in each county. The federal implementing agency was to be the U.S. Office of Education (USOE). At the state level, state departments of education were responsible for implementation.

USOE approached its task of controlling states and local school districts with little enthusiasm. Regulations were drafted attempting to ensure that Title I money actually went to educate low-income children. The states and the NEA complained of federal intrusion; the federal guidelines were revised. Two years after enactment of the law USOE issued final guidelines specifying criteria to be used in distributing the money. Again the states complained, members of Congress complained, USOE clarified the guidelines to the extent that it admitted that they were not to be interpreted as being binding but only as advisory. USOE was responding to its state and local constituency, and the result was vague, meaningless, unenforced, and unenforceable regulations.

Unfortunately for USOE, its actual environment for Title I enforcement was more inclusive and less harmonious than initially appeared. One major complicating factor was the existence of the HEW audit agency which had responsibility to determine if federal funds were being spent in compliance with federal law and regulations. Its comprehensive reviews of Title I expenditures from 1965 to 1969 were extremely critical of USOE and the states. The audits estimated that over 15 percent of Title I funds were being improperly used in violation of the law. Yet USOE made no attempt to recover the funds or to control their future use. Civil rights groups and groups representing the poor were equally critical of USOE allowing Title I to be changed from a poverty program into a general aid to education program.

Later reauthorizations of Title I were to make its intent more explicit, but its success as a program to equalize educational opportunities for poverty children has been limited. What the early implementation of Title I illustrates most clearly is that states and local units of government can play a determinative role in the formulation and enforcement of federal regulations that directly affect them. They are active, they are organized, they are vocal, and they can be extremely powerful when they act in concert. It should also be noted that despite five successive internal audits alleging noncompliance with the law, USOE did not even attempt to terminate or recover funds from states found to be in violation of the law. The implications for federal regulatory agencies are clear. They must pay serious attention to these units of government in formulating regulations and attempt to incorporate their demands. Failure to do so results in unenforceable regulations and intense political opposition

THE PRESS AND THE PUBLIC

You know it's going to be a bad day when . . . you walk into your office and find a 60 Minutes news team waiting for you.

AUTHOR UNKNOWN

For many regulatory agencies the above quotation aptly summarizes their impression of the role the media play in their environment. For the most part, regulatory agencies are ignored by the media; their procedures are viewed as arcane and incomprehensible and their work and outputs as boring or inconsequential. The unfortunate regulatory agency may find itself propelled out of this obscurity into an unwelcome notoriety only when it attempts highly controversial regulation or acts, or fails to act, in a manner that is viewed as unsatisfactory by the media. The FDA rarely receives coverage for the thousands of routine inspections of food processors it makes, for the new drug applications approved, or for the dangerous food additives it disallows. It invariably receives publicity, however, when it delays approval of DMSO which many people believe to be a wonder drug for the treatment of arthritis, bursitis, and various other diseases, or when it insists that laetrile has not been proven effective as a cancer treatment, or when it suggests that saccharin is far from being a safe food additive. From the perspective of the news media, good news is no news and bad news is good copy.

The importance of the media is magnified by its role as the major, perhaps the only, source of information that the general public has concerning government regulatory agencies. For most people the alphabet soup of government agencies is of low salience; what they do, how they do it, and why they do it is seldom understood. When the public is made aware of the consequences of the regulatory process, all too frequently it is of its negative consequences. The failure of the EPA to require that Love Canal be cleaned up, the economic cost of OSHA regulations, and the FAA's role in the DC-10 disaster all received extensive media coverage. This negativism in press coverage is viewed as unfair and unfortunate by many regulatory agency personnel. It makes their jobs more difficult; enforcement is complicated by lack of public support and this same lack of public support may result in an agency becoming more dependent on regulatees for political survival.

There is, however, another and vitally important aspect of critical media coverage of regulatory agencies: It serves as a real, although informal, check on regulatory behavior. An agency which behaves arbitrarily or fails to protect the public interest should be brought to public attention, and agencies should realize that their behavior cannot and should not be kept secret from the public. While it is unfortunate that the "good" work of agencies receives little attention from the media, that is one of the side effects of a free press. Some agency personnel have learned that the press is not always detrimental to their efforts. Without press coverage, Dr. Kelsey and the FDA would probably not have been able to prevent the marketing of thalidomide, and without media coverage on the real hazards of toxic waste disposal, the EPA would not have been given the legal authority and political support to attempt regulation in that area.

Overall, the role of both the press and the public in the regulatory process is sporadic. Normally, agencies may pursue their objectives without arousing any great concern among the public or the press. But the existence of both press and public as inactive but potentially involved actors in regulatory decisions serves as a viable check on such decisions.

CLIENTELE GROUPS

Unlike the environmental actors we have considered to this point, clientele groups are an omnipresent factor in the day-to-day operations of agencies. Every agency has at least one clientele group—the individuals, corporations, or organizations toward whom its regulatory activities are directed. The nature and number of these clientele groups are as diverse as the nature and number of regulatory agencies. Some agencies, such as the CAB, the Federal Maritime Commission, the Veterans' Administration, and the Nuclear Regulatory Commission have a single industry or primary group of individuals as a clientele. Some agencies, such as the Food and Drug Administration (food processors and pharmaceutical manufacturers), have a multiple but not competitive clientele. Some agencies, such as the NLRB and OSHA, have two distinct and normally competitive clientele groups. Other agencies with across-the-economy regulatory authority (EPA, SEC, FTC) have a diversified clientele that varies depending on the specific regulatory action contemplated. Given this diversity of clientele group situations, generalizations are difficult and frequently misleading. One commonality does unite all of these diverse situations: Because the agency's action directly affects the economic well-being of clientele group members, the groups are constantly active, informed, and involved in the agency's day-to-day operations.

The first two types of agency-clientele situations have been the most controversial and criticized, since it is this situation that leads most frequently to regulatory capture. The airlines, at least in the past, had to be continually concerned with the CAB since it controlled the relevant aspects of their economic existence: their routes, their rates, the services they provided, whether they could merge with another airline. Naturally in the course of the CAB's existence, the airlines or their representatives had day-to-day contact with the staff and members of the agencies. Just as naturally, Board members attended industry conferences and spoke at industry conventions. Frequently, when appointments were being made, the logical choice for a nominee was someone "familiar with the industry," i.e., someone from the industry. Just as frequently, when a Board or staff member sought new employment, he/she found a willing employer in one of the airlines. The resulting relationship was a close and all too compatible one. At the same time, no one else needed to be much concerned with the CAB's operations; passengers were generally unorganized, the press uninvolved, and the President unconcerned. Congress was aware of the CAB's existence annually at appropriations time, but hearing no complaints and made aware of the airlines' political support of the Board through various methods, it had little reason to be concerned with the agency. The result was a closed environment and the only voices the CAB heard were those of airlines. If the Board listened to those voices it was understandable, and if the regulatory actions that the Board took favored the airlines, that also was understandable. This scenario could be repeated with regulatory agency after regulatory agency and led critics to conclude that regulation in the public interest was impossible.

In some ways the relationship was/is even closer and more dependent than just portrayed, since the regulatees frequently control the most important regulatory resource of all: the information on which decisions must be based. No regulatory agency better exemplifies this than the FDA in its new drug licensing procedures. The FDA does not test new drugs to determine their safety or effectiveness. Instead it requires the drug manufacturer to do the testing and submit its research with the new drug application. FDA staff members then review the company's research and, normally, based on this research, recommend whether the drug is to be licensed. Given such a relationship of dependency the impartiality of agency decisions is certainly open to debate and has frequently been criticized.

Agencies with competing clienteles have a far less comfortable existence than that just discussed. The National Labor Relations Board is a classic example of an agency caught between two hostile clientele groups: unions and business. The result has not been a neutral board rigorously impartial in its dealings with the two groups but rather a board that has vacillated between being prolabor (usually when nominees of a Democratic President dominated) and probusiness (when dominated by Republican appointees). One prime example of this fluctuation was the Board's interpretation of the "employer free speech" provision of the Taft-Hartley Act. The Truman NLRB, through the "Bonwit-Teller" doctrine, interpreted this provision to mean that an employer could speak against unions only if he granted equal time to union spokesmen. The Eisenhower NLRB interpreted the provision to allow unlimited, unqualified free speech for employers. The Kennedy NLRB reversed this interpretation, reiterated the Bonwit-Teller doctrine, and enforced it strictly.[42] To the extent that such agencies are likely to be dominated by their clientele, it is likely to be cyclical and highly dependent on political control of both the presidency and Congress.

The impact of clientele relationships on agencies like the FTC, SEC, and EPA is even more variable than those of the competing clientele agencies. All three agencies have jurisdiction over a wide diversity of businesses and industries. For the FTC and EPA this has resulted in an inability to generate organized and supportive clientele; the best they could hope for was an inactive and neutral clientele response to their activities. Until recently the FTC achieved this by regulatory inactivity which earned it a reputation as a weak, ineffective agency that was generally useless as a protector of consumer interests. FTC activism mobilized its business clientele, but in a direct assault on the Commission. The EPA has also encountered severe problems in generating a supportive clientele and has increasingly found itself berated by businessmen and bemoaned by environmentalists. The SEC, on the other hand, has managed to survive and carry out its mission relatively successfully in a multiple-clientele environment.

There is a final type of agency–clientele situation which is even more complicated than those already discussed, and that is the situation where the target group is not necessarily the actual clientele. Technically, the poor are the target group for Medicaid and Food Stamps and the elderly are the target group for Medicare. Realistically, the ultimate beneficiaries of these programs are very different; the health industry—physicians, hospitals, laboratories, and nursing homes—are the real beneficiaries of Medicaid and Medicare, and agricultural producers and food retailers are the ultimate beneficiaries of Food Stamps. The target group may be poorly organized, or even if well organized, politically powerless. The real beneficiaries tend to be well organized and powerful. The interests of the two groups, while not directly contradictory, are not necessarily compatible either. Regulations that negatively affect one are likely also negatively to affect the other. Yet to protect the target group, the beneficiaries must be regulated; to fail to regulate health care providers jeopardizes the quality of health care that the poor receive. To regulate fraud and abuse in the Medicaid program requires regulation of providers, but such regulation may make them antagonistic toward the poor and unwilling to serve them. For the agency caught in the middle, the situation of a single-interest regulatory agency must be enviable.

Obviously not all clientele groups are equal. Industry groups are well organized and financially powerful. They can and do have the best legal representation that money can buy, and for that matter the best pressure group techniques. They are articulate and experienced in regulatory politics and legal procedures. Veterans' groups, education groups, unions, and professional groups have the same advantages in dealing with their clientele agencies. Where these clientele groups are the only voices the regulatory agency hears, almost inevitably the emerging regulations will favor the group. Where the clientele group is poorly educated, poorly organized, inexperienced in regulatory procedures, and politically powerless—welfare recipients or food stamp recipients, for example—regulatory capture is seldom mentioned and even less seldomly occurs. When the group composition of an agency's environment is diverse and competitive, predictions about regulatory outcomes are difficult, if not impossible.

THE RISE AND IMPACT OF PUBLIC INTEREST GROUPS

One of the most significant changes that has occurred in the environment of many regulatory agencies in the past twenty years has been the increase in the number, activism, and power of public interest groups. The first problem in discussing these groups is to define what the term "public interest group" includes. Anyone familiar with the recent literature in intergovernmental relations is likely to assume that public interest groups, PIG's as they are referred to, are the Big Seven intergovernmental associations, which include the Council of State Governments, the National Association of Counties, the National League of Cities.[43] Without arguing with the characterization of these groups as public interest groups, they are not primarily what most people think of when they visualize public interest representation. For the purpose of this discussion, we will use the following definition of a public interest group:

> an organizational entity that purports to represent very broad, diffuse, non-commercial interests which traditionally have received little explicit or direct representation in the processes by which agencies, courts, legislatures make public policy.[44]

Under this definition consumer groups, environmental groups, taxpayers' associations, concerned citizens' groups, and groups representing the poor are considered to be public interest groups. As the definition states, in the past such groups were under- or unrepresented in regulatory agency processes, although it should be noted that many public interest groups have been in existence for decades. Despite this, their constant attention to and involvement in regulatory processes is a relatively recent phenomenon. The reasons for this sudden upsurge in their activity are complex; as Wilson suggests, the availability of funding from foundations and computerized mass solicitations have been important in their rise to prominence.[45] Other factors have been equally important: the emergency of effective, dedicated leadership exemplified by Ralph Nader, widespread and favorable media coverage of their activities, broad-based public approval of their issues, industry overkill in attempting to nullify their growing power, and as a consequence of all these, increasing receptivity to their demands by elected officials.

Money and publicity make all things possible in regulatory politics, and they have made it possible for public interest groups to engage in a broad spectrum of activities in the regulatory process. They have been able to petition, with considerable success, for agency rules in all types of government activities: Nader's petition which resulted in the CAB requiring nonsmoking sections on airplanes is a classic example. They have been able to sue to compel agency action and to reverse agency actions of which they disapprove. They have become continuous participants in agency rule-making processes, from the EPA to the FTC to the Nuclear Regulatory Commission. They have persuaded both agencies and the courts to expand the definition of "interested parties" so that they may participate in agency adjudicatory proceedings and court cases. They have become active in legislative politics and election campaigns. They have had their representatives appointed to key regulatory positions—as the appointment of Joan Claybrook, former director of Nader's Congress Watch, as head of National Highway Traffic Safety Administration illustrates. They have even persuaded Congress to fund their participation in some regulatory agency proceedings. They have changed the once placid environment of many regulatory agencies.

They have also been the most ungrateful of participants in the process. Because they are issue-based groups they tend to take clear, coherent, and uncompromising positions on what constitutes acceptable regulatory action. Regulatory decision makers, as has been shown, exist in a highly political environment and are frequently beset with competing and conflicting demands from various participants in the process. Political survival and legal restrictions require that they must juggle all of these demands and come up with a compromise that is satisfactory or at least acceptable to most of the participants. For example, when the EPA finally decided to ban aldrin/dieldrin for use as a pesticide, it had to weigh the economic arguments presented by chemical manufacturers and agricultural producers along with scientific arguments about the health hazards associated with the pesticide's use. The final EPA decision was a compromise which infuriated environmental groups: It banned the pesticide but did not include in the ban stocks of aldrin/dieldrin produced prior to the issuance of notice of intent to suspend registration.[46] From the public interest groups' perspective the agencies never act soon enough or strongly enough to protect consumers, the environment, the poor, the sick, or workers.

Public interest groups tend to feel that they are the least powerful of the actors in the regulatory process, and that they lack the economic resources that have made industry groups so dominant. To prove their case, they are likely to point to the decisions where they have failed to achieve the result they desired. Whether one agrees with their contention or not, it is necessary to recognize that their activism has changed—broadened and diversified—the environment in which many agencies operate. They have increased the visibility of many regulatory decisions and by so doing have increased the level of conflict in the regulatory process. If they have seldom won total victories, at least they have compelled the agencies to listen to and consider viewpoints that before would not have been presented or would have been ignored.

CONCLUSION

One of the most frequent and serious criticisms of regulatory agencies is that they have not only come to exercise vast and sweeping powers but also that they do so in the absence of meaningful control by the elective, representative branches of government.

The result has been the creation of a "headless fourth branch" of government which undermines the democratic nature of the entire political process. The initial part of the criticism, the extent of regulatory agencies' power, is unarguably accurate; the accuracy of the second half of the criticism is much more difficult to ascertain. As we have seen in this chapter, the elective branches, Congress and the President, possess a variety of formal powers over the agencies that in the aggregate constitute the necessary and sufficient means to control every aspect of their behavior. However, this has not necessarily resulted in the exercise of those powers in a meaningful fashion. Several aspects of the general political situation may undermine the effectiveness of both congressional and presidential control and complicate ascertaining the extent to which meaningful control over the agencies is actually maintained.

The first complicating factor is the extent to which power over the agencies is shared by Congress and the President. When the two branches disagree over how and in what direction power should be exercised, a stalemate may result and at least in the short run neither branch may be able to establish dominance. During such periods of congressional–presidential conflict, the agencies function without meaningful direction, vacillating between the contradictory demands emanating from the two branches. Currently, many regulatory agencies are operating in such an environment, and determining who, if anybody, is in control is an almost impossible task.

A second complicating factor occurs in situations in which both congressional and presidential attitudes toward regulation are characterized by "benign neglect." Confronted with a multitude of responsibilities, issues, and demands, Congress and the President can devote only a limited amount of their time and attention to any one specific area. Frequently, regulatory agencies are allowed to operate for long periods of time without either Congress or the President paying any substantial attention to them or making any attempt to oversee or intervene in their activities. Although from one perspective this may indicate an abdication of political control, from another perspective it may prove the effectiveness of such control. The absence of formal attention may indicate that the agencies have so attuned themselves to the wishes of Congress and the President that overt exercises of power are unnecessary.

The evaluation of the effectiveness of formal controls must also include consideration of the existence and use of informal pressures by the President and Congress and the extent to which this enhances their overall control of the agencies. Both branches have used a variety of informal pressures to persuade the agencies to respond to their wishes. These informal pressures have made the exercise of formal control less necessary; the existence of the formal powers has made the informal pressures more effective. Formal political controls, informal pressures, and regulatory agency responsiveness to them does not necessarily constitute proof that the requirements of democratic theory have been satisfied. Even total agency responsiveness to political control is a meaningless indicator unless the political controls are democratic in orgin and nature. If the controls exerted by Congress and the President do not reflect majority preferences or are contrary to the public interest, democracy has not been achieved simply because a bureaucratic agency responded to those pressures.

Democracy may also be measured by procedural aspects of a policy-making process: the fairness of the procedures and the extent to which the process is open to both public participation and inspection. Congress, the presidency, and the judiciary have devoted a great deal of time and effort to establishing "fair" regulatory procedures and to ensuring that agencies adhere to those procedures. Judicial review has emerged as an increasingly important control on both procedural and substantive aspects of the regulatory process. The existence of judicial review has compelled the agencies to be concerned constantly with establishing and following fair procedures and has limited substantive agency action by restricting arbitrary and capricious exercises of power. The regulatory process, at least those aspects covered by the Administrative Procedure Act, is relatively open to public participation and the major limitations on participation are similar to the limitations on participation in the general political process: the availability of money, time, expertise, and organization. Particularly since the passage of the Freedom of Information Act, most regulatory decisions and procedures are open to public inspection.

Whether the expansion of administrative regulation has undermined the procedural aspects of the American democratic system must and will be determined by each individual who examines the regulatory process. What has been established in this chapter is that regulation is subject to political control and is carried on in a complex environment populated by a constantly changing set of actors and attitudes, and that the specific components of that environment differ from agency to agency and decision to decision.

NOTES

1. Arthur Snow and Burton A. Weisbrod, "Consumerism, Consumers, and Public Interest Law," in B. Weisbrod, Joel F. Handler, and Neil Komesar, eds., *Public Interest Law* (Berkeley: University of California Press, 1978), p. 408.

2. "CAB Studies Overbooking Rules," *Aviation Week and Space Technology*, 104 (April 26, 1976), 32.

3. See Frank J. Goodnow, *Politics and Administration: A Study in Government* (New York: MacMillan, 1900), and Woodrow Wilson, "The Study of Administration," 2 *Political Science Quarterly* (June 1887), 197–222, for examples of this school of thought.

4. Joel D. Aberbach, "Congressional Oversight," in David C. Kozak and John D. MacCartney, eds., *Congress and Public Policy* (Homewood, Ill.: Dorsey Press, 1982), p. 390.

5. Ibid.

6. "On the Regulatory Circuit," *National Journal*, April 3, 1982, p. 602.

7. Florence Heffron, *The Independent Regulatory Commissioners*, Unpublished Ph.D. dissertation, Dept. of Political Science, University of Colorado, 1971, p. 395.

8. "DMSO Is No Big Worry for FDA," *Spokesman-Review* (Spokane, Washington), September 12, 1980, p. 23.

9. Judy Sarasohn, "FTC Fund Bill with Legislative Veto Clears," *Congressional Quarterly*, May 24, 1980, p. 1407.

10. *Writers' Guild of America, West, Inc. v. Federal Communications Commission*, 423 F Supp 1075 (S.D. Cal. 1976).

11. Quoted in "Bellar-Dirksen Exchange," *Administrative Law Review*, 12, (Winter 1959–60), 132–33.

12. Richard Pious, *The American Presidency*, (New York: Basic Books, 1979), p. 159.

13. Harold Seidman, *Politics, Position, Power*, 3d ed. (New York: Oxford University Press, 1980), p. 262.

14. See *Humphrey's Executor v. United States*, 295 U.S. 602 (1935), and *Wiener v. United States*, 357 US 349 (1958).

15. Peter Woll, *American Bureaucracy*, 2d ed. (New York: Norton, 1977), p. 245.

16. Jeremy Rabkin, "Office of Civil Rights," in James Q. Wilson, ed., *The Politics of Regulation* (New York: Basic Books, 1980), p. 319.

17. Harrell Rodgers III and Charles Bullock III, *Law and Social Change* (New York: McGraw-Hill, 1972), p. 89.

18. Quoted in Rodgers and Bullock, p. 91.

19. Samuel Bernstein and Patrick O'Hara, *Public Administration: Organizations, People, and Public Policy* (New York: Harper & Row, 1979).

20. Louis Kohlmeier, *The Regulators* (New York: Harper & Row, 1969), p. 41.

21. Richard Berner, *Constraints on the Regulatory Process: A Case Study of Regulation of Cable Television* (Cambridge, Mass.: Balinger, 1976) pp. 45–47.

22. See Carl McFarland, *Judicial Review of the ICC and the FTC* (Cambridge: Harvard University Press, 1934), p. 175.

23. *Vermont Yankee Nuclear Power Corp. v. Natural Resources Defense Council Inc.*, 435 U.S. 519 (1978). This case will be discussed fully in chapter 11.

24. 347 U.S. 672 (1954).

25. 360 U.S. 378 (1959).

26. See Daniel Froino, "Regulating the Natural Gas Producing Industry: Two Decades of Experience," in James E. Anderson, ed., *Economic Regulatory Policies* (Lexington, Mass.: Lexington Books–D.C. Heath, 1976), pp. 89–103.

27. Rodgers and Bullock, *Law and Social Change*, p. 83.

28. John M. Pfiffner and Robert Presthus, *Public Administration*, 5th ed. (New York: Ronald Press, 1967) pp. 131–32.

29. Ibid., p. 133.

30. Randall Ripley and Grace Franklin, *Congress, the Bureaucracy, and Public Policy*, rev. ed. (Homewood, Ill.: Dorsey Press, 1980), p. 151.

31. S. A. Lawrence, "The Battery Additive Controversy," in *Inter-University Case Program* (University: University of Alabama Press, 1962).

32. Gabriel Kolko, *The Triumph of Conservatism* (New York: Free Press, 1963), pp. 98–108.

33. Pendleton Herring, *Public Administration and the Public Interest* (New York: McGraw-Hill, 1936), p. 215.

34. See Environmental Defense Fund and Robert Boyle, *Malignant Neglect* (New York: Vintage Books, 1980), pp. 117–20.

35. "Reauthorization Bills Reported for Insecticide Program," *Congressional Quarterly*, June 7, 1980, p. 1586.

36. David Howard Davis, *Energy Politics*, 2d ed. (New York: St Martin's, 1978), p. 127.

37. U.S. Bureau of Census, vol. 1, no. 1, pt. 1, 1977, *Census of of Governments* (Washington, D.C.: GPO, 1977).

38. Harold Hughes, "From the Governor's Chair," in Donald Herzberg and Alan Rosental, eds., *Strengthening the States* (Garden City, N.Y.: Doubleday and Anchor, 1972), p. 114.

39. Conversation with an administrator, Idaho State Department of Health and Welfare, July 1978.

40. Charles S. Bullock and Harrell Rodgers, *Coercion to Compliance* (Lexington, Mass.: Lexington Books, 1976), pp. 26–27.

41. The following discussion is based on Norman C. Thomas, *Education in National Politics* (New York: David McKay, 1975), and Jerome T. Murphy "The Education Bureaucracies Implement Novel Policy," in Allan Sindler, ed., *Policy and Politics in America* (Boston: Little, Brown, 1973), pp. 160–99.

42. Herbert Northrup and Gordon Bloom, *Government and Labor* (Homewood: Richard D. Irwin, 1963), p. 70.

43. See Deil S. Wright, *Understanding Intergovernmental Relations* (North Scituate: Duxbury Press, 1978), p. 62.

44. Peter Schuck, "Public Interest Groups and the Policy Process," *Public Administration Review*, March/April 1977, p. 133.

45. James Q. Wilson, "The Politics of Regulation," in Wilson, ed., *The Politics of Regulation*, p. 385.

46. Environmental Defense Fund and Boyle, *Malignant Neglect*, p. 129.

Chapter 6

Regulatory Theory

To this point we have examined the growth and scope of regulatory power and the general constitutional, legal, and political environment in which regulation occurs. Although to a certain extent each regulatory action is unique and can be fully understood only by examining it in terms of the specific circumstances in which it occurred, one of the more enduring concerns of political scientists has been the attempt to develop general theories of the regulatory process. Political theory is a "body of thought that seeks to evaluate, explain and predict political phenomena."[1] Empirical theory specifically attempts to "explain, predict, guide research and organize knowledge through the formulation of abstract models and scientifically testable propositions."[2] When the political phenomenon under consideration is regulation, theory is and has been directed at explaining

1. Why regulatory policies have been adopted;
2. Why regulatory agencies, once created, behave as they do; and
3. The determinants of outcomes of the regulatory process.

Although a multitude of theories have been developed to explain these aspects of regulation and the regulatory process, the theories differ widely in their conclusions and no uniformly accepted theory has yet emerged. To cover all the theories that have been advanced would require a full-length book. Those who would like such an overview would be well advised to consult Mitnick's *The Political Economy of Regulation*.[3] This chapter will consider only a few of the most commonly cited theories of regulation and the regulatory process.

THEORIES OF REGULATORY ORIGIN

As has been pointed out frequently in this book, various types of regulation exist. They were created at different times in response to widely differing situations and problems, and their scope, impact, and goals similarly vary. Treating such diverse types of regulation as a single phenomenon for theoretical purposes has proven unproductive and the starting point for many theorists has been the attempt to develop typologies of regulation. One of the most common typologies is the distinction between "economic" or "old style" regulation and "new style" "social" regulation.

The old style economic regulation or traditional "Regulation I"[4] typically "focuses on markets, rates, and the obligation to serve"[5]; it is concerned "primarily with the prices charged in individual industries and with entry by new producers into those industries."[6] Thus it deals largely with economic questions and the scope of the old style regulatory agencies is usually confined to regulation of particular industries or specific sectors of the economy. Often the expressed purpose of economic regulation is to promote, protect, or restore competition within a single industry. It encompasses the regulatory activities of such agencies as the Interstate Commerce Commission, the Federal Maritime Commission, and the Securities and Exchange Commission.

The new style social regulation or Regulation II is a more recent phenomenon which has been initiated largely in the last two decades and is concerned more with social policy than economic matters. It also has very substantial economic effects just as the "economic" regulation has a substantial impact on human welfare. "The new-style social regulation effects the conditions under which goods and services are produced and the physical characteristics of products that are manufactured . . . [and] also extends to far more industries and ultimately affects far more consumers than the old-style regulation, which tends to be confined to specific sectors."[7] It includes environmental protection regulation, regulation to protect the health and safety of workers, pure food and drug regulation, and regulation concerned with the safety of automobiles, airplanes, and various other consumer products. Social regulation, although the smaller type, is the faster growing area and concerns business more, since it often involves government in the internal affairs of the corporation. White notes that most social regulatory agencies are within the executive branch (OSHA, EPA, FDA) while most old style economic regulations are administered by independent regulatory commissions (ICC, FCC, FMC).

A slightly different typology is offered by Ripley and Franklin who distinguished between "competitive" regulatory and "protective" regulatory policy. "Competitive" regulation limits "the provision of specific goods to only one or a few designated deliverers chosen from a larger number of potential or actual competitors."[8] Although it overlaps considerably with Regulation I, it excludes "regulation of the conditions under which competition in the business world can take place"[9] and rate-setting activities. Both of these are included in "protective" regulatory policy which is "designed to protect the public by setting conditions under which various private activities can occur."[10] It includes environmental regulation, antitrust regulation, the activities of the FTC, and food and drug regulation. Competitive regulatory policy is a low-visibility type of policy handled primarily by the implementing agency which determines who gets cotrol of relatively limited resources such as airplane, trucking, or railroad routes, or television or radio station licenses. Protective policy is characterized by higher visibility, greater conflict, and many more active participants in the policy determining process.

Just as the purpose and scope of the two kinds of regulations differ, so too do the origins of social and economic regulatory agencies. In many cases old style regulation came about at the behest of clients or the industries themselves as attempts to enhance competition or to limit entry by new producers into the field. New style social regulation has often been promoted by consumer-type groups, sometimes with the help of an outside entrepreneur or leader, in an attempt to advance a conception of the public interest. The next section describes various theories of the origin of economic and social regulation.

Economic Regulation: Origins

A number of scholars, particularly Marver H. Bernstein and Herbert Kaufman, contend that economic regulatory agencies are created at the behest of "injured parties" or groups.[11] "Agencies come into existence in response to demands for service from politically mobilized segments of society, both inside and outside the government."[12] The creation of the agency is usually the culmination of a lengthy struggle between those who argue that there exists a public problem which requires public regulation and those (particularly the industry which is due for regulation) who argue that the status quo should be maintained. The struggle occurs in a political arena in which a great number of actors participate. Many of these actors will continue to play a major role in the future agency's environment but the gestation struggle also attracts the concern of actors who will have little to do with the agency after it has been created. Often the President takes a personal interest during this phase and may lead the battle for enactment and agency creation. The entire Congress may be drawn into the struggle to enact enabling legislation. The public as a whole may be made aware of the demand for a new agency through the media. The specific interest groups involved or industries to be regulated are very active at this stage and, Bernstein argues, usually powerfully resist regulation. They may be overcome only by strong advocacy by reformers. The gestation of an old style regulatory agency may require several decades as affected groups or customers become organized and make demands on government for regulation of the industry. Only because of strong advocacy by reformers and/or as the result of critical conditions is the statute passed over the objections of the industry which is to be regulated, and because that statute is the product of compromise it is usually vague and may be out of date by the time of enactment. Merle Fainsod makes the same general argument. He suggests that regulation "has been initiated by particular groups to deal with specific evils as they arose." Economic regulation comes about at the demand of injured groups who want government controls over "felt abuses."[13] According to this theory, for example, farmers and shippers who were adversely affected by monopolistic and unfair practices of the railroads sought government regulation and were the primary motivating force in the creation of the Interstate Commerce Commission.

Bernstein's theory of the gestation of regulatory agencies has been subjected to extensive and intensive criticism. A large body of research indicates that far from being born out of the desires of public interest proponents or demands from those injured by industry behavior, many agencies were unfortunately born in sin, out of the desires of the potential regulatees to protect their favored interests.[14] No set of regulatory agencies better exemplifies this than occupational licensing boards and agencies at the state level. Currently, over 100 occupations are subject to licensing requirements in one or more states. The occupations covered range from medicine and law to architecture, embalming, beekeeping, barbering, and horseshoeing. As Gellhorn has noted, "virtually the only people who remain unlicensed in at least one of the United States are clergymen and university professors, presumably because they are nowhere taken seriously."[15] These boards are invariably created at the behest of members of the profession and are staffed and completely controlled by members of that profession who argue that the only ones that can determine competence and professional standards are members of the profession in question. Once established, these professional boards exercise monopoly control over their profession. Regulator and regulatee are, from the start, synonymous. Many federal regulatory agencies had similar origins. The CAB, the FCC, federal meat inspection, and the Atomic Energy Commission most certainly were created at the urging of the affected industry.[16] Both the FTC and ICC also had business support in their initiation.

Another school of thought on the origins of economic regulatory agencies may be called the "public interest" theory. This theory assumes "that regulation is established largely in response to public-interest-related objectives" as screened through and advocated by agents like public interest groups and entrepreneurial politicians.[17] There may be disagreement over what comprises *the* public interest but public interest theorists argue that those seeking regulation are attempting to champion their conception of the public interest. Cushman's well-researched study of *The Independent Regulatory Commissions* concludes that the old style economic regulatory agency was created to solve major economic problems and that Congress acted largely with the public interest at heart in passing enabling legislation. "A major purpose in creating a commission was to provide machinery to secure the accurate and expert information necessary to the solution of that (economic) problem."[18] Richard Posner suggests that economic regulation may be initiated to serve the public interest function of redistributive taxation; regulation permits internal subsidies which compel "the provision of certain services in quantities and at prices that a free market would not offer."[19]

A third explanation of the origin of economic regulation might be termed the "industry protection" theory. This theory argues that the industry itself desires regulation in order to protect the established producers and limit entry by others. The most extreme proponent of this view is Gabriel Kolko who argues that the act setting up the Interstate Commerce Commission was sought mainly by railroad executives to protect their own interests in an increasingly unstable economic environment. The railroads primarily wanted protection with a minimal amount of regulation, consequently, the Interstate Commerce Act was very weak and contained few provisions requiring competition among the established railroads.[20]

The last theory of the origin of old style economic regulation which we will cover is that of James Q. Wilson, who suggests a "politics of regulation" approach.[21] Wilson presents a fourfold typology of regulation proposals classified in terms of the perceived distribution of their costs and benefits. Both costs and benefits may be monetary or nonmonetary and may be widely distributed or narrowly concentrated. If both costs and benefits are widely distributed (such as in the social security and national defence areas) "majoritarian" politics result. Although no interest groups form to oppose such policies, they can be passed only when popular opinion supports them in sufficient breadth to make up for the lack of intensity. When both costs and benefits are narrowly concentrated, "interest group" politics arises. A subsidy or regulation may confer benefits on a relatively small, identifiable group at the expense of a different identifiable group. The public may not believe it will be affected and therefore may not be concerned. The two opposing groups, however, will perceive the importance of the issue to them and will organize in an attempt to exercise political influence to pass or prevent the regulation. Regulation that results from interest group politics, such as most labor legislation, usually is a compromise and contains a "charter" defining the obligations and rights of each side. Under a proposed regulatory policy involving concentrated benefits but widely distributed costs such as most professional licensing, "client" politics will emerge. This may be thought of as very similar to the industry protection origin theory; the small, identifiable group that is likely to benefit from the regulation or subsidy or entry restriction will organize to push for its passage. Since costs are dispersed, no single individual is strongly affected and little opposition to the creation of the regulation occurs.

Social Regulation: Origins

The new style social regulation usually has different origins from economic regulation. The last category of James Q. Wilson's classification of costs and benefits—distributed benefits with concentrated costs—offers one theory of the origin of social regulation. Wilson suggests that the passage of a regulation that will confer general benefits to a large group at the expense of a small, identifiable group is the result of "entrepreneurial" politics. A policy entrepreneur of the general public must pull together a legislative majority on behalf of the diffusely affected constituency. This may be accomplished by mobilizing latent public opinion in favor of regulation promoting widely shared values. A scandal in the industry to be regulated, a perceived or real crisis, or the support of the media or other political activists may help the entrepreneur defeat the organized opposition, which will use the many access points of the political system to attempt to slow or block passage of the social regulation. If the political environment is right, the entrepreneur may succeed in getting such a social regulation implemented; even though no individual will receive large benefits, the "public interest" has been advanced.

THEORIES OF REGULATORY BEHAVIOR

The previous sections have described several of the more prominent theories of regulatory origin. Once a regulatory agency is established, the next aspect we are interested in is the behavior of that agency. This section will discuss attempts by several scholars to develop coherent theories that explain and predict the behavior of regulatory agencies. Two points should be kept in mind. First, the origins of the regulation may have a significant, possibly determining influence over the behavior of the agency. And second, the theories suggest that the political environment is a major factor in regulatory behavior. The two theories of regulatory behavior which will be considered and evaluated are the life cycle theory and the theory of subgovernment formation or "capture" theory.

The Life Cycle Theory

Several authors, particularly Marver H. Bernstein in *Regulating Business by Independent Commission* and Anthony Downs in *Inside Bureaucracy*, have argued that administrative agencies pass through a life cycle similar to that of human beings: They are created, grow, mature, and age, but unlike human beings, only infrequently die. Although the rate at which agencies progress through this life cycle varies and although there are unique elements in the experience of each agency, all agencies go through distinct and similar phases. Just as the maturing process affects human behavior, so too does it affect the agencies' ability and desire to regulate. For Bernstein many of these changes in agency behavior are directly related to a diminution in the number of relevant actors in the agency's environment. He argues that there are four phases in the natural and regulatory life cycle: gestation, youth, maturity, and old age:

1. *Gestation.* This phase was covered in the discussion of theories of origin of economic regulation. As was pointed out, Bernstein believes that regulation is a result of the desires of those who are adversely affected by business activity to secure government intervention and protection and is opposed by the affected industry. High-level conflict is thus characteristic of regulatory policy creation, and Congress has a major role in mediating the conflict. Instead of resolving specific issues, however, Congress will delegate power and responsibility in broad, sweeping terms to an administrative agency. The will to reform is satisfied, but the specifics of that reform and regulatory effort are left to the agency to determine. The scene of the usually bitter and prolonged conflict over regulation shifts to the agency.
2. *Youth.* "Characteristically, the great federal regulatory agencies in the early years of their existence have been fired with an inspiration to achieve the goals laid down for them by Congress."[22] The newly created agency will usually push aggressively to promote the public interest that it was created to protect. This occurs because the agency is likely to be staffed initially by individuals whom Downs calls zealots and advocates.[23] These officials are loyal to the expressed goals of the new regulatory agency and push aggressively for both substantive regulation and agency growth. The youth of an agency is usually the only phase where rapid growth is possible since the opportunity to demonstrate that the agency is needed and is accomplishing important tasks clearly exists.

    Obstacles to growth soon appear: competition for scarce resources, inability to produce new and impressive results, and conflict among the climbers in the agency impede the agency's ability to expand and to pursue regulatory goals with its initial zeal.[24] These obstacles and the lessened newness of the agency may bring about important changes in its personnel and its political environment. Often the zealots become restless when progress is stymied. They begin to move on to new programs. The public begins to lose interest; the President and the Congress as an entity are no longer involved or interested in the day-to-day decisions of the agency.[25] The agency's relevant political environment narrows considerably. The public and the media lose interest and turn their attention to new issues. The groups that pushed for legislation assume that the battle has been won and that implementation will occur automatically. Fewer individuals and institutions are concerned with the agency's programs. The regulated industry accepts the agency as a fait accompli and decides that it must learn to coexist with it. The initial pattern of relationships between the agency and the industry—the regulator and the regulated—changes. That which was guarded and cautious becomes cooperative and harmonious.

3. *Maturity*. "The process of devitalization"—the agency gradually loses its drive to regulate in the public interest and becomes more concerned with political survival. Its prior public and political support has faded. The only actors who are still concerned with the agency actions and who attend appropriations/oversight hearings are the regulated industries. Consequently, personal relationships develop between the employees of the agency and the affected industry's personnel. Often an interchange of personnel between industry and agency occurs. The agency starts to "understand" better the needs and problems of the industry and loses its regulatory zeal. The best and frequently only supporters of the agency in its political struggles for appropriations and power become industry representatives. In maturity, the regulatory agency often concentrates less on regulation than on promotion and protection of the industry.

Since the industry is its biggest defender and usually the only external voice that the agency hears, the agency becomes more concerned with the health of the industry and less concerned with the larger public interest, for the public is neither supportive nor interested.[26]The narrowing of the political environment leads to a narrow point of view by the agency and its staff, who tend to become what Downs terms "conservers."

4. *Old age*. Bernstein describes Phase Four as one of debility and decline. The agency is passive or stagnant; it loses whatever small concern it ever had with the public or consumer interest. It is concerned only with maintaining the status quo of the "regulated" industry and its protective relationship with that industry. Bernstein notes that this debility does not go unnoticed by the executive and the legislative branches. Budgets and staffs are cut, which makes the agency even more dependent upon the industry for support and staff, which further reinforces the status quo and accelerates the process of decline. Bernstein does recognize the possibility that due to scandal, crisis, or renewed public attention the drive to regulate can be ignited again and that same "old" agency may be rejuvenated as the cycle starts again.

5. *Death*. Normally old agencies do not die, they fade into comfortable obscurity. But in a relatively few instances, the decline of the regulatory agencies may result in their death. Kaufman in *Are Government Organizations Immortal?* reported that some government agencies do die, notwithstanding popular mythology. Ironically, however, it is not "old" agencies that die, but rather more recently created organizations. Kaufman's empirical study therefore backs up Down's theory that few governmental bureaus "disappear once they have passed their initial survival thresholds."[27] He argues that this is so because older

agencies are willing to shift functions (e.g., from regulation to promotion) in order to survive and because the client groups (i.e., regulated industries) continue to maintain political pressure to continue the agencies for their own benefit.

The basic problem with the life cycle theory is that it is based on a false analogy. Organizations, public and private, are not analogous to individual biological organisms, whether they be human or protozoan. While organizations do exhibit some of the characteristics of their individual human components, they have separate and distinct characteristics of their own. Certainly one of the most important of these is longevity and the ability to survive and prosper long after the initial human members of the organization have disappeared. This is crucial to the understanding of some current regulatory agencies which should have long since lapsed into permanent old age. New personnel, sometimes only a few top crucial members of an organization, can change its direction and orientation. Regulatory agencies can be born again. A moribund FTC can become after 56 years of lassitude a zealous defender of consumer interests; a complacent CAB can vigorously undertake deregulation of the airlines and prod a reluctant Congress to acquiesce; and a stagnant ICC can move aggressively to inject competition into railroad rate determinations although for 32 years rail price fixing has had government approval. Another problem with the theory is that the length of the stages is not specified and the differences between them are not precise. Bernstein never specifies whether youth can last for forty years or maturity pass extremely quickly. Nor does he explain the difference between the lack of congressional support in maturity and its reduction of funding for the agency in "old age."[28] Further, even a superficial examination of the original appointees to some agencies indicates that zealots and advocates were notably lacking. According to Gabriel Kolko the initial members of the ICC chosen by President Grover Cleveland were directly tailored to suit the railroads' taste: "The railroads themselves could not have chosen a more sympathetic regulatory body."[29] Similarly, the initial appointees to the FTC caused consternation among Progressives and led one of them, Louis Brandeis, to remark that Wilson had ruined the Commission by his choice of administrators.[30] If agencies are in fact created in this type of environment, they need traverse no life cycle to arrive at instant senility.

At the other side of the argument, there are those who criticized the life cycle theory from the point of view that often the regulated industry never does gain control over the agency and the agency never undergoes "devitalization."[31] Rather, a conception of the "public interest" may be the major factor in agency behavior. Some regulatory agencies have never degenerated into senility but have pursued their activities with continued enthusiasm and zeal; the Internal Revenue Service and the Immigration and Naturalization Service are prime examples.

At best the life cycle theory has only limited applicability to the diverse spectrum of regulatory agencies. It is directed exclusively at economic regulatory agencies with only one clientele group and, as we have seen, many agencies do not fit this situation. Ultimately, the basic problem with the life cycle theory is that it assumes that the environment of regulatory agencies quickly becomes limited and stagnant. It fails to recognize that the environment of an agency is subjected to rapid change and expansion as new issues arise, as new groups develop and become active, and as new politicians are elected to office. Accepting one of the basic tenets of life cycle theory, that agencies desire to survive politically, means accepting that an agency, when confronted with such environmental changes, will either adapt or perish. If survival requires tilting toward consumers or environmental groups, then it should not be surprising to see an agency respond to them.

Subgovernment/Regulatory Capture Theories

The concept of subgovernments is in some respects a logical derivative of the life cycle theory, and it, too, is concerned with describing and explaining the impact of the political environment of administrative agencies. Subgovernments or subsystems, "triumvirates," "whirlpools," or "cozy triangles"[32] or the "eternal triangle" all refer to the same concept: that in many areas of public policy routine decisions are actually made by a very limited set of actors—members of Congress from the committees or subcommittees that "have principal or perhaps exclusive jurisdiction over the policy area,"[33] who also often have a direct constituency concern with the area; committee staff members; bureaucrats from the agency which has regulatory authority; representatives of the economic interest group which will be directly affected by the decision:

> Together Congress, interest groups, and bureaus have all the necessary resources to satisfy each other's needs. Bureaus supply services or goods to organized groups but need resources to do so. Congressional committees supply the bureau with resources but need electoral political support to remain in office and political support to win policy disputes in Congress. The interest group provides the political support that the member of Congress needs, but the interest group needs government goods and services to satisfy members' demands. The result is a tripartite relationship that has all the resources necessary to operate in isolation from politics if no great crises occur.[34]

Because of the fragmented nature of American politics, the subgovernment usually acts in semi-isolation. The media, the public, and other political leaders are not concerned with the "routine" administrative regulatory decisions. The result is that these routine matters are left to the subgovernment which is familiar with and affected by those matters. Ripley and Franklin note that there are three ways that the "normally closed, low-profile operations of a subgovernment can be opened up to 'outsiders' ": If the subgovernment participants fundamentally disagree on a point, this may be publicized and stimulate attention from nonmembers; if outside political actors decide to inquire into subgovernment activities using formal or informal resources such as legislative oversight or personal influence; or if a new issue which is controversial is injected into the routine of subgovernment policy decisions.[35] Over time these "routine" decisions become public policy for that set of issues.

The concept of subgovernment resembles the "maturity" phase of the life cycle theory. Both perceive regulatory policy as being formulated in a closed environment with a limited number of participants who share common views, information, and interests. The agency's bonds with the regulated industry are constantly strengthened as personnel are interchanged, and a relationship of interdependency is fostered between the agency and the regulatee. The congressional subcommittees also function as part of the subgovernment. Although the subgovernment may have originated in the agency's "youth," it reaches its zenith in the mature phase and lasts through the "old age" phase of the agency's existence. Agency action is aimed at maintaining the supportive relationship among the subgovernment's actors and ensuring the survival of the agency. The agency has become "captured" by the interests it was designed to regulate.[36]

Mitnick offers a different theory for explaining regulatory capture which is based primarily on the agency's need for information to regulate. Since industry possesses the most vital information required by the regulatory agency a condition of "information impactedness"[37] develops. The industry's primary interest is self-protection: It supplies information selectively and with that interest uppermost in its concern. Industry's power over regulators is enhanced by its control over rewards sought by the regulators: "status, prestige, friendship and future job goals." The result is the creation of an incentive system for regulators to respond to the wishes of the regulatees. The impact of the incentive system is magnified by the tendency to recruit regulators from industry, by close personal association of regulators with regulatees and high turnover rates for regulators. Regulatory capture, the tendency of regulators to identify with regulatees and to shape regulation to fit their preferences, is the end result of this incentive system.[38]

The concept of subgovernments shares many of the weaknesses of the life cycle theory. Its applicability is greatest for regulatory or promotional policies directed toward a single, well-organized economic interest. One of the most impenetrable subgovernments has been, and remains, the Veterans' benefits subgovernment. Other well-established subgovernments have experienced some disruption of their placid environments recently. Agricultural policy determination is a prime example of such a subgovernment. Commodity stabilization policies—that mix of programs which includes price supports, marketing quotas, acreage allotments and commodity loans— is determined by the Agricultural Stabilization and Conservation Service in the Department of Agriculture, farm groups (farmers actually administer the program at the local level and vote on marketing quotas), and the relevant subcommittees of the two Agriculture Committees. Despite the tenacity of the particular subgovernment, it has been subjected to new environmental pressures in the 1970s and 1980s. As inflation affected food prices, consumer groups began to complain, and their complaints were registered by members of Congress and the President. The subgovernment remains intact but considerably more vulnerable than it has been in decades. Increasingly, such policy areas have attracted "outside" observers such as "watchdog" groups or public interest associations and the subgovernment has been subject to pressure from these interests.

Subgovernments have only rarely, if at all, developed in areas of social policy where the clientele is the poor. The Food Stamp Program administered by the Food and Nutrition Service of the Department of Agriculture has been regarded as an unwanted stepchild by its administrators and congressional overseers. Tolerated because it does increase demand for food products and indirectly channels money to the "real" clientele, the Food Stamp Program administrators have never developed close ties to their primary recipients and regulations aimed at these recipients have not been made through close consultation with them. Further, while it may be customary to have someone closely associated with agribusiness appointed as Secretary of Agriculture, it is unlikely that a food stamp recipient will ever be appointed administrator of the Food and Nutrition Service.

James Q. Wilson, among others, argues that the regulatory capture concept is much too simplistic. In reality, regulators act from a variety of motives and agencies must deal with and respond to a variety of interests in their environment—clientele, institutions, and public, as well as their own professional norms. His book *The Politics of Regulation* contains several case studies of various regulatory agencies. A few of them appear to be "captives" of their clientele but others respond to different interests.

Despite their lack of universal applicability, the concepts of subgovernments and regulatory capture are valuable tools in understanding the behavior and outputs of many administrative regulatory agencies. Unlike the requirements of the life cycle theory, subgovernment formation and capture can occur at any stage in any agency's existence, including its creation. Further, there is no theoretical bar to a subgovernment being temporarily disrupted or a captive agency escaping. Currently, we are in a period of time where many subgovernments are being shaken: The ICC has defied the railroads on rate regulation, the CAB displeased the airlines on deregulation, the Nuclear Regulatory Commission must daily contend with vocal opponents to nuclear power, and even the most impenetrable of subgovernments, the Corps of Engineers and water projects, has been attacked head-on by a President and environmentalist groups. It is unlikely that any of these will result in the permanent and irrevocable destruction of the subgovernment, however. The resources of the new intervenors—public interest groups, Presidents, and the press—are limited; the number of potential policy issues is limitless. As participants change, and as new problems surface, the intervenors will move on and the subgovernments will be left to regroup—shaken, perhaps, but still basically intact.

Theories of Individual Regulators' Behavior

Another approach to explaining regulatory behavior is to focus on the actions and motivations of individual regulators. We have already mentioned Downs's description of advocates, zealots, and conservers (he also lists climbers and statesmen, who are loyal to their own careers and the broader public interest, respectively), and Mitnick's incentive theory. A number of other scholars have also suggested types of regulators, of which the two general types are "politicians" and "bureaucrats."[39] Politicians seek to maximize their goals (which may be personal or policy) by behavior which attracts support from the major actors in their environment. Bureaucrats seek to preserve their position and thus the position of the agency and tend to favor clientele interests in their decision making. Thus an agency populated or led by bureaucrats is more prone to "capture." The key to all such theories of individual motivation is that agency behavior is the result of individual regulators' motivations and rational decision making in reaching those goals.

This view also has validity; individuals do attempt to maximize their preferences. But as with all such psychological theories, it is difficult to specify precisely the characteristics of any type or to determine which individuals fit into a specific category. Equally difficult and usually unspecified in these theories is the determination of whether an agency has to be populated entirely by one type or has to have one type in all the leadership positions in order for the agency's behavior to be in conformity to the theory. At this time, empirical evidence to support the theories as lacking.

SYSTEMS APPROACH TO REGULATORY ANALYSIS

General Systems Theories

This section deals with a different type of theory. Rather than attempting to explain a specific type or origin or behavior, the open-systems approach provides a general model or framework for understanding the regulatory agency in its totality. Open-systems theory views organizations as adaptive systems which must continuously interact with their environments and which are totally dependent on successful interactions with their environment for survival.[40] As open systems, organizations seek equilibrium or a stable state wherein those actors in the environment which seek change are counterbalanced by those who desire either no change or a change in the opposite direction.[41] The organization must react to certain "inputs" (which may be demands or supports) from the major forces in its environment and convert those inputs into outputs (policy). Those outputs have an impact which is fed back as more inputs into the organization.[42] When the organization's environment changes sufficiently to unhinge the established equilibrium the organization will modify its behavior in an attempt to reestablish equilibrium.

An organization's environment may be broken into two basic components: the general environment or the broad societal conditions that are potentially relevant for organizational functioning and the specific environment which is composed of those organizations, groups, and individuals with which the organization is in direct interaction. The general environment includes technological, legal, political, economic, demographic, ecological, and cultural conditions.[43] Changes in the general environment may affect the organization both directly and indirectly by modifying the complexity and intensity of the specific environment.

Terreberry has classified organization environments into four basic types. Type I is a Placid-Random environment characterized by a low degree of change and low interconnection between environmental parts and actors. Type II environments are Placid-Clustered, composed of stable environmental actors that are divided into recognizable and potentially powerful coalitions. Type III environments are Disturbed-Reactive, and Type IV environments are Turbulent, marked by accelerating change and complexity that exceed the organization's ability to predict and control the consequences of its actions. A Type IV environment puts extreme pressure on organizational decision makers, reduces their freedom of choice, and decreases their ability to anticipate the behavior of other organizations and actors.[44] Turbulence compels the organization to search constantly for methods to establish an equilibrium.

Organizational responses to turbulence include inspirational efforts, attempts to decrease the complexity of the environment, compartmentalization of the environment, development of routines to formalize relations with and among environmental actors, and domain modification. Domain modification is a dominant strategy for managing organization-environment relations. Its use depends on the organization's domain choice flexibility—the extent to which it is free to alter its domain by determining "what aspects of the environment are to be of concern, what phenomena should be noticed and what variables should be introduced into the criterion function for the organization's performance."[45] Although public organizations have less domain choice flexibility than private firms[46] since their domain is determined and limited by legal mandate, those mandates have always permitted agencies broad discretion as to whether, when, and how to enforce the law.

Regulatory Agencies as Open Systems: The FTC as an Example   Regulatory agencies are a special type of open system. Agencies receive inputs from any number of sources: clientele, legislatures, the public, other agencies, the executive, and the judiciary. They must respond to at least some of these inputs and convert them into policy decisions. Those outputs have some type of an impact on the environment and feedback may result. The environment of regulatory agencies, as has been discussed, is of great importance to the agency and influences agency behavior.[47]

No agency better exemplifies the impact of environmental change on regulatory policy than the Federal Trade Commission. Created in 1915, the FTC is one of the oldest of the independent regulatory commissions and in its 65-year history has been criticized, condemned, calumnied, and even, recently, praised. It exemplifies neither the life cycle theory nor the subgovernment concept but it well illustrates the importance of environmental influences as well as the problems and perhaps the impossibility of effectively regulating business in this country.[48]

The FTC: Creation and the Early Years   The environment in which the FTC was created was a turbulent, Type IV environment populated by diverse and competing groups. Progressives, consumers, small businessmen, big corporations, and muckrakers all supported the concept of an independent commission with authority to maintain fair competition in interstate commerce. If the FTC was created with the support of potential regulatees, they were certainly not its only advocates, and if they had a rather different view of what regulation entailed than the other proponents, it was not until after the FTC was in operation that they made this view clear.

The roots of the FTC go back at least as far as 1890 and the passage of the Sherman Anti-Trust Act which was intended to prevent unreasonable combinations in restraint of trade. The Sherman Act was enforced by the antitrust division of the Justice Department through civil or criminal charges brought in the federal courts. The Sherman Act quickly ran into problems when it was challenged in the Supreme Court, which at that time was hostile to any governmental regulation of business. In 1895, the Court ruled that the Sherman Act did not apply to manufacturing.[49] In 1911, in *United States v. American Tobacco Co.*,[50] the Court held that the Sherman Act was not intended to prohibit all monopolies but only those that were unreasonable. The Sherman Act had been rendered useless and if competition were to be restored or maintained, some other method would have to be devised.

The method Congress devised was to create a commission and because of the high level of political conflict surrounding this issue, to provide it broad but undefined powers over competitive practices. Since there was no agreement among supporters of both the Federal Trade Commission and Clayton Acts as to what constituted "unfair methods of competition," Congress did not attempt to define them, leaving that determination to the discretion of the FTC. The Commission was given the power to investigate business practices, to issue cease and desist orders, and to publicize violations. The agency was to be headed by five commissioners with seven-year terms, appointed by the President and confirmed by the Senate. No more than three commissioners were to be from the same political party and commissioners could be removed only for due cause.

The "youth" of the FTC was remarkably short, terminated by some rather unfortunate choices for commissioners,[51] an unfriendly Congress, and a hostile Supreme Court. As Bernstein pointed out, one characteristic of the youth phase is repeated legal challenges of the agency's powers and procedures:

> The regulatory commission soon discovers that it can accomplish little until the Supreme Court has passed on the validity and constitutionality of its powers and authority. . . . The trial by legal combat gives most of the advantages to the private parties.[52]

In 1920, in *FTC v. Gratz*,[53] the Supreme Court limited the FTC's jurisdiction to those unfair methods of competition that had been identified prior to 1914 and ruled that the final determination of what constituted unfair competition was to be a judical not administrative one. In 1924, in *FTC v. American Tobacco*,[54] the Court severely curbed the agency's investigatory powers. After dismissing an FTC attempt to examine records as "a fishing expedition," the Court put the Commission in the same position as criminal enforcement agencies: no probable cause, no warrant; no warrant, no inspection of documents. Congress's resentment of the FTC's investigation of the meatpacking industry and its subsequent rebuke have already been discussed.

Whatever regulatory enthusiasm the FTC might have had quickly dissipated in this hostile environment. Unlike some regulatory agencies, the FTC had no built-in clientele that it could turn to for support. Its clientele was too diverse, too preoccupied with other matters, and perceived too few benefits to attempt regulatory capture. The FTC's clientele is the entire spectrum of business rather than one specific industry; the FTC had little to offer in terms of subsidies, favorable rate determinations, or protection from competitors. Consumer groups at this time were poorly organized, poorly funded, and relatively inactive, and a "what's good for business" mentality dominated American society throughout the 1920s. It was the worst of times for the FTC. If Wilson's nominees to the commission had been suspect, those of his Republican successors were worse. The appointment of William Humphrey to the Commission in 1925 confirmed the FTC's lapse into premature senility. Dominated by a conservative Republican majority, the Commission was determined "to help business help itself."[55] Survival required domain contraction; this was accomplished by the FTC adopting a passive, noninterventionist style of policy implementation. As the number of relevant actors in its environment decreased, the environment became Type I, Placid-Random.

The rewards of old age are many, and even if the FTC aged too rapidly, it was rewarded. The more passive it became, the more legislation Congress gave it to enforce: the 1918 Export Trade Association Act (Webb-Pomerene), the Robinson-Patman Act, the Wheeler Act, the Wool Product Labelling Act, the Lanham Trademark Act, the Fur Products Labelling Act, the Flammable Fabrics Act, the Textile Fiber Products Identification Act, the Fair Packaging and Labelling Act, the Consumer Credit Protection and Truth in Lending Act, and the Cigarette Labelling and Advertising Act. If there was logic in all of this, it was political logic.

One potentially disruptive aspect in the FTC's environment was the extent to which its jurisdiction overlapped and conflicted with that of other regulatory agencies. In maintaining competition the FTC shares responsibility with the Antitrust Division of the Department of Justice and the specific economic regulatory commissions such as the ICC, the FCC, and the CAB. In the false and deceptive advertising area, the FTC shares jurisdiction with the FCC in broadcast advertising, the FDA in food, drugs, and cosmetic advertising, and the Department of Agriculture in food products advertising. Passivity, however, prevented overt conflict and hostility from developing.

Politics in every sense of the word has been a continual factor in the FTC's regulatory performance. By the 1930s, politics had reduced the FTC to an ineffectual and largely useless, if benign, regulator of business. The election of Franklin Roosevelt as President introduced a disruptive new element into the FTC's environment. Roosevelt, in an attempt to establish presidential supremacy in removal of all executive officials, succeeded in further demoralizing the agency. In an attempt to remake the FTC in his own image, he decided to remove (fire) one of the commissioners, congressional restrictions notwithstanding. Roosevelt asked William Humphrey to resign from the commission so that a commissioner more in tune with FDR's policies could be appointed. Humphrey refused, and Roosevelt "removed" him in 1933, and "Humphrey—who never acquiesced and continued thereafter to insist that he was a member of the FTC—sued for his salary."[56] There ensued several years of warfare between Roosevelt and Humphrey, with the FTC caught in the middle. The President had the locks on Humphrey's door changed so he could not enter his office and told the other commissioners not to communicate any FTC decisions to Humphrey. The suit for back pay continued after Humphrey's death and was pursued by his executor to the Supreme Court. The Court, in *Humphrey's Executor (Rathbun) v. United States*,[57] agreed with Humphrey's argument and held that the President could not remove a commissioner of an independent regulatory commission where Congress had stated that removal could be only for cause. Clearly recognizing the quasi-legislative and quasi-judicial powers of such a nonpartisan independent commission, the Court held that it was not directly subject to presidential control.

Until recently, little that was favorable has ever been said about the FTC and its commissioners. Excoriated by business and consumers alike, it also fared badly in more impartial studies of regulatory agencies. The Hoover Commission report of 1949 was particularly critical of the FTC; it stated that the Commission had accomplished little in maintaining competition and its commissioners had been primarily political hacks with little interest or experience in areas of FTC jurisdiction.[58] The evaluation of the FTC changed little from 1949 to 1961, when James Landis, who had been appointed by President-elect John Kennedy to make recommendations on improving the regulatory process, reported that the FTC was a weak and ineffective agency. Landis found that like the other commissions, the FTC had become so bogged down in judicial procedures that it had been unable to "fabricate clear standards out of its melange of generalities."[59] In the summer of 1968, Nader's Raiders singled out the FTC for special consideration and condemnation. After an extensive investigation they concluded that the FTC was characterized by

> cronyism, . . . alcoholism, spectacular lassitude, and office absenteeism, incompetence by the most modest standards, and a lack of commitment to the regulatory mission. . . . [The Chairman] has trundled along . . . [60]

In 1969, the American Bar Association reviewed the FTC's performance and generally agreed with the Nader critique of the personnel and procedures of the Commission. Its report stated that the FTC should have been at the forefront of consumer protection at the federal level but that instead it was a failure. It suggested that a new federal consumer protection agency be established.

Despite the continual flow of criticisms the FTC survived but seemed to be destined for continuing decline. By the mid-1970s, however, consumer groups were praising the FTC and Ralph Nader rated it as one of the most responsive of federal regulatory agencies. On the other hand, business had come to view the FTC as anathema and was pressuring Congress to curtail its powers. The Commission, whose existence had never neatly paralleled the life cycle theory, added a new phase—rejuvenation. Changes in the FTC's environment put new demands on it and resulted in internal changes, particularly in the agency's top-level personnel. Consumer and public interest groups emerged as continuing actors that constantly pressured the agency to become more aggressive in enforcing the laws assigned to its jurisdiction. Much of the credit (or blame) for this rejuvenation can also be traced to the appointment by Richard Nixon of two chairmen who turned the FTC into an active consumer protection agency. The first was Caspar Weinberger who served only seven months (from January through August of 1970) before he was appointed Secretary of HEW. During his brief tenure Weinberger began important changes. He opened the staff recruitment process, designed new procedures to encourage public participation, and delegated a great deal of responsibility to regional offices, allowing them to make independent investigations. He was followed as chairman by Miles Kirkpatrick, who had chaired the ABA committee which had the year before investigated and criticized the FTC. He continued the direction that Weinberger had charted and implemented some of the reforms suggested by the ABA Report including a greater emphasis on consumer affairs. Kirkpatrick served until January of 1973 when he resigned in opposition to Nixon's request that he suspend certain regulatory actions. Kirkpatrick was followed in quick succession by three chairman, who if they broke no new ground, at least did not reverse the direction the FTC had taken. It remained for Jimmy Carter to appoint a chairman so committed to consumer protection and to an activist FTC that he had been denounced by business leaders as a "radical," a "socialist," and "the most dangerous man in America."[61] Michael Pertschuk had served as chief counsel to the Senate Commerce Committee prior to his appointment to the FTC. As chief counsel he had worked on various consumer protection bills including the FTC Improvement Act of 1974. Under Pertschuk the FTC moved ever more vigorously into the consumer protection area and in the process managed to antagonize some of the most powerful businesses and business groups in the country: the Bar Association, the American Medical Association, the insurance, television, advertising, automobile, drug, and funeral home industries.

Reaction and retaliation were swift. The FTC's environment became increasingly turbulent. The business groups, the professional associations, the U.S. Chamber of Commerce, and the National Association of Manufacturers joined forces to pressure Congress to restrict the FTC. Members of Congress, already sensitive to what they perceived to be a growing anti-government sentiment within the electorate, were responsive. Despite counterpressure from consumer groups who strongly backed the FTC, Congress appeared determined to reverse the FTC's direction. The President and consumer groups seemed equally determined to protect the Commission. Finally, on May 28, 1980, after forcing the FTC to close down operations because of lack of funds, the competing forces reached a compromise. Congress got its legislative veto over all FTC rules; the FTC and its supporters got in return an assurance that it would be allowed to complete all pending investigatory and rule-making proceedings. Pertschuk was typically undaunted by Congressional reaction: "The most serious threats to the agency's ability to protect consumers have not materialized."[62]

The FTC's history illustrates many different aspects of the role that political environment plays in affecting regulatory outcomes. The Commission does not fit easily into the life cycle theory; its creation was not opposed by potential regulatees because no one knew what the Commission was supposed to do. Its first foray into regulatory activism was sharply rebuked by Congress. The Commission lapsed into lethargy, and as long as it remained passive it had amicable relationships with Congress, despite constant criticism from observers. During this long period of lethargy, the Commission failed to generate a supportive clientele group: Business viewed it as impotent and lacking in rewards for support, and consumer and public interest groups were not active or powerful and at any rate regarded the Commission as useless. When the FTC undertook a campaign of vigorous regulation its existence was immediately in jeopardy. Business quickly mobilized to oppose it, and consumer protection groups, which did attempt to support it, learned quickly how weak they were in pressure politics at the federal level. Already badly beaten by the defeat of their attempts to secure creation of a consumer protection agency, these groups now were unable to prevent a weakening of the FTC. Unless both the FTC and the public interest groups which are its most likely supporters learn better to protect their interests, the prognosis for a vital and assertive FTC is dim.

The political environment in which administrative regulation occurs shapes and determines regulatory outcomes. As we have seen, each agency and each issue has a distinct environment populated with institutions, individuals, and groups which attempt to influence regulatory decisions. Under certain circumstances, the political environment may be narrow, and subgovernments may effectively control policy with little outside interference. Ultimately, however, we must conclude that an agency's environment is not static and new actors may change an agency's orientation towards its mission.

To understand the regulatory process, the politics of that process must also be understood. Why an agency was created, the nature of the mandate with which it was provided, and how it interpreted and enforced that mandate are determined by its political environment. At the same time, the role of the legal environment favors certain political actors' attempts to influence regulation. These actors in turn struggle to shape the legal environment so that it magnifies their influence. The result is a complex and constantly changing blend of factors that shape and determine regulatory outcomes.

CONCLUSION

Summary

This chapter has presented a variety of theories of regulation—both "old style" economics and "new style" social regulation. A number of theories have been proposed to explain the origins of economic regulation; some suggest injured parties demand regulation while others propose that the industry itself push for regulation. Public interest theorists argue that regulations are initiated to serve a public interest. James Q. Wilson proposes that the origin of regulation varies according to the dispersion of costs and benefits. New style social regulation may come about when an entrepreneur is able to mobilize general public support for the regulation of a particular sector. There are also a variety of theories which attempt to explain regulatory behavior. These range from the life cycle theories, which analogize agency development to individual development, to theories of subgovernment formation and agency capture. Behavior is also explained as a result of differing motivation and characteristics of individual regulators. Finally, we described the open-systems approach to regulation which proposes that agencies' outputs are largely the result of adaption to their environment.

Difficulties of Theory Construction

"It would be marvelous if there were an agreed upon general theory of the politics of regulation. . . . Unfortunately, as yet no such accepted theory exists."[63]Just as in general political theory, there is no consensus on the "correct" explanation of the complex phenomena under consideration. Oftentimes a theory which does a good job of explaining one aspect of regulation or one regulatory agency's behavior is inapplicable (or irrelevant) to other aspects or other agencies. A theory which sounds intuitively correct may not be validated by empirical study. Critics are much more successful at demolishing theories than constructing ones of their own. In the complex area of regulatory behavior with constantly shifting political forces and changing ideas, it is difficult for any one theory to predict accurately what will occur in regulation—and prediction is one major responsibility of theory.

Need for Eclecticism

Does this mean that regulatory theory is irrelevant and theory construction impossible? To the extent that we expect a general theory of regulation which explains all regulatory behavior to emerge, the answer is probably yes. "A single explanation theory of regulatory politics is about as helpful as a single explanation of politics generally, or of disease. Distinctions must be made, differences examined."[64]Rather than accepting any single explanation of the regulatory process, a more reasonable approach would be to use the relevant and significant portions of various theories and to recognize the diversity of regulatory origin and regulatory behavior. Only then can we come to a general theory which accepts and deals with the diversity, and perhaps to a real understanding of the complexity of the administrative regulatory process.

NOTES

1. Jack Plano, Robert Riggs, and Helenan Robin, *The Dictionary of Political Analysis*, 2d ed. (Santa Barbara: ABC–CLIO, 1982), p. 109.

2. Ibid.

3. Barry M. Mitnick, *The Political Economy of Regulation* (New York: Columbia University Press, 1980).

4. A. Lee Fritschler and Bernard Ross, *Business Regulation and Government Decision-making* (Cambridge, Mass.: Winthrop Publishing, 1980), p. 41.

5. William Lilley III and James C. Miller III, "The New 'Social Regulation,' "*The Public Interest*, 47 (1977), 54.

6. Lawrence J. White, *Reforming Regulation: Processes and Problems* (Englewood Cliffs, N.J.: Prentice-Hall, 1981), p. 41.

7. Lilley and Miller, "The New Social Regulation," p. 5.

8. Randall Ripley and Grace Franklin, *Bureaucracy and Policy Implementation* (Homewood, Ill.: Dorsey Press, 1982), p. 72.

9. Ibid.

10. Ibid.,p. 73.

11. Marver H. Bernstein, *Regulating Business by Independent Commission* (Princeton: Princeton University Press, 1951), chapter 3, and Anthony Downs, *Inside Bureaucracy* (Boston: Little, Brown, 1966), chapter 2. In addition, Herbert Kaufman's *Are Government Organizations Immortal?* (Washington D.C: The Brookings Institution, 1976) provides some interesting insights into the birth and death of public organizations, and William H. Starbuck's article "Organizational Growth and Development," in *Handbook of Organizations*, ed. James G. March (Chicago: Rand McNally, 1964), discusses general theories of organizational growth.

12. Kaufman, *Are Government Organizations Immortal?* , p. 66.

13. Merle Fainsod and Lincoln Gordon, *Government and the American Economy* (New York: Norton, 1941), p. 226.

14. See, for example, Paul Sabatier, "Social Movements and Regulatory Agencies: Toward a More Adequate—and Less Pessimistic—Theory of Clientele Capture," *Policy Science*, 6 (September 1975), 30–42, and George W. Hilton, "The Consistency of the Interstate Commerce Act," *Journal of Law and Economics*, 9 (October 1966), 87–113.

15. Walter Gellhorn, "The Abuse of Occupational Licencing," *University of Chicago Law Review*, 44 (1976), 6.

16. Sabatier, "Social Movements and Regulatory Agencies," Mitnick, *The Political Economy of Regulation*, chapter 3.

17. Mitnick, *The Political Economy of Regulation*, p. 91.

18. Robert E. Cushman, *The Independent Regulatory Commissions* (New York: Oxford University Press, 1941), p. 64.

19. Richard Posner, "Taxation By Regulation," 2 *Bell Journal of Economics and Management* (1971), 22, 41.

20. Gabriel Kolko, *Railroads and Regulation, 1877–1916* (Princeton, N.J.: Princeton University Press, 1965). Mitnick, p. 158, provides the term "industry protection origin theories."

21. James Q. Wilson, "The Politics of Regulation," in Wilson, ed., *The Politics of Regulation* (New York: Basic Books, Inc., 1980), chapter 10, and Wilson, chapters 14 and 15 in *American Government: Institutions and Policies* (Lexington, Mass.: D.C. Heath and Company, 1980).

22. Kenneth C. Davis, *Administrative Law* (St. Paul, Minn.: West Publishing Co., 1951), p. 164.

23. Downs, *Inside Bureaucracy*, p. 5.

24. Ibid., p. 12.

25. Bernstein, *Regulating Business by Independent Commission*, p. 81, quoting Emmette S. Redford, *Administration of National Economic Control* (New York: MacMillian, 1952), p. 386.

26. Starbuck reports that mature organizations are more willing to modify their formal original goals in order to survive. Starbuck, "Organizational Growth and Development," p. 473.

27. Downs, *Inside Bureaucracy*, p. 22.

28. Mitnick, *The Political Economy of Regulation*, pp. 49 and 73.

29. Gabriel Kolko, *Railroads and Regulation* (Princeton, N.J.: Princeton University Press, 1949), p. 47.

30. Arthur Link, *Wilson and the Progressive Era* (New York: Harper and Bros., 1954). p. 47.

31. See Wilson, "The Politics of Regulation," p. 360, and Mitnick, *The Political Economy of Regulation*, p. 49.

32. These terms are used by, among others, respectively, Randall B. Ripley and Grace A. Franklin, *Congress, the Bureaucracy and Public Policy* (Homewood, Ill.: Dorsey Press, 1980), p. 8; J. Lieper Freeman, *The Political Process: Executive Bureau–Legislative Committee Relations* (Garden City, N.Y.: Doubleday and Company, Inc., 1955), p. 1; Kenneth J. Meier, *Politics and the Bureaucracy* (North Scituate: Duxbury Press, 1979), p. 51; Ernest S. Griffith, *The Impasse of Democracy* (New York: Harrison-Hilton Books, 1939), p. 182; and R. H. Davidson, "Breaking Up Those 'Cozy Triangles': An Impossible Dream?" in S. Welch and J. G. Peters, eds., *Legislative Reform and Public Policy* (New York: Praeger, 1977). The Ripley and Franklin section is often used in this discussion.

33. Ripley and Franklin, *Congress, the Bureaucracy and Public Policy*, p. 8.

34. Meier, *Politics and the Bureaucracy*, p. 51.

35. Ripley and Franklin, *Congress, the Bureaucracy and Public Policy*, p. 9.

36. For more on regulatory capture, see Mitnick, *The Political Economy of Regulation*, pp. 206ff.

37. Mitnick, *The Political Economy of Regulation*, p. 209.

38. Ibid., p. 210–24.

39. Ibid., pp. 120ff, and Wilson, "The Politics of Regulation," add some different categories.

40. Daniel Katz and Robert Kahn, *The Social Psychology of Industry* (New York: Wiley, 1966), pp. 15–20.

41. Frederick Mosher, "Some Notes on Reorganizations in Government Agencies," in Frederick S. Lane, *Managing State and Local Government* (N.Y.: St. Martin's, 1980), p. 129.

42. David Easton, *A Systems Analysis of Political Life* (New York: Wiley, 1965), is the classic political science work.

43. Robert Miles, *Macro Organizational Behavior* (Santa Monica: Goodyear, 1980), pp. 189–96.

44. Shirley Terreberry, "The Evaluation of Organization Environments," *Administrative Science Quarterly*, 12 (1968), 590–613.

45. William McWhinney, "Organization Form, Decision Modalities, and the Environment," *Human Relations*, 21 (1968), 272.

46. Gary Wamsley and Mayer Zeld, *The Political Economy of Organizations* (Boston: Lexington Books, 1973), p. 58.

47. See the discussions of regulatory agencies as an open system in Edwin G. Krasnow, et al., *The Politics of Broadcast Regulation*, 3d ed. (New York: St Martin's, 1982), chapter 4, and Florence Heffron, "The Politics of Deregulation," paper presented at the Western Political Science Association Conference, Denver, Colorado, 1982.

48. This discussion is drawn from several sources, including E. Pendleton Herring, *Public Administration and the Public Interest* (New York: Harper & Row, 1967), and Glen O. Robinson and Walter Gellhorn, *The Administrative Process* (St. Paul, Minn.: West Publishing, 1974), pp. 371ff. See also Edward F. Cox, et al., *The Nader Report on the Federal Trade Commission* (New York: Grove Press, 1969), and Robert A. Katzmann, *Regulatory Bureaucracy: The FTC and Antitrust Policy* (Cambridge: MIT Press, 1980). For an excellent discussion of the politics of a particular FTC policy, see F. Lee Fritschler, *Smoking and Politics* (Englewood Cliffs, N.J.: Prentice-Hall, 1975).

49. *U.S. v. E. C. Knight*, 156 US1 (1895).

50. 221 US 106 (1911).

51. See page 286 infra.

52. Bernstein, *Regulating Business by Independent Commission*, p. 81.

53. 253 US 421 (1920).

54. 264 US 298 (1924).

55. Herring, *Public Administration and the Public Interest*, p. 137.

56. Robinson and Gellhorn, *The Administrative Process*, p. 377.

57. 295 US 602 (1935).

58. Commission on Organization of the Executive Branch, *Appendix N: Task Force Report on Regulatory Commissions* (Washington, D.C.: GPO, 1949), p. 122.

59. U.S. Congress, Senate Committee on the Judiciary, *Report on Regulatory Agencies to the President Elect*, 86th Congress, 2d Session, 1960, p. 81.

60. Cox, *The Nader Report on the Federal Trade Commission*, p. 170.

61. Alan Barlow, "Business Wants Congress to Limit Powers of Agency," *Congressional Quarterly*, August 11, 1979, p. 1648.

62. Quoted in *Congressional Quarterly's Federal Regulatory Directory*, 1980–81 (Washington, D.C.: CQ Inc., 1980), p. 331.

63. Krasnow, *The Politics of Broadcast Regulation*, p. 134.

64. Wilson, "The Politics of Regulation," p. 393.

PART II

Basic Administrative Processes

Chapter 7

Collecting the Facts: Administrative Investigatory Procedures

Census forms, income tax returns, Affirmative Action–Equal Employment Opportunity compliance forms, airport screenings of passengers and carry-on luggage, and health inspections of restaurants are examples of administrative investigatory activities: the methods used by agencies to collect information needed to carry out their responsibilities. Although these activities are an essential antecedent to all other forms of administrative activity, they have become one of the most controversial aspects of the regulatory process. Their scope has become so broad that no resident of the United States is beyond their reach and in many instances they involve intrusion into the most personal and private aspects of individuals' lives. Compliance with administrative demands for information has become an irritating and time-consuming activity that costs industry billions of dollars a year. Presidents, Congress, the General Accounting Office, the Office of Management and Budget have all criticized the costs, the intrusiveness, and in many instances the uselessness of administrative information collection. Nevertheless, the administrative quest for information continues unabated.

This chapter will examine the various types of administrative investigatory activities and the legal and practical problems currently involved in carrying them out. It will also be concerned with judicial attitudes toward investigations and the major constitutional restraints on their conduct. Current public and political dissatisfaction with investigations and suggestions for reforming and restricting their scope and procedure will also be discussed.

THE FUNCTIONS OF ADMINISTRATIVE INVESTIGATIONS

In one sense, at least, administrative agencies do not differ from other institutions: their effectiveness is determined by the information they have or can acquire. Whatever the administrative action, whether formal or informal, its scope and impact is conditioned by the information the agency obtains by its prior investigation.[1]

As Gellhorn and Robinson indicate, the quality and effectiveness of any administrative activity is only as good as the information on which it is based and administrative agencies have developed numerous types of fact-finding procedures to ensure that they have the requisite information to perform their functions. Frequently, the information they seek is provided voluntarily, but almost invariably if it is not, the agency can compel its production. Most individuals, for example, "voluntarily" provide the Internal Revenue Service with the information it needs to determine their tax liability, but those who do not are likely to discover that the IRS has ways of compelling the release of the information and of punishing the recalcitrant or reluctant.

The IRS tax return illustrates the most common purpose for which agencies seek information: routine enforcement of the laws assigned to them. For OSHA to protect the health and safety of workers, it must have information on hazards in the workplace that endanger workers' health and safety. For the FAA to ensure that all aircraft are airworthy, it must have firsthand information on the airworthiness of individual airplanes. The purpose of most routine physical inspections is to protect the public health and safety by deterring the development of dangerous situations. No agency can enforce the laws under its jurisdiction unless it has direct knowledge of the situations and circumstances in which the law is applicable, and as these examples indicate, much information collection is aimed at prevention rather than punishment. Similarly, when the information collected does reveal violations, most administrative agencies, unlike criminal law enforcement agencies, allow voluntary correction and compliance before they resort to formal action.

If voluntary compliance is not forthcoming, and the agency decides to prosecute the individual or business, then it must gather even more information concerning the violation, since successful prosecution in either an adjudicatory hearing or courtroom will require "substantial evidence." Information gathering at this point usually proceeds from voluntary submission to the use of compulsory processes to obtain records and testimony and the scope of the information sought will be considerably broader than for routine enforcement activities.

Agency rule making also requires that the agency obtain information concerning the particular situation toward which a proposed rule will be directed. The breadth of impact of a rule, the level of controversy surrounding it, the technical complexity of the situation being regulated, and the "age" of the regulatory activity determine both the type of information gathering techniques that will be used and the amount of information that will be sought prior to promulgation. The regulations interpreting and enforcing Title IX of the Education Act, discussed in chapter 1, had a widespread impact, were extremely controversial, and involved a relatively new area of regulatory activity. Consequently, the information gathering process that preceded their adoption was lengthy, involved a variety of techniques, and encouraged wide participation in providing input. On the other hand, rules promulgated by the Agricultural Stabilization and Conservation Service regarding the Beekeeper Indemnity Payment Program are likely to be of low public interest and visibility, limited in impact, and relatively noncontroversial. Consequently, the information gathering process will be similarly restricted in scope and participation. In established, old-line regulatory areas where rules involve technical considerations and the agency has accumulated voluminous information as a result of past regulatory activities, the search for information will usually be limited to the agency's technical staff and the technical staff of the industry affected. No matter how technical the subject matter, if it is controversial, as is nuclear energy, then the information gathering process will be extended and extensive.

Other administrative actions which require information collection include licensing, granting contracts and benefits, and recommending legislation to Congress. The granting of a license requires the agency to determine the competence of the individual or firm applying for it and in many cases to determine if the "public interest" will be served by granting the license. Before an agency can grant an individual government benefits, whether Social Security payments, Veterans' Benefits, or AFDC payments, it must have information provided to it so that it can determine the eligibility of the individual applicant. Similarly, prior to the awarding of a government grant or contract, an agency must determine if the potential grantee has the resources and capability of carrying out the terms of the grant or contract. Administrative agencies also play a major role in the legislative process by proposing changes in current law or recommending new laws. Frequently these proposals for change are based on the analysis of information collected for routine enforcement purposes. At other times, recommendations for legislation result from special investigations conducted by the agency into policy areas that have not been subject to regulatory attention.

Investigatory actions, then, are an essential part of all administrative activity. Although they are frequently viewed as leading to punitive action, in reality they rarely do, and in many cases they protect not only the public but also individuals and firms that have been unfairly or erroneously accused of wrongful behavior. "Ill-considered agency action could result in wasted public funds and energies, as well as in grave consequences to private parties. The mere filing of a complaint by a government agency can have severe repercussions. In this respect, the acquisition of information by an agency is necessary for protection of private interests."[2]

MAJOR TYPES OF INVESTIGATORY ACTIVITIES

Records, Reports, Red Tape

In 1976, the federal bureaucracy had 4,418 different forms that various organizations and individuals were required to fill out. It was estimated that this took 143 million hours a year,[3] at a total cost of $100 billion. The federal government alone spent approximately $1 billion a year in developing and distributing the forms, another billion on directions on how to fill them out, $15 billion processing them, and $1.7 billion filing and storing them.[4] Surely, critics argued, this proved that the administrative quest for information had become uncontrollable, and no individual, business, or unit of government could avoid the unpleasant and expensive necessity of filling out an endless stream of government reports. Individuals must fill out income tax returns and census forms. State and local government agencies must fill out reports on employment practices (Affirmative Action), on how they have spent the federal money they have received, and the extent to which they have complied with federal environmental laws. Businesses must fill out forms for OSHA, for the EEOC, for the IRS, for the EPA, for the Consumer Product Safety Commission, and any other administrative agency with jurisdiction over their activities.

The problems and costs of these required forms were dramatically illustrated in an evaluation by the General Accounting Office of Department of Agriculture paperwork. GAO discovered that the meat industry was required to fill out 87 different forms for USDA annually, and that much of the information collected was unused. One required form certifying that cattle had not been exposed to carcinogens before slaughter was routinely thrown away by inspectors. GAO estimated the cost of compliance for the meat industry in filling out these forms at $750,000 annually.[5]

The amount of information gathered is voluminous. Unquestionably, it assists agencies to perform the otherwise impossible task of enforcing laws with limited personnel, but it is equally unquestionable that the proliferation of government forms has imposed real economic costs on those compelled to fill them out. In 1974, Congress created the Commission on Federal Paperwork to investigate the problem and recommend ways of alleviating the burden imposed on individuals and businesses. The Commission's experiences indicate some of the problems of trying to eliminate or reduce government reports. The AFL-CIO representative withdrew from Commission participation in 1976 when organized labor became concerned that modifying reporting requirements would erode workers' rights in areas such as OSHA, pension laws, and other labor programs. President Ford felt compelled to veto a law based on a Commission recommendation which would have required agencies to use standardized forms for grants and contracts on the grounds that it was too simplistic.[6] Congress was not too enthused when the Commission identified it as the major cause of the problem. The Commission estimated that Congress adds 300–500 reports a year that agencies must submit to the legislative branch. The agencies in turn must collect ever-increasing amounts of information from the public to satisfy Congressional demands.[7]

Although some of these required reports are unnecessary, many are redundant, others are frivolous, and all are costly, still others are not only essential to agency decision making, but also result in cost savings for the taxpayers. Prototypical of this type of form is the New Drug Application (NDA) on which the Food and Drug Administration bases its decision to approve or disapprove marketing of a new prescription drug. The New Drug Application must include a full report of research and testing that the pharmaceutical company has done on the drug to demonstrate that the drug is both safe and effective. One alternative to this procedure would be to have the FDA do the research and testing itself. This would undoubtedly save the pharmaceutical industry money but would transfer the burden to the federal taxpayer. Ironically, this FDA procedure is heavily criticized by consumer groups and illustrates a major problem of agency reliance on regulatee-submitted information: the danger that the information is less comprehensive and accurate than it should be.

Frequently, agencies will not require that forms be filled out and sent in but will instead require a regulatee to permit them access to routine records. The normal business records of regulated industries—airlines, railroads, trucking firms, for example—are subject to periodic examination by relevant regulatory agencies. As enforcement devices these periodic checks of business records can be an efficient if not always completely effective procedure. During the 1970 wage-price freeze, for example, the enforcing agencies, the Cost of Living Council and IRS, had massive responsibility for monitoring the entire economy and ensuring that wage-price stability was achieved.

Rather than requiring all firms to file wage-price reports, they selected a primarily reactive enforcement strategy: responding to complaints and questions. IRS did engage in some proactive enforcement by spot-checking business records during tax audits.[8]

In addition to inspection of normally maintained business records, some regulatory agencies have the power to compel business firms to maintain specified types of records which must be accessible for agency personnel on request. Heavily regulated industries such as firearms dealers, liquor distributors and retailers, and pharmacies are required to maintain detailed records on all business transactions. Similarly, pursuant to issuance of a cease and desist order or a consent agreement, an agency may require that the business involved keep certain kinds of records accessible for inspection so that the agency can more easily monitor compliance with the order.

Finally, in 1980, in response to the recommendation of the Commission on Federal Paperwork, Congress passed the Paperwork Reduction Act. The Act created an Office of Information and Regulatory Affairs (OIRA) within the Office of Management and Budget and charged it with reviewing and approving all information requests of federal agencies, and reducing the overall burden imposed by federal paperwork by 25 percent by 1984. In addition, OIRA was instructed to establish policy for federal statistical activities, privacy of records, records management activities, and use of technology for managing information resources. The only agency exempted from OIRA approval for information requests was the Federal Election Commission, although independent regulatory commissions could, by majority vote, override an OIRA rejection of proposed information gathering activities. The Act also created a Federal Information Locator System to establish and maintain a comprehensive index to information sources within the federal government.[9]

Physical Inspections

Appearances to the contrary, not all the information that agencies need can be or is gathered through records and reports. The second major category of administrative investigatory techniques is physical inspection of residences, places of business, and facilities and equipment. In the majority of cases the purpose of these physical inspections is the protection of public health and safety through the prevention, detection, and correction of situations that endanger public safety. Such physical inspections are carried out at all levels of government. At the local level, compliance with fire codes, building codes, electrical and sanitation codes is ensured through inspections by various administrative agencies. At the state level, inspections are conducted to ensure compliance with child labor laws, fair working conditions, AFDC program requirements, to ensure healthful conditions in the dairy and meat-packing industries, and for various other purposes. At the federal level, OSHA inspects workplaces; the FDA inspects food processors, drug manufacturers, and cosmetics producers; the Federal Aviation Administration inspects aircraft and airport landing facilities; the Mine Safety and Health Administration inspects mines; and the Nuclear Regulatory Commission inspects all nuclear power facilities. This list is lengthy but is a very incomplete catalog of the physical inspections conducted by administrative agencies.

Although few people would deny the importance of these inspections, many would contest the degree to which they violate the privacy of individuals and businesses. Physical inspections unquestionably involve a direct intrusion by administrators into the lives, homes, and businesses of Americans, and despite procedural safeguards to limit the timing and conduct of these inspections the conflict with privacy rights can never be completely resolved. Individual privacy rights must be balanced against the necessity of protecting the public from fires, rats, unsanitary conditions, hazardous building conditions, unhealthful and dangerous food, meat, drugs, and cosmetics.

From another perspective, the major objection to inspections is not that they are so intrusive, but that they are so ineffective. Despite frequent inspections, the industrial accident rate continues unchanged, Three Mile Island still happened, and cattle are still fed DES-supplemented food immediately prior to slaughter. The job of an administrative inspector is complicated, confusing, and frustrating, and frequently inspectors are under tremendous pressure from industry, labor, and hierarchical superiors to ignore violations. The problems involved in ensuring maximum effectiveness in protecting the public result partially from these complications and partially from the inability of administrators to enforce laws when voluntary compliance is withheld by large numbers of potential regulatees.

This brings us back to the by now familiar problem of many regulatory agencies. In comparison with the numbers, wealth, and/or power of persons over whom they have jurisdiction, the agencies are relatively small in terms of both personnel and funding. OSHA is a classic example: In 1978 it employed 2,818 people, 1,250 of whom were inspectors who had to cover an estimated 4 million business establishments. Compounding the inspection problem, there were over 4,000 safety consensus standards that OSHA had adopted, and in an attempt to limit discretion of inspectors, OSHA had required them to enforce all regulations and cite all violations detected.[10] OSHA's method for dealing with the impossibility of inspecting all establishments was initially preventive: 70 percent of their inspections were scheduled inspections performed primarily in five target industries with the highest injury rates and inspectors were encouraged to concentrate on the largest establishments. As a preventive device this procedure was not particularly effective. It led to an overemphasis on safety as opposed to health standards and limited OSHA to preventing only those injuries caused by detectable work-related injuries.[11] In 1976, OSHA adopted a more reactive inspection policy, emphasizing inspections based on complaints received from industrial workers and unions. The change in policy was due to criticism of OSHA's failure to investigate an informal complaint concerning one of the most hazardous workplaces in the country, the Kepone plant at Hopewell, Virginia.[12]

If OSHA's inspection problems have been caused by too many rules to enforce over too many regulatees, other administrative agencies have encountered similar problems which have been compounded by the development of unethical, if not illegal, relationships between inspectors and inspectees. The FAA and its long and tangled involvement with the DC-10 illustrates the human consequences of inspection systems that fail. From the time of its development, the DC-10 has been a troubled airplane, but one that until June 1979 passed FAA safety inspections. The initial safety problem with the DC-10 centered on its cargo door latch system. McDonnell-Douglas, the plane's manufacturer, responding to a request from American Airlines, one of the major purchasers of the DC-10, had ordered its subcontractor, Convair, to change the design from a hydraulic to an electric door latch system. Despite objections from Convair engineers that the electric latch system "was less than desirable," and that were the door to blow out in flight, the passenger cabin floor would collapse, McDonnell-Douglas insisted on the specified design.

Initially, the FAA, which was required to inspect and certify the safety of the DC-10, was completely coopted by McDonnell-Douglas. Lacking sufficient manpower to conduct all mandated inspections, the FAA routinely deputizes employees of the airplane manufacturers to grant certification. In this case, it was an engineer from Douglas who was deputized to certify the DC-10, and despite Convair's objections, which were not revealed to the FAA, the certification was granted.

In 1972, an American Airlines DC-10 blew a cargo door and the rear section of the cabin floor dropped. That time, no one was killed and FAA field personnel attempted to rectify past mistakes. They drafted an airworthiness directive which would have required Douglas to make modifications. The directive was never issued; the president of Douglas went to the top of the FAA and worked out an informal agreement. The FAA would not issue the directive and Douglas would fix the doors. In 1974, the cargo door on a Turkish Airlines DC-10 blew and this time 346 people were killed.[13] Although the door problem was finally corrected, the DC-10 was still far from safe.

In May 1979, an American Airlines DC-10 taking off from O'Hare Airport in Chicago crashed, killing 275 people. The left engine and pylon had ripped away during takeoff, and once again the FAA found itself in a decidedly uncomfortable position. It grounded the DC-10s and ordered inspections of their pylon assemblies. They were recertified and back in the air when the National Transportation Safety Board indicated that the inspection process may have compounded the problem by damaging vital parts. The FAA vacillated, but after a federal court granted, then delayed a grounding decree, it acted decisively. It indefinitely lifted the design certificate of the DC-10, and assigned more than 100 FAA investigators to work with Douglas to solve the problem.[14] Ultimately, the FAA determined that the probable cause of the accident was a series of modifications in American Airlines' maintenance processes that escaped notice by FAA inspectors and that were not reported by the airline to the agency. Although Douglas had recommended that engine and pylon be removed separately for maintenance and inspections, an American Airlines supervisor developed a new timesaving technique for removing the two simultaneously by forklift. Although FAA regulations require that it be notified of any "major" changes in maintenance procedures this modification was considered to be minor and was not reported. Compounding the problem, American Airlines subsequently transferred all DC-10 maintenance operations to Tulsa, Oklahoma, where in some instances mechanics were not given adequate training on DC-10 procedure and reversed recommended maintenance procedures which may have resulted in cracking the aft-bulkheads that supported the pylon and engine.[15]

The Three Mile Island nuclear plant accident in March 1979 also raised questions concerning the impartiality and effectiveness of inspections when regulators must exist in close and cooperative proximity with regulatees. The Nuclear Regulatory Commission regularly inspects nuclear power plants to ensure compliance with safety regulations. Prior to TMI, the General Accounting Office had criticized NRC inspectors for overrelying on test results provided by the companies; after TMI a different problem was identified: Inspectors live too close and become too familiar with the power companies, working with them constantly day after day, and in this case at least, familiarity bred understanding and a willingness to tolerate violations.[16]

A final case well illustrates the complexity of the administrative inspector's situation. On October 8, 1971, 40 federal meat inspectors were indicted for having "accepted things of value" from meat packers. Unquestionably, tainted or adulterated meat is dangerous to public health, and meat that has been injected with water or contains excessively high levels of fillers is an expensive and profitable form of consumer fraud. Those are the primary reasons we have federal meat inspection, and inspectors accepting favors or things of value from meat packers raises serious questions about the reliability of the inspection process. At the same time, the regulations that meat inspectors must enforce are incredibly detailed and complex and it is widely recognized that if all the regulations were enforced, the meat-packing industry would be driven out of business. The USDA offers no official guidance on the exercise of discretion by inspectors nor does it routinely back inspectors in disputes with meat packers. One of the meat inspectors described their situation:

> Look, we are . . . required to go out among the regulated to do our job. We
> don't just visit them periodically, we just about marry them. Day after day, night
> after night, we are in the lion's den alone with the lion. How are we supposed to
> get along? USDA doesn't tell us. How are we supposed to resist the barrage of
> threats and temptations the packers constantly direct at us? USDA doesn't tell us.
> . . . If you tag too many violations, your supervisor will frequently say you are
> being too antagonistic and rigid. Then when you let some minor violations go,
> . . . he blames it on you, not the packer.[17]

Most of the inspectors were convicted of accepting meat; none of the packers were even indicted: they were granted immunity from prosecution for testifying against the inspectors.

One type of inspection where this problem seldom occurs is with the welfare case workers' "home visits" to AFDC recipients. In fact, until specifically prohibited by federal regulations, these inspections were carried out with considerable zeal and not infrequently in the middle of the night. The midnight raiders were inspecting to determine if there were a man in the house so that undeserving AFDC recipients could be removed from the welfare rolls and the taxpayers' money spent only on the deserving poor. Although after-business-hours inspections are no longer common, routine home visits to recipients are. The expressed purpose of such visits is to determine eligibility and to check on the well-being of the intended beneficiaries of AFDC payments—the children. Although highly controversial and not subject to the same judicial restrictions as other types of investigations, these home visits have also been criticized for being too few and far between to protect the abused or neglected child:

> With some frequency, however, neglect in an AFDC home is brought before the
> court only through a fortuity rather than by a welfare worker. . . . [I]n
> reviewing the backgrounds of juvenile delinquents from AFDC homes,
> unreported neglect during early years often appears to be an important cause of
> delinquency. Thus, a Family Court judge may hope from a child welfare
> standpoint—for more, rather than fewer, welfare home-visits.[18]

Legislative-Type Hearings

Although an agency will generally have extensively investigated a situation before it proposes new rules, occasionally it will hold public hearings to permit interested persons to submit their viewpoints and information. In complex, technical areas, such hearings may result in providing the agency with new and useful information.[19] In other areas, such hearings may generate little new information and a great deal of redundant material. Appearance at such hearings is voluntary and normally anyone who wishes to testify is allowed to do so. Although the agency may limit oral testimony, it seldom limits the volume of written testimony.

The procedure followed in these hearings is similar to that used in a congressional committee hearing. Infrequently, these hearings may be presided over by an administrative law judge; more frequently a member of the agency's staff will preside. If the issue under examination is highly visible or controversial, the agency director or the commissioners themselves may preside. Like congressional hearings, most agency rulemaking hearings are rather mundane, low key, and not very stimulating affairs. Sometimes however, as in the case of the cigarette advertising hearings and the Kid Vid (Children's Television Advertising) hearings before the FTC, the opposite is true. Conflicting witnesses become emotional, tension increases, and a great deal of heat (if little light) is generated.

The utility of these hearings as information-gathering devices is questionable. Although a voluminous amount of testimony is frequently taken, rarely does it include information that the agency did not already possess or that it could not have obtained in less costly and time-consuming fashion, most notably through the normal notice and comment procedure where written documentation only is submitted to the agency. The real utility of hearings lies more in the areas of enforcement, securing voluntary compliance, and compiling a record which may be useful in ensuring that the rule will be able to withstand judicial challenges.

Body Searches: Physical Inspections of Individuals

Although physical searches of individuals may not normally be thought of as administrative investigatory techniques, they are routine activities for some agencies, most notably the U.S. Customs Service and the Immigration and Naturalization Service. The Customs Service is charged with collecting taxes on imported merchandise, with detecting and preventing smuggling and fraud, and with processing carriers, persons, baggage, cargo, and mail entering the United States. In the process of carrying out those responsibilities the Customs Service has and frequently uses the power to search the persons of individuals. Similarly, INS has and uses the power to conduct physical searches of aliens entering the country, as well as illegal aliens apprehended and detained. Further, since aliens with certain, specified communicable diseases are not eligible for entry into this country, INS also has and uses the authority to compel suspected persons to submit to medical examination by a physician.

For many Americans one of the most familiar administrative searches of persons and property is the routine scanning of carry-on luggage and passengers boarding commercial airlines. These airport searches, first instituted on a mandatory basis in 1972, clearly illustrate not only the scope and primarily preventive nature of investigatory power, but also the ability of agencies to formulate, adopt, and implement policy prior to explicit congressional authorization. Unfortunately, they also illustrate the extent to which investigatory power may result in intrusion into matters that were once considered to be private. The searches were instituted by order of the Federal Aviation Administration in 1972 in an attempt to curb aircraft hijackings which had become increasingly common and dangerous. From 1969 to 1972, there were 277 incidents of aircraft hijackings, 113 of which occurred in the United States.[20] Initial attempts by the FAA to deal with the problem had proven to be unsuccessful, and when two hijackings in the fall of 1972 resulted in one death and five injuries, the FAA, acting pursuant to an emergency executive order of the President, issued the rules currently in effect. Magnetometers, detection devices used for screening, were required at every boarding gate in every airport; airlines were required to screen all passengers and carry-on luggage; and state and local governments were required to supply law enforcement officers at boarding gates. To help defray the costs the FAA rechanneled $3.5 million which had been allocated to the sky marshall programs into funds for the purchase of electronic detection devices, and the Civil Aeronautics Board authorized airlines to impose a surcharge of $.34 per passenger to cover the costs of screening.[21] The thoroughness and effectiveness of these procedures were indicated by FAA reports covering the first eight months of 1973: 894 guns were seized, 1,337 arrests were made, 1,505 passengers who refused to submit to a search were denied boarding, and there were no reported incidents of aircraft hijacking. Not until July 1, 1974, did Congress explicitly grant legislative authorization and approval of the FAA's procedures.[22]

Subpoenas

As has been indicated, most of the information that agencies request is voluntarily supplied by the affected individual or business. If it is not, virtually all regulatory agencies have been authorized to compel the production of necessary information through the issuance of subpoenas—administrative commands to appear and/or produce specified documents (subpoena duces tecum). The Federal Trade Commission Act is a typical example of explicit congressional authorization of the power to issue subpoenas and the normal procedure used to enforce them:

> The Commission shall have the power to require by subpoena the attendance and testimony of witnesses and the production of all such documentary evidence relating to any matter under investigation. Any member of the commission may sign subpoenas. . . .
> In case of disobedience to a subpoena the Commission may invoke the aid of any court of the United States. . . . Any of the district courts . . . may in case of contumacy or refusal to obey subpoena . . . issue an order requiring such person to appear before the Commission or to produce the documentary evidence . . . and any failure to obey such order of the court may be punished by such court as a contempt thereof.[23]

The Administrative Procedure Act deals generally and briefly with agency subpoena procedures. Section 555(c) specifies that "Process, requirement of a report, inspection or other investigative act or demand . . . may not be issued, made or enforced except as authorized by law." Section 555(a) grants "a person compelled to appear in person before an agency" the right "to be accompanied, represented and advised by counsel." Section 555(b) deals with judicial enforcement of subpoenas: "On contest, the court shall sustain the subpoena or similar process or demand to the extent that it is found to be in accordance with law," and provides for enforcement through contempt of court procedures.

Although contempt of court procedure is the most common method for punishing those who refuse to obey a lawfully issued agency subpoena, some statutes also make failure to comply a crime. The FTC Act provides that

> Any person who shall neglect or refuse to attend and testify . . . or to produce documentary evidence, if in his power to do so, in obedience to the subpoena, . . . shall be guilty of an offense and upon conviction . . . shall be punished by a fine of not less than $1,000 nor more than $5,000 or by imprisonment for not more than one year or both.[24]

The Administrative Investigation

The investigatory techniques that have been examined to this point may be and are used individually by agencies, but any combination of them may also be used in certain situations. For purposes of clarity this will be referred to as an administrative investigation. To illustrate the effectiveness of using multiple investigatory techniques, two types of administrative investigations will be examined: aircraft accident investigations and FTC investigations of possible violations of antitrust laws.

Flying, we are regularly told, is one of the safest forms of transportation, and statistics support this contention. But even in statistically safe modes of transportation, accidents do happen and when the accident involves a commercial passenger aircraft, the loss of life and property can be exceedingly high. Since most accidents are preventable, investigating those that do occur to determine their causes and then ensuring that those causes are eliminated are essential in maintaining the safety of air travel. Currently, two federal agencies have authority to investigate major aircraft accidents: the Federal Aviation Administration and the National Transportation Safety Board. Although this may appear to be another case of needless duplication, in this instance it is justified. Although the FAA clearly has needed expertise for such investigations and may ultimately have to issue new regulations or change procedures as a result of investigation, its impartiality may be suspect since it certifies both aircraft and pilots. The procedures that the two agencies follow in investigating an accident are painstakingly thorough, comprehensive, time-consuming, and usually include the entire gamut of investigatory techniques. A full-scale investigation can take over a year to complete and may involve over 100 investigators.

The investigation normally begins within minutes of a crash: written statements are taken from crews of other airplanes that were in the vicinity concerning weather and approach conditions, air traffic control equipment is inspected, controllers are questioned, and airport tapes of the approach are reviewed. The airline will be required to supply voluminous amounts of information on the particular flight, on the airplane's operational history, and the flight crew's training, qualifications, and personnel record. The records of the aircraft's manufacturer and its subcontractors will be equally subject to thorough examination, as will all FAA records and documents relating to the aircraft and its crew. Every scrap of physical evidence that survived the crash will be collected, intensively examined and tested, and where possible, the remains of the aircraft reassembled to provide investigators a clearer picture of what happened. Aircraft of the same model will be intensively inspected, tested, and retested. Any survivors will be questioned and the final tape recordings from the cockpit of the plane will be reviewed. The culmination of the investigatory process will be a public hearing where the evidence is put on the record and a variety of witnesses are permitted and compelled to testify under oath and may be subject to rigorous questioning. The final outcome will be the aircraft accident report, the agency's official determination of the cause of the accident. Whether determination is mechanical failure or human error, the FAA will then move to ensure that corrective procedures are undertaken to prevent future accidents.[25]

From most perspectives FTC antitrust investigations are considerably less dramatic and emotionally charged than those of aircraft accidents, unless, of course, one happens to be an executive of the corporation being investigated. These investigations consist of three distinct phases: the pre-preliminary investigation, the preliminary investigation, and the formal or seven-digit (for the file numbers of such cases) investigation.[26] The pre-preliminary investigation is usually instituted in response to a letter of complaint received by the Commission. The letter is assigned to a staff attorney who does rather limited research to determine if the complaint has validity. This research commonly involves library research of sources such as the *Wall Street Journal* and SEC documents and phone conversations with the complainant. The attorney then makes a recommendation to the Bureau Chief as to whether the investigation should be pursued. If a recommendation to continue is accepted, then the preliminary investigation begins and frequently takes two to three months to complete. At this stage, all information submission is voluntary. Attorneys send out letters of inquiry to competitors, conduct interviews with executives of firms who may be willing to supply information, and attempt to gather as much data as possible. Smaller firms tend to be more cooperative than large firms, although the large firms frequently assert that they are being cooperative. Their cooperation, however, may take the form of a corporate equivalent of "Go Fish." The agency is given only the information specifically identified and requested and that, usually, only after a considerable delay. As one FTC attorney described it:

> They'll stall for time, hoping to wear us down. As soon as they've readied their own case, which they'll present in the event we serve a subpoena, they'll drop the pretense of cooperation.[27]

Once the preliminary investigation is concluded, it is up to the members of the FTC to determine if a formal investigation is warranted. Only if a majority of the commissioners approves will such an investigation be undertaken, and unless such an investigation is approved, the staff attorneys do not have the power to subpoena records, documents, and testimony. A formal investigation involves a thorough and time-consuming data gathering process. Its final result may be either a recommendation to take formal action against the industry involved or to terminate the inquiry without further action. Prior to 1970, once a formal investigation was opened, it tended to remain that way long after reason and logic should have closed it. In 1969, however, the Commission created the Garbage Committee (Special Committee on Caseload Screening) and based on its recommendations, authorized closing 700 of the 1,000 open investigations.[28]

As these examples indicate the outcomes of administrative investigations are as diverse as the techniques employed. Sometimes they result in recommendations for change; sometimes they result in orders requiring change; sometimes they lead to formal agency action; and sometimes they lead to nothing. Whatever their outcome, however, they have served their primary purpose. They have provided the agency with information it felt it required to carry out its statutory responsibilities.

JUDICIAL ATTITUDES TOWARD ADMINISTRATIVE INVESTIGATIONS

So common have administrative investigatory techniques become that most of us tend to view them as an inherent if intrusive part of government. What we tend to forget is that as forms of government action, they are very recent in development. Traditionally, the only form of government investigation was the criminal investigation. A law had been broken—a crime committed, and law enforcement investigators sought to determine who had committed it and to apprehend and try the alleged guilty culprit. To reiterate, administrative investigations frequently start from entirely different premises and have entirely different purposes. Their newness and their differences have frequently perplexed and amazed the federal courts when they had to review and determine their permissibility and decide which, if any, of the procedural protections found in the Bill of Rights were applicable to their conduct.

The Supreme Court, in particular, struggled long and hard with the questions raised by the increasing scope of investigatory power. Its attitude towards those investigations has evolved from an initial tendency to view them as completely unacceptable and unconstitutional, through an "anything goes" approach, to its current cautious and inconsistent attempts to impose procedural safeguards on their conduct without destroying their effectiveness as an administrative procedure.

The Period of Restrictiveness: 1880–1940

The first period of judicial consideration of administrative investigations was characterized by the Supreme Court's attempt to prohibit all administrative investigations, even those specifically authorized by Congress. To the Supreme Court of the 1880s, the only permissible (and familiar) type of investigation was the criminal investigation. As the justices perceived it, no crime meant no investigation was permissible. This attitude was exemplified in the 1881 case of *Kilbourn v. Thompson*,[29] which dealt with the power of Congress to investigate for the purpose of legislating and to issue and enforce a subpoena to acquire information in the course of such an investigation. The Court held that Congress did not have a general power of investigation unless it was relevant to the investigation of a specific crime. Neither house "possesses the general power of making inquiry into the private affairs of the citizen." The implication of *Kilbourn* was, of course, that Congress certainly could not delegate a general investigatory power which it did not itself possess to administrative agencies.

Apparently unimpressed by the *Kilbourn* decision, in 1887 Congress authorized the ICC to investigate for the general purposes of rule making and recommending legislation and authorized it to use subpoenas to compel testimony. This congressional authorization was challenged in 1908 in *Harriman v. ICC*.[30] Pursuant to an investigation undertaken for the purpose of recommending legislation to Congress, the ICC issued a subpoena duces tecum to Harriman, a railroad magnate. He refused to comply, arguing that an administrative agency had no power to issue and enforce subpoenas in an investigation with the sole purpose of recommending legislation. The Supreme Court agreed that agencies have no general investigatory power: "The power to require testimony is limited . . . to only those cases where the sacrifice of privacy is necessary—those where the investigations concern a specific breach of the law."[31] Without evidence of a crime there could be no investigation and no subpoena could be issued.

This argument was also rejected by Congress and the enabling legislation for the FTC granted it general power of investigation. In the early 1920s, the Senate passed a resolution calling for an investigation of unfair competitive practices in the tobacco industry by the FTC. In the process of the investigation the FTC subpoenaed communications between the American Tobacco Company and its customers. Displaying considerable reluctance to clash head on with Congress, the Court refused to require the production of the documents on the grounds the FTC had not been authorized by the FTC Act to violate the Fourth Amendment's right of privacy:

> Anyone who respects the spirit as well as the letter of the Fourth Amendment would be loath to believe that Congress intended to authorize one of its subordinate agencies to sweep all our traditions into the fire and to direct fishing expeditions into private papers on the possibility that they may disclose evidence of crime. We do not discuss the question whether it could do so if it tried, as nothing short of the most explicit language would induce us to attribute to Congress that intent. . . . It is contrary to the first principles of Justice to allow a search through all the respondents' records, relevant or irrelevant, in the hope that something will turn up.[32]

For sixty years the judiciary held fast to the view that the regulatory process could not violate the traditional constitutional standards for investigation: without "probable cause" there could be no investigations. Ensuring compliance with regulatory orders or recommending legislation were not sufficient grounds to investigate and violate privacy; no general power of investigation ("fishing expeditions") was upheld by the Court. Congress never accepted these views of the proper role of administrative investigations and when the New Deal regulatory agencies were created in the 1930s and 1940s they were endowed with broad and sweeping investigatory powers.

Period of Permissiveness: 1941–1965

The Court responded, beginning in the 1940s, with a complete reversal of its previous decisions. It became increasingly willing to allow almost all administrative investigations to proceed, even in the face of the Fourth and Fifth Amendment objections. *Endicott Johnson Corporation v. Perkins*[33] began the new era and abolished the probable cause standard of the past. The Walsh-Healy Public Contracts Act required that government contractors observe certain minimum employment standards or be penalized by losing the contracts. In order to ensure compliance, the Secretary of Labor, Frances Perkins, was authorized to investigate contractors and given subpoena power. Endicott Johnson had a contract to sell shoes to the government, but the Secretary of Labor subpoenaed records of companies owned by Endicott Johnson which were not specified in the contract. The Department of Labor was on a fishing expedition—it "had reason to believe" that some employees of those subsidiaries were engaged in contract work and it wanted to determine if it had jurisdiction over them. Endicott Johnson refused to comply, arguing that these subsidiaries were outside of the administrator's jurisdiction. The Supreme Court ruled that the subpoena was valid and should have been enforced by the District Court. The Secretary had broad investigatory authority to determine compliance with the Act, and the Secretary, not the District Court, was the one to determine whether a company was subject to Department of Labor jurisdiction. The Court went on to specify the limits on District Court review of administrative subpoenas:

> The District Court had no authority to control the procedure or to condition enforcement of her subpoenas upon her first reaching and announcing a decision on some of the issues. . . . Nor was the District court authorized to decide the question of coverage itself. The evidence sought was not plainly incompetent or irrelevant. . . . [A]nd it was the duty of the District Court to order its production for the Secretary's consideration.[34]

Three years later, a majority of the Supreme Court clearly affirmed that they not only understood but accepted and approved of administrative investigations. *Oklahoma Press Publishing Co. v. Walling*[35] continues to be the definitive statement of the Court on the constitutionality of administrative subpoenas and the limited protection provided by the Fourth and Fifth Amendments against subpoenas. The Fair Labor Standards Act of 1938 had established minimum wage and maximum hour standards for businesses operating in interstate commerce and had authorized the Wage and Hours Administration to "investigate and gather data," and to enter and inspect records of affected businesses. Payroll records of Oklahoma Press Publishing Co. had been subpoenaed and the company had refused to comply arguing that an agency proceeding without a prior charge and probable cause was a fishing expedition which violated Fourth Amendment protection against unreasonable searches and seizures. It also argued that requiring the company to turn over its records violated the Fifth Amendment protection against self-incrimination. The Supreme Court disagreed on all counts. Administrative agencies did not need to charge that a specific violation of law has occurred in order to launch an investigation: "It is enough that the investigation be for a lawfully authorized purpose within the power of Congress to command. . . . The very purpose of the subpoena and of the order, as of the authorized investigation, is to discover and procure evidence, not to prove a pending charge." The argument that the subpoena violated the Fourth Amendment fared no better: "The short answer to the Fourth Amendment objections is that the records in these cases present no question of actual search and seizure. . . . No officer or other person has sought to enter petitioners' premises against their will, to search them or to seize or examine their books, . . . otherwise than pursuant to orders of court authorized by law." The longer answer was no more supportive:

> It is not necessary . . . that a specific charge or complaint of violation of law be
> pending. . . . The requirement of probable cause . . . is satisfied by the court's
> determination that the investigation is authorized by Congress for a purpose
> Congress can order, and the documents sought are relevant to the inquiry.
> Beyond this the requirement of reasonableness, including particularity in
> describing the places to be searched and the persons or things to be seized, . . .
> comes down to specification of the documents to be produced adequate, but not
> excessive, for the purposes of the relevant inquiry.[36]

Further, the court made it very clear that the Fifth Amendment protection against self-incrimination does not apply to corporate records. "The Fifth Amendment affords no protection by virtue of the self-incrimination provisions, whether for the corporation or its officers. . . . The only records or documents sought were corporate ones. No possible element of self-incrimination was therefore presented."

In 1948, the Supreme Court again narrowed the scope of Fifth Amendment protections against administrative investigations of businesses engaged in interstate commerce. The Price Control Act in force during World War II had not only authorized the administrator of the Office of Price Administration to set maximum prices for commodities but also authorized him to require dealers to keep records on prices charged which were to be available for inspection and copying by OPA investigators. Shapiro, a fruit and produce wholesaler, was subpoenaed to appear before OPA and bring the required records with him. When he appeared, his attorneys asked if he was being granted immunity from prosecution. They were told he was "entitled to whatever immunity which flows as a matter of law from the production of these books and records which are required to be kept pursuant to price regulations." The records were turned over and Shapiro was prosecuted and convicted for violation of the law. He claimed violations of his Fifth Amendment rights. The Supreme Court upheld the conviction and specified that required records were exempt from Fifth Amendment protection:

> the privilege which exists as to private papers cannot be maintained in relation to
> records required by law to be kept in order that there may be suitable
> information of transactions which are the appropriate subjects of governmental
> regulation and the enforcement of restrictions validly established.[37]

The court did point out that "there are limits which the government cannot constitutionally exceed in requiring the keeping of records," but it did not specify what those limits were.

The Court reaffirmed and strengthened its support of administrative investigations in *U.S. v. Morton Salt Co.*[38] The FTC had ordered Morton Salt to file special reports with it demonstrating that the company was in compliance with a previously issued cease and desist order. Morton Salt declined and argued one more time that administrative fishing expeditions were prohibited by the Fourth Amendment. Once again the Supreme Court rejected the argument:

> This case illustrates the difference between the judicial function and the function the Commission is attempting to perform. The respondents argue that since the Commission made no charge of violation either of the decree or the statute it is engaged in a mere "fishing expedition" to see if it can turn up evidence of guilt. We will assume for the argument this is so. . . . We must not disguise the fact that sometimes, especially early in the history of the federal administrative tribunal, the courts were persuaded to engraft judicial limitations upon the administrative process. The courts could not go fishing and so it followed neither could anyone else. Administrative investigations fell under the colorful and nostalgic slogan "no fishing expeditions." It must not be forgotten that the administrative process and its agencies are relative newcomers in the field of law and that it has taken and will continue to take experience and trial and error to fit this process into our system of judicature. More recent views have been more tolerant of it. . . . The only power that is involved there is the power to get information from those who best can give it and who are most interested in not doing so. . . . Even if one were to regard the request for information in this case as caused by nothing more than official curiosity, nevertheless law enforcing agencies have a legitimate right to satisfy themselves that corporate behavior is consistent with the law and public interest.[38]

The Court reiterated that corporate records are public records not protected by the Fifth Amendment ban against self-incrimination and also reiterated that the agency demand for information must not be "too indefinite," and that it must be "reasonably relevant." The extent to which these requirements limited agency fishing expeditions was clarified in 1957. The Civil Aeronautics Board had issued a subpoena in an enforcement proceeding calling for voluminous and only generally identified information from affected companies: "all bank statements and cancelled checks," "all correspondence, contracts, agreements and options between any of the following corporations." To the Court of Appeals this appeared to be "practically all records, books, and documents of or concerning the companies, for a period of 38 months." Although the Court of Appeals found this to be a little too indefinite and asserted the power and responsibility of the courts to determine relevancy,[39] the Supreme Court agreed with the district court which had initially upheld and enforced the subpoena: "as we read the order of the District Court, it duly enforced the Board's right to call for documents relevant to the issues of the Board's complaint, with appropriate provisions for assuring the minimum interference with the conduct of the business of respondents."[40]

The Supreme Court continued to narrow the protection the Fifth Amendment self-incrimination clause provides against administrative investigations through the 1970s. Papers or records turned over to a third party, even if that third party were one's tax accountant, were held not to be protected by the Fifth Amendment:

> The Fifth Amendment privilege is a personal privilege; it adheres to the person not to information which may incriminate him.[41]

The Court reiterated the *personal* nature of the protection in 1976 when it upheld the seizure of records from an individual's office since he "was not asked to do or say anything,"[42] and held that bank records, even those of individual transactions, were also not protected.[43]

Further, the Court has agreed that if the administrative agency offers immunity from prosecution, the protection against self-incrimination becomes irrelevant and documents and testimony must be rendered at the agency's request. Forty-four different statutes authorize most major regulatory agencies to grant immunity in order to compel testimony. Since 1970, such grants have required approval of the attorney general. Failure to testify after such a grant is punishable by fines of up to $1,000 and/or one year imprisonment. The Supreme Court has held that such grants of immunity need not be absolute (transactional). As long as they protect against direct or derivative use of compelled testimony, the Fifth Amendment is satisfied.[44]

In 1959, the Court loosened another Fourth Amendment restriction on administrative inspections in *Frank v. Maryland*.[45] An ordinance of the city of Baltimore permitted warrantless health inspections whenever the health commissioner had "cause to suspect that a nuisance exists in any house, cellar, or enclosure." The Court found that the ordinance provided reasonable safeguards. There had to be grounds for suspicion of a nuisance, the inspection had to be made in daytime, and the inspector could not force entry. Consequently, the lack of requirement for a warrant was not an impermissible violation of the Fourth Amendment: "In light of the long history of this kind of inspection and of modern needs, we cannot say that the carefully circumscribed demand which Maryland here makes on appellants' freedom has deprived him of due process of law."

Clearly, the Supreme Court had done a complete about-face on its initial unwillingness to allow administrative investigations. The Fourth Amendment had been discarded as a prohibition against such investigations, whether conducted by physical inspections or subpoenaed documents or testimony. The Fifth Amendment self-incrimination protection had been defined not to apply to corporate records, labor union records, partnership records, records turned over to an accountant, required records, or testimony compelled after a limited grant of immunity. The lower federal courts had been left little discretion on enforcing administrative subpoenas: As long as the agency asserted that the investigation was for some legally authorized purpose, the information requested was reasonably clearly identified and provisions were made not to disrupt the normal conduct of business the district courts had to enforce. By the late 1960s, however, the court was beginning to demonstrate some concern with the almost total lack of constitutional protections that its about-face had created. Consequently, slowly, somewhat inconsistently, and not very vigorously, it began to modify its permissiveness, primarily in the area of physical inspections and the Fourth Amendment.

The Contemporary Period: Redefining the Fourth Amendment: 1966–Present

In *Frank v. Maryland*, the Court had given rather limited and cautious approval to warrantless administrative inspections. The vast majority of health, fire, and building code inspections were authorized to be and were conducted without search warrants. Then, in 1967, the Supreme Court explicitly overruled the *Frank* decision and decided that warrants were required for such inspections if the owner or resident of a building refused to consent to the inspection. The first of these cases, *Camara v. Municipal Court*,[46] involved a routine annual inspection by public health officials for compliance with the city's housing code. Camara refused on three separate occasions to allow the inspector to enter his apartment without a search warrant. He was charged with a violation of the Municipal Code which imposed penalties for failure to permit inspection. He then challenged the code's authorization of warrantless inspections as a violation of the Fourth Amendment. In agreeing with his argument, the Court noted that the basic purpose of the Fourth Amendment was to "safeguard the privacy and security of individuals against arbitrary invasions by governmental officials," and no matter how well intended inspections might be, they constituted "significant intrusions upon the interests protected by the Fourth Amendment." The Court then went on to hold that such warrantless searches were unconstitutional and "that the reasons put forth in *Frank v. State of Maryland . . .* for upholding these warrantless searches are insufficient to justify so substantial a weakening of the Fourth Amendment's protections."

The Court refused, however, to apply the strict standards for probable cause that are required for criminal search warrants, and substituted instead a test of "reasonableness." Magistrates could issue "area search warrants" to an agency if "reasonable legislative or administrative standards for conducting an area inspection are satisfied." Experience, the passage of time since the last inspection, or the conditions of the area could be used to prove reasonableness. The peculiarity of "this newfangled warrant system" was noted by Justice Clark in his dissent in *See v. Seattle*[47] which applied the same requirements to inspections of business premises:

> This boxcar warrant will be identical as to every dwelling in the area, save the street number itself. I daresay they will be printed up in pads of a thousand or more—with space for the street number to be inserted—and issued by magistrates in broadcast fashion as a matter of course.
>
> I ask: Why go through such an exercise, such a pretense? . . . Why the ceremony, the delay, the abuse of the search warrant?

Neither *Camara* nor *See* had completely disallowed warrantless inspection. In *Camara*, emergency inspections had been specifically excluded from the warrant requirement and in *See*, the Court excluded "licensing programs which require inspections prior to operating a business or marketing a product." When the Court was called upon to review federal warrantless inspection, it repeated these exemptions from the warrant requirement. In *Colonnade Catering Corporation v. United States*,[48] it upheld warrantless inspections of federally licensed liquor dealers, although it did disallow forcible entry by Bureau of Alcohol, Tobacco and Firearms (BATF) agents since Congress had not explicitly authorized it. In both *Colonnade* and *Biswell v. U.S.*,[49] the Court referred to heavily or "pervasively regulated businesses," and explicitly held that inspections of these businesses were exempt from the warrant requirement.

In 1971, the Court considered whether state welfare agencies could "deny, reduce or terminate AFDC benefits to otherwise eligible persons who refuse to allow caseworkers to enter their homes without a warrant, issued upon probable cause."[50] The *James* case had been preceded by considerable adverse publicity about midnight raids on the homes of welfare recipients and at least one state supreme court decision had held such raids to be unconstitutional.[51] The home visit required by the New York City Social Services Department was of a considerably different nature. A written request for an appointment during the day was sent to the AFDC recipient. There was no forcible entry or entry under false pretenses and the only penalty for refusing the request for a home visit was termination of payments. Although on the surface this might appear to distinguish home visits from the building inspections in the *Camara* case, appearances can be as deceiving as the terminology used. Visitors do not usually have the power to deprive one of "the very means by which to live,"[52] if one refuses to admit them. "Visitors" do not have the power to ask "questions concerning personal relationships, beliefs and behavior,"[53] and compel an answer. In the real world of the welfare recipient, the home visit of a caseworker is an inspection by an authority figure that is just as intrusive and considerably more threatening to personal survival than was at issue in either *Camara* or *See*. For Barbara James it may have been even more serious, since this was not really a fishing expedition. Mrs. James's case record indicated that her child had had a fractured skull, dented head, and apparent rat bites. Child abuse and neglect is a crime, and so is welfare fraud.

In spite or perhaps because of these facts, the Supreme Court saw clear differences between the visit in the James' case and the inspections involved in *Camara* and *See*:

> If, however, we were to assume that a caseworker's home visit, before or subsequent to the beneficiary's initial qualification for benefits somehow (perhaps because the average beneficiary might feel she is in no position to refuse consent to the visit), and despite its interview nature, does possess some of the characteristics of a search in the traditional sense, we nevertheless conclude that the visit does not fall within the Fourth Amendment's proscription. This is because it does not descend to the level of unreasonableness.[54]

Much of the reasonableness that the Court found in welfare inspections related to the nature of the AFDC program and the public's (the states) need to check up on the use of taxpayers' funds to insure that they were being used properly.

One of the most puzzling sections of the decision, particularly if compared to the *Camara* and *See* cases, dealt with the reasons why a warrant could not and should not be required:

> The warrant procedure . . . is not without its seriously objectionable features in the welfare context. If a warrant could be obtained (the appellees afford us little help as to how it would be obtained), it presumably could be applied for ex parte, its execution would not be so limited as those prescribed by home visitation. The warrant necessarily would imply conduct either criminal or out of compliance with an asserted governing standard. . . . it would have to rest upon probable cause, and probable cause in the welfare context . . . requires more than the mere need of the caseworker to . . . have assurance that the child is there and is receiving the benefit of the aid which was authorized for it. In this setting the warrant argument is out of place.[55]

Perhaps it is, but not much more so than it was in *Camara* and *See*.

When, if, and what kind of warrant issued under what circumstances was required for administrative inspections was still not clear when Congress passed the Occupational Safety and Health Act of 1970. Section 8(a) of that act had authorized OSHA inspectors to search the work area of any business under its jurisdiction. In 1975, an OSHA inspector entered Barlow's Inc., an electrical and plumbing installation business in Pocatello, Idaho, and informed the owner that he wished to inspect the premises. After ascertaining that the inspector did not have a warrant, Barlow refused to permit the inspection. When OSHA sought a court order to compel admission, Barlow sought injunctive relief against the warrantless search. In defense of these warrantless searches, in *Marshall v. Barlow's Inc.*,[56] the Department of Labor made at least as persuasive an argument of their necessity and permissibility as had been presented in the *James* case. It argued that "all businesses involved in interstate commerce have long been subjected to close supervision of employee safety health conditions" (heavily regulated businesses), that the "enforcement scheme of the act requires warrantless searches and that the restrictions on search discretion contained in the Act and its regulations already protect as much privacy as a warrant would."

The Court was not persuaded. The existence of federal regulation of working conditions in industry since 1936 did not make all industries "heavily regulated." "The degree of federal involvement in employee working circumstances has never been of the order of specificity and pervasiveness that OSHA mandates, . . . nor can any but the most fictional sense of voluntary consent to later searches be found in the single fact that one conducts a business affecting interstate commerce." Nor did the Court believe that effective enforcement required warrantless searches. "We are unconvinced, however, that requiring warrants to inspect will impose serious burdens on the inspection system, or the courts will prevent inspections necessary to enforce the statute or will make them less effective." But having established the necessity of a warrant, the Court in reality provided no more meaningful protection than it had given in *See* or *Camara*:

> Whether the Secretary proceeds to secure a warrant or other process, with or without prior notice, his entitlement to inspect will not depend on his demonstrating probable cause to believe that conditions in violation of OSHA exist on the premises. Probable cause in a criminal sense is not required. For purposes of an administrative search such as this, probable cause . . . may be based . . . on a showing that "reasonable legislative or administrative standards for conducting an . . . inspection are satisfied with respect to a particular establishment" [Camara]. A warrant showing that a specific business has been chosen for an OSHA search on the basis of a general administrative plan for the enforcement of the Act derived from sources such as, for example, dispersion of employees in various types of industries . . . and the desired frequency of searches . . . would protect an employer's Fourth Amendment rights.[57]

The Court was not unaware of the criticisms that had been made of the meaninglessness of such warrants, and in one of the more interesting sections of the Barlow decision addressed itself to those criticisms:

> Nor do we agree that the incremental protections afforded the employer's privacy by warrant are so marginal that they fail to justify the administrative burdens that may be entailed. . . . A warrant . . . would provide assurances from a neutral

officer that the inspection is reasonable under the Constitution, is authorized by statute and is pursuant to an administrative plan containing neutral criteria. Also a warrant would then and there advise the owner of the scope and objects of the search, beyond which limits the inspector is not expected to proceed.[58]

A careful rereading of this section of the decision indicates the logic of the apparently meaningless warrant requirement. The Court, perhaps unintentionally, put physical inspections under the same standards for judicial scrutiny as administrative subpoenas. Fishing expeditions are still acceptable, whether they be conducted through an inspection or a broadly framed subpoena, but in both instances courts will be able to determine if the expedition is statutorily authorized and to ensure that it is not unreasonable in scope and intent. In neither case is administrative power unduly curbed, nor are individual rights completely disregarded. At least symbolically, judicial supremacy has been established and if the actual impact is meaningless, the symbolic value should not be discounted.

The *Barlow* decision was far from being the Supreme Court's final decision on the permissibility of warrantless administrative searches. In 1976, the Court upheld routine, warrantless searches of automobiles by the U.S. Border Patrol: The searches were reasonable since they were limited in scope, occurred at fixed and known border locations so that no element of surprise was involved, and in general the agency provided sufficient administrative safeguards to protect privacy interests.[59] In 1981, in *Donovan v. Dewey*,[60] the Court upheld the constitutionality of warrantless searches conducted under the Federal Coal Mine Health and Safety Act of 1977. In the course of the decision, the Court attempted to distinguish between mine safety inspections and inspections of private homes and other types of businesses:

> The expectation of privacy that the owner of commercial property enjoys differs significantly from the sanctity accorded an individual's home. The interest of the owner of commercial property is not one of being free from any inspections. Rather the Fourth Amendment protects the interest of the owner of the property in being free from unreasonable intrusions onto his property.[61]

The differences between mining and other types of businesses fully justified the differences in warrant requirements for inspections: The mine safety act, unlike OSHA law, "applies to an industrial activity with a notorious history of serious accidents and unhealthful working conditions." In recognition of this the act required that all mines be inspected at least four times a year and the Court agreed that not only were surprise inspections necessary for the effective administration of the law but also that the "overwhelming government interest in protecting the lives and health of mine employees" was sufficient to justify whatever infringement of the mine owners' privacy occurred.

In other cases involving administrative investigatory techniques, the contemporary Supreme Court has been as permissive as its 1940s–1950s predecessors. Airport screenings have frequently resulted in turning up a great deal more than handguns, weapons, and bombs. Apparently, a considerable number of passengers carry their own remedies for fear of flying, most notably, marijuana, hashish, and heroin. If all goes well, these substances will pass through the magmetometers and X-ray screening devices without detection, but Murphy's Law at point, frequently things go wrong. The equipment breaks down, a suspicious shape appears on the screen, or pocket change or keys set off the detectors. A hand search of luggage and person may follow, conducted by airport personnel under the watchful eye of the back-up law enforcement personnel, and if illegal substances, even if not those that the search is conducted to discover, turn up, the individual will likely be arrested and charged. To the individual charged and for many others this may appear to be not only unfair but also a violation of the Fourth Amendment's ban against unreasonable searches. The federal courts do not view it from that perspective. Although there have been a multitude of cases at the district and court of appeals level, the Supreme Court has not heard arguments on this issue. In 1979, it did deny certiorari to such a case and basically reaffirmed what has become the dominant approach at the lower court level.

The standards were best expressed in *United States v. Edwards.*[62] After Edward's bag had activated the magnetometer, it was hand searched and heroin was discovered. He was charged and convicted and the Court found nothing unreasonable about the search; it met the three tests of a valid search: (1) good faith, (2) reasonable in scope, (3) advance notice with opportunity to withdraw. The 1979 case, *U.S. v. DeAngelo,*[63] involved similar but slightly different circumstances. DeAngelo submitted his briefcase for X-ray screening. When a large portion of the case appeared black on the screen, he was told that the case would have to be hand searched. He protested, stating that he would prefer not to fly rather than submit to such inspection. Over his objections, security officers opened the case and found marijuana and hashish. His arguments were no more successful than those of Edwards. Reiterating the voluntary nature of such searches (implicit consent), the Court held that there were adequate warning signs about the X-ray machine and possible physical searches provided, so that all passengers should have been aware of them. Consequently, when DeAngelo voluntarily entered the screening process, he acquiesced to its full scope. Allowing him to withdraw after that point would frustrate the purpose of the regulations which was to deter hijacking. Therefore, "Having consented to the search, DeAngelo could not withhold permission after the first step of the process disclosed that he was attempting to carry aboard the aircraft articles that were concealed from X-ray."

One other area in which the Court attempted to impose modest limitations on investigatory power in this period was to clarify the limits of what kind of records agencies could require individuals and businesses to keep. From an administrative perspective, requiring records of all types of activities subject to regulation is appealing. As one of the dissenters in *Shapiro* remarked: "It would no doubt simplify enforcement of all criminal laws if each citizen were required to keep a diary that would show where he was at all times, whom he was with and what he was up to."[64] Such a legal requirement could also place the individual in a Catch-22 situation: If he kept records of an illegal activity he could be prosecuted, but if he failed to keep the records he could also be prosecuted. Such was the situation that Congress created by requiring persons who engaged in the business of accepting wagers to file detailed information with IRS and to pay an occupation tax. Engaging in such a business was a violation of both federal and most states' laws. In *Marchetti v. U.S.,*[65] the Supreme Court struck down the requirement, and specified the limits on required records:

1. They must be "of a kind customarily kept";
2. The records must have "public aspects";
3. They must be in "an essentially noncriminal and regulatory area of activity."

Consequently, requiring records of illegal gambling activities and requiring registration of illegal firearms were held to be violations of the Fifth Amendment.[66]

Although we have repeatedly stressed that most administrative investigations do not end in criminal prosecutions, most have the potential of doing so and some actually do. IRS tax audits, for example, usually end with IRS either accepting the taxpayer's arguments or requiring the payment of back taxes. But tax fraud is a crime and if the auditor perceives intent to defraud he or she may recommend criminal charges be filed. All of which raises the question as to when, if ever, administrative investigators must inform subjects of their Miranda rights to silence and to retain counsel. The somewhat unsatisfactory answer that the Supreme Court has given to that question is, if a person is already in jail he/she should be informed of their Miranda rights before any questioning occurs. The decision specifically concerned a routine IRS tax investigation of an individual who was in a state prison. The IRS investigator had not informed the individual of any rights to remain silent and both documents and statements obtained from him were introduced as evidence in a subsequent hearing for filing false information on tax returns. Carefully limiting the scope of the decision, the Supreme Court held that

> Tax investigations which frequently lead to criminal prosecution are not immune from the *Miranda* warning requirement to be given to a person in custody, whether or not such custody is in connection with the case under investigation.[67]

One final decision of the Supreme Court in 1980 indicates how little it has actually deviated from the attitude of permissiveness toward investigatory techniques. In the late 1970s, IRS began an investigation into the financial activities of U.S. citizens in the Bahamas. As not infrequently happens, as the investigation progressed, IRS attention was attracted to a particular individual, Jack Payner, who IRS suspected had falsified his tax returns. This suspicion, and the subsequent criminal charge, was based on the belief that Payner had obtained money through a loan agreement based on funds deposited in the Castle Bank and Trust Company of Nassau, Bahama Islands, which had never been reported to IRS. Evidently unable or unwilling to collect the information through normal IRS methods, the agent in charge hired a private investigator to uncover information about Castle Bank. The private investigator developed an amicable relationship with a vice president of Castle Bank and introduced him to an attractive woman acquaintance (who also happened to be a private investigator). The vice president came to Miami to visit his new female acquaintance and when he took her out to dinner left his briefcase in her apartment. In their absence, the other investigator entered the apartment, removed the briefcase and gave it to the IRS agent who photographed its contents. The photographs included the loan agreement which was subsequently use to convict Payner, the guilty bystander, of income tax fraud.

To this point, the Payner case illustrates many aspects of contemporary investigative techniques. Certainly, it proves that IRS is both innovative and persistent in its investigations and it does seem to indicate that IRS is not overly concerned with "fairness" or procedural niceties when it is trying to collect tax revenues. Just as certainly, it indicates that there are multitudinous methods used to defraud the United States government in tax cases. The district court and the court of appeals both held that IRS had gained the evidence illegally and could not use it to prove criminal charges. The Supreme Court disagreed and put the Fourth Amendment's protection on the same personal basis that it had previously established for the Fifth Amendment. "Our Fourth Amendment decisions have established beyond the doubt that the interest in deterring illegal searches does not justify the exclusion of tainted evidence at the instance of a party who was not the victim of the challenged practices."[68]

The Court did note that the behavior by IRS was, if not illegal, at least reprehensible:

> No court should condone the unconstitutional and possibly criminal behavior of those who planned and executed this "briefcase caper." . . . [But], the suppression of probative but tainted evidence exacts a costly toll upon the ability of courts to ascertain the truth in a criminal case.[69]

The moral of this case is as perplexing as that of the airport searches cases: If administrative agencies want information that they cannot acquire legally, their best recourse is to hire a private agency to collect it illegally, and if an individual has information that may incriminate him, he had best keep it to himself, in his own home, in a personal diary. Otherwise, the Constitution provides no meaningful protections against "official curiosity."

Although the Supreme Court has imposed minimal restrictions on a limited number of administrative investigations in the contemporary period, its overall attitude has not perceptibly changed from the era of anything goes. The warrant requirement for physical inspections has by definition become as meaningless as judicial supervision of subpoenas. Although agencies have been barred from requiring individuals and businesses to keep records of explicitly defined illegal behavior, they have not been at all restricted from requring records of normal activities that can, will be, and are used against individuals in criminal prosecutions. In the Court's defense, administrative investigations remain a deviation from traditional government procedures. They truly are an innovation or deviation, depending on one's perspective, from traditional government activities, and as such they are only peripherally, if at all, subject to a constitution drafted at a time when they were unfamiliar techniques with unknown and unaccepted purposes.

ADMINISTRATIVE INVESTIGATIONS: CONCLUSION

Despite mounting criticism and resentment, administrative information gathering continues to be an essential aspect of the regulatory process. Congress, the courts, and Presidents have struggled, rather unsuccessfully, to find a satisfactory resolution to the conflict between the administrative need for the information and the costs, tangible and intangible, that this need imposes on individuals and businesses. All three branches have found the problem far more complex to solve than is indicated by current political rhetoric. The investigatory techniques that have been covered in this chapter are not only essential for enforcing the laws and protecting the public health and safety but they also are one of the most cost-effective methods. The alternatives to reports, records, and inspections are more personnel, and in the public sector which is already heavily labor intensive, additional personnel costs are politically impractical in a period of fiscal scarcity.

Congressional attempts to resolve the problem have been limited. In 1979, Congress did minimally limit OSHA's inspection coverage by prohibiting it from inspecting businesses with 10 or fewer employees *unless* they were in industries with injury rates of over 7 percent or to investigate health hazards or when substantial hazards were involved, when an employee made a complaint, or there had been an accident leading to hospitalization or death. If that was a rather modest accomplishment, congressional attempts to reduce federal paperwork have been even more so. Unable to agree on substantive legislation, Congress finally passed legislation in 1980 creating the Office of Information Regulatory Affairs within OMB (another bureaucratic agency). The new office was required to identify duplication in information collection and develop methods for eliminating it, to establish a Federal Information Locator System, to develop controls to improve information processing, and to make recommendations to Congress and administrative agencies.

Congress's inability to deal with the problem is also indicated by its failure to deal with investigatory procedures in the Administrative Procedure Act and with its own propensity for requiring agencies to gather even more data. As mentioned previously, the APA deals only briefly with investigatory procedures, primarily with the issuance and enforcement of subpoenas by the courts. Beyond that, attention is directed to authorizing statutes, and these have not only encouraged but also required the vast bulk of administrative information collection. Further, when agencies have engaged in warrantless inspections they have generally done so with congressional approval.

Presidents have had even less success in curbing agencies' demands for information. Both Ford and Carter bemoaned the time, costs, and efforts these demands required. Both issued impressive executive orders requiring agencies to curtail their efforts. Both discovered that this was easier said than done, and once said, best forgotten.

The Supreme Court has also grappled with the problem, and its proposed solutions have equaled those of the other two branches: Courts will not really limit investigations but they do wish to be consulted. Subpoenas must be brought to them for enforcement; contested inspections must have warrants. Both, however, will be issued on a pro forma basis at the request of the agency. All of which may assure the courts' full employment but none of which really addresses the central conflict.

In reality, that conflict has long since been resolved. The need to protect the public and to enforce the laws in an urban industrial society has long been accepted as limiting the right of the individual to pollute, to maim workers, to live in a rat-infested fire trap, to produce and sell life-endangering foods, drugs, and consumer products, to cheat the government out of legally required taxes, or to carry bombs, knives, and handguns aboard commercial aircraft. The result of administrative investigatory techniques aimed at preventing these and other equally serious problems may offend those who believe justice is defined only procedurally. For those who believe that substantive justice should be the goal of a political system, they appear in a very different light. Ironically, those who support the latter concept of justice find equally serious problems with information gathering techniques: They are too sporadic, too few, and too much reliant on the honesty of the regulated. Given this rather different set of criticisms, it might seem we have achieved Pareto optimality in adminstrative investigations: It is impossible to change the current situation without making someone worse off as a result of the change.

NOTES

1. Glen O. Robinson and Ernest Gellhorn, *The Administrative Process* (St. Paul, Minn.: West Publishing Co., 1974), p. 385.

2. Ernest Gellhorn, *Administrative Law and Process in a Nutshell* (St. Paul, Minn.: West Publishing Co., 1972), p. 77.

3. Ted Vaden, "Paperwork Commission into High Gear," *Congressional Quarterly*, March 26, 1977, p. 533.

4. P. H. Abelson, "Curtailing Federal Growth," *Science*, December 24, 1976, p. 1379.

5. "GAO Paperwork Study," *Congressional Quarterly*, March 29, 1980, p. 82.

6. Vaden, "Paperwork Commission into High Gear," pp. 554–55.

7. Elizabeth Wehr, "Federal Paperwork: Congress Is the Culprit," *Congressional Quarterly*, July 30, 1977, p. 1608.

8. Robert Kagan, *Regulatory Justice* (New York: Russell Sage Foundation, 1978), p. 29.

9. "Act Reduces Paperwork under OMB Management," *Public Administration Times*, January 15, 1981, pp. 1 and 6.

10. John Mendeloff, *Regulating Safety* (Cambridge: MIT Press, 1979), p. 41.

11. Mendeloff, *Regulating Safety*, p. 87.

12. Mendeloff, *Regulating Safety*, p. 199.

13. This section is based on "One Airplane and Three Institutional Actors," in Samuel Bernstein and Patrick O'Hara, *Public Administration: Organizations, People, and Public Policy* (New York: Harper &Row, 1979), pp. 227–30.

14. "Debacle of the DC-10," *Newsweek*, June 18, 1979, pp. 14–15.

15. "Behind the Crash: FAA Inquiry Charges Many Errors in Manufacturing and Maintenance of DC-10 Airliners," *The Wall Street Journal*, July 17, 1979, pp. 1 and 25.

16. "Watching the Watchdogs," *Newsweek*, April 16, 1971, p. 31.

17. Phillip E. Present, *People and Public Administration* (Pacific Palisades, Calif.: Palisades Publishers, 1979), p. 69.

18. Nanette Dembitz, "The Good of the Child versus the Rights of the Parents," *Political Science Quarterly*, September, 1971, p. 391.

19. Lee Fritschler, *Smoking and Politics* (Englewood Cliffs, N.J.: Prentice-Hall, 1968), p. 83.

20. Alona E. Evans, "Aircraft Hijacking: What Is Being Done," *American Journal of International Law*, 67 (October 1973), p. 641.

21. Evans, "Aircraft Hijacking," p. 643.

22. "Aircraft Hijacking," *Congressional Quarterly*, July 27, 1974. p. 1983.

23. 15 U.S.C.A. 49.

24. 15 U.S.C.A. 50.

25. One of the best detailed descriptions of an aircraft accident investigation is Morton Hunt, "The Case of Flight 320," *The New Yorker*, April 30, 1960, pp. 119ff.

26. See Robert A. Katzmann, *Regulatory Bureaucracy: The Federal Trade Commission and Antitrust Policy* (Cambridge: MIT Press, 1980), p. 24.

27. Quoted in Katzmann, p. 65.

28. Ibid., p. 119.

29. 103 US 168 (1881).

30. 211 US 407 (1900).

31. 211 US 419 (1900).

32. Ibid.

33. 317 US 501 (1943).

34. 317 US 501 (1943).

35. 327 US 186 (1946).

36. Ibid.

37. *Shapiro v. United States*, 335 US 1 (1948).

38. *U.S. v. Morton Salt Co.*, 338 US 632 (1950).

39. *Hermann v. CAB*, 237 F2d 359 (9th Circuit, 1956).

40. *CAB v. Hermann*, 353 US 322 (1957).

41. *Couch v. United States*, 409 US 322 (1973).

42. *Andreson v. State of Maryland*, 427 US 463 (1976).

43. *U.S. v. Nuller*, 425 U.S. 435 (1976).

44. *Kastigar v. United States*, 406 US 441 (1972); *Zicarelli v. New Jersey State Commission of Investigation*, 406 US 472 (1972).

45. *Frank v. Maryland*, 359 US 360 (1959).

46. *Camara v. Municipal Court*, 387 US 523 (1967).

47. *See v. Seattle*, 387 US 541 (1967).

48. *Colonnade Catering Corporation v. United States*, 397 US 72 (1970).

49. *Biswell v. United States*, 406 US 311 (1972).

50. *Wyman v. James*, 400 US 309 (1970).

51. *Parrish v. Civil Service Commission*, 66 Cal 2d 260 (1967).

52. *Goldberg v. Kelley*, 397 US 254 (1970).

53. *Wyman v. James*, 400 US 309 (1970).

54. Id. at 318.

55. Id. at 323.

56. *Marshall v. Barlow's Inc.*, 436 US 307 (1978).

57. Id. at 320.

58. Id. at 322.

59. *United States v. Martinez-Fuerte*, 428 US 543 (1976).

60. 452 US 594 (1981).

61. *Donovan v. Dewey*, 452 US 594, 598 (1981).

62. *United States v. Edwards*, 498 F. 2d 496 (2d Circuit, 1974).

63. *U.S. v. DeAngelo*, 584 F. 2d 46 (D.C. Circuit, 1979); cert. denied, 440 US 935 (1979).

64. 535 US 1 (1948).

65. Marchetti v. U.S., 390 US 39 (1968).

66. See also *Grosso v. U.S.*, 390 US 62 (1968), and *Haynes v. United States*, 390 US 85 (1968).

67. *Mathis v. U.S.*, 391 US 1 (1968).

68. *U.S. v. Payner*, 447 U.S. 727, 735 (1980).

69. Id. at 733, 734.

Chapter 8

Informal Actions

On November 25, 1978, the British medical journal *Lancet* published an article by Dr. James Todd, a researcher at the University of Colorado, which reported that Todd and his colleagues had identified "what appears to be a new and severe, acute disease," whose symptoms included high fever, low blood pressure, nausea, diarrhea, and a generalized rash which resembled sunburn. The disease, toxic shock syndrome (TSS), was caused by a common bacteria, Staphyloccocus aureus. TSS was and is a relatively rare illness with only 408 reported cases and 40 deaths from 1975 to 1980, and it received little attention outside of the medical community until May 1980. In January of that year Dr. Jeffrey Davis, chief epidemiologist of the Wisconsin State Health Department, had contacted the Federal Center for Disease Control in Atlanta, Georgia, to report that he had found seven cases of TSS in his state and that apparently there had been an additional five cases reported in Minnesota. In May, 68 additional TSS cases were reported to CDC and throughout the summer, the number of reported cases continued to increase reaching a high of 120 cases in August.

The Center for Disease Control, one of whose functions is to identify causes of disease and to protect the public against disease outbreaks, established a "toxic shock task force" to collect information on the causes and extent of the illness. On May 23, 1980, the CDC published its first report of TSS in its *Morbidity and Mortality Weekly Report*. For some reason, the report attracted national publicity and became the subject of a Senate committee hearing chaired by Edward Kennedy. The CDC continued research, as did Dr. Davis and other scientists. The data collected indicated that TSS primarily affected women. Of the over 400 cases that had been reported, only 14 were in men or boys. Davis's research and a survey taken by CDC of women who had survived the disease also indicated that women who used tampons during their menstrual periods ran a much higher risk of contracting TSS than those who did not. The June 25, 1980, *Morbidity and Mortality Weekly Report* suggested that women should consider alternating use of tampons with sanitary napkins.

Throughout the summer research continued. The CDC's own data was confirmed by a study conducted by the Utah State Department of Health: Approximately 70 percent of the female TSS victims had used one particular brand of tampon, Rely, manufactured by Procter and Gamble company. On September 11, CDC director William Loege contacted officials of the Food and Drug Administration to inform them of the newest research results. Although the FDA had been monitoring the situation and had had a series of informal talks with tampon manufacturers following the June report, it had taken no official position on the problem. On September 12, FDA officials flew to Atlanta to confer with CDC researchers. The following Monday, September 15, FDA officials contacted officials of Procter and Gamble and informed them of the newest research findings. Representatives from Procter and Gamble immediately flew to Atlanta to review the results and consult with CDC officials. On September 17, the CDC and FDA jointly issued a press release, warning that women who used Rely tampons ran a high risk of contracting toxic shock. The following day Safeway stores, the nation's largest supermarket chain, announced that it was removing Rely from its 2,000 stores.[1]

On September 22, Procter and Gamble announced that it had decided to suspend sales of Rely and was recalling supplies that had already been distributed. Company officials were careful to stress that they were not conceding that Rely was in fact at fault and that removal of the product from the market would not eliminate the threat of the disease. "This is being done despite the fact that we know of no defect in Rely tampons and despite evidence that withdrawal of Rely will not eliminate the occurrence of toxic shock syndrome," stated Edward G. Harness, chairman and chief executive officer of Procter and Gamble.[2]

Already confronted with several multimillion dollar lawsuits brought by TSS victims and their families, Procter and Gamble's problems were far from resolved by the voluntary recall (which it termed a "withdrawal") of their product. On September 23, officials of the company met with FDA staffers. The result of that meeting was a consent agreement under which Procter and Gamble was required not only to recall Rely but also to launch a massive and expensive nationwide advertising campaign warning of the dangers of TSS, the connection with tampon and particularly Rely usage, and offering a refund for unused Rely tampons.[3] "We have acceded to every request made by the government in an effort to remove Rely and the company from the TSS controversy," stated Procter and Gamble chairman Edward Harness.[4]

On October 1, the FDA sent telegrams to the five other major tampon manufacturers "strongly recommending" that they add a warning label to boxes of their products "as a responsible consumer protection step on your part." The agency suggested the wording for the warning label:

> Toxic shock syndrome (TSS) is a rare but serious disease that can occur in menstruating women. TSS can cause death. The disease has been associated with the use of tampons. You may therefore want to consider not using tampons or alternating tampons with napkins.

The telegram also requested the manufacturers to meet with the agency to discuss actions that they were planning to take "for labeling, educating the public and conducting research."[5]

The meeting with the manufacturers was held on October 6. All of the manufacturers agreed to include a warning statement in or on boxes of their products. In addition, Tampax corporation agreed to publish a series of newspaper and magazine advertisements describing the disease, and Kimberly Clark, manufacturer of Kotex tampons, agreed to send letters to 260,000 doctors describing TSS and how to recognize and treat it.[6]

On October 19, 1980, the FDA issued a notice for proposed regulations requiring mandatory labels on all tampon packages.

INFORMAL ACTION: THE LIFEBLOOD OF
THE ADMINISTRATIVE PROCESS

Webster's Dictionary defines informal as "not formal; conducted or carried out without formal, regularly prescribed, or ceremonious procedure,"[7] and that definition has substantial relevance to the definition of informal administrative actions. Their informality relates not to the seriousness of their consequences, since many informal actions, such as emergency seizures of contaminated food, have severe adverse consequences for affected parties, but to the fact that they are not covered by formal procedural restrictions specified in the Administrative Procedure Act.

Any administrative action which is not formal adjudication or formal or §553 rule making is classified as an informal administrative action. Every action taken by the Food and Drug Administration prior to October 19 was "informal," and the toxic shock case partially illustrates the scope, importance, impact, and advantages of informal regulatory actions. Publicity, consultation, negotiation, advice, voluntary recall, and a consent agreement were the informal methods used by the FDA in dealing with Procter and Gamble and the other tampon manufacturers. The actions taken by the agency were not covered by formal procedural restrictions specified in the Administrative Procedure Act. They allowed the agency great flexibility in dealing with a serious problem and permitted it to act with great speed; only ten days elapsed from the time it first became convinced that Rely posed a serious health hazard to the withdrawal of the product from the market. The financial consequences of these actions were considerable: Procter and Gamble estimated the loss from sales of Rely at $75 million plus the substantial cost involved in the nationwide advertising campaign. As the publicity and media coverage of the TSS-tampon linkage continued, other tampon manufacturers saw sales of their products similarly decrease as more women switched products. At the same time, however, both the companies and the agency saved substantial amounts of money that would have been involved in a protracted contested case. How many lives were saved and cases of illness averted because of the prompt action is unknown, as is the number of private lawsuits that Procter and Gamble avoided by prompt compliance. These informal actions were always backed by the possibility that the FDA could have resorted to formal actions, and when it finally did so after the immediate problem had been solved, the formal action was considerably facilitated by the informal procedures that had preceded it.

To the list of informal actions used by FDA could be added "initiating, investigating, . . . settling, contracting, dealing, . . . threatening, . . . concealing, planning, recommending, supervising," issuing policy statements, awarding grants, licensing, processing applications, claims, and tax returns,[8] emergency seizures of private property to protect public health or safety, deciding not to enforce, not to regulate, and not to prosecute. The importance of informal action has long been recognized. As the Final Report of the Attorney General's Committee on Administrative Procedure in 1941 stated, "informal procedures constitute the vast bulk of administrative adjudication and are truly the lifeblood of the administrative process." These informal acts account for at least 90 percent of the work of government agencies,[9] and in many instances private parties are more seriously affected by informal actions than by formal agency actions. Despite their recognized importance, until recently informal actions were given scant attention in most administrative law textbooks. The primary reason for this inattention was that there was very little law—statutory, constitutional, or agency-made—regarding informal procedures. Although this has slowly begun to change, informal actions still remain subject to considerably fewer legal restraints than formal actions.

This chapter will provide an overview of some of the most important informal actions, their advantages and disadvantages, current restrictions on their use, and recommendations for improving agency procedures relating to them.

INFORMAL ACTIONS

Summary Action

The Federal Insecticide, Fungicide and Rodenticide Act Amendments of 1972 require that all herbicides must be registered with the Environmental Protection Agency (EPA). EPA is then responsible for monitoring the use of these herbicides, and if it determines that a herbicide poses an "imminent hazard" and "serious harm" would occur it may invoke an emergency suspension of the herbicide's registration. Between 1973 and 1979 an average of 3 million kilograms per year of the herbicide 2, 4, 5-T (commonly known as dioxin) was sprayed on the farms, ranches, forests, and roadsides of the United States. Although research had proven that dioxin was highly toxic and had teratogenic (fetus deforming), oncogenetic (miscarriage producing), and carcinogenic (cancer causing) effects on animals, it became the most widely used herbicide in this country.

In April 1978, Bonnie Hill, a 33-year-old schoolteacher in Alsea, Oregon, wrote EPA. From 1973 to 1978, she and seven other women in Alsea had had a total of 13 miscarriages, which she believed were a direct result of the extensive spraying by the U.S. Forest Service and the Bureau of Land Management of 2, 4, 5-T on the hills and forests surrounding the community. The EPA responded and launched a ten-month investigation which included epidemiological studies, analysis of medical and hospital records, interviews, analyses of soils, water, deer, and elk meat and human mother's milk samples collected in the Alsea area. On March 1, 1979, Deputy EPA Administrator Barbara Blum invoked an emergency suspension of 2, 4, 5-T's registration just as the spring spraying season was about to begin.[10]

Dow Chemical, the largest manufacturer of 2, 4, 5-T, immediately filed suit against the EPA alleging that the suspension was unwarranted and based on invalid and incomplete scientific evidence. Although the District Court judge agreed that if it had been his decision, he would not have invoked the emergency suspension, he still upheld the EPA action. In the opinion of the court, the EPA had considered "relevant factors," had made no clear error of judgment, and had had sufficient evidence of potential serious harm to justify its decision to suspend 2, 4, 5-T's registration prior to a formal hearing.[11]

Summary actions are actions taken by an administrative agency "pending an adjudicatory hearing, sometimes called emergency or temporary action."[12] They include the seizure and destruction of unwholesome food, animals, and illegal goods, the suspension of licenses, the seizure of assets and property, and the takeover of banks which are believed to be on the brink of insolvency. What characterizes these actions is that the agency is allowed to act immediately before allowing the affected party an opportunity for a hearing. Generally, the courts will uphold the permissibility of such actions if explicit statutory authorization for the action has been granted or if it was taken in an "emergency situation."

As the Supreme Court made clear in 1978, the statutory authorization for such actions must be explicit. The Securities Exchange Act of 1934 had authorized the SEC "summarily to suspend trading in any security . . . for a period not exceeding ten days if in its opinion the public interest and the protection of investors so require." The SEC had initially summarily suspended trading in the common stock of Canadian Javelin Ltd., and for over a year, every ten days had again summarily suspended trading of the stock. In holding that the agency had acted in excess of statutory authority, the Court noted:

> The power to summarily suspend trading in a security even for 10 days, without any notice, opportunity to be heard or findings based upon a record, is an awesome power with a potentially devastating impact on the issuer, its shareholders and other investors. A clear mandate from Congress such as that found in §12(K) is necessary to confer this power. No less clear a mandate can be expected from Congress to authorize the Commission to extend virtually without limit, these periods of suspension. But we find no such unmistakeable mandate.[13]

What constitutes an emergency situation justifying such peremptory administrative actions may not always be obvious to ordinary persons and is subject to court interpretation. Some of the circumstances that courts have found to justify summary action are the need to protect national security during wartime, the need to protect the public health against impure food and drugs, and the need to protect the public against economic injury. In those situations, courts have permitted agencies to seize property without prior hearing. As the Court noted in *Bowles v. Willingham*, "national security might not be able to afford the luxuries of litigation and the long delays which preliminary hearings have traditionally entailed."[14]

Although the seriousness of these situations may be readily agreed upon as requiring prompt administrative action, other "emergency" situations are considerably more open to question. One of the most controversial of these is "the need of the government promptly to secure its revenues"[15] by making jeopardy assessments. Whenever the Commissioner of IRS believes that the assessment or collection of a deficiency will be jeopardized by delay he may seize the taxpayer's assets and freeze them until the taxes are paid. Although such seizures may impose considerable hardship on the affected individual the Court has upheld such summary tax collection procedures as having been long accepted and necessary. Similarly, the Court has allowed tenured civil servants to be dismissed prior to a hearing[16] and permitted the FDA to seize misbranded (but not dangerous or harmful) food supplements.[17]

Summary actions are dramatic and they enable agencies to prevent tremendous and irreparable harm to the public. They also have the capacity to injure wrongfully. The very speed which characterizes them means they also have a high risk of error since they are likely to be based on incomplete information.[18] Businesses have been destroyed, reputations permanently damaged, and individual lives seriously disrupted by wrongful summary actions. Unquestionably, however, the existence of such power, like most other informal powers and actions, tremendously facilitates agency enforcement of the law.

Publicity

Sunshine, as the advocates of open government point out, is the best disinfectant, and when that is extended to include the power of administrative agencies to publicize their actions, it is also one of the most potent of informal enforcement devices. Agencies use publicity for various purposes, most commonly to provide information and warnings to the public and regulatees, as a sanction to deter unlawful conduct, as a substitute for formal action, and/or to force a transgressor to negotiate.[19] The FDA, for example, used press releases not only to inform the public of the dangers of toxic shock syndrome, potentially averting an unknown number of illnesses and deaths, but also to pressure Proctor and Gamble to take the "voluntary" action of withdrawing Rely from the market.

Similar to summary actions, publicity can have devastating consequences for the regulatees. The publicity surrounding TSS was not limited in impact to Proctor and Gamble. It also cost other tampon manufacturers millions of dollars in lost sales. The announcement of the FCC in 1965 that it was instituting an investigation of AT&T is estimated to have resulted in a decline of the market price of AT&T stock of $3.5 billion in the succeeding three month period.[20] On November 9, 1959, Secretary of Health, Education and Welfare Arthur Flemming announced that a portion of the cranberry crop in Washington and Oregon had been contaminated with a chemical weed killer. Although less than 1 percent of the crop was affected, millions of Americans decided to have their Thanksgiving dinner without cranberries. Only $9 million of the estimated $21.5 million lost by the cranberry growers was ultimately indemnified by Congress.

Unquestionably, publicity by administrative agencies protects the public in an efficient and expeditious manner, but just as unquestionably it has the potential of wrongfully and irremediably damaging companies which are its focus. Occasionally, careless or erroneous use of publicity is obvious; in other cases it is more difficult to determine if the agency acted precipitously or unfairly. An example of the former was provided by the FDA in 1979. In August 1979, company auditors of Sterling Cooperative Inc. discovered that a batch of Sterling pumpkin pie filling had been underprocessed, leaving the possibility of bacterial contamination. Although local (Buffalo, New York) public health officials assured the company that baking the pie filling would destroy any harmful bacteria, the company sent letters to its customers telling them to pull the pie filling from their shelves. The company also notified the FDA and over the next two months the FDA determined that a recall had occurred and assigned it a classification number. Unfortunately the FDA did not complete all of its paperwork on the case until November 1. At that time it sent the completed notice to its publication department for inclusion in the weekly FDA enforcement bulletin. The announcement was routinely scheduled for publication in the November 21 (the day before Thanksgiving) bulletin. The news media immediately picked up on the announcement and all day and night before Thanksgiving, radio stations in the Sterling distribution areas announced the recall. The reports frequently failed to include information that the recall had been conducted three months earlier or that, in fact, the recalled pie filling had actually been distributed as much as two years before the recall. The amount of damage inflicted on the company was inestimable.[21]

Another example involved Bon Vivant Inc. Bon Vivant was a manufacturer of gourmet food products, including vichysoisse. In 1971, a man and his wife became seriously ill after consuming Bon Vivant vichysoisse. The man ultimately died and the cause of death was determined to be botulism contracted from consuming the Bon Vivant soup. The FDA immediately issued publicity warnings concerning the soup and the manufacturer recalled all Bon Vivant vichysoisse. Although ultimately only five cans were found to be contaminated, the company's sales sagged tremendously and eventually it went bankrupt. Five contaminated cans of soup may seem a minor problem to have caused the bankruptcy of a company but neither Bon Vivant nor the FDA knew the extent of the contamination when the publicity was released and even five cans of soup could have caused multiple deaths.

The FDA, unlike some other federal agencies, has been given explicit statutory authority to disseminate adverse publicity. Section 705 of the Food, Drug and Cosmetic Act authorizes the FDA to warn the public "of imminent dangers to health" or gross deception. This statutory power to use publicity forms the basis for most product recalls that have occurred under FDA auspices.[22] The FDA has two classes of product recalls: Class I are products which constitute an immediate threat to public health (Bon Vivant); Class II recalls cover products which constitute a serious or potential threat to health (Rely). All recalls are announced by the FDA through the release of a weekly "public recall list." The power of publicity is indicated by the fact that although the FDA has the power to seize dangerous products and remove them from the market, most product removals are, like Rely and Bon Vivant, "voluntary recalls."

The statutory framework for other agency usage of publicity is weak and in most cases nonexistent. Most agencies have not been given explicit authority to use publicity but have assumed its existence as an implicit aspect of their responsibility to protect the public and facilitate their enforcement processes.[23] In at least one instance, Congress has restricted agency use of publicity. The EEOC is forbidden from publishing complaints until conciliation efforts have failed and formal charges have been filed. Overall, however, Congress has provided little specific guidance as to the proper use of or limits on agency publicity. Although some agencies, the FTC for example, have established procedural manuals or rules governing the use of publicity, the majority have not.

The courts have infrequently addressed the problems and legality of agency publicity. Most agencies routinely issue press releases concerning enforcement actions. The FTC, for example, issues a press release immediately after filing a complaint and frequently calls a press conference to explain the release. Adversely affected parties term such publicity actions "trial by media." In 1967, the FTC issued a complaint against Cinderella Career and Finishing Schools, Inc., charging it with deceptive advertising. The issuance of the complaint was announced in a routine press release. Cinderella immediately challenged the issuance of the press release contending that the FTC was not authorized by law to issue such releases, and that the release had caused it "irreparable damage, . . . public disrepute, scorn, and loss of business." Although the Court of Appeals sympathized with Cinderella's plight, "where much has been said, something will be believed," it still upheld the FTC's authority and obligation to issue press releases. The Court held that Congress had authorized the Commission to make public information obtained by it and that the press releases "constitute a warning or caution to the public, the welfare of which the Commission is in these matters charged." Further, although the damage to Cinderella may have been unfortunate, it did not constitute a transgression of legal rights.[24]

Advice and Advisory Opinions

Every day employees of federal agencies are asked questions by telephone, by letter, and by personal visits by individuals seeking information about agency interpretations of the laws they enforce. "Will this transaction be taxable or this expenditure deductible? . . . Must this employee be given minimum wage? . . . Does my grant permit me to spend money on this item? . . . Would this kind of advertising be misleading?"[25] Every day the agencies answer these questions, advising private citizens and businesses as to what the agency considers to be legal and permissible conduct.

Although advice-giving is a major aspect of most regulatory areas, during the wage-price freeze of 1971 it emerged as the primary form of regulatory action. The 90-day wage-price freeze was imposed by Executive Order on August 15, 1971. The implementing agencies, the Cost of Living Council, the Office of Emergency Preparedness, and the Internal Revenue Service, were given no lead time to prepare for the massive job of enforcing the freeze across the national economy and almost immediately they were bombarded with inquiries from businesses, consumers, labor unions, and individual employees. In the 90-day period, they responded to over 750,000 inquiries.[26] Almost all of these inquiries were answered on the basis of the information provided by the requesting party; no hearings were held, no attorneys were involved, and no notification of interested parties occurred. The agencies avoided formal procedures and relied exclusively on informal advice to resolve problems, answer questions, and enforce the freeze.[27]

Advice-giving activities range all the way from verbal responses to inquiries, to the more "formal" letter rulings of IRS and letters of comment and no-action letters of the SEC. Every year the IRS commissioner issues over 32,000 letter rulings on private tax liability in response to specific inquiries, and countless thousands more private rulings are issued by IRS branch offices. The SEC uses letters of comment to speed up the securities registration process. When a registration statement is received it may be subjected to a summary review by the staff and a determination made that it is either well prepared or requires only a few "comments." If the suggestions made in these comments are adhered to by the registrant, immediate clearance is normally granted for registration. If summary review is not granted or the comments not accepted, the time lapse between receipt of the initial registration and the final effective date frequently exceeds six months.[28] "No action" letters are responses to inquiries in which the SEC staff indicates that it would not recommend enforcement action if a transaction is carried out as described in the initial letter of inquiry.

Advice-giving is unquestionably one of the most common forms of informal actions used by regulatory agencies, and its advantages to both the agency and affected parties are impressive. It is fast, and in a regulatory process frequently criticized for its slowness, this is no small factor. Since frequently time is money, advice-giving saves both regulatees and agencies vast amounts of money. Advice, if taken, may prevent irreparable damage to the regulatee and the public. It decreases the agencies' formal workloads and facilitates their formal processes, in many instances making it possible for an agency to handle otherwise impossibly large workloads. In new regulatory areas where the agency has had neither the time nor expertise to develop "formal" rules, advice allows them to guide regulatee behavior until formal guidelines can be established.

The statutory law controlling and guiding advice-giving by agencies is almost non-existent, but several agencies have established procedural guidelines for giving or in some cases not giving advice. The SEC, for example, has formal procedural rules governing the issuance of letters of comment.[29] Both the IRS and FTC have published extensive explanatory material on their advice-giving procedures and both have also specified the issues and conditions under which they will not provide advice.[30] Even so, it remains unclear in most agencies who is authorized to give advice or how to go about getting it.

The informality of the advice-giving process, the lack of binding effect of the advice on the party requesting it, and its lack of finality has meant that for the most part it is not subject to judicial review. In 1970, a Court of Appeals did hold that SEC "no action" letters were reviewable. The Medical Committee for Human Rights which owned stock in Dow Chemical sought to compel the company to include in its forthcoming proxy statement a resolution which would have required Dow to stop making napalm. After Dow refused to include the statement, the Committee requested the assistance of the SEC's Division of Corporation Finance. What the Committee got was a no action letter from the Division: The Division would not recommend any action against Dow for the refusal. Although the court upheld the SEC, it did establish that the no action letter was final agency action and thus reviewable.[31] This case, however, remains the exception and most advisory actions are not reviewable by the courts.

Policy Statements

When an agency wishes to clarify its position in regard to a specific subject under its jurisdiction but does not wish to make that position as legally binding on itself or others as an officially promulgated regulation would be, it can issue a policy statement. Policy statements are explicitly exempted from Administrative Procedure Act rule-making procedures by §553(b)(3)(A) of the Act, and agencies have considerable leeway in structuring the process by which they are formulated.

During the 1970s, the Federal Communications Commission was frequently caught in the middle of an ongoing and constantly escalating conflict between broadcasters and public interest groups. The public interest groups were extremely dissatisfied with the content and quality of much of the programming on television and radio and attempted to compel the FCC to take a more active role in policing the air waves. The FCC, which has traditionally been broadcaster-oriented, was truly a "reluctant regulator,"[32] but the public interest groups were persistent. In 1966, the District of Columbia Court of Appeals, which has been given jurisdiction by Congress over all broadcast license cases, made it clear that public interest groups qualified as "interested parties" who had the right to intervene in licensing decisions and to challenge FCC actions.[33] In an attempt to placate these public interest groups which it could no longer ignore, the FCC resorted to a variety of informal actions, relying heavily on the issuance of policy statements.

When Action for Children's Television (ACT) compelled the FCC to become involved in consideration of the quality and quantity of children's programming, the Commission's response was to institute a lengthy inquiry into children's television which culminated in the issuance of a policy statement in 1974. The policy statement included the FCC's interpretation of what "the public interest" might require as far as advertising, timing, and quantity in the area of children's programming, but it mandated no new changes. As a symbolic gesture, the policy statement failed to placate its intended audience. ACT was dissatisfied and challenged it, unsuccessfully, in the Court of Appeals.

Similarly, when environmental groups successfully challenged the FCC's refusal to apply its Fairness Doctrine to require a licensee to air viewpoints opposing paid advertisements for high-powered cars and high-test gasoline,[34] the FCC resorted to a policy statement to clarify its position:

> We do not believe . . . that the usual product commercial can realistically be said to inform the public on any side of a controversial issue of public importance.
> . . . In the future we will apply the Fairness Doctrine only to those commercials which are devoted in an obvious and meaningful way to the discussion of public issues.[35]

The FCC's usage of policy statements is illustrative of their general utility to a regulatory agency. Such statements permit the agency to state its position on an issue without going through a lengthy, highly structured rule-making procedure. It can follow whatever procedure it deems appropriate, allow limited participation, give the appearance of being responsive, and since the statement is not legally binding, no one is compelled to obey it. As the FCC discovered, however, when an agency relies on one of its policy statements as the justification for an action, the substance of the policy statement is judicially reviewable. In 1974, the D.C. Court of Appeals had ruled that when a significant segment of the listening audience station objected to a program format change, the FCC was required to hold a hearing.[36] The FCC's response to that decision had been the issuance of a policy statement which unequivocally disagreed with the court and argued that "the public interest . . . is best served by unregulated competition among licensees."[37] The policy statement also urged the Court of Appeals to change its "policy." When the FCC attempted to rely on the policy statement to dismiss a challenge to a program format change, the Court of Appeals not only held the policy statement to be of no force or effect but also lectured the FCC on the difference between policy and law, especially the FCC's references to the Court's decisions: "We should have thought that *WEFM* represents not a *policy* but rather the *law* of the land as enacted by Congress and interpreted by the Court of Appeals and as it is to be administered by the Commission."[38] The Supreme Court, however, ultimately preferred the FCC's "policy" to the Court of Appeals "law," and the validity of the policy statement was upheld.[39]

Negotiated Settlements

Negotiated settlements are one of the few types of informal actions required by the Administrative Procedure Act. Section 554(c) requires agencies to give respondents in complaint cases an opportunity for settlement "when time, the nature of the proceeding and the public interest permit." When an agency has investigated a complaint, decided that it has merit, and intends to take formal action before adjudication begins, affected parties are allowed to meet with agency representatives to attempt to arrive at an informal agreement. If such an agreement can be negotiated without resort to a formal hearing, both the agency and the party involved will be spared a lengthy and expensive process. The utility and essentiality of these informal, negotiated settlements was explained by Ray Garrett, former chairman of the SEC:

> Settlements are important almost everywhere in the law. They are especially important in securities regulation. If our staff had to fight each case all the way through, the Commission's enforcement program would grind to a halt. It does not have and probably never will have, the resources for so stupendous a litigation effort.[40]

Although every agency has its own procedures for negotiating settlements, those followed by the FTC in deceptive advertising practices cases are fairly typical. Of the approximately 13,000 complaints a year the FTC receives in this area, approximately half lead to FTC action. The vast majority of these are settled through informal procedures which result in oral or written promises from the business involved to "voluntarily comply" with FTC suggestions. About 250 cases a year are settled through consent agreements. If voluntary compliance is not forthcoming, the FTC notifies the affected firm and includes in that notification a proposed order. At that point negotiations between the two are begun. If a settlement is negotiated, it is reviewed by the full Commission. If the Commission accepts it, the offer is made public for comment and views of interested parties. Usually 30 days are allowed for such comments and the FTC will then either issue a consent order or withdraw the offer for settlement.[41] A consent order waives all procedural rights, accepts agency authority, and requires the respondent not to engage in specified practices. Although arrived at through informal procedures, such an order has the same effect as an order issued as a result of an adjudicatory hearing.

In 1972, *Reader's Digest*, after protracted negotiations with the Federal Trade Commission, signed a consent order requiring it to stop engaging in certain practices connected with the "sweepstakes" which it used as a promotional device to sell subscriptions. *Reader's Digest* was prohibited from "using or distributing simulated checks, currency, or using or distributing any confusingly simulated item of value." The FTC soon became convinced that the *Digest* had reneged on the informal agreement, and alleged that in 1973 it mailed consumers more than $13.8 million in "Travel Checks" and more than $4 million in "Cash Convertible Bonds" to increase sales. In November 1978, the U.S. District Court in Wilmington, Delaware, agreed with the FTC that the consent agreement had been violated and finally in 1981 levied a civil fine of $1.75 million against the *Digest*.[42] Although the *Digest* immediately appealed the fine, the case once again demonstrates that informal actions can have formal and very expensive consequences.

Few informal actions irritate public interest groups as much as negotiated settlements. The issues at stake are frequently extremely significant to these groups and just as frequently, they allege, they are excluded from meaningful participation in the negotiations. At the FTC, for example, although "interested parties" are allowed to file motions to intervene at any time during the negotiations, "the FTC has never approved a motion to intervene in an ongoing consent negotiation."[43] Women's and minority groups have been particularly critical of Equal Employment Opportunity Commission (EEOC) negotiated settlements which have been arrived at without participation by groups representing affected employees. They point specifically to the EEOC's settlements with the steel industry and AT&T as examples of how the informal process works to their disadvantage.

The steel industry settlement was a massive and highly expensive agreement under which industry agreed to pay more than $30 million in back-pay awards to employees who had been discriminated against. But women's groups and the NAACP charged that they "were not permitted to participate in the steel negotiations. . . . They were not even consulted or notified of the progress of the talks."[44] The agreement between the EEOC and the steel industry was interesting: Workers who received back-pay awards were required to sign releases waiving the right to sue for further awards and the EEOC agreed to intervene on the side of the steel industry if a worker or group attempted to seek further relief. The agreement was to be monitored by a tripartite committee consisting of one representative from the unions, one from management, and one from government. To the affected and excluded public interest groups the steel industry settlement was an object lesson of how "a firm with an extensive history of discrimination could buy its way out of legal trouble at a small price."[45]

The AT&T settlement, although financially the most expensive for a single company that the EEOC had achieved, was no more satisfactory to women's and minority groups. Initially, AT&T had been prepared to sign an agreement with the General Services Administration and the Wages and Hours Division of the Department of Labor that would have provided no back pay and little affirmative relief. The National Organization for Women was able to block that settlement and to force EEOC to enter the conflict. But once EEOC became involved these groups were excluded, and although the final settlement appeared impressive in financial terms, NOW and minority group representatives were not pleased with it. Although AT&T agreed to pay $15 million in back pay to persons illegally discriminated against and also to provide $23 million per year to equalize wages, the back-pay awards averaged only $400 per employee. Further, the EEOC agreed to drop all existing charges against AT&T, to declare that the company was in conformance with federal law, and neglected to establish goals or timetables for the actualization of equal opportunity for women or minorities.[46]

The FTC and EEOC are most certainly not the only federal agencies which systematically exclude public interest groups from negotiations with businesses that have been charged with violations of law. During the summer of 1980 the Department of Energy (DOE) excluded consumer groups from negotiations with 37 major oil companies which had been accused of overcharging under federal price control laws. Despite protests from the consumer groups that the law required the money be rebated directly to consumers or be placed in a trust fund and used for projects to relieve the impact of high energy prices, the consent agreements signed by the companies and DOE provided that the companies would pay the federal government $1.4 billion which would be used to reduce future oil prices and to help the companies increase their future exploration budgets.[47]

As the preceding examples indicate, negotiated settlements are not normally open to participation by anyone other than the corporation or individual that is the subject of agency action. The agreements are arrived at in closed sessions and their substance frequently equals and even exceeds in importance the output of the formal processes. Although "secret decisions, secretly arrived at" are normally offensive to democratic theory, closed negotiations are not that unusual in the American political and economic processes. Labor-management negotiations are seldom open to public participation. When a prosecuting attorney meets with a defense attorney and a plea bargain is arranged, neither the public nor the victim is invited to the session, and until 1975, conference committees between the House and Senate which worked out compromises on major legislation were conducted completely in secret with no record being kept of their deliberations. Both agencies and corporations contend that allowing public intervention in negotiations might have serious negative consequences. Firms might refuse to negotiate and agencies would be compelled to take all cases to adjudication. If so, then the time and expense involved in handling cases would increase and agencies would be able to handle far fewer cases than they currently do.[48] Even so the secrecy surrounding negotiations remains a troublesome and controversial issue.

Applications

Every year the Social Security Administration processes 5 million applications for benefits; the Internal Revenue Service processes 100 million tax returns; the FDA handles hundreds of applications to license new drugs and therapeutic devices; and a variety of other federal agencies from the Veterans' Administration to the Department of Agriculture accept, reject, or respond in other ways to applications from individuals and businesses for the almost endless variety of benefits, permissions, and approvals provided by the federal government. Initially, all of these applications are handled "informally" and in the vast majority of cases the disposition made at the informal stage is the final disposition.

In some cases, the applications-approval process flows swiftly and smoothly. Since 1914, meat processors have been required to have prior USDA approval of their labels before they can sell their products. In fiscal 1980, the eight-member label section of the Division of Meat and Poultry Standards received 104,826 label applications, 95 percent of which were processed in less than one week. Many were approved immediately when they were brought to the USDA by personal representatives of the meat companies. The process moves *too* fast for some consumer advocates who claim that the labels, particularly those for new meat products like substitute bacon, are misleading, incomplete, or erroneous, and USDA seldom checks for accuracy.[49]

In other cases, most notably FDA approval of new drug applications, the process moves, if at all, with glacial speed. When a drug company wishes to market a new drug, it must first do initial screening and testing of the drug on animals and then secure permission from the FDA to test the drug on humans through submission of a Notice of Claimed Investigational Exemption for a New Drug (IND). Once (if) the FDA grants the IND, research can begin using human subjects. When the research is completed, the company submits the New Drug Application (NDA). Technically, the FDA has 180 days to act on the application but in reality delays of from two to three years are not unusual.[50] The result, according to some critics, has been a "drug lag" in the United States which has deprived Americans of effective medical treatment available in other countries and has increased the overall costs of health care.[51]

An example of an application process that is not only slow but evidently permeated with inaccuracy and unfairness is the handling of disability claims under the Social Security Administration. To a certain extent the delays in the process are attributable to the procedure specified for handling applications in Title II of the Social Security Act. A claimant must first apply for disability benefits at the district Social Security office. That office determines if the claimant is covered by Social Security and if so forwards the application to a *state* agency, where medical and vocational evidence are developed and analyzed. The state agency makes an initial determination on the claim and notifies both the SSA and the claimant. If the claim is denied and SSA affirms the denial, the claimant is entitled to de novo reconsideration of the claim by the state agency. Denial at this stage is appealable to the Social Security Administration where a full-scale adjudicatory hearing will be held. The accuracy of the initial application process is questionable: From January to June, 1974, 49 percent of the denials appealed to the SSA were reversed by its administrative law judges.[52] The inconsistency of the process is unarguable. "Indeed, it is widely believed that the outcome of cases depends more on who decides the case than on what the facts are."[53]

Authorizing statutes frequently specify both application procedures and the grounds for granting or denying an application. In addition, the Administrative Procedure Act may require that an agency supply a rejected applicant with a statement of the reasons for the denial of the application. Section 555(e) of the APA states:

> Prompt notice shall be given of the denial in whole or in part of a written application, petition or other request of an interested person made in connection with any agency proceeding. Except in affirming a prior denial or when the denial is self-explanatory, the notice shall be accompanied by a brief statement of the grounds for denial.[54]

The key words, however, are "agency proceeding" which is defined in §551(12) as an agency process defined by paragraphs (5) [rule making], (7) [adjudication], and (9) [licensing]. The Attorney General's manual strictly interprets the section as being applicable only to the three specified proceedings, but increasingly the courts and the agencies themselves have begun to interpret it as requiring them to supply a statement of reasons for denial of applications and other informal actions.[55] Even the Immigration and Naturalization Service, at the suggestion of Kenneth Davis, has relented and has begun to supply a brief statement of reasons to aliens whose applications have been denied.[56] The courts have had little to say about initial agency processes for handling applications partly because the initial disposition of an application is usually not considered final agency action since most agencies provide an internal appeals process.

Friendly Persuasion

When the President of the United States wants to persuade a labor union to moderate its wage demands in the collective bargaining process or a corporation to hold the line on price increases, he jawbones. He uses the entire panoply of informal presidential powers and techniques, backed always by the formal powers of the office, to talk the union or the corporation into doing what he believes to be in the public interest. Regulatory agencies also use jawboning to persuade regulatees to do what the agency thinks is in the public interest. Like presidential jawboning, agency efforts at friendly persuasion are also backed by the possibility of formal action if the subject of the persuasion effort fails to see things the agency's way.

In the early 1970s, various groups, including the national PTA, became concerned about the excessive amount and explicitness of sex and violence on television. These groups communicated their concern to Congress and in 1974, the House Appropriations Committee directed the Federal Communications Commission to report to it by December 31, 1974, what actions the Commission had taken or planned to take in response to the problem. The FCC had been aware of the problem for some time but had in fact done nothing about it, at least partly because some of the members of the Commission, including its Chairman, Richard Wiley, believed "that constitutional, statutory and prudential considerations dictated that the government had no role to play."[57] Wiley, in particular, believed that both the First Amendment and the Communications Act of 1934 prohibited the FCC from excessive tampering and involvement with program content of broadcasters. Nevertheless, Congress or a very important part of it had spoken, and Wiley decided the FCC must respond.

Ultimately, the response the FCC decided on was a jawboning approach suggested by the FCC staff. The Commission members would make it clear to licensees that the FCC was becoming convinced that too much sex and violence in programming was not in "the public interest," the crucial criteria for license renewal. On October 10, 1974, Chairman Wiley addressed the Illinois Broadcasters Association. The speech centered on the question of violence and obscenity on television, reminded broadcasters of their responsibilities as licensees, and urged them to undertake self-regulation in this area. On November 7, 1974, Wiley met with the vice presidents of CBS, NBC, and ABC to encourage the networks to draw up their own policies on sex and violence.

He suggested that the policies should include not only warnings to the viewing audience concerning objectionable program content but also that programs containing such content should be scheduled for later in the evenings.

Throughout November and December, 1974, Wiley and FCC staffers held several meetings with network executives. Throughout the meetings, Wiley adopted a consistent approach:

> He did not want to "threaten" anyone. . . . But if the networks were to be so unwise as not to act, the Commission (probably but not necessarily with his support) would be forced by the circumstances . . . to take action. . . . The bottom line, however, remained the same, in substance if not in tone—"Do something to curb the 'offensive' material or we, the FCC, will be forced to take action."[58]

In early January 1975, the National Association of Broadcasters (NAB) entered the picture, primarily at the urging of CBS, to consider whether the NAB code should be modified. Informal pressure from the FCC continued and several more meetings with network executives were held. Similar pressure was exerted on the NAB to do something before the FCC was compelled to take formal action. Finally, in April 1975, the NAB did something. It adopted an amendment to the NAB Code for Television Broadcasters:

> Entertainment programming inappropriate for viewing by a general family audience should not be broadcast during the first hour of network entertainment programming in prime time and in the immediately preceding hour.[59]

The "Family Hour" was born.

Depending on one's perspective, FCC behavior in this case amply illustrates informal action at either its best or worst. To television producers like Norman Lear, whose "All in the Family" was bumped from its original time slot to a later hour, and Larry Gelbart, producer of "M*A*S*H," and to writers of program scripts who felt compelled to censor their programs, the FCC's behavior was abominable and illegal. The Federal District Court, Central District of California, agreed with them. In addition to finding the FCC's action incompatible with the First Amendment, the district court held that FCC actions reflected "a total disregard of the procedural protections afforded by the APA. Without providing public notice and without affording any opportunity for interested parties to be heard, the Commission, acting through its chairman, negotiated to form a new policy for television."[60]

On the other hand, supporters of the FCC and Family Hour would point out that with minimal government expenditure, involvement, and time, a worthwhile and essential policy change occurred. For better or worse, the District Court decision was reversed by the Court of Appeals.[61] Most assuredly, the case illustrates the integral relationship between formal and informal actions. Informal pressure was successful because it was backed by the possibility, even if in this instance it was remote, of formal action being taken through either rule making or licensing. The availability of informal methods, however, spared the FCC from initiating what would have been a lengthy, involved, and extremely controversial formal process.

INFORMAL ADMINISTRATIVE ACTIONS IN THE ADMINISTRATIVE PROCESS

Informal action encompasses the vast majority of administrative actions: everything that administrative agencies and administrators do except adjudication and legislative rule making is informal. Obviously, the above examples constitute only a minute sampling of the universe of informal action, but they do serve to illustrate their importance and advantages to the public, the regulatees, and the agency. Without informal action, the regulatory process would be impossible, the formal processes so overburdened and lacking in credibility that they would be ineffective.

Most informal actions share certain characteristics. They are marked by a seeming absence of compulsion; either the regulatee or client initiates the contact with the agency "voluntarily" (requesting advice, applying for benefits, seeking a negotiated settlement) or the agency's action does not compel the regulatee to take or refrain from taking any action (publicity, policy statements). Additionally, the regulatee may reject or ignore the advice given or the settlement offered. At the same time, however, informal actions are always backed and made effective by the possibility of formal action: charges being filed, subpoenas being issued, advice and policy statements being made into rules and regulations. Informal actions are also marked by the absence of a formal record and are usually taken on an individual, case-by-case basis, which means that they may be lacking in uniformity. Finally, they are not covered by the Federal Administrative Procedure Act.

Their advantages over the formal processes from the regulatee/client's perspectives are many. Informal processes are faster, less cumbersome, and more flexible than formal actions. Many informal actions are preventive in nature. Advice may be given immediately, saving the individual uncertainty, anguish, and time, and if favorable, allowing the individual to proceed on a proposed course of action without delay. If the advice given warns against taking a proposed course of action, the individual may have avoided irreparable harm or at least a costly and damaging formal action. Both the speed and flexibility of informal actions make them less expensive for the affected individual. It is usually not necessary to hire an attorney in informal administrative actions, but even if it is, the time and expense will be considerably less than in a formal action. For lower-income persons, or individuals or businesses not used to dealing with government agencies, informal procedures are considerably less intimidating than adjudicatory hearings. Because informal processes are not limited by strict procedural requirements, they are flexible and may be modified on an individual basis to respond to the needs of clients. Their lack of uniformity permits individualized decisions that may be more equitable and fairer than general rules which cannot take into account differences in situations and circumstances of individuals and businesses.

From the agencies' perspective informal actions are equally beneficial and even more essential than from the perspective of affected individuals. In many respects their advantages to the agencies are the same as to individuals. They are less expensive; they allow agencies to respond quickly to potentially dangerous problems; they allow agencies to experiment with different types of procedures and action in order to improve fairness, efficiency, and accuracy. Even more importantly, informal procedures allow chronically understaffed, underfunded, and overloaded administrative agencies to perform what would otherwise be impossible tasks. Rules could not be formulated to cover every minute situation in an agency's jurisdiction; hearings could not be held on every application and formal charges could not be filed and administratively prosecuted against every infraction of the laws or rules. The existence of the informal processes makes the formal processes more effective by limiting their use to only major or recurring problems, identifying problems requiring general action, and providing information essential to their performance. In new regulatory areas, reliance on informal action is especially necessary since the agency will not have had time to formulate rules or standards.

The public also benefits from the informal administrative actions. Summary seizure of contaminated food or hazardous products allows immediate protection of public health and safety. The use of publicity by an agency provides the public with essential information that may prevent injury, death, economic loss, or unfair treatment by businesses or employers. Problems that directly affect the public may be solved in an expeditious and inexpensive manner through the use of informal actions. The existence of informal processes helps make agencies more accessible and responsive to the public and the flexibility of those processes frequently makes them more comprehensible to the average person than the arcane and complex formal procedures.

INFORMAL ACTION: DISADVANTAGES AND PROBLEMS

Unfortunately, informal actions are characterized by as many disadvantages as advantages. In an administrative and judicial system which tends to equate justice with procedure, one of the most alarming aspects of informal actions is the lack of procedural safeguards surrounding their use. As has been mentioned frequently the Administrative Procedure Act scarcely mentions and is not applicable to most informal actions. Section 553 explicitly exempts policy statements from the general requirements for agency rule making. Section 554(c) does require agencies to give respondents in complaint cases an opportunity to negotiate a settlement, but is silent on the procedures to be used and creates no obligation for the agency to accept offers of settlement. Section 555(e) has emerged as the most important and relevant provision of the APA as far as informal actions are concerned. Its requirement that "a brief statement of the grounds for denial" of applications be given has through court interpretations compelled administrators to provide reasons and justifications for certain categories of informal action or inaction.

The silence of the APA has left most informal actions unrestricted by uniform procedural guidelines. Constitutional due process requirements for informal action remain unclear and in some instances nonexistent. In giving or not giving advice, in using publicity as an informal sanction, in negotiations, in the application process, due process depends almost entirely on the inclination of the individual agency, and while some agencies have established procedural guidelines for their employees in these situations, most have not. Nor do most authorizing statutes establish procedural requirements for informal actions. The result is that due process offers considerably less protection to individuals and businesses in informal processes than in the formal ones.

This lack of uniform, legislated procedural safeguards is compounded by the lack of availability of judicial review for most informal actions. Many informal actions are considered to be "committed to agency discretion" (§5 U.S.C.A. 701(a)(2)), and consequently are exempt from review. The refusal of an agency to give advice or accept an offer of settlement, for example, are not judicially challengeable. Since many other types of informal action do not constitute final agency action they also are not judicially challengeable. Damaging publicity may appear to be final agency action, but as the *Cinderella* case indicated, the courts do not offer much protection in this area either. Compounding this problem, many informal actions are also exempt under the Federal Tort Claims Act, and even if the action is wrongful and inflicts harm, an injured party may not recover damages. This is most particularly true in the case of government publicity. Even if Cinderella Finishing School were found not to have engaged in deceptive advertising, it could not have recovered·its monetary losses from the Federal Trade Commission, nor could Sterling Cooperative, Bon Vivant, or Proctor and Gamble recover their losses from the Food and Drug Administration. The discretionary nature of other types of informal actions also exempts them from tort claims coverage. Although recently the federal courts have indicated a willingness to review certain limited informal actions, for the most part these actions continue to be conducted beyond the scrutiny of the judicial branch of government. In general, the more informal the action, the less likely the courts will review it; the more final the action, the more likely the courts will review it.

The lack of scrutiny of many of these actions is not limited to the courts. Because of their pervasiveness and their low visibility (invisibility in some instances), informal actions may not even be subject to review by higher levels of the agency involved. Unquestionably, many lower-level administrative personnel give advice that may or may not be accurate, but it will never be appealed within the agency and supervisory personnel will never realize it has been given. In some instances, applications will be denied wrongfully but in an overworked welfare agency no one will ever be aware of what occurred. Similarly, within the Internal Revenue Service, district offices all over the United States interpret the tax code for citizens and in the vast majority of instances whether the advice is accurate or inaccurate, it will not be checked by anyone in the higher levels of the agency.

Informal actions are rarely subject to review by Congress and the President. Because of their flexibility, nonuniformity, and low visibility, only rarely will informal actions come to the attention of the President. Ironically, however, informal administrative actions constitute one of the major burdens for individual members of Congress. A large portion of the casework which occupies a vast amount of the time and effort of the staffs of members of Congress consists of requests from individual constituents for legislative intervention with administrative agencies, primarily in informal actions. Applications that have been denied, lost, or misplaced, advice that has been given but not accepted, benefits that have been reduced or terminated constitute a large portion of the complaints for which individuals seek congressional assistance. It is equally ironic that in handling these problems on an individual basis, members of Congress compound the inequity and lack of uniformity that characterizes informal actions. Just as overreliance on individualized, nonstandardized informal actions impedes the development of uniform, general standards in the administrative process, individualized congressional responses delay the development of general, uniform legislative standards to guide the agencies.

The low visibility of informal processes creates additional problems. In some instances low visibility becomes secrecy. As pointed out earlier, negotiations are normally conducted in secret, foreclosing participation by public intervenors, and are beyond the purview of press, public, and politicians. But even where secrecy in the decision process is not involved, many informal actions are not subject to public disclosure under the Freedom of Information Act. Policy statements, advisory opinions, and "interpretations which have been adopted by the agency," in contrast, are covered by the Freedom of Information Act.

Increasingly, both agencies and the federal courts have moved to make written, informal opinions subject to public inspection. Internal Revenue issues over 32,000 private letter rulings a year. IRS's initial reaction was that such rulings were not covered by the FOIA. In 1974, however, the Court of Appeals held that IRS must make such rulings available for public inspection.[62] Subsequently, IRS has digested approximately 750 of what it considers to be the most significant of these and publishes them annually in its *Cumulative Bulletin*.[63] Similarly the SEC has made public its no-action and other advisory letters.

What remains exempt from disclosure is oral advice given by an agency and inter- and intragency memoranda or letters "which would not be available by law to a party . . . in litigation with the agency."[64] This exemption has proven to be particularly difficult to interpret. As the final Senate Report on the FOIA explained this exemption, and the Supreme Court agreed, the purpose of the exemption was to protect

> the decisionmaking processes of government agencies. . . . The frank discussion of legal or policy matters in writing might be inhibited if the discussion were made public and that the "decisions" and "policies formulated" would be the poorer as a result. . . . As we have said in another context, "human experience teaches that those who expect public dissemination of their remarks may well temper candor with a concern for appearances . . ." (*U.S. v. Nixon* 418 U.S. 683, 1974). The lower courts have uniformly drawn a distinction between predecisional communications which are privileged and communications made after the decision and designed to explain it.[65]

In the preceding case the Court held that memoranda from the NLRB General Counsel concluding that no complaint should be filed were subject to disclosure (final action) but those directing the filing were not (did not constitute final agency action). Subsequent court decisions have not clarified what information, particularly relating to informal action, is exempt from disclosure. For example, in 1977, the Washington, D.C., Court of Appeals held that "predecisional matters are not exempt merely because they are predecisional; they must also be part of the deliberative process within a government agency."[66]

One of the biggest problems concerning administrative advice is its accuracy and reliability. Obviously, if advice is accurate, there is no problem with its reliability. Where problems develop is when an employee of an agency gives advice, an individual relies on it, and subsequently the advice proves to have been erroneous. IRS has perhaps the worst reputation of any federal agency for providing inaccurate advice. "IRS Told You What? Uh, that might be right, but . . ." as one newspaper article expressed it. The article was based on an experiment run by the *Washington Post* which had asked 110 questions of various IRS offices throughout the country. Thirty-seven of the answers given to the *Post* were wrong. "It disturbs me . . . but does not surprise me that we give wrong answers. . . . [This is] the result of human failing and very complex tax laws," was the explanation offered by Stanley Goldberg, director, IRS Taxpayer Service Division.[67] As far as the government is concerned, however, good faith reliance on erroneous IRS advice does not relieve a taxpayer of tax liability if at some future date the error is discovered, and quite frequently, the individual may be charged interest on tax owed as a result of the error. IRS's official position that it may deviate from advice given in private rulings if they are erroneous has been upheld by the courts.[68] Further, its *Cumulative Bulletin* states clearly that "private rulings will not be relied on, used or cited as precedents by service personnel."[69] Although IRS insists that it has discretion to change a ruling to a taxpayer's detriment, in reality, it only does so "in rare and unusual circumstances."[70]

Most federal agencies will stand by erroneous advice that has been relied on by individuals. Asimow found that although most agencies have no written policies on reliability, it was considered "almost unthinkable that anyone who relied in good faith on staff advice would suffer any detriment."[71] The advisory rulings of several agencies have been made binding by statute. For example, rulings by the Wage and Hour Administration and the General Counsel of the EEOC are statutorily binding.[72] Other agencies, however, will not stand by erroneous advice given by employees, and at that point the affected individual may take his case to court. The federal courts, however, have been reluctant to apply the doctrine of equitable estoppel to government agencies. Estoppel is a legal doctrine which prevents a party from asserting a claim inconsistent with a previous position which has been relied on by another party and that party will suffer damage from the new position. In 1917, the Supreme Court held that the federal government could not be estopped by acts of its employees:

> It is enough to say that the United States is neither bound nor estopped by acts of
> its officers or agents in entering into an arrangement . . . to do . . . what the law
> does not sanction or permit.[73]

This view was reiterated in 1947 in one of the lead cases on estoppel of government agencies, *Federal Crop Insurance Corp. v. Merrill.*[74] The Merrill brothers had applied for federal crop insurance making full disclosure that the crop had been reseeded. Although published regulations of the FCIC barred reseeded crops from being insured, the county committee accepted the Merrill brothers' application and premium. When their crop was wiped out by drought, the Merrills tried to collect on the insurance. Upon ascertaining that the crop was reseeded the FCIC refused to pay. The Merrills sued, alleging that the action of the authorized agent of the FCIC estopped the government from refusing to pay the premium. The Supreme Court disagreed:

> The case no doubt presents phases of hardship. . . . But . . . anyone entering into
> an arrangement with the Government takes the risk of having ascertained that he

who purports to act for the government stays within the bounds of his authority.
. . . Men must turn square corners when they deal with government.[75]

In 1951, however, without using the language of estoppel, the Supreme Court held that assurances from the State Department and the Swiss Legation that a Swiss alien would not be debarred from U.S. citizenship for refusing to serve in the army, despite an explicit law to the contrary, prevented the Immigration and Naturalization Service from barring him from citizenship.[76] In 1957, the Court held that "equitable estoppel is not a bar to the correction by the Commissioner [of Internal Revenue] of a mistake of law."[77] On the other hand, in 1973, the Court held that a company that had relied on regulations and long-standing interpretations of the Corps of Engineers, although contrary to the Rivers and Harbors Act of 1913, could not be prosecuted for violating the act: "Thus, to the extent that the regulations deprived PICCO of fair warning as to what conduct the Government intended to make criminal, we think that there can be no doubt that traditional notions of fairness in our system of criminal justice prevent the Government from proceeding with the prosecution."[78]

The lower federal courts have used what some commentators have perceived as a "balancing approach," which measures "the harm suffered by a private party against the damage to the public interest by allowing estoppel."[79] The balance seems to tilt more to the private party in cases involving government property dealings[80] and toward the government in other types of cases. For example, a widow who had been told by a Social Security Administration employee that she would not lose her benefits if she remarried before age 60 relied on this advice and remarried two months before her 60th birthday. She was then notified by the Social Security Administration that her benefits were terminated pursuant to specific terms of the Social Security Act. Her argument that the government was estopped by the employee's advice was rejected by a Court of Appeals:

> estoppel cannot be set up against the Government on the basis of an authorized representation or act of an officer or employee who is without authority in his individual capacity to bind the government. . . . The government could scarcely function if it were bound by its employees' unauthorized representations.[81]

In addition to their occasional inaccuracy and lack of reliability, informal actions may also lead to inconsistency and inequity in administrative treatment. The advice that a taxpayer receives from IRS depends on which agent in which office gives that advice. For example, in response to the question, "Last year, I bought a $100 calculator which I use at work. Can I deduct that as a business expense?" two IRS officers said "no," seven said "yes," but suggested deductions ranging from $20 to $100.[82] Informal action magnifies administrative discretion and all of the problems associated with unguided discretion, ultimately fostering arbitrariness and lack of accountability.

An individual contemplating requesting advice from an administrative agency should consider one additional factor. If the agency's advice is sought, its attention has been directed to a matter that otherwise might have escaped its notice. If the advice given is supportive of the contemplated action, nothing has been lost or gained. If the agency advises against the action, however, the possibility of being able to proceed with it and escape agency attention has been sharply diminished.

The speed which characterizes informal action and constitutes one of its major advantages may also lead to hasty decisions based on insufficient information. In some instances informal action has taken the form of "shooting first and asking questions later." Advice may be given without carefully checking the law or agency regulations, publicity disseminated as soon as charges are filed, and products seized without first ascertaining whether they are in fact dangerous. In many informal actions no record is developed on which decisions are based. At this time, the exact relationship between Rely tampons and TSS has still not been ascertained and although Rely has been removed from the market, its "guilt" has never been proven.

Finally, agencies may find it more expedient to rely on informal processes than to formulate general and uniform standards. The result may be a neglect of the formal processes and a failure to develop consistent regulations and equitable standards.

RECOMMENDATIONS FOR IMPROVING AND CONTROLLING INFORMAL ACTIONS: A CRITIQUE

Informal actions will always be an essential and beneficial part of the administrative regulatory process, and while improvements are needed great caution should be exercised not to destroy the very real advantages that they offer. Any reforms of these actions should be directed at preserving their advantages and minimizing their disadvantages. It should also be recognized that lawyers are likely to suggest reforms that administrators may not find palatable.

One of the most commonly suggested reforms is that agencies should be compelled to state findings and reasons for most informal actions.[83] Since the federal courts appear to be moving in the direction of requiring this for many administrative decisions, administrative agencies that currently do not provide such reasons would be well advised to initiate the practice. Although specifying reasons may increase administrative workloads and might inhibit some agencies from using informal actions, if reasons are ultimately going to be required by the courts, specifying them initially may actually save time. This reform is closely tied to suggestions that most informal actions should be made subject to judicial review. Besides further enriching the legal profession this might compel administrators to be more consistent, fair, and accurate in their informal decisions. It might also deter them from relying on informal processes and add to the cost, complexity, and time of the administrative process.

Gellhorn has suggested several controls on agency use of publicity. He suggests that agencies should establish clear procedures on when, how, and by whom adverse publicity should be released. Additionally, he recommends that the Federal Tort Claims Act be amended to allow suits for damages resulting from erroneous agency publicity. His final recommendation, that respondents be given the option of discontinuing an allegedly harmful action in lieu of prehearing publicity,[84] is not as acceptable from the perspective of the public interest as the first two. For example, in the case of false and misleading advertising the public should have the right to be informed that past claims made by a company may be false even though the company no longer makes those claims. Any restrictions on agency public information activities should be evaluated in terms of its impact on the public's right to know. Censorship of agency speech and press is no more advisable than censorship of private speech and press.

Many recommendations have been suggested to improve agency advice-giving processes. One of the most interesting is Asimow's suggestion that agencies should charge fees for written advice.[85] If it is true that one gets what one pays for, charging for agency advice might improve its quality and reliability and in all probability would decrease the number of requests for such advice, thus decreasing agency workload. Certainly in the private sector advice from professionals is seldom, if ever, free. Serious theoretical and practical problems do exist with this suggestion. Considerations of equity and fairness should be carefully weighed before any such suggestion is adopted and the ultimate net social benefits of this proposal are uncertain. Deterring businesses and individuals from seeking informal advice might result in increasing the formal workloads of agencies and in increasing citizen and business hostility toward government agencies and activities.

More consistency, uniformity and openness in agency advice-giving is desirable. Procedures specifying who gives advice and how to obtain it should be established. Similarly, advice given to one individual or business should be made available for all others and for general public inspection. This would do more to improve the accuracy and reliability of advice than almost any other suggested change. It would ensure that higher levels of an agency could check the accuracy of advice given at lower levels and that political executives and Congress, if they wished, could also check and control these activities.

Applying the doctrine of estoppel to government agencies is a tempting idea that should be rejected. Although on an individual case-by-case basis this seems only fair, from the broader perspective of the need for political control and dominance of the administrative process, it is unwise. Lower- and higher-level administrative officials should not be given authority to commit the government to policies that contravene those adopted by Congress. Government is not just another litigant in the judicial process. Ultimately, it is better for the health of the political system that some individuals suffer because of erroneous administrative advice than to establish a system whereby administrators through ignorance or duplicity can countermand the laws. As Thompson points out, applying estoppel to governmental actions might promote fraud and collusion, cause losses to the public treasury, and negatively affect administrative efficiency and flexibility.[86]

Finally, many commentators have suggested that an ombudsman or ombudsmen be established to investigate, oversee, and handle complaints from citizens about administrative agencies. Sweden has had an ombudsman since 1809; Denmark has had one since 1955. As of 1979, 20 countries in the world, 18 states in this country, various American cities, the U.S. Department of Commerce, and the Internal Revenue Service had created ombudsman offices.[87] Other than the normal concerns about creating Super Bureaucrat, suggestions for establishing ombudsman offices raise questions about the size, expense, and administrative location of such offices. At the national level in the U.S. such suggestions have also raised little enthusiasm from members of Congress who perceive such offices as undermining the necessity of their constituency casework and ultimately their chances for reelection.

Regardless of criticisms, praises, or suggestions for reform, informal actions still constitute the bulk of the administrative process and in all probability will continue to do so. For the vast majority of Americans, individuals, and businesses, these informal actions and decisions are the most important aspect of the regulatory process. And despite the criticisms, informal action remains the most flexible, expeditious, inexpensive, and accessible aspect of the regulatory process.

NOTES

1. Charles Seabrook, "The Toxic Shock Syndrome Story," *Seattle Post-Intelligencer*, October 12, 1981, p. A18.

2. Michael King and Mark Nodosh, "Proctor and Gamble Tampon is Withdrawn from Stores," *Wall Street Journal*, September 23, 1981, p. 2.

3. "Maker Agrees to Advertise Warning on Rely Tampons," *Spokane Spokesman-Review*, September 28, 1980, p. 2.

4. Nancy Yoshihara and Pamela Moreland, "A Successful Product Meets a Baffling Disease," *Spokane Spokesman-Review*, October 2, 1980, p. 2.

5. "FDA Wants Warning Labels on All Boxes of Tampons," *Spokesman-Review*, October 1, 1980, p. B14.

6. "The Way Tampons Are Made Won't Be Changed," *Seattle Post-Intelligencer*, October 12, 1980, A18.

7. Philip Babcock Gone, ed., *Webster's Third New International Dictionary of the English Language, Unabridged* (Springfield, Mass.: G. & C. Merriam Co., 1976).

8. Kenneth Davis, *Administrative Law: Cases-Text-Problems* (St. Paul, Minn.: West Publishing Co., 1977), p. 441.

9. Warner Gardner, "The Procedures by Which Informal Actions Are Taken," 24 *Administrative Law Review*, 155 (1972).

10. *New Yorker*, April 23, 1979.

11. *Dow Chemical v. Blum*, 469 F. Supp. 892 (D.D.C. 1979).

12. James O. Freedman, *Crisis and Legitimacy: The Administrative Process and American Government* (Cambridge: Cambridge University Press, 1978), p. 207.

13. *Securities Exchange Commission v. Sloan*, 436 U.S. 112 (1978).

14. 321 U.S. 502, 521 (1944).

15. *Phillips v. Commissioner of Internal Revenue Service*, 283 U.S. 589 (1931).

16. *Arnett v. Kennedy*, 416 U.S. 134 (1974).

17. *Ewing v. Mytinger and Casselberry, Inc.*, 339 U.S. 594 (1950).

18. Freedman, *Crisis and Legitimacy*, p. 235.

19. Ernest Gellhorn, "Adverse Publicity by Administrative Agencies," 86 *Harvard Law Review*, 1383 (1973).

20. Davis, *Administrative Law*, p. 441.

21. "Pumpkins: Food and Drug Administration Makes a Blunder in the Pie Caper," *The Daily Idahonian* (Moscow, Idaho), November 27, 1979, p. 11.

22. Gellhorn, "Adverse Publicity by Administrative Agencies," p. 1408.

23. Ibid., p. 1383.

24. *Federal Trade Commission v. Cinderella Career and Finishing Schools, Inc.*, 404 F2d 1308 (D.C. Cir. 1968).

25. Michael Asimow, *Advice to the Public from Federal Administrative Agencies* (New York: Mathew Bender, 1973), p. v.

26. Robert Kagan, *Regulatory Justice* (New York: Russell Sage Foundation, 1978), p. 28.

27. Ibid., p. 3.

28. Jeremy Wiesen, *Regulating Transactions in Securities* (St. Paul, Minn.: West Publishing Co. 1975), p. 48.

29. Davis, *Administrative Law*, p. 515.

30. Asimow, *Advice to the Public from Federal Administrative Agencies*, p. 23.

31. *Medical Committee for Human Rights v. SEC*, 439 F2d 659 (D.C. Cir. 1970).

32. See Barry Cole and Mae Oettinger, *Reluctant Regulators: The FCC and the Broadcast Audiences* (Reading, Mass.: Addison-Wesley, 1978).

33. *Office of Communications, United Church of Christ v. FCC*, 358 F2d 994 (D.C. Cir. 1966).

34. *Friends of the Earth v. FCC*, 449 F2d 1164 (D.C. Cir. 1971).

35. *Handling of Public Issues*, 48 FCC 2d 26 (1974).

36. *Citizens Committee to Save WEFM v. FCC*, 506 F2d 246 (D.C. Cir. 1974).

37. 60 FCC 2d, 858 (1976).

38. *WNCN Listeners' Guild v. FCC*, 610 F2d 838 (D.C. Cir. 1979).

39. *FCC v. WNCN Listeners' Guild*, 455 US 914 (1981).

40. Wiesen, *Regulating Transactions in Securities*, p. 28.

41. Arthur Snow and Burton Weisbrod, "Consumerism, Consumers, and Public Interest Law," in Burton A. Weisbrod, Joel Handler, and Neil Komesar, eds., *Public Interest Law* (Berkeley: University of California Press, 1978), p. 419.

42. *New York Times*, July 4, 1980, section 4, p. 2.

43. Snow and Weisbrod, "Consumerism, Consumers, and the Public Interest," p. 420.

44. Joel Handler, with George Edgar and Russell Settle, "Public Interest Law and Employment Discrimination," in Weisbrod, *Public Interest Law*, p. 267.

45. Ibid.

46. Ibid.

47. *Newsweek*, September 8, 1980, p. 15.

48. Snow and Weisbrod, "Consumerism, Consumers, and the Public Interest," p. 420.

49. Molly Sinclair, "Imitation Products Provoke Debate," *Spokesman-Review*, October 22, 1980, p. B2.

50. Paul Quirk, "The Food and Drug Administration," in James Q. Wilson, *The Politics of Regulation* (New York: Basic Books, 1980), p. 208.

51. Ibid., p. 226.

52. Jerry Mashaw, Charles Goetz, Frank Goodman, Warren Schwartz, and Paul Vierkiel, *Social Security Hearings and Appeals* (Lexington, Mass.: D.C. Heath, 1978), p. 3.

53. Ibid., p. xxi.

54. 5 U.S.C. §555(e).

55. P. R. Verkuil, "A Study of Informal Adjudication Procedures," 43 *University of Chicago Law Review*, 739 (1976).

56. Walter Gellhorn, Clark Byse, and Peter L. Strauss, *Administrative Law: Cases and Comments*, 7th ed. (Mineola, N.Y.: Foundation Press, 1979), p. 367.

57. *Writers Guild of America, West, Inc. v. FCC*, 423 F. Supp. 1064 (C.D. Cal. 1976).

58. *Writers Guild v. FCC*, 423 F. Supp. 1064, 1074 (C.D. Cal. 1976).

59. *Writers Guild v. FCC*, 423 F. Supp. 1064, 1981 (C.D. Cal. 1976).

60. *Writers Guild v. FCC*, 423 F. Supp. 1064, 1983 (C.D. Cal. 1976).

61. *FCC v. Writers Guild*, 609 F2d 355 (9th Cir. 1979).

62. *Tax Analysts and Advocates v. IRS*, 505 F2d 350 (D.C. Cir. 1974).

63. Asimow, *Advice to the Public from Federal Administrative Agencies*, p. 88.

64. Exemption 5, Freedom of Information Act. 5 USC §552(b)(5).

65. *NLRB v. Sears, Roebuck*, 421 U.S. 132, 157 (1975).

66. *Mead Data Control, Inc. v. U.S. Department of Air Force*, 562 F2d 242 (D.C. Cir, 1977).

67. *Spokesman-Review*, March 20, 1980, p. 38.

68. *Tax Analysts and Advocates v. IRS*, 505 F2d 350 (D.C. Cir. 1975).

69. Davis, *Administrative Law*, p. 25.

70. Asimow, *Advice to the Public from Federal Administrative Agencies*, p. 162.

71. Ibid., p. 7.

72. Ibid., p. 30.

73. *Utah Power and Light Company v. U.S.*, 243 U.S. 389 (1917).

74. 332 U.S. 380 (1947).

75. 332 U.S. 380, 383 (1947).

76. *Moser v. United States*, 341 U.S. 41 (1951).

77. *Automobile Club of Michigan v. Commissioner*, 353 U.S. 180 (1957).

78. *United States v. Pennsylavania Chemical Corporation*, 411 U.S. 655 (1973), p. 674.

79. David Thompson, "Equitable Estoppel of the Government," 79 *Columbia Law Review*, 551 (1979).

80. *U.S. v. Georgia Pacific Co.*, 421 F2d 92 (9th Cir. 1970); *U.S. v. Lazy FC Ranch*, 481 F2d 985 (9th Cir. 1973).

81. *Goldberg v. Weinberger*, 546 F2d 477, (2d Cir. 1976); cert. denied, 431 U.S. 937 (1977).

82. *Spokesman-Review*, March 20, 1980, p. 38.

83. Davis, *Administrative Law*, p. 455; Freedman, *Crisis and Legitimacy*, p. 245.

84. Ernest Gellhorn, *Administrative Law and Process in a Nutshell* (St. Paul, Minn.: West Publishing Co., 1972), p. 112.

85. Asimow, *Advice to the Public*, p. 127.

86. Thompson, "Equitable Estoppel of the Government," p. 554.

87. Donald D. Barry and Howard R. Whitcomb, *The Legal Foundations of Public Administration* (St. Paul, Minn.: West Publishing Co., 1981), p. 261.

Chapter 9

Rules and Rule Making

As the FDA's response to Toxic Shock Syndrome and tampon usage illustrates, administrative processes are closely interrelated and blend together; investigation may result in an agency taking a variety of informal actions. These informal actions may in turn lead to an agency decision to promulgate rules and those rules may form the basis for an adjudicatory action. As the TSS case also illustrates, the rule-making process is not necessarily a speedy one. The FDA first published the notice for proposed regulation of tampon labeling on October 21, 1980. The original notice allowed 30 days for public comment. On January 12, 1981, the FDA announced that it was reopening the comment period for additional public input because circumstances directly relevant to the proposed rule had changed, requiring more time and information to evaluate those changes. The incidence of TSS had begun to decline and manufacturers had raised valid questions on the statistical relationship between TSS and specific brands of tampons. Even the extended comment period proved to be insufficient and once again on April 28, 1981, the FDA reopened the comment period on the proposed regulation.

DEFINITIONAL PROBLEMS: A RULE IS A RULE IS A RULE UNLESS IT'S AN ORDER OR A RULING OR . . .

Rule making has been called "the distinctive administrative process"[1] and "one of the greatest inventions of modern government."[2] Unfortunately for those who prefer definitional and linguistic precision, however, there is no agreed upon definition of what a "rule" is, and in many instances a rule by any other name may still be a rule. Just as there is "no bright line between rulemaking and adjudication,"[3] there is no bright line between informal policy statements and rules. Agencies maintain their own distinctive terminologies: The Treasury Department calls its rules "decisions"; other agencies call rules "orders"; still others, such as the Civil Aeronautics Board, call rules "policy statement" regulations. "Standards," "guidelines," "opinions," "final reports," and "orders" may in fact be rules depending on the agency that issues them. Further complicating the situation there are different types of rules, each of which has different legal impact and which are promulgated through different types of processes. There are interpretive rules, procedural rules, and substantive rules. Substantive rules may be formulated through the informal rule-making process (§553 of the Administrative Procedure Act), the formal rule-making process (rule making "on the record," following procedures outlined in §§556 and 557 of the APA), or by a "hybrid process" specified in an agency's authorizing legislation. Interpretive and procedural rules may also be formulated pursuant to the APA, although they are not required to be, or through some other process of the agency's own devising.

The Administrative Procedure Act defines a "rule" as "the whole or part of an agency statement of general or particular applicability and future effect designed to implement, interpret or prescribe law or policy or describing the organization, procedure or practice requirements of an agency."[4] As the definition indicates, rules are not clearly distinguishable from other types of administrative activity. Similar to adjudicatory orders, some rules may be of very limited (particular) applicability, and similar to informal policy statements, they may be primarily concerned with "interpreting" the law.

The general characteristics which distinguish rules from other types of agency action are their future orientation, the process by which they are formulated, the agency's perception of the nature of the action, and the reviewing courts' perception of that action. Although the facts on which a rule is based may result from past or present behavior or situations (as adjudicatory decisions also do), a rule is concerned with prescribing future conduct and not with judging the legality of past behavior. The proposed FDA tampon labeling regulation clearly illustrates the future orientation of rules: Its concern is with establishing a required standard of behavior for manufacturers that will be applicable only after the rule has been finally published. Further, for an action to be properly classified as a rule, it must have been properly formulated through a statutorily defined rule-making process, and the agency must generally recognize the outcome as a "rule" binding on itself and affected parties. Finally, for the action to be classified as a legitimate rule, reviewing courts must accept it as such. Any administrative action which possesses all, most, or some of the above characteristics is a "rule," regardless of how it is labeled. The remainder of this chapter will further clarify the meaning of "rules" and the nature of the rule-making process.

Rule Making vs. Adjudication

Rule making is that part of the administrative process which most resembles the legislative process, while adjudication most resembles the judicial process. As such, rule making is a flexible process which allows maximal public input and participation and is normally concerned with establishing future standards for required conduct that are of general applicability. Because of these characteristics administrative rule making has the same advantages as a policy-making device over adjudication that legislation has over judicial decisions. Informal rule making, in particular, is quicker, less expensive, fairer, and more democratic than adjudication.[5] It is proactive and may be initiated by the agency before harm or injury has occurred to individuals or the general public. Rules may be stated in general terms, based on general facts, and made generally, rather than specifically, applicable. Rules are the essence of due process since they make known in advance of prosecution the standards of behavior that are expected of affected parties. Particularly in situations where legislative standards are vague, meaningless, or absent, rules are an excellent means of structuring administrative discretion and ensuring equal treatment under the law. Rule making also tends to facilitate congressional guidance and input into the administrative process since members of Congress and congressional committees are allowed to intervene freely in the rulemaking process where such intervention in an adjudication would be considered impermissible.[6]

Closer scrutiny of the two processes, however, tends to diminish their differences. Although notice of proposed rule making, unlike adjudications, must be published in the Federal Register, and this in theory makes rule making more public than adjudication, as Robinson points out, the visibility of that publication is not high and actual public awareness of rulemaking proceedings may be no greater than is true of adjudications.[7] Most agencies also now permit rather extensive public participation in adjudicated cases. The distinction between the future impact of rules and adjudicatory decisions is not all that clear since decisions in many adjudicatory cases are aimed primarily at prescribing future conduct. A cease and desist order, for example, imposes no immediate punishment for past behavior and results in sanctions only if it is violated subsequent to its issuance.[8] When formal rule making is considered, the procedural advantages of rule making over adjudication are substantially diminished.

Ultimately, the choice between the preferability of two forms of administrative action is reduced to a choice between making policy on an ad hoc, case-by-case basis or making policy by uniform standards of general applicability. That choice lies within the discretion of the individual administrative agency. Although individual justices have expressed displeasure with agency policy making through adjudication, the Supreme Court has consistently, if reluctantly, upheld the right of the agencies to make the choice. In *Securities and Exchange Commission v. Chenery Corp*,[9] after establishing that the SEC had both rule-making and adjudicatory authority, the Court refused to require the Commission to use rulemaking procedures to formulate new standards of conduct:

> problems may arise in a case which the agency could not reasonably foresee,
> problems which must be solved despite the absence of a relevant general rule. . . .
> And the choice between proceeding by general rule or by individual, ad hoc
> litigation is one that lies primarily in the informed discretion of the administrative
> agency.[10]

As it has done repeatedly in subsequent cases, however, the Supreme Court did point out that rule making was preferable to adjudication for establishing general standards of conduct: "The function of filling in the interstices of regulatory statutes should be performed, as much as possible, through this quasi-legislative promulgation of rules to be applied in the future."[11]

The National Labor Relations Board is a classic example of an administrative agency which has eschewed its rulemaking authority to rely on policy making through adjudication. Prior to 1969, the NLRB had never used its rulemaking authority to establish policy, choosing instead to make and change broad policy decisions on a case-by-case basis. In 1966, the Board announced the Excelsior "rule." Union representatives had objected to the certification of union election results at Excelsior Underwear, Inc., because the companies involved had refused to supply them a list of eligible employees. At the time of the election there was, of course, no NLRB rule which specified that management was required to do this. Consequently, the issue had to be resolved through adjudication. During the Excelsior hearing the NLRB invited "certain interested parties" to participate. The final Board decision in Excelsior specified that in the future such lists must be provided to the unions, but the Board refused to apply the "rule" to the companies involved in the Excelsior case.

Three years after Excelsior, the Supreme Court considered the permissibility of the NLRB's failure to promulgate rules through required APA rulemaking procedures. The case involved the Excelsior "rule" and the NLRB's application of that rule to a contested union election at the Wyman–Gordon Company. The Court made it very clear that it did not approve of the NLRB's avoidance of rule making and that rule making was preferable to adjudication as a policy formulation process:

> The rulemaking provisions of that Act [the APA], which the Board would avoid, were designed to assure fairness and mature consideration of rules of general application. . . . They may not be avoided by the process of making rules in the course of adjudicatory proceedings. . . . Apart from the fact that the device fashioned by the Board does not comply with statutory command, it obviously falls short of the substance of the requirements of the Administrative Procedure Act. The "rule" created in Excelsior was not published in the Federal Register, . . . only selected organizations were given notice. . . . Under the Administrative Procedure Act, the terms or substance of the rule would have to be stated . . . and all interested parties would have an opportunity to participate.
>
> The Board did not even apply the rule it made to the parties in the adjudicatory proceedings, the only entities that could properly be subject to the rule.[12]

Despite its disapproval of NLRB procedures, however, the Court upheld the Board's application of the Excelsior "rule" to the specific facts of the case involved in Wyman–Gordon.

With its case-by-case approach seemingly upheld, even if disapproved of, by the Supreme Court, the NLRB apparently felt little compulsion to utilize rulemaking procedures. In 1974, it was again challenged in the courts for announcing new policy in an adjudicatory case and was again upheld by the Supreme Court: "the Board is not precluded from announcing new principles in an adjudicative proceeding. . . . the choice between rule making and adjudication lies in the first instance within the Board's discretion."[13]

Although policy making by adjudication is not necessarily always inferior to policy making by rule making, the experience of the NLRB illustrates some of the negative consequences of agency failure to establish general rules. Slowness, case overload, and backlogs are an inevitable concomitant to failure to establish general rules. Since principles announced in adjudicatory cases are applicable only to the specific parties and facts of individual cases, uncertainty as to expected behavior and unfairness in treatment are likely results. The outcome of the Excelsior case is a horrible example: Although the union position was upheld, the union got no relief from the decision in the case. The consequences for employers are equally unfair: "the employer comes to the adjudicative procedure without a clear notion of precisely what actions are required or prohibited on his part and . . . [then] ignorance of the behavior expected . . . is compounded by the failure of the Board's inconsistent and confusing decisions to provide clear and instructive precedents for future cases."[14] While it may be understandable for a newly created agency in a new regulatory area to proceed cautiously on a case-by-case basis, the NLRB has had 46 years of experience in labor-management relations—surely sufficient time to acquire familiarity with its regulatory responsibilities to be able to establish general rules and regulations.

Rule Making vs. Informal Action

Just as the NLRB has avoided rule making by reliance on adjudicatory decisions, many other agencies have avoided rule making by reliance on informal actions. As was discussed in chapter 8, informal action from the agency's perspective has several advantages over rule making: It is faster, more flexible, less expensive, and easier to change than rule making. These advantages become disadvantages when viewed from the perspective of regulated interests or the public. Lack of publicity and openness and limited opportunity for participation in the decision process characterize informal action just as notice, openness, and participation characterize rule making. While the courts have reluctantly allowed agencies to substitute adjudication for rule making, they have been far less willing to allow agencies to replace rule making with reliance on informal action. Certain types of informal actions such as policy statements and interpretation are not considered by the courts to be legally binding on affected parties or on the courts.

In 1974, the Supreme Court disallowed an attempt by the Bureau of Indian Affairs (BIA) to make binding general policy informally. The BIA was authorized by the Snyder Act[15] and the Appropriations Act of 1968 to expend money to provide welfare services and assistance to American Indians. Although the BIA's Staff Manual provided that eligibility for general assistance was limited to Indians living *on* reservations, that provision had not been formulated pursuant to APA rule-making procedures, nor had it been published in the Federal Register. When the BIA sought to rely on the Staff Manual as a basis for denying benefits to a Papago Indian who lived 15 miles from the reservation, the Supreme Court refused to allow it to rely on the manual. After asserting that the BIA had both the power and the responsibility to establish eligibility standards for benefits, the Court stressed that BIA had an obligation to formulate those standards as legislative-type rules pursuant to the APA:

> The power of an administrative agency to administer a congressionally created and funded program necessarily requires the formulation of policy and the making of rules to fill any gap left, implicitly or explicitly by Congress. . . . This agency power to make rules that affect substantial individual rights and obligations carries with it the responsibility not only to remain consistent with the governing legislation, but also to employ procedures that conform to law. . . . The determination of eligibility cannot be made on an ad hoc basis by the dispenser of funds. . . .
>
> The conscious choice of the Secretary not to treat this extremely significant eligibility requirement, affecting rights of needy individuals, as a legislative type rule renders it ineffective. It is essential that the legitimate expectation of these needy Indians not be extinguished by what amounts to an unpublished ad hoc

determination of the agency that was not promulgated in accordance with its own procedures to say nothing of those of the Administrative Procedure Act.[16]

Rules and rule making are different from and, at least in the Supreme Court's opinion, superior to other forms of administrative action as methods for establishing general policy. Although the definition of a "rule" remains unclear and rule-making procedures are subject to endless variation, in the remainder of this chapter we will attempt to differentiate among categories of rules and explore the three major types of rule-making procedures.

THE MAJOR VARIETIES OF ADMINISTRATIVE RULES

Procedural Rules

All administrative agencies have inherent authority to establish rules governing their own procedures.[17] Procedural rules describe an agency's organization, its basic methods of operation, and specify procedures that it uses in various types of administrative action including rule making and adjudication. For example, procedural rules define who is allowed to intervene in adjudicatory cases, under what circumstances, and specify whether public intervenors are eligible for public funding to support their intervention. Procedural rules are exempt from the requirements of §553 of the APA: "Except when notice or hearing is required by statute, this subsection does not apply— A. to interpretative rules, general statements of policy, or rules of agency organization, procedure or practice."[18] Although agencies are allowed to devise their own procedures for adoption of such rules, most agencies consult interested parties before they write procedural rules. Once adopted, these rules must be published in the Federal Register:

> Each agency shall separately state and currently publish in the Federal Register for
> the guidance of the public—(A) descriptions of its central and field organizations, . . .
> (B) statements of the general course and method by which its functions are
> channeled and determined, including the nature and requirements of all formal
> and informal procedures available, (C) rules of procedure.[19]

Several agencies, although they were under no obligation to do so, have established procedural rules that are considerably more demanding than the APA or authorizing statutes. Once established and published, these procedural rules become binding on the agency and its decisions will normally be reversed by the court if the agency fails to comply with them.[20] "He that takes the procedural sword shall perish with it."[21] If the rules do not "confer important procedural benefits on individuals," the Supreme Court has occasionally permitted agencies to deviate from them: "it is always within the discretion of a court or an administrative agency to relax or modify its procedural rules adopted for the orderly transaction of business before it when in a given case the ends of justice require it."[22]

The Nixon Administration was wounded badly, if not fatally, by the procedural sword during the Watergate investigation. When Attorney General Elliot Richardson appointed Archibald Cox as Special Prosecutor, he also issued a regulation which specifically empowered the Special Prosecutor to conduct court proceedings and to contest claims of executive privilege if he determined it was necessary. The regulation also provided that the Special Prosecutor would not be removed from office except for "extraordinary improprieties on his part."[23] Although normally the President has unquestioned power to dismiss purely executive, political appointees, in this instance the voluntary issuance of a restrictive procedural regulation limited the dismissal power of both the President and the Attorney General. When Special Prosecutor Cox persisted in his attempts to secure the White House tapes over presidential objections, the President ordered the Attorney General (actually three Attorneys General in very quick succession) to fire him. Although there was no assertion that Cox had committed any extraordinary improprieties, Acting Attorney General Robert Bork finally complied with presidential orders and Cox was fired. When the dismissal was challenged the District of Columbia District Court held it to have been illegal on the grounds that the Attorney General "chose to limit his own authority in this regard by promulgating the Watergate Special Prosecutor regulation. . . . It is settled beyond dispute that under such circumstances an agency regulation has the force and effect of law and is binding upon the body that issues it. . . . The firing of Archibald Cox in the absence of a finding of extraordinary impropriety was in clear violation of an existing Justice Department regulation having the force of law and was therefore illegal."[24]

That same regulation played a major role in *U.S. v. Nixon*. When the new Special Prosecutor, Leon Jaworski, attempted to subpoena the White House tapes, the President sought to have the subpoena quashed arguing that what was involved was an intrabranch dispute beyond the jurisdiction of the judiciary. A unanimous Supreme Court disagreed:

> The Attorney General has delegated the authority to represent the United States in these particular matters to a Special Prosecutor. . . . The regulation gives the Special Prosecutor explicit power to contest the invocation of executive privilege in the process of seeking evidence. . . .
>
> So long as this regulation is extant it has the force of law. . . . [I]t is theoretically possible for the Attorney General to amend or revoke the regulation defining the Special Prosecutor's authority. But he has not done so. So long as this regulation remains in force the Executive Branch is bound by it.[25]

Interpretive Rules

Even if Congress does not explicitly authorize an agency to promulgate rules having the force of law, the agency still has power to interpret the laws it enforces and to issue those interpretations in the form of "guidelines," "standards," "policy statements," and interpretive rules. Although interpretive rules are exempt from §553 APA rulemaking procedures, they must be published in the Federal Register. Interpretive rules are distinguished from procedural rules primarily by their content and subject matter. Like procedural rules, interpretive rules are binding on the agency and may be formulated through whatever type of process the agency deems suitable. Frequently, agencies will "open" up the process for interpretive rule making, allowing public comment and participation.

In some instances, the only type of rules that an agency may promulgate is interpretive. For example, when Congress passed the Fair Labor Standards Act, it made a clear decision not to confer rule-making power on the Administrator. Similarly, Title VII of the Civil Rights Act conferred no rule-making authority on the Equal Employment Opportunity Commission, which might partially explain why that agency is so seriously backlogged with individual complaints and cases. In other instances it may not be clear as to whether an agency's rules are substantive or interpretive. Until 1973, the Federal Trade Commission's authority to issue substantive rules was doubtful and opponents of the Commission argued that it could issue only interpretive rules.

When the FTC attempted to establish the rule requiring a health-warning label on cigarettes, the tobacco industry's major legal argument was that the FTC had not been given substantive rule-making authority.[26] The FTC had issued no substantive rules prior to 1964 and the Federal Trade Commission Act was somewhat vague. Although it directed the FTC "to prevent" unfair methods of competition and unfair or deceptive acts, it also specified that this was to be done by issuing complaints, holding hearings, and issuing cease and desist orders.[27] It was only in a later section of the Act[28] that the Commission was given authority to make "rules" for the purpose of carrying out the provisions of this title. In 1973, the D.C. Court of Appeals overruled a District Court decision and held that the FTC did have the power to issue substantive rules.[29] Congress further clarified FTC authority in the Federal Trade Commission Improvement Act of 1975 by giving it power to issue both interpretive rules and substantive rules.

Interpretive rules are also characterized by the procedure the agency follows in promulgating them. No matter what the agency's power or authority may be, unless §553 APA procedures have been complied with in formulating a regulation, that regulation will be considered by the courts as interpretive. Similarly, if an agency wishes a rule to be classified as interpretive, it may deliberately bypass §553. In 1969, the Internal Revenue Service, which has clear statutory authority to issue substantive rules, issued a ruling without opportunity for notice and comment which allowed hospitals to qualify as charitable organizations without having to provide free or below cost care for the indigent. Although the ruling substantially modified IRS regulations and affected millions of indigent persons, a Court of Appeals held it to be "interpretive . . . and not subject to the requirements of §553 of the APA."[30]

Whether a rule is interpretive or substantive might appear to be insignificant; however, the legal impact of the two different types is significantly different. Interpretive rulings are not binding on the courts or affected parties; they are advisory in nature. In discussing the interpretations of the Fair Labor Standards Administration, the Supreme Court explained the legal status of these interpretations: "We consider that the rulings, interpretation and the opinions of the Administrator under this Act, while not controlling upon the Courts . . . do constitute a body of experience and informed judgment to which courts and litigants may properly resort for guidance."[31]

Normally the courts will give full weight to interpretive regulations which satisfy one or more of the following conditions:

1. The regulation is issued in an area where there is considerable agency expertise and equal lack of court expertise;

2. The regulation has been reenacted by the legislature;
3. The regulation was issued contemporaneously with the passage of the statute it interprets; or
4. The regulation is long standing.

The Supreme Court, however, has not always liked the "guidance" provided by interpretive regulations and when it does not it feels quite free to substitute its own interpretation for that of the agency. In 1972 the EEOC issued a "guideline" which interpreted §703(a)(1) of Title VII of the 1964 Civil Rights Act to require employers to include disabilities resulting from pregnancy. childbirth, and abortion in their health insurance plans. Justice Rehnquist, writing for the majority, rejected the EEOC's interpretation and refused to grant it legal deference:

> It should first be noted that Congress, in enacting Title VII did not confer upon the EEOC authority to promulgate rules. . . . This does not mean that EEOC guidelines are not entitled to consideration in determining legislative intent. . . . But it does mean that courts properly may accord less weight to such guidelines than to administrative regulations which Congress had declared shall have the force of law. . . . The EEOC guideline . . . is not a contemporaneous interpretation of Title VII. . . . The guideline flatly contradicts the position which the agency had enunciated at an earlier date.[32]

Interpretive rules, then, are agency statements on what they believe a law or substantive rules mean. Although these rules lack the full legal force of substantive rules, they do provide an indication of what the agency believes individuals and businesses should do to avoid prosecution, and although they are not binding on the courts, judges will normally accord them considerable deference.

Substantive Rules

Unlike procedural or interpretive rules or policy statements, substantive rules have the same legal effect as a law of Congress. Despite their importance, there is no short or clear definition of substantive rules and they are defined as much by what they are not as by what they are. The Supreme Court has on several occasions discussed the distinction between substantive rules and other forms of administrative action. One of the more recent and lengthy of such discussions is found in the opinion of *Chrysler Corporation v. Brown*. At issue were regulations of the Office of Federal Contract Compliance Programs (OFCCP) concerning disclosure of corporate equal employment opportunity records under the Freedom of Information Act. The regulations had been issued pursuant to Executive Orders 11246 and 11375 and the agency contended that they were substantive regulations having the force of law. Chrysler and the Supreme Court disagreed:

> It has been established in a variety of contexts that properly promulgated, substantive agency regulations have the "force and effect of law." This doctrine is so well established that agency regulations implementing federal statutes have been held to pre-empt state law under the Supremacy Clause. . . .
> In order for a regulation to have the "force and effect" of law it must have

certain procedural requisites. The central distinction among agency regulations found in the Administrative Procedure Act (APA) is that between "substantive rules" on the one hand and "interpretive rules, general statements of policy, or rules of agency organization, procedure or practice" on the other. A "substantive rule" is not defined in the APA and other authoritative sources essentially offer definitions by negative inference. But in *Morton v. Ruiz*, we noted a characteristic inherent in the concept of a "substantive rule." We described a substantive rule— or a "legislative-type rule,"—as one "affecting individual rights and obligations." This characteristic is an important touchstone for distinguishing those rules that may be "binding" or have the "force of law."

That an agency regulation is "substantive," however, does not give it the "force and effect of law." The legislative power of the United States is vested in Congress, and the exercise of quasi-legislative authority by governmental departments and agencies must be rooted in a grant of such power by the Congress and subject to such limitations as that body imposes. . . . Likewise the promulgation of these regulations must conform with any procedural requirements imposed by Congress. For agency discretion is not only limited by substantive, statutory grants of authority, but also by the procedural requirements which "assure fairness and mature consideration of rules of general application." The pertinent procedural limitations in this case are those found in the APA.[33]

For a rule to be considered "substantive" and have the full force of law, it must satisfy three criteria: (1) it must affect individual rights and obligations; (2) it must have been properly promulgated through statutorily specified procedures, either those in the APA or those in the authorizing statute; and (3) it must have been made pursuant to a grant of legislative authority by Congress. "This is not to say that any grant of legislative authority . . . must be specific. . . . What is important is that the reviewing court reasonably be able to conclude that the grant of authority contemplates the regulations issued."[34] In *Chrysler*, the OFCCP regulations "perished by the procedural sword." Not only had the Secretary of Labor specifically referred to the regulations as interpretive rather than substantive rules, but the OFCCP had also not complied with the APA in promulgating them.

The procedure followed in promulgating rules is a crucial determinant for classifying those rules as substantive. Three major types of procedures for formulating substantive rules have been established by Congress: the formal and informal rule-making procedures outlined in the Administrative Procedure Act and hybrid procedures found in authorizing statutes of specific agencies.

RULE-MAKING PROCEDURES

Formal Rule Making

When rules are required by statute to be made on the record after opportunity for an agency hearing, sections 556 and 557 of this title apply.[35]

Formal rule making, also known as rule making on the record, requires that an agency must hold a trial-type hearing on the proposed rule, follow all the procedural requirements for such a hearing specified in §§556 and 557 of the APA, and base the final rule on "substantial evidence in the record" of the hearing. As the APA makes clear, an agency is required to follow 556–557 procedures in rule making only if explicitly instructed to do so by an authorizing statute. Currently, 16 federal statutes mandate the use of such procedures. In some instances, such as the Fair Package and Labelling Act of 1966 and §371(e)(3) of the Food, Drug and Cosmetic Act of 1938, the statutory requirement for formal rule making is unambiguous, but in other cases the statutory language is less clear and subject to interpretation. The Coal Mine Health and Safety Act of 1969 and the National Traffic and Motor Vehicle Safety Act of 1966, for example, provide for notice and comment in rule making but also specify that on request by an interested party, "a public hearing for the purpose of receiving relevant evidence" shall be held. Both also require "findings of fact" and judicial review in accordance with the "substantial evidence in the record" rule. Yet neither affected agency interprets this as requiring trial-type hearings or formal rule making.

The Supreme Court has made it clear that it will consider an agency bound to follow formal rule making procedures only if the statutory commandment to do so is clear and unambiguous. The Esch Car Service Act, §1(14)(a) of the Interstate Commerce Act, provided that "The Commission may, after hearing, . . . establish reasonable rules, regulations and practices with respect to car service by common carriers." The Supreme Court disagreed with the railroads' and district court's contention that this required the Interstate Commerce Commission to promulgate such rules through formal rule making procedures:

> Appellees claim that the Commission's procedure here departed from the provisions of 5 U. S. C. §556 and 557 of the Act [the APA]. Those sections, however, govern a rulemaking proceeding only when 5 U. S. C. §553 so requires . . . "when rules are required by statute to be made on the record after opportunity for an agency hearing. . . ." The Esch Act . . . does not require such rules "be made on the record." . . . Sections 556 and 557 need be applied "only [w]here the agency statute, in addition to providing a hearing, prescribes explicitly that it be 'on the record.'" *Seigel v. Atomic Energy Commission*, 130 US App D. C. 307 (1978). . . .
>
> Because the proceedings under review were an exercise of legislative rulemaking power rather than adjudicatory hearings . . . and because 49 U. S. C. §1(14)(a) does not require a determination "on the record" the provisions of 5 U.S.C. §556, 557 were inapplicable.[36]

The Supreme Court further clarified the statutory requirements necessary to mandate formal rule making in 1973 in *United States v. Florida East Coast Railway Co.* ICC rule making under §1(14)(a) of the Interstate Commerce Act was once again at issue and the Supreme Court once again explained that the "hearing" required by that section did not require rule making on the record:

> The term "hearing" in its legal context undoubtedly has a host of meanings. Its meaning undoubtedly will vary, depending on whether it is used in the context of a rule making-type proceeding or in the context of a proceeding devoted to the adjudication of particular disputed facts. . . . [I]t cannot be doubted that a statute that requires a "hearing" prior to rulemaking may in some circumstances be satisfied by procedures that meet only the standards of §553 (of the APA)[37]

The "hearing" required by the Interstate Commerce Act did not "by its own force require the commission to hear oral testimony, to permit cross-examination of Commission witnesses, or to hear oral argument."[38]

When agencies must use formal rule-making procedures, the results are not necessarily beneficial. Such rule making tends to be extremely tedious and drawn out. The establishment of the standard for peanut butter by the FDA, which took nine years, is, as Davis termed it, "a horrible example."[39] The negative consequences of required formal rule making were summarized by R. W. Hamilton:

> At worst, these procedures have warped regulatory programs or resulted in virtual
> abandonment of them. . . . The primary impact of these procedural requirements
> is often not as one might otherwise have expected, the testing of agency
> assumptions. . . . Rather these procedures either cause the abandonment of the
> program (as in the Department of Labor), the development of techniques to reach
> the same regulatory goal but without a hearing (as the FDA is now trying to do)
> or the promulgation of noncontroversial regulations by a process of negotiation
> and compromise (as FDA historically has done and Interior is encouraged to
> do).[40]

Informal Rule Making

APA Requirements   Fortunately for administrative agencies, the vast majority of substantive rules that they promulgate may be formulated following the "notice and comment" procedures specified in §553 of the Administrative Procedure Act. Those procedures are basically (and perhaps deceptively) simple:

1. A notice of the proposed rule making must be published in the Federal Register specifying the legal authority under which the rule is proposed, the terms or substance of the proposed rule, and the time, place, and nature of public rule-making proceeding. Although the notice need not contain the exact content of the proposed rules, it must not omit an explanation of the basic issues and elements involved in those rules.
2. An opportunity for interested persons to participate in the rule making must be provided, but this may be satisfied by allowing either written or oral comments.
3. The agency must incorporate in the final rule a concise general statement of its basis and purpose.
4. The final rule must be published 30 days before its effective date.

Even these relatively unrestrictive procedures may be dispensed with if "the agency for good cause finds (and incorporates the finding and a brief statement of reasons therefore in the rules issued) that notice and public proceedings thereon are impracticable, unnecessary or contrary to the public interest."[41] This emergency rule making procedure has been used only rarely by agencies. Lower federal courts have held that such emergency rules may not be continued indefinitely.[42] Consequently, if an agency wished them to become permanent it must repromulgate them using regular §553 procedures.

THE PRACTICAL MECHANICS OF THE RULE-MAKING PROCESS

Initiation of Proposed Rules   Most rules are proposed at the initiative of the agency involved, but the APA also requires each agency to "give an interested person the right to petition for the issuance, amendment or repeal of a rule."[43] This provision has been used frequently by industry, public interest groups, and individuals to encourage agencies to consider proposing rules in areas where the agencies might otherwise not have acted. The Federal Communications Commission, for example, was pressured into considering (although not adopting) regulations governing all programming for children by Action for Children's Television (ACT). Until 1970, the FCC had exhibited little interest in becoming involved in regulating children's television programming, but constant pressure from ACT, culminating in a petition for proposed rule making, finally led the Commission to institute an inquiry into the subject on January 26, 1971.[44] An inquiry is equivalent to a pre-preliminary investigation; the agency is simply investigating and collecting information to determine if there is a need for proposing rules. In this instance the FCC decided not to propose rules but instead to adopt a policy statement.[45] Although ACT was far from satisfied with the FCC failure to promulgate rules, the case illustrates that agencies do take petitions for rule making seriously even if they do not adopt the requested rules.

Although agencies are not required by the APA to adopt or even seriously to consider rules proposed by petition, they must respond to the petition: "Prompt notice shall be given of the denial in whole or in part of a written application, petition, or other request of an interested person made in connection with any agency proceeding. Except in affirming a prior denial or when the denial is self-explanatory, the notice shall be accompanied by a brief statement of the grounds for denial."[46] Some statutes provide more demanding standards for responding to petitions. The Consumer Product Safety Act explicitly permits individuals to petition for adoption, repeal, or amendment of a safety standard, and if the petition is denied, the Act permits appeal to the District Court which may order the Commission to initiate the action petitioned for. Although not explicitly required by statute, individuals submitting petitions for proposed rule making would be well advised to put the petition in the same form that an agency would have to use in issuing the notice and to provide substantial supporting evidence on the need for the rule.[47]

Notice and Comment Procedures   Publication of the notice of proposed rule making in the Federal Register satisfies the requirement of the APA. The low visibility and limited circulation of the Register have encouraged many agencies to utilize additional methods of publication to help ensure that all interested persons are informed and aware of proposed regulations. The Federal Trade Commission, for example, routinely issues press releases and mails letters of intent to those parties it presumes to be interested in proposed rules.[48]

Although the APA does not specify how much time must elapse between the publication of notice for proposed rule making and issuance of final rules, agencies normally allow ample time for public comment. For controversial regulations that arouse a great deal of public or interest group attention, such as the HEW Title IX regulations or the

FDA tampon labeling regulations, it is not unusual for the notice and comment period to extend over several months or, in some cases, years. On the other hand, the courts have upheld a notice and comment period of less than a week. On September 19, 1947, the Department of Interior issued a notice of proposed rule making to prohibit the killing of wild geese in certain areas of Illinois. The final rules were signed and published on September 25, 1947. Despite the brevity of the notice period, the Court of Appeals found that the APA had not been violated.[49]

The notice for proposed rule making must specify the manner in which public comments may be submitted. Since the APA does not require agencies to hold hearings on proposed rules, it is within the agency's discretion to determine whether it wishes to do so. In the vast majority of cases, agencies do not hold rule-making hearings and only written comments are solicited. When an agency does decide to hold hearings, the purpose is seldom to secure substantive information and only rarely does a hearing actually change anybody's mind on the advisability of the proposed rules.[50] If this is the case, and particularly since hearings are expensive, one might wonder why they are held at all. From a legal perspective, a closely related question also arises: If hearings rarely change administrators' minds, does this not indicate the rule makers are impermissibly biased?

For highly controversial rules, those that are vehemently opposed by affected interests and/or those that have wide geographical, social, and economic impact, hearings are essential. Perhaps most importantly, the hearings will result in an extensive public record which the agency can use, if judicially challenged, to prove that public comment was solicited and that competing views were at least heard (if not accepted). The hearing allows open, reciprocal, and immediate communication among the agency, supporters, and opponents of proposed rules, resulting, it is hoped, in better understanding by all parties of the various impacts and ramifications of the rules. Hearings also serve to educate the agency, the media, affected parties, and the public on the issues and problems involved. They also may result in the agency being supplied with information that it did not previously have. Theoretically at least, open and extensive hearings should result in greater public acceptance of the final rules and facilitate their enforcement. Presumably, if the affected interests have full opportunity to participate in the rule-making process, they should more willingly accept its final outcome even if they do not agree with the outcome.

Conversely, hearings also have certain disadvantages when used in rule-making proceedings. They do add substantially to the cost of rule making and they frequently result in further delaying an already slow process. Full, free, and open participation by all comers may also result in large amounts of trivial, redundant testimony leading to information overload and obscuring vital information. Further, hearings frequently degenerate into adversary proceedings where the primary concern becomes not the exploration of general social, economic, and legal situations and facts, but the presentation of specific adjudicatory facts and arguments by opposing parties. The result is that the legislative nature of the proceeding becomes obscured or lost and the desired flexibility of the rule-making process undermined.

The D.C. Court of Appeals summarized the utility and limitations of hearings in *Pacific Coast European Conference v. United States*:

> In rulemaking hearings the purpose is to permit the agency to educate itself and not allow interested parties to choose the issues or narrow the scope of the proceedings. The purpose of the notice is to allow interested parties to make useful comment and not allow them to assert their "rights" to insist that the rule take a particular form. The agency, in rulemaking, can look beyond the particular hearing record, since it otherwise would be unable to draw upon its own expertise.[51]

Formal public input into the rule-making process may be through oral testimony at a hearing or written submissions, but whatever form it takes, informed participation is likely to be costly. The average cost for participation in a single rule-making proceeding before the FDA has been estimated at $30–40,000.[52] Individuals and public interest groups can seldom match the financial capabilities for sustained participation exhibited by regulated industries. In 1976, during the Civil Aeronautics Board proceedings on airline deregulation, the 11 major airlines spent $2.85 million plus expenses for in-house counsel. The only active public interest group, Consumer Action Group, spent $20,000, which was half of its 1976 budget.[53] This pronounced financial inequity between business interests and consumer and public interest groups led to the development of what has become one of the most controversial aspects of the contemporary rule-making process—public intervenor funding.

Congress first specifically authorized agency funding for public intervenors in the 1974 Moss-Magnuson FTC Improvement Act. The FTC was authorized to pay attorney and expert witness fees and expenses by parties otherwise unable to participate in rule making. The only other agencies given explicit authorization for funding such participation in rule making were the Federal Energy Regulatory Commission and the EPA for the toxic substance control program. Other agencies, including the Food and Drug Administration, the Consumer Product Safety Commission, and the Department of Agriculture, funded such participation under implied authority. Although only a total of $2 million had been spent on such funding since 1972, business interests vigorously and successfully opposed it in the 96th Congress.

Business's main argument against such funding was that it was improper for the government to pay taxpayers' money to special interest groups; consumer groups were typical nonrepresentative special interests. In addition, the critics (the U.S. Chamber of Commerce, the National Association of Manufacturers, and the Business Roundtable) charged that agencies, the FTC in particular, stacked the deck by providing funding only to groups that supported regulation, limited funding to a few, very unrepresentative California and Washington organizations and gave money to groups, like ACT, which should have been able to raise their own funds. Most of the criticisms were partly true and largely irrelevant. Although an Administrative Conference of the United States (ACUS) study did confirm that the majority of compensated witnesses in FTC rule making were prorule, it concluded that this was primarily because antirule groups seldom sought such funding.[54] Further, while 65 percent of the funding went to only eight groups, many individuals also received funding, and even the concentration in funding was not detrimental to the purposes of such funding: "it seems efficient to prefer groups and lawyers who already know the ropes and have demonstrated competence in prior proceedings."[55] Nevertheless, Congress specifically prohibited the

Federal Energy Regulatory Commission, the National Highway Traffic Safety Administration, the CAB, and the Nuclear Regulatory Commission from expending any of their appropriated funds for FY 1981 on public intervention activities.

The FDA and various other federal agencies including the Bureau of Land Management have special procedures to ensure relatively broad-based participation in their rule-making processes. The FDA uses a system of advisory committees composed of representatives from the scientific community, industry, and consumer interests to provide expertise and to allow interested parties opportunity for full participation in agency decision making. By 1974, there were 66 active advisory committees utilized by the FDA. Members of the committees are nominated by professional, industry, and consumer groups and are selected by the FDA Commissioner. From the FDA's perspective these committees have been extremely useful in providing knowledge, in increasing the legitimacy and credibility of agency decisions, and in strengthening the agency's position in court challenges. Industry has been equally satisfied with the operation of these committees, but consumer groups have been less so, feeling that the system is biased in favor of regulatees.[56]

Ex Parte Contacts in Rule Making   Up to this point the forms of public participation that have been discussed have been "formal," i.e., the information and opinions supplied have become part of the "record" on which a rule is based. But frequently during rule making, participation extends to "informal" methods of participation—informal consultation, conversations, meetings, phone calls, suggestions, and advice offered off the record. Such informal communication had traditionally been considered not only innocuous, but based on the analogy to the congressional process, an important and useful part of the democratic legislative process.

In 1977, however, the D.C. Court of Appeals reevaluated these assumptions and denied the permissibility of ex parte contacts during rule making. At issue in the case were the FCC's "pay cable" rules which sharply restricted programming on subscription television. One of the objections to the validity of the rules was the extent of ex parte contacts between Commission members and a wide variety of groups and individuals throughout the rule-making process. When ordered by the court to produce a list of such contacts, the FCC submitted a 60-page list that read like the Who's Who of Broadcasting. In *Home Box Office Inc v. FCC* such contacts were held to violate both the Government in the Sunshine Act and §553 of the APA:

> Even the possibility that there is here one administrative record for the public and
> this court and another for the Commission and those "in the know" is
> intolerable. Whatever the law may have been in the past, there can now be no
> doubt that implicit in the decision to treat the promulgation of rules as a "final
> event" . . . is an assumption that an act of reasoned judgment has occurred, an
> assumption which further contemplates the existence of a body of material—
> documents, comments, transcripts, and statements in various forms declaring
> agency expertise or policy—with reference to which such judgement was
> exercised . . . Against this material, "the full administrative record that was before
> [an agency official] at the time he made his decision," (*Citizens to Preserve Overton
> Park v. Volpe*, 401 US 420) it is the obligation of this court to test the actions of the

Commission for arbitrariness. . . . The public record must reflect what representations were made to an agency. . . .

In the Government in the Sunshine Act, for example, Congress has declared it to be "the policy of the United States that the public is entitled to the fullest practicable information regarding the decisionmaking processes of the Federal Government. . . . [I]nformation gathered ex parte from the public which becomes relevant to a rulemaking will have to be disclosed at some time. . . . Once a notice of proposed rulemaking has been issued, . . . any agency official or employee who is or may reasonably be expected to be involved in the decisional process of the rulemaking proceeding, should "refuse to discuss matters relating to the disposition of a [rulemaking proceeding] with any interested private party, or an attorney or agent for any such party, prior to the agency's decision" (Executive Order 11 920). . . . If ex parte contacts nonetheless occur, we think that any written document or summary of any oral communication must be placed in the public file."[57]

The ban on ex parte contacts during rule making was new law and law that could not really be traced to §553 of the APA, custom, tradition, or other judicial precedents. If it were valid new law, it would change the nature of informal rule making to rule making on the record. It also proved to be very controversial law and was not accepted by other judges, even on the D.C. Court of Appeals. Later that same year, a different panel on that court was asked to review the FCC's policy statement and its failure to promulgate children's television programming. One of the objections raised by ACT to the statement was the extent of ex parte contacts allowed by the Commission during the policy formulation process. The Court of Appeals decision in *ACT v. FCC* explicitly disagreed with the *Home Box Office* decision barring ex parte contacts during all rule-making proceedings. The court, referring to an earlier decision in *Sangammon Valley Television Corp v. US*,[58] which had held that ex parte contacts might be impermissible in certain rule-making proceedings, limited the holding to proceedings which involved "resolution of conflicting private claims to a valuable privilege" (allocation of a television channel):

If we go as far as Home Box Office does in its ex parte rulings in ensuring a "whole record" for our review, why not go further to require the decisionmaker to summarize and make available for public comment every status inquiry from a Congressman, or any germane material—say a newspaper editorial—that he or she reads or their evening hour ruminations? . . . The problem is obviously a matter of degree, and the appropriate line must be drawn somewhere. In light of what must be presumed to be Congress' intent not to prohibit or require disclosure of all ex parte contacts during or after the public comment stage, we would draw that line at the point where the rulemaking proceedings involve "competing claims to a valuable privilege."[59]

As both *Home Box Office* and *ACT v. FCC* made clear, ex parte contacts are widespread in notice and comment rule making. Technically, any time an official sees, hears, reads, or talks to anyone about a subject in a pending rule-making proceeding, an ex parte contact has occurred. Trying to prevent such contacts would be impossible and the results would not necessarily be beneficial. "Impartial does not mean uninformed, unthinking, or inarticulate,"[60] and rules formulated on such a basis are not likely to be good policy. As long as the final rule is based on solid information from whatever source gained, and *as long as that information is clearly explained and presented* in the basis and purpose statement accompanying it, administrators should be allowed considerable latitude in ex parte contacts during informal rule making.

Bias in Rule Making

When the Federal Trade Commission first proposed to regulate cigarette advertising in 1964, it was logical to conclude that a majority of Commission members had already decided that such regulation was both necessary and proper and that the subsequent hearings were unlikely to change their minds on the issue. Similarly, in many rule-making proceedings, particularly those undertaken at the agency's initiative, agency administrators have determined in advance of the hearing that the proposed rules are necessary. In an adjudicatory proceeding, such determinations in advance of a hearing would probably be considered a disqualifying bias, but rule making is not adjudication and a predisposition toward certain policy issues is not sufficient to require administrators to disqualify themselves from participation. After all, members of Congress are not judges; legislating is fundamentally different from judging the facts in a particular case, and when administrators are making rules, they are legislating. Faithful implementation of the law requires administrative bias in favor of the law. A Federal Trade Commissioner who believes that false advertising is good constitutes a far more serious deviation from norms of democratic accountability than one who believes rules should be promulgated defining what practices in cigarette advertising are sufficient to avoid charges of false advertising.

The distinction between bias in rule making and bias in adjudication was explored and explained by the D.C. Court of Appeals in *Association of National Advertisers, Inc. v. FTC*. The Federal Trade Commission had become involved in the Kidvid controversy, but with considerably more enthusiasm than had characterized the FCC's involvement. Prior to the issuance of notice of proposed rule making on advertising on children's television in April 1978, FTC Chairman Michael Pertschuk had made several speeches, written articles, and even sent an official memo to the Commissioner of the FDA clearly indicating that he believed advertising on children's television was inherently unfair. The Association of National Advertisers immediately petitioned the FTC requesting that Pertschuk disqualify himself from the pending proceeding. He and the Commission refused the request. Although the rule-making procedure required by the FTC is a hybrid procedure (to be discussed later), the Court of Appeals chose to regard it as primarily a legislative procedure:

> When a proceeding is classified as a rulemaking, due process ordinarily does not demand procedures more rigorous than those followed by Congress.
>
> The legitimate functions of a policymaker, unlike an adjudicator, demand interchange and discussion about important issues. We must not impose judicial roles upon administrators when they perform functions very different from those of judges.[61]

The court recognized that the FTC Improvement Act required the Commission to formulate judgments on proposed rules since the notice for proposed rules was required to state "with particularity the reason for the proposed rule prior to the comment stage of the proceeding." Obviously, an initial determination on the necessity of the rules had to be made, and although Commissioners were expected to be impartial, "impartial does not mean uninformed, unthinking or inarticulate." The standard for disqualifying an administrator from a rule-making proceeding because of bias was a stringent one: "An agency member may be disqualified from such a proceeding only when there is a clear and convincing showing that he has an unalterably closed mind on matters critical to the disposition of rule making."[62] With his right to participate legally vindicated, Chairman Pertschuk voluntarily withdrew from the case.

The Rule-Making Record   While §553 requires agencies to solicit public comment on proposed rules, it says nothing about what the agency is required to do with those comments or how seriously it is supposed to consider them. Nor on its face does it require that agencies must compile a record of the proceedings. What it does require is that the agency incorporate in the final rules "a general statement of their basis and purpose." Initially, it was left to the agencies to interpret this section and develop methods to comply with it. The Attorney General's Manual on the Administrative Procedure Act issued in 1947 informed agencies that it interpreted the provisions as meaning that "findings of fact and conclusions of law are not necessary. Nor is there required an elaborate analysis of the rules or of the considerations upon which the rules were issued. Rather, the statement is intended to advise the public of the general basis and purpose of the rules."[63] For the most part federal agencies followed the Attorney General's guidelines and received homogenized and digested comments, weighed them against agency expertise, and issued final rules with relatively brief explanations.

Then in 1971, the Supreme Court handed down the *Overton Park* decision.[64] *Overton Park* dealt with a determination by the Secretary of Transportation on the provision of federal highway funds for construction of a highway through a public park. Among other things, the court opinion made clear that administrative officials had best be prepared to present the full record on which administrative decisions were based if the decision were judicially challenged as arbitrary, capricious, or an abuse of discretion, and although it did not deal with §553 rule making, *Overton Park* came to be increasingly used by lower federal courts to require more and more detailed records for informal rule making. Slowly but surely, the courts of appeals, dissatisfied as much with the substance of agency rules as with administrative procedure, began to rewrite §553, expanding the requirements for an acceptable rule making record.[65] Agencies were increasingly required to respond to and rebut critical comments, to compile more and more data, and to make findings that increasingly resembled those in adjudicatory cases if they wished their rules to withstand challenges. In 1974, the Administrative Conference of the United States (ACUS) recommended that agencies compile and, if their rules were challenged, supply to a reviewing court the following information:

1. the initial notice;
2. all comments and documents received;

3. all transcripts of hearings;
4. any additional factual information considered;
5. reports of advisory committees;
6. final statement of basis and purpose.

The Federal Register was one victim of such increased procedural requirements as agencies began to publish along with the final rules, summaries of comments received and agency responses to those comments. That neither ACUS nor the agencies were overreacting was confirmed in *National Welfare Rights Organization v. Mathews*. In striking down HEW regulations limiting the amount of capital resources that families may retain and still be eligible for AFDC payments, the court emphasized the insufficiency of the record on which the regulations were based:

> Judicial review is meaningless where the administrative record is insufficient to determine whether the action is arbitrary and capricious.[66]

For that record to be sufficient, the Court held that the basis and purpose statement must be "sufficiently detailed and informative to allow a searching judicial scrutiny of how and why the regulations were actually adopted." Satisfying these record requirements would be neither simple nor short, since the Court held that "adequate record for §553 rule making will reflect all of the relevant views and evidence considered by the rule maker from whatever source."[67]

The courts of appeals had created what has been called "a paper hearing procedure," and were gradually eliminating the distinction between informal and formal rule making. Although the lower courts had constantly cited *Overton Park* as proof of Supreme Court requirements for these new procedures, in reality, the Supreme Court had never applied such stringent requirements as the lower courts were purporting to § 553 rule making, and in both *Allegheny-Ludlum Steel* and *Florida East Coast Railroad* had indicated that it would require agencies to hold trial-type hearings in rule making only if a statute clearly and unequivocally commanded them to do so.

In 1978, the Supreme Court, in an opinion written by Justice Rehnquist, attempted to set the record straight on what §553 actually required of federal agencies in the rule-making process. At issue were rules promulgated in 1974 by the Atomic Energy Commission (whose powers were later transferred to the Nuclear Regulatory Commission) involving the analysis and evaluation of the environmental effects of spent fuel processing for nuclear power reactors. The rule-making process used by the AEC had followed the specifications of §553. Subsequent to issuance of notice, a rule-making hearing had been held but neither discovery nor cross-examination had been allowed at the hearing. As closely as the Supreme Court could tell (and it had great difficulty in determining this) the Court of Appeals had invalidated the rule because of procedural inadequacies of the AEC process. The Supreme Court held that the Court of Appeals had misconstrued both the APA and previous Supreme Court decisions:

> In 1946, Congress enacted the Administrative Procedure Act, which as we have noted elsewhere was not only "a new, basic and comprehensive regulation of the procedures of many agencies," *Wong Yang Sun v. McGrath*, 339 US 33, . . . but was also a legislative enactment which settled "long-continued and hard-fought

contentions, and enacts a formula upon which opposing social and political forces have come to rest" Id., . . . [T]he Act established the maximum procedural requirements that Congress was willing to have the courts impose upon agencies in conducting rulemaking procedures. Agencies are free to grant additional procedural rights in the exercise of their discretion, but reviewing courts are generally not free to impose them if the agencies have chosen not to grant them.

Even apart from the Administrative Procedure Act this Court has for more than four decades emphasized that the formulation of procedures was basically left within the discretion of the agencies to which Congress had confided the responsibility for substantive judgments . . .

It is in the light of this background of statutory and decisional law that we granted certiorari to review two judgments of the Court of Appeals for the District of Columbia circuit because of our concern that they had obviously misread or misapplied this statutory or decisional law cautioning reviewing courts against engrafting their own notions of proper procedures upon agencies entrusted with substantive functions by Congress.

The Court [of Appeals] . . . examined the rulemaking proceedings and, despite the fact that it appeared that the agency employed all the procedures required by 5 U.S.C. §553 (1976 ed.), and more, the court determined the proceedings to be inadequate and overturned the rule. . . .

But this much is absolutely clear. Absent constitutional constraints or extremely compelling circumstances the "administrative agencies should be free to fashion their own rules of procedure." . . .

[I]f courts continually review agency proceedings to determine whether the agency employed procedures which were in the court's opinion, perfectly tailored to reach what the court perceives to be the "best" or "correct" result, judicial review would be totally unpredictable. And the agencies . . . would undoubtedly adopt full adjudicatory hearings in every instance. . . .

Informal rulemaking need not be based solely on the transcript of a hearing. . . . Indeed the agency need not even hold a formal hearing. . . . Thus, the adequacy of the "record" in this type of hearing is not correlated directly to the type of procedural devices employed, but rather turns on whether the agency has followed the statutory mandate of the APA. . . .

In short, nothing in the APA, NEPA, the circumstances of the case, the nature of the issues being considered, past agency practice or the statutory mandate under which the Commission operates permitted the court to review and overturn the rulemaking proceeding on the basis of the procedural devices employed (or not employed) . . . so long as the Commission employed at least the statutory minima, a matter about which there is no doubt in this case.[68]

Although *Vermont Yankee* unequivocally instructed lower federal courts to stop creating their own procedures in lieu of the APA for agency rule making, it did little to clarify what constitutes an adequate record for §553 rule making. While the lower courts could no longer tell the agencies *how* they must compile that record, they were still left free to determine if it was sufficient to justify the rule, which could in many circumstances lead to precisely the same result that the Supreme Court had seemingly prohibited:

There remains, of course, the question of whether the challenged rule finds justification in the administrative proceedings that it should be upheld by the reviewing court. . . . There are also intimations in the majority opinion which suggest that the judges . . . may have thought the administrative proceedings an insufficient base upon which to predicate the rule in question. We accordingly remand so that the Court of Appeals may review the rule in question as the Administrative Procedure Act requires.[69]

In other words, it is quite possible that following the minimal procedures of the APA, an agency might come up with an insufficient "basis and purpose" statement and an incomplete record. To avoid the rule being struck down in court, the agency had best make sure that this does not occur. In order to do that it might want to adopt more rigorous procedures.

Section 553 remains the basic source of required procedure, but its more vague and ambiguous provisions remain subject to interpretation. In the first instance this will be done by the agencies and the Attorney General, increasingly with presidential guidance. The courts will still review the outcome of the procedures for adequacy and ultimately Congress itself will have the final say on the acceptability of the procedures.

HYBRID RULE-MAKING PROCEDURES

Procedures are never neutral; change the procedures and you can change the outcome of the game—winners can become losers, losers can become winners. The courts are unquestionably aware of this fact and so are politicians and opponents of substantive regulatory outcomes. In the late 1970s and early 1980s such opponents found many members of Congress were increasingly responsive to their demands to check the growth of regulatory power. One of the major responses of Congress was to modify rule-making procedures for specific regulatory agencies, and to establish "hybrid rule-making" procedures for those agencies. In biology, a hybrid is the offspring of a cross between two different breeds, varieties, species, or genera of animals or plants. When undertaken deliberately by breeders, the goal is to produce a hybrid which combines the best features of the two breeds that have been crossed. In administrative rule making, a hybrid procedure is the offspring of a combination of formal and informal rule making. Such procedures have been created by Congress in the CPSC Act, the Occupational Safety and Health Act, the FTC Improvement Act, the Coal Mine Health and Safety Act, the National Traffic and Motor Vehicle Safety Act of 1966, the Toxic Substances Control Act, the SEC amendments of 1975, and the Department of Energy Organization Act of 1977. As frequently happens with first generation hybridization, no two of the offspring are exactly the same.

What most of the hybrid rule-making procedures have in common is a requirement for some kind of oral hearing under certain conditions. The Occupational Safety and Health Act, the Coal Mine Health and Safety Act, and the National Traffic and Motor Vehicle Safety Act, for example, allow notice and written comment rule making but specify that on request of an interested person a public hearing for the purpose of receiving relevant evidence must be held.[70] The Acts require findings of fact and stipulate that the final rule must be based on substantial evidence in the record. None of the agencies interpret this as requiring formal rule making and they have been upheld in the courts on this contention. OSHA has provided through its own procedural rules for cross-examination "on crucial issues" at the hearing.[71] The Toxic Substance Act and SEC amendments require not only an oral hearing but mandate the right to cross-examination if there are "disputed issues of material facts." The DOE Organization Act allows the use of straight §553 procedures unless the Secretary determines that a "substantial issue of law or facts exists. If he determines thusly, then an opportunity for oral presentation of views, data and argument shall be provided."[72]

The Federal Trade Commission Improvement Act (Moss-Magnuson Act) which established a hybrid rule-making procedure for FTC Trade Regulation Rules concerning unfair and deceptive practices was the result of a compromise between those who wanted to curb the FTC's consumer protection propensities and those who wanted to protect them. The result was to give the FTC the authority to regulate those practices if it could figure out how to do so within the mandated procedures. The Act included several modifications of §553 rule making including a requirement that the notice for proposed rule making must state "with particularity the reason for the proposed rules," all comments received must be made available for public inspection, and require the FTC to provide an opportunity for an informal hearing. According to the statute an opportunity for cross-examination and rebuttal by interested persons is required at the hearing only if the Commission determines "there are disputed issues of material fact" and if the Commission determines that cross-examination is "appropriate" and "required for a full and true disclosure with respect to such issues."[73] The final rule is required to be based on "substantial evidence in the record," and the requirements for the basis and purpose statement are also specified: It must include an assessment of the prevalance of the actions involved, the manner and context in which they are unfair, and their economic effect. Although preenforcement judicial review is explicitly authorized, the contents and adequacy of the statement of basis and purpose "shall not be subject to judicial review in any respect."

The FTC had serious problems initially in implementing its hybrid procedures. After four years of operation, the FTC had promulgated few rules under the new procedures and it was castigated by a House Committee for "delay, postponement and extension at every level of the process."[74] The delays were at least partially attributable to the FTC's uncertainty about the precise requirements of the new procedure. Two of the major uncertainties involved the type and conduct of hearing required and the extent to which the new procedures required Commissioners to behave as judges rather than legislators. The FTC attempted to resolve the first uncertainty by establishing a two-stage hearing process. The first stage would be an informal legislative-type hearing, and if disputed material facts arose a second stage hearing allowing cross examination and rebuttal would be held.[75] The second uncertainty was a major issue in the FTC's proposed Kidvid advertising regulations and was addressed by the D.C. Court of Appeals in *Association of National Advertisers, Inc. v. FTC.*[76]

As discussed earlier the Court of Appeals held in that case that the new procedures did not convert FTC rule making into an adjudicatory proceeding and consequently the standards for proper administrative behavior were those required for §553 rule making, with the exception of the requirement to hold trial-type hearings to resolve "disputed issues of material fact." Although the court referred to Davis's distinction between legislative (general) facts and adjudicative (specific to a particular case) facts, and to the House report on the legislation which stated that disputed issues of material fact were characterized "as issues of specific fact in contrast to legislative fact," it nevertheless held that the "material facts" mentioned in the statute were "a category of legislative fact."[77] All of which, of course, makes the hybrid proceeding more legislative than judicial.

If the hybrid procedures provided for the FTC created uncertainty and slowed the rule-making process down, those initially created for the Consumer Product Safety Commission rendered it, if not sterile, at least remarkably unproductive. Although the Consumer Product Safety Act authorized the Commission to adopt mandatory safety standards, it was not allowed to develop those standards. Instead, once the Commission determined that a particular product presented an unreasonable risk of injury and that a product standard was required, it was required to request, in the Federal Register, offers from the public to develop the standard. Only if no acceptable outside offers were made was the Commission allowed to formulate the standard. To encourage participation by other than industry groups, the CPSC was authorized to underwrite some of the costs involved in the development of standards. In developing the standard the offerer was required to provide all interested parties an opportunity to participate. Once the offerer had developed the standard, the Commission was to review and evaluate it and to provide opportunity for public oral comment. At that point, the CPSC was authorized to issue a notice for proposed rule making in the Federal Register and to follow §553 procedures. It was required, however, to provide additional opportunity for oral comment. For the final rule, findings are required, and the rule must be supported by substantial evidence in the record.

Under the offerer system a wide variety of private groups, including Consumers Union, Underwriters Laboratory, the National Consumers League, and the National Swimming Pool Institute, have been authorized to develop safety standards.[78] Unquestionably the system goes the furthest of any of the federal agency public participation programs toward turning actual rule-making authority over to private groups, and combined with the other required elements of the standard setting process results in a process that is more mutant than hybrid. The Commission has had serious problems implementing the process and was criticized by the GAO in 1977 for the slowness of its procedures which had resulted in only three safety standards being issued in four years. In spite or perhaps because of this, when Congress reauthorized the CPSC in 1978 the only substantial procedural change provided was to allow the Commission to participate directly in developing standards.

Hybrid procedures reflect congressional ambivalence about both the substance and process of administrative rule making. Having vested administrative agencies with the power to make rules having the force of law, Congress has become increasingly reluctant to allow some agencies the same informality that characterizes its own legislative process. At the same time it has also been reluctant to impose on those agencies the restrictive procedures of the judicial process. The result has been the development of procedures that require more opportunity for public participation in the rule-making process, that require agencies to consider, weigh, and respond to that participation and to reach their final rule-making decision almost but not exactly like a judge deciding a contested case.

PRESIDENTIAL MODIFICATIONS OF RULE-MAKING PROCEDURES

Presidents have also recognized that procedural modifications can also result in modifications in substantive regulatory outcomes. One President may seek to change the rule-making procedures so that habitual losers—consumers, environmentalists, minorities, women—can have a better chance to win. Another President may change the procedures to ensure that those who do not like this competition—affected corporations—can resume their winning ways. Jimmy Carter was a President who changed the procedures to give the losers an expanded opportunity, if not always to win, at least to participate more effectively in the rule-making process, but also changed other procedures to benefit big business.

In January 1978, Carter established the Regulatory Analysis Review Group (RARG), an interagency group to be composed of representatives from each cabinet department (except State and Defense) and officials from OMB, the CEA, EPA, and OSTP. All "significant" proposed regulations, those having an estimated economic impact in excess of $100 million, were to be submitted to RARG, whose staff would review the economic impact analysis that agencies were required to submit with each regulation. RARG's analysis and comment would then become part of the public record compiled for the proposed rule. Critics challenged the legality of this new arrangement on both substantive and procedural grounds. The procedure required agencies, which had not been instructed to do so by Congress, to weigh the costs and benefits of new regulations. Further, it slowed down the rule-making process and apparently discouraged some agencies from proposing new rules.[79]

In March 1978, Carter issued Executive Order 12044 which required additional and substantial modifications in the informal rule-making procedures. EO #12044 reiterated the requirement that all significant proposed regulations be submitted to an economic analysis and required agencies to develop new procedures to ensure that the need for and purpose of all regulations was clearly established. Agencies were required to publish semiannual agendas of all regulations likely to be proposed and to provide an opportunity for public comment. Regulations were to be written in clear and simple English. The real crux of EO #12044, however, was the requirement that agencies must develop improved methods to ensure early and meaningful opportunity for public comment in the rule-making process. The order recommended that agencies consider issuing an advance notice of proposed rule making, hold open conferences or public hearings, send notices to publications other than the Federal Register, and allow a minimum of 60 days for public comment.

These recommended procedures further lengthened the rule-making process, although in some agencies similar procedures were already in effect. Since 1976, pursuant to a memo from Secretary Donald Mathews, DHEW agencies had been required to issue a Notice of Intent to promulgate regulations. The issuance of such an advance notice allows public input and participation in the initial stages of agency rule making before regulations have taken final form. Allowing participation in the drafting of regulations increases the meaningfulness and impact of such input. The result, however, is a lengthier, more drawn-out process, since regardless of the extent of prenotice participation, APA requirements for postnotice comment must still be followed.

From a legal perspective, the most questionable of the procedural reforms instituted by the Carter Administration involved postcomment review of regulations. In 1978, the Administration asserted the right of the Executive Office of the President to review proposed regulations and communicate with the agencies after the public comment period had closed.[80] The propriety, fairness, necessity, and wisdom of this practice were questionable, and it was antithetical to the supposed broadening of public participation. The meaningfulness of expanded public participation is diminished if the results of that participation can be nullified by ex parte pressure from the Executive Office of the President (EOP) to ignore it—particularly when no opportunity is provided for counterbalancing those closed communications. If such communications are not part of the record but shape the final rule, judicial review is also made less meaningful. Why it should be necessary, given the extensive prenotice and notice and comment opportunity for providing presidential input, was also unclear. The legality of the procedure has been challenged by both environmental groups and labor unions, and in 1979, EOP began to keep logs of contacts and to place its information and contacts on the public record.[81]

Considerably less controversial was the establishment of the Regulatory Council which was charged with reducing duplication and conflict in regulations and with publishing a semiannual calendar of Federal Regulations listing all upcoming significant regulations. The Council was composed of representatives from all executive branch regulatory agencies and was provided a permanent staff.

If Carter's procedural modifications substantially changed §553 rule makings, Reagan's have come close to eliminating them. One of his first acts as President was to impose a 60-day freeze on pending and new regulations. The RARG was disbanded, but created in its place was a regulatory reform task force headed by Vice President George Bush to review existing and proposed regulations and recommend changes. By executive order all agencies were required to do cost-benefit analysis on all proposed and existing major rules and to pick the least costly alternative. To make sure agencies did the analyses properly and to further concentrate power in the presidency, compliance with the Executive Order was to be monitored by the OMB. Not only did these initial changes substantially modify the intent and practice of the APA, they also nullified large portions of substantive law. These changes are also of questionable legality. While the President has authority to oversee execution of the laws by the executive branch, his constitutional authority is "to take care that the laws be faithfully executed," not to devise procedures that make executive agency enforcement of the laws difficult if not impossible. Nor does the President have unilateral authority to write legislation, which is precisely what some of the Reagan changes have done.

At this point, informal rule making, conducted pursuant to the procedures outlined in §553 of the Administrative Procedure Act, appears to be an endangered species. What Davis termed "one of the greatest inventions of modern government" is being warped beyond recognition by procedural changes mandated by the presidency which are aimed at either delaying or destroying substantive regulation.

FEDERAL RULE-MAKING PROCEDURES: CHANGES AND REFORMS

In a subsequent chapter, the consequences and impact of various federal regulations will be discussed. Currently, the impact of those regulations is being condemned and castigated by various individuals and groups. One line of attack being taken by opponents to the substance of these rules is to demand changes in the rule-making process. As we said earlier, procedures are never neutral and any proposed procedural change has real potential to modify the substance of agency regulation. During the 1960s and 1970s, it was most frequently the "public interest" groups that challenged rule-making procedures. They argued that the process was tilted against them. They could not afford meaningful participation; when they did participate, the agencies did not take their presentations seriously. They found a sympathetic ear in Congress, the courts, the presidency, and many regulatory agencies. Rule-making procedures were modified to facilitate public interest participation. Inevitably, substantive outputs of those procedures began to reflect the demands of public intervenors. Regulatory agencies and their regulations began to be perceived by a new (old) set of institutions—corporations, universities, and industry groups and associations—as dangerous and detrimental.

The first choice of these critics of regulations is to do away with them—modify, repeal, or not enforce them. Their second choice is procedural changes that will accomplish the same results. Funding for public intervenors should be abolished; no more government funding for "self-appointed consumer advocates" is an initial step in the right direction, according to James P. Carty of the National Association of Manufacturers.[82] "We need to get business in on the front end" of regulation, according to M. Kendall Fleeharty, Director of the Chamber of Commerce Regulatory Action Center.[83] Conservative business groups, their supporters in Congress, and the Reagan administration agree that the procedural changes necessary to produce these desired results include mandatory cost-benefit analyses (to be discussed later), expanded control of the OMB over agency rules, and expanded opportunities for court review and overturning of agency rules. Conservative members of Congress also support congressional power to veto any regulation that makes it through the altered processes previously discussed.

The existing §553 rule-making procedure is fair, open, and still allows room for agency expertise in establishing rules. It could be improved without unduly attacking the substance of regulations by the following modifications:

1. Making the definitions of rules and terminology used by federal agencies concerning rules and rule making uniform;
2. Eliminating the exemptions in the APA, particularly the interpretive rule exemption;
3. Providing meaningful congressional standards to guide rule making;
4. Eliminating formal rule making;
5. Requiring and funding public intervenor participation in all rule-making proceedings;
6. Limiting judicial review to procedural aspects in accordance with the above; and

7. Requiring all interventions, whether from business groups, the President, Congress, the EOP, or public interest groups, to be recorded and reported.

To reiterate, procedure is not neutral; if Congess, which, at least theoretically, is the legislative branch of government, wishes to abolish regulation, then it and its 535 voting members should do so openly and aboveboard. It should not opt for the alternative of destroying "the greatest invention of modern government." Section 553 is a valid procedural enactment; if it has not produced perfect substantive results it has at least provided an open process for the formulation of administrative rules that is in many respects fairer and more democratic than the congressional process.

NOTES

1. Glen O. Robinson, Ernest Gellhorn, and Harold Bruff, *The Administrative Process*, 2d. ed. (St. Paul: West, 1980), p. 30.

2. Kenneth C. Davis, *Administrative Law: Cases-Texts-Problems*, 6th ed. (St. Paul, Minn.: West Publishing Co., 1977), p. 241.

3. *Bell Telephone Co. v. FCC*, 503 F2d 1250, 1268 (3d Cir. 1974).

4. 5 U.S.C. §551 (4).

5. Kenneth Davis, *Discretionary Justice* (Baton Rouge: Louisiana State University Press, 1969), p. 66.

6. Ibid.

7. Glen O. Robinson, "The Making of Administrative Policy: Another Look at Rulemaking and Adjudication and Administrative Procedure Reform," 118 *University of Pennsylvania Law Review* 485, 514 (1970).

8. Ibid., 516.

9. 332 US 194 (1947).

10. Ibid., at 203.

11. Ibid., at 202.

12. *NLRB v. Wyman-Gordon Co.*, 394 US 759, 764 (1969).

13. *NLRB v. Bell Aerospace Co.*, 416 US 267, 294 (1974).

14. Charles Bulmer and John Carmichael, "The NLRB and the Duty to Bargain in Good Faith: Consistency or Confusion?" in James E. Anderson, *Economic Regulatory Policies* (Lexington, Mass.: D.C. Heath, 1976), p. 136.

15. 25 U.S.C. §13.

16. *Morton v. Ruiz*, 415 US 199, 231–236 (1974).

17. Bernard Schwartz, *Administrative Law* (Boston: Little, Brown, 1976), p. 153.

18. 5 U.S.C. §553(b)(3)(A).

19. 5 U.S.C. §552(9)(1).

20. *Service v. Dulles*, 354 US 363 (1957).

21. *Vitarelli v. Seaton*, 359 US 535, 547 (1959).

22. *American Farm Lines v. Black Ball Freight Service*, 397 US 532, 539 (1970).

23. 38 *Federal Register* 14688 (1973).

24. *Nader v. Bork*, 366 F. Supp. 104, 108 (D.D.C. 1973).

25. *US v. Nixon*, 418 US 683, 694–696 (1974).

26. A. Lee Fritschler, *Smoking and Politics* (Englewood Cliffs, N.J.: Prentice-Hall, 1969), p. 87.

27. 15 U.S.C. §45.

28. 15 U.S.C. §46.

29. *National Petroleum Refiners Assoc. v. FTC*, 482 F2d 672 (D.C. Cir. 1973).

30. *Eastern Kentucky Welfare Rights Organization v. Simon*, 506 F2d 1278 (D.C. Cir. 1974).

31. *Skidmore v. Swift and Co.*, 323 US 134, 140 (1944).

32. *General Electric Co. v. Gilbert*, 429 US 125, 141 (1976).

33. *Chrysler Corporation v. Brown*, 441 US 281, 295 (1979).

34. Ibid., at 308.

35. 5 U.S.C. §553(c).

36. *United States v. Allegheny-Ludlum Steel Corp.*, 406 US 742, 756 (1972).

37. *U.S. v. Florida East Coast Railway Co.*, 410 US 224, 239 (1973).

38. Ibid., at 241.

39. Davis, *Administrative Law*, p. 245.

40. Robert W. Hamilton, "Procedure for the Adaptation of Rules of General Applicability: The Need for Procedural Innovation in Rulemaking," 60 *California Law Review* 12, 76 (1972).

41. 5. U.S.C. §553(b)(B).

42. *US v. Vail*, 252 F. Supp. 823 (D.C. Ohio 1969).

43. 5 U.S.C. §553(e).

44. 36 *Federal Register* 14219 (1971).

45. 50 FCC 2d 1 (1974).

46. 5 U.S.C. §555 (e).

47. James R. Michael, ed., *Working on the System: A Comprehensive Manual for Citizen Access to Federal Agencies* (New York: Basic Books, 1974).

48. Fritschler, *Smoking and Politics*, p. 80.

49. *Lansden v. Hart*, 168 F2d 409 (7th Cir.); cert. denied, 335 US 858 (1948).

50. Fritschler, *Smoking and Politics*, p. 80.

51. 350 F2d 197, 205 (D.C. Cir. 1965).

52. Peter Schuck, "Public Interest Groups and the Policy Process," *Public Administration Review*, March/April 1977, p. 137.

53. Judy Sarasohn, "Critics Successful in Reducing Funds for Public Participation," *Congressional Quarterly*, November 1, 1980, p. 3274.

54. Ibid., p. 3276.

55. Ibid.

56. Robert S. Friedman, "Representation in Regulatory Decisionmaking: Scientific, Industrial, and Consumer Input to the FDA," *Public Administration Review*, May/June 1978, pp. 205–13.

57. *Home Box Office, Inc. v. FCC*, 567 F2d 9, 54 (D.C. Cir. 1977); cert. denied, 438 US 839 (1978).

58. 269 F2d 22 (D.C. Cir. 1959).

59. *ACT v. FCC*, 564 F2d 458, 477 (D.C. Cir. 1977).

60. *Association of National Advertisers, Inc. v. FTC*, 627 F2d 1151, 1174 (D.C. Cir. 1979).

61. Ibid., at 1165.

62. Ibid., at 1170.

63. Quoted in Walter Gellhorn, Clark Byse, and Peter L. Strauss, *Administrative Law: Cases and Comments*, 7th ed. (Mineola, N.Y.: Foundation Press, 1979) p. 373.

64. *Citizens to Preserve Overton Park v. Volpe*, 401 US 402 (1971).

65. See, for example, *General Telephone Co. v. U.S.*, 449 F2d 846 (5th Cir. 1971); *Kennecott*

Copper Corp. v. EPA, 462 F2d 846 (D.C. Cir. 1972); *Amoco Oil v. EPA*, 501 F2d 722 (D.C. Cir. 1974), *Portland Cement Assoc. v. Ruckelshaus.* 486 F2d 375 (D.C. Cir. 1974).

66. 533 F2d 637, 648 (D.C. Cir. 1976).

67. Ibid.

68. *Vermont Yankee Nuclear Power Corp. v. Natural Resources Defense Council, Inc.*, 435 US 519, 523 (1978).

69. Ibid., at 549.

70. Davis, *Administrative law*, p. 246.

71. 29 CFR 1911.15.

72. See P.R. Verkuil, "The Emerging Concept of Administrative Procedure," 78 *Columbia Law Review* 258 (1978).

73. 15 U.S.C. §557(a).

74. U.S. Congress, H.R. Report #95–472, *FTC Oversight—Rulemaking Advertising and Consumer Access* (95th Congress, 1st session, 1977).

75. Robinson, Gellhorn, and Bruff, *The Administrative Process*, p. 553.

76. 627 F2d 1151 (D.C. Cir. 1979).

77. Davis, *Administrative Law*, p. 276.

78. Judy Hermanson, "The Implications of the CPSC's Offerer System," *Public Administration Review*, March/April, 1978, p. 153.

79. *Federal Regulatory Directory, 1980–1981* (Washington, D.C.: Congressional Quarterly, 1980), p. 37.

80. Lawrence White, *Reforming Regulation: Processes and Problems* (Englewood Cliffs, N.J.: Prentice-Hall, 1981) p. 22.

81. Ibid., p. 25.

82. Sarasohn, "Critics Successful in Reducing Funds," *Congressional Quarterly*, p. 3273.

83. Quoted in Laura Weiss, "Reagan, Congress Planning Regulatory Machinery Repair," *Congressional Quarterly*, March 7, 1981, p. 412.

Chapter 10

Adjudicatory Procedures

Although setting food standards, establishing requirements for product packaging and labeling, granting or revoking nuclear power plant licenses, denying Social Security disability benefits, terminating AFDC benefits, determining that a company has engaged in false advertising, expelling a student for misconduct from public school, firing a tenured civil servant, and ordering a company to reinstate employees dismissed for engaging in union organizing activities are disparate administrative activities, they share one common characteristic: They require the agency involved to provide interested parties an opportunity to be heard at some point in the administrative process. Although the exact nature and timing of the hearing provided will differ for each of the above actions, all will involve the use of adjudicatory procedures and at the federal level must be conducted in accordance with §§554–557 of the Administrative Procedure Act.

The same diversity that characterized agency terminology for "rules" is also found in terminology for adjudicatory procedures and their output. The APA defines an "order" as the "whole or part of a final disposition, . . . of an agency in a matter other than rule making but including licensing." This is immediately qualified by the definition of "adjudication"—"agency process for the formulation of an order."[1] "Fair hearing," "evidentiary hearing," "contested case," "trial-type hearing," and "hearing on the record" all refer to an adjudicatory hearing. As with rules, the crucial determinant of whether an action is an adjudicatory proceeding is not what an agency calls it, but the actual procedure the agency was required to follow in taking the action. If the agency was required to make its decision "on the record after opportunity for an agency hearing," the agency must prove if the decision is challenged that it followed adjudicatory procedures.

Actual adjudicatory procedures are subject to considerable variation ranging from relatively informal oral proceedings up through highly formalized hearings that involve most of the procedural aspects of a trial. The precise nature of the procedures followed depends on whether the hearing was statutorily mandated or was required by the courts, and on the specific rules of the agency involved. Such hearings involve at a minimum the presentation of evidence and the provision of an opportunity to rebut that evidence. The decision, based on the record compiled at the hearing, is made by an impartial person. Like trials, adjudicatory hearings are best suited for determining the specific facts of an individual case, what Davis has called "adjudicatory facts."[2] The essential fairness of these procedures which allow an individual who has been accused of violating a specific law or regulation to counter those claims in an open and adversary proceeding is vital to the continued legitimacy of the administrative process.

Those same procedural aspects limit the utility of adjudicatory hearings for other types of administrative actions. The adversarial nature of hearings, their limits on participation, and their restrictions on the use of agency expertise become disadvantages in general rule making. The expense involved and the opportunities for tremendous delay implicit in adjudicatory procedures further limit their effectiveness and efficiency for other administrative actions. When, if, and in what form they should be used has become one of the most controversial questions in contemporary administrative regulation. As discussed in chapter 8, Congress has increasingly required agencies to provide some kind of hearing in rule making. Similarly, the federal courts have, in the past decade, required administrative agencies at all levels of government to provide an opportunity to be heard in a wide variety of situations where previously administrators had been allowed broad discretion in choosing procedures.

THE OPPORTUNITY TO BE HEARD: WHEN REQUIRED

Statutory Requirements

The Administrative Procedure Act states that an agency must follow adjudicatory procedures "in every case of adjudication required by statute to be determined on the record after opportunity for an agency hearing."[3] Whether the actual nature of the action is rule making, licensing, testing, or determining an individual's compliance with the law, if by statute Congress requires an on-the-record hearing, the agency must provide for one. As was pointed out in the preceding chapter, however, the Supreme Court has held that in rule making the statutory language must be explicit before it will require an agency to hold an adjudicatory hearing. Statutory requirements for a hearing for other types of administrative actions need not be and seldom are quite so explicit. The Federal Communications Act, for example, states that in the case of contested applications for broadcast licenses, "The Commission . . . shall formally designate the application for hearing on the ground or reasons then obtaining."[4] Similarly, the Federal Trade Commission Act states that when the Commission believes a corporation has engaged in unfair methods of competition or deceptive acts, "it shall issue and serve upon such person . . . a complaint . . . containing a notice of hearing."[5] In both instances the hearing required is an adjudicatory one.

Constitutional Requirements for a Hearing

The first place to look, then, to determine if an agency must provide an opportunity to be heard is the agency's authorizing statutes. Statutory silence or failure to require a hearing, however, does not necessarily mean that one is not required. The Fifth and Fourteenth Amendments prohibit government from depriving a person "of life, liberty or property without due process of law" and have been interpreted by the courts to require the provision of an opportunity to be heard in various administrative situations.

One of the first Supreme Court decisions to arrive at such a conclusion was *Londoner v. Denver*. The Colorado legislature had authorized the City of Denver to order the paving of streets, to apportion the cost of that paving among property owners on the street, and assess each property owner on the basis of benefits received. Although property owners were allowed to file written complaints, they were not provided an opportunity to be heard. The Court held that this violated the due process clause of the Fourteenth Amendment:

> Where the legislature of a State, instead of fixing the tax itself, commits to some subordinate body the duty of determining whether, in what amount and upon whom it shall be levied, . . . due process of law requires that at some stage of the proceedings before the tax becomes irrevocably fixed, the taxpayer shall have the opportunity to be heard.[6]

What *Londoner v. Denver* seemingly established was that whenever an administrative action was specific and particularized in impact and when it adversely affected a legal right, an opportunity to be heard had to be provided whether required by statute or not. The decision laid the groundwork for the due process explosion of the 1970s that required both courts and administrators to define "legal rights" and to determine which of the myriad of benefits, grants, and privileges that government provided were protected rights that could not be taken away without an opportunity for a hearing. Legal rights obviously include both explicit and implicit constitutional rights discussed in chapter 3,[7] but they have also come to include many of the benefits and opportunities provided by government as was discussed in chapter 4.[8]

The greatest expansion in legal rights has come from the transformation of government benefits into property interests, bringing them squarely under the protection of the due process clauses. The process necessary to transform a benefit into such a constitutionally protected property interest and the consequences of the conversion were explained by the Supreme Court in *Board of Regents of State Colleges v. Roth*:

> The Fourteenth Amendment's procedural protection of property is a safeguard of the security of interests that a person has already in specific benefits. These interests—property interests—take many forms.
>
> To have property interest in a benefit a person clearly must have more than a unilateral expectation of it. He must instead have a legitimate claim of entitlement to it. It is a purpose of the ancient institution of property to protect those claims upon which people rely in their daily lives, reliance that must not be arbitrarily undermined. It is a purpose of the constitutional right to a hearing to provide an opportunity for a person to vindicate these claims.
>
> Property interests, of course, are not created by the Constitution. Rather they are created and their dimensions are defined by existing rules or understandings that stem from an independent source such as state law, rules or understandings that secure certain benefits and that support claims of entitlement to those benefits.[9]

The key to turning a benefit into a protected property interest remains a specific legal enactment—state constitution or law, federal law or administrative regulation—stating or at least interpretable as stating that an entitlement has been created. Among the federal benefit programs that the courts have held to create property interests for eligible individuals are AFDC payments,[10] Social Security disability benefits,[11] and unemployment compensation.[12] Similarly, by virtue of statutory language, Food Stamps, Veterans Benefits, public housing, Social Security, Medicare, and Medicaid create entitlements for eligible individuals. The establishment of these benefits programs as creating legal rights has led both the courts and administrative agencies into a due process quandary. Among the complex questions that have arisen are

1. Are applicants who are denied benefits entitled to the same opportunity to be heard as recipients whose benefits are reduced or terminated?
2. Does any administrative action which adversely affects beneficiaries require providing them an opportunity to be heard?
3. Are the timing and nature of the hearing the same for all benefits programs?

The answers that have been given by the courts to these questions are not likely to satisfy those who value consistency and uniformity. In the absence of specific statutory requirements, denied applicants do not have the same right to a hearing that actual recipients do. "It has long been settled that a party aggrieved by loss of a preexisting right or privilege may enjoy procedural rights not available to one denied the right or privilege in the first instance."[13] In 1980, the Ninth Circuit Court of Appeals applied the ethic of cost-benefit so popular in national politics to applicants whose claims for welfare benefits had been denied. Although the court agreed that applicants had a statutory entitlement protected by due process, in determining required procedures, "costs to the public must be weighed against benefits to both the individual and the public."[14] In this instance the costs were held to outweigh the benefits.

The Supreme Court addressed the second question in 1980 in *O'Bannion v. Town Court Nursing Center*.[15] Pursuant to its own regulations and those issued by the Department of Health, Education and Welfare, the Pennsylvania Department of Public Welfare had revoked the authority of the nursing center to be reimbursed for patient care under Medicaid and Medicare. The consequences of that revocation was the displacement of patients who were Medicaid or Medicare recipients. They argued that they were entitled to a prerevocation hearing. Although the Supreme Court conceded that the revocation would have an adverse impact on the recipients, the enforcement proceeding did not directly affect their constitutional or legal rights since they had no property interest in receiving treatment at a particular facility. Although the result of the revocation may be considerable hardship and in some instances a lack of ability to receive care, the injury to their protected interest was too indirect and incidental to establish a right for an opportunity to be heard.

The timing and nature of a court-imposed hearing will be discussed at length in the following section. When and what kind of a hearing must be provided is subject to endless variation depending on the nature of the interest involved and the courts' perception of the severity of the injury to that interest.

The Supreme Court's approach to determining which governmentally granted benefits are rights has been cautious and somewhat inconsistent, demonstrating considerable reluctance either to accept or to reject completely the old dichotomy between rights and privileges. One area where the Court's caution and inconsistency have been amply illustrated has been the status of public employment. In 1956, the Court held that a public college professor who had explicitly been granted tenure was entitled to procedural due process (a hearing) before dismissal.[16] In 1972, the Court expanded this procedural due process protection to a public college professor employed by a college which had no tenure system:

> A person's interest in a benefit is a "property" interest for due process purposes if there are rules or mutually explicit understandings that support his claim of entitlement.[17]

In that case the Court held that an understanding could form the basis of an entitlement to continued employment which required providing the affected individual an opportunity for hearing prior to dismissal.

In 1976, in *Bishop v. Wood*, the Court held that local government employees have a property interest in their jobs only if such an interest has been specifically granted by statute or ordinance. A city ordinance of Marion, North Carolina, provided that city employees became permanent employees after six months and that permanent employees could be removed for specified causes. The ordinance did not require that a hearing be provided for permanent employees who were dismissed. The Court held that the granting of permanent employment status did not create a property interest in the job so long as the ordinance did not so specify:

> The ordinance may also be construed as granting no right to continued employment by merely conditioning an employee's removal on compliance with certain specified procedures.[18]

The closing sentence in the *Bishop* decision offered little comfort to public employees who might be erroneously or unfairly dismissed from their jobs: "The Due Process Clause of the Fourteenth Amendment is not a guarantee against incorrect or ill-advised personnel decisions."

Although state and local government employees are thus apparently dependent on specific statutory language granting a right to a hearing when they are dismissed for cause, federal employees have been given such a right. Title II of the Civil Service Reform Act of 1978 provides that employees of covered agencies have the right to appeal an adverse personnel action to the Merit System Protection Board (MSPB). The MSPB is required to grant all appellants a hearing and allow them to be represented by an attorney at the hearing. In cases involving unacceptable performance, the MSPB must find the agency action to be supported by substantial evidence. In all other cases, the agency must be supported by a preponderance of evidence.

The status of students in public educational institutions is nearly as ambiguous as that of public employees. In 1961, the Fifth Circuit Court of Appeals held that students at tax-supported colleges were entitled to notice and an opportunity for some kind of hearing before they were expelled for misconduct.[19] Although the Court of Appeals found that there was no right to attend a public college and that published Board of Education regulations specified the college could at any time decline to provide service to any student, the court nevertheless held that due process was applicable and "the

State cannot condition the granting of even a privilege upon the renunciation of the constitutional right to procedural due process." The Supreme Court remained silent on the subject until 1973, when it held that there was no federal constitutional right to an education at public expense.[20] In 1975, in *Goss v. Lopez*,[21] however, the Court held that a state could by statute create an entitlement to a public education, and if it did so, students had a property interest in education that they could not be deprived of without due process, subject, however, to certain qualifications. At issue in *Goss v. Lopez* was a 10-day suspension of students for disruptive conduct. The Court explicitly limited its holding to suspensions for misconduct, although normally the reason that a state or the federal government has for depriving an individual of a right is not determinative of whether they must follow due process. Further, the procedural requirements established were not particularly demanding: "Students facing suspension and a consequent interference with a protected property interest must be given *some* kind of notice and afforded *some* kind of hearing."

The Supreme Court never expanded the due process protections provided students in *Goss v. Lopez* and has rather severely circumscribed the situations in which hearings must be provided for them. In 1977, the Court held that schools need not provide an opportunity to be heard before inflicting corporal punishment on students[22] and in 1978, the Court explicitly refused to require hearings for dismissals for academic reasons. After emphasizing the "distinct differences" between educational actions taken for disciplinary and academic reasons, the Court expressed the same weariness with and wariness of involvement in educational administration that it had expressed with public personnel administration. "We decline to further enlarge the judicial presence in the academic community and thereby risk deterioration of many beneficial aspects of the faculty–student relationship. We recognize as did the Massachusetts Supreme Judicial Court over 60 years ago, that a hearing may be 'useless or even harmful in finding out the truth as to scholarship.' "[23]

Although government grants and contracts constitute a major portion of some businesses' and universities' financial well being, the courts and Congress have shown little enthusiasm for establishing them as property interests and no hearing is usually needed if they are not awarded. The Court in 1940, in *Perkins v. Lukens Steel Co.*,[24] held that "no legal rights" were violated when the government refused to purchase steel from a particular company. The only exception that has been made in this area is that some courts of appeals' decisions have held that the government could not permanently debar a person or company from receiving contracts without a full hearing to ensure government was not acting arbitrarily.[25]

The status of licenses held by individuals and businesses varies depending on the type of license involved. A license is a permit issued by government allowing the recipient to engage in a specified activity. Activities that are subject to licensing in the United States include but are not limited to driving a car, practicing medicine, law, and a host of other occupations, selling liquor, operating a pool hall, a radio, or television station or a nuclear power plant. The suspension, denial, or revocation of such licenses can obviously have an immediate, negative, and severe impact on affected individuals. In some instances, particularly at the federal level, Congress has expressly required license-granting agencies to provide potential or actual licensees opportunity for hearing in any situation which may negatively affect them. The Administrative Procedure Act expressly addressed the procedures that agencies must generally follow in licensing: "When application is made for a license required by law, the agency . . . shall set and complete proceedings required to be conducted in accordance with sections 556 and 557 of this title."[26] The APA also requires that before instituting "proceedings" to withdraw, suspend, revoke, or annul a license the agency must provide the licensee with written notice and opportunity to demonstrate or achieve compliance with all lawful requirements.

State and local licensing procedures, which affect far more individuals and businesses, are not necessarily so clearly stipulated or protective of the right of licensees to a hearing, and the concept of a license as a "mere privilege" retains some viability. In the area of occupational licensing, federal and state courts originally established a distinction between the respectable, "learned," "dignified" callings (law, medicine) and those which they perceived to be less dignified, respectable, and learned (selling liquor, operating pool halls). The distinction was recognized by the Supreme Court in 1873 when it held that before a state could disbar an attorney it was required to provide him notice and "ample opportunity of explanation and defence. . . . All courts have agreed that some classes of licensees do indeed have genuine rights of which they cannot be deprived without opportunity to be heard."[27] Courts have been far more reluctant to extend procedural due process rights to those engaged in the "undignified" professions or to licensees for engaging in what they perceive to be nonessential activities. Drivers' licenses, which in many areas of the United States are as essential to survival as a job or welfare benefits, appear to have made the transition from being mere privileges to quasi-rights which under certain circumstances may not be suspended without an opportunity for hearing.[28] The Model State Administrative Procedure Act further clarifies the status of licensees and provides them the same procedural protections as accorded by the federal act.

Due process also protects liberty interests and unquestionably many administrative actions may result in restricting or denying such liberty interests. The federal courts, however, have been more reluctant to require agencies to provide an opportunity for hearings when the appellant alleges that the action infringes a liberty interest than if a property interest is at stake. In *Roth*, *Kennedy*, and *Bishop*, for example, the dismissed employees argued that their terminations also infringed protected liberty interests. All three argued that their dismissals wrongfully stigmatized them and limited their freedom to seek other employment. Although the Supreme Court in *Roth* reiterated its commitment to a broad definition of liberty as

> not merely freedom from bodily restraint but also the right of the individual to contract, to engage in any of the common occupations of life, to acquire useful knowledge, to marry, establish a home and bring up children, to worship God . . . and generally to enjoy those privileges long recognized . . . as essential to the orderly pursuit of happiness by free men (*Meyer v. Nebraska*, 262 U.S. 390),[29]

it did not find that the challenged administrative actions in the three cases had violated liberty interests. From the Court's perspective the major relevant liberty interest in the cases was the individual's right to protect his "good name, reputation, honor, or integrity." In *Roth*, the Court found that the administrative action imposed no stigma on the individual's reputation; in *Kennedy*, it found that the existence of a posttermination hearing was sufficient to allow the individual to clear his name; and in *Bishop*, since the reasons for discharge had not been made public, no stigma severely damaging to Bishop's reputation had occurred. In *Board of Curators v. Horowitz*, the Supreme Court declined even to consider if Charlotte Horowitz's termination from medical school had deprived her of a liberty interest since she had "been awarded at least as much due process as the Fourteenth Amendment requires."

The Supreme Court further refined and limited its definition of "liberty" interests that require an opportunity to be heard before agencies restrict them in *Paul v. Davis*.[30] In 1971, the Court had held in *Wisconsin v. Constantineau*[31] that "where a person's good name, reputation, honor or integrity is at stake because of what government is doing to him, notice and opportunity to be heard are essential." A Wisconsin statute had prohibited the sale or delivery of alcoholic beverages to persons who "were determined to have become hazards to themselves, to their family or to the community by reason of their excessive drinking." Constantineau had been so "posted" without an opportunity for a hearing, and the Court held this to be a violation of due process. In *Paul v. Davis*, the police had distributed a flyer "of subjects known to be active shoplifters" and had included in that flyer the photograph and name of Edward Davis who had been charged but never tried or convicted of shoplifting. Ultimately, the charges against him had been dropped. The Supreme Court, however, held that no liberty interest had been infringed and in its opinion clearly differentiated the action from that involved in *Constantineau*. The distinction rested on the phrase "because of what the government is doing to him," which it held "referred to the fact that the governmental action taken in that case [Constantineau] deprived the individual of a right previously held under state law—the right to purchase or obtain liquor. . . . 'Posting,' therefore, significantly altered her status as a matter of state law, and it was that alteration of legal status which, combined with the injury resulting from defamation, justified the invocation of procedural safeguards. The 'stigma' resulting from the defamatory character of the posting was doubtless an important factor . . . but we do not think that such defamation, standing alone, deprived Constantineau of any 'liberty' protected by the procedural guarantees of the Fourteenth Amendment."[32]

The key to this rather complex tangle as to when adminstrative agencies must provide an opportunity to be heard where liberty interests are negatively affected now appears to be the phrase "standing alone." Infringement of a property interest, "standing alone," requires an opportunity to be heard. The infringement of certain types of liberty interests, "standing alone," however, does not. Only if the infringement of these interests results in the infringement of some other clearly defined legal right (such as a property interest) is an opportunity to be heard required.

One area in which the Supreme Court has held that the infringement of liberty interests "standing alone" may require an opportunity to be heard has been in the area of postconviction treatment of criminals. In 1972, in *Morrissey v. Brewer*,[33] the Court held that before a state could finally revoke an individual's parole it had to provide him both a preliminary and final revocation hearing, and in 1973, it applied the same requirements to revocation of probation.[34] In 1974, the Court held that disciplinary actions within state prisons were also subject to requirements for due process. Specifically, the Court found that the taking of "good time" involved deprivation of a liberty interest which required prison officials to provide affected prisoners with the opportunity for a modified form of hearing.[35]

By 1976, the Court had pursued the protection of liberty interests of prisoners about as far as it cared to go. Six prisoners at the Massachusetts Correctional Institution had been transferred from the facility to other state prisons after having been accused of criminal involvement in several fires that had occurred at the institution. The prisoners had not been provided the opportunity to appear at a hearing and defend themselves prior to the transfers and consequently alleged they had been deprived of due process. The Supreme Court disagreed, primarily because it could find no "liberty interest" that had been violated. As the Court noted, conviction had already deprived the individual of his liberty interest and it could find nothing in the due process clause which protected a prisoner from transfers within a state prison system.[36] As it had done in other administrative areas the Court expressed its disinclination toward being involved in the mundane details of administration: "Holding that arrangements like this are within the reach of the procedural protections of the Due Process Clause would place the Clause astride the day to day functioning of state prisons and involve the judiciary in issues and discretionary decisions that are not the business of federal judges." In 1979, the Court limited the reach of the due process clause decisions involving the granting or denying of parole to eligible inmates. In *Greenholtz v. Inmates of the Nebraska Penal and Correctional Complex*,[37] the Court ruled that due process did not require that every eligible inmate be given a hearing, be allowed to participate in parole board hearings, or even be informed of the evidence upon which the board based a decision to deny parole. In 1980, however, the Court did hold that a state could not declare a prison inmate mentally ill and place him against his will under psychiatric treatment without providing him with a hearing. Unlike transfers from one prison to another, the transfer from a prison to a mental institution did involve the violation of a liberty interest since an inmate could have a reasonable expectation that he would not be moved to such a facility.[38]

Although the doctrine of privileges has been considerably modified and the Supreme Court seldom uses the term any longer in determining whether an opportunity for hearing must be provided, reports of its complete and total demise are exaggerated. In the first place, some government actions clearly remain privileges that may in fact be denied without a hearing. The most unblemished example of such an action remains the admission of aliens into the United States. Neither Congress nor the Supreme Court has ever modified the Court's holding in *Knauff v. Shaughnessy*: "Admission of aliens to the United States is a privilege . . . granted only upon such terms as the United States shall prescribe."[39] The Supreme Court held steadfast on that issue even when it involved an alien who had lived in the United States for 25 years and had left the country to visit his dying mother. The subsequent refusal to readmit him resulted in his being confined on Ellis Island for nearly two years without being given reasons for the refusal to readmit him. Both the detention and failure to provide an opportunity for a hearing might be unfortunate but they were not unconstitutional: "Whatever the procedure authorized by Congress is, it is due process as far as an alien denied entry is concerned."[40] In the second place, recent Supreme Court decisions have been increasingly restrictive in their definition of what kinds of liberty interests are protected by due process in administrative actions and similarly reluctant to extend property interests in the absence of express legislative language creating such a right.

Adjudication versus Rule Making

Even if an administrative agency is required by statute or the Constitution to provide an opportunity for hearing, it may still bypass that requirement in some instances by promulgating rules of general applicability. Seven years after the Supreme Court handed down its decision in *Londoner v. Denver*, it was once more confronted with the question of what due process required in administrative actions increasing property taxes. At issue this time, however, was an administrative decision that increased the value of *all* taxable property in Denver by 40 percent. As was true in *Londoner*, no opportunity to be heard was provided to taxpayers, but the Supreme Court approached the issue from a different perspective: "The question then is whether all individuals have a constitutional right to be heard before a matter can be decided in which all are equally concerned."[41] The answer was "no." "Where a rule of conduct applies to more than a few people it is impracticable that everyone should have a direct voice in its enactment," and if the decision had been made by the state legislature, "no one would suggest that the Fourteenth Amendment was violated unless every person affected had been allowed an opportunity to raise his voice against it. . . . There must be a limit to individual argument in such matters if government is to go on."[42]

Just as in some instances agencies have eschewed general rule making in favor of adjudicatory policy making, in other instances agencies have eschewed a case-by-case approach in favor of general rule making. The Supreme Court has been as tolerant of the latter as of the former. In 1943, in *United States v. Storer Broadcasting Co.*,[43] the Court upheld the power of the Federal Communications Commission to promulgate rules of general applicability and to deny an adjudicatory hearing to license applicants whose applications demonstrated a violation of the qualifications established by the rule. The Storer Doctrine was reaffirmed in *FPC v. Texaco*:

> The statutory requirement for a hearing . . . does not preclude the Commission
> from particularizing statutory standards through the rulemaking process and
> barring at the threshold those who neither measure up to them nor show reasons
> why in the public interest the rules should be waived.[44]

Storer and *Texaco* upheld the power of agencies to establish through rule-making procedures general standards and qualifications and to deny hearings to applicants who failed to satisfy those qualifications. The Second Circuit Court of Appeals in *Airline Pilots Association v. Quesada*[45] held that an agency could by rule making alter or even abolish existing property rights without providing affected individuals an opportunity for hearing. The Federal Aviation Act provided that before an airman's license could be revoked an adjudicatory hearing must be provided. In 1958, the FAA issued general regulations barring individuals over the age of sixty from serving as pilots. The result of that regulation was not only to modify the license rights of all pilots but also to revoke automatically the licenses of all pilots over the age of sixty. The Court of

Appeals upheld the FAA's rules and the automatic revocation of some licenses without a hearing:

> The administrator's action does not lose the character of rulemaking because it modified the plaintiff pilots' claimed property rights in their license and their contractual rights under collective bargaining agreements. . . . Administrative regulations often limit in the public interest the use that persons may make of their property without affording each one affected an opportunity to present evidence upon the fairness of the regulation.[46]

Basically, then, when an administrative action adversely affects a specific, individual legal or constitutional right and the application of that action depends on the determination of specific, particularized facts of the cases, a hearing must be provided. Otherwise, unless a statute so requires, the agency is allowed to use other forms of administrative action to accomplish its purposes.

TIMING OF THE HEARING

Although it might seem that if a hearing is required, it should be held before the affected individual has been adversely affected, this is not always the case. In many instances agencies are allowed to take initial actions which have immediate adverse and serious consequences and to provide a hearing sometime later in the administrative process.

One of the major categories of situations in which an agency is permitted to act first and provide a hearing later are emergency situations in which the public health or safety is threatened. As discussed in chapter 8, the courts have almost invariably allowed administrative agencies to act quickly to protect the public through summary and other types of informal actions in a variety of situations. In those situations, the hearing, where one is provided, will come well after irrevocable and adverse action has taken place.

Similarly, in many government benefits programs when a recipient is believed to be ineligible for further payments, benefits may be suspended immediately with the opportunity for hearing provided only after the initial termination. The constitutional propriety of such arrangements was the actual issue in contention in *Goldberg v. Kelly*.[47] The procedural regulations of the New York City Department of Social Services did provide welfare recipients whose benefits were terminated with the right to a "fair hearing," but the hearing was to be provided only after the initial termination of benefits. If the recipient prevailed at the hearing, then she was entitled to receive all benefits erroneously withheld. Specifically limiting its decision to welfare recipients, the Supreme Court held the posttermination hearing procedure to be an unconstitutional violation of due process:

> For qualified recipients, welfare provides the means to obtain essential food, clothing, housing, and medical care. . . . [T]ermination of aid pending resolution of a controversy over eligibility may deprive an eligible recipient of the very means by which to live while he waits. Since he lacks independent resources, his situation becomes immediately desperate. . . .
>
> Moreover, important governmental interests are promoted by affording

recipients pre-termination evidentiary hearing. . . . Public assistance, then, is not mere charity, but a means to "promote the general Welfare and secure the Blessings of Liberty to ourselves and our posterity." The same governmental interests which counsel the provision of welfare, counsel as well its uninterrupted provision to those eligible to receive it; pre-termination evidentiary hearings are indispensable to that end.[48]

The Court noted in *Goldberg* that it found the "crucial factor" in requiring the pretermination hearing to be the immediate physical and economic desolation that an eligible welfare recipient would face if his/her benefits were cut off. The Court also noted this was "a factor not present in the case of a blacklisted government contractor, the discharged government employee, the taxpayer denied a tax exemption, or virtually anyone else whose governmental largesse is ended." While the Court's legal logic may be sound, its assumption about the financial position of recipients of other government benefits programs is arguable. Nevertheless, in subsequent cases it has adhered to the reasoning in *Goldberg*: In situations involving the termination of government benefits, even if those benefits are a property right, a pretermination hearing is required only if the desperation of the recipient outweighs the legitimate government interest in prompt action.

In 1974, a badly divided Supreme Court held that nonprobationary federal employees were not entitled to a hearing prior to dismissal but there was little agreement among the justices as to why this was so. Two of the justices in the majority held that the provision of a posttermination hearing satisfied due process requirements while the three other justices in the majority contended that since no property interest was involved due process requirements were not relevant.[49] In *Mathews v. Eldridge*,[50] the Supreme Court further clarified the circumstances under which pretermination hearings were required. At issue in this case were the procedures followed in terminating Social Security disability benefits. The Social Security Act specified that to be eligible for disability benefits a worker must have shown that he was unable "to engage in any substantial gainful activity by reason of any medically determinable physical or mental impairment which can be expected to result in death or which has lasted or can be expected to last" for at least 12 months.[51] As had been true of the New York City Social Service regulations, the only opportunity for a hearing provided to disability recipients was after their benefits had been terminated. Although the Secretary of HEW conceded that on average a delay of over a year between the cutoff of benefits and a decision in a hearing was likely, the Supreme Court did not find the necessary degree of desperation to require a pretermination hearing: "the hardship imposed upon the erroneously terminated disability recipient may be significant. Still the disabled worker's need is likely to be less than that of a welfare recipient." Three factors were to be weighed in determining whether a pretermination hearing was required:

First, the private interest that will be affected by the official action; second, the risk of an erroneous deprivation of such interest through the procedures used, and the probable value, if any, of additional or substitute procedural safeguards; and finally, the Government's interest, including the function involved and the fiscal and administrative burdens that the additional or substitute procedural requirement would entail.[52]

On all three factors, disability benefit recipients fell short. Their interest in continued payments was not one of desperate necessity; the procedures already provided by the SSA were sufficiently fair to safeguard against flagrant error, and the "Government's interest, and hence that of the public in conserving scarce fiscal administrative resources" was a weighty and significant one.

In 1977, the Court applied its three-factor test to the automatic revocation of drivers' licenses when the license had been suspended three times within ten years. Once again the Court held that the government's interest in administrative efficiency when compared to the risk of erroneous deprivation and the severity of that deprivation was sufficient to justify the lack of an opportunity for pretermination hearings,[53] particularly since a posttermination hearing was provided.

In those situations where the Court has allowed a required hearing to be held after action has been taken, it has usually carefully scrutinized the nature of preliminary procedures both in terms of their potential for avoiding error and their essential fairness. Where it has determined the procedures to be inadequate on those two counts, it has been reluctant to allow prehearing action unless the agency acted to protect public health or safety. Even when the Court has required a prior opportunity for hearing, it has not necessarily required a full-blown adjudicatory hearing.

WHAT KIND OF HEARING?

As Justice Rehnquist noted in *United States v. Florida East Coast Railway Co.*, "The term 'hearing' in its legal context undoubtedly has a host of meanings."[54] The meanings of the term are not limited to the distinction between rule making and adjudicatory hearings but include a wide diversity of procedures that may be used to satisfy a requirement for some kind of hearing. At the federal level, if the hearing is required by statute, the basic procedures to be followed are those specified in the Administrative Procedure Act. When the hearing is one that is required by court decision, however, the court frequently will specify just how much process is due to satisfy its notion of procedural fairness. The required procedures range from providing an informal opportunity to the affected individual to present his side of the case to providing him with a full-scale, trial-type hearing.

Before discussing the hearing process, it should be noted that even though an agency may be obligated to provide an opportunity to be heard, the adversely affected person is not obligated to take advantage of that opportunity. As with other rights, the right to a hearing may be waived by the individual and in the overwhelming majority of cases is. Although precise figures vary from agency to agency, generally at the federal level less than 5 percent of the cases in which an opportunity to be heard exists actually result in a full-scale hearing.[55]

Although the general procedural requirements for an on-the-record hearing are specified by §§554–557 of the Administrative Procedure Act, specific procedures followed will vary from agency to agency. In addition to those general legislative requirements, specific procedural guidelines for agency hearings are derived from three other sources:

1. Procedural rules of the agency, which in many cases are more demanding than the APA requirements and like other procedural rules are binding on the agency involved;
2. Authorizing statutes in which Congress has modified APA requirements for specific agencies or specific actions; and
3. Court decisions defining or interpreting constitutional and statutory provisions and agency procedural regulations.

The actual procedure followed in an adjudicatory hearing is a composite of the requirements emerging from these four sources. The existence of these multiple sources of requirements ensures considerable diversity in actual hearing procedures from agency to agency and in some instances within an individual agency depending on the nature of the issue or even of the parties involved in the hearing.

Notice

Persons entitled to notice of an agency hearing shall be timely informed of:
> (1) the time, place, and nature of the hearing;
> (2) the legal authority and jurisdiction under which the hearing is to be held; and
> (3) the matters of fact and law asserted.[56]

Once an agency has decided to take action against a specific person, the first and most obvious thing it must do is to notify that person. Unquestionably, the business or individual that is the subject of the proposed adverse action is "entitled to notice," but the APA leaves unresolved the question whether any other persons are also similarly entitled. Further, unlike notices for proposed rule making, notices of adjudicatory proceedings are not required by the FOIA to be published in the Federal Register. Since most authorizing statutes are also silent as to who besides the party named in the action is entitled to notice, any expansion of the notice requirement apparently lies within agency discretion. Responding to this situation, some federal agencies have developed procedures to publish notice generally in the Federal Register and newspapers and to provide specific notice to public interest groups, competitors, or other groups they feel may be interested in a case. The FCC, for example, requires licensees to publicize license renewal proceedings.

The time and place of the hearing are determined by the agency unless authorizing statutes specify otherwise. The APA does require that "due regard shall be had for the convenience and necessity of the parties." As far as the timing of the hearing is concerned, this requires that the agency must provide the individual adequate time to prepare for the case. What constitutes adequate time, however, is subject to agency and court interpretation. In *Goldberg v. Kelly*,[57] for example, the Supreme Court gave qualified approval to seven-days advance notice: "We are not prepared to say that the seven-days notice . . . is constitutionally insufficient per se, although there may be cases where fairness would require that a longer time be given." In *Wolff v. McDonnell* (a prison disciplinary action case), the Court shortened the required notice period considerably: "[N]o less than 24 hours . . . should be allowed for the inmate to prepare."[58]

In *Goss v. Lopez*, it shortened it still more: "There need be no delay between the time 'notice' is given and the timing of the hearing."[59] In general, the more complex the legal and factual issues involved in a case, the more time the agency must allow for preparation after serving notice. Conversely, an agency which excessively delays the scheduling of a hearing runs the risk of being challenged in court by an interested party. Section 706 of the APA provides that a reviewing court "shall compel agency action unlawfully withheld or unreasonably delayed," and some lower federal courts have used that as a basis for judicial review of agency nonscheduling of hearings.[60] The location of the hearing is also within the agency's discretion and as long as the agency has not acted arbitrarily, capriciously, or in total disregard for the convenience of the individual moved against, the courts will uphold the choice.

An additional factor that agencies must consider in scheduling hearings is the requirement for consolidation established by the Supreme Court in *Ashbacker Radio Corp. v. FCC.*[61] Where a decision in one case effectively precludes a decision in another case, the agency must combine the two cases and hear them simultaneously. One of the most common situations in which this problem might arise is, as was true in *Ashbacker*, in applications for broadcast licenses when the grant of a license to one applicant would foreclose the possibility of such a grant to another applicant.

Right to Counsel

Although the Sixth Amendment guarantees defendants in criminal cases the right to be represented by counsel, administrative hearings are not criminal cases and consequently there is no constitutional right to counsel in hearings. Even in those situations where the Supreme Court has required agencies to provide an opportunity to be heard it has been noticeably reluctant to impose any uniform requirement for those adversely affected to be represented by retained counsel and even more reluctant to require agencies to provide counsel for indigents. In *Goldberg*, the Court did require that the welfare agency allow the recipient to retain an attorney, but did not require the agency to provide one. In *Gagnon v. Scarpelli*, it stated that in most probation revocation hearings the presence of an attorney would be "undesirable," but refused to establish a uniform requirement on that point: "We think rather that the decision as to need for counsel must be made on a case-by-case basis. . . . [A]lthough the presence and participation of counsel will probably be both undesirable and constitutionally unnecessary in most revocation hearings, there will remain certain cases in which fundamental fairness . . . will require the State to provide at its own expense counsel."[62] The Court did indicate in *Gagnon* that where the individual requested an attorney, appeared to be incapable of speaking for himself, and put forth a colorable claim of either innocence of the charges or mitigating circumstances, the agency should seriously consider providing an attorney. If the request for an attorney was denied, "the grounds for refusal should be stated succinctly in the record." In cases involving the involuntary transfer of a prison inmate to a mental institution, although the Court did not require the State to provide the inmate with an attorney, it did require that it must provide him a qualified, independent advisor to assist at the hearing.[63] In *Wolff v. McDonnell*, it denied inmates subject to disciplinary actions the right to either retained or appointed counsel;

and in *Goss v. Lopez*, it similarly denied high school students the right to retain counsel.

The Administrative Procedure Act, however, provides that "A person compelled to appear in person before an agency or representative thereof is entitled to be accompanied, represented, and advised by counsel, or, if permitted by the agency, by other qualified representative. A party is entitled to appear in person or with counsel or other duly qualified representative in an agency proceeding."[64] Although the language of the APA appears to be unequivocal, the right to be represented by counsel remains only a statutory right that may be and has been considerably modified by other statutes. The most common type of federal statute that in reality limits the right to counsel either explicitly limits the fees that may be paid to counsel ($10 for adjudication of veterans' claims)[65] or allows the agency to set such fees.[66] Although such fee limits may make it extremely difficult, if not impossible, to retain an attorney, the Supreme Court has consistently upheld the limitations.[67] Further, the language of the APA does not necessarily mean that agencies are obligated to provide counsel at their expense to indigent parties, and the Supreme Court has not compelled agencies to do so.

Public Intervenors

The APA, as discussed above, does not clearly define who should be considered "parties" entitled to participate fully in all stages of an adjudicatory case. Prior to 1966, most federal agencies took a very restrictive view of who had standing to intervene in adjudicatory cases. To establish such standing potential intervenors had to show invasion of a legally protected interest or substantial and direct injury greater than that suffered by members of the general public. That definition was usually sufficient to disqualify public interest groups from any right to be admitted as parties in adjudicatory hearings. Using this standard, the FCC for example, refused to permit viewers of a television station standing to intervene as parties in a license renewal proceeding. In a groundbreaking decision, the D.C. Court of Appeals overruled the Commission and ordered it to allow "some audience participation" in license renewal proceedings.[68]

The issue of allowing public intervenors as full parties in adjudicatory proceedings is considerably more controversial than allowing such participation in rule making. Although not criminal cases, many adjudicatory cases can result in rather heavy sanctions being imposed on the individual named in the case. In analagous criminal situations, full participatory rights are limited to the accused and the state. While many public interest groups argue that their participation is highly desirable in cases involving corporate misconduct, in other situations other groups, as well as the named party in the cases, would contest the desirability of such intervention. For example, the desirability, as well as the fairness, of allowing the Citizens United to Eliminate Cheats on Welfare full intervention rights in a welfare termination hearing is questionable.

Most agencies, like the FCC, have resisted extending the right to intervene on the grounds that it might result in a "a host of parties" descending on them, clogging, delaying, and stalling the adjudicatory process.[69] Although their fears on this point have been overstated, the expanded rights of participation, particularly in nuclear power plant licensing decisions, may have contributed to "analysis paralysis."[70] The courts, however, have not found that argument persuasive:

> The fears of regulatory agencies that their processes will be inundated are rarely borne out. Always a restraining factor is the expense of participation in the administrative process.[71]

Further, the courts have consistently recognized the power of the agencies to limit unnecessary delays, repetition, and obstructions through procedural regulation.

In 1971, the Administrative Conference of the United States adopted guidelines for the role and rights of public intervenors in federal agency proceedings. Although generally supportive of allowing and encouraging full public participation in hearings, the guidelines also addressed the necessity of protecting the rights of the named party: "Public participation in adjudications where the issue is whether the charged respondent has violated a settled law or policy should be permitted only after close scrutiny of the effect of intervention . . . on existing parties."[72] Currently, most agencies readily permit public intervenors to participate freely and fully at the hearing stage of the process and some have reimbursed public intervenors for their expenses.

Prehearing Conference

> The agency shall give all interested parties opportunity for—
> 1. The submission and consideration of facts, arguments, offers of settlement, or proposals of adjustment when time, the nature of the proceeding and the public interest permit.[73]

> Subject to the published rules of the agency and within its powers, employees presiding at hearings may—
> (6) hold conferences for the settlement or simplification of the issue by consent of the parties.[74]

Once notice has been served, the agency is more or less obligated to allow interested parties opportunity to make an offer for negotiated settlement. As discussed in chapter 8, the procedures followed at this stage are informal. Agencies have strictly limited participation, and they are under no obligation to accept an offer of settlement. The prehearing stage frequently involves one or more informal conferences at which the agency explains the charges, the evidence on which they are based, and who will be called as witnesses. Although administrative agencies are not required to follow Federal Rules of Civil Procedure relating to discovery, following recommendation by ACUS in 1970, they must have adopted rules of procedure that in modified form do provide for the most of the elements of discovery.[75] If no settlement is arrived at, the respondent may request that the agency issue subpoenas in his or her behalf. Unlike court procedure, the agency does not have to comply with that request without some reassurances as to the relevance of the evidence sought. The APA authorizes agencies to adopt procedural rules requiring parties to show the general relevance and resonableness of scope of evidence sought through the requested subpoenas.

The Presiding Officer

> There shall preside at the taking of evidence—
> 1. the agency;
> 2. one or more members of the body which comprises the agency; or

3. one or more administrative law judges appointed under section 3105 of this title.[76]

Although agency heads may preside at hearings, they are likely to do so only rarely. In the overwhelming majority of adjudicatory hearings the presiding officer will be an administrative law judge. Administrative law judges are appointed at level of GS 15 and above by the agencies from lists supplied by the Office of Personnel Management (see Table 10.1 below). Minimum qualifications for the position require that an applicant must be an attorney with at least seven years' experience presenting cases before federal

TABLE 10.1. Total Number of ALJ's by Grade and Agency: 1980

Breakdown by grade

GS–15	729
GS–16	349
GS–17	11
	1,089

Breakdown by agency	GS–15	GS–16	GS–17
Agriculture		5	
Civil Aeronautics Board		7	
Coast Guard	14	1	
Commerce	1		
Commodity Futures Trading Commission		4	
Drug Enforcement Administration		1	
Environmental Protection Agency		7	
Federal Communications Commission		12	1
Federal Energy Regulatory Commission		21	1
Federal Labor Relations Authority		10	1
Federal Maritime Commission		7	
Federal Mine Safety and Health Review Commission		16	1
Federal Trade Commission		11	1
Food and Drug Administration		1	
Housing and Urban Development	1		
Interior		12	1
Internal Revenue Service	1		
	GS–15	GS–16	GS–17
International Trade Commission		2	
Interstate Commerce Commissions		50	1
Labor	58	12	1
Maritime Administration		3	
Merit Systems Protection Board		1	
National Labor Relations Board		107	1
National Transportation Safety Board		6	
Nuclear Regulatory Commission		1	
Occupational Safety and Health Review Commission		44	1
Postal Service		1	
Securities and Exchange Commission		6	1
Social Security Administration	654	1	
	729	349	11

courts or federal agencies. Frequently, agencies will specify experience in the general area of regulation that they deal with as an additional desired qualification. Once appointed the judges are relatively insulated from direct agency control. Any disciplinary action against a judge goes directly to the Merit System Protection Board (MSPB) which must provide a full adjudicatory hearing on the complaint before any action can be taken against the judge. They are removable only for cause as determined by the MSPB. Their salaries are prescribed and their advancement is determined by OPM "independently of agency recommendations or ratings." On internal administrative matters, such as specific case assignments, the judge is subject to agency decision making. The APA also specifies that administrative law judges must "be assigned to cases in rotation so far as practicable, and may not perform duties inconsistent with their duties and responsibilities" as judges.

A "fair trial by an unbiased and non-partisan trier of the facts is of the essence of the adjudicatory process."[78] Several provisions of the APA are designed to ensure the impartiality of the administrative law judge. She is barred from ex parte contacts during the course of a hearing and may not be subject to supervision of anyone "engaged in the performance of investigative or prosecuting functions of the agency."[79] In addition, persons who have engaged in either investigation or prosecuting a case may not participate in the decision.

The APA also provides that a presiding officer "may at any time disqualify himself" by filing an affidavit of personal bias with the agency, which then determines if disqualification is necessary.[80] The APA does not, however, define what constitutes a disqualifying bias and the courts have distinguished among several types of bias, not all of which are considered to require a presiding officer to withdraw from a case. Philosophical or policy bias, a predisposition in favor of the law the agency enforces, for example, is not considered to be disqualifying bias. On the other hand, prejudgment of the specific issues of a case is usually considered to be a disqualifying bias. An agency may determine and announce that certain kinds of behavior will in the future be considered violations of the law. Officials and employees of the agency may well express agreement with that policy, and then proceed against individuals or businesses that they believe have engaged in the specified behavior without having exhibited a disqualifying bias.[81] However, if a deciding officer, whether an administrative law judge or an agency head, had announced in advance of trying a case that a named party was most assuredly guilty, that would in all likelihood constitute a disqualifying bias. Similarly, expressing personal animosity, favoritism, or prejudice toward a party to a proceeding prevents an impartial hearing and violates due process.

"The words 'personal bias or prejudice' carry with them the idea of such personal dislike of a litigant as an individual or party to the suit, or such personal favoritism or regard for some opposite party to the suit, as that the mind of the judge will be swayed or prevented by the one or the other from an impartial consideration of the merits of the controversy."[82] Paul Rand Dixon, the FTC Chairman, was disqualified for this reason in *Texaco Inc. v. FTC*[83] because, while a charge against Texaco was pending, he had made a speech naming Texaco as one of the companies who engaged in "price fixing, price discrimination, and overriding commissions on accessories sold to its retail dealers."

Finally, if the deciding officer has a conflict of interest, a financial or personal stake in the outcome of the hearing, this will also usually be a disqualifying bias. "No man shall be a judge in his own cause."[84] The Supreme Court has held that a mayor who received compensation from the fines of convicted defendants or whose city received much of its revenue from fines could not act as an impartial tribunal.[85] In 1973, in *Gibson v. Berryhill*,[86] the Supreme Court ruled that the Alabama Board of Optometry which regulated professional conduct of optometrists was disqualified from deciding cases alleging that optometrists employed by corporations were engaging in unprofessional conduct. The Board consisted only of members of the Alabama Optometric Association which barred from its membership optometrists employed by corporations. The Court held that the Board members' financial interests in the outcome of these cases constituted a disqualifying bias.

Although an individual with a disqualifying bias usually must remove himself from a case, there is an exception to this: the "rule of necessity." The rule, which goes back at least to the 1840s and Chancellor Kent,[87] provides that "when the only tribunal that has authority to act in a proceeding allegedly is biased, it will be permitted to act nevertheless because the alternative would mean nonenforcement of the law entirely."[88]

The problem of bias in presiding officers is usually most pronounced at the top of the agency and is compounded at that level by the combination of functions in agency heads and commissioners. As noted previously the APA requires strict separation of investigative and prosecutorial personnel from those who act as presiding officers in adjudicatory hearings, but explicitly exempts "the agency or a member or members of the body comprising the agency."[89] The result is that at the Federal Trade Commission, for example, Commission members determine whether formal antitrust investigations should be launched in a specific case; when the investigation is completed they determine whether a formal complaint should be issued; and if the case goes to a hearing either may preside at it or in any case will act as the ultimate administrative court of appeals for that case. Although this intermixing and combining of functions has been judicially challenged numerous times, the Supreme Court has not found it to be offensive to due process nor to constitute a disqualifying bias in adjudicatory cases.

The Court specifically addressed the permissibility of combination of functions in *Withrow v. Larkin* in 1975.[90] In 1973, Duane Larkin, a licensed physician in Milwaukee, Wisconsin, had received a notice from the state medical examining board that it would hold an investigative hearing "to determine whether he had engaged in certain proscribed acts. . . . Based upon evidence presented at the hearing, the Board would decide whether to warn, or reprimand," or to institute action to revoke his license. On July 12 and 13, 1973, an investigatory hearing with Board members presiding was held. On September 18, the Board notified Larkin that a "contested hearing" would be held before it to determine whether his license should be suspended. Alleging an unconstitutional violation of due process Larkin immediately sought and was granted an injunction from a federal district court restraining the holding of the contested hearing. The Board appealed, and the Supreme Court overruled the district court:

> The contention that the combination of investigative and adjudicative functions necessarily creates an unconstitutional risk of bias in administrative adjudication

has a much more difficult burden of persuasion to carry. It must overcome a presumption of honesty and integrity in those serving as adjudicators; and it must convince that under a realistic appraisal of psychological tendencies and human weakness, conferring investigative and adjudicative powers on the same individuals poses such a risk of active bias or prejudgment that the practice must be forbidden if the guarantee of due process is to be adequately implemented. . . . The accepted rule is to the contrary. . . .

Without a showing to the contrary, state administrators "are assumed to be men of conscience and intellectual discipline, capable of judging a particular controversy fairly on the basis of its own circumstances." *United States v. Morgan*, 313 U.S. 409.[91]

In arriving at this conclusion, the Supreme Court noted both the federal APA exemption from required separation of functions for agency heads and the common practice in criminal cases of allowing the same judge to issue an arrest warrant, preside at the preliminary hearing and at the trial where, in the absence of a jury, he would make the determination of guilt or innocence. "The combination of investigative and adjudicatory functions does not, without more, constitute a due process violation."

Congress has expressed considerable ambiguity on the necessity for separation of functions in adjudicatory proceedings. A year after the passage of the APA, the Taft-Hartley Act was passed establishing a strict separation of functions for the National Labor Relations Board. The Act established a separate and independent general counsel who was given sole authority to investigate and prosecute unfair labor practices. The arrangement has not been particularly successful and one of the most frequent criticisms of the post-Taft-Hartley NLRB has been that the creation of the independent general counsel clouded jurisdictional responsibilities and resulted in conflicts between the counsel and the Board which have hampered the enforcement of labor policy.[92] Congress leaned in the opposite direction in 1952, however, by specifically exempting the INS from APA adjudicatory procedures and allowing its "inquiry officers" to be subject to control by investigating and prosecuting officials. This arrangement was upheld by the Supreme Court in *Marcello v. Bonds*.[93]

Another aspect of ensuring the impartiality of the presiding officer on which there has been far less ambiguity from either the courts or Congress has been to bar ex parte contacts during adjudicatory proceedings. The Government in the Sunshine Act now explicitly bars all such contacts in on the record proceedings. The law prohibits "interested persons outside the agency" from making ex parte contacts during such proceedings with "any member of the body comprising the agency, administrative law judge or other employee who is or may reasonably be expected to be involved in the decisional process."[94] Those involved in the decisional process are similarly barred from contacting interested persons unless the substance of such contacts is made part of the public record. What the law does not prohibit, however, is ex parte contacts from persons not "interested" in the proceeding, such as members of Congress or other agencies in the executive branch, and §557(d)(2) provides that "This subsection does not constitute authority to withhold information from Congress."

Although the powers of presiding officers at an adjudicatory hearing are similar to those of a judge in a trial, their role and functions are different. The APA provides that presiding officers may:

1. administer oaths
2. issue subpoenas
3. rule on evidence
4. take depositions or have them taken
5. conduct the hearing
6. hold prehearing conferences
7. rule on procedural motions
8. make or recommend decisions; and
9. take any other action authorized by the agency.[95]

Unlike judges, however, presiding officers, whether administrative law judges or agency members, frequently take a very active role in the conduct of the hearing. Administrative law judges at the NLRB are authorized to "call, examine and cross-examine witnesses and to introduce into the record documentary or other evidence."[96] In the Social Security Administration, the government is not even represented by separate counsel; the administrative law judge is solely responsible for developing the record on which the decision will be based."[97]

Evidence

Any oral or documentary evidence may be received, but the agency as a matter of policy shall provide for the exclusion of irrelevant, immaterial or unduly repetitious evidence. A sanction may not be imposed or a rule or order issued except on consideration of the whole record or those parts thereof cited by a party and supported by and in accordance with the reliable, probative and substantial evidence.[98]

The APA clearly establishes the admissibility of hearsay evidence, statements "made other than by a witness while testifying at the hearing."[99] What the APA does not so clearly establish is whether hearsay evidence alone is sufficient to constitute the substantial evidence on which to base a decision. At the federal level, the Supreme Court has defined the required substantial evidence as being "more than a mere scintilla. It means such relevant evidence as a reasonable mind might accept as adequate to support a conclusion."[100] In *Richardson v. Perales*, the Court held that hearsay evidence in the form of written reports could constitute the required substantial evidence for a decision:

We conclude that a written report by a licensed physician who has examined the claimant and who sets forth in his report his medical findings in his area of competence may be received as evidence in a disability hearing, and despite its hearsay character and an absence of cross examination, and despite the presence of opposing direct medical testimony and testimony by the claimant himself, may constitute substantial evidence supportive of a finding by the hearing examiner adverse to the claimant, when the claimant has not exercised his right to subpoena the reporting physician.[101]

The Model State APA similarly allows the admission of hearsay evidence, "if it is of the type commonly relied upon by reasonably prudent men in conduct of their affairs."[102] Although some state courts routinely refer to the residuum rule—the requirement that a decision totally unsupported by evidence admissible in a jury trial must be set aside[103]—most will, in fact, uphold an administrative decision based on uncontroverted hearsay.[104]

Just as the agency is entitled to introduce evidence and cross-examine witnesses, so is the party "entitled to present his case or defense by oral or documentary evidence, to submit rebuttal evidence and to conduct such cross-examination as may be required for a full and true disclosure of facts."[105] All of the evidence thus presented is recorded and becomes part of the final record of the hearing.

The Initial Decision

After all of the evidence has been presented, the hearing draws to a close and if the case was heard before an administrative law judge, he "shall initially decide the case unless the agency requires, either in specific cases or by general rule, the entire record to be certified to it for decision."[106] Even in the latter instance, the administrative law judge "shall first recommend a decision."[107] In arriving at a decision, the administrative law judge weighs the evidence presented. "Except as statutes otherwise provide, the proponent of a rule or order has the burden of proof."[108] Since usually the agency will have been the proponent, it is required to have presented "substantial evidence" to prove its allegations. Some statutes do provide otherwise; in false advertising cases, for example, the burden is on the advertiser to prove the truth of his claims.

In actually arriving at a decision, most judges will likely consider more than just the evidence presented at the hearing. In administrative agencies where the deciding officer may have years of experience and expertise in the substantive area of regulation, he or she inevitably brings the knowledge gained by that experience to the hearing and the decision process. When that factual knowledge is relied on in making an administrative decision it is referred to as taking "official notice." In addition to personal knowledge, presiding officers frequently take official notice of information in books, journals, manuals, other decisions, and a variety of other sources. The APA clearly permits this kind of activity but specifies that "When an agency decision rests on official notice of a material fact not appearing in the evidence in the record, a party is entitled, on timely request, to an opportunity to show the contrary."[109] As long as facts officially noticed are made part of the record and interested parties are given an opportunity to respond, both the APA and due process have been satisfied.

The APA requires that parties be given an opportunity to submit "proposed findings and conclusions," exceptions to the initial decision, and supporting reasons for each which become a part of the record. The initial decision must include "findings and conclusions . . . on all the material issues of fact, law or discretion . . . and the appropriate rule, order, sanction, relief or denial thereof."[110] If the agency presided at the hearing, this initial decision becomes the agency's final decision. Similarly, "unless there is an appeal to, or review on the motion of the agency within time provided by rule,"[111] the initial decision becomes the final decision.

Court-Mandated Hearing Procedures

To this point the procedures discussed have been those associated with a hearing conducted under the Administrative Procedure Act. As was discussed earlier, when the

Supreme Court requires an agency to provide the opportunity to be heard, it frequently specifies the minimum acceptable procedures for such hearings. The major common requirement for court-mandated hearings has been the requirement that the affected individual must be informed of the charges against him and given an opportunity to counter those charges orally.

In *Londoner v. Denver*, for example, although the Supreme Court required an opportunity to be heard, the type of hearing it mandated was not necessarily a full-blown adjudicatory hearing and the Court accepted that "many requirements essential in strictly judicial proceedings may be dispensed with in proceedings of this nature." What it did require in that case in addition to written notice was that the person entitled to the hearing be given the opportunity to present oral evidence and "to support his allegations by argument however brief, and if need be by proof, however informal."

Goldberg v. Kelly provides a classic example of a court-mandated hearing procedure that resembles but is not identical to a full-blown adjudicatory hearing. Although the pretermination hearing required by the Court in *Goldberg* "need not take the form of a judicial or quasi-judicial trial," it must include the following procedural safeguards:

a. "timely and adequate notice detailing the reason for a proposed termination";
b. "an opportunity to confront and cross-examine witnesses";
c. "an opportunity to present his own arguments and evidence orally";
d. "the evidence used to prove the Government's case must be disclosed to the individual";
e. "the recipient must be allowed to retain an attorney if he so desires";
f. "the decisionmaker's conclusion as to a recipient's eligibility must rest solely on the legal rules and evidence adduced at the hearing";
g. "the decisionmaker should state the reasons for his determination and the evidence he relied on";
h. "and of course, an impartial decisionmaker is essential."[112]

Although the required procedures are very similar to an APA mandated adjudicatory hearing, they do not require a full record or an opinion with findings of fact and conclusions of law.

The hearing procedures for students expelled for misconduct from public educational institutions are considerably less stringent than those required for welfare terminations. In *Dixon v. Love*, [113] the Fifth Circuit Court of Appeals, after establishing the students' right to some kind of hearing, specified that the hearing provided could be relatively informal as long as it included "the rudimentary elements of fair play": The student must be given written notice of charges, provided with names of witnesses against him and an oral or written report of their testimony, and be given an opportunity to present his own testimony and that of witnesses in his behalf. If the hearing were not held before the Board, a report of the findings had to be made available for the student's inspection. The procedures required for suspending high school students in *Goss v. Lopez*[114] were still less restrictive: oral or written notice of the charges, an explanation of the evidence, and an opportunity for the student to present his side of the story.

The type of hearing required in cases involving the restrictions of the rights of persons convicted of crimes also varies considerably depending on the nature and severity of the restriction involved. In parole and probation revocation cases, the affected individual is entitled to a hearing that encompasses all the requirements specified in Goldberg except one: the right to retain counsel. In other types of prison disciplinary actions, the procedural requirements for the required hearing are more limited. Advance written notice, a minimum of 24 hours to prepare a response, a limited right to call witnesses and present documentary evidence, and a written statement of the evidence relied on are sufficient in such cases. Neither confrontation nor cross-examination of witnesses is required and the inmate "has no right to either retained or appointed counsel in disciplinary proceedings."[115] The Court did hold that if an affected inmate were illiterate or incapable of preparing or presenting his case he must be allowed either to seek the aid of fellow prisoners or be provided assistance by the staff.

In determining the precise nature of a hearing required by the due process clause, the Court appears to have used the same criteria that it uses to decide if a hearing is required in advance of administrative action. The nature of the interest involved, "the risk of erroneous deprivation through the procedures already used," the nature of the governmental function involved, and the burdens imposed by new or additional procedures are weighed by the Court on a case-by-case basis. The more serious the deprivation of interest and the higher the risk of error resulting from existing procedures, the more likely it is that the Court will impose extensive procedural requirements for the hearing, unless the governmental function involved would be severely disrupted or to do so would impose serious financial or administrative hardship on the affected agency. While this ad hoc approach does not result in procedural uniformity and leaves both affected individuals and agencies with considerable uncertainty as to how much process is due in varying situations, its flexibility contributes greatly to the fairness and viability of the administrative process.

INSTITUTIONAL DECISIONS

In the majority of cases the initial decision of the administrative law judge will be appealed by either the party or the agency. What happens at that point varies tremendously from agency to agency, since each agency establishes its own internal appeals procedures. In the Social Security Administration, for example, initial decisions made by ALJ's of the Bureau of Hearing Appeals may be appealed to the Appeals Council; in the Department of Agriculture appeals go to a Judicial Officer. In both agencies the decisions by the appeals officers are final agency decisions. The FCC has a two-step appellate process: Initial decisions may be appealed to a review board of staff officials and that decision may under certain circumstances be appealed to the Commission. The ICC provides for appellate review by divisions consisting of three commissioners with only a very limited number of cases entitled to appeal beyond that for full commission review. The CAB has no intermediate appeal level; the full Board acts as the appellate tribunal.[116]

Appeal procedures are also determined by the agency. Only rarely will an agency provide for a hearing de novo on appeal and only slightly more frequently is an opportunity for oral argument provided. The most common practice is for the written record to be certified to the appellate officer(s) for review. Whatever the procedure, the APA makes clear that the agency retains full power to make its own decisions on appeals:

> On appeal from or review of the initial decision, the agency has all the powers which it would have in making the initial decision except as it may limit the issues on notice or by rule.[117]

The initial decision becomes part of the record, a part that must be carefully considered but that is in no way binding on the agency. The Supreme Court has consistently held that the final decision power rests with the agency:

> The responsibility for decision thus placed on the Board is wholly inconsistent with the notion that it has power to reverse an examiner's findings only when they are "clearly erroneous." Such a limitation would make so drastic a departure from prior administrative practice that explicitness would be required.[118]

At the appellate level, the agency decision truly becomes an "institutional decision," a decision made not by an identifiable individual but rather one made by the organization as a collective, utilizing the composite skills, experience, expertise, and memory of that organization. Although the final decision will ultimately be signed by the agency head, in arriving at that decision he or she will usually have consulted with various staff members of the agency. The precise decision process varies and in most instances remains unknown, as does the thoroughness of the review of the hearing record. The Supreme Court struggled with the question of how thorough this review must be and how courts could determine if the review had been sufficiently thorough in the *Morgan* cases. The cases involved the procedures followed by the Secretary of Agriculture in issuing a final order determining maximum rates for livestock transactions of the Kansas City Stockyards. The hearing record consisted of over 10,000 pages of testimony plus 1,000 pages of statistical evidence. The Secretary had not presided at the hearing; the examiner had issued no initial decision; and although oral argument was allowed, it was held before the acting Secretary. The first time the Morgan case reached the Supreme Court, it found the decision process fatally defective and stated that deciding officers had a clear personal responsibility to weigh carefully and thoroughly the evidence presented at the hearing:

> It is not an impersonal obligation. It is a duty akin to that of a judge. The one who decides must hear.
>
> The necessary rule does not preclude practicable administrative procedure in obtaining the aid of assistants in the department. . . . But, there must be a hearing in a substantial sense. And to give the substance of a hearing . . . the officer who makes the determinations must consider and appraise the evidence which justifies them.[119]

Precisely what the Supreme Court intended to require of agency heads in deciding complex adjudicatory appeals was not really clear in *Morgan I*. On retrial of the case in district court, the Secretary of Agriculture was required to testify in person concerning the procedure he used to arrive at his decision. The second time the Morgan cases reached the Supreme Court, the issues involved different aspects but the Court noted in passing that it had never intended to subject agency heads to this kind of judicial scrutiny:

> [W]e agree with the Government's contention that it was not the function of the Court to probe the mental processes of the Secretary in reaching his conclusions if he gave the hearing which the law required. The Secretary read the summary . . . and he conferred with his subordinates. . . . We assume that the Secretary sufficiently understood its purport.[120]

In 1941, the fourth time around for the Morgan cases, the Court reiterated that the courts should not have "probed the mental processes of the Secretary," and that the courts had an obligation to respect "the integrity of the administrative process."[121]

Since *Morgan*, the courts have avoided strict scrutiny of the actual decision process used by agency heads in deciding appeals and have instead focused on the adequacy of the actual decision, particularly on findings of basic and ultimate facts, the extent to which those findings are based on substantial evidence in the record, and the agency's reasons, its conclusions as to law. "The orderly functioning of the process of review requires that the ground upon which the administrative agency acted be clearly disclosed and adequately sustained."[122]

FINAL ORDERS

The final decision of the agency in a contested case will normally include the agency's findings of fact and law, its decision, and the order entered. The order is the agency's determination as to what subsequent action is required by or in respect to the affected party. It also includes the sanction imposed or relief granted. To withstand judicial challenge, the order must be reasonably related to the findings upon which it rests and "must state with reasonable specificity the acts which the respondent is to do or refrain from doing."[123] Agencies are authorized to impose a wide variety of sanctions which are defined by the Administrative Procedure Act as

> the whole or part of an agency—
> (A) prohibition, requirement, limitation or other condition affecting the freedom of a person;
> (B) withholding of relief;
> (C) imposition of penalty or fine;
> (D) destruction, taking, seizure or withholding of property;
> (E) assessment of damages, reimbursement, restitution, compensation, costs, charges or fees;
> (F) requirement, revocation or suspension of a license; or
> (G) taking other compulsory or restrictive action.[124]

In those cases where the individual has prevailed the forms of relief that may be provided include:

(A) grant of money, assistance, license, authority, exemption, exception, privilege or remedy;

(B) recognition of a claim, right, immunity, privilege, exemption or exception or;

(C) taking or other action on the application of and beneficial to, a person.[125]

One of the most common forms of negative orders issued by agencies is the cease and desist order which commands the affected party to stop engaging in certain practices which have been found to be illegal. Figure 10.1 is an excerpt from a cease and desist order issued by the Federal Trade Commission.[126] The order was issued subsequent to the determination that Warner-Lambert's advertising claims that Listerine would prevent or cure the common cold constituted false and misleading advertising. Part I of the order was a traditional cease and desist command; Part III established a new power for the Commission in such orders by going beyond the usual negative language and requiring affirmative action by the company to inform consumers of inaccuracies in past advertising. Warner-Lambert challenged the order alleging that the FTC had not been given statutory authority to issue such an order. In support of this allegation the company pointed out that for the first 50 years of its existence the Commission had never referred to a power to require corrective advertising in any of its orders. In upholding the FTC's order, the D.C. Court of Appeals rejected the contention that failure to assert a power constitutes proof of its absence and reaffirmed the long established doctrine that the choice of sanctions is within the discretion of the agency:

> The Commission is the expert body to determine what remedy is necessary to eliminate the unfair or deceptive trade practices which have been disclosed. It has wide latitude for judgment and the courts will not interfere except where the remedy selected has no reasonable relation to the unlawful practices found to exist.[127]

In this instance, the Court found the FTC's requirement for corrective advertising "entirely reasonable," but it did hold that requiring such advertisements to be prefaced by "Contrary to prior advertising," to be unnecessary.[128]

The Supreme Court has also held that allowing agencies to impose fines after determining an individual has violated the law does not violate the Seventh Amendment requirement that "in suits at common law where the value in controversy shall exceed twenty dollars, the right to trial by jury shall be preserved." The Occupational Safety and Health Act authorized the imposition of civil penalties by the Secretary of up to $10,000 for violations of health and safety standards. The constitutionality of this procedure was upheld in *Atlas Roofing Co., Inc. v. Occupational Safety and Health Review Commission*:[129]

> [W]hen Congress creates new statutory "public rights," it may assign their adjudication to an administrative agency with which a jury trial would be incompatible, without violating the Seventh Amendment's injunction that jury trial is to be "preserved" in "suits at common law." Congress is not required by the Seventh Amendment to choke the already crowded federal courts with new types of litigation or prevented from committing some new types of litigation to

In the Matter of
Warner-Lambert Company

ORDER, OPINION, ETC., IN REGARD TO ALLEGED VIOLATION OF THE FEDERAL TRADE COMMISSION ACT

Docket 8891. Complaint, June 27, 1972—Order, Dec. 9, 1975
Order requiring a Morris Plains, N.J., manufacturer and distributor of "Listerine" mouthwash preparation, among other things to cease misrepresenting the medicinal therapeutic qualities, beneficial effects, and germicidal nature of its product. Respondent is futher required to include a corrective advertising disclosure in its advertisements. The order dismisses the complaint allegation regarding the effects of "Listerine" on children who gargle with it twice a day.

PART I

It is ordered, That respondent Warner-Lambert Company, a corporation, its successors and assigns and respondent's officers, agents, representatives and employees, directly or through any corporation, subsidiary, division or other device, in connection with the labeling, advertising, offering for sale, sale or distribution of Listerine or any other nonprescription drug product in or affecting commerce, as "commerce" is defined in the Federal Trade Commission Act, do forthwith cease and desist from:

1. Representing, directly or by implication, that any such product will cure colds or sore throats;
2. Representing, directly or by implication, that any such product will prevent colds or sore throats;
3. Representing, directly or by implication, that users of any such product will have fewer colds than nonusers.

. . .

PART III

It is further ordered, That respondent Warner-Lambert Company, a corporation, its successors and assigns, and respondent's officers, agents, representatives and employees, directly or through any corporation, subsidiary, division or other device, do forthwith cease and desist from disseminating or causing the dissemination of any advertisements for the product Listerine Antiseptic unless it is clearly and conspicuously disclosed in each such advertisement in the exact language below that:

Contrary to prior advertising, Listerine will not help prevent colds or sore throats or lessen their severity.

administration agencies, with special competence in the relevant field . . . [T]he right to a jury trial turns not solely on the nature of the issue to be resolved but also on the forum in which it is to be resolved."[130]

Once an order has been entered it is immediately enforceable unless an appeal is filed and a stay is granted. The agency may at its discretion grant a stay while an appeal is pending or the court may grant a stay. For a court to grant a stay, it will generally insist that four separate standards be met. It must be satisfied that (a) the case is likely to prevail on its merits; (b) the petitioner has shown that without a stay it will suffer irreparable injury; (c) other interested parties would not be substantially harmed by a stay; and (d) the "public interest" would not be adversely affected by a stay.[131] If no appeal is filed, the order becomes enforceable. Failure to comply with a valid administrative order is in many instances a felony punishable by fine and/or imprisonment. This requires that a criminal enforcement action be taken to the court; initiation of such actions may be by the agency, an aggrieved party, or the Justice Department.

CONCLUSION

The adjudicatory process is the most "formal" of administrative processes and the one where procedures have been most extensively prescribed by legislatures and the courts. Although adjudicatory procedures initially were required in only a limited number of situations, the due process explosion greatly expanded the circumstances under which individuals were entitled to an opportunity to be heard before final administrative action could be completed.

The expansion of the requirements to provide a hearing and the concomitant increase in the judicialization of the administrative process have been defended as constitutionally required and necessary to protect individual rights. In some cases, particularly given the severity of the sanctions that may be imposed by an agency, this is unarguably true. But the expanded requirements for a hearing on the record have also resulted in making the administrative process more expensive and more time-consuming.

No administrative area better illustrates the complexity and nature of the tradeoffs between procedural propriety and substantive justice than welfare administration. From FY 1968 to FY 1976, total government expenditures on need-based (welfare) programs increased 289 percent to an estimated $62.6 billion per year. In 1975, DHEW estimated 6.9 percent of the families receiving AFDC payments were ineligible and 15.3 percent were receiving excess payments; in 1977, the GAO estimated the federal government was losing $590 million a year in food stamp overpayments.[132] At the same time, sizable proportions of those who were actually eligible for the programs were not receiving benefits. With the current cutbacks in welfare funding at all levels of government the tradeoff between procedure and substance is bleak and ultimately unfortunate: Every dollar that an agency allocates for administrative procedure is one dollar less that could be paid in benefits to, in the Reagan administration's terminology, the "truly needy." Similarly, every dollar paid to ineligible recipients also reduces the amount available for payment to eligible recipients. If the requirements for hearings worked well in protecting the intended beneficiaries, the tradeoff might still be considered acceptable, but there is far from universal agreement that this has occurred. Welfare recipients by definition are low income, frequently uneducated, and commonly intimidated by formal procedures. Ironically, the judicialization of the welfare system (or the educational system) tends to transform the system into an adversarial process which further undermines its ability to aid its clientele—its primary goal.

In administrative areas such as welfare and educational administration where the regulatory aspect of the programs is a secondary function undertaken to assist in the accomplishment of some primary nonregulatory goal, excessive judicialization may well be counterproductive. In administrative areas where the primary goal is regulation, adjudicatory procedures are frequently necessary, fair, and effective methods for accomplishing that goal. Although in an ideal world it might be otherwise, the "pure" regulatory situation frequently involves adversarial relationships between regulator and regulatee, and adjudicatory procedures serve to formalize and regularize those relationships. Further, the individuals moved against in this type of situation are usually businesses who are not easily intimidated and who can well afford to retain expert legal counsel. The expenditure of agency resources on adjudication does not result in such a serious diversion of resources from accomplishing the agency's goals as occurs in "nonregulatory" programs, and frequently contributes directly to the accomplishment of agency goals.

The Supreme Court and Congress have tried to balance the need for individual protection against the need for agency effectiveness. Although further decisions on this area undoubtedly will occur, it seems the Court at least is increasingly unwilling to go much further in specifying new procedures.

NOTES

1. 5 U.S.C. §552(6) and (7).
2. Kenneth Davis, *Administrative Law and Government* (St. Paul, Minn.: West Publishing Co., 1975), p. 135.
3. 5 U.S.C. §554(a).
4. 47 U.S.C. §309(e).
5. 15 U.S.C. § 45(b).
6. *Londoner v. Denver*, 210 U.S. 373, 385 (1908).
7. See pp. 64–70 above.
8. See pp. 104–108 above.
9. *Board of Regents of State Colleges v. Roth*, 408 U.S. 564, 576 (1972).
10. *Goldberg v. Kelly*, 397 U.S. 254 (1970).
11. *Mathews v. Eldridge*, 424 U.S. 319 (1976).
12. *Sherbert v. Verner*, 374 U.S. 389 (1963).
13. *Sumpter v. White Plains Housing Authority*, 29 N.Y. 2d 420; cert. denied, 406 U.S. 928 (1972).
14. *Griffeth v. Detrich*, 603 F2d 113 (9th Cir. 1980).
15. 447 U.S. 773 (1980).
16. *Slochower v. Board of Education*, 350 U.S. 551 (1956).
17. *Perry v. Sindermann*, 408 U.S. 593, 601 (1972).

18. *Bishop v. Wood*, 426 U.S. 341 (1976).

19. *Dixon v. Alabama State Board of Higher Education*, 294 F2d 150 (5th Cir. 1961); cert. denied, 368 U.S. 930 (1961).

20. *San Antonio Independent School District v. Rodriquez*, 411 U.S. 1 (1973).

21. 419 U.S. 565 (1975).

22. *Ingraham v. Wright*, 430 U.S. 651 (1977).

23. *Board of Curators of the University of Missouri v. Horowitz*, 435 U.S. 78, 90 (1978).

24. 310 U.S. 113 (1940).

25. *Gonzalez v. Freeman*, 118 U.S. App D.C. 180, 334 F2d 570 (D.C. Cir. 1969), and *Scanwell Laboratories v. Shaffer*, 137 U.S. App. D.C. 371, 424 F2d 859 (D.C. Cir. 1970).

26. 5 U.S.C. §558(c).

27. *Ex parte Robinson*, 86 U.S. 505 (1873).

28. *Bell v. Burson*, 402 U.S. 535 (1971), and *Dixon v. Love*, 431 U.S. 105 (1977).

29. *Board of Regents of State Colleges v. Roth*, 408 U.S. 564, 572 (1972).

30. 424 U.S. 693 (1976).

31. 400 U.S. 433 (1971).

32. *Paul v. Davis*, 424 U.S. 693, 708 (1973).

33. 408 U.S. 471 (1972).

34. *Gagnon v. Scarpelli*, 411 U.S. 778 (1973).

35. *Wolff v. McDonnell*, 418 U.S. 539 (1974).

36. *Meachum v Fano*, 427 U.S. 215 (1976).

37. 442 U.S. 1 (1979).

38. *Vitek v. Jones*, 455 U.S. 480 (1980).

39. 338 U.S. 537 (1950).

40. *Shaughnessy v. United States ex rel. Mezei*, 345 U.S. 206 (1953).

41. *Bi-Metallic Investment Co. v. Colorado State Board of Equalization*, 239 U.S. 441, 445 (1915).

42. Ibid.

43. 319 U.S. 190 (1943).

44. *FPC v. Texaco*, 377 U.S. 33, 39 (1964).

45. 276 F2d 892 (2d Cir. 1960); see also *American Airlines v. Civil Aeronautics Board*, 359 F2d 634 (D.C. Cir. 1966).

46. *Airline Pilots Association v. Quesada*, 276 F2d 892, 896 (2d Cir. 1960).

47. *Goldberg v. Kelly*, 397 U.S. 254 (1970).

48. Ibid., at 264.

49. *Arnett v. Kennedy*, 416 U.S. 34 (1974).

50. 424 U.S. 319 (1976).

51. 42 U.S.C. §423(d)(1)(A).

52. *Mathews v. Eldridge*, 424 U.S. 319, 335 (1976).

53. *Dixon v. Love*, 431 U.S. 105 (1977).

54. 410 U.S. 224 (1973).

55. See Bernard Schwartz, *Administrative Law* (Boston: Little, Brown, 1976), pp. 193–94.

56. 5 U.S.C. §554(b).

57. 397 U.S. 254 (1970).

58. 418 U.S. 539 (1974).

59. 419 U.S. 565 (1975).

60. See *Templeton v. Dixie Color Printing Co.*, 313 F. Supp. 105 (N.D. Ala 1970), *Environmental Defense Fund Inc. v. Hardin*, 428 F2d 10933 (D.C. Cir. 1970), and *NLRB v. J.H. Rutter Rex Mfg. Co.*, 396 U.S. 258 (1969).

61. 326 U.S. 327 (1946).

62. *Gagnon v. Scarpelli*, 411 U.S. 778, 790 (1973).

63. *Vitek v. Jones*, 445 U.S. 480 (1980).

64. 5 U.S.C. §555(b).

65. 38 U.S.C. §3404.

66. Social Security Act, 42 U.S.C. §406.

67. See *Gendron v. Levi*, 423 U.S. 802 (1975); *Randolph v. United States*, 389 U.S. 570 (1968).

68. *Office of Communication of the United Church of Christ v. FCC*, 359 F2d 994 (D.C. Cir. 1966).

69. Ibid.

70. Lester Thurow, *The Zero Sum Society* (New York: Penguin, 1981), p. 13.

71. *Office of Communication of the United Church of Christ v. FCC*, 359 F2d 994 1006 (D.C. Cir. 1966).

72. 1 CFR 305, 71–6.

73. 5 U.S.C. §554(c).

74. 5 U.S.C. §556(c).

75. Walter Gellhorn, Clark Byse, and Peter Strauss, *Administrative Law: Cases and Comments*, 7th ed. (Mineola, N.Y.: Foundation Press, 1979), pp. 681–82.

76. 5 U.S.C. §556(b).

77. Personal letter from Marvin H. Morse, Director, Office of Administrative Law Judges, Office of Personnel Management, September 18, 1980.

78. *NLRB v. Phelps*, 136 F2d 562 (5th Cir. 1943).

79. 5 U.S.C. §554(d)(2).

80. 5 U.S.C. §556(b).

81. *FTC v. Cement Institute*, 333 U.S. 683 (1948).

82. *Saunders v. Piggly Wiggly Corp.*, F2d 582, 584 (W.D. Tenn 1924).

83. 336 F2d 754 (D.C. Cir. 1964).

84. *In re Larsen*, 86 A 2d 430, 435 (N.J. Super. 1952, Brennan, concurring).

85. *Tumey v. Ohio*, 273 U.S. 510 (1927), and *Ward v. Village of Monroeville*, 409 U.S. 57.

86. 411 U.S. 564 (1973).

87. *In re Leefe*, 2 Barb. Ch. 39 (N.Y. 1846).

88. James O. Freedman, *Crisis and Legitimacy: The Administrative Process and American Government* (Cambridge: Cambridge University Press, 1978), p. 200.

89. 5 U.S.C. §554(d)(c).

90. 421 U.S. 35 (1975).

91. Ibid., at 47.

92. See *Report on Regulatory Agencies to the President-Elect*, Senate Judiciary Committee, 86th Congress, 2d Session, 1960.

93. 349 U.S. 302 (1955).

94. 5 U.S.C §557(d)(1)(A).

95. 5 U.S.C. §556(c).

96. 29 CFR §102.35(k).

97. Gellhorn, Byse, Strauss, *Administrative Law*, p. 756.

98. 5 U.S.C. §556(d).

99. Uniform Rule of Evidence G-3, quoted in Steven Gifis, *Law Dictionary* (Woodbury, N.Y.: Barrow's Educational Series, 1975). p. 94.

100. *Consolidated Edison v. NLRB*, 305 U.S. 197 (1938).

101. *Richardson v. Perales*, 402 U.S. 389, 402 (1971).
102. Section 10.
103. See *Carroll v. Knickerbocker Ice Co.*, 218 NY435 (1916).
104. See Gellhorn, Byse, Strauss, *Administrative Law*, pp. 748–51.
105. 4 U.S.C. §556(d).
106. 5 U.S.C. §557(b).
107. Ibid.
108. 5 U.S.C. §556(d).
109. 5 U.S.C. §556(e).
110. 5 U.S.C. §557(c).
111. 5 U.S.C. §557.
112. *Goldberg v. Kelly*, 397 U.S. 252, 267, 268, 269, 270, 271 (1970).
113. 294 F2d 150 (5th Cir. 1961).
114. 419 U.S. 565, (1975).
115. *Wolff v. McDonnell*, 418 U.S. 539, 570 (1974).
116. Gellhorn, Byse, Strauss, *Administrative Law*, p. 781–83.
117. 5 U.S.C. §557(b).
118. *Universal Camera Corp. v. NLRB*, 340 U.S. 474 (1951). The Supreme Court reached an identical conclusion in *FCC v. Allentown Broadcasting Corp.*, 349 U.S. 358 (1955).
119. *Morgan v. United States*, 298 U.S. 468, 481 (1936).
120. *Morgan v. U.S.*, 304 U.S. 1, 18 (1938).
121. *United States v. Morgan*, 313 U.S. 409 (1941).
122. *SEC v. Chenery Corp.*, 318 U.S. 80 (1943).
123. *NLRB v. Express Publishing Co.*, 312 U.S. 426 (1941).
124. 5 U.S.C. §551.
125. Ibid.
126. 86 FTC 1513 (1973).
127. *Jacob Siegel Co. v. FTC*, 327 U.S. 608, 612–613 (1946).
128. *Warner-Lambert v. FTC*, 562 F2d 749 (D.C. Cir. 1977); cert. denied, 435 U.S. 950 (1978).
129. 430 U.S. 442 (1977).
130. Id. at 455, 460.
131. *Virginia Petroleum Jobbers Association v. FTC*, 259 F2d 921 (D.C. Cir. 1958).
132. Grover Starling, *The Politics and Economics of Public Policy* (Homewood, Ill.: Dorsey Press, 1979), p. 558.

PART III

Judicial Controls

Chapter 11

Judicial Review

The proliferation of social and economic problems in the United States has resulted in a proliferation of laws to deal with those problems and a concomitant expansion of the number, size, and power of administrative agencies. This growth of administrative power has, in turn, required the development of a variety of formal and informal checks to ensure that power is exercised constitutionally, legally, and responsibly. Judicial review has become one of the most significant formal safeguards against the arbitrary and improper use of administrative power. This chapter examines the scope, nature, and limitations of judicial review as a check on administrative power.

JUDICIAL REVIEW: AVAILABILITY

Judicial review is the power of a court to determine the legality and constitutionality of an action of a government official, agency, or legislative body. Not all actions are subject to judicial review; whether a court in fact has the power of review over a specific action depends initially on whether it has jurisdiction over the case which challenges the action. Jurisdiction, the power of a court to hear and decide cases, may be either original, the power to hear a case in the first instance, or appellate, the power to hear the case on appeal. The jurisdiction of the federal courts is controlled by the Constitution and Congress. Article III of the Constitution clearly specifies the original jurisdiction of the Supreme Court. Its appellate jurisdiction, however, is made subject to "such exceptions and under such regulations as the Congress shall make." The existence, structure, and jurisdiction, original and appellate, of the lower federal courts is established and defined by Congress. This legislative control over appellate jurisdiction is generally the rule in the states as well.

At the federal level, whether an administrative action is judicially reviewable, and, if so, which court shall review it, depends on Congressional action or, in some cases, inaction. The Administrative Procedure Act deals only generally and somewhat inconsistently with reviewability of administrative actions. Section 701 of the Act exempts from judicial review those actions where "statutes preclude judicial review" or which have been "committed to agency discretion by law." Section 704 provides that "Agency action made reviewable by statute and final agency action for which there is no other adequate remedy in a court are subject to judicial review." Although superficially §704 appears to establish an independent base for judicial review of certain administrative actions, the Supreme Court ruled in 1977 that this was not so: "The APA is not to be interpreted as an implied grant of subject matter jurisdiction to review agency actions. . . . it merely tells the reviewing court what to do after it has obtained jurisdiction under some other statute."[1] Authorizing statutes may specify which actions are not reviewable, and for those that are, whether the case should be taken to the district courts or the courts of appeals. The Federal Trade Commission Act of 1914, for example, provides that challenges to FTC orders may be filed with either the D.C. Court of Appeals or the Court of Appeals in the circuit in which the petitioner resides or has his principal place of business. The Federal Communications Act provides that appeals from FCC decisions in almost all broadcast license cases are to be taken only to the D.C. Court of Appeals. Other statutes provide for review by the district courts.

UNREVIEWABILITY

Legislative Preclusion

The constitutional power of Congress over the federal courts has generally been interpreted to mean that if Congress wishes to exempt an action from judicial review, it may do so, and in a number of statutes it has done exactly that. One of the most explicit preclusions of judicial review is provided for decisions of the Veterans' Administration on benefit claims: "the decisions of the administrator on any question of law or fact under any law administered by the Veterans' Administration providing benefits for veterans shall be final and conclusive and no other official or any court of the United States shall have power to review any such decision."[2] In other statutes, the wording has been somewhat less explicit, providing only that the decisions of the agency "shall be final."[3]

Historically, the federal courts have vacillated considerably as to the extent to which Congress may preclude judicial review of administrative actions and the degree of congressional explicitness required to establish such preclusion. Until the twentieth century, congressional silence on reviewability was usually interpreted by the courts as precluding review. In 1840, in refusing to review the denial of a pension to a veteran's widow where the statute made no mention of reviewability, the Supreme Court noted:

> The interference of the Courts with the performance of the ordinary duties of the executive departments of the government would be productive of nothing but mischief and we are quite satisfied that such a power was never intended to be given them.[4]

Later courts developed a greater taste for mischief and by the 1940s the opposite interpretation of congressional silence held sway in the federal courts: Silence meant reviewability.[5] The passage of the APA was interpreted by the Supreme Court as establishing a "basic presumption in favor of judicial review," and "only upon a showing of clear and convincing evidence of a contrary legislative intent should the courts restrict access to judicial review."[6]

The courts progressed from interpreting silence as permission to review, to requiring that the legislative preclusion be explicit and clear and even then strictly interpreting its applicability. One of the most common methods Congress had used to preclude judicial review had been to declare the decisions of the agency to be "final." Gradually, the courts came to interpret "final" as not necessarily precluding judicial review of the action. In *Shaughnessy v. Pedreiro*,[7] the Supreme Court interpreted the finality clause of the Immigration and Naturalization Act as allowing review: "It is more in harmony with the generous review provisions of the Administrative Procedure Act to construe the ambiguous word 'final' . . . as referring to finality in administrative procedure rather than as cutting off the right of judicial review in whole or in part." The precise and somewhat lengthy preclusion clause in the Veterans' Administration Act was not merely an exercise in congressional verbosity, but rather a result of congressional awareness of the courts' changed attitudes towards preclusion clauses. In 1970, Congress had reacted strongly against the willingness of federal district courts to permit review of termination of veterans' benefits through a loose interpretation of the less explicit preclusion clause.

Even the unequivocal preclusion of review in the 1970 statute has been interpreted by the Supreme Court as not completely cutting off review. In *Johnson v. Robinson*,[8] the Court held that although the *Administrator's* decisions under the Veterans Administration statute were unreviewable, *Congressional* decisions in creating the act, if they involved constitutional questions, were reviewable. Similarly, where the plaintiff alleges that the agency acted in excess of its statutory mandate[9] or clearly departed from its statutory mandate,[10] the Supreme Court has held the action reviewable even in the face of legislative preclusion.

Action Committed to Agency Discretion

Although §701 of the APA clearly precludes judicial review where "agency action is committed to agency discretion by law," §706(2)(A) expressly provides that courts, in reviewing agency action, may "hold unlawful and set aside agency action, findings and conclusions found to be—(A) arbitrary, capricious, an abuse of discretion." These two sections have presented the courts with two separate problems in determining reviewability of administrative actions: first, determining what constitutes an action "committed to agency discretion" and second, determining which of these discretionary actions might be reviewable under §704 language.

The Supreme Court addressed the first problem in *Citizens to Preserve Overton Park v. Volpe*.[11] The Federal Highway Act and the Department of Transportation Act of 1966 had specified that the Secretary of Transportation could not authorize the expenditure of federal funds to construct a highway through a public park if a "feasible and prudent" alternative route existed. If no alternative existed, construction could be approved only if "all possible planning to minimize harm" to the park had occurred. The City of Memphis, Tennessee, had requested federal funds to construct a six-lane interstate highway through a 340-acre municipal park and the Department of Transportation approved the request. Citizens to Preserve Overton Park, a public interest group, brought suit to stop the construction on the grounds that the Secretary of Transportation had not supported his decision with formal findings, that there were feasible and prudent alternatives available, and that the current plan did not include "all possible methods for reducing harm to the park." The government contended that the Secretary's decision was a discretionary action exempt from judicial review.

The Supreme Court disagreed. After determining that neither of the two authorizing statutes precluded judicial review of the Secretary's action, the Court determined that the statutes had also not specifically committed the action to agency discretion. In the absence of such explicit congressional language, an action could be classified as discretionary only in very limited circumstances: "The legislative history of the Administrative Procedure Act indicates that it is applicable in those rare instances where 'statutes are drawn in such broad terms that in a given case there is no law in ascertaining the existence of Congressional standards.' Plainly there is 'law to apply,' and thus the exemption for 'action committed to agency discretion' is inapplicable."

In 1975, in *Dunlop v. Bachowski*,[12] the Supreme Court attempted to resolve the apparent contradiction between §701 and §706. The attempt was only partly successful. The Labor-Management Reporting and Disclosure Act of 1959 (LMRDA) required the Secretary of Labor to investigate complaints brought under the law and to decide whether to bring civil action against offenders. In 1973, the United Steel Workers of America held district elections and Bachowski, an incumbent defeated in the elections, subsequently filed a complaint under LMRDA with the Secretary of Labor. After investigation, the Secretary determined "that civil action to set aside the challenged election is not warranted." Bachowski filed suit requesting that the Secretary's action be set aside as "arbitrary and capricious" (APA, §706). The district court held the action was an unreviewable action committed to agency discretion (APA, §701(a)). The court of appeals not only held the action reviewable but also held that a "trial type inquiry into the factual bases of the Secretary's conclusion" was authorized. The Supreme Court agreed with neither; instead it held that although the Secretary's decision was discretionary, it was reviewable, but the review was to be limited in scope.

In determining reviewability, the Court chose to ignore §701(a) of the APA and concentrated on legislative intent of the LMRDA. It found there neither an explicit prohibition of review nor

> any congressional purpose to prohibit judicial review. Indeed there is not even the
> slightest information that Congress gave thought to the matter of preclusion of
> judicial review. The only reasonable inference is that the possibility did not occur
> to the Congress. . . . [However] since the statute relies upon the special
> knowledge and discretion of the Secretary for the determination of both the
> probable violation and the probable effect, clearly the reviewing court is not
> authorized to substitute its judgment for the decision of the Secretary.

What the Secretary must do when his decision is judicially challenged is to provide the court with a statement of reasons supporting his decisions: "When action is taken by [the Secretary] it must be such as to enable a reviewing Court to determine with some measure of confidence whether or not the discretion, which still remains in the Secretary, has been exercised in a manner that is neither arbitrary nor capricious. . . . [I]t is necessary for [him] to delineate and make explicit the basis upon which discretionary action is taken."[13]

The decision does not completely answer the question of whether discretionary actions are reviewable or not, but does create a presumption of their reviewability under §706 of the APA unless Congress has explicitly precluded review in an authorizing statute. It does not, and no court decision can, resolve the contradiction between §701 and §706. Only congressional action can do that and to this point Congress has not been inclined to clarify the intent of the two sections. The combined impact of *Overton Park* and *Bachowski* has been to require agencies to be prepared to support all actions and some inaction with a written statement of reasons. Preferably, that statement of reasons should be prepared and available at the time a decision is announced, but if the agency fails to do that, it must provide the courts and the complainant with the statement if the decision is judicially challenged.

Action Unsuited for Review

Courts may also decline to exercise review of an action on the ground that the issue raised is unsuitable for judicial review. Two of the most important of these types of action are "political questions" and foreign policy decisions. The basis for the unreviewability of political questions is the Court's determination that some issues are best left to the other branches of government to resolve.[14] The Supreme Court has used three criteria to determine what constitutes a political question. The first criterion is based on the doctrine of separation of powers and provides that where the Constitution has committed the determination of an issue to another branch of government, the courts should not intervene. A second criterion is if no "judicially manageable standards" to resolve the issue exist and/or there are no adequate judicial remedies to deal with the situation, the courts should not become involved. The third criterion is more amorphous and "suggests that the political questions notion is essentially a problem of judicial discretion, of prudential judgments that some issues ought not to be decided by the courts because they are too controversial or could produce enforcement problems or other institutional difficulties."[15]

Using these criteria, the Supreme Court has held that questions regarding the organization of the national guard were not reviewable because the Constitution commits that authority to Congress;[16] that the issue of whether a constitutional amendment has been properly ratified is unreviewable because there were no judicially discoverable standards for guidance;[17] and that it was best for courts not to get involved in political party convention credential disputes[18] or attempts to define what the guarantee of a "republican form of government" implies.[19] Similarly, prior to 1962, the Supreme Court had held that legislative districting and reapportionment were unreviewable political questions. The Court reversed itself on this question in *Baker v. Carr* and held that reapportionment was not a political question since the Constitution had not excluded the courts from the issue and review standards and remedies did exist.[20]

The unreviewability of most foreign policy decisions has been based on the Supreme Court's perception of them as "political questions." The Court has usually held that the Constitution assigns responsibility for foreign affairs to the President and the Congress and has refused to become involved in foreign policy making. Consequently, it refused to hear cases questioning the constitutionality of the Vietnam "conflict"[21] and declined jurisdiction over the issue of whether the President could terminate a treaty with Taiwan without the Congress's (or the Senate's) approval.[22] Essentially, the Court has applied its own version of §702 of the APA to foreign policy decisions: Where it determines that the Constitution has committed some action to the discretion of another branch, it will refuse to exercise judicial review.

Sovereign Immunity

> An action in a court of the United States seeking relief other than money damages and stating a claim that an agency or an officer or employee thereof acted or failed to act in an official capacity or under color of legal authority shall not be dismissed nor relief therein denied on the ground that it is against the United States or that the United States is an indispensable part.[23]

Prior to the addition of the preceding amendment to the Administrative Procedure Act in 1976, sovereign immunity constituted a major and, if invoked, usually insuperable barrier to judicial review of governmental action. The doctrine of sovereign immunity which holds that government (the sovereign) may not be sued without its consent originated in England based on the belief that "the king can do no wrong." The transplant of a monarchical doctrine to a republican form of government was not made by the Constitution or Congress but rather by the American courts. Precisely why or when the courts transplanted it is unclear, as the Supreme Court conceded in 1882: "While the exemption of the United States and of the several states from being subjected as defendants to ordinary actions in the courts . . . has been repeatedly asserted here, the principle has never been discussed or the reasons for it given, but it has always been treated as established doctrine."[24]

The existence of sovereign immunity as a bar to judicial intervention resulted in some patently unfair and absurd judicial decisions. If the government chose to invoke sovereign immunity (it did not always choose to do so), and if the court accepted the government's claim (it did not always choose to do so), regardless of the injustice committed, the suit would be dismissed. For example, a government employee alleged that he had been denied promotion for 11 years because of ethnic discrimination and attempted to challenge an administrative finding that no discrimination had occurred. The government invoked sovereign immunity and the court dismissed the case without reaching the question.[25]

Even though the courts had created sovereign immunity, they were not always content to honor it and developed methods to circumvent it when they chose to do so. One of the major methods used to allow a party to circumvent sovereign immunity was to allow suit to be brought against an *official* who had acted in excess of statutory authority or who had enforced an allegedly unconstitutional statute. The logic behind this circumvention was that an official acting in such a manner was "stripped of his official or representative character" and could be subjected "in his person to the consequences of his individual conduct."[26] The courts were not always consistent in applying this rule, however, and frequently cases brought against officials were dismissed when the government invoked sovereign immunity.

The 1976 amendments terminated sovereign immunity in nonmonetary cases at the federal level. They did not terminate it for cases involving monetary damages as will be discussed in the following chapter, and they did not in any way modify other statutes precluding judicial review.

> Nothing herein (1) affects other limitations on judicial review . . . or (2) confers authority to grant relief if any other statute that grants consent to suit expressly or impliedly forbids the relief which is sought.[27]

Similarly, sovereign immunity has not been abolished at the state level, although it has been modified and restricted as a defense in a majority of the states.

STANDING

Even if a court has jurisdiction over an agency's action, the court may still dismiss a case if the individual challenging the action does not have "standing." Standing is a complex matter related to the adversarial nature of the judicial process, which at the federal level is based on the constitutional specification that the judicial power extends to "cases" and "controversies."[28] A case or controversy has been interpreted by the courts as requiring two adverse parties, one of which must have suffered an actual injury to some legally protected interest at the hands of the other.

The question of who has standing to challenge an administrative action has been addressed by the federal courts in a multitude of cases and the answers they have given have been inconsistent and frequently unsatisfactory. The inconsistency had resulted from diverse interpretations of what constitutes "actual injury" and "legally protected interest." Congress attempted to clarify the meaning of these two terms as far as challenging administrative action was concerned in §702 of the APA:

> A person suffering legal wrong because of agency action, or adversely affected or aggrieved by agency action within the meaning of a relevant statute, is entitled to judicial review thereof.[29]

Unfortunately, the clarification attempt was unsuccessful and federal courts have struggled as much with determining standing under §702 as they had prior to its passage.

Prior to the passage of the APA, a person seeking standing to challenge governmental action had to show direct, personal injury to a specific legal right, and the concept of legal right was very narrowly interpreted by the courts. In 1937, for example, 18 private power companies which alleged they had been adversely affected by competition from the Tennessee Valley Authority sought to challenge its constitutionality. The Supreme Court dismissed the case on the grounds that the companies lacked standing; they had not established an actual injury to a legal right—"one of property, one arising out of contract, one protected against tortious invasion, or one founded on a statute."[30] Unfair competition from an allegedly unconstitutional government agency which lessened profits and affected a business's financial position was not sufficient to establish standing.

Consumers and government contractors were no more successful than competitors in establishing standing. When consumers who had to pay more for coal because of a minimum price order which applied to coal retailers sought to challenge the order, the Supreme Court held that they suffered no direct damage to any legal rights. Therefore they had no standing to challenge the price order.[31] In *Perkins v. Lukens Steel Co.*,[32] the Court ruled that a government contractor lacked standing to challenge conditions imposed by the agency contract because no legal rights were affected. The contractors, "to have standing, in court, must show an injury or threat to a particular right of their own."

Suits brought by taxpayers seeking to challenge government expenditures met a similar fate. In 1921, Congress passed the Maternity Act which provided federal aid to state programs to reduce infant mortality. Mrs. Frothingham, a federal taxpayer and private citizen, sued, contending that the "effects of the appropriations complained of will be to increase the burden of future taxation and thereby take her property without due process of law." The Court held that Frothingham lacked standing because she had shown no direct personal injury; individual taxpayers' contributions to federal expenditures were so minute that no real interest was shown. "The party must be able to show, not only that the statute is involved, but that he has sustained or is immediately in danger of sustaining some direct injury as a result of its enforcement, and not merely that he suffers in some indefinite way in common with people generally."[33] For 45 years, *Frothingham* "stood as an absolute bar to federal taxpayer suits."[34]

The Supreme Court did make some exceptions to this narrow interpretation of standing in the early 1940s. In *FCC v. Sanders Brothers Radio Station*,[35] the Supreme Court interpreted §402(b) of the Federal Communications Act which allowed any "person aggrieved or whose interests are adversely affected" by a Commission decision to appeal as sufficient to grant standing to an existing broadcaster seeking to challenge a license grant to another station. As long as the existing station could show potential economic injury which might result in diminished public service, the Communications Act requirement for standing had been satisfied. The Court arrived at a similar conclusion in *Scripps-Howard Radio, Inc. v. FCC*.[36]

In 1966, the D.C. Court of Appeals went even further in broadening standing under the Communications Act to challenge FCC decisions. Section 309(d) of the Act allowed "any party in interest" to intervene in FCC licensing decisions. The Court of Appeals found that sufficient to grant a group representing listeners' interest the right to intervene not only in FCC proceedings but also to establish standing to challenge an adverse decision in court.[37]

Not until 1968, however, did the Supreme Court liberalize its general requirements for standing in other types of cases challenging government decisions. The first major loosening of standing requirements came in the Court's decision in *Flast v. Cohen*.[38] Seven federal taxpayers sought to challenge the Elementary and Secondary Education Act of 1965 alleging that it violated the First Amendment prohibition against establishment of religion by providing public funds to religious schools. Although the suit seemed to be barred by *Frothingham*, the Court stated that a "taxpayer may or may not have the requisite personal stake in the outcome, depending upon the circumstances of the particular case."

For taxpayers to establish standing to challenge a governmental action, they have to pass a two-part "logical nexus" test. First, they must show a "logical link" between their status as taxpayers and "the type of legislative enactment attacked." This essentially limited taxpayer challenges to congressional actions "under the taxing and spending clause of Art. I, § 8. . . . Secondly, the taxpayer must establish a nexus between that status and the precise nature of the constitutional infringement alleged. . . . the taxpayer must show that the challenged enactment exceeds specific constitutional limitations."[39]

The decision in *Flast v. Cohen* signaled a major change in the Supreme Court's attitude on standing and it became the reference point for subsequent decisions in which the Court further loosened requirements for standing. In 1970, a group of tenant farmers sought to challenge a change in U.S.D.A. regulations under the Upland Cotton Program which they alleged made it possible for their landlords to subject them to irreparable economic injury. The changed regulations had allowed tenant farmers to assign their subsidy payments for rent, a practice which had previously been prohibited. Landlords had translated permission into a requirement that either the farmers assigned their payments or they were denied a lease. The Court granted the farmers standing to challenge the regulations:

> Although *Flast v. Cohen* was not a case challenging agency action, its determination of the basis for standing should resolve that question for all cases. . . . "[T]he gist of the question of standing" is whether the party seeking relief has alleged such a personal stake in the outcome of the controversy as to assure concrete adverseness. . . . "In other words," we said in Flast, . . . "the question is whether the person whose standing is challenged is a proper party to request an adjudication of a particular issue" and not whether . . . on the merits, the plaintiff has a legally protected interest which the defendant's action invaded. . . .
>
> In light of Flast, standing exists when the plaintiff alleges as the plaintiffs in each of these cases alleged, that the challenged action has caused him injury in fact, economic or otherwise. He thus shows that he has the requisite "personal stake in the outcome." . . . Recognition of his standing to litigate is then consistent with the Constitution and no further inquiry is pertinent to its existence.[40]

The same day the Court handed down *Barlow v. Collins*, it also handed down *Association of Data Processing Service Organizations v. Camp*, which overruled *Tennessee Power Co. v. TVA* and granted competitors standing to challenge administrative actions which they allege adversely affect their competitive status. The test for standing specified in that case was two-pronged:

1. Does the plaintiff allege that the challenged action has injured him in fact? and.
2. Does the interest sought to be protected fall within "the zone of interests to be protected or regulated by the statute or constitutional guarantee in question"?[41]

The Court stated that the zone of interests that might be protected was broad. "Aesthetic, conservational and recreational" interests were included, as were "First Amendment values." "We mention these noneconomic values to emphasize that standing may stem from them as well as from the economic injury on which petitioner relies here."[42]

Although these cases definitely liberalized the requirements to establish standing, in 1972 the Supreme Court signaled that no further liberalization was likely to be forthcoming. The Sierra Club had sought to challenge a decision by the Forest Service to allow construction of a multimillion dollar recreation complex in Mineral King Valley in Sequoia National Park. The Sierra Club, however, deliberately failed to allege "injury in fact," hoping to establish precedent for an even greater broadening of standing than had already occurred. It claimed standing on the grounds that it has "special interest" in conserving National Parks and Forests, and that, the Supreme Court held, was simply not sufficient:

> A mere "interest" in a problem, . . . is not sufficient by itself to render the organization "adversely affected" or "aggrieved" within the meaning of the APA. . . .
>
> The requirement that a party seeking review must allege facts showing that he is himself adversely affected does not insulate executive action from judicial review. . . . It does serve . . . to put the decision as to whether review will be sought in the hands of those who have a direct stake in the outcome.[43]

Thwarted in its attempt to liberalize standing requirements, the Sierra Club did modify its complaint in the district court, alleging injury in fact to the recreational and aesthetic interests of its members, and was then granted standing.[44]

In 1973, the Supreme Court reiterated its commitment to the "injury in fact" test as a threshold determinant of standing and stretched it beyond previous cases when it allowed an environmental association composed of law students to challenge an ICC rate order allowing railroads to impose an emergency 2.5 percent surcharge on freight rates. The "injury in fact" alleged by the association, Students Challenging Regulatory Agency Procedures (SCRAP), was that the surcharge would increase the cost of shipping recyclable materials (freight rates for shipping "virgin" materials, previously unused natural resources such as timber and mineral ore, are lower than rates for other materials as a result of congressional action and ICC regulation). This, SCRAP alleged, would discourage recycling and result in further environmental damage to the forests, streams, and mountains which its members used and enjoyed. SCRAP had shown sufficient injury in fact to have standing. Being granted standing is far from winning a case, however, and in this instance when the Supreme Court reached the merits of the arguments, SCRAP lost. The Court ruled that the Interstate Commerce Act has vested exclusive power in the ICC to determine interim emergency rates.[45]

Without modifying its holdings on standing, the Supreme Court began in 1973 to staunch the flood of cases that resulted from the liberalized standing requirement. The initial restrictions were aimed at class action suits, those brought by an individual or organization seeking to represent the interests of all members of a class that has been adversely affected by an action. Many of these class action suits had been used to secure judicial review of utility rate determinations, public welfare cases, and environmental and consumer actions. In *Zahn v. International Paper Co.*,[46] the Court required that each member of a class represented in such a suit must have suffered a minimum of $10,000 damage to qualify under federal jurisdiction of damage actions. In *Eisen v. Carlisle and Jacquelen*,[47] the Court required that notice must be sent to all identifiable members of the class, no matter how large. Although the opinion did not apply to class actions seeking injunctive relief, it severely limited other class action challenges. In

Alyeska Pipeline Service Co. v. The Wilderness Society,[48] the Supreme Court reversed a Court of Appeals decision awarding attorney's fees to environmental groups which challenged the Department of the Interior's approval of an oil pipeline through Alaska. The lower court reasoned that the environmental groups had acted to vindicate "important statutory rights of all citizens" and, in doing so, had acted as "private attorneys general." The Supreme Court reversed, holding that it would be inappropriate judicial policy making.

In 1974, the Supreme Court clarified the *Flast v. Cohen* requirements for establishing standing in taxpayer suits. In *United States v. Richardson*,[49] a federal taxpayer had asserted that the secrecy of the CIA's budget violated Article I, §9, clause 7 of the Constitution: "a regular statement of Account of the Receipts and Expenditures of all public money shall be published from time to time." Richardson claimed standing under *Flast v. Cohen* but Chief Justice Burger's majority opinion denied the claim, holding that there was "no claim that appropriated funds are being spent in violation of a specific constitutional limitation upon the [taxing and spending power]" as *Flast* required. Burger argued further that Richardson alleged no "particular concrete injury" but only a "generalized grievance" suitable for determination by the political process. The decision in a companion case, *Schlesinger v. Reservists' Committee to Stop the War*,[50] "reemphasized the majority's determination to maintain standing as a significant barrier to access to federal courts, despite the erosion of that concept in prior years."[51]

Asserting standing as taxpayers and citizens, members of the Reservists' Committee challenged the membership of some 103 members of Congress in the military reserve as violative of the Incompatibility clause: "no person holding any office under the United States, shall be a member of either house during his continuance in office," and as depriving taxpayers and citizens of the faithful discharge of the congresspersons' duties because of inconsistent obligations. Burger's opinion held that the plaintiffs lacked standing: As taxpayers they failed to satisfy the first nexus of *Flast* since they did not challenge an enactment under the taxing and spending clause, and as citizens because they asserted only a "generalized citizen interest," not a concrete personal injury.

In 1975 and 1976, the Supreme Court began to modify its liberalized standing concept and to move back to a more restrictive view. In *Warth v. Seldin*,[52] a group of low-income citizens and a building contractors' association were denied standing to challenge a restrictive zoning order which effectively excluded low-income, multifamily housing from a locality. The test used by the Court to determine and deny standing was to clarify the necessary "injury in fact" and to add a new specification—the "but for" test. The injury had to be a *direct* result of the action challenged, and in addition the challenger had to demonstrate that "but for" the action (statute, ordinance, rule, or decision) complained of the injury would not have occurred, or that "judicial relief"—invalidation of the action—"would remove the harm." The low-income citizens could satisfy neither of these tests: the injury claimed was not a direct result of the ordinance, and even if the ordinance were invalidated relief would not be immediate but would depend on the subsequent actions of third parties (developers) not named in the case. The builders' association has similarly "failed to show the existence of any injury to members of sufficient immediacy and ripeness to warrant judicial intervention."

This same two-part test was used in *Simon v. Eastern Kentucky Welfare Rights Organization*. Organizations representing indigents sought to challenge a modification of an Internal Revenue Service ruling which eliminated the requirement that a hospital must provide free care "to the extent of its financial ability" to indigents in order to qualify for tax exempt status. Although the plaintiffs were able to show that indigent individuals had been denied free care by tax exempt hospitals, the Supreme Court denied them standing to challenge the IRS ruling. The "injury in fact" they suffered was not (at least as the Supreme Court viewed it) a direct injury inflicted by IRS but rather one inflicted by hospitals who were not defendants in the case, and the indigents had failed to show that but for the IRS regulation they would have received treatment:

> The principle of . . . Warth controls this case. . . . [I]ndirectness of injury, while not necessarily fatal to standing may make it substantially more difficult to meet the minimum requirement of Art. III: to establish that, in fact, the asserted injury was the consequence of the defendants' actions, or that prospective relief will remove the harm.[53]

Applying this two-part standing test is not always easy and the current Supreme Court has not always applied it in a restrictive (or consistent) manner. In 1977, the Court applied the test to a case that a disinterested observer might feel was similar to *Warth v. Seldin*, but this time standing was granted. At issue was a restrictive zoning ordinance of the Village of Arlington Heights which was challenged by the Metropolitan Housing Development Corporation (MHDC) and three black individuals. MHDC had contracted to purchase land in the village with the intent to construct low-income, multifamily housing. The contract was contingent upon Arlington Heights rezoning the land, which it refused to do. The blacks alleged that they had been denied housing because of the ordinance which constituted a denial of equal protection. MHDC was granted standing: "clearly MHDC has met the constitutional requirements and it therefore has standing to assert its own rights. Foremost among them is MHDC's right to be free of arbitrary or irrational zoning actions" (direct injury). "The challenged action of the petitioners stands as an absolute barrier to constructing the housing MHDC has contracted to place [there], . . . If MHDC secures the injunctive relief it seeks, that barrier will be removed." As for the blacks, "at least one individual . . . has demonstrated standing. . . . Respondent Ransom, a Negro, works at the Honeywell factory in Arlington Heights. . . . he seeks and would qualify for the housing MHDC wants to build. . . . The injury Ransom asserts is that his quest for housing nearer his employment has been thwarted by official action that is racially discriminatory. If a court grants the relief he seeks, there is at least a substantial probability . . . that the . . . project will materialize, affording Ransom the housing opportunity he desires."[54]

The Supreme Court stretched its direct injury—but for—standing test to even more generous limits in *Duke Power Co. v. North Carolina Environmental Group, Inc.* in 1978. Environmental groups and 40 individuals sought to sue Duke Power Company and the federal Nuclear Regulatory Commission seeking as relief a declaration that the Price-Anderson Act which limits total liability for a single nuclear power plant accident to $560 million was unconstitutional. Duke Power Company had applied for and been granted a license by the Nuclear Regulatory Commission (actually by its predecessor the AEC) to construct two nuclear power plants in North and South Carolina. In an opinion, written by Chief Justice Burger, the Court held that the environmental groups and the individuals had standing; they had demonstrated both direct injury and that "but for" the Price-Anderson Act that injury would not occur:

> We turn first to consider the kinds of injuries the District Court found the appellees suffered. It discerned two categories of effects which resulted from the operation of nuclear power plants in potentially dangerous proximity to appellees' living and working environment. The immediate effects included (a) the production of small quantities of non-natural radiation . . . (b) a "sharp increase" in the temperature of two lakes . . . (c) interference with the normal use of the waters of the Catawba River; (d) threatened reduction in property values. . . . (e) "objectively reasonable" present fear and apprehension. . . . It is enough that several of the "immediate" adverse effects were found to harm appellees. . . .
>
> The more difficult step in the standing injury is establishing that these injuries "fairly can be traced to the challenged action of the defendant." . . . The District Court discerned a "but for" causal connection between the Price-Anderson Act . . . and the construction of the nuclear power plants which the [appellees] view as a threat to them." . . . The District Court concluded that "there is a substantial likelihood that Duke would not be able to complete the construction and maintain the operation of the . . . plants but for the protection provided by the Price-Anderson Act.[55]

Justice Burger agreed with the District Court, and then proceeded to address the question as to whether the decision in this case conflicted with the decision in *Flast v. Cohen*. He saw no conflict and limited the "logical nexus" text to general taxpayers' suits:

> We . . . cannot accept the contention that, outside the context of taxpayers' suits, a litigant must demonstrate anything more than injury in fact and a substantial likelihood that the judicial relief requested will prevent or redress the claimed injury to satisfy the "case or controversy" requirement of Article III.[56]

To reiterate an earlier point, being granted standing is not synonymous with prevailing on the merits of the case, and in this case the environmental groups lost.

In 1982, the Supreme Court further refined and restricted the guidelines for taxpayer's establishing standing to challenge administrative actions. In 1976, the Department of Health, Education and Welfare had transferred over $500,000 worth of federal surplus property to Valley Forge Christian College, a church-supported institution. Americans United For Separation of Church and State sought to challenge the transfer as a violation of the First Amendment Establishment clause which resulted in denying its members the right to have their tax dollars used in a constitutional manner. The Supreme Court denied standing to the organization on the grounds that Americans United had failed to show "injury in fact" to a protected interest. "The federal courts were simply not constituted as ombudsmen of the general welfare."[57] Establishing standing to challenge a governmental action requires more than claiming that one's constitutional rights require a certain kind of conduct; it requires a positive showing of specific injury and this Americans United had not accomplished. Their suit was dismissed for lack of standing, and the possibility of future taxpayers suits challenging government spending programs was sharply diminished.

Determining who has standing to challenge a governmental action remains a complex, controversial, and complicated subject. Generally, under the Burger Court's guidelines, a person seeking standing must show (1) an actual or threatened personal injury-in-fact to a legally cognizable interest, either (a) a legal or constitutional right or (b) an interest protected by a statute, and (2) a causal relationship between the challenged action and the injury such that a favorable judicial decision overturning the action would result in relief from the claimed injury. The only clear and noncontroversial aspect of standing is that without it, an individual cannot contest a governmental action no matter how patently unfair, illegal, or unconstitutional that action may be.

PRIMARY JURISDICTION, EXHAUSTION, RIPENESS

If the issue is reviewable, and if it falls within federal jurisdiction, three additional hurdles must be overcome before judicial review is granted. These hurdles are the requirements for exhaustion and ripeness and the doctrine of primary jurisdiction. While the major question of standing was *who* may ask for judicial review of agency action, the question of these three concepts is *when* will judicial review take place.

Normally a court will require that an individual must exhaust all available administrative remedies before seeking judicial relief:

> [T]he long settled rule of judicial administration that no one is entitled to judicial relief for a supposed or threatened injury until the prescribed administrative remedy has been exhausted.[58]

The Administrative Procedure Act reinforces the requirement for exhaustion by specifying that unless statutes provide otherwise *"final* agency action" is subject to judicial review.[59] That is, until the agency has completed its consideration of the matter and has had time to correct any errors or satisfactorily resolve the issue, courts are not to interfere.

Some major exceptions to the "long settled rule" do exist. If the challenge is to the jurisdiction of the agency, i.e., whether the agency has power to take action in the first place, then courts may agree to determine the issue before final agency action. Similarly, if the agency's action is challenged as invalid on its face, the courts may step in and enjoin the proceeding before the agency has completed its action.[60] If the challenge is brought under §1983 of the Civil Rights Act of 1871, alleging that a "person acting under color of state authority" has deprived the individual of a federal constitutional or legal right, the federal courts will not necessarily require the aggrieved party to exhaust state administrative procedures. Finally, if there are no clearly defined administrative remedies to exhaust, the courts may agree to review prior to final agency action.

The requirement that a case be "ripe" before judicial review is granted arises from the Article III limitation of the judicial power to "cases" and "controversies." Consequently, ripeness is closely related to both standing and the requirement to exhaust administrative remedies before seeking judicial review. An administrative action is ripe for review if it involves two bonafide adverse parties, one of which alleges injury in fact (has standing) as a result of *final* agency action (exhaustion). The rationale for the requirement of ripeness was explained by the Supreme Court in *Abbott Laboratories v. Gardner*.[61] Ripeness is necessary to prevent the courts, through avoidance of premature adjudication, from entangling themselves in abstract disagreements over administrative policies, and also to protect the agencies from judicial interference until an administrative decision has been formalized and its effects felt in a concrete way by the challenging parties.

Two of the central questions in determining ripeness are (1) assuming the complaining party has standing, how final must agency action be, and (2) must the complainant have actually suffered the injury or is grave and probable threat of injury sufficient? In answer to the second question, the Supreme Court held in *United Public Workers of America v. Mitchell*[62] that "a hypothetical threat is not enough." Several federal employees who desired to engage in partisan political activity had brought suit to enjoin the Civil Service Commission from enforcing the Hatch Act which forbids such activities. The situation as the Court saw it was too speculative to decide.

Ripeness is particularly difficult to determine when the action challenged is the promulgation of an administrative regulation. The difficulty involves determining whether the actual promulgation of the rule constitutes final action which may be challenged by persons against whom it may be enforced or whether finality requires actual enforcement and the imposition of sanctions against the person.

Congress had attempted to solve the problem faced by a person who believed an administrative action to be unauthorized, but who did not wish to risk punishment by violating it, by passing the Federal Declaratory Judgment Act of 1934. The Act provided that:

> In a case of actual controversy within its jurisdiction . . . any court of the United States . . . upon the filing of an appropriate pleading, may declare the rights and other legal relations of any interested parties seeking such declaration, whether or not further relief is or could be sought. Any such declaration shall have the force and effect of a final judgment or decree and shall be reviewable as such.

Although the Supreme Court in *Aetna Life Insurance Co. v. Haworth*[63] held the Act constitutional since such judgments meet the "case" or "controversy" test, the Act failed to resolve the basic problem of determining at what point in the administrative process an action truly becomes final.

In three companion cases decided in 1967 the Court resolved those difficulties with an unequivocal "It all depends." In the first case, *Abbott Laboratories v. Gardner*,[64] the Court held that a regulation could be considered final action and ripe for review prior to enforcement against a specific party. In that case, the FDA acting under the authority of the Food, Drug and Cosmetic Act, had promulgated a regulation requiring the labels of prescription drugs to include the generic drug name as well as the brand name. Complying with the regulation would have entailed considerable expense for pharmaceutical manufacturers. Failure to comply might have resulted in an enforcement action involving civil and criminal penalties and loss of public confidence.

Alleging that the FDA had exceeded its statutory authority the companies sought preenforcement review. The Supreme Court held the case was ripe for review. In determining ripeness, the Court established another two-part test: The "problem is best seen in a twofold aspect, requiring us to evaluate both the fitness of the issues for judicial decision and the hardship to the parties of withholding court consideration." The issue is purely legal (interpretation of the statute) and the regulation is a "final agency action" within the meaning of the APA. Further, the regulation involved hardship on the drug firms because they had to resolve the dilemma of either complying at great cost or risking severe penalties. Since both aspects of the twofold test were present, judicial review of the regulations could commence even though no enforcement had occurred.

In the second case, *Gardner v. Toilet Goods Association*,[65] the Court reached a similar conclusion. In the third case, however, *Toilet Goods Assoc. v. Gardner*, it arrived at the opposite conclusion. Although the regulation challenged, which required manufacturers of color additives to allow free access to FDA inspectors or suffer immediate suspension of their FDA certification, was accepted by the court as "final" agency action, the potential hardship for the Toilet Goods Association for disobeying the regulation was not sufficient to justify preenforcement judicial review:

> The test of ripeness . . . depends not only on how adequately a court can deal with the legal issue presented, but also on the degree and nature of the regulation's present effect on those seeking relief. . . . This is not a situation in which primary conduct is affected. . . . [N]o irremediable adverse consequences flow from requiring a later challenge to this regulation. . . . a refusal . . . would at most lead only to suspension of certification . . . that can be promptly challenged through an administrative procedure.[66]

As the 7th Circuit Court of Appeals phrased it in 1976, "Determination of ripeness is, as we have said, a commonsense judgment."[67]

Determining primary jurisdiction involves somewhat different considerations from either ripeness or exhaustion decisions. The need to determine primary jurisdiction arises in situations where both an agency and the courts have been given jurisdiction by Congress to resolve a particular issue. In such situations if a party seeks initial relief in court, the court must determine "whether enforcement of the claim requires the resolution of issues which, under a regulatory scheme, have been placed within the special competence of an administrative body; in such a case the judicial process is suspended pending referral of such issues to the administrative body for its view."[68]

For example, §9 of the Interstate Commerce Act provided that any person "claiming to be damaged by any common carrier" subject to regulation under the Act, could either "make complaint to the Commission . . . or bring suit . . . in any District or Circuit Court." In 1907, Abilene Cotton Oil Company sued Texas and Pacific Railway Company in court seeking to recover $1,951.83 for what it alleged had been unreasonable rates charged by the railroad. Despite the statutory provision that allowed such suits, the Supreme Court held that the ICC had primary jurisdiction: "a shipper seeking reparation predicated upon the unreasonableness of the established rate . . . must *primarily* invoke redress through the Interstate Commerce Commission."[69] In order to ensure uniformity and fairness, the Court held that the reasonableness of rates must be determined in the first instance by the ICC.

Generally, if an issue involves technical determinations where the expertise of the administrative agency is particularly relevant, the courts will hold the agency has primary jurisdiction even if statutes provide for concurrent jurisdiction. If the issue involved does not require "the expert and specialized knowledge"[70] of the agency to resolve or involve violation of agency regulations, the individual may be permitted to bypass the agency and bring suit in court. In *Nader v. Allegheny Airlines, Inc.,*[71] the Supreme Court addressed "the question whether a common law tort action based on alleged fraudulent misrepresentation by an air carrier subject to regulation by the Civil Aeronautics Board must be stayed pending reference to the Board for determination whether the practice is "deceptive" . . . [under] the Federal Aviation Act." The "deceptive" practice involved was the airlines' policy of overbooking and Allegheny's unfortunate bumping of Ralph Nader from one of its flights. At the time the CAB had no regulation regarding overbooking. Consequently, the Court held that there was "no irreconcilable conflict between the statutory scheme and the persistence of common law remedies," and that "The standards to be applied to an action for fraudulent misrepresentation are within the conventional competence of the courts and the judgment of a technically expert body is not likely to be helpful in the application of these standards to the facts of this case."

Primary jurisdiction, exhaustion, and ripeness are the major "timing" requirements for challenging administrative actions in court. Usually, if all administrative remedies have not been exhausted, if the issues are not ripe for judicial review, and/or resolution of the issues requires the technical expertise of the agency, courts will not accept a case but will instead remand it to the relevant agency for resolution. Such a remand does not foreclose future judicial review after final agency action has occurred.

SCOPE OF REVIEW

After all of the preceding requirements for securing judicial review have been satisfied, the next major issue to be resolved is determining the proper scope of review of the challenged action. Scope of review refers to the extent to which the court will inquire into the administrative determination: "the breadth and the depth of judicial scrutiny of the agency's action."[72] As Davis has pointed out, "the scope of judicial review of administrative action ranges from zero to one hundred per cent."[73] The scope of review varies depending on both the substantive and procedural nature of the action being challenged. Currently, §706 of the Administrative Procedure Act provides the basic framework for the scope of review of agency actions:

> To the extent necessary to decision and when presented, the reviewing court shall
> decide all relevant questions of law, interpret constitutional and statutory
> provisions, and determine the meaning or applicability of the terms of an agency
> action. The reviewing court shall—(1) compel agency action unlawfully withheld
> or unreasonably delayed; and (2) hold unlawful and set aside agency action,
> findings, and conclusions found to be— (A) arbitrary, capricious, an abuse of

discretion, or otherwise not in accordance with law; (B) contrary to constitutional right, power, privilege, or immunity; (C) in excess of statutory jurisdiction, authority, or limitations, or short of statutory right; (D) without observance of procedure required by law; (E) unsupported by substantial evidence in a case subject to sections 556 and 557 of this title or otherwise reviewed on the record of an agency hearing provided by statute; or (F) unwarranted by the facts to the extent that the facts are subject to trial de novo by the reviewing court. In making the foregoing determinations, the court shall review the whole record or those parts of it cited by a party, and due account shall be taken of the rule of prejudicial error.[74]

One of the basic determinants of the scope of review is whether the question raised is a question of law or a question of fact. As §706 makes clear, all questions of law are reviewable and are subject to thorough and intense scrutiny by the court. Examples of questions of law include whether the agency has exceeded statutory authority, whether it has violated constitutional provisions, whether it has followed legally mandated procedures, and whether it has applied proper standards in making its decision (§706(2)(A), (B), (C), (D)). When such questions are at issue, judicial review proceeds independently of the agency's determination. Questions of fact are subject to more limited scope of review under the APA primarily by the standards specified in §706(2)(A), (E), and (F). Unfortunately, the distinction between law and fact is not always clear-cut, and some issues involve a mixture of the two. In such cases, the scope of review varies depending on the precise nature of the mixture.

Adjudicatory Decisions: The Substantial Evidence Test

The primary question of fact involved in judicial review of many adjudicatory decisions is whether the agency decision is supported by "substantial evidence" in the record. For a court to determine this, it must have the entire record of the agency proceeding to review, and the court will evaluate the reasonableness of the agency's decisions in light of the entire record. Since most adjudicatory proceedings are adversary in nature, their records will usually contain contradictory and conflicting testimony. Determining what constitutes substantial evidence in such situations is seldom easy and judicial guidelines are not exactly models of clarity: "[S]ubstantial evidence is more than a mere scintilla. It means such relevant evidence as a reasonable mind might accept as adequate to support a conclusion."[75] The Supreme Court expanded on this definition of substantial evidence in *Universal Camera Corp. v. NLRB*. In reviewing an administrative order, the courts were to weigh the agency decision in light of the entire record, not "merely on the basis of evidence which in and of itself justified" the decision, but also "taking into account contradictory evidence or evidence from which conflicting inferences could be drawn." After conceding that the substantiality test was not "a calculus of value," the Court summarized its meaning:

> The Board's findings are entitled to respect; but they must nonetheless be set aside when the record before a Court of Appeals clearly precludes the Board's decision from being justified by a fair estimate of the worth of the testimony of witnesses or its informed judgment on matters within its special competence or both.[76]

Since reasonable persons have been known to disagree on a very large number of issues, what constitutes substantial evidence remains unclear. What is clear, however, is that a reviewing court will scrutinize the entire record in deciding cases involving such questions.

The second standard for review of factual questions is found in §702(2)(F) which allows the courts to set aside an agency action which is "unwarranted by the facts *to the extent that the facts are subject to trial de novo by the reviewing court*" (emphasis added). This standard is applicable only to a limited category of cases. "De novo review . . . is authorized by §706(2)(F) in only two circumstances. First, such de novo review is authorized when the action is adjudicatory in nature and the agency fact-finding procedures are inadequate. And, there may be independent judicial fact-finding when issues that were not before the agency are raised in a proceeding to enforce nonadjudicatory agency action."[77]

Scope of Review: Rule Making

The scope of review for formal rule making (rule making on the record) is identical to the scope for adjudicatory orders. In addition to full review of questions of law, courts will also review formal rules to ensure that they are based on substantial evidence in the record. The scope of review for informal rules, those made pursuant to §553, particularly for questions of fact, is different and under §706, considerably narrower. Although on questions of law (to reiterate, questions involving procedure, statutory basis, constitutionality) §706 provides for identical scope of review for the two types of action, it specifically limits the substantial evidence test to cases subject to §§556 and 557 of the act. The scope of review for questions of fact in §553 rule making is limited to determining if the rule is "arbitrary and capricious."

In the 1970s, the federal courts of appeals increasingly used the "arbitrary and capricious" standard to require agencies to resort to stricter procedures for informal rule making than mandated by §553, frequently requiring a "paper hearing." The results of this "quasi-hearing" were in turn used to apply a "quasi-substantial evidence" test to informal rules. The decision by the D.C. Court of Appeals in *National Welfare Rights Organization v. Mathews* exemplifies how the "arbitrary and capricious" standard was used to broaden the scope of review of informal rules and subsequently to modify informal rule-making procedure. At issue was a regulation promulgated by DHEW limiting the amount of assets that could be reserved by families receiving AFDC payments. The court invalidated the regulation:

> [J]udicial review is meaningless where the administrative record is insufficient to determine whether the action is arbitrary and capricious. . . . Even within the narrow scope of review mandated in this case, support for the Secretary's actions must appear in the record. . . .
>
> We agree that the regulation does clearly express policy decisions. . . . The choice of limitation, however, "turns crucially on factual issues" and therefore requires "sufficient attention to these in the statement to allow the fundamental rationality of the regulations to be ascertained." *Amoco Oil v. EPA*, 501 F2d 722 (1974). . . .
>
> The "basis and purpose" statement . . . must be sufficiently detailed and

informative to allow a searching judicial scrutiny of how and why the regulations were adopted.[78]

Substance and procedure were becoming almost interchangeable in judicial review. Although the courts were not supposed to substitute their judgment on matters of substance for that of the agency, they felt increasingly free to require agencies to modify procedures so that they would come to the "correct" substantive decision. This judicial tendency to create extrastatutory procedures was the primary issue addressed by the Supreme Court in *Vermont Yankee Nuclear Power Corp. v. Natural Resources Defense Council*. As discussed in chapter 8, the Court's opinion in Vermont Yankee reprimanded lower federal courts for requiring agencies to use procedures in excess of those mandated by Congress in the APA and other statutes, and while it certainly clarified the scope of review of procedural questions, it left unclear the scope of review for substantive questions:

> There remains, of course, the question of whether the challenged rule finds sufficient justification in the administrative proceedings that it should be upheld by the reviewing court. . . . [T]he validity of that action must "stand or fall on the propriety of that finding, judged, of course, by the appropriate standard of review. If that finding is not sustainable on the administrative record made, then the . . . decision must be vacated. . . . ." *Camp v. Pitts*, 411 U.S. 138 (1973). . . .
>
> Fundamental policy questions appropriately resolved in Congress and in the state legislatures are not subject to reexamination in the federal courts under the guise of judicial review of agency action. . . . In the meantime courts should perform their appointed function. . . . Administrative decisions should be set aside in this context, as in every other, only for substantial procedural or substantive reasons as mandated by statute . . . not simply because the court is unhappy with the result.[79]

Absent specific statutory provisions, presumably the scope of review for substantive question involving informal rules, is limited to a determination as to whether they are arbitrary and capricious. Since this is also the standard for reviewing informal actions, its meaning will be discussed at greater length in the following section.

The scope of review of both legal and factual questions in hybrid rule making depends primarily on the specific authorizing statute mandating the procedure. OSHA health and safety standards for example are, by statute, subject to review under the substantial evidence test,[80] as are FTC rules relating to unfair or deceptive acts or practices.[81]

Scope of Review: Informal Action

The scope of review of informal actions is considerably narrower than for either rule making or adjudication. Even on questions of law, review is less comprehensive with informal actions because usually there is less law to apply to the action. Procedures for informal actions are not specified in the APA and usually are not covered in authorizing statutes either. Many informal actions are not considered "final agency actions" so they are not even subject to judicial review. Finally, informal actions constitute the bulk of those actions "committed to agency discretion" which are also exempt from judicial review.

The scope of review for substantive informal actions that are reviewable is governed by the "arbitrary, capricious or abuse of discretion" standard in the APA. The Supreme Court opinion in *Overton Park* included an excellent discussion of the scope of review for informal actions:

> The Court is first required to decide whether the Secretary acted within the scope of his authority. . . .
>
> Scrutiny of the facts does not end, however, with the determination that the Secretary has acted within the scope of his authority. Section 706(2)(A) requires a finding that the actual choice made was not "arbitrary, capricious, an abuse of discretion. . . ." To make this binding the court must consider whether there has been a clear error of judgment. . . . [T]he ultimate standard of review is a narrow one. The court is not empowered to substitute its judgment for that of the agency.
>
> The final inquiry is whether the Secretary's action followed the necessary procedural requirements.[82]

The Court noted that APA requirements for findings were not applicable to the Secretary's decision.

In 1973, in *Camp v. Pitts*,[83] the Supreme Court reiterated the limited scope of review under the arbitrary and capricious standard, holding that the courts should limit their consideration to "the administrative record already in existence, not some new record made initially in the reviewing court." Although these decisions did result in requiring agencies to defend certain informal actions which previously had not been subject to review, they stopped short of requiring either findings or a record for such actions. To withstand judicial challenge, the agency had to demonstrate that the decisions made were not "clearly erroneous" or totally irrational. In *Dunlop v. Bachowski*, the Supreme Court further clarified the scope of review under the arbitrary and capricious standard:

> The necessity that the reviewing court refrain from substitution of its judgment for that of the Secretary thus helps define the permissible scope of review. . . . [T]he court's review should be confined to examination of the "reasons" statement, and the determination whether the statement, without more, evinces that the Secretary's decision is so irrational as to constitute the decision arbitrary and capricious. . . . "If . . . the Court concludes there is a rational and defensible basis [stated in the reasons statement] or [the Secretary's] determination, then that should be an end to this matter." . . . DeVito II.[84]

To the extent that informal actions are subject to judicial review, the "depth, breadth and intensity" of that review is considerably less than is characteristic of review of more "formal" types of administrative action.

JUDICIAL REVIEW AS A CHECK ON ADMINISTRATIVE POWER

The availability of judicial review provides a vital and essential check on the exercise of administrative power. Its very existence ensures that agencies must constantly maintain vigilance in following legally and constitutionally required procedures, be prepared to justify the reasonableness and rationality of their actions, and respect the constitutional and legal rights of individuals. Despite its importance and efficacy, judicial review has severe limitations as a check on administrative power. As we have pointed out in this chapter, not all administrative actions are subject to judicial review; of those that are reviewable the thoroughness of the review varies considerably with some actions subject to only superficial review. The concept of standing results in further limiting the availability of review; not everyone who is injured by an administrative action will be permitted by the courts to challenge it. The requirements for exhaustion, ripeness, and primary jurisdiction frequently result in requiring that an individual must suffer severe injury before judicial relief will be granted.

At best judicial review is a sporadic check on administrative power. Of the hundreds of thousands of administrative decisions made in a year, only a minuscule proportion will ever be challenged. Of those that are, final judicial decision may be delayed for years. No method currently has been developed to determine how many of the vast majority of actions that are not challenged are legal, constitutional, and proper. At worst, judicial review is a check that works best for the wealthy and powerful. Pragmatically, the poor, the weak, and the unorganized are severely disadvantaged in securing relief by the realities of the judicial process which is expensive, time-consuming, and complex. Only those who can afford the entry fees can play the game—and the entry fees for judicial review are high.

Even when judicial review is available and is granted, the outcome is unpredictable. Courts do not necessarily favor the interests of the poor, nor do they have a monopoly on commitment to fairness and justice, and most assuredly when they become too deeply enmeshed in "Monday morning quarterbacking" of administrative decisions they do not make better technical decisions than the agencies. Occasionally, when courts make "compassionate" decisions, as in *Goldberg v. Kelly*, they do not recognize the tradeoffs inherent in the decision they have made. In evaluating the impact of *Goldberg*, for example, Gellhorn points out: "In effect Goldberg traded off the interests of those entitled to benefits but not enrolled for the interests of those on the rolls . . . facing termination. From a public interest perspective, it is by no means clear that the benefits of this tradeoff exceeded its costs."[85] The plurality opinion in *Marshall v. American Petroleum Institute*[86] struggling with OSHA's benzene standard clearly indicated the limitations of judges and lawyers in understanding and evaluating cost-effectiveness analysis.

The propriety of judicial activism and the proper scope of judicial review of administrative actions has been a recurring controversy in American politics. The controversy has resurfaced and intensified with the Reagan Administration. In a speech to top lawyers of the executive branch of government on October 29, 1981, Attorney General William French Smith accused the federal courts of "constitutionally dubious and unwise intrusions upon the legislative domain," and specifically criticized them for assuming "greater power of review over governmental action" in various administrative areas by deciding cases which they should have avoided by invoking judicial doctrines such as "standing, ripeness, mootness and the presence of a political question."[87] "Satisfactory" resolution of that controversy has evaded the reach of many presidential administrations, including that of Franklin Roosevelt, and probably will evade that of

Ronald Reagan. For all its weaknesses, inadequacies, and unfairness, judicial review remains an essential check on the excesses of the executive branch of government.

NOTES

1. *Califano v. Sanders*, 430 U.S. 99, 105 (1977).
2. 39 U.S.C. §211(a).
3. Immigration and Naturalization Act, 8 U.S.C. §1252(b).
4. *Decatur v. Paulding*, 39 U.S. 497, 515 (1840).
5. *Stark v. Wickard*, 321 U.S. 288 (1944).
6. *Abbot Laboratories v. Gardner*, 387 U.S. 136, 141 (1967).
7. 349 U.S. 48 (1955).
8. 415 U.S. 361 (1974).
9. *Harmon v. Bruckner*, 355 U.S. 579 (1958).
10. *Oestereich v. Selective Service System Local Board No. 11*, 393 U.S. 233 (1968).
11. 401 U.S. 402 (1971).
12. 421 U.S. 560 (1975).
13. *Dunlop v. Bachowski*, 421 U.S. 560 (1975).
14. For more detailed discussion of the doctrine of political questions, see Gerald Gunther, *Cases and Materials on Constitutional Law* (Mineola, N.Y.: Foundation Press, 1980), pp. 1688ff, and Howard Ball, *Courts and Politics* (Englewood Cliffs, N.J.: Prentice-Hall, 1980), p. 133ff. See also Alexander M. Bickel, *The Least Dangerous Branch* (Indianapolis: Bobbs-Merrill, 1972), and Philippa Strum, *The Supreme Court and "Political Questions"* (University: University of Alabama Press, 1974).
15. Gunther, *Cases and Materials*, p. 450.
16. *Gilligan v. Morgan*, 413 U.S. 1 (1973).
17. *Coleman v. Miller*, 307 U.S. 433 (1939).
18. *O'Brien v. Brown*, 409 U.S. 1 (1972).
19. *Luther v. Borden*, 7 Howard 1 (1849).
20. 369 U.S. 186 (1962).
21. *Mora v. McNamara*, 389 U.S. 934 (1967).
22. *Goldwater v. Carter*, 444 U.S. 256 (1979).
23. 5 U.S.C. §702.
24. *United States v. Lee*, 106 U.S. 196, 207 (1882).
25. *Gnotta v. United States*, 415 F.2nd 1271 (8th cir., 1969).
26. *Ex Parte Young*, 209 U.S. 123 (1908).
27. 5 U.S.C. §702.
28. Art. III, Sec. 2.
29. 5 U.S.C. §702.
30. *Tennessee Electric Power Co. v. TVA*, 306 U.S. 111 (1937).
31. *Atlanta v. Ickes*, 308 U.S. 517 (1939).
32. 310 U.S. 113 (1940).
33. *Frothingham v. Mellon*, 262 U.S. 447, 488 (1923).
34. William Smith, "Standing To Sue in Taxpayer Suits," 46 Mississippi Law Journal 361 (1975).
35. 309 U.S. 470 (1940).
36. 316 U.S. 4 (1942).

37. *Office of Communication, United Church of Christ v. FCC*, 359 F.2d 994 (D.C. Cir., 1966).

38. 392 U.S. 83 (1968).

39. Ibid., at 102.

40. *Barlow v. Collins*, 397 U.S. 159, 170 et seq. (1970).

41. 397 U.S. 150, 152 et seq. (1970).

42. Ibid., at 154.

43. *Sierra Club v. Morton*, 405 U.S. 727 (1972).

44. *Sierra Club v. Morton*, 348 F. Supp. 219 (N.D. Cal. 1972).

45. *United States v. SCRAP*, 412 U.S. 669 (1973).

46. 417 U.S. 219 (1973).

47. 417 U.S. 156 (1973).

48. 421 U.S. 240 (1975).

49. 418 U.S. 166 (1974).

50. 418 U.S. 208 (1974).

51. Gunther, *Cases and Materials on Constitutional Law*, p. 1628.

52. 442 U.S. 490 (1975).

53. *Simon v. Eastern Kentucky Welfare Rights Organization*, 426 U.S. 26, 44 (1976).

54. *Village of Arlington Heights v. Metropolitan Housing Development Corp.*, 429 U.S. 252, 264 (1977).

55. *Duke Power Company v. North Carolina Environmental Group Inc.*, 438 U.S. 59, 72 et seq. (1978).

56. Ibid., at 79.

57. *Valley Forge Christian College v. Americans United for Separation of Church and State,*—U.S.—(1982).

58. *Myers v. Bethlehem Shipbuilding Corp.*, 303 U.S. 41, 50 (1938).

59. 5. U.S.C. §704.

60. *Public Utilities Commission of Ohio v. United Fuel Gas Co.*, 317 U.S. 456 (1943).

61. 387 U.S. 136 (1967).

62. 330 U.S. 75 (1947).

63. 300 U.S. 227 (1937).

64. 387 U.S. 136 (1967).

65. 387 U.S. 167 (1967).

66. *Toilet Goods Association v. Gardner*, 387 U.S. 158, 164 (1967).

67. *Bethlehem Steel Corporation v. United States Environmental Protection Agency*, 536 F.2d 156 (7th Cir., 1976).

68. *United States v. Western Pacific Railroad Company*, 352 U.S. 59, 64 (1956).

69. *Texas Pacific Railway Co. v. Abilene Cotton Oil Co.*, 204 U.S. 426 (1907).

70. *U.S. v. Western Pacific Railroad*, 352 U.S. 59 (1956).

71. 426 U.S. 290 (1976).

72. Glen O. Robinson and Ernest Gellhorn, *The Administrative Process* (St. Paul, Minn.: West Publishing Co., 1974), p. 219.

73. Kenneth Davis, *Administrative Law: Cases-Texts-Problems* (St. Paul, Minn.: West Publishing Co., 1977), p. 75.

74. 5 U.S.C. §706.

75. *Consolidated Edison Co. v. National Labor Relations Board*, 305 U.S. 197, 229 (1938).

76. *Universal Camera Corp. v. NLRB*, 340 U.S. 474, 490 (1951).

77. *Citizens to Preserve Overton Park, Inc. v. Volpe*, 401 U.S. 402 (1972).

78. *National Welfare Rights Org. v. Mathews*, 533 F.2d 637, 648 (D.C. Cir., 1976).

79. *Vermont Yankee Nuclear Power Corp. v. Natural Resources Defense Council*, 435 U.S. 519, 549 et seq. (1978).

80. 29 U.S.C. §665(f).

81. 15 U.S.C. §57(a).

82. *Citizens to Preserve Overton Park, Inc. v. Volpe*, 401 U.S. 402, 415 et seq. (1971).

83. 411 U.S. 138 (1973).

84. *Dunlop v. Bachowski*, 421 U.S. 560, 572 (1975).

85. Walter Gellhorn, Clark Byse, and Peter Strauss, *Administrative Law: Cases and Comments*, 7th ed. (Mineola, N.Y.: Foundation Press, 1979), p. 447.

86. 448 U.S. 607 (1980).

87. "Smith to Move against Judicial Activism," *Spokane Spokesman Review*, October 29, 1981, p. 6.

Chapter 12

Obtaining Monetary Redress from Government

Congress shall make no law . . . abridging the right of the people . . . to petition for redress of grievances.

THE FIRST AMENDMENT

Obtaining judicial review of administrative action is never automatic and seldom simple; obtaining monetary compensation for injury inflicted by government action, agencies, or employees is considerably more difficult and complicated. The primary source of the difficulties and complications is the doctrine of sovereign immunity which remains as a bar to monetary claims brought against government unless it has consented to the suit. Neither the federal nor the state governments have provided for a blanket waiver of sovereign immunity in cases seeking monetary damages. The 1976 amendments to the Administrative Procedure Act which waived sovereign immunity as a defense in other types of action explicitly limited that waiver to cases "seeking relief other than monetary damages." Congress and the states have consented to some monetary suits for certain actions in certain circumstances and courts have created other circumstances under which monetary relief may be gained, but many exemptions to such suits remain and consistency and uniformity are conspicuously lacking in this area.

Sovereign immunity, as was explained in the preceding chapter, was derived from the English common law concept that the king (the sovereign) can do no wrong. Even sovereigns, and especially agents of the sovereign, did, however, engage in activities which inflicted injury on others. Under English common law a method was developed for those who had been injured by government action to recover monetary damages. A petition for redress could be submitted to the Crown, eventually to Chancery court, and if the Crown felt the petition meritorious, redress would be granted.

Both the concept of soverign immunity and, as the First Amendment indicates, the method for obtaining redress were transplanted to the United States. Since there was no Crown to receive the petitions, the honor and the power were assumed by Congress. Although the constitutional basis for sovereign immunity in cases involving other than monetary damages is nonexistent, in monetary cases the Constitution does provide a possible basis for such immunity. Early Congresses interpreted Art. I, § 9, "no money shall be drawn from the Treasury, but in consequence of appropriations made by law," as meaning that only Congress could grant monetary relief for claims against the government.[1] Consequently, petitions for redress could only be submitted and responded to by the Congress. Until 1855, regardless of the nature or size of the claim against the government, the injured party had only one recourse—the benevolence and generosity of Congress. Even today, although many cases requesting monetary relief can go to the courts for resolution, others, if relief is to be obtained, must go to Congress. Private bills, the method Congress uses to respond to these "petitions for redress," continue to constitute, in numbers at least, a sizable proportion of the legislative output of Congress.

Monetary claims against the government can arise from various circumstances: contract disputes, illegal collection of taxes, taking of property for public use, or pay disputes with employees. From an administrative perspective one of the most important categories of claims are those arising out of torts committed by administrative agencies or employees. Basically, a tort is a civil wrong, usually a willful or negligent act which results in injury to another's person, property, or reputation, for which the law requires compensation. Although from one perspective administrative responsibility would seemingly require that agencies and administrators should be held strictly liable for torts against citizens, Congress and the courts have been reluctant to adopt this perspective. Although tort liability (and immunity) will be discussed later in the chapter, some terms can be clarified at this point. If and when there is liability for torts committed by government, that liability may be either

1. agency (government) liability—the suit is brought directly against the government (federal, state, or local) entity that has committed the alleged tort, and monetary damages, if awarded, are paid by the governmental entity; or
2. officer liability—the suit is brought against the individual government official (employee) and the monetary damages are assessed against him personally.

Immunity from such suits ranges all the way from absolute immunity (suit is barred) to no immunity (the government agency or official has no more protection from being sued than a private individual would have). The middle ground is qualified immunity which permits suit to be brought but allows the agency or official to use "good faith" as a defense. If government or the official can show that the action was taken in good faith, even if injury resulted, no monetary damages will be awarded. Petitioning the Crown for redress of grievances may not always have been satisfactory, but it certainly was easier to explain than the current hodgepodge of methods that exist for securing relief.

OBTAINING REDRESS: FEDERAL LAW FOR FEDERAL ACTIONS

Government Liability

The United States Court of Claims　In 1855, Congress created the Court of Claims to assist it in handling claims based on a "law of Congress, regulation of an executive department or a contract with the United States government."[2] The Court could receive claims, investigate them, and make initial awards of damages. Its decisions were not final and could be revised by either Congress or the Secretary of Treasury. Not until 1887 and the passage of the Tucker Act was the Court of Claims given the power to make final decisions and not until 1953 did Congress make it an Article III (constitutional) court.

Currently, the Court of Claims has jurisdiction to hear and decide all claims founded on the Constitution, a law of Congress, an administrative regulation, or a government contract. Specifically excluded from its jurisdiction, however, are claims arising from pensions or torts, and it may hear only cases involving monetary damages. It has concurrent jurisdiction with the district courts for claims under $10,000 and tax refund cases. All claims in excess of $10,000 must be brought before the Court of Claims. Since the passage of the Tucker Act, its jurisdiction has been expanded to include claims for damages by persons unjustly convicted and imprisoned by the United States, claims against the United States Department of Agriculture for destruction of animals to suppress livestock diseases, certain claims by providers of services for reimbursements under Medicare, claims against Internal Revenue Service for intentional and willful violation of laws relating to disclosure of tax return information, Indian claims against the United States, and claims for reimbursement for cleanup of oil spills brought under the Water Quality Improvement Act of 1970. Congress overcame its qualms about the implications of the Appropriations clause by providing a standing appropriation to pay any final judgment against the United States entered by either the Court of Claims or the district courts. In 1976–77, for example, the Court of Claims awarded over $72 million in damages and interest against the federal government.[3]

In many respects the Court of Claims is unique among the constitutional courts. It currently consists of seven judges who act primarily as an appellate tribunal. Cases are initially heard by trial judges who are not Article III judges but resemble administrative law judges very closely in terms of powers and procedures. The trial judges hear the cases, rule on all motions, conduct pretrials, receive evidence, make findings of fact and conclusions of law, and make initial determinations. Court of Claims judges hear only oral argument when the decisions of trial judges are appealed. Jury trials are not permitted at any point in the Court of Claims despite the Seventh Amendment provision that "In suits at common law, where the value in controversy shall exceed twenty dollars, the right of trial by jury shall be preserved." The Supreme Court dismissed constitutional objections to this procedure early in the history of the Court of Claims using the logic that it has used to dismiss objections to the lack of juries in administrative hearings: Suits against government are not "suits at common law," and were, in fact, barred by common law. Such suits required a special waiver of sovereign immunity by Congress and it was well within Congress's power to establish special procedures and special courts when it decided to allow such suits.[4]

Both Congress and the Supreme Court have strictly limited the jurisdiction of the Court of Claims. In *United States v. Testan*,[5] the Supreme Court ruled that the Court of Claims has no jurisdiction in equitable matters, nor did the Tucker Act create any substantive rights to sue the United States for money. Only when Congress has by statute explicitly waived sovereign immunity and provided the right to sue does such a right exist. In only one instance has Congress provided that the Court of Claims may grant other than monetary relief. In 1972, it was given the authority to order reinstatement of dismissed federal employees who had prevailed in a case seeking monetary judgment for back pay.

The Court of Claims constitutes the first major waiver of sovereign immunity by Congress. The bulk of the cases handled by that court involve contract disputes, the taking of property under the Fifth Amendment, suits for tax refunds, and monetary disputes between the government and its employees. This waiver of immunity was only partial and torts committed by government remain outside the jurisdiction of the Court of Claims. Congress provided a grudging, relatively limited waiver of tort immunity through the Federal Tort Claims Act of 1946.

Federal Tort Claims Act[6] Tort claims against the government may be brought in either the district court where the plantiff resides or where "the act or omission complained of occurred." Similar to claims cases, the court decides without a jury and is authorized to grant monetary relief only "on account of damage to or loss of property or on account of personal injury or death caused by the negligent or wrongful act or omission of any employee of the Government while acting within the scope of his office, . . . under circumstances where the United States, if a person, would be liable. . . . in accordance with the law of place where the act or omission occurred . . . the United States shall be liable . . . in the same manner, and to the same extent as a private individual." The act then proceeds to exempt a wide and sweeping variety of actions from its coverage. Specifically exempt are claims

a. based on an act or omission of an employee "in the execution of a statute or regulation, whether or not such statute or regulation be valid, or based upon the exercise or performance or the failure to exercise or perform a discretionary function or duty";
b. "arising out of assault, battery, false arrest, malicious prosecution, abuse of process, libel, slander, misrepresentation, deceit or interference with contract rights";
c. for damages caused by the fiscal operations of the Treasury;
d. arising out of combatant activities during wartime.

Even a brief casual reading of those provisions indicates some of the problems the courts have had in deciding whether an action was covered by the law and that individuals have had in trying to secure redress for many injuries caused by governmental action. One of the first problems with the law is that it establishes no uniform, national standards. Whether an action which causes an injury is compensable depends on the state in which it took place, as does the amount of compensation for wrongful injury. Even disregarding the specific exemptions from liability, it is far from clear which acts or omissions are included in the Act, since it states that the government is liable "if a private person would be liable." Government, however, is not a private person and engages in many activities (besides the exemptions) in which private persons do not.

Arguably, and the government has frequently argued this point somewhat less than persuasively, all those are also exempt. The specific exemptions leave injured individuals with no judicial recourse for injuries suffered as a result of those activities. Finally, the exemption of "discretionary" functions, which as usual are undefined, has compelled the courts to struggle with determining what Congress meant to include (or exclude) from the act.

"Discretion" and "discretionary" are terms that appear with great frequency in administrative law and are likely to have slightly (or sometimes very) different meanings depending on the context in which they appear. In interpreting their meaning in the context of the Federal Tort Claims Act, the Supreme Court has attempted to establish a dichotomy between planning (discretionary) and operational (non-discretionary) administrative actions. The results of this attempt are far from satisfactory, and one of the most unsatisfactory Court decisions on this ground was handed down in *Dalehite v. United States.*[7] In the period after World War II, 15 government-owned ordinance plants were converted to fertilizer production as part of the American attempt to aid in postwar agricultural recovery of Europe and Japan. The plants were operated under the "supervision, direction, control and approval of the Army." The main ingredient in the fertilizer produced was ammonium nitrate, which was also a component in explosives. For some reason, the fact that fertilizer produced from an explosive chemical might itself also be explosive seemed not to have occurred to anyone connected with the program. On April 16, 1947, two ships loaded with the fertilizer and other cargo, including explosives, caught fire and exploded in the harbor in Texas City, Texas. Five hundred sixty people were killed, 3,000 were injured, and millions of dollars of property damage occurred. The plaintiffs sought to sue the federal government alleging negligence in practically every phase of the fertilizer program, from the decision to use an explosive base, to improper packaging, shipping, storing, and sending the material into a "congested area without warning of the possibility of explosion." In disallowing the suit, the Supreme Court ruled that all government actions challenged as negligent were discretionary functions:

> It is enough to hold, as we do, that the "discretionary function or duty" that cannot form a basis for suit under the Tort Claims Act includes more than the initiation of programs and activities. It also includes determinations made by executives or administrators in establishing plans, specifications or schedules of operations. Where there is room for policy judgment and decision there is discretion. It necessarily follows that acts of subordinates carrying out the operations of government in accordance with official directions cannot be actionable.[8]

Consequently all actions challenged, from the decision to use ammonium nitrate as fertilizer through the failure to provide warnings, were planning (discretionary) decisions and hence exempt under the Tort Claims Act.

The distinction the Court used between planning and operational activities is neither precise nor clear. In 1964, the Ninth Circuit provided a summary of governmental activities that previous cases had established as being discretionary and non-discretionary:[9]

Discretionary	*Nondiscretionary*
1. to undertake fire-fighting, lighthouse, rescue or wrecked ship marking services	1. to conduct such operations negligently
2. to admit a patient to an army hospital	2. to treat the patient in a negligent manner
3. to establish a post office	3. to negligently fail to install handrails
4. to establish control towers at airports	4. to conduct the same negligently
5. to reactivate an airbase	5. to construct a drainage and disposal system thereon in a negligent fashion
6. to conduct a survey in a low flying airplane	6. for pilots thereof to fly negligently

Using the logic implicit in that classification, it seems quite reasonable to classify a decision to produce explosive fertilizer as discretionary, if unwise, but to conduct the production operation negligently as nondiscretionary and equally unwise.

The Supreme Court in *Dalehite* also established that the Tort Claims Act exempted governmental functions from its coverage: "Congress exercised care to protect the government from claims, however negligently caused, that affected the governmental functions." The result was that the alleged failure of the Coast Guard in fighting the Texas City fire was also exempt. "If anything is doctrinally sanctified in the law of torts it is the immunity of communities and other public bodies for injuries due to fighting fire."

In subsequent cases, the Supreme Court modified its view on the governmental function exemption. In *Indian Towing Co. v. United States*, the Government sought to escape liability for allegedly negligent failure to maintain a Coast Guard beacon light by arguing that lighthouse operation was a "uniquely governmental function." The Supreme Court rejected the argument:

> The Government reads the statute as if it imposed liability to the same extent as would be imposed on private person "under the same circumstances." But the statutory language is "under like circumstances," and it is hornbook tort law that one who undertakes to warn the public of danger and thereby induces reliance must perform his "good Samaritan" task in a careful manner.[10]

In *Rayonier, Inc. v. United States*,[11] the Court further restricted the governmental function exemption and held that firefighting activities undertaken by the Forest Service were not exempt from the Tort Claims Act, and "to the extent there was anything to the contrary in the Dalehite case, it was necessarily rejected by Indian Towing."

The specific exemptions in the Tort Claims Act have also been subject to extensive and occasionally bizarre interpretations by the courts. For example, a case alleging negligence on the part of a Veterans' Hospital surgeon who amputated the wrong leg of a patient was dismissed because the action was held to be an "assault."[12] Severe injury or even death which results from abuse of military recruits in basic training has also been ruled exempt as "assault."[13] An erroneous report by the FDA that spinach had been contaminated by the chemical heptachlor and which resulted in several hundred thousand dollars loss was held to fall under the "mis-representation" exemption.[14]

Congress has modified both the procedure and substance of the Tort Claims Act since its passage. Two of the most important modifications were the 1966 amendments which authorized administrative settlements of claims and the 1974 amendments which modified the exemptions applicable to the behavior of the investigative and law enforcement personnel. The 1966 amendments allow administrators to settle claims of any amount without going to court. Any settlement in excess of $25,000 must have prior approval of the Attorney General. One of the largest settlements made under this procedure was made by the Public Health Service in 1975 when it agreed to pay $9 million to the survivors and their heirs of its Tuskegee experiment. The experiment was begun in the 1930s to determine the long-run effects of untreated syphillis. The subjects were 600 black males and the experiment was not terminated until 1972. The results of long-term untreated syphillis include blindness, spinal cord deterioration, and death.

The 1974 amendments were added following several well-publicized instances of overzealous behavior by federal narcotics officers who demonstrated a rather cavalier disregard of constitutional niceties. The amendments were also a response to the Supreme Court decision in *Bivens v. Six Unknown, Named Agents of the Federal Bureau of Narcotics*[15] (discussed below) which held that lacking any other remedy, the officers who committed the unconstitutional acts might be held personally liable for damages. The amendments provided "That with regard to acts or ommissions of investigative or law enforcement officers of the United States Government . . . this chapter . . . shall apply to any claims arising out of assault, battery, false imprisonment, false arrest, abuse of process or malicious prosecution." Investigative and law enforcement officers were defined as any officer "empowered by law to execute searches, to seize evidence, or to make arrests."[16]

The Tort Claims Act, even as amended, still exempts a wide variety of government actions from tort liability. For an individual injured as a result of an exempt activity, two possible recourses remain—private laws and/or personal suit against the official who committed the action.

Private Laws   Private laws are a special category of Congressional legislation. Their applicability is usually limited to one or a very few specifically identified individuals. In each session of Congress between 2,000 and 3,000 such bills are introduced and usually only a little over 100 of them will pass. Almost all private bills can be classified into one of two categories:

    a. those which direct payment to private individuals adversely affected by government action or
    b. those granting exemptions from immigration and naturalization laws and regulations.[17]

Private bills remain one of Congress's primary methods for responding to individual "petitions for redress of grievances," and for individuals who have been denied relief by administrative agencies and the courts their final opportunity to obtain such relief.

After losing their case in the Supreme Court, the victims of the Texas City fertilizer explosion turned to Congress. Eventually, Congress granted $17,000,000 in relief.[18] Similarly, after Mizokami's (the spinach grower) case against FDA was held barred, Congress passed a private bill awarding the growers over $300,000. In 1975, Congress awarded the family of Dr. Frank Olson, a civilian physicist who committed suicide after consuming a drink in which CIA agents had put LSD, $750,000 in compensation.[19] Individuals are not the only parties Congress has been willing to provide relief for through private legislation. In 1978, Congress generously authorized the Court of Claims to indemnify losses suffered by children's sleepwear manufacturers who had, at least from their perspective, unfairly lost millions of dollars because of regulations promulgated by the Consumer Product Safety Commission. The manufacturers had been compelled by a 1971 federal regulation to make sure that children's sleepwear was made flame resistant. This they had done by treating the sleepwear with Tris, a chemical flame-retardant, which unfortunately was later proven to be a carcinogenic agent. In 1977, CPSC banned the sale of Tris-treated fabrics and garments. With their suit barred under the Tort Claims Act, the manufacturers turned to Congress. Unfortunately for the manufacturers, President Carter disagreed with congressional generosity and pocket-vetoed the legislation as "an unprecedented and unwise use of taxpayers funds," particularly since "the actions of the Government were fully justified."[20]

The vast majority of private bills that are introduced into Congress are never passed, and undoubtedly those that are introduced represent a small and nonrandom sample of all the deserving claims that are barred from relief through the court system. While private legislation is a valuable "court of last resort," it is considerably less fair and uniform a method of relief than a revised Tort Claims Acts with fewer exemptions would be. Although Congress has published no criteria as to how it decides which bills pass and which fail, or how members decide whether to introduce such bills, the suspicion is strong that publicity value and political utility play a major role. Unfortunately not all valid claims have either publicity value or political utility.

Officer Liability

Under common law, public officials could be held personally liable for tortious acts committed in the line of duty and early court decisions in this country frequently levied heavier penalties on public officers than on private citizens for similar actions. In the 1800s, courts were not adverse to holding such officials liable for actions that were neither negligent nor willful.[21] The result was that even if an injured party could not sue the government because of sovereign immunity, frequently he could sue the official who carried out the policy. The courts, however, never extended this personal liability to judges since to do so, they alleged, would destroy the integrity of the judicial system and the ability of the courts to administer justice.

In 1896, the Supreme Court held that high-level administrative officials were also entitled to absolute immunity from suit for actions performed in the line of duty. In *Spalding v. Vilas*, the Court ruled that the Postmaster General was immune from such suits:

The same general considerations of public policy and convenience which demand

> for judges . . . immunity from civil suit for damages arising from acts done by
> them in the course of performance of their judicial functions apply to a large
> extent to official communications made by heads of Executive Departments when
> engaged in the discharge of duties imposed on them by law. . . . It would
> seriously cripple the proper and effective administration of public affairs as
> entrusted to the executive branch of the government, if he were subjected to any
> such restraint.[22]

From granting absolute immunity to top administrative officials, the courts proceeded to extend that immunity further and further down the hierarchy until all federal employees, as long as they were acting in an official capacity, were equally immune.

The magnitude of the atrocities that this allowed officials to commit without any fear of recourse was amply illustrated by the decision of the second Circuit Court of Appeals in *Gregoire v. Biddle*. The defendants in the case included two Attorneys General, two directors of the Enemy Alien Control Unit, and the Director of Immigration. During World War II, Gregoire was arrested under the pretext that he was an enemy alien (German). Although the Enemy Alien Hearing Board determined that he was French and not an enemy alien, he was imprisoned for four years. Gregoire brought personal suit against the officials. The district court dismissed his suit on the grounds that "the defendants had an absolute immunity from liability, even though their unlawful acts had been induced only by personal ill-will." The Court of Appeals agreed:

> We . . . think that the complaint should not stand, even though . . . the
> defendants arrested the plaintiff "maliciously and willfully." . . . Officers of the
> Department of Justice, when engaged in prosecuting private persons, enjoy the
> same absolute privilege as judges. . . . To submit all officials . . . to the burden of
> trial and to the inevitable danger of its outcome would dampen the ardor of all
> but the most resolute, or the most irresponsible, in the unflinching discharge of
> their duties.[23]

Ardor for lawless and unconstitutional behavior perhaps should be dampened, if not drowned, in the interests of justice, fairness, and responsible government. The Court, however, felt that it was "better to leave unredressed the wrongs done by dishonest officers than to subject those who try to do their duty to the constant dread of retaliation."[24]

The Supreme Court gave its blessing to the growing inclusiveness of official immunity in *Barr v. Matteo*. Two suspended federal employees attempted to sue their superior for press releases he had made, alleging that the press releases had defamed and injured them. As the Supreme Court viewed the suit, it had to weigh "the protection of the individual citizen against pecuniary damages caused by oppressive or malicious action on the part of officials of the Federal Government," against the "protection of the public interest by shielding responsible governmental officers against the harassment and inevitable hazards of vindictive or ill-founded damage suits."[25] The individual citizen lost. Absolute immunity was necessary so that "officials of governments should be free to exercise their duties unembarrassed by the fear of damage suits . . . which would consume time and energies which would otherwise be devoted to governmental service and the threat of which might appreciably inhibit the fearless, vigorous and effective administration of policies of government." Such immunity was not limited to top administrative officials but extended down the hierarchy. "We cannot say that these functions become less important simply because they are exercised by officers of lower rank in the executive hierarchy."[26]

Official immunity was thus not only apparently all-inclusive, but was also absolute. Regardless of whether an official knowingly, willfully, maliciously, or even viciously committed a wrongful act, as long as he did it in his official capacity he was immune from suit. More likely than not, in light of the multitudinous exemptions of the Tort Claims Act, the government was equally immune. Whether this really protected the public interest was questionable; that it resulted in a blatant failure to protect individual rights was unquestionable.

In 1971, the Supreme Court indicated that it was willing to reconsider the scope of official immunity for federal employees. The reconsideration resulted in considerable lessening of that immunity. As is appropriate with such reversals, the Court began by shrinking immunity at the bottom of the administrative hierarchy and gradually worked its way to the top, perhaps the very top of the executive branch. *Bivens v. Six Unknown, Named Agents of the Federal Bureau of Narcotics*[27] initiated the trend away from official immunity. Bivens had been the victim of a warrantless search and arrest conducted in the early morning hours by the narcotics agents. His home had been thoroughly searched, he had been arrested, interrogated, and strip-searched, and since no evidence was found, eventually released. He sought personal monetary damages against each of the agents. The Supreme Court responded by creating what has come to be known as a "Bivens tort." An individual whose constitutional rights, in this instance Fourth Amendment rights, had been violated was not barred from seeking redress through a tort action brought against the official who had committed the violation.

> Of course, the Fourth Amendment does not in so many words provide for its enforcement by an award of money damages for the consequences of its violation. But "it is . . . well settled that where legal rights have been invaded and a federal statute provides for a general right to sue for such invasion, federal courts may use any available remedy to make good the wrong done."[28]

The Supreme Court remanded to the Court of Appeals the question as to whether the agents were immune from suit. The Second Circuit held that the primary determinant of immunity was not the official position of the individual who had committed the challenged action but whether the action itself was discretionary: whether it was "the result of a judgment or decision which it is necessary that the Government be free to make without fear or threat of vexatious or fictitious suits and alleged personal liability."[29] Discretionary actions remained immune. The actions of the narcotics agents were held to be nondiscretionary and consequently the agents had only qualified immunity. To avoid liability, the officers would have to prove that when they violated the individual's constitutional rights they believed "in good faith" that their conduct was lawful *and* that this belief was reasonable.

Bivens left many questions about official liability in cases where a plaintiff alleged that the official had violated his or her constitutional rights unanswered. In 1978, the Supreme

Court clarified which federal officials, under what circumstances, were subject to suit for violation of an individual's constitutional rights. *Economou v. Butz*[30] seemingly established that top-ranking executive officials, including cabinet officers, were entitled to only qualified immunity in suits alleging violation of constitutional rights. After reviewing all the cases that had held that state and local officials, up to and including governors, had only qualified immunity under 42 USCA §1983 (see discussion below), the Court applied the same principle to federal administrators: "Surely, *federal* officers should enjoy no greater zone of protection when they violate *federal* constitutional rules than do state officers. . . . to create a system in which the Bill of Rights monitors more closely the conduct of state officials than it does federal officials is to stand the constitutional design on its head."[31] In determining which officials, if any, remained immune from suit, the *Economou* decision went one step beyond the Court of Appeals decision in *Bivens*, extending personal liability to officials exercising discretion:

> If, as the Government argues, all officials exercising discretion were exempt from personal liability, a suit under the Constitution could provide no redress to the injured citizen. . . .
> The extension of absolute immunity . . . would seriously erode the protection provided by basic constitutional guarantees. . . . It makes little sense to hold that a Government agent is liable for warrantless and forcible entry into a citizen's house in pursuit of evidence, but that an official of higher rank who actually orders such a burglary is immune simply because of his greater authority. Indeed the greater power of such officials affords a greater potential for a regime of lawless conduct.[32]

Consequently, "federal executive officials exercising discretion" have only qualified immunity in suits alleging constitutional violations, "subject to those exceptional circumstances where it is demonstrated that absolute immunity is essential for the conduct of public business."[33]

The personal liability the Court imposed on executive officials was not, however, to be imposed on their quasi-judicial subordinates: "There are some officials whose special functions require a full exemption from liability."[34] Hearing examiners, the Judicial Officer of the Department of Agriculture, and the prosecuting attorney were entitled to absolute immunity so that they could "perform their respective functions without harrassment or intimidation."[35]

The *Economou* decision seemingly implied that no executive official, regardless of rank, was entitled to absolute immunity in "constitutional tort" suits. If the Secretary of Agriculture could be sued, probably other cabinet officials could be sued and maybe even the President of the United States could be sued. The first major opportunity that the Supreme Court had either to extend or limit *Economou* was in *Kissinger v. Halperin*.[36] Morton Halperin, who had served as a National Security Council staff member during the Nixon Administration, had filed suit against ex-Secretary of State Henry Kissinger, ex-Attorney General John Mitchell, and ex-President Richard Nixon alleging that they had violated his Fourth Amendment rights by placing an illegal wiretap on his home telephone in 1969 and leaving it in place for 21 months. The D.C. Court of Appeals ruled, basing their reasoning on *Economou*, that all three officials had only qualified immunity. The Supreme Court deadlocked 4–4 on the case allowing the lower court decision to stand. The tie vote resulted from Justice Rehnquist's decision to disqualify himself from the case since he had served as assistant attorney general under Mitchell. The issue was not resolved and immediately resurfaced.

On November 30, 1981, the Supreme Court heard arguments on two cases involving the extent of immunity of high level executive officials: *Nixon v. Fitzgerald*[37] and *Harlow and Butterfield v. Fitzgerald*.[38] A. Ernest Fitzgerald, one of the most famous federal whistleblowers, had brought suit seeking monetary damages from Nixon and various presidential aides for blatantly and frequently violating his constitutional rights and ultimately causing him to be illegally dismissed from his job at the Pentagon. The illegality of the dismissal had already been adjudicated, and under court order he was reinstated in the federal service. The case attracted a wide assortment of "interested parties" from the ACLU to the Mountain States Legal Foundation and several members of Congress, all of whom argued that the President should be entitled to only qualified immunity. The Supreme Court, by a 5–4 vote, ruled that although presidential aides are entitled to only qualified immunity, the President has absolute immunity from damage suits:

> We consider this immunity a functionally mandated incident of the President's unique office, rooted in the constitutional tradition of the separation of powers and supported by our history. . . . Because of the singular importance of the President's duties, diversion of his energies by concern with private lawsuits would raise unique risks to the effective functioning of government. This immunity extends to acts within the "outer perimeter" of his official responsibility.[39]

Members of Congress discovered in 1973 that their immunity was not quite as absolute as they had previously thought it to be. In *Tenney v. Brandhove*,[40] the Supreme Court had held that state legislators had absolute immunity for even improperly motivated acts. The Speech and Debate clause of Article I ("and for any speech or debate in either house they shall not be questioned in any other place") had been interpreted as providing federal legislators with broad immunity from damage suits. In 1973, in *Doe v. McMillan*, the Supreme Court affirmed that members of Congress "are absolutely immune when they are legislating. But when they act outside the 'sphere of legitimate legislative activity,' they enjoy no special immunity."[41] As Senator William Proxmire learned, issuing newsletters and press releases on the Golden Fleece Awards was outside "the sphere" and he had no special immunity from a personal damage suit.[42] In *Holton v. Benford*,[43] the Court rejected the claim of congressional committee investigators that they were immune from damage suits based on actions undertaken in pursuit of their official duties during the course of a congressional investigation.

One of the primary justifications that the Supreme Court had offered in *Bivens* and *Economou* for expanding the personal liability of federal officials was the lack of alternative remedies for one whose constitutional rights had been violated, since the actions involved in those cases fell within the exemptions of the Tort Claims Act. The implication appeared to be that if suit could be brought against the Government under that act, the official would not be personally liable. In *Carlson v. Green*,[44] the Supreme Court put that notion to rest and further expanded the potential personal liability of officials. The mother of a man who died in federal prison, allegedly as the result of improper medical care for chronic asthma, brought a personal damage suit against Norman Carlson, the director of the Federal Bureau of Prisons on the grounds that he had violated the Eighth Amendment stricture against cruel and unusual punishment. Carlson and the Justice Department argued that since the suit could have been brought under the Tort Claims Act, a personal suit against the administrator was barred. The decision reaffirmed the right of individuals whose constitutional rights have been violated by a federal official to sue that official unless special factors "counsel . . . hesitation in the absence of action by Congress" or Congress has provided an effective substitute. The Tort Claims Act was not an effective substitute since a personal suit which holds the official rather than government liable is a more effective deterrent to unconstitutional behavior. The Tort Claims Act was a complimentary but not an exclusive means for remedying the injury.

Both the concepts of sovereign immunity and official immunity have undergone considerable transformations at the federal level since the adoption of the Constitution. Despite the transformations, however, sovereign immunity continues to maintain considerable legal viability. The government still cannot be sued without its consent and although Congress has granted standing consent to sue for various actions there are still many situations for which consent has not been granted and sovereign immunity stands as a bar to any suits which might arise out of those situations. Official immunity has traversed an interesting path from being nonexistent to being absolute to its current status of qualified immunity when constitutional rights are infringed. Even members of Congress have seen the sphere of their official immunity circumscribed by court decisions. Only Presidents, judges, their administrative counterparts, and prosecutors have been left with absolute immunity from suit.

Government should not be above the law and even a primordial sense of justice indicates that individuals who have suffered injury from lawless and unconstitutional actions of government or its officials should be entitled to redress. Serious questions have been raised and are still unanswered, however, as to whether the recent trend towards official liability evidenced in Supreme Court decisions is the best or wisest way to provide that redress. Whether administrative responsibility, responsiveness, and effectiveness may suffer from these decisions is one of the more serious of these questions. Equally serious is the question of fairness to the affected employees. The Court willingly concedes that judges need to be free from the "harrassment" and intimidation of possible lawsuits in order to perform their duties in an impartial and conscientious manner. Perhaps the old argument that administrators need equal freedom in order to perform their duties in a conscientious manner also contained some merit. If constitutional rights were engraved on stone tablets, expecting federal officials to know and honor them might be just. Unfortunately, this is not so; constitutional rights are defined in Supreme Court decisions and as was pointed out earlier, their meaning changes from year to year and, some administrators would contend, from day to day. If individual administrators at all levels must be constantly and individually responsible for each and every action taken, hierarchal control and responsibility is weakened, and excessive timidity in administrative behavior is a possible result.

Governmental liability is a better solution. It not only guarantees that the victim will be ensured of adequate compensation (federal employees are not necessarily wealthy), but also places responsibility precisely where it belongs—with Congress and top executive officials who hopefully will be motivated to create and maintain a climate throughout the government that individual rights must be respected. Responsibility for failure to achieve this could then reside directly in Congress and the President. An impetus would exist for creating and enforcing uniform policies throughout the federal bureaucracy; administrative sanctions could be imposed on individual employees who violate those policies; injured individuals would always be ensured of a legal recourse; and individual administrators could devote their attention to the effective implementation of public policy without fear of personal liability. Presidential liability presents different problems but the same solution is appropriate. If government is liable for his unconstitutional behavior and Congress must appropriate the money to pay for his transgressions, Congress might be compelled to take a more responsible role in restricting unconstitutional presidential behavior before too many serious injuries have been inflicted upon individuals.

Judges should be made as liable for their unconstitutional behavior as administrators are. If administrators, who "knew or reasonably should have known" that their conduct violated constitutional rights, are liable, judges should know even better and should be equally responsible for such conduct. It would be the ultimate irony if we should finally abandon the belief that "the king can do no wrong" to substitute for it the concept that "only judges can do no wrong."

OBTAINING REDRESS FROM STATE AND LOCAL GOVERNMENTS

> If injured by the state in fact,
> Your first remedy is its Tort Claims Act;
> If through its loopholes, your suit's denied,
> Section nineteen-eighty three should then be tried.
> A KNOWN, UNNAMED, ADMINISTRATIVE LAW STUDENT

State Law

Obtaining monetary redress for injuries resulting from state or local government action involves many of the same barriers and complications confronted at the federal level, although the precise nature of those barriers and complications depends on the state in which the injury occurred and on the nature of the injury suffered. Unless the injury involved a violation of federal constitutional or legal rights, redress must be sought at the state level and whether it will be obtainable depends on the extent to which sovereign immunity has been waived by the specific state in which the injury occurred. Sovereign immunity at the state level was initially propounded by the judiciary based on the same justification, or lack thereof, that characterized federal court decisions. State sovereign immunity has similarly been modified, reinterpreted, and occasionally abolished through state court decisions and state legislative action.

One of the earliest distinctions developed by state courts to separate actions for which governmental units could be held liable from those which were immune was the "governmental–proprietary" distinction. Governmental functions were immune; proprietary functions were not, and the only remaining problem was identifying which functions performed by government were nongovernmental functions. As the Supreme Court noted in *Indian Towing Co. v. U.S.*[45] when it abandoned the distinction under the Federal Tort Claims Act, the definition of the two terms was far from uniform among the states. "A comparative study of cases in the forty-eight states will disclose an irreconcilable conflict. More than that, the decisions in each of the states are disharmonious and disclose the inevitable chaos when courts try to apply a rule of law that is inherently unsound."[46] If drawing distinctions between the two types of functions was difficult in 1955, the accelerating trend toward contracting out for the provision of municipal services from garbage collection to fire protection has further diminished the actual distinctions between the two.

Gradually, some state courts grew dissatisfied with the governmental–proprietary distinction and moved to eliminate the distinction. For example, the California Supreme Court in 1961 in *Muskopf v. Corning Hospital*[47] abolished governmental immunity for torts committed by state agents. Some state legislatures have followed Congress's example and have passed Tort Claims Acts which closely resemble the federal law as far as definitions, applicability, and exemptions are concerned. Other state legislatures have approached the question of governmental liability on a piecemeal basis, passing individual statutes waiving immunity for specifically identified actions.

The result of all this has been a notable lack of uniformity on tort liability among the states. Which actions are covered, procedures to be followed in obtaining redress for covered actions, and even limits on the amounts that may be obtained differ from state to state and year to year. One survey made in 1977 estimated that 18 states had completely waived immunity and 13 states retained absolute immunity, that procedures for granting redress ranged from hearings before administrative tribunals or special courts of claims to trials in regular state courts.[48] The state of Idaho, for example, allows tort actions against governmental entities to be filed in state district courts but limits the amount that may be granted in any specific case regardless of the injury to $200,000, the amount of individual liability insurance that government agencies and entities are required by law to carry. Private laws continue to constitute a significant form of redress in all states. The resulting variety proves that diversity in the federal system is alive and well, at least as far as sovereign immunity is concerned.

Federal Law

Every person, who under color of any statute, ordinance, regulation, custom or usage, of any State or Territory, subjects or causes to be subjected, any citizen of the United States or other person within the jurisdiction thereof to the deprivation of any rights, privileges or immunities secured by the Constitution and laws, shall be liable to the party injured in an action at law, suit in equity or other proper proceeding for redress. (The Civil Rights Act of 1871, 42 USCA §1983)

Section 1983 was only a small section of the Civil Rights Act of 1871, which in turn was only one of the multitude of laws passed by Congress following the Civil War to enforce the provisions of the Fourteenth Amendment. For nearly ninety years §1983 lay dormant and unused, but by 1981 it had become one of the most controversial and least liked portions of federal law as far as state and local government officials were concerned. Its elevation to such prominence is partially illustrated by the following statistics:

- in 1961, 261 §1983 cases were filed in federal courts;
- by 1972, 8,000 §1983 cases had been filed;
- in 1976, 12,911 §1983 actions were pending;
- in 1979, 2,500 new §1983 actions were filed; and
- from June 1980 to January 1981, 400 §1983 actions were filed against the City of New York *alone*.[49]

The evolution of a relatively obscure provision of a hundred-year-old statute into a frequently utilized method to gain monetary redress from state and local officials and subsequently governmental units is a legal development equal in impact to the due process explosion which followed the decision in *Goldberg v. Kelly*. Section 1983's rise to prominence began with the Supreme Court's decision in *Monroe v. Pape* in 1961.[50]

Official Liability under §1983   *Monroe v. Pape* involved behavior by members of the Police Department of the City of Chicago which bore striking similarity to the behavior engaged in by the federal narcotics agents in the *Bivens* case. The Chicago policemen had broken into a private residence, engaged in a violent and warrantless search, subjected the residents to physical and verbal abuse, detained the family head, and ultimately released him without filing charges. A §1983 suit was filed against both the City of Chicago and the police officers. Although the Supreme Court held that cities were *not* "persons" under §1983, it did not accept the argument that the lawless behavior of the police officers put them outside the coverage of the section, nor did it accept the argument that relief must first be sought in the state court:

> Misuse of power, possessed by virtue of state law and made possible only because the wrongdoer is clothed with the authority of state law is action taken "under color of State Law." . . . The Civil Rights Act is supplementary to the state remedy, and the latter need not be first sought and refused before the federal one is invoked.[51]

From street-level local government employees, the Supreme Court gradually expanded the personal liability of state and local administrative officials under §1983 to include even state governors. In *Scheur v. Rhodes*,[52] suit was brought against the Governor of Ohio, the adjutant general of the National Guard, various Guard Officials, and the president of Kent State University by victims and families of victims who had been shot by National Guard members during an anti-Vietnam War demonstration on the Kent State campus. The Court held that the officials named, including the governor, had only a qualified immunity from the suit under §1983.

> A qualified immunity is available to officers of the executive branch of government . . . dependent upon the scope of discretion and responsibilities of the office and all the circumstances as they reasonably appeared at the time of the action on which liability is sought to be based. It is the existence of reasonable grounds for the belief formed at the time and in light of all the circumstances, coupled with good-faith belief, that affords a basis for qualified immunity of executive officers for acts performed in the course of official conduct.[53]

In 1975, qualified immunity only was held applicable to school board members in *Wood v. Strickland*[54] and to state hospital administrators in *O'Connor v. Donaldson*.[55] In Wood, the Court explained the standard for an official to claim qualified immunity:

> The official must be acting sincerely and with a belief that he is doing right, but an act violating a . . . constitutional right can no more be justified by ignorance or disregard of settled indisputable law . . . than by the presence of actual malice. . . .
>
> A school board member is not immune from liability . . . if he knew or reasonably should have known that the action he took . . . would violate the constitutional rights of the student affected or if he took the action with the malicious intention to cause a deprivation of constitutional rights.[56]

In 1978, the Court further refined and narrowed the scope of qualified immunity in *Procunier v. Navarette*,[57] holding that prison administrators were liable under §1983 and that even qualified immunity was unavailable "if the constitutional right allegedly infringed . . . was clearly established at the time of the challenged conduct, if the officials knew or should have known of the right, and if they knew or should have known that their conduct violated the constitutional norm."[58] Bluntly, ignorance of constitutional rights is not an acceptable excuse for violating them and does not entitle a governmental official to any immunity from §1983 suits. If the right is specified in the Constitution or has been "read into" the Constitution by Supreme Court decision, all officials *should know* of its existence and may be held liable for actions which violate it. Even if an official is entitled to qualified immunity, the burden is on the official to plead and prove good faith in his defense if he is sued under §1983. The plaintiff does not have to allege bad faith. "By the plain terms of §1983, two—and only two—allegations are required to state a cause of action. . . . First the plaintiff must allege that some person has deprived him of a federal right. Second, he must allege that the person who has deprived him of that right acted under color of state or territorial law."[59]

Although §1983 clearly states that "*any* person" acting under color of state authority is liable for violating another's constitutional rights, the Court has held three categories of such persons immune from suit: state legislators, judges, and prosecutors. The same year, 1951, that the Supreme Court held police officers liable under §1983 it held state legislators to be absolutely immune from such suits on the grounds that it was one of "the presuppositions of our political history" that legislators "must be free to speak and act without fear of criminal or civil liability." As long as they were acting in an official capacity, immunity was absolute. Even if they acted maliciously and in bad faith, they were still "immune from deterrents to the uninhibited discharge of their legislative duty, not for their private indulgence but for the public good."[60]

Judges were accorded the same immunity from §1983 suits in *Pierson v. Ray*.[61] A group of white and black clergymen had been arrested and convicted of disorderly conduct for unofficially but peacefully desegregating a segregated waiting room in a Mississippi bus terminal. They ultimately filed a §1983 suit against the policemen who arrested them and the judge who convicted and sentenced them. If ever a suit aptly corresponded to the original intent of §1983, theirs did, but as the Supreme Court saw it, only the police officers were liable; the judge was not—he was only doing his duty.

> It is a judge's duty to decide all cases brought before him. His errors may be corrected on appeal but he should not have to fear that unsatisfied litigants may hound him with litigation. Imposing such a burden on judges would contribute not to principled or fearless decision making but to intimidation.[62]

Although the Supreme Court systematically expanded the liability of administrative officials under §1983 throughout the 1970s, it refused to modify its position on judicial immunity. In 1978, in *Stump v. Sparkman*,[63] the Court illustrated how far the bounds of judicial immunity extended. In 1971, Judge Stump had approved a petition for the compulsory sterilization of a 15-year-old girl who may or may not have been retarded. The petition was filed by her mother who was having problems controlling her teenage daughter. The judge granted the petition the same day it was filed "without notice to the minor, without a hearing, and without the appointment of a guardian ad litem."[64] After the petition was granted, Linda Sparkman was hospitalized, having been told that she was going to have her appendix removed, and was sterilized. Not until her marriage and the subsequent discovery that she could not have children, did Ms. Sparkman realize the nature of the operation to which she had been subjected. The Court of Appeals ruled that the judge was not immune from suit for two reasons:

1. There was "a clear absence of all jurisdiction" in Judge Stump's court to consider the sterilization petition. Although state law (Indiana) did provide for the sterilization of *institutionalized* persons under narrowly defined circumstances, following specific statutory procedures, it provided no such authorization for sterilization of non-institutionalized individuals. Consequently, the judge was not authorized to consider the petition and was not acting in a "judicial capacity."
2. Even if the action taken by him was not foreclosed under the Indiana statutory scheme, it would still be an illegitimate exercise of common law power because of his failure to comply with elementary principles of due process.[65]

The dissenting opinion filed by Supreme Court Justice Potter Stewart elaborated both points in arguing for liability. "There was no case. . . . There were no litigants. There was and could be no appeal. And there was not even the pretext of principled decision making. . . . The conduct complained of in this case was not a judicial action."[66] The majority of the Supreme Court disagreed. Even though the judge's action was not authorized by state law, "it is more significant that there was no Indiana statute and no case law in 1971 prohibiting a circuit court[67] . . . from considering a petition of the type presented to Judge Stump."[68] A judicial act is "a function normally performed by a judge," and since approving petitions relating to the affairs of minors is a normal act for judges, the approval of the sterilization petition was a judicial act. The lack, or total absence, of even rudimentary due process safeguards was irrelevant: "A judge is absolutely immune for his judicial acts even if his exercise of authority is flawed by the commission of grave, procedural errors."[69] If an administrator had done what Judge Stump did (and regrettably some have) he or she would have been held liable and qualified immunity would have been of little protection since an administrator could "reasonably have been expected to know"[70] that the action was a clear violation of constitutional rights. Judges are different:

> Both the Court of Appeals and the respondents seem to suggest that, because of the tragic consequences of Judge Stump's actions, he should not be immune. . . . Despite the unfairness to litigants that sometimes result, the doctrine of judicial immunity is thought to be in the best interests of "the proper administration of justice . . . since it allows a judicial officer, in exercising the authority vested in him, to be free to act upon his own convictions, without apprehension of personal consequences to himself." *Bradley v. Fisher*, 13 Wallace 347.[71]

Prosecutors were accorded absolute immunity from §1983 liability in *Imbler v. Pachtman*.[72] They also needed absolute immunity in order to perform their duties properly, even if unconstitutionally. As a majority of the Supreme Court saw it, making prosecutors liable for violating individuals' constitutional rights "would disserve the broader public interest. It would prevent the vigorous and fearless performance of the prosecutor's duty that is essential to the proper functioning of the criminal justice system." In 1981, the Court held that public defenders, even though they were public employees, were not necessarily acting "under color of state law," and consequently were not subject to suit under §1983. In *Polk County v. Dodson*,[73] Russell Dodson alleged that the public defender of Polk County, Iowa, had failed to represent him adequately on his appeal of a robbery conviction. He sought to sue under §1983 on the grounds that he had been denied due process and the right to counsel. The majority opinion written by Justice Powell used a unique interpretation of the traditional governmental–proprietary distinction to arrive at the conclusion that because a nongovernmental function was involved, suit under §1983 was barred. The function of representing a client against the state "is essentially a private function, traditionally filled by retained counsel, for which state office and authority are not needed."[74] At least in that case, the Court held that the nature of the function rather than official position determined whether an action had been committed "under color of State law."

The immunity that the Supreme Court has accorded to legislators, judges, and prosecutors from §1983 suits is inequitable and unfair both to administrative officials who enjoy no such privilege and to individuals whose constitutional rights are violated by immune officials. School board members, who are usually part-time elected officials, are liable for damages if they knew or "reasonably should have known" they were violating a constitutional right, so are policemen on the beat, public hospital administrators, prison officials, welfare administrators, university administrators, and governors. Yet judges and prosecutors who are trained attorneys, who might "reasonably be expected" to know better than any other group in society what the Constitution requires, are not held to the same standard of behavior. From the perspective of democratic control, the immunity of judges is unfair and unwise. Their protection from "political" control and direct hierarchial control translates into considerably greater individual discretion to violate individual rights without fear of retaliation. Ironically, that same protection grants them far more leeway to refuse to enforce unconstitutional laws or to engage in unconstitutional behavior without fear of hierarchal sanctions or political reaction than is true for administrative officials. The Supreme Court has created an incongruous situation in which a legislator may knowingly and maliciously propose and secure passage of an unconstitutional law, a prosecutor may with equal malice and knowledge seek out individuals to be tried under that law, and a judge may hear the case, convict the defendant and sentence him to prison knowingly and maliciously, and the only official in the entire gamut of that policy process who can ever be held liable under §1983 is the police officer who, perhaps even conscientiously thinking it his duty, makes the arrest. That, to rephrase the Supreme Court in *Economou v. Butz*, comes close to standing "the constitutional design" and the protection of the Bill of Rights on their heads.

Governmental Liability under §1983   *Monroe v. Pape* held that governmental entities were immune from suit under §1983; that municipalities, for example, were not "persons" under the law. This interpretation had compounded the vulnerability of administrators referred to above: if an allegedly unconstitutional law or policy was adopted by the governmental entity administrators had two choices (assuming they knew the policy was unconstitutional): enforce the policy and be personally liable for §1983 suits or refuse to enforce the policy and be subject to administrative disciplinary actions up to and including dismissal. An individual whose constitutional rights were violated as a result of enforcement of such policy had only one path to secure monetary redress under §1983: sue the individual administrator who enforced the policy and hope that administrator had saved enough money to pay any monetary damages that might be awarded.

In 1978, the Supreme Court overruled *Monroe* and held that local government entities, specifically cities, could be directly sued under §1983. In *Monell v. New York City Department of Social Services*,[75] women employees brought suit directly against the city alleging that its policy of requiring pregnant women to take unpaid leave from city jobs earlier in pregnancy than was medically necessary violated the Fourteenth Amendment. After examining the legislative history of the 1871 Civil Rights Act, the Court held that Congress had not intended that cities should be immune from §1983 suits, rather "Congress *did* intend municipalities and other local government units to be include among those persons" who could be sued. "Local governing bodies, therefore, can be sued directly . . . for monetary, declaratory or injunctive relief where, as here, the action that is alleged implements or executes a policy statement, ordinance, regulation or decision officially adopted and promulgated by the body's officers."[76] Only if the alleged injury was "inflicted solely" by city employees or agents did the city retain immunity from suit.

The major question left unanswered by the Monell decision was whether municipalities were entitled to qualified immunity in defending themselves in a §1983 action. That question was answered negatively in *Owen v. City of Independence*,[77] which held that neither history, tradition, nor policy provided any support for the argument that Congress had intended cities to enjoy qualified immunity in such suits. An injury inflicted by a municipality's unconstitutional conduct was intended to be fully redressable under §1983; although local officials were still entitled to "good faith" immunity, the locality itself was not. The result of the abolition of such immunity from the Supreme Court's perspective would inevitably be a greater respect for constitutional rights on the part of both municipal employees and municipal governing bodies. "The knowledge that a municipality will be liable for all its injurious conduct whether committed in good faith or not should create an incentive for officials who harbor doubt about the lawfulness of their conduct to err on the side of protecting citizen's constitutional rights."[78]

State Governments

The judicial power of the United States shall not be construed to extend to any suit in law or equity commenced or prosecuted against one of the United States by citizens of another state, or by citizens or subjects of any foreign state.

THE ELEVENTH AMENDMENT

The Eleventh Amendment has long provided state governments with protection from being sued in federal courts. Although the actual words of the amendment do not appear to bar suits brought against a state by its own citizens, the Supreme Court ruled in 1890 that such suits were in fact barred by the amendment.[79] The immunity of state governments, however, did not extend to their employees who could be enjoined in their official capacity[80] or sued for monetary damages under §1983.[81] Gradually the Supreme Court has narrowed the immunity of even state governments. In 1974, the court ruled that the states were not protected by the Eleventh Amendment from suits requesting injunctive relief, although suits for monetary damages were still barred.[82] In 1976, in *Fitzpatrick v. Bitzer*,[83] the Court ruled that the state immunity granted by the Eleventh Amendment had to a certain extent been overruled by the Fourteenth Amendment, which authorized congressional enforcement of its provisions and allowed Congress to choose appropriate methods for such enforcement.

42 USC §1988 provides that in any action or proceeding to enforce a provision of §§1981, 1982, 1983, 1985, and 1986 of the law "the court in its discretion may allow the prevailing party . . . reasonable attorney's fees." In 1978, in *Hutto v. Finney*,[84] the court held that awards of attorney fees against a state in cases brought under the 1871 Civil Rights Act were not barred by the Eleventh Amendment. But in *Quern v. Jordon*,[85] the Court decided that §1983 suits for monetary damages could not be brought directly against a state in federal court. The states were given little time to rejoice in their newly reaffirmed immunity, however, since in 1980 the Court decided that §1983 cases could be brought in state courts, and if they were, the Eleventh Amendment offered the state no protection against awards of monetary damages.[86] The states thus could be sued for injunctive relief in federal court and/or for monetary redress in the state courts, if it were alleged that the state had violated an individual's constitutional

rights. Regardless of where suit was brought, if the state lost, it could be ordered to pay the plaintiff's attorney's fees. §1983 had always provided that deprivation of rights secured by *law* also constituted grounds for suit, but until 1980 state and local governments assumed that this was limited to civil rights or equal protection laws. Their assumption was erroneous. *State of Maine v. Thiboutot*[87] extended §1983's coverage to include the entire range of federal legal rights, particularly federal entitlement programs. The case involved allegations that the state of Maine had wrongfully deprived a couple of welfare benefits to which they were entitled under federal law. The Court had previously ruled in *Rosado v. Wyman*[88] that suits for injunctive relief in federal court under §1983 were "proper to secure compliance with the provisions of the Social Security Act on the part of participating states," and in *Thiboutot* it unequivocally extended this coverage to other entitlement programs:

> The question . . . is whether the phrase "and laws" means what it says or whether it should be limited to some subset of laws. Given that Congress attached no modifiers to the phrase, the plain language of the statute undoubtedly embraces respondents claims that petitioners violated the Social Security Act.[89]

The Supreme Court had already held that in suit for injunctive relief involving violation of Fourteenth Amendment rights, the Eleventh Amendment did not bar awards of attorney's fees against a state. Since *Thiboutot* had been brought in state court, the court did not consider whether this extended to cases involving violations of legal rights brought in federal court. The decision in *Maher v. Gagne*[90] held that in any case in which the plaintiff prevails on a wholly statutory claim in which substantial violations were alleged but not adjudicated, the Eleventh Amendment did not bar the award of attorney's fees against the state.

Currently, state governments enjoy only limited immunity from §1983 suits. Although they may not be sued directly for compensatory damages in federal courts, their officials may be so sued; the state government may be sued for injunctive relief in federal court, attorney fees may be awarded against the state if the plaintiff prevails, and if plaintiff brings suit in state court, direct monetary damages may be awarded against the state. Further, the liability of state governments extends to suits involving violations of not only federal constitutional rights but also of the entire gamut of federal legal rights.

THE KING CAN DO NO RIGHT: CONSEQUENCES OF EXPANDED GOVERNMENTAL LIABILITY

The problems created by expanding official liability have already been examined. Replacing official liability with governmental liability solves some of these problems but does not solve them all, and in fact creates additional ones particularly at a time when public funds are increasingly limited. The majority of §1983 cases involve procedural allegations that the states or local governments have violated due process in restricting or abridging a right. The moral for those affected governmental units is to concentrate time, effort, and money on developing and following proper and elaborate procedures.[91] At a minimum, it suggests that governments should develop training programs to ensure that personnel are fully aware of constitutional and legal rights. Unfortunately, this inevitably translates into more money being spent on procedures and less being available for substantive program benefits—another version of the tradeoff exemplified by the *Goldberg v. Kelly* decision. The emphasis on elaborate procedures in turn results in a proliferation of the same proceduralism and bureaucratic red tape which have infuriated so many hapless citizens who have had to attempt to contend with government agencies in the past. Ultimately, one wonders who really wins from all this litigation: not the administrators who increasingly feel alienated from their programs and their clients; not the courts who are flooded with suits when they already were seriously backlogged; not the taxpayers whose money is diverted from substantive purposes to legal defense funds; not the clients of benefits programs who pay for increased proceduralism through lower benefits. Perhaps the ultimate and only beneficiaries are the lawyers who at least get their legal fees and employment in a profession with an increasingly high unemployment rate.

Ironically, despite its blatant injustices and unfairness, sovereign immunity may well be a doctrine in need of a logical rational basis that the American courts which established it neglected to provide. Under the Constitution, government, at every or any level, is not king, but neither is it a private citizen or business. Government is different; its goal is to serve the public interest and to do that it must occasionally develop new procedures and depart from history and precedent established in a world where AT&T, Agent Orange, and AFDC payments were unknown. In doing so, government and its officials may inflict injuries of a different nature and for different reasons from private actors. How those injuries can best be compensated is a problem that merits serious consideration. Most assuredly, holding individual officials liable is not the solution, particularly when they are enforcing policy officially adopted by the elected representatives of the people. Conversely, allowing government to violate individual rights without fear of recourse seems an equally unacceptable solution.

From the standpoint of equity and efficiency, the following principles merit consideration, if not enactment into policy:

1. Where an official at any level or in any branch of government personally and in "bad faith" violates an individual's legal or constitutional rights, the official should be held liable. "Bad faith," however, should extend only to rights that were clearly established and recognized by the courts at the time the challenged action occurred.
2. Governmental liability should be similarly defined and limited: An individual official should never be held personally liable for conscientiously enforcing officially established policy and governmental entities should never be held liable for violating "rights" that had not been defined or established at the time the challenged policy was adopted.
3. Injunctive relief should always be available to protect newly established rights.
4. Financial responsibility should be assumed by the highest level of government involved in implementation of a contested program.
5. Financial responsibility should be assumed by the relevant legislative body: The legislatures adopt the policies and they should assume continuous responsibility

for proper enforcement of the policy. Only if they are compelled to review on a regular basis the true costs for enforcing those policies can their enforcement be constitutional and legal. Only through regular and public review of the constitutional and legal problems that arise from the enforcement of legislative policy can legislative control be assured, and, by virtue of that, public accountability.

NOTES

1. Wilson Cowen, Philip Nichols, Jr., and Marion Bennett, *The United States Court of Claims: A History*, part II: *Origin-Development-Jurisdiction* (Washington, D.C.: Committee on the Bicentennial of Independence and the Constitution of the Judicial Conference of the United States, 1978), p. 5.
2. Ibid., p. 7.
3. Ibid., p. 165.
4. *McElrath v. United States*, 102 U.S. 426 (1880).
5. 424 U.S. 392 (1976).
6. The Tort Claims Act is found in several sections of the U.S. Code: 28 USCA§§1291, 1346, 1402, 1504, 2110, 2402, 2412, 2671–2678, and 2680.
7. 346 U.S. 15 (1953).
8. Ibid., at 35.
9. *United Air Lines v. Wiener*, 335 F2d 379, 393 et seq. (9th Cir. 1964); cert. denied, 379 U.S. 951 (1964).
10. *Indian Towing Co. v. United States*, 350 U.S. 61, 64 (1955).
11. 352 U.S. 315 (1957).
12. *Moos v. United States*, 225 F2d 705 (8th Cir. 1955).
13. *Pendarvis v. United States*, 241 F Supp 8 (E.D.S.C. 1965).
14. *Mizokami v. United States*, 414 F2d 1375 (Ct. Cl. 1969).
15. 403 U.S. 388 (1971).
16. 28 USC§2680(h).
17. Walter Oleszek, *Congressional Procedures and the Policy Process* (Washington, D.C.: Congressional Quarterly Press, 1978), p. 85.
18. Donald Barry and Howard Whitcomb, *The Legal Foundations of Public Administration* (St. Paul, Minn.: West Publishing Co., 1981), p. 85.
19. Ibid.
20. *Congressional Quarterly Weekly Report*, November 18, 1978, p. 3327.
21. Walter Gellhorn, Clark Byse, and Peter Strauss, *Administrative Law: Cases and Comments*, 7th ed. (Mineola, N.Y.: Foundation Press, 1979), p. 1073.
22. 161 U.S. 483, 498 (1896).
23. *Gregoire v. Biddle*, 177 F2d 579, 580 et seq. (2d Cir. 1949).
24. Ibid., at 581.
25. *Barr v. Matteo*, 360 U.S. 564, 565 (1959).
26. Ibid., at 573.
27. 403 U.S. 388 (1971).
28. Ibid., at 396.
29. 456 F2d 1339, 1346 (2d Cir. 1972).
30. 438 U.S. 478 (1978).

31. Ibid., at 501.
32. Ibid., at 505.
33. Ibid., at 527.
34. Ibid., at 508.
35. Ibid., at 512.
36. 452 U.S. 713 (1981).
37. —— U.S. —— (1982).
38. —— U.S. —— (1982).
39. —— U.S. —— (1982).
40. 341 U.S. 367 (1951).
41. *Doe v. McMillan*, 412 U.S. 306, 312 (1973).
42. *Hutchinson v. Proxmire*, 443 U.S. 11 (1979).
43. 661 F2d 917 (4th Cir. 1981); cert. denied 454 U.S. 1060 (1981).
44. 449 U.S. 904 (1980).
45. 350 U.S. 61 (1955).
46. Ibid., at 65.
47. 55 Cal 2d 211 (1961).
48. "The State as a Party Defendant: Abrogation of Sovereign Immunity in Tort in Maryland," 36 *Maryland Law Review* 653–70 (1977).
49. Walter Groszyk and Thomas Madden, "Managing without Immunity: The Challenge for State and Local Government Officials in the 1980's," *Public Administration Review*, March/April 1981, pp. 272, 277.
50. 365 U.S. 167 (1961).
51. Ibid., at 184.
52. 416 U.S. 232 (1974).
53. Ibid,, at 247.
54. 420 U.S. 308 (1975).
55. 423 U.S. 563 (1975).
56. 420 U.S. 308, 321 (1975).
57. 434 U.S. 555 (1978).
58. Ibid., at 562.
59. *Gomez v. Toledo*, 446 U.S. 635 (1980).
60. *Tenney v. Brandhove*, 341 U.S. 367 (1951).
61. 386 U.S. 547 (1967).
62. Ibid., at 554.
63. 435 U.S. 349 (1978).
64. Ibid., at 360.
65. 552 F2d 172, 174 et seq. (7th Cir. 1977).
66. 435 U.S. 349, 368 (1976).
67. Ibid., at 358.
68. Ibid., at 362.
69. Ibid., at 359.
70. Ibid., at 356.
71. Ibid., at 363.
72. 424 U.S. 409 (1976).
73. 454 U.S. 312 (1981).
74. Ibid., at 319.
75. 436 U.S. 658 (1978).
76. Ibid., at 690.

77. 445 U.S. 622 (1980).
78. Ibid., at 651.
79. *Hans v. Louisiana*, 134 U.S. 1 (1980).
80. *Ex Parte: Edward T. Young, Petitioner*, 209 U.S. 123 (1908).
81. *Scheuer v. Rhodes*, 416 U.S. 232 (1974).
82. *Edelman v. Jordon*, 415 U.S. 651 (1974).
83. 427 U.S. 445 (1976).
84. 437 U.S. 678 (1978).
85. 440 U.S. 332 (1979).
86. *Martinez v. California*, 444 U.S. 277 (1980).
87. 448 U.S. 1 (1980).
88. 397 U.S. 397 (1970).
89. 448 U.S. 1, 4 (1980).
90. 448 U.S. 122 (1980).
91. Groszyk and Madden, "Managing without Immunity," p. 272

PART IV

Regulation: Consequences and Reforms

Chapter 13

The Consequences of Regulation

As the American economy became increasingly industrialized, mechanized, and inter-dependent it generated a variety of problems for a society and political system that was completely unprepared to handle such problems. The unpreparedness was largely attributable to what Charles Schultz called the "rebuttable presumption" which has long been dominant in the United States, the belief that the unrestricted market system would automatically result in the best of all possible worlds economically and socially.[1] When the largely unrestricted market system resulted in unanticipated problems, no theoretical solutions to these problems were apparent. When competition led to merg-ers and the growth in the size of enterprises, frequently to the point where many of these enterprises were largely immune to market forces, no obvious solution was avail-able. When technology generated, along with all its many benefits, increasing air and water pollution and processes and products that posed serious and frequently hidden hazards to workers, consumers, and the public, the market appeared incapable of handling those problems. As racial and sexual inequality persisted and increased, the inadequacy and irrelevance of the market to achieve long-range equity became more and more obvious. The consequential loss of individual self-sufficiency which is an inevitable aspect of industrialized society, accompanied by new and more serious forms of unemployment, poverty, and destruction of traditional family responsibility for the elderly and, subsequently, the young, further challenged reliance on the beneficent and automatic operations of the market system.

As the problems proliferated, more and more individuals, groups, and businesses sought government intervention to mitigate the hardships associated with an unre-stricted market system. Gradually, government came to be perceived by the majority of Americans as having responsibility for solving all the social and economic problems confronting the nation. Unfortunately, government has failed to solve those problems, but by accepting responsibility for their solution it has become the target of public frustration and anger. Increasingly, government is blamed not only for failing to solve problems but also for exacerbating them and in some instances for creating new ones through its misguided attempts at economic and social intervention.

Regulation, which has been one of the dominant means of government interven-tion, has become a scapegoat, the symbol on which most of the frustration and anger has come to center. Conservatives, liberals, big businessmen, small businessmen, labor, environmentalists, universities, the poor, the rich, lawyers, and economists all castigate the regulatory activities and agencies of government. The reasons for this castigation are the major topic of this chapter. Assessing the consequences of regulation on American society and economy is a controversial and difficult task, but before attempting to assess these consequences, the general nature of regulation needs to be reiterated. Regulation is control, a restriction on someone's choices and/or behavior. Consequently, regulation is never going to be universally popular. Those who are negatively affected by the imposition of the restrictions will oppose them. By definition regulation involves "losers," which will make it less than universally popular. A further characteristic of American regulation also contributes both to its lack of popularity and to the difficulty of assessing its consequences: the failure on the part of Congress and society to agree on and consequently to specify the goals of regulation. This results in both public and interest group misunderstanding and creates almost insuperable problems in determining if the goals of regulation have been met.

Total objectivity in assessing the consequences of regulation is impossible to attain. As Weidenbaum noted in 1978, "proponents of governmental intervention stress the benefits that are expected to flow . . . The costs which are involved tend to be discounted or even ignored."[2] What Weidenbaum failed to note was that opponents tend to err in the opposite direction, emphasizing costs and ignoring benefits. What is even more confusing is that opponents and proponents also tend to use very different methodologies, data, and data sources in determining regulatory impacts. Both proponents and opponents approach their evaluations from ideological perspectives. Proponents start from the presumption that government must assume responsibility for achieving social justice and equity. Opponents base their objection on, for them, the nonrebuttable presumption that only the market system can maximize individual preference satisfaction, which is frequently their sole criterion of justice. Maintaining objectivity under such circumstances is impossible. The bias of this chapter is that most of the implicit goals of regulation are desirable, that most of those goals cannot be achieved through the market system, but that regulation as it has traditionally been conceived and conducted in this country does not appear to have been much more successful in attaining them than the market system.

The assessment of the consequences of government regulation requires that its impact be evaluated both in terms of specific individual regulatory policies and second in terms of its aggregate impact on the American economic and political systems. To evaluate the hundreds of separate regulatory policies in a single chapter is impossible. Therefore the approach taken in this chapter will be to examine the three basic types of regulation, identify consequences generally attributed to those types, and then within each type to examine a limited number of regulatory policies.

Although most typologies of regulation emphasize only two distinct categories of regulation, a third and equally important category of regulation exists. The two most commonly recognized categories, Regulation I, old-style economic regulation, and Regulation II, the "new" social regulation,[3] were discussed in chapter 6. The third type of regulation, Regulation III, encompasses those regulatory activities which are undertaken as a necessary method of accomplishing the primary goal of a nonregulatory program or policy. It includes all those regulations that direct and control the implementation of federal benefit programs as well as regulatory activities like those of the

Internal Revenue Service and the Immigration and Naturalization Service. These three types of regulation have different impacts on different segments of the economy and society.

Policy evaluation is an imprecise craft. Its primary concerns are determining the extent to which the policy/program being evaluated has succeeded in accomplishing its goals and how efficiently it has utilized resources. A variety of techniques and methodologies are currently used to evaluate policies, but one of the most controversial is cost-benefit analysis. One of the major controversies surrounding cost-benefit analysis relates directly to the specifics of the technique: There is no standard, accepted method for performing a cost-benefit analysis and two analysts given the exact same policy to evaluate will quite frequently come up with widely differing assessments of its actual impacts. The lack of agreement permeates every phase of cost-benefit analysis and keeps it from determining what should be included as costs and benefits, how they should be measured, over what period of time, and at what discount rate. Other controversies involve the political and moral acceptability of putting dollar values on intangibles such as human life, health, and aesthetics, and the inherent tendency of the technique to relegate goal attainment to a secondary, if not irrelevant consideration. Despite these controversies and the imperfections of the technique, it has come to dominate discussions of the impact of regulation (specifics of cost-benefit analysis will be discussed in the following chapter) and evaluations of the desirability of regulatory actions. Consequently, a general cost-benefit framework will be used in this chapter. The general desirability of identifying costs and benefits of regulation is recognized and accepted as are the limitations of the technique and the need to adopt a broader perspective on making political and social decisions which have direct and widespread impact on the lives of human beings.

REGULATION I: ECONOMIC REGULATION

Regulation I is primarily concerned with the market aspects of industrial behavior—rates, quality and quantity of service, competitive practices within a specific industry or, in some instances, segment of the economy.[4] Railroad and trucking regulation by the ICC, airline regulation by the CAB, and communications regulation by the FCC exemplify one subcategory of Regulation I: regulation which focuses on a specific industry and is implemented by an agency which has no other responsibilities or duties. A second subcategory is antitrust regulation which is economy-wide rather than industry specific. A third subcategory of Regulation I involves regulation of marketing activities such as false and misleading advertising, unfair and deceptive trade practices, and requiring disclosure of full and accurate information on a product or service. Agencies with enforcement responsibility for these two subcategories include the Federal Trade Commission, the Antitrust Division of the Justice Department, and the Securities and Exchange Commission.

Single-industry regulation has been criticized by almost everyone who has evaluated it. It has also been staunchly defended by the industries which have been its subjects. Ultimately such regulation restricts competition and guarantees a limited number of firms stable and sizable profits. The costs involved in such regulation are distributed throughout society and a large portion of those costs are those imposed on the taxpayers who must support the regulatory agencies. These are the most obvious and easiest costs to measure. Considerably more difficult to measure are the costs that result from consumers having to pay higher prices for goods and services produced by the noncompetitive regulated industries. Other costs imposed by such regulation include costs to workers which result from elimination of jobs and restrictions on creation of new jobs, costs to the economy through the loss of smaller businesses, and costs to society from a reduced flow of new and better products and loss of technological innovation. In his 1976 study of the cost of federal regulation, Weidenbaum estimated that price and entry regulations of the FCC, ICC, and the CAB plus tariff protection against imports cost consumers $62.3 billion a year.[5]

The Interstate Commerce Commission has frequently been singled out as "bloated, rigid, senile and the worst of all major commissions."[6] The total cost of ICC regulation of railroads *only* has been estimated at $2 billion a year.[7] The costs of trucking regulation have at least equaled, if not exceeded that amount. The ICC also exemplifies another problem typical of single industry regulation—impeding of technological innovation within the industry. The ICC's long and finally unsuccessful attempt to prevent Southern Railroad from charging lower freight rates on its experimental and efficient Big John hopper grain cars is a textbook example of how to discourage innovation in an industry.

The ICC may be the worst but it is certainly not the only economic regulatory agency to impose burdens on consumers and the economy. The Federal Communications Commission deserves full credit for its misguided attempts to obstruct "the introduction of new technologies that threatened the positions of favored industries . . . quite clearly damaging general interests."[8] The impact of CAB regulation on airlines has been estimated to have caused those rates to be from 30 to 50 percent higher than they would have been in an unregulated situation.[9] Conversely, in regulating the price of natural gas the Federal Power Commission erred in the opposite direction with equally unfortunate long-run results. By keeping the price of natural gas well below market level throughout the 1970s, the FPC discouraged badly needed new exploration, encouraged efforts to avoid regulation, and directly contributed to shortages and ultimately higher long-range price levels.[10]

The case against single-industry economic regulation is persuasive but not completely as one-sided as its severest critics portray it. Those critics are generally economists whose primary criterion in evaluating a policy is economic efficiency. In a comprehensive evaluation, however, two other criteria are equally relevant: equity and effectiveness. To measure effectiveness, the goal of a policy must first be determined, and that goal must be derived from authorizing statutes. In examining the authorizing statutes of the ICC, the FCC, and the CAB an interesting set of goals emerges. Distributional considerations, equity, emerge as important concerns for Congress and the regulatory agencies. What is to be sought is a sound, *national* air transport system, railroad system, and communications system. For Congress and its members that means that not only New York, Chicago, and Los Angeles were to have air and rail service and television stations but that smaller towns and cities were also entitled to such service even if its provision was not truly economically efficient. Congress has not been one of the true believers in the market system when constituency interests are at stake. Real tradeoffs were involved for the industries that got regulatory protection. In return for guaranteed profits, protection from competition, and a stable, predictable environment, they had to provide service on a nationwide basis. Regulatory protection simultaneously resulted in establishing and maintaining economic stability within regulated industries which contributed to the development of *sound* national systems in vital service sectors. Competition and economic efficiency emerged as secondary goals.

What resulted in many regulatory areas was a form of cross-subsidization. Consumers in major population centers were compelled to pay higher rates to subsidize service to consumers in small cities.[11] The result in both rail and air transport was a national transport system that maximized geographical equity at tremendous efficiency costs. The existence of these multiple goals complicates evaluation of these regulatory policies. What is clear is that one category of beneficiaries of these policies has been established in firms and their employees and quite rationally those two groups oppose efforts to deregulate their industry. The other major beneficiaries have been localities and their residents who have received below-cost services from regulated industries. They also have opposed deregulation.

Single-industry economic regulation is also the regulatory category that is most subject to "regulatee capture."[12] Both the nature of the functions performed and the long-term specific environments of the agencies involved make them peculiarly susceptible to such capture. Charged by authorizing statutes with assuring the orderly development of the industries under their jurisdiction, the agencies tended to place higher priority on development than on regulation, a tendency which was facilitated by the close and continuing contacts between them and industry representatives. Until recently, the lack of other participants in the agencies' environments served to confirm their perception that no conflict between the regulatees' interest and the public interest existed. The economic regulatory agencies have also developed the most elaborate procedures with heavy reliance on adjudication, which some critics suggest contributed to their proindustry bias.[13] Such an emphasis results in obscuring broader public concerns in regulation and in detracting the attention of potential intervenors, including the Presidents, press, and public interest groups from the regulatory arena. Conversely, however, the meticulous attention these agencies have paid to developing and following proper procedures has contributed to the legitimacy of the regulatory decisions.

The second subcategory of Regulation I, antitrust regulation, is primarily the responsibility of the Justice Department and the Federal Trade Commission, although each of the economic regulatory commissions has primary jurisdiction over mergers and combinations within their industries. The goal of antitrust policy is the maintenance or restoration of competition which is essential to the proper functioning of the market system. Monopolistic or oligopolistic control of a market imposes real costs in the form of higher prices to consumers, inefficiency in production, and increased perceptions of unfairness by consumers and workers. The primary benefits of a successful antitrust policy would be to decrease or eliminate those costs. Not surprisingly, assessments of the effectiveness of federal antitrust regulation vary considerably. While monopoly (one firm controlling a dominant share of the market in a specific sector) is not common, oligopoly (market control by a very limited number of firms) is. In 1972, the Census Bureau estimated that out of 422 categories of product markets, 100 were oligopolies.[14] Increasing numbers of corporate mergers and takeovers have occurred with the knowledge and approval of both the FTC and Justice Department. From 1973 to 1977, 217 mergers with a purchase price of $100 million or more occurred, and by 1977 the 200 largest manufacturing corporations controlled over 60 percent of the manufacturing assets in the United States.[15]

Why this has occurred and the consequences of this increasing concentration are not totally clear. Nevertheless, several factors associated with these conditions are evident. For example, the resources available to both the Antitrust Division and the FTC are minuscule compared to those available to the corporations involved:

> the [Antitrust] Division's yearly budget is less than . . . *one week's* profit at
> stake—and therefore available for resistance efforts—in several major industries.[16]

The FTC with all of its diverse responsibilities is scarcely better funded. Delays inherent in the legal process can tie up a major portion of the agencies' resources, limiting the number of cases that they can be involved in at any one time. Little political support from within Congress or from the President is provided for vigorous antitrust activity. Even when an anti-trust suit is successfully prosecuted, the penalties levied are so minor that the deterrent effect is minimal. General Motors lost several antitrust suits between 1935 and 1970, but the largest fine imposed was $56,000.[17] Inadequacies in the antitrust laws also have played an important role in recent mergers, the majority of which have been conglomerate takeovers. Mobil Oil may be barred from taking over Marathon Oil since that would be classified as a horizontal merger which conceivably could result in a lessening of competition within the petroleum industry. When U.S. Steel, however, attempts to take over Marathon, proving that a substantial lessening of competition and thus a violation of antitrust law has occurred is considerably more difficult, if not impossible. Consequently, conglomerate takeovers are rarely challenged by either the FTC or the Antitrust Division. Conglomerates, typified by ITT, are unquestionably big, but not necessarily bad. "No one has ever shown that aggregate concentration results in anything."[18] Although conclusive empirical evidence may be lacking, critics of conglomerates allege that bigness does equate with badness, that the growing concentration of economic power in fewer and fewer corporations results in an increasing concentration of political power in the same hands and growing immunity from both market forces and legal sanctions. The increase in oligopoly control of various segments of the economy may also be a contributing factor to the chronic and seemingly incurable inflation that has been plaguing the American economy. For example, an FTC staff report alleged that from 1958 to 1972, oligopoly control in the breakfast-food industry cost consumers over $1 billion in overcharges.[19] Prices in oligopolistic industries appear to be immune to demand shifts; despite decrease in demand for the product, prices in oligopolies have actually increased in recent years.[20]

The final subcategory of economic regulation, regulation of marketing behavior, has recently become one of the most criticized and controversial of regulatory actions. Conservatives, in particular, have come to view this type of regulation as burdensome, odious, and unfair and have concentrated their wrath on the FTC's attempts to require advertisers and businesses to tell consumers the truth, the whole truth, and nothing but the truth. This is, however, one regulatory area where critics of regulation have not stressed cost-benefit analysis, although much has been said about the costs of truthful advertising. Consumer fraud is a multimillion-dollar-a-year problem. When a consumer buys a used car for $1000, believing that the car is mechanically sound, drives it for 50 miles at which point the car ceases to function, and then is compelled to pay an additional $700 in repair bills, that consumer has been subjected to one of the more common and unfair experiences of contemporary life. On September 10, 1981, the Federal Trade Commission submitted to Congress a regulation that would require used-car dealers to place a sticker on every used car offered for sale stating whether a warranty was offered and specifying any known defects in the car. The FTC estimated the stickers would cost 18 cents each; it did not estimate how much money consumers might save by avoiding defective automobiles. The regulation was the first to be subjected to a congressional veto under the 1980 FTC Act amendments. Whether the regulation was cost-beneficial was irrelevant to the major participants in the decision, although savings to consumers would have more than balanced costs imposed on dealers. The National Automobile Dealers' Association opposed the rule and it contributed over $1 million to political candidates in 1980 elections. The current chairman of the Federal Trade Commission, James Miller III, opposed the rule because he believed it interferes with the operations of the free market.[21]

Requiring sellers to provide full and accurate information on their products might appear to be perfectly compatible with the market system. It contributes to individual consumer rationality and should alleviate the need for other more intrusive types of regulation. It has, however, become as unpopular as social regulation as far as some critics who view it as unacceptable intervention in the market system are concerned. Such critics are ignoring the reality that the market system itself is created by law and not by nature. Without laws establishing and protecting property rights, and rules governing the exchange process, a market system could not exist. Possession would be the law and possession could be established by force. If the free market is to function properly, participants must follow certain rules. When participants cease to obey those rules, when, for example, instead of paying for a desired item, an individual simply steals it or pays for it with counterfeit (false) money, someone, government, has to step in and enforce the rules. Full and accurate disclosure about a product are rules that the FTC is trying to impose on sellers. The questions left unanswered by those who oppose this type of regulation is, if the free market has rules that buyers can be compelled to follow, why should there not be similar rules for sellers?

Overall, economic regulation is based on the recognition that the unrestricted operations of the free market do not necessarily result in desired outcomes for either sellers or buyers. Both the successes and failures of economic regulation make it difficult to evaluate on a cost-benefit basis. While some of its costs and benefits are tangible and can be assigned monetary values with minimal difficulty, others, perhaps the most important, are intangibles whose monetary value is difficult, if not impossible, to ascertain. All three types of economic regulation are attempts to maintain the basics of the private enterprise system and at least a partial semblance of a market system. All three types have been criticized from a variety of perspectives for failing to accomplish what proponents intended, for unconscionable meddling in the operations of the market system, and for failing to curb the growth of economic concentration. At the same time, economic regulation has placated those most aggrieved by perceived inadequacies of the market system, controlled the grossest abuses of that system, and forestalled the more drastic government intervention or nationalization of certain types of enterprises that has occurred in other countries.

REGULATION II: SOCIAL REGULATION

Social regulation is directed at controlling the nature and types of goods and services produced and the processes by which they are made. The two major goals of social regulation are to control or eliminate socially harmful impacts that occur as a by-product of the productive process and to protect consumers and the public from unsafe or unhealthy products. Included under this category are environmental regulations, regulations relating to working conditions, and regulations relating to food, drug, and product safety. If Regulation I is unpopular with conservatives, Regulation II is anathema. As Weidenbaum at one point conceded, however, the goals of these social regulations are laudable and many of them enjoy widespread public support:

> We must recognize that it is difficult to criticize the basic mission of these new regulatory agencies. Only a Scrooge would quarrel with the intent . . . [of] safer working conditions, better products for the consumer, elimination of discrimination, reduction of environmental pollution . . . We must recognize that the programs were deliberately established by Congress in response to a surge of rising public expectations about corporate performance. Each of these programs has yielded significant benefits to society as a whole and at times to business specifically.[22]

The primary case against Regulation II revolves around the contention that it has been neither effective nor efficient, imposing massive costs for minuscule benefits. To a large extent the battle over reauthorization of the Clean Air Act in 1981–82 typifies the complexities of evaluating and identifying costs and benefits for Regulation II. Although the original Clean Air Act was passed in 1955, not until 1970 were significant national enforcement powers provided. At that time there was widespread agreement among scientists and the American public that the quality of the nation's air, particularly that over urban areas, was rapidly deteriorating. The major sources of air pollution were also well known. Heading the list was the automobile, followed by emissions from factories and utilities. If air pollution were to be controlled, emissions from those three sources had to be controlled.

Air pollution is not cost free; it imposes extremely high costs on society and individuals. Air pollution is a classic example of a negative externality—a cost of the productive process that is not reflected in market price, but is widely distributed throughout society. The major categories of costs imposed by air pollution are

1. Damage to health and subsequent medical costs, lost work time, and decreased productivity;
2. Damage to property—buildings, automobiles, vegetation, and livestock.

The difficulties in identifying these costs and assigning dollar values to them are illustrative of the general problems involved in applying cost-benefit analysis to this type of policy area. Some of the health hazards associated with air pollution are known:

> Exposure to sulfur oxides in combination with particulate matter has been associated with increased mortality . . . aggravated symptoms in persons with heart and lung disease . . . [They] are also associated with coughs, and colds, asthma, bronchitis and emphysema.[23]

Some air pollutants are carcinogenic; others retard fetal development; others aggravate coronary heart disease and various respiratory illnesses. One study on the effects of "acid dust" estimated that it may account for as many as 187,686 deaths per year in the United States.[24] As many as 67 million Americans, 30 percent of the population, may be "sensitive" to air pollution. Buildings deteriorate more rapidly, historic structures are lost forever, paint blisters and peels on buildings and automobiles in the presence of serious air pollution. Many of the costs remain unknown, and many are not measurable. The more intensified and frequent angina attacks suffered by coronary disease victims imposes costs other than direct medical bills; pain and suffering are rarely included in traditional cost-benefit analyses. Even so the known and measurable costs of pollution are enormous. The most conservative estimates of those that are measurable place them at $24.9 billion *per year.*[25]

One of the major categories of measurable benefits for air pollution reduction is savings achieved by reduction of the preceding costs. Other benefits resulting from pollution regulation include the creation of new technologies, new companies, and new jobs. Counterbalancing these benefits are the direct costs imposed on industry to comply with regulations, the loss of jobs that may result from plants and factories closing because they are unable to meet direct costs, loss of productivity, and the particular vulnerability of smaller businesses which may fail, leaving behind a more concentrated industry structure.[26] An additional category of costs imposed by environmental as well as other types of regulation is avoidance costs: resources expended by those subject to regulation to acquire additional information, hire attorneys, engage in litigation and various other activities to prevent enforcement of the regulations.[27]

To determine if pollution regulation has been cost-beneficial two additional steps are necessary. First, the actual monetary costs imposed must be determined, and second, the extent of pollution reduction attributable to regulation must be identified and the consequent benefits monetarily valued. Neither step has proven easy and several studies have produced conflicting results. A study conducted by Batelle Laboratories for EPA estimated the total cost of compliance with the Clean Air Act between 1970 and 1986 at $291.6 billion (1977 dollars). A Business Roundtable study estimated the cost to be $414.6 billion for the same period. University of Wisconsin economist Robert Haveman attributed 8–12 percent of the decline in American productivity to environmental regulations,[28] but a study by Data Resources, Inc., indicated that their impact on productivity was miniscule. Although air pollution control has been accused of contributing to inflation, proving that accusation has also been difficult. If compensating cost savings are achieved, the overall inflationary impact of such controls may be neutral or even negative. Since health care costs have increased at a rate far exceeding the general rate of inflation and they constitute one of the largest costs of pollution, any reduction of those costs is anti-inflationary. Data Resources estimated that air pollution controls had had only a minor impact on inflation (0.1 to 0.2 percent inflation increase) and had actually decreased unemployment slightly (0.2 to 0.3 percent annually).[29] Estimates of the actual impact of the regulations on pollution levels and subsequent benefits are as diverse. A study released by the Brookings Institution in November 1981 concluded that although some progress has been made in curbing air pollution, very little of that progress is attributable to regulation under the Clean Air Act.[30] That report argued that most of the progress against pollution was caused by the switch from coal to oil and gas by many industries during the 1960s. Conversely, a study released by the Center for Policy Alternatives at MIT contended that environmental regulation has lessened pollution and that the monetary benefits of that lessening ranged from $5 to 58 billion annually.[31]

The state of the art of cost-benefit analysis is obviously not advanced enough to permit definitive conclusions about the impact of air pollution regulation. Although economists are currently controlling the terms of debate about the efficacy and propriety of environmental regulation, in reality the ultimate issues involved therein and in other regulatory areas are political, not economic, questions and will be answered by political and not economic logic. Political logic accords public opinion a weighty role. Economics, cost-benefit analysis, and policy evaluations notwithstanding, the public strongly supports air pollution regulation; pollster Louis Harris found in polls conducted in October 1981 that 80 percent of the American public opposes changes in existing federal regulation of air pollution. Testifying before the Senate Environment and Public Works Committee, Harris explained, "Clean air happens to be one of the sacred cows of the American people, and the suspicion is afoot that there are interests in the business community and among Republicans and some Democrats who want to keelhaul that legislation. And people are saying, 'Watch out. We will have your hide if you do it.' "[32]

Occupational safety and health may not be a sacred cow for the American public but it comes close to being that for organized labor. Not surprisingly, then, the same diversity that characterized assessments of air pollution regulation also exists for OSHA regulations. The major categories of costs and benefits are readily identifiable. The major costs are those imposed on industry to install new equipment, change processes, and to provide medical diagnostic examinations and checkups, and direct administrative costs. The major potential benefits include savings of resources used in treatment and rehabilitation of occupational injuries and diseases, administrative savings on workmen's compensation, vocational, rehabilitation programs, savings from avoidance of tort suits for injuries, increased worker morale and productivity, and greater enjoyment of life by those not injured or maimed.[33] Costs of compliance range from the Business Roundtable's $184 million for 48 major corporations in 1977,[34] through Weidenbaum's estimated $3 billion per year,[35] to the Chamber of Commerce's estimate that from 1970 to 1981 industry spent $116.2 billion on worker safety and health expenses.[36] Less susceptible to quantification in monetary terms are the costs imposed by the loss of management freedom and the intrusive presence of inspectors which some businessmen contend violates their constitutional rights. Conversely, the total costs associated with occupational accidents and illnesses are also exorbitant. The National Safety Council estimated that such accidents involved costs of $25.2 billion in 1979 and occupational diseases imposed costs of over $3 billion per year on Social Security and government welfare programs.[37]

Estimates of OSHA's effectiveness in reducing job-related injuries and illnesses vary considerably. Table 13.1 summarizes comparative data compiled by the Bureau of Labor Statistics for 1972 and 1979.[38] As the table indicates, although injuries and fatalities have decreased, lost workdays have increased. Estimates on incidence of occupational illnesses are unreliable since such illnesses frequently take years to develop and diagnose. However, BLS estimates that there has been a decline in such illnesses since 1975.

The uncertainties and the controversies that characterize the costs and benefits of air pollution and occupational safety and health regulation can be and have been replicated in every other social regulation policy arena. The Food and Drug Administration has been regularly condemned for delaying the introduction of potentially life-saving drugs from the market and praised for protecting the United States from Thalidomide-type disasters. The National Highway Traffic Safety Administration has been credited with saving lives and reducing the costs of accident-related automobile repairs,[39] and for adding hundreds of dollars to the price of an automobile.[40] Affirmative Action has been alternately singled out as "reverse discrimination" and the only available method for reversing centuries of discrimination and achieving equal opportunity. Social regulatory agencies have been accused of acting both too slowly and too rapidly, too zealously and too haphazardly.

The reasons for the vociferous opposition to social regulation are not difficult to ascertain. Unarguably, such regulation does impose real costs; those costs are highly visible, relatively easy to measure, and their initial impact falls on vocal, powerful, and well-organized interests. The benefits of this type of regulation are mostly intangible, extremely difficult to measure, not easily susceptible to monetary valuation, and widely distributed among beneficiaries who may be ignorant of the extent of benefits received. Organized groups which purport to represent the interests of beneficiaries are likely to be as critical of social regulation as opponents, for different reasons. Consumer groups, environmental groups, civil rights groups are likely to charge that social regulatory agencies have done too little, too late, and too timidly. The result is to create for those agencies a generally unsupportive, if not directly hostile, environment. Neg-

TABLE 13.1. Worker Injuries–Fatalities

	Total Private Sector		Construction Industry	
	1972	1979	1972	1979
Injuries[1]	10.5	9.2	18.4	16.0
Lost Workdays[1]	47.9	67.7	88.5	120.4
Fatalities[2]	10.0	9.0	53.0	31.0

[1] Per 100 workers
[2] Per 100,000 workers

ative evaluations are as likely to be made by beneficiaries as they are by those on whom the costs of regulation are imposed.

Opponents of social regulation view its political consequences as negatively as its economic consequences. Although no one has accused social regulatory agencies of being subject to regulatee capture, the agencies have been accused of being staffed by individuals who are overly committed to the regulatory goals of their agencies. "Regulatory agencies tend to lure personnel who 'believe' in regulation. It is not surprising, for example, that EPA has a reputation for having a staff composed of 'environmentalists.' . . . many officials behave as though driven by a desire to 'punish' a transgressor. Understandably, kicking around some company because it has done something wrong can be fun."[41] The potential result is to create an antagonistic relationship between government and business that makes the accomplishment of governmental functions more difficult and contributes to negative attitudes towards government and politics generally.

Regulation II has also been criticized for vastly expanding the power and intrusiveness of the federal government and for at least potentially dangerously expanding presidential power.[42] Most social regulatory programs are administered by agencies that are directly subject to presidential control. A President could use the vast powers of those social regulatory agencies to punish or pressure an industry or individual firm to comply with presidential aims unrelated to regulation. Similarly, as both Carter and Reagan have demonstrated, a President can use his powers over those agencies to affect sweeping changes in national policy directions without the advice or consent of Congress.

From a different perspective, Regulation II might be viewed as the savior of the free enterprise system that has prevented even greater expansion of governmental power into the economic system. As pointed out earlier, the problems that social regulations are directed at alleviating are serious problems and are perceived as such by a majority of the public. While government and politics may not be held in particularly high esteem by the American public, big business is not well liked or trusted either. Even if regulation does not solve the problems, it may well satisfy the public's sense of fair play, diminishing the likelihood that more intrusive types of governmental involvement, such as government ownership, will be supported. Just as the New Deal helped save capitalism from itself during the depression, largely through symbolic reassurances and action, Regulation II may well provide the safety valve that can save capitalism from itself during periods of increasing social unrest.

REGULATION III: SUBSIDIARY REGULATION

Regulation III encompasses all the regulatory activity that is engaged in as a necessary concomitant of the implementation of policies whose primary goal is other than regulatory. It includes all the regulations and regulatory activity associated with Social Security, Medicare, Medicaid, AFDC, Food Stamps, and veterans' benefits programs, Internal Revenue Service regulatory activities, and the "strings" on categorical grant programs. Regulation III affects more individuals directly than either Regulation I or

II, and court cases involving Regulation III have become increasingly common in the last decade. The subsidiary, or as some critics allege, hidden, nature of Regulation III has contributed to its receiving less explicit attention from regulatory analysts who usually concentrate on the more obvious forms of regulation.

The initial targets of Regulation III are usually either individuals or state and local government agencies. Although businesses are indirectly affected by these regulations, only rarely, as with some Medicare regulations which are aimed at hospitals, are they the direct targets. Throughout this book, frequent references have been made to the impact of regulations on the lives of beneficiaries of government largesse. The student, the veteran, the welfare recipient, the government employee, and the Social Security recipient pay a high price in terms of lost privacy and liberty for the benefits they receive. The total costs of Regulation III would have to include consideration of the aggregate societal loss of freedom and innovation and the decline in individual responsibility that has been a consequence of this type of regulation. If determining the monetary value of clean air, human life, and wilderness is difficult, placing monetary value on privacy, liberty, and human dignity is considerably more so. Perhaps the tradeoff is even; payment for benefits is less or equal to the amount received. Perhaps it is not, but Regulation III is as difficult to evaluate using cost-benefit logic as were Regulations I and II.

The regulations themselves are a by-product of a changed society and economy which have made individual self-sufficiency difficult, if not impossible, and has pitted individual economic freedom against individual economic survival. Once the survival of the individual became dependent on the functionings of an economy which has been continuously subject to cyclical patterns of recession–inflation and the survival of that economy become dependent on the prolonged willingness of the mass of society to tolerate perpetual insecurity, government intervention to help maintain stability was inevitable. Once government intervention to ensure that the "truly needy" did not perish was accepted, regulation to guide the distribution of largesse became equally inevitable.

Public reaction to Regulation III is characterized by considerable ambivalence. On one side, the belief that there is no such thing and should not be such a thing as a free lunch is widely held. Suspicion, mistrust, and hostility toward freeloaders, welfare cheats, and Food Stamp chiselers is also fairly widespread. On the other hand, almost all Americans receive or anticipate receiving benefits from government whether it be through claiming deductions or credits on their income tax to receiving Social Security, Unemployment Compensation, or Veterans' Benefits. The opportunities for cheating are almost limitless in benefit programs unless clear and specific regulations to prevent such cheating are made and enforced. Big government comes in many forms and one way of getting government off the people's back is to get the people out of the government's pocketbook. The appeal of that alternative, however, is always greater when applied to groups to which one does not currently belong.

Regulation III also weighs heavily on the lower levels of government in the American federal system. Just as businesses find that regulations limit their freedom in terms of internal management practices and resource allocation, so increasingly have lower levels of government found themselves similarly restricted. Like their counterparts in the private sector, government officials have chosen not to suffer in silence. In response to the Reagan administration's publication of what it considered the 20 most burdensome regulations on the private sector, the National Association of Counties (NACO) published its own 20 most burdensome list. Included on NACO's list were five regulations involving implementation of the CETA program, Davis-Bacon Act regulations, and the conflicting and duplicating regulations issued by USDA for the Food Stamp program and DHHS regulations for AFDC programs.[43] NACO's resistance is relatively minor when compared to that of college athletic directors in their reaction to HEW's Title IX regulations, which have been accused of endangering everything from intercollegiate football to the entire concept of athletic integrity. Beguiled by the availability of federal funds to alleviate problems within their jurisdictions for which they lack the resources or the will to solve, state and local governments are compelled to accept the regulations that inevitably accompany those funds. The price they pay is high. They lose flexibility, power, and discretion to solve problems. They are committed to endless red tape, excessive paperwork. They must allocate increasingly scarce resources and personnel to compliance with and enforcement of federal regulations. They run the risk of incurring the anger and frustration of their residents, who are likely to attribute any inadequacies or problems arising out of these programs not to the federal government but to the unit of government that administers the programs and that they hold responsible for the alleged inadequacies of the programs. Increasingly, these units of government and their personnel find themselves legally liable for alleged injuries that result from the administration of these programs. Increasingly, too, the lower levels of government find themselves locked into the same legalistic, proceduralistic rigidity that has come to characterize the federal-level regulatory process. That these lower levels of government usually lack the personnel, the resources, the experience, and the capabilities to maintain a legalistic administrative process is irrelevant to both the federal agencies and courts. The states, counties, cities, school districts, too, have done the crime—they agreed to participate in the federal program; they also must do the time, or at least pay the fine.[44]

Beyond these two groups primarily affected by Regulation III lie the indirect beneficiaries of the programs and consequently the ultimate subjects of many regulations. Nursing homes increasingly rely on Medicaid payments as a major source of income; they are also increasingly subject to the regulation that is an inevitable consequence of being a recipient of those funds. Everything from the qualifications of their personnel to the quality and quantity of food served for breakfast, lunch, and dinner come under regulatory scrutiny or direction. Hospitals, pharmacies, and even physicians are similarly affected and equally displeased with the interference of their normal operating procedures.

Regulation III has also provided considerable benefits..It has ensured that there is a least common denominator in procedures followed in implementing national policies which in its absence would most assuredly have been lacking. As burdensome as those regulations may be they have provided some uniformity in procedural fairness throughout the United States. Many of these regulations have been aimed at achieving equal protection, a standard mandated by the Constitution and one that had not even come close to approximation prior to the institution of federal regulations, and one which the unfettered market system seemed unlikely ever to achieve. Despite the burdens these regulations have imposed on state and local government, they have also provided them with real benefits also. In many instances they have mandated preformed national procedures that have already withstood legal-constitutional challenges. If the states and localities have encountered liability problems because of these federal programs, they have also probably been spared additional legal challenges and the consequent expense of those challenges by Regulation III. Due process requirements are constitutional; they will not disappear with the elimination of Regulation III.

Cost savings from reduction of fraud and abuse in many government benefit programs have also occurred as a result of Regulation III. While such fraud and abuse continue, in the absence of regulation the financial losses attributable to fraudulent activities would be much higher. While general statements prohibiting such behavior may be philosophically admirable, they are usually legally unenforceable and widely ignored. Only when very specific statements defining what is prohibited and what is permissible exist is enforcement possible. Specificity requires detail which results in proliferation of number and coverage of federal regulations. Some critics of these programs, or at least the abuses associated with them, feel that more, rather than less, regulation would be appropriate in this area.

As was true with Regulations I and II, assessments of the consequences of Regulation III are diverse, contradictory, and value laden. In many respects, the costs and benefits of this type of regulation are even less susceptible to quantification than the other two categories. The costs that have been discussed are largely intangible: They have no readily apparent market value. Similarly, many of the benefits, which range from excluding ineligibles from benefit programs to providing equal sports opportunities for women in college and equal educational opportunity to the handicapped, are difficult to value in monetary terms. Many categories of Regulation III have no identifiable beneficiaries and consequently no identifiable supporters. Regulations concerning eligibility for food stamps are not likely to engender strongly supportive interest groups, nor are outspoken supporters of Medicaid nursing home regulations easy to find. Similar to other types of regulation, Regulation III is loved by no one but in its absence millions would be adversely affected.

GENERAL CONSEQUENCES OF REGULATION

Taken separately, each of the three major types of regulation have had an impressive, if not completely measurable, impact on the economy, the society, and the polity of the United States. Taken together, the three types of regulation have had an even more impressive and more difficult to measure impact on American life. Regulation has become a symbol in political and journalistic rhetoric for all the ills currently afflicting the body economic, politic, and social. It is blamed for inflation, recession, the demise of the family, of individual initiative and the federal system. Assessing the aggregate consequences of the expansion of government regulation is not an easy task, and a good policy analyst approaches it with full awareness of the likelihood of committing E_{III}— an error of the third kind, defining the wrong problem.[45]In all likelihood blaming government regulation for the varieties of problems currently besetting us is E_{III}; it is mistaking the symptoms for the causes of the problems. To the extent that that assumption is accurate, alleviating the symptoms, decreasing or eliminating the scope and magnitude of administrative regulation will not solve the basic problems. At best it will provide short-term relief while the problems themselves continue to exist and possibly worsen.

Symptom or cause, solution or palliative of social and economic problems, the expansion of administrative regulatory power has been one of the most important developments in the American political system since the adoption of the Constitution. Although assessing the impacts of specific regulatory areas provides some indication of the consequences of this development, the aggregate consequences may well constitute a situation in which the whole is greater than the sum of the individual parts. Unfortunately no empirically verifiable comprehensive assessment of those consequences exists. What follows is a largely conjectural attempt at such an assessment.

Economic Impact

The American economy is a regulated economy and governmental restrictions on private sector management freedom have proliferated in recent years. On that point most economists and analysts agree, although they sharply disagree on the relative extent and aggregate impact on the economy of regulatory activity:

> The encroachment of government power in the private sector in recent years has been massive. . . . [G]overnment intervention on an increasing scale has interfered with and inhibited the ability of the typical business enterprise to meet the needs of the consumer.[46]

> We probably have fewer regulations than any other industrialized country in the world.[47]

Although these two points of view are not completely incompatible, they do form the basis for distinctive assessments of the impact of regulation on economic performance. Currently, the American economy is not performing very satisfactorily; both inflation and unemployment are high and the last four presidential administrations have had little success in finding long-term solutions to these problems.

Although economists and politicians differ sharply over the basic causes of inflation and unemployment, government regulation has been singled out by many of them as a major cause. Others, Thurow, for example, point out that the correlation between regulation and economic problems is neither direct nor simple. Other economies, West Germany and Japan, for example, which are more extensively regulated than ours, have experienced less severe economic problems than we have.

The extent to which regulation has contributed to inflation in the United States is difficult to measure. Weidenbaum reported to the Joint Economic Committee that the total costs imposed by federal regulation in 1976 were over $65 billion, distributed as indicated in Table 13.2.[48] By 1979, he estimated that such costs had escalated to $102.7 billion. He believes that these costs are passed directly on to the consumer, resulting in higher prices paid for goods and services. He estimated, for example, that in 1978 federal regulations added $666 to the price of an average automobile. He also believes that regulation has contributed to inflation by decreasing industrial productivity.[49]

Purchasing magazine in its June 7, 1978, issue confirmed and expanded Weidenbaum's conclusions. It estimated that the total cost of compliance with federal regulations for 1979 would be $134.8 billion. A study conducted by the Business Roundtable in 1979 estimated the cost of compliance for 48 corporations with regulations of only *six* federal agencies would be $2.6 billion.[50] Countless studies have confirmed that regulatory activity imposes multibillion dollar costs on the American economy. Without more, the case against regulation based on its inflationary impact appears persuasive. There is more, however, and at least two additional concerns must be met and satisfied before valid conclusions can be drawn. Specifically, the two concerns that must be addressed are:

1. Is the data on which the cost estimates are based accurate?
2. Are there compensatory cost savings which reduce or eliminate the upward price spirals attributed to regulation?

The data on which cost estimates are based are supplied by affected corporations, and frequently those corporations are opposed to regulation. Public interest groups have alleged that many of those corporations are guilty of what they call "crosstown hypocrisy," submitting very different cost data to OMB and the regulatory agencies and to the Securities Exchange Commission in their financial disclosure statements. Congress Watch offered a prime example of one corporation that reported to EPA that compliance with proposed hazardous waste rules would cost it $115 million but stated in a SEC filing that compliance costs would only be $40–66 million.[51] Weidenbaum's 1979 estimates are equally suspect since they were based on his "multiplier of 20," which he derived from his 1976 data. In 1976, the cost of estimated compliance had been $62.3 billion or 20 times the $3.1 billion of direct federal expenditures for the 41 regulatory agencies included in his study. As his data in Table 13.2 indicate, however, his multiplier is not at all uniform, and using it as a basis to make projections is of questionable validity. Although regulation has unquestionably increased the costs of

TABLE 13.2. Annual Cost of Federal Regulation, by Area, 1976 (in millions of dollars)

Area	Administrative cost	Compliance cost	Total
Consumer safety and health	1,516	5,094	6,610
Job safety and working conditions	483	4,015	4,498
Energy and the environment	612	7,760	8,372
Financial regulation	104	1,118	1,222
Industry specific	474	26,322	26,796
Paperwork	—[1]	18,000	18,000
TOTAL	3,189	62,309	65,498

SOURCE: Center for the Study of American Business
[1] Included in other categories

production in many industries, accurate and reliable data on the amount of the increase do not exist at this time.

As was pointed out earlier, each of the cost increases attributable to regulation may well have been counterbalanced by benefits resulting from those regulations. Benefits assessments would include cost savings, productivity increases, and cross-subsidization savings. Regrettably, the data on the total benefits resulting from regulation has not been assembled. From the limited information available from specific regulatory areas, those benefits would total in the tens and possibly hundreds of billions of dollars. Determining the inflationary impact of regulation is a complex and uncertain activity given the lack of comprehensive and accurate data of both its costs and benefits. Equally uncertain is the impact that deregulation would have on prices and overall inflation. The causes of the current inflation are multiple, with energy price increases, deficit spending, and high interest rates contributing factors. Regulation cannot be completely dismissed as a cause of inflation, but what evidence is available indicates that it has played a relatively minor role.

Increased unemployment has also been attributed to regulation. Economic regulation prevents new businesses, and hence new jobs, from developing. Social regulation drives marginal firms which cannot afford the costs of compliance out of business. It also reduces new capital formation and forces a rechanneling of investment funds away from new business establishment into complying with regulations.[52] By increasing labor costs, regulation also encourages firms to eliminate jobs and automate more rapidly than might otherwise be the case. Conversely, regulation has ensured that some jobs which from an economic perspective should be eliminated are preserved, has created thousands of jobs for lawyers and government employees, restored public confidence in the banking industry, and prevented the collapse of financially troubled banks and savings and loan institutions, has led to the development of new business (environmental regulations), and has expanded employment opportunities for the two groups, women and minorities, in the labor force with the chronically highest unemployment rates (Affirmative Action). Those firms or facilities that have gone out of business because they could not afford to comply with regulation were without exception economically marginal and in all probability would not have survived in an unregulated, competitive economy (U.S. Steel, Gary, Indiana).

Various other economic ill-effects have been attributed to regulation: It has discouraged innovation and new product development; it has been particularly destructive of small businesses which cannot afford to comply or to fight and which consequently have been driven to bankruptcy or dissolution, with the ultimate result that economic power has become increasingly concentrated. Although specific examples of each of the preceding can be produced, so can counterbalancing examples. Regulation can and has forced beneficial technological innovation. Automobile safety devices, environmental compliance technology are only two examples of innovations that developed in response to regulatory compulsion. It is true that "necessity is the mother of invention": regulation has sometimes resulted in the necessity to invent new products and processes that the unregulated market would not have encouraged. Similarly, many of the new firms that have developed in the environmental control areas are small businesses.

One of the more intangible consequences of government regulation has been the maintenance of the confidence of the American public in the economic system. Businessmen who are particularly hostile to government regulation should bear in mind that from the perspective of the American public, big business is not one of the more popular or trusted institutions in the country. In 1975, for example, only 19 percent of the public had "a great deal of confidence" in the major American companies, and from 1975 to 1977 the percentage of people who agreed that "the country has the most to fear from big business" doubled.[53] Countless surveys have confirmed the widespread public dislike and fear of unrestrained big business. While the public is equally distrustful of government regulatory agencies—81 percent of the respondents in a 1977 poll agreed that "large companies have a major influence on the government agencies regulating them"[54]—the existence of that regulation provides symbolic reassurance that the worst of business excesses and abuse are being curbed and ultimately defuses demands for more radical control or restructuring of the economy. Further, the public does not share the adamant opposition to regulation of some of its more vocal critics in the business community. Consistent majorities have supported and continue to support maintaining or increasing the amount of government regulation of business.[55] Ironically, one of the consequences of regulation may well have been to forestall more regulation.

Similarly, the existence of labor-oriented regulation—OSHA, NLRB, fair labor standards enforcement—may have placated organized labor and satisfied its demands at a relatively inexpensive price economically and politically. Since such regulation is at least theoretically uniform across the economy, it also minimizes the unfair competitive edge that might be gained by firms that mistreat and endanger labor and consumers, and protects the position of the conscientious firm. Regulation of quality and safety of products has also protected the export position of many American firms and ensured that American products are not banned by other countries that wish to protect consumers.

In the aggregate, the impact of government regulation on the economy has been mixed. While it has imposed costs on industry, restricted management freedom, curtailed the operations of the free market, it has also protected and expanded the basic free-market nature of the economy, reassured the public, and protected workers and consumers from a variety of the hazards and externalities that result from its operation.

Political Consequences of Regulation

The growth of administrative regulatory power has changed responsibilities and relationships among the branches and levels of government. Although Congress created the regulatory statutes and the agencies which enforce them, increasingly Congress has come to feel that it no longer has control over its creations, and that it has lost power within the political system. Congress has long recognized the potential loss of its power to the President that regulatory expansion might entail. One of the major reasons it created independent regulatory commissions was to limit presidential control over specific regulatory areas. Recent congressional frustration with the activist Federal Trade Commission indicates that while the IRC's may limit expansion of presidential power, they do not necessarily preserve or enhance congressional power. Regulatory areas and agencies that do fall within the nominal span of control of the presidency are more numerous and in the aggregate have power over far more activities, organizations, and individuals than the commissions, and from the congressional perspective they pose an even greater threat to its power.

In absolute terms Congress has not lost power as a result of the expansion of federal regulatory activity. The growth of regulatory power has resulted in a general expansion of governmental power from which Congress has not been excluded. But measuring power is similar to measuring poverty; perceptions are more important than reality and relative situations are more important than absolutes. Congress believes it has lost power and that it has not shared proportionately in the general expansion of governmental power. Although Congress expanded its power by creating regulatory agencies, once created, the agencies and the executive branch received the largest share of the ongoing power. Congress is suffering not from an actual loss of power but from "relative deprivation." The growth of administrative regulatory power presents to both Congress and the President a paradox of power: The fewer subordinates or activities that one must supervise, the closer and more intensive can be the scrutiny and control that is exercised over them; conversely, the more subordinates and activities that one must supervise, the greater the scope and domain of one's power but the less likely it is that each activity or subordinate can be closely and constantly controlled. The fewer executive agencies that Congress had to oversee, the more intensive could be congressional oversight. Congressional power was increased by increasing the number of executive agencies and statutes, but its oversight of those agencies was destined to be much more superficial. If Congress were to provide for a legislative veto of all regulations, it would again be confronted with the same paradox. Superficially, congressional power would be expanded because more regulatory activities would be brought under direct congressional scrutiny, but that very expansion would reduce the time and intensity available for all legislative activities.

Although from a congressional perspective the expansion of regulatory power may appear to have resulted in a diminution of its power and an increase in presidential power, recent Presidents have felt as frustrated over their inability to control and command the regulatory apparatus as Congress has. Theoretically, presidential power appears to have expanded as a direct result of the growth of regulatory power. With the exception of the IRC's, regulatory agencies are directly in the President's chain of command and any increase in their number and powers theoretically increases presidential power. Realistically, however, Presidents have faced the same paradox that Congress has confronted. As the presidential power domain has expanded, the effective control of specific segments of that domain has decreased. Although potentially, "regulatory activity in the health, safety and environmental areas concentrates enormous amounts of power in the Presidency,"[56] creating the possibility that a President bent on punishing "enemies" could use the regulatory powers of agencies under his command to harass them, actually this seldom occurs.

The resistance that Nixon encountered from the Internal Revenue Service when he attempted to pressure it into punishing his enemies is illustrative of the limits that administrative regulatory power places on the presidency generally. Beyond the problems of viable control of the vast and sprawling administrative regulatory apparatus, Presidents encounter further limits from two additional aspects of administrative regulatory process: divided loyalties, and chains of command and procedural restrictions on the agencies and ultimately on presidential control of them.

The basic system of separated but shared powers has ensured that regulatory power would be similarly divided between Congress and the presidency and that regulatory agencies would be responsive and responsible to both. It also ensured that over time both would feel aggrieved and short changed by the division of power. A major restriction on presidential power over the agencies has been the procedural restrictions imposed on regulatory activities by both Congress and the Courts. The mandated procedures that agencies must follow in their regulatory activities, whether derived from the APA, authorizing statutes, or Supreme Court restrictions, constitute an obstacle to the exercise of presidential control over the agencies. As the barrage of legal challenges to Carter's attempts to change outcomes of the regulatory process through procedural modifications illustrate, due process constitutes a viable limitation on presidential control of the regulatory agencies. The President acting alone cannot change the legally required procedures, nor can he command or determine the overall substantive outcome of the process.

Presidents have frequently expressed their displeasure over the expansion of regulatory agency power and their inability to control those agencies. Congress, collectively and through individual members, has indicated similar feelings. Regulatory power and the agencies that exercise that power have become one more battlefield in the ongoing war between President and Congress over control of the federal government. Neither seems to feel it has won any significant or lasting victories. Both claim that the only winner in the struggle is the bureaucracy, "the headless fourth branch of government," as the Brownlow Committee in 1937 portrayed it.[57]

If the bureaucracy is the winner, it is a battered and embattled victor. Although it has grown in both size and power as a result of the expansion of federal regulatory activities, the bureaucracy has also grown in visibility to the point where it has become a convenient scapegoat for a multitude of problems which it lacks ability to solve. All the bureaucratic regulatory agencies have come to fit the description that William Cary once applied to the independent regulatory commissions: "Stepchildren whose custody is contested by Congress and the Executive, but without very much affection from either side."[58] Neither stepparent has hesitated to blame the agencies for inflation, overzealousness, abuse of individual rights, failing to act aggressively to solve problems assigned to their jurisdiction. Ironically, although regulatory agencies are frequently accused of exercising power without responsibility, they are increasingly held responsible for situations that they lack the power to solve. The social-regulatory agencies in particular have long found themselves to be in the most unenviable situation of all the agencies. Positioned between two adverse groups, they have been able to satisfy neither, and consequently unable to build reliable and consistent support for the constant political and legal battles in which they have been embroiled.

As has been pointed out repeatedly in this book, many aspects of the regulatory process have become increasingly legalistic and as the reach of that process has expanded, so has the involvement of the judiciary. The courts have become increasingly involved as administrative participants. Responding to a flood of lawsuits, contemporary judicial decisions not only enforce but direct executive actions in policies dealing with the environment, prisons, education, housing, welfare payments, civil rights, health and many other fields. At the end of the 1950's for example, the secretary of health, education and welfare had several hundred lawsuits pending against him; at the end of 1975 he faced approximately 10,000 lawsuits, a large portion of which challenged some use of executive discretion.[59]

The quotation highlights three additional aspects of the political consequences of regulation: Agencies have not actually gained as much power as has been attributed to them; programmatic responsibility is so fragmented in the regulatory process as to be impossible to determine and the courts have been subject to the same nominal expansion of power from the expansion of regulation as have the other branches.

The courts have gained power from regulatory expansion but only to a limited extent and in much the same fashion as the other branches of government. The Supreme Court best exemplifies the paradox of power for the judiciary. While it has been asked to resolve more issues, handle more cases, and become involved in a constantly expanding sphere of substantive policies, the Court has simultaneously become more overloaded and pushed into more and more controversial "political" areas. Several recent Supreme Court decisions that have been covered in preceding chapters have included explicit recognition of the growing weariness of the Court at having to resolve the myriad of grievances that arise from the regulatory process. Chief Justice Burger has been the most outspoken on the increasing inability of the court system to handle the workload and the responsibility that has been placed on it: "It is now clear that neither the federal nor the state court systems are capable of handling all the burdens placed upon them."[60]

Given the legalistic, procedural emphasis characteristic of the regulatory process, the extensive involvement of the courts in that process was and is inevitable. As the scope of the regulatory process expanded, so also did the number and complexity of issues that the courts were expected to resolve. From establishing the constitutional legitimacy of the regulatory process through the endless series of delegation cases to determining the precise requirements of due process in a variety of specific regulatory situations, the judicial system shaped and affected the regulatory process. In turn, the judiciary's caseload became increasingly shaped by that process. The courts became, frequently unwillingly, involved in the day-to-day details of administration. The conflict and frustrations that are an integral part of regulation were taken to the courts for resolution and the courts increasingly came to share with the agencies the dissatisfaction and criticism of the "losers" in the regulatory process.

The judicialization of the administrative regulatory process has curtailed management freedom. It has forced the reallocation of administrative resources from substantive goal accomplishment to procedural arrangements and personnel. It has caused delays and a general slowdown in the administrative process, and has led to an increasing preoccupation with procedure to the detriment of substantial outputs. By ensuring that substantive actions can and increasingly are judicially challenged on procedural grounds, this judicialization has further fragmented and obscured responsibility for programmatic goal accomplishment. Determining who was responsible for regulatory outputs has always been complex when ultimate responsibility was divided among Congress, the President, and the agencies. When the courts began to act as Monday-morning quarterbacks, the determination became even more difficult. Truman may have believed that the buck stopped at the presidency, but with regulatory policy the buck just keeps on passing.

The expansion of regulation, particularly Regulation III, has also affected relationships in the federal system. In return for the expansion of their capabilities to provide needed or desired services to their citizens made possible by federal funds, the states and localities were required to submit to extensive and direct interference by the federal government in the implementation of those benefit programs. The states and localities, too, have been caught in a different version of the paradox of power; they have had to surrender freedom from federal interference and administrative flexibility in order to gain the power that results from provision of federally funded services. The decision in *Maine v. Thiboutot*[61] which made states financially liable in suits alleging deprivation of rights under federal benefit programs has further restricted their power and sovereignty.

Many categories of Regulation II—meat and dairy inspection, occupational safety and health protection, pollution control, for example—have presented the states with a similar either–or situation. They may either accept responsibility for implementation of those regulatory programs and consequently maintain or expand their power, or they may avoid the financial burdens imposed by acceptance of such responsibilities and allow federal agencies to implement the programs within their borders. Whatever the choice, the states have lost significant control over their own policy agencies; the policy items they must consider are selected by the federal government, which has also delineated the alternatives that may be adopted as responses to those items.

Overall, the political consequences of the growth of the regulatory state have been varied. Total governmental power over the economy and society has increased as the number and kind of activities subject to regulatory control have expanded. All branches and levels of government have shared in the expansion of power, but each has also paid for its new powers by loss of old powers. Overall, with increased power has come increased responsibility for the total well-being of society. This increased responsibility is reflected in public expectations that government can and should solve all economic and social problems that arise. Unfortunately, old problems have not been solved and many have worsened; new problems have arisen. Government and regulation have become the prime targets for.blame. The recurring refrain is to "get government off the people's backs."

Assessing the consequences of the growth of the regulatory state is a complex and subjective undertaking. Many of the costs and benefits associated with it have been indirect, unintended, and unmeasurable. While it has imposed very real costs on American society, those costs are outweighted by the benefits it has provided. Regulatory activity has tempered some of the worst excesses of the economic system, has allowed us to advance toward a more humane society that values human life, health, and dignity; it has created the image of a political system that can and will respond to the demands of workers, blacks, the poor, consumers, and various other public interest groups. Reforming regulation should be approached cautiously with full recognition of the benefits, social and political as well as economic, that regulation entails, and its major goal should be to preserve the benefits while reducing the costs.

NOTES

1. Charles Schultz, *The Public Use of Private Interest* (Washington, D.C.: Brookings Institution, 1977), p. 13.

2. Murray Weidenbaum, *The Costs of Government Regulation of Business: Report to the Joint Economic Committee of Congress* (Washington, D.C.: Government Printing Office, 1978), p. 1.

3. See Lawrence White, *Reforming Regulation: Processes and Problems* (Englewood Cliffs, N.J.: Prentice-Hall, 1981), pp. 29–31; James Q. Wilson, *The Politics of Regulation* (New York: Basic Books, 1980), chapter 10; William Lilley III and James C. Miller III, "The New 'Social Regulation,'" *The Public Interest*, Spring 1977, pp. 49–61.

4. Murray Weidenbaum, *The Future of Business Regulation: Private Action and Public Demand* (New York: AMACOM, 1980), p. 6.

5. Weidenbaum, *The Costs of Government Regulation of Business*, p. 12.

6. William Shepherd and Clair Wilcox, *Public Policies toward Business*, 6th ed. (Homewood, Ill.: Richard Irwin, 1979), p. 389.

7. Ibid., p. 389.

8. Paul J. Quirk, *Industry Influence in Federal Regulatory Agencies* (Princeton, N.J.: Princeton University Press, 1981), p. 4.

9. Theodore Keeler, *Domestic Trunk Airline Regulation in U.S. Senate, Government Operations Committee: A Framework for Regulation* (Washington, D.C.: Government Printing Office, 1978).

10. Lester Thurow, *The Zero Sum Society* (New York: Penguin, 1981), p. 143.

11. Ibid., p. 135.

12. See chapter 6 infra.

13. See Quirk, *Industry Influence in Federal Regulatory Agencies*, p. 11, and Theodore Lowi, *The End of Liberalism* (New York: Norton, 1969), pp. 134ff.

14. See Ovid Demaris, *Dirty Business: The Corporate–Political Money–Power Game* (New York: Harper & Row, 1974), pp. 30–36.

15. Carl Chelf, *Public Policymaking in America* (Santa Monica: Goodyear Publishing Co., 1981), p. 22.

16. Shepherd and Wilcox, *Public Policies toward Business*, p. 91.

17. Ralph Nader, Mark Green, and Joel Seligman, *Taming the Giant Corporations: How the Largest Corporations Control Our Lives* (New York: Norton, 1976), p. 22.

18. J. Fred Weston, quoted in Lawrence Mosher, "Conglomerate Mergers—A Threat or a Blessing?" *National Journal*, March 24, 1979, p. 481.

19. The Spokane *Spokesman–Review*, October 3, 1980, p. 27.

20. Howard Sherman, "The New Monopolies: How They Affect Consumer Prices," *Consumer Reports*, June 1975, p. 378.

21. Michael Wines, "Miller's Directive to the FTC—Quit Acting like a Consumer Cop," *National Journal*, December 5, 1981, p. 2149.

22. Murray Weidenbaum, *Business, Government, and the Public* (Englewood Cliffs, N.J.: Prentice-Hall, 1977), p. 15.

23. *The Clean Air Act* (Washington, D.C.: National Clean Air Coalition, 1981), pp. 9–10.

24. Kathy Koch, "Pollutants from Coal Burning Plants . . . and the Spread of Acid Rain-

fall," *Congressional Quarterly*, May 30, 1980, p. 1490.

25. Weidenbaum, *Business, Government, and the Public*, p. 80.

26. Ibid., p. 82.

27. Roland McKean, "Enforcement Costs in Environmental and Safety Regulation," *Policy Analysis*, Summer 1980, p. 570.

28. Laurence Mosher, "The Clean Air That You're Breathing May Cost Hundreds of Billions of Dollars," *National Journal*, October 10, 1981, p. 1817.

29. *Federal Regulatory Directory: 1980–1981* (Washington, D.C.: Congressional Quarterly, 1980), p. 52.

30. Lester Lave and Gilbert Omenn, *Report on the Clean Air Act* (Washington, D.C.: Brookings Institution, 1981).

31. *Regulatory Directory*, p. 81.

32. Kathy Koch, "Senate Committee Begins Clean Air Revision," *Congressional Quarterly*, November 7, 1981, p. 2192.

33. Weidenbaum, *Business, Government, and the Public*, p. 63.

34. *Regulatory Directory*, p. 47.

35. Weidenbaum, *The Costs of Government Regulation of Business*.

36. Michael Wines, "They're Still Telling OSHA Horror Stories, but the Victims Are New," *National Journal*, November 7, 1981, p. 1980.

37. Ibid.

38. Ibid., p. 1987.

39. *Regulatory Directory*, p. 52.

40. Weidenbaum, *The Costs of Government Regulation of Business*, p. 14.

41. Lilley and Miller, "The New 'Social Regulation,' " p. 54.

42. Ibid., p. 51.

43. *Public Administration Times*, November 1, 1981, p. 12.

44. See George Hale and Marian Lief Palley, *The Politics of Federal Grants* (Washington, D.C.: Congressional Quarterly Press, 1981).

45. Howard Raiffa, *Decision Analysis* (Reading, Mass.: Addison-Wesley, 1968), p. 264.

46. Weidenbaum, *The Future of Business Regulation*, p. 4.

47. Thurow, *The Zero Sum Society*, p. 122.

48. Weidenbaum, *The Cost of Government Regulation of Business*, p. 16.

49. Ibid., p. 18.

50. *Regulatory Directory*, p. 47.

51. "Inside O.M.B.," November 19, 1981, p. 3.

52. Weidenbaum, *The Future of Business Regulation*, p. 23.

53. Ibid., p. 59.

54. *Regulatory Directory*, p. 75.

55. See Steven Kelman, "Regulation That Works," *The New Republic*, November 25, 1978.

56. Lilley and Miller, "The New 'Social Regulation,' " p. 52.

57. U.S. President's Committee on Administrative Management, *Report of The Committee*, 74th Congress, 2d Session (Washington, D.C.: Government Printing Office, 1937), p. 40.

58. William L. Cary, *Politics and the Regulatory Commissions* (New York: McGraw-Hill, 1967), p. 4.

59. Hugh Heclo, *A Government of Strangers* (Washington, D.C.: Brookings Institution, 1977), p. 18.

60. Chief Justice Burger, speech to the American Bar Association, quoted in the Spokane *Spokesman–Review*, January 25, 1982, p. 3.

61. 448 U.S. 1 (1980).

Chapter 14

Regulatory Reform

Regulatory reform has become a highly visible item on the national policy agenda. Economists, lawyers, judges, members of Congress, Presidents, and pressure groups have put forth a variety of proposals for modifying regulation and the regulatory process. Many of the reform proposals stem directly from the reformer's perception of the intended goals of regulation, the desirability of those goals, and the assessment of how well or poorly those goals have been achieved. For example, an evaluator who approaches assessment of OSHA with the belief that its overriding goal is to protect worker health and safety and who believes that that goal is desirable will first assess the extent to which OSHA has actually protected workers' health and safety. That evaluator's reform proposal will be primarily directed at increasing OSHA's effectiveness as a protective agency. A different evaluator who believes that protecting worker health and safety is only one of OSHA's goals and one that is restricted by the necessity of limiting private costs of regulation will likely arrive at very different evaluative conclusions and reform suggestions.

Regulatory reform proposals cannot be separated from the reformer's assessment of the consequences of goverment regulation and the desirability of that regulation. Consequently, one person's reform may be anathema to another person equally committed to reform. Although this is most obvious with substantive reform proposals, such as proposals for deregulation, it is equally true of procedural reforms and reforms which involve changing the current pattern of political controls over regulatory activity. This chapter will examine the substantive, procedural, and political reform proposals that have received the most serious attention from analysts and politicians.

SUBSTANTIVE REFORM PROPOSALS

As has been pointed out several times in this book the dividing line between substance and procedure in regulatory actions is frequently nonexistent and to a certain extent this is equally true of regulatory reform proposals. The overt and primary intention of substantive reform proposals is to change the outcomes of regulation. Although this may frequently involve procedural modifications, they are incidental to the substantive reforms. The specifics of substantive reforms vary for Regulations I, II, and III but many of these proposals share a common goal: a desire to deregulate. "Deregulation"

372

has been defined to include "the removal of govermental restrictions on economic activity," the elimination of specific regulations, or the reduction in the effectiveness of a specific regulatory program.[1] All the meanings, however, point toward a reduction in the role, powers, and responsibilities of federal government regulatory agencies. At the opposite end of the reform spectrum are those proposals aimed at increasing the level and effectiveness of regulatory programs. They, too, inevitably involve procedural modifications as a subsidiary part of their reform approach.

Regulation I

Economic regulation is the area where economists are most likely to recommend sweeping deregulation in the sense of complete termination of regulatory control. Underlying those economic proposals is a substantive assumption equivalent to the procedural assumptions of some lawyer-reformers who argue that by extending and perfecting the adversary process substantive justice and equity can be better achieved. Economist reformers tend to believe that deregulation, the elimination of government controls on rates and service, will achieve similar results.[2] Competition, the law of supply and demand, and the unfettered operation of the market system will, in their estimation, result in more desirable outcomes than government control.

The proponents of single-industry economic deregulation have won some significant victories in the political process. In 1976, Congress passed the Railroad Revitalization and Regulatory Reform Act which attempted to encourage rate flexibility in ICC regulation of the railroads. Over the objections of some airline industry members, in 1978 Congress instructed the CAB to deregulate and to place "maximum reliance" on competition in interstate airline passenger service. That same year, Congress also provided for the gradual deregulation of the price of new natural gas. In 1980, Congress deregulated the trucking and household goods transportation industries, removing barriers to new service providers, and requiring rates to be determined competitively rather than set by cooperative rate bureaus. Also in 1980, Congress allowed the railroads even greater flexibility in establishing their own rates. In January 1981, President Reagan decontrolled the price of crude oil and gasoline. Additionally, acting without legislative authorization, the Federal Communications Commission moved to deregulate substantial portions of the broadcast and telecommunications industry. Currently, Congress is also considering deregulation of intercity buses and large segments of the banking industry.

Clearly, economic deregulation is a reform whose time in the political process has definitely come. Whether it will deliver the promised results, however, is far from clear. Deregulation in the airline industry has not resulted in quite the consumers' bonanza that some proponents had predicted. Although problems in the airline industry have definitely been exacerbated by the air controllers' strike and subsequent mass firing which resulted in mandatory cutbacks on some of the airlines' most profitable routes, even prior to the strike the results of deregulation from the consumers' and the airlines' perspective were disappointing. Air fares had risen rapidly: Between late 1979 and late 1980 they had increased by 30 percent, 10 percent in constant dollar terms.[3] Although discount fares were available, they were mainly limited to the most heavily travelled routes, and ascertaining their availability was a task so complicated that even travel agents with sophisticated computer systems had difficulty tracking the best deal for passengers.[4] Passengers and smaller communities had begun to complain about decreased service availability. The airlines estimated that in 1980 they experienced a 5 percent decline in revenue passenger miles and operating losses of about $200 million.[5] Competition had initially increased as new carriers entered the field, but how long it would be maintained was questionable since the financial problems of the major air carriers indicated that bankruptcy or requests for mergers seemed likely. The bankruptcy of Britain's Laker Airways and America's Braniff Airlines indicated that maintaining competition on profitable routes was going to prove difficult.

Similar outcomes were anticipated for the railroad industry, with some analysts predicting an increase in the number of mergers that would ultimately reduce the current 25 rail systems in the country to 5–10 railroads.[6] Trucking deregulation had bogged down under Reese Taylor, Reagan's ICC chairman who showed little enthusiasm for deregulation, particularly in the face of trucker resistance.[7] The FCC's attempts at broadcast deregulation had drawn loud complaints from public interest groups who challenged the legality of broadcast deregulation in the courts, and from the National Association of Broadcasters who similarly challenged cable television deregulation.[8] The FCC has largely abandoned its deregulatory efforts in the area of broadcast competition.[9]

The ability of deregulation to accomplish the intended goals of its proponents depends heavily on the maintenance, or in some instances, creation, of competition in the deregulated industry. This in turn would seem to require vigorous enforcement of the antitrust laws, but both the desirability and possibility of this occurring are debatable. Although the implementing agencies and procedures differ, antitrust action still involves government regulation. Ultimately, then, one form of regulation is substituted for another, and as the antitrust case against IBM illustrates, the substitute may be even more inefficient than economic regulation. The Justice Department initially filed suit against IBM in 1969; thirteen years later the suit was abandoned.[10] In the interim both the government and IBM devoted extensive amounts of time, effort, and money for what turned out to be an exercise in futility. Thurow believes that if the United States is to maintain a competitive position in the international economy it will be necessary to allow growth in the size of industries. He also points out that historical experience proves "that the antitrust laws do not, in fact, produce competitive industries. At best the laws break one very large firm into two or three large firms."[11] Consumers do not necessarily benefit equally from antitrust efforts. As was pointed out in the last chapter, regulated monopolies or oligopolies use their protected positions to cross-subsidize services and consumer categories in order to provide services that would otherwise be economically unfeasible. Deregulation combined with antitrust action will result in the termination of such crosssubsidization. The recent antitrust settlement with AT&T clearly illustrates this type of reaction. Under the terms of the consent agreement signed by AT&T with the Justice Department, AT&T was compelled to divest itself of its 22 local operating telephone companies. In return AT&T will be permitted to expand its operations into unregulated fields of data processing and electronic information. The major losers in the AT&T settlement are local service telephone customers who can anticipate paying substantially higher rates, and possibly IBM, who will face competition from one of the largest industrial firms in the world.[12]

What is equally clear from both the AT&T and IBM antitrust cases is that such actions are lengthy and expensive processes for both government and the corporations concerned. Millions of dollars were spent on legal fees which might better have been spent on research and development, particularly since the estimated long-range impact of the settlements on competition in the American economy appears to be minuscule.

Deregulation and more extensive antitrust enforcement are reforms based on the belief that a competitive market system can be reestablished and maintained in oligopolistic industries and that this will result in the "best" long-run results for consumers, the economy, and society. A reform proposal that is 180 degrees apart from this position calls for the nationalization of many of the industries that are subject to economic regulation. Proponents of nationalization fully agree with deregulation proponents that regulation has not worked to serve the public interest and that middle-range reforms aimed at changing procedures will not correct the basic problems of the regulatory process. They hold an equally firm conviction that the market system will render no better substantive results for the masses of consumers or the protection of the public interest. Nationalization, public takeover, and operation of industry has as its greatest potential benefit, "that the conflict between public goals and corporate profit maximizing goals *could* disappear since there is *theoretically* no further role for the latter."[31] The problems with nationalization as a viable regulatory reform range from its almost total lack of political feasibility at this point to highly critical evaluations of publicly owned enterprises currently in existence, which indicate that public ownership results in neither improved efficiency nor improved commitment to the public interest.[14]

A mid-range substantive reform that has been proposed by Ralph Nader would involve restructuring the American corporation through federal chartering of corporations that would require their adherence to a "Corporate Bill of Obligations." These obligations would include expansion of corporate democracy, the appointment of public interest directors, mandatory worker participation in management decision making, replacing corporate secrecy with corporate disclosure, and applying constitutional obligations currently operative only against government to corporations.[15] Again, political feasibility seems to stand as an insuperable obstacle to the adoption of such a proposal. Whether the reforms, if adopted, would result in a furthering of the public interest remains unclear and Nader provides little empirical evidence to indicate that this would occur.

Regulation I clearly has been the subject of substantive reform efforts, some of which, mainly in the area of deregulation, have already been adopted. To the extent that deregulation does not deliver anticipated results and this in turn results in negative public and political feedback, further demands for changes can be anticipated. Many of the industries which have been subject to Regulation I and subsequent deregulation appear to be experiencing severe financial problems. The airlines and the railroads are far from being financially healthy. Other Regulation I industries, such as the banking and savings and loan industry, which have not yet been deregulated, are also experiencing financial problems, which do not appear to be soluble by deregulation and might be exacerbated by it. If deregulation turns out not to be the answer, some of the other suggested reforms may become more politically feasible than they currently are.

Regulation II

To the extent that we have problems with externalities, competitive markets are no solution at all.[16]

Market mechanisms do not address most of these issues. They ignore them![17]

Regulation II—social, environmental, and health regulation directed at minimizing the social costs (externalities) of the industrial system—has been the target of a variety of reform proposals. Although economists and analysts agree that competition and the market system will not achieve the substantive results sought through this type of regulatory activity, deregulation, the elimination or reduction of regulations, has received increasing political attention and support. Other major substantive reforms suggested for Regulation II include (1) requiring that all proposed and existing regulations be subjected to cost-benefit and/or cost-effectiveness analyses and that only those regulations proven to be cost-beneficial be adopted or allowed to remain on the books; (2) substituting charges/fees for traditional regulations; (3) substituting performance standards for the elaborate and specific design standards that characterize many current regulations in this area; (4) requiring businesses to provide more extensive and accurate information on potentially undesirable or dangerous products and allowing consumers to make their own decisions as to whether to purchase the products; (5) increasing reliance on private liability suits.

Under the Carter administration deregulation efforts had been concentrated on Regulation I activities; under the Reagan administration, deregulation activities have been concentrated primarily on Regulation II and III activities. For example, the Task Force on Regulatory Relief headed by Vice President George Bush announced in August 1981 that it had targeted thirty regulations as especially burdensome and prime targets for elimination.[18] All thirty of those regulations were Regulation II; the hit list included regulations forbidding sex discrimination in college sports programs (Title IX), EPA regulations requiring a reduction in the amount of lead in gasoline, and regulations aimed at preventing or eliminating discrimination against the handicapped. Environmental regulations have been prime targets for other deregulatory efforts within the Reagan administration. For example, under OMB Office of Information and Regulatory Affairs review procedures, EPA has been pressured into withdrawing rules covering stationary source pollution, disposal of hazardous chemical wastes, and planning for cleanup of toxic chemical dumps.[19] Budget and personnel cutbacks and the appointment of top-level administrators unsupportive of EPA's regulatory mission have similarly resulted in *de facto*, if not *de jure*, deregulation.

If the consequences of economic deregulation are uncertain and dependent on the efficiency of the market to self-regulate, the consequences of social/health deregulation are regrettably less uncertain. The activities that are the subject of those regulations are not subject to market forces; they are externalities or irrelevancies, and competition may in fact exacerbate the problems associated with those activities. If a firm can improve its competitive position (reduce costs) by decreasing expenditures on pollution control, on maintaining healthy and safe working conditions, the probability is high that it will be compelled to do so. Substantive deregulation in this area will likely result in the abandonment of these concerns and controlling their harmful impacts on society as goals of public policy. This inevitable and unfortunate result has already been illustrated in the area of coal mine safety. De facto deregulation was accomplished by a decrease in the number of inspectors at the Mine Health Safety Administration, fewer inspections, and a changed agency management climate emphasizing "cooperativeness" rather than enforcement. In 1981, 155 miners died in mine accidents, an increase of 17 percent over 1980 and the highest number of fatalities since 1972.[20]

One of the already emerging consequences of federal deregulation which businesses view with increasing alarm is "regulatory balkanization."[21] As the federal government has decreased its regulatory activities, many state governments have increased theirs in areas such as environmental protection, hazardous materials transportation, worker safety, consumer fraud protection, and product reliability. From 1980 to 1981, the number of administrative regulations proposed at the state level increased from 25,000 to 30,000.[22] Many state laws and regulations are stricter than federal requirements and the prospects of having to ascertain and comply with varying state, and in some instances local, standards rather than with a uniform national standard has caused some multistate corporations to oppose any further federal deregulatory activities.[23]

The suggestion that regulations be subjected to cost-benefit analysis has received increased attention and support since President Ford established the Inflation Impact Statement Program in 1974 and required that all major regulations must be accompanied by an assessment of their overall economic impact. Currently, under the provisions of Executive Order #12292, issued in February 1981, agencies are directed not to issue regulations if their costs exceed their benefits. Although the agencies are allowed to do the cost-benefit analysis in the first instance, final review of the adequacy and accuracy of their analyses has been given to OMB. The legality of this presidentially mandated procedure is under review in both Congress and the courts. Congress also moved in the direction of requiring agencies to consider the economic impact of regulation with the passage of the Regulatory Flexibility Act of 1980 (PL 96–354) which required agencies to include an assessment of the impact of proposed regulations on *small* businesses, individuals, and governments in their notice for proposed rule making.

Determining the costs and benefits of regulations is a complex and complicated technique. As was pointed out in the preceding chapter, numerous attempts have already been undertaken to determine the aggregate and individual costs and benefits of existing regulations and those attempts have yielded widely differing estimates. Although from a technical perspective Weidenbaum's assessment of cost-benefit analysis as a "neutral concept" with "the same weight given to a dollar of costs as to a dollar of benefits" is accurate,[24] from a pragmatic perspective determining what should be counted as costs and benefits and what dollar weight should be assigned to those impacts that do not have currently established market values is seldom neutral.

Superficially, cost benefit analysis is a straightforward technique that requires only that for a given regulation or program all the costs and benefits associated with the regulation be identified, assigned monetary values, added up, and compared. If total dollar benefits exceed total dollar costs, the regulation should be regarded as acceptable;

if costs exceed benefits, the regulation should be abandoned. Unfortunately, such straightforwardness vanishes when the specifics of the technique are examined. Among the most complicated specific determinations involved in a cost-benefit analysis are

1. Ascertaining *all* the costs and benefits—direct and indirect, tangible and intangible, associated with a given regulation;
2. Deciding over what time period the analysis should extend;
3. Selecting the discount rate to be used on monetary values;
4. Deciding which intangibles should be converted to dollar values and what methods should be used for the conversion;
5. Deciding how to handle intangibles that are not converted to dollar amounts.

Although determining all of the impacts of regulation prior to its implementation is desirable, human limitations of the predictive capabilities of analysts frequently make it impossible to identify all the possible or probable consequences of an action. For example, one of the responses to the energy shortage was the adoption and implementation of policies to compel utilities and industrial plants to switch to coal as a fuel source.[25] Unfortunately, one of the unintended costs of encouraging the use of coal-fired generators has been an increase in acid rain and dust, both of which have been associated with increased human mortality rates, destruction of the ecosystems of lakes, and adverse effects on agricultural crop yield.[26] Although an accurate analysis would have recognized and valued those costs, what was not known at the time of policy adoption and still is not known with any degree of scientific precision is the exact quantitative relationship among increased coal burning, increased acid dust and rain, and increased levels of the identified negative impacts. Conceivably, at some time in the future, computer predictive capabilities may be improved to the point where most of the significant costs and benefits of a regulation may be identified, but at present that capability is lacking, and even the most thorough analysis is unlikely to be completely accurate. Identifying the long-range costs and benefits of the abandonment of regulatory attempts to eliminate discrimination against women, minorities, and the handicapped is a task which should humble the most arrogant cost-benefit analyst.

Most regulations are not short-term, one-shot policies; they are long-range policies whose costs and benefits extend over several years. OSHA's cotton dust (brown lung) standard exemplifies the complications this aspect of regulation poses. Although costs of compliance tend to be concentrated in the initial enforcement period, benefits (decreased health costs, increased productivity) will be dispersed over an extensive time period of twenty years or more. A valid cost-benefit analysis covers the entire existence of a program, not just the start-up period. Determining the length of a regulatory program, however, involves a judgment on the part of the analysts and makes a real difference in terms of the ultimate evaluation of the program's effect.

The long-range nature of most regulatory actions also requires that a discount rate must be selected and used. A basic rule of cost-benefit analysis is that net benefits must be stated in present-value terms. One dollar in benefits immediately is worth more than one dollar in benefits ten years from now. How much more, however, depends on the discount rate used. If the discount rate selected is 1 percent, the present value of $1 of benefits 10 years from now is $.905. If the discount rate is 10 percent, the present value drops to $.386. The logic of discounting is simple, as is the procedure for converting benefits to present value:

$$PV = \frac{1}{(1+r)^n} \times \text{dollar value}$$

PV = Present Value
r = Discount Rate
n = Number of Years

What is neither simple nor agreed upon is the procedure to be used in selecting a discount rate.[27] The higher the discount rate selected, the lower the long-range benefits of regulation will be. When an inflation rate must be selected and included in a long-range analysis, the reliability of that analysis is further conditioned on the accuracy of the inflation rate selected.

When the benefits or costs of a regulation are intangible—anything for which no current market price exists—cost-benefit analysis becomes even more fallible and subject to manipulation. Intangibles include human life, aesthetic values, robins and bald eagles, and pain and suffering. Many, perhaps most, of the benefits associated with Regulation II are intangible and converting those benefits into monetary amounts is not only analytically difficult but, as some critics allege, morally unacceptable. Lives saved (deaths averted) are clearly one of the major categories of benefits of environmental and health and safety regulation. Moral objections notwithstanding, cost-benefit analysis has developed several methods for placing a dollar value on a human life.[28] All of the most common techniques use age, earning capabilities, or economic status of the affected individual in determining that individual's value. The methods used for valuing other intangibles are somewhat less controversial but no more precise than those used for valuing life. Shadow pricing, attempting to determine what price consumers would pay for a benefit (more pleasant smelling air, satisfaction, snail darters) if it were offered for sale in the marketplace, involves the use of various methods such as prices for sample items (where available) in the marketplace.

Some cost-benefit analysts feel that not all intangible costs and benefits can or should be converted to dollar values. Unfortunately, consensus on which intangibles this includes and how to treat nonqualified intangibles is noticeably lacking. This raises an additional question as to how cost-benefit analysis can or should be used in deciding which regulations may or should be adopted or implemented. For example, an OSHA regulation might have as a major category of benefits the prevention of 10,000 cases of chronic, although not fatal, lung disease. One analyst (working for OSHA) might decide that the avoidance of pain and suffering can and should be converted into monetary values and uses one of the controversial techniques available to determine such a value. His analysis shows the regulation to have net benefits of $500,000 (present value). Another analyst (working for OMB) disagrees and includes no monetary benefits resulting from decreased pain and suffering. He does include a narrative statement recognizing that such benefits exist. His analysis shows negative net dollar benefits (costs) for the regulation. Who makes the decisions as to whether the regulation is cost beneficial and what criteria should be used to make that decision is certainly not answered by most of the political rhetoric that supports mandatory cost-benefit analysis for regulations.

A final concern involved in performing cost-benefit analyses on social regulations is the extent to which distributional (equity) effects should be included in such analyses. One of the major characteristics of Regulation II is that the direct costs tend to be concentrated on industry and the direct benefits distributed broadly among workers, consumers, and disadvantaged groups in society. In impact these regulations may be the most redistributive policies in existence at the federal level. Society may place special value on redistribution, and to the extent that it does, a complete cost-benefit analysis would have to include valued redistributional effects. Valuing intangibles is simple and noncontroversial compared to valuing redistributional impacts.

The imperfections of cost-benefit analysis are illustrated by the ongoing battle over mandatory federal automobile bumper standards. Since the standards were first adopted in 1971, the automobile industry, the auto insurance industry, and the National Highway Traffic Safety Administration have collected and analyzed masses of data on the costs and benefits of requiring bumpers to withstand 5-mph crashes without apparent damage. The automobile industry contends that the standards add from $19 to $67 in manufacturing costs to the price of an automobile and with the added weight of the bumper also reduce's gas mileage, increasing lifetime fuel costs by $35 to $100. The insurance companies insist that the bumpers have held insurance costs down and estimate that that has saved individual drivers approximately $257 over the life of a car. NHTSA estimated in 1979 that the bumpers saved individual car owners $200 over the life of a car, reduced that figure to $29 in 1980, and to negative benefits (costs) of $2 in 1981. Depending on which analysis was examined, the 5-mph bumper was definitely cost-beneficial, imposed costs in excess of benefits, or no firm conclusions could be drawn based on the data available.[29]

This explanation and critique of cost-benefit analysis of regulations is not intended to disparage the technique but to illustrate some of the problems involved in adopting any reform proposal that would require regulations to be cost-beneficial. Proponents in Congress, the Carter and the Reagan administrations have not openly addressed how they propose to resolve the ambiguities and controversies that abound in the existing methodology of cost-benefit analysis. If they do not resolve these problems and such analysis is mandated, the intriguing question as to how and who will resolve them arises. Unquestionably the courts would soon be confronted with cases challenging the adequacy and accuracy of cost-benefit analysis methodologies, and how they would arrive at any decision is almost beyond comprehension. Closer examination of some of the reform proposals which purport to require cost-benefit analysis indicate that this is not actually what their proponents seek. For example, OMB's regulatory analysis worksheets that are used in the Reagan administration to estimate consequences have no space for specifying benefits; they include two columns for costs—private and public sector costs.[30] Similarly, proposals that would require agencies to prepare regulatory budgets such as that proposed by Senator Lloyd Bentsen are concerned only with the specification of costs and not with the specification of benefits.[31]

Requirements that agencies use cost-effectiveness analysis to choose among different regulatory proposals has also been proposed as a reform directed at minimizing societal costs of regulation. Cost-effectiveness analysis is an offshoot of cost-benefit analysis that avoids some of its methodological difficulties but raises other equally difficult value choices. Cost calculations are performed in an identical fashion to those in cost-benefit analysis; benefits do not have to be stated in monetary terms. They must, however, be reduced to a single, quantitative measure: deaths averted, accidents avoided, persons placed in jobs. Consequently, from a theoretical perspective, cost-effectiveness is a less comprehensive and less accurate method of measuring and comparing the impacts of a regulatory action. For example, environmental regulations have various categories of benefits ranging from health benefits to reduction of property damage and improvement of aesthetic qualities of the environment. If a given environmental regulation imposed total societal costs of $10 billion, a cost-effectiveness analysis would require that one category of benefits be selected—for example, reduction in number of deaths attributable to pollution—and the cost per unit of reduction be calculated. If the proposed regulation averted 10,000 deaths, its cost-effectiveness ratio would be $1 million per death averted or life saved, depending on one's perspective. An alternative regulation which averted 1,000 deaths at a cost of $90 million has a cost-effectiveness ratio of $90,000 per death averted and if the most cost-effective regulation is to be chosen, is the preferable alternative. Nine thousand will die but they were too expensive to save, unless, of course, one switches to marginal cost-effectiveness analysis, which uses different decision rules. Once again, however, the responsibility for determining the specifics of the technique must be assumed by Congress or else the courts will be flooded with policy determinations that far exceed their capabilities and competence to make.

Requiring that regulations must be cost beneficial or that an agency must choose the most cost-effective regulatory alternative has superficial appeal that obscures the magnitude of the value decisions implicit in them and the problems involved in making such determinations. As Justice Rehnquist pointed out in his opinion in *Industrial Union Department, AFL-CIO v. American Petroleum Institute,*[32] such requirements entail a decision that life and health have only monetary value; if as a society we want to go on record as supporting that approach, it should be done openly, honestly, and through the political process. It should not be done covertly and without clearly stating the value premises that underlie such an approach. If we wish to expand the approach to include placing only monetary value on the dignity of handicapped persons, the liberty and equality of minorities and women, and the beauty of untouched wilderness areas, presumably as a society we have that power. Presumably also, if as a society we decide that employed white middleclass males who only live to be 35 but have three cars, four stereos, and two recreation vehicles is the ultimate societal good, we have the power to pursue that good with unmitigated dedication. In fairness to all those who will not share the benefits, however, we should at least specify our value preferences and explain how our chosen methodologies support those preferences.

Not all proposals for reforming Regulation II are directed at eliminating it; some seek to improve its effectiveness as well as its efficiency. One such proposal is to switch from what has become the tendency of regulations to deal in specific design/procedural standards to performance standards. Many regulations—environmental, worker health and safety, affirmative action—although directed at achieving some desired result go beyond specifying what that result is to mandating *how* the result must be achieved. OSHA and EPA, for example, in the past tended to specify engineering design standards and controls that industry was compelled to adopt. Similarly, regulations that were aimed at improving the access of the handicapped to public transportation and facilities became increasingly concerned with not just goal achievement but with the details of how the goal was to be achieved. The results have been to discourage innovativeness on the part of regulatees and resistance of the regulatees and a disregard of the imposition of unnecessary costs. The switch to general performance standards leaves the regulatees flexibility to determine how best to achieve the stipulated goal and also frees the regulatory agency from becoming mired in the minutiae of technical problems and allows it to concentrate on monitoring results.[33]

Some federal agencies have already begun to switch to performance standard regulation. The Interior Department has changed its approach to enforcing the strip-mining law to emphasize performance standards approach; OSHA is in the process of revising its workplace noise regulations to minimize required engineering controls and allow employers greater flexibility in determining how best to protect workers. EPA's "bubble concept," which views an industrial facility as a single entity within a bubble which must meet overall emission standards . . . permits considerable variation in emissions within the bubble is another example of the move towards performance standards.[34] Although such standards have obvious advantages, they are not without critics who allege that in the absence of specific and detailed procedural guidelines, regulatees will take the cheapest and easiest route, which ultimately will result in nonattainment of goals.

A different approach to substantive reform favored by many economists, particularly in the area of environmental regulation, is the imposition of charges on unwanted or hazardous outputs. This approach to regulation requires that undesirable outputs be identified and then a charge be imposed on each unit of that output. To control air pollution, for example, a tax/charge would be imposed on each pound of sulfur dioxide, carbon monoxide, and particulate matter released into the air.[35] The charges would be set high enough to discourage pollution by making it too expensive. A similar approach could be used to control water pollution, industrial accidents, or any form of behavior which results in socially undesirable outputs. The standard objections to such an approach are that "firms will simply pay rather than reduce pollution or accidents," "that [costs] will simply be passed on to the consumer," and that this type of regulation is unfair since it "allows the rich to buy the right to pollute or cause accidents."[36] To an economist these objections are not only irrelevant but based on ignorance of the operation of the price system.[37] From an economic perspective prices must ultimately reflect costs; if the cost of pollution is high enough, the price of goods produced by polluting industries will become prohibitive. To maintain consumer demand and survive, costs (pollution) will have to be reduced so that prices can be reduced.

Whether the economists are correct in their assessment of how cost/price adjustments would actually work is far from as certain as they assert, but what the economists overlook is the fundamental and horrendous administrative problems that the effluent-charge proposal entails. Not being administrators, economists tend to be a little vague on the administrative specifics of how charges would be determined, monitored, and enforced on the tens of thousands of point-source polluters in the United States. If the system were to work, it would have to depend heavily on voluntary compliance, just as in reality the current system does. However, the charges imposed would create a strong incentive for a polluter to avoid compliance and to fight the enforcing agency, whether it be EPA or the Internal Revenue Service.

The charge approach is a punitive approach to regulation and it creates incentives to avoid enforcement; a modification involves offering rewards (subsidies) for reducing pollution, or industrial accidents, or discrimination. Although this approach to regulation is not without enforcement problems, primarily preventing an increase in the undesirable activity so that rewards could be collected for subsequent reduction, the biggest objection to it is lack of political acceptability. Rewards may be a more potent motivator than punishment but politically the idea of paying someone not to pollute, or discriminate, or injure workers is even more offensive than allowing them to pay to produce the undesirable output.

One of the major objectives of Regulation II is to protect individuals from various hazards in the workplace and in the marketplace. One of the primary methods used to accomplish this objective has been to require industry to remove the source of the hazard. The result has been, in the area of consumer protection, for example, that hazardous products have been either removed from the market or made safer but at considerable expense or inconvenience to all consumers. An alternative approach to this type of regulation that has received support from Weidenbaum[38] and numerous other economists is the information strategy:[39] Consumers should be provided with full and accurate information covering the potential hazards involved with use of a particular product, but allowed to assess the risks and determine for themselves whether they wish to accept the risk. For example, rather than impose costly design changes on power lawnmowers which the Consumer Product Safety Commission at one point proposed, the information strategy would require that full disclosure of all dangers associated with product use be made and the consumer would be left the choice of accepting the risks of a lower-priced product or demanding a safer but higher-priced lawnmower.

If consumers actually prefer the safer product, market pressures will force producers to provide it. The full-disclosure approach to regulation is seldom popular with industry, as is exemplified in the current struggle of the food-processing industry against the FDA's attempt to require mandatory labeling of sodium content in packaged foods and the used-car dealers' successful battle to persuade Congress to veto FTC regulations requiring that all known defects of used cars be disclosed to potential purchasers. Sodium is a potentially dangerous ingredient in foods, particularly for those 60 million Americans who suffer from hypertension. Although one FDA study estimates that mandatory labeling of sodium content could decrease the health care costs associated with hypertension treatment by $400 million to $1 billion a year, the food industry has countered both in agency proceedings and in Congress that it would also impose costs of $50–200 million on them to test and redesign labels. Although this would still make the labeling cost beneficial and impose minimal restrictions on the industry, its acceptability to them is lacking.[40] Many consumer advocates are no more supportive of the informational strategy than is industry. From their perspective once a product which poses a clear danger to human health or safety has been identified, it should be removed from the market; to expose individuals to the possibility of injury, disfigurement, or death is unacceptable even if the individual is warned of the dangers prior to using a product.

Increased reliance on private liability suits against producers and employers for injuries suffered by consumers and employees has also been suggested as a method for improving the effectiveness of certain types of social regulation. The current system of tort liability serves as a remedial supplement to many forms of social regulation. The suits brought against Procter and Gamble by victims of Toxic Shock Syndrome and the multitudinous suits that have been and are being brought by workers suffering from asbestosis against Johns-Manville exemplify the role of private liability suits in the total regulatory scheme. The private liability system has several theoretical advantages as a form of regulation. Since the monetary awards made by judges and juries are frequently far higher than any fines that could be imposed by a regulatory agency, the possibility of such suits should serve as a powerful deterrent to the undesirable activity. Producers and employers are allowed almost unfettered flexibility in determining how injuries can best be avoided since only results, not specific procedures or methods, are relevant. Even if injury has already occurred, compromises on settlements can be arranged to the mutual satisfaction of both parties. Further, judges and juries have been largely immune from "regulatory capture."[41]

The disadvantages of the current system of private liability to accomplish regulatory goals counter most of these theoretical advantages. The legal process is very slow and very costly. When the victims are poor, ignorant, uneducated, they may not realize they have a cause for action, may be intimidated by the legal process or unaware of how to obtain legal assistance. Similarly, when the injury suffered is relatively small but there are multiple victims, suit may never be brought since individual victims may not feel it worth the time and effort involved. Current limitations on class action suits also make such suits more difficult to bring. The deterrent effect of such suits is blunted by two factors. The existence of liability insurance diminishes pressures on businesses to take corrective action[42] to avoid suit, and deterrent theory implies that businesses are fully informed about risks and does not take into account the reality that many injuries are inflicted out of ignorance and/or human error.[43] Finally, if the health care industry is typical, increased reliance on private liability suits may be an extremely costly and ineffective method for preventing injury. The number and the size of monetary awards in medical malpractice suits has increased dramatically in recent years. One study indicated that "defensive medicine," the health-care industry's attempt to take all possible actions to avoid potential malpractice suits, has added $2.3 billion per year to health-care costs, has not reduced medical malpractice, and in some instances has resulted in doctors avoiding high risk but potentially beneficial procedures.[44]

Various reforms have been suggested to alleviate some of these problems and improve the utility of private liability suits as a means for accomplishing substantive regulatory goals. To reduce both the expense and time involved in such suits and increase administrative expertise of the deciding officials, special administrative tribunals could be created to hear these cases. The burden of proof which currently rests with the injured party could be modified to require only that "plausible evidence" be presented to prove that the injury resulted from corporate action and the defendant corporation would then have to prove that the injury resulted from other causes.[45] An even more radical modification would be to change the laws to provide for no-fault liability.[46] "Second wave" suits could use evidence from the original suits and current limitation on class-action suits could be modified. Without minimizing the importance of private liability suits as a form of controlling undesirable activity, it seems likely even if these reforms are made, they can at best serve as a supplement to direct regulatory activity.

As was true with Regulation I, reform proposals abound for modifying Regulation II activities. Some of those proposals are aimed at eliminating or reducing regulatory activity and effectiveness; others are directed at improving its effectiveness. One of the characteristics that distinguishes Regulation II reform attempts is the intense emotional reaction to deregulation attempts. This is partially attributable to the recognition that any reduction in Regulation II activity involves substantive goal abandonment, since not even from a theoretical perspective can it be contended that these goals could be accomplished through the unrestricted operation of the market system. The intensity of response to deregulation proposals also reflects the conflict that has been an indigenous aspect of large portions of Regulation II activity. Environmental regulation, worker health and safety and consumer protection, and attempting to achieve equal opportunity have continuously involved higher levels of conflict than characterized economic regulation. That conflict predictably carries over to the regulatory reform arena. Consequently, achieving substantive reform in this area is likely to be more politically difficult and potentially dangerous than was true in the less visible Regulation I arena.

Regulation III

Regulation III is composed primarily of the mass (or morass) of regulations involved with the implementation of government benefit programs. Many of those regulations are imposed by the national government on lower levels of government which actually administer federal programs. The Reagan Administration's New Federalism, if it were to be adopted by Congress, would theoretically involve sweeping reforms of Regulation III. Reagan's New Federalism is based on the turnback of over 40 federal programs including AFDC and Food Stamps, to the states, and Federal takeover of the Medicaid program. Although the specifics of the proposal are understandably lacking at this point, from the perspective of the state and local governments the turnback should mean the elimination of volumes of federal regulations and paperwork resulting in a sweeping deregulation of the administration of these programs. Federalization of Medicaid would further free the states from federal regulations.[47]

As was true with other regulatory reform proposals, Reagan's New Federalism has advantages and disadvantages, and raises questions concerning scope and magnitude of impact that at this point are unanswerable. To the extent that it actually involves deregulation, the proposal appears to benefit the state and local governments. Their reaction, however, has been somewhat less than enthusiastic and resembles that of industries that have been targeted for deregulation:

> Many private firms have become dependent on regulatory agencies to protect them from competition, and the Federal grants process works the same way: in effect to insulate public programs from having to compete for local or state funding. Thus, in both the public and private arenas we find officials trying to have their cake and eat it too; that is publicly criticizing Federal intrusion while simultaneously resisting proposals to deregulate activities or terminate Federal funding.[48]

The apprehension of the state and local government also stems from the uncertainty surrounding the magnitude of the loss of federal funds and the amount of actual deregulation that would occur. The actual amount of deregulation that would occur, at least during the interim period in which federal funding would still be provided (1984–1991), appears to be limited, since the administration has indicated that maintenance-of-effort provisions would be included in the transition. The ultimate price that the states would pay for whatever new freedom results is the loss of federal funds for all of the turnback programs and a consequent necessity to increase their own taxes. They will also find themselves compelled to take an even more active and expensive role in writing, enforcing, and adjudicating their own regulations.

From a societal perspective, the costs and benefits of the turnback are not as clear nor as easily calculated as first appears. For the beneficiaries of these programs the turnback will likely involve serious negative consequences. Presumably, they would lose federal legal rights and the procedural protections that had been attached to those rights. With the termination of federal funds and the consequent necessity for each state to rely on its own resources and willingness to finance programs, greater unevenness and inequities that characterize the current benefit system are likely to occur.

Other reform approaches in Regulation III that would involve more limited deregulation would include increased reliance on block grants which would maintain federal funding but decrease the number and restrictiveness of regulations accompanying the funds and/or increasing general revenue sharing which involves even fewer regulations. Consolidating regulations imposed by different federal agencies could also simplify compliance for the affected governments. Similarly, allowing greater regulatory flexibility, substituting results-oriented performance standards (as has been recommended for Regulation III), would also lessen the burdens of compliance without abandoning the goals of the regulatory effort.[49]

As was true with the other regulatory areas, Regulation III reform proposals are not all directed at deregulation. The federalization of Medicaid could involve another type of regulatory reform: increased regulatory activity to minimize fraud and abuse in the program. The growing suspicion that most benefit programs, not only AFDC and Medicaid, but also higher education and veterans' programs, are riddled with fraud and abuse has led many of the same people who are pushing for other types of deregulation to urge a tightening up, an increase of regulation in these programs.[50] With the funding cutbacks for social welfare programs that have recently occurred have come a tightening in the eligibility standards for such programs and an accompanying increase in the regulations spelling out those new standards. The possible reach of those new regulations was illustrated by amendments that the House of Representatives added to the Food Stamps authorization bill for 1982: Banks and distributors of food stamps were made liable for food-stamp losses if they failed to follow strict new procedures for identifying eligible recipients and Agriculture Department investigators were authorized to carry guns, issue warrants for arresting violators, and under certain circumstances to arrest violators without warrants.[51]

Substantive regulatory reform proposals range all the way from those which support increasingly encompassing regulatory activity to those which advocate termination of large areas of such regulation. Although the current political climate would seem to be more supportive of deregulation than increased regulation, appearances are deceiving. While deregulation in all three regulatory areas has considerable support, it also has substantial opposition. Further complicating the situation is the tendency of the same political actors to support deregulation in some areas but to support increased regulation in other areas. The suggestion that regulations be proven cost-beneficial can support either side depending on how costs and benefits are determined and measured. Substantive regulatory reform involves all the same political questions and actions that the creation and implementation of regulation did. That it has become a highly visible policy agenda item indicates the failure of regulation to resolve the basic conflicts and problems. Whatever policies *are* ultimately adopted, the one certainty is that they too will fail to resolve those conflicts and problems, thus guaranteeing regulation and regulatory reform a permanent position on the national policy agenda.

PROCEDURAL REFORMS: CHANGING PATTERNS OF POLITICAL CONTROL

One of the most frequent criticisms of regulation has been that it has vested great power in administrative agencies that are immune from political control. Although the validity of that criticism is arguable, given the panoply of controls vested in Congress, the presidency, and the courts, one of the most commonly recurring themes in regulatory reform has been the need to strengthen the controls of the "legitimate" branches of government over the regulatory process. What has also characterized this category of reform proposals has been the lack of agreement as to just whose control should be strengthened. Presidents have tended to feel that presidential control should be increased; Congress has sometimes agreed but recently has tended to feel that Congress's control should be strengthened or that judicial control should be improved. Although impressive constitutional and legal principles may be invoked to support any (and all) sides in this controversy, the political realities involved in resolving it were concisely summarized by Senator Thomas Eagleton in 1979 in response to a proposal to strengthen presidential control over regulatory agencies:

> The dilemma I face on the Presidential intervention business is that if the
> President is one whom I politically favor and if he intervenes in issues that pander
> to my voice . . . then I am going to give him all kinds of rights of authority to
> intervene. . . .
>   Conversely, if it is a President of an opposite political persuasion and of an
> opposite philosophy, then I don't want him intervening.[52]

Procedure and substance are inextricable.

The two most frequent reform proposals put forward to strengthen congressional control over the regulatory process have been sunset laws and extension of the legislative veto to include all administrative regulations. A third proposal which receives less attention from Congress but which would also increase its control in a constitutionally unassailable manner would be for Congress to provide clear, meaningful standards to guide agency action.

Proposals requiring some kind of sunset provision have taken various forms. One form of sunset would require that Congress authorize all programs/agencies for only a limited period of time—5 or 10 years. When a program's authorization expired, unless Congress took positive action to reauthorize it, the program, the agency, and all its regulations would be terminated, or more poetically, fade off into the sunset. A more limited version of sunset reforms would make it applicable only to administrative regulations. A still more limited version is the "high noon" approach, which would require *review* of regulations or programs or agencies every few years but would not be accompanied with a sudden-death provision.

Theoretically, sunset legislation would require Congress to take a more active and involved role in reviewing and evaluating the impact of regulatory programs and would require agencies to be more responsive to Congress. Congress can, of course, review any program at any time and legislatively modify or repeal it; it rarely does so, however. Sunset proposals recognize and attempt to overcome one of the major aspects of congressional behavior—the squeaking wheel syndrome. As long as no undue pressure is put on Congress to act, it will usually allow a program, once created, to continue into perpetuity. Sunset laws would compel regular congressional action on programs regardless of a lack of pressure. What sunset proposals overlook is the reason Congress behaves as it does, and it is not primarily because of congressional lassitude, apathy, or misfeasance. Time pressures, overload of duties, issues and problems that must be contended with as they arise, and the political realities of elected officials leave members little time for routine oversight of programs which are not perceptibly malfunctioning. One of the major objections to mandatory sunset proposals is that if their goal is to increase congressional control they may actually be counterproductive since they will limit congressional flexibility and ability to control its own policy agenda and determine its own priorities. Automatic sunset also gives advantage to minorities in the Senate who could filibuster an agency or program to death despite majority support for its continuation. High noon proposals are less restrictive of Congressional prerogatives. A limited version of high noon proposal did pass in 1980. The Regulatory Flexibility Act of 1980 imposed on agencies, although not on Congress, a requirement to review all major regulations every ten years. Full-scale sunset proposals have been less successful. Although in 1978 the Senate did pass a 10-year sunset law for almost all federal programs, the House failed to concur.[53]

The experience of state governments with sunset laws amply illustrates their strengths and weaknesses as a "regulatory reform device" (see Figure 14.1). By 1982, 35 states had adopted sunset laws, and from 1976 to 1981, 1,500 state agencies had been reviewed. One in every five agencies reviewed had been terminated and state legislative oversight of administrative agencies had unquestionably increased.[54] Sunset review, however, entailed some serious and predictable problems: In a survey conducted by

Common Cause, cost, time, increased influence of regulated interests were cited by state legislative staff personnel as the most common problems.[55] The average per-agency cost of a sunset review was estimated at $12,000. Public participation and interest in the review process had been minimal, but regulated interest and participation had been extremely high. The final most commonly cited problem with sunset review was the lack of adequate measurement information to evaluate agencies' performance. Given the considerable increase in the cost of review, and since the benefits of the review process remained unclear, the wisdom of denoting more scarce public resources to the process is questionable.[56]

FIGURE 14.1[57]   Scope of Coverage of State Sunset Laws

Regulatory Agencies Only	Regulatory & Selected Other Agencies	Comprehensive Review
Florida	Alabama	Arizona
Georgia	Alaska	Arkansas
Hawaii	Colorado	Indiana
Illinois	Connecticut	Louisiana
Maryland	Delaware	Maine
Montana	Kansas	New Hampshire
New Mexico	Mississippi	Rhode Island
South Carolina	Nebraska	Tennessee
Utah	Nevada	Texas
Vermont	North Carolina*	Washington
	Oklahoma	
	Oregon	
	Pennsylvania**	
	South Dakota	
	West Virginia	
	Wyoming	

* Sunset mechanism repealed in 1981
** Law enacted in December 1981

The mandatory submission of all regulations to Congress prior to enforcement, with Congress having the power to veto any regulation, involves considerably more constitutional problems than sunset proposals. In the past two Congresses, Representative Elliot Levitas of Georgia has introduced legislation, most recently with 160 cosponsors, which would subject all regulations to a one-house veto. Once a regulation was submitted, Congress would have 60 days to take action; if it failed to act the regulation would become effective. Under his proposal one house could vote to block a regulation; the other house could overrule that veto. In April 1982, the Senate passed legislation that would subject all major administrative regulations to a two-house veto.[58] As of September 1982, however, the House had failed to act on that proposal. Although intended to increase congressional control over the regulatory process, the across-the-board legislative veto could have the same unintended effect of ultimately limiting congressional power that sunset legislation might have: overload and loss of flexibility and control of agenda.

The constitutional objections to such intrusive congressional involvement in the executive process are far from resolved. In *Chadha v. Immigration and Naturalization Service*,[59] the Ninth Circuit Court of Appeals held that a one-house legislative veto of a quasi-judicial proceeding was an unconstitutional violation of separation of powers that involved an intrusion of Congress into the powers of both the executive and the judicial branches. In *Chadha*, an immigrant from Kenya had appealed a deportation order under a provision of the 1952 Immigration and Naturalization Act which allowed INS to grant aliens who would suffer "extreme hardship" from deportation permission to remain in the country. A special inquiry officer of INS had heard Chadha's appeal and granted his request to be allowed to remain in the United States. The House of Representatives under legislative veto provisions of the 1952 act, overruled INS and ordered the deportation. The particular veto provision was held to render the executive's power and duty to enforce the law meaningless; to have made the role of judicial review "equally nugatory," and to have subjected both to the "unfettered discretion" of a single house of Congress. In January 1982, the D.C. Court of Appeals also held that a one-house veto of administrative regulations was unconstitutional. In *Consumer Energy Council v. Federal Energy Regulatory Commission*,[60] the Court ruled that the legislative veto "contravenes the fundamental purpose of the separation of powers doctrine. Congress gains the ability to direct unilaterally, and indeed unicamerally, the exercise of agency discretion in a specific manner considered undesirable or unachievable when the enabling statute was first passed." Bluntly, the court held that what Congress has done by statute, it can only undo by another statute or "may in the future enact more specific delegations." Both cases have been scheduled for argument in the Fall 1982 Supreme Court term.

Public interest groups object to the legislative veto on two additional grounds: First, it would further slow down an already tedious and time-consuming regulatory process, and second, it would add to their expense by compelling them to maintain their participatory efforts and stretch their already thin resources to include participation in whatever review process Congress created. They also allege that the existence of the veto would impair the fairness of the rule-making process by causing the agencies to give undue weight to the perceived political (congressional) power of pressure groups. Ultimately the veto might also result in agencies abandoning the rule-making process with all its inherent advantages in favor of the less uniform, slower, and less satisfactory case-by-case approach.

The legislative veto is definitely a controversial method for reestablishing Congressional control over the regulatory process. Congress could assert more meaningful control at the time of creation of regulatory programs if it would provide specific guidelines to structure and restrict administrative discretion. Theoretically, such Congressional goal clarification is desirable, but realistically, valid reasons have always existed for Congressional vagueness (see chapters 1 and 2), and those reasons remain as valid today as they were in the early 1900s. Rapidly changing technology, increasing social and economic complexity, escalating changes in social values make it increasingly difficult to establish specific and uniformly applicable congressional standards in many areas without dooming legislation to anachronistic irrelevancy. At least partially, congressional recognition of the difficulty of providing adequate legislative standards has contributed to its desire for increased post-enactment control of regulations through the legislative veto process. Whether the Supreme Court will accept the constitutionality of this desire has yet to be decided. If the Court rejects the legislative veto, Congress may have no choice, if it wishes to exert control, other than by providing more meaningful standards.

Presidents and their supporters seek different goals and have offered their own solutions to the regulatory control "problem." The primary solution is to increase presidential control over the agencies and their outputs. One method for achieving this has been the suggestion proposed by every presidential study commission from the Brownlow Commission Committee in 1937, through both Hoover Commissions, the Landis Report of 1960, and the Ash Council study in 1971 that the independent status of regulatory agencies be abolished and all such agencies be placed directly in the President's chain of command. Presidential commissions and recommendations notwithstanding, Congress has shown little enthusiasm for such proposals and has continued to resort to the independent commission form when it has created new regulatory functions (CPSC, EEOC, FEC) and when it has reorganized existing regulatory functions: Both the Nuclear Regulatory Commission which replaced the Atomic Energy Commission in 1974 and the Federal Energy Regulatory Commission which replaced the Federal Power Commission in 1977 were given independent status.

Unable to secure elimination of the independent agencies, Presidents have sought other methods to make those agencies more responsive to their control. One of these methods has been to seek increased control over personnel matters within these agencies, most commonly seeking authorization from Congress to designate the chairmen of the commissions. Congress has been considerably more willing to allow this limited expansion of presidential control than it has been to allow other types of presidential control reforms. Currently, the President is allowed to designate the chairmen of all the independent regulatory commissions except FERC, the Federal Reserve Board, and NRC. If no vacancy on the commission exists, however, an incoming President must designate the chairman from among those members already on the commission. On the three major agencies not subject to presidential designation, the chairman is appointed by the President for a fixed term. The chairman of the Federal Reserve Board, for example, is appointed for a four-year term which for the current chairman, Paul Volcker, will not expire until August 1983. Similarly, Congress has granted some commission chairmen considerable power to control agency management, personnel, and operations (FTC, ICC, for example) but has failed to do so for others (NLRB). Another personnel reform that could result in strengthening presidential control over the regulatory agencies' permanent staff was the proposal submitted to Congress by the Carter administration that would have provided seven-year terms for administrative law judges and would have made their performance subject to review by the Administrative Conference.

Another approach that has been suggested for increasing presidential control over regulatory output is to develop methods to improve coordination among the agencies and to reduce overlapping and duplicative functions of various agencies. Specific methods for achieving this include the suggestion of the Moss Committee that all consumer health and safety functions which are currently distributed among the CPSC, FDA, NHTSA, and HUD be lodged in a single agency.[61] Similarly, the Ash Council proposed that the transportation regulatory functions exercised by the ICC, CAB, and FMC should also be transferred to a single transportation agency. At least theoretically, such consolidation would simplify presidential control and direction. Congress has shown little interest in creating such superregulatory agencies and recent Presidents developed their own procedures for coordinating regulatory output and minimizing duplication.

Under the Nixon and Ford administrations a Quality of Life Review procedure was implemented which required agencies in the health and safety fields to submit proposed rules to OMB and other affected agencies for review and comment.[62] In the Carter Administration, review and coordination functions were assigned to the Regulatory Action Review Group (RARG) and the Regulatory Council. RARG was an interagency group composed of members from EPA, EOP agencies, and all cabinet departments except State and Defense. It was chaired by the Council of Economic Advisors and administered by the Council on Wage-Price Stability. Its function was to review economic impact analyses of proposed regulations and to make suggestions for improving their quality. The Regulatory Council was also an interagency group specifically charged with minimizing duplication and conflict among regulations. This was to be accomplished by requiring agencies to submit proposed rules for review to the Council which also published the Calendar of Federal Regulations, a twice-yearly summary of proposed regulations.[63] President Reagan abolished RARG but continued the Regulatory Council. He also created the Task Force on Regulatory Relief chaired by Vice-President George Bush which was also charged with review of existing and proposed regulations to eliminate duplicative, conflicting, and unnecessarily burdensome regulations, and authorized OMB's Office of Information and Regulatory Affairs to review all pending and proposed regulations to ensure they were cost effective.[64]

Although Presidents tend to feel that such attempts to assert control and direction over regulation are both necessary and proper, public interest groups and some members of Congress have questioned the legality of such attempts in the absence of specific congressional authorization. Thus far, at least, these ad hoc coordinating mechanisms have been limited to informal pressure and publicity as enforcement mechanisms and not been granted command authority over the regulatory agencies. While this mitigates the arguments against their legality, it also indicates their limitations as methods for asserting presidential dominance. If their role is to be other than advisory and withstand legal challenge, Congress will have to provide legislative authorization.

Various reform proposals have also been offered to increase and/or modify judicial control of the regulatory process. One of the perennially recurring reform proposals has been that special administrative courts should be created to review the decisions of the regulatory agencies. Many of these proposals are modeled on the French legal system which has a separate system of administrative courts staffed by judges who receive specialized training in administrative law.[65] Such courts would provide for more expert and hopefully speedier review of administrative decisions while at the same time reducing the burden and workload of the regular federal courts. Precedents for the creation of such specialized courts include the U.S. Tax Court , the Court of Customs and Patent Appeals, and the Court of Claims. Congress, which would have to create such special courts, has preferred to expand the size of the existing district courts and courts of appeals.

Currently one judicial review reform proposal which is receiving serious consideration in both the House and the Senate is a proposal submitted by Senator Dale Bumpers. The "Bumpers Amendment" would expand the scope of judicial review of rule making; it would abolish existing case law precedent that has presumed that an agency is correct in its interpretation of the law, and would require all rules to be supported by "substantial evidence in the record" and subjected to judicial review on that basis.[66] The courts would be given increased power of review of questions of fact in rule making, and almost inevitably would be increasingly involved in the substance of regulatory decisions. Unless such an expansion of judicial workload were accompanied by an expansion in the number of courts and judges the already overburdened judicial system would probably be incapable of handling the burden in a timely fashion. The result would be increased delays, increased expense for litigants, and a stultifying of the rule-making process. The current Supreme Court, with its move away from judicial activism, has not welcomed the suggestion that the courts become more deeply involved in the administrative process.

INTERNAL AGENCY REFORMS: PROCEDURES AND PERSONNEL

As with every other aspect of regulation, proposals to reform administrative procedures abound. Many of these reform proposals have been considered in preceding chapters dealing with specific aspects of the regulatory process and will not be repeated at this point. Proposals addressing the rule-making process range from changes that would streamline the process to those that would slow it down and include changes that would increase or decrease citizen/public interest group participation in the process. One of the proposed reforms submitted by the Carter Administration to Congress in 1979 would have required agencies to set deadlines for completion of action on proposed rules. The proposal would also have largely eliminated the requirement for formal rule-making hearings.[67] At the other extreme are proposals that would require formal hearings for an increased number of rule-making procedures. Mid-range proposals (similar to the Bumpers Amendment) would require that agencies expand the opportunity for oral presentations in rule making and require that rules be based on the record compiled during the rule-making proceeding.[68] Some proposals also look to an expansion of the hybrid rule-making process similar to that which Congress imposed on the FTC in the Moss-Magnuson FTC Improvement Act. Conversely, other proposals for rule-making reform have argued that on-the-record procedures only add to the expense and slowness of rule making and should be replaced "whenever possible" by informal notice and comment procedures.[69]

An interesting, if controversial, proposal suggested by Vice President Bush's Task Force on Regulatory Relief would involve the use of third-party mediation in the initial stages of rule making. Based on a view of rule making as an adversary process, the proposal would use the officers of the Federal Mediation and Conciliation Service to bring opposing parties together to work out a compromise position in the initial stages of rule making.[70] The proposal, however, has brought little positive response from FM&CS which already has an extensive workload mediating conventional labor-management disputes.

In 1977, the Senate Committee on Governmental Operations reported the results of its study on the adequacy of public participation in the regulatory process.[71] The committee found that regulatory proceedings were dominated by participants from the regulated industries and that the major barrier to nonindustry participation was the cost of such participation and the lack of financial ability of public intervenors to fund such participation. The major alternatives proposed to alleviate such problems have been the creation of a separate consumer agency, an extension of the financial compensation programs for public intervenors in agency proceedings.

Proposals for creation of an independent consumer agency authorized to represent consumer interests in all regulatory proceedings received serious consideration in Congress throughout the 1970s. The House passed legislation to create such an agency in three separate sessions but the Senate failed to accept the House proposal. A single consumer agency would have ensured that consumer interests could always be heard in any regulatory proceeding and would have provided a single point of contact for consumer groups with all government agencies. Caught in the rising tide of antiregulation feelings within Congress, the Carter administration's bill to create such an agency was defeated in the House in 1978. In 1979, by executive order Carter did create an interagency Consumer Affairs Council to help develop uniform consumer involvement programs and policies.[72]

Recently, Congress has indicated more interest in cutting back those compensation programs for public intervenors that already exist than in expanding such programs. In 1980, for example, both the House and Senate FTC authorizing legislation included restrictions on that agency's public participation funding program. Similarly, the Senate's 1982 reform bill barred agencies from using appropriated funds to pay the expenses of persons participating in agency proceedings unless specifically authorized to do so by statute.[73] Weidenbaum and other conservatives not only oppose such funding but contest the representativeness of what he has termed "so-called and self-appointed public interest groups," which "know little and care less about the poor, the black and the unemployed." He proposes that what is needed is the development of a "new breed" of public interest groups similar to the Mountain States Legal Foundation[74] with which Secretary of the Interior James Watt was associated prior to his appointment. Everyone, it seems, has his own definition of the public interest.

Foremost among the changes suggested for adjudicatory proceedings is that they be relied on less and that quicker, less cumbersome, and less expensive procedures be substituted whenever possible.[75] Depending on both the nature of the parties and the issues involved, a formal hearing could be replaced by either written procedures or informal oral procedures. Where the affected party is a business represented by counsel and the issues are legalistic or technical, a written hearing could be substituted for oral proceedings. In those situations where the affected party is poor, uneducated, or in any manner likely to be disadvantaged by written procedures, oral procedures similar to those used in small-claims courts could be substituted. Such substitution might also have the advantage of being less intimidating for individuals and allowing them to better present their side of the case.

One of the recurring suggestions for improving the quality and fairness of informal actions is that a "concise statement of reasons" for informal decisions be supplied whenever requested.[76] Davis has also recommended more openness and publicity in the informal processes and the creation of an ombudsman who could intervene to assist individuals and business who have complaints concerning informal actions. For the most part these procedural reforms of the informal process are receiving considerably less attention in the political process than substantive reforms or reforms aimed at increasing congressional, judicial, or presidential control over the regulatory process.

Both the selection process and the quality and impartiality of the individuals selected to head regulatory agencies have frequently been criticized. Most commonly, the regulators have been accused of being overly sensitive to industry needs and pressures and unconcerned with consumers, labor, or the public interest. Business groups, after having to deal with some Carter administration regulators such as Charles Ferris at the FCC, Michael Pertschuk at the FTC, and Joan Claybrook at NHTSA, had a different set of grievances about the quality of regulatory appointments. One recent study of the Federal Trade Commission and the Federal Communications Commission came to the same conclusion that countless earlier studies of the regulatory commissions had also reached: Politics and political considerations were more relevant concerns in making regulatory appointments than professional competence and impartiality.[77] As long as top-level regulators are appointed by the President and confirmed by the Senate, political and ideological considerations are inevitably going to dominate the process. Reforms of the appointment process range from suggestions that presidential control over the process be strengthened to suggestions that executive controls be weakened and more emphasis placed on the development of career staffs and nonpolitical appointments.[78] Suggestions for improving the appointment process have included proposals for developing evaluation procedures for nominees, the involvement of citizen advisory committees in their selection and evaluation,[79] strengthening the Senate's confirmation role, and even creating an ABA committee to rate and screen regulatory agency nominees as is currently done with federal judicial nominees.[80] Since not all regulators are or should be lawyers and since their skills at cost-benefit analysis may increasingly be more important than legal background, perhaps the screening should be done by the American Economic Association.

In 1978, Congress attempted to slam the "revolving door" that has been associated with the "regulator–regulatee" cycle but found it necessary to reopen the door at least a crack. The 1978 Ethics in Government Act barred former federal government employees from representing anyone before their former agencies on any matter that the employee had personally participated in while working for government, barred them from appearing before their agencies for two years on any matter that was under their formal authority, and barred all officials, GS–17 and above, from contacting their agencies on any matter for one year after leaving the government and from "assisting in representing" another person before their agency on matters dealt with as federal employees for two years. The Ethics Act was to become effective July 1, 1979; Congress amended it on June 15, 1979. Critics had charged that the law went too far, that it was encouraging a mass exodus of high-ranking federal employees prior to its effective date, and that it would discourage qualified individuals in the private sector from coming to work for the government. Whether the critics were right or not, Congress chose not to find out. The amended version of the act restricted the applicability of the "assisting in representing" to only those matters in which the individual had participated "personally and substantially," and reinterpreted it to prohibit only personal appearances before the agency[81]

THE PROSPECTS FOR REGULATORY REFORM

Regulation as it is currently conducted is under fire from all sides. Its substance, its procedures, its impact on the economy and traditional power relationships within the political system have been criticized by various interest groups and individuals. Regulation has become the focal point for those who are increasingly frustrated with the performance of the American economy and who believe, rightly or wrongly, that the government is responsible for its unsatisfactory performance. For many, regulation has been singled out as a scapegoat, a basic cause of the problems of the economy, which if removed will result in an immediate improvement in its performance. Similarly, those who believe that government must correct the inequities, the injustices, and the dangers to human health and safety that have been an integral part of industrialization have also become disenchanted with the results of government regulation.

Regulation is an intensely political process deeply concerned with the "authoritative allocation of values," real and symbolic. Regulatory reform is no less political. All proposals for regulatory reform are based on the reformer's perception of what is "wrong" with the current process and substance of regulation and what the reformer believes is the "right" way to regulate or the "right" regulatory result. Identify your preferences and countless reform proposals have already been developed which their authors believe will satisfy those preferences. What will actually happen in terms of actual changes, particularly long-term statutory changes, in regulation is unclear. For every "opponent" of regulation or regulatory procedures there is usually a proponent of that same regulation. Even at the peak of public interest and interest-group involvement in the area, regulatory reform is not a glamorous political issue likely to hold the enduring interests of the public or the media. Even directly and adversely affected interest groups have demonstrated ambivalent feelings about pursuing regulatory reform. Congress which must actually decide which, if any, of the reform proposals will be adopted is an overloaded institution and at least in the short run has far more pressing, visible, and politically rewarding or punishing issues to resolve than regulatory reform. Although the Senate did manage to pass a comprehensive regulatory reform act in 1982, the House, distracted by more pressing issues of budget cutting and increases, has yet to do so. Much sound and fury has already characterized Congress's most recent involvements in regulatory reform; ultimately they too may signify nothing.

The Supreme Court under Chief Justice Burger has clearly signaled its desire to opt out of the substantive issues of regulation. The presidency of Ronald Reagan may soon, too, tire of the conflicts and diminishing rewards of the regulatory reform policy arena. It is an area in which injuries are easily inflicted but in which rewards are uncertain. The Reagan administration has already experienced some of the more unpleasant side effects of intervening in complex regulatory issues that resulted from its attempt to invalidate Internal Revenue Service regulations denying tax-exempt statutes to educational institutions that discriminate on the basis of race. The attempt infuriated civil rights groups, liberals, and various other organizations that find racial discrimination repulsive and unconstitutional; the administration's post hoc arguments that the action was taken to protest the unauthorized exercise of rule-making power by an administrative agency convinced no one and subjected the administration to additional charges of ignorance, bigotry, and disregard of the law. Each further action taken to change the regulatory process will also alienate groups and individuals and the President may come to question the utility of such conflict and tension-increasing actions.

All of this does not mean that regulatory reform will not occur. What it does indicate is that sweeping and comprehensive reform with clear specific and stated goals will not be achieved. Instead, Congress will enact incremental substantive and procedural changes, Presidents will implement some relatively limited changes by executive orders, the agencies themselves will formally and informally modify their behavior, and the courts will continue to require modifications in the regulatory process on a case-by-case basis. The long-range impact of this kind of reform is likely to be extensive. Fortunately for practitioners, regulatees, regulators, consumers, workers, and the public, the short-range impact will be limited and will allow time for adjustment, reaction, and opportunity to work for reforms that they believe negatively affect them.

NOTES

1. Barry Mitnick, *The Political Economy of Regulation* (New York: Columbia University Press, 1980), pp. 418–19.

2. See Paul MacAvoy, *The Regulated Industries and the Economy* (New York: Norton, 1979), pp. 122–24; Murray Weidenbaum, *The Future of Business Regulation: Private Action and Public Demand* (New York: Amacom, 1980); and Lawrence White, *Reforming Regulation* (Englewood Cliffs, N.J. Prentice-Hall, 1981).

3. Randall Ripley and Grace Franklin, *Bureaucracy and Policy Implementation* (Homewood, Ill.: Dorsey Press, 1982), p. 124.

4. Ibid., p. 125.

5. Judy Sarasohn, "Intercity Buses May Become the Next Target for Deregulation," *Congressional Quarterly*, January 17, 1981, p. 143.

6. Ibid., p. 145.

7. Michael Wines, "Rhetoric and Reality," *National Journal*, October 10, 1981, p. 1824.

8. *Broadcasting*, January 19, 1981, p. 32.

9. Michael Wines, "Reagan's Reforms Are Full of Sound and Fury, but What Do They Signify?" *National Journal*, January 16, 1982, p. 94.

10. Michael Wines, "Experts Flash Caution Lights on AT&T, IBM Antitrust Settlements," *National Journal*, January 16, 1982

11. Lester Thurow, *The Zero Sum Society* (New York: Penguin, 1981), p. 127.

12. Wines, "Experts Flash Caution Lights on AT&T, IBM Antitrust Settlements," p. 125.

13. Alan Stone, "Economic Regulation, the Free Market, and Public Ownership," in James Anderson, ed., *Economic Regulatory Policies* (Lexington, Mass.: Lexington Books, 1976), p. 199.

14. See Harold Seidman, "Government Sponsored Enterprise in the United States," in Bruce L. R. Smith, ed., *The New Political Economy: The Public Use of the Private Sector* (New York: Wiley, 1975), pp. 83–108; Annmarie Hauck Walsh, *The Public's Business: The Politics and Practices of Government Corporations* (Cambridge: MIT Press, 1978); and Gordon Adams, "Public Ownership and Private Benefits," in Philip Brenner, Robert Borosage, and Methany Weidner, eds., *Exploring Contradictions: Political Economy in the Corporate State* (New York: David McKay, 1974), pp. 183–204.

15. Ralph Nader and Mark Green, "Federal Chartering and Corporate Accountability," in Brenner, Borosage, and Weidner, *Exploring Contradictions*, pp 169–82.

16. Thurow, *The Zero Sum Society*, p. 127.

17. Guy Benveniste, *Regulation and Planning: The Case of Environmental Politics* (San Francisco: Boyd Fraser, 1981) p. 163.

18. "Ax Is Honed For Federal Regulations," *Spokane Spokesman-Review*, August 13, 1981, p. 1.

19. Wines, "Reagan's Reforms Are Full of Sound and Fury, But What Do They Signify?" p. 97.

20. Michael Wines, "Listening on the Roof," *National Journal*, February 27, 1982, p. 82.

21. David Gottlieb, "Business Mobilizes as States Begin to Move into the Regulatory Vacuum," *National Journal*, July 31, 1982, p. 1340.

22. Ibid.

23. Ibid., p. 1342.

24. Weidenbaum, *The Future of Business Regulation*, p. 38.

25. *Energy Supply and Environmental Coordination Act of 1974*, PL 93–319, and *The Powerplant and Industrial Fuel Use Act of 1978*, PL 95–620.

26. Kathy Koch, "Pollutants from Coal Burning Plants... and the Spread of Acid Rainfall," *Congressional Quarterly*, May 31, 1980, pp. 1490–91.

27. See Mark Thompson, *Benefit-Cost Analysis for Program Evaluation* (Beverly Hills: Sage Publications, 1980), pp. 26ff.

28. See Victor Fuchs, *Who Shall Live? Health, Economics, and Social Choice* (New York: Basic Books, 1974), and E. J. Mishan, "Evaluation of Life and Limb: A Theoretical Approach," *Journal of Political Economy*, Fall 1971, pp. 687–705.

29. Michael Wines, "Automobile Bumper Standard Crumples as Cost-Benefit Analysis Falls Short," *National Journal*, January 23, 1982, pp. 145–49.

30. Wines, "Reagan's Reforms Are Full of Sound and Fury, but What Do They Signify?" p. 98.

31. Christopher DeMuth. "Constraining Regulatory Costs, Part Two: The Regulatory Budgets," *Regulation*, March/April 1980, pp. 29–44.

32. *Industrial Union Department, AFL-CIO v. American Petroleum Institute*, 448 U.S. 607 (1980).

33. MacAvoy, *The Regulated Industries and the Economy*, p. 122.

34. "Even Deregulation Can Mean More Regulation," *National Journal*, January 23, 1982, p. 166.

35. Charles Schultz, *The Public Use of Private Interest* (Washington, D.C.: Brookings Institution, 1977), p. 50.

36. Thurow, *The Zero Sum Society*, p. 152.

37. Schultz, *Public Use of Private Interest*, p. 83.

38. Murray Weidenbaum, *The Costs of Government Regulation of Business: Report to the Joint Economic Committee of Congress* (Washington, D.C.: Government Printing Office, 1978), p. 25.

39. See George S. Day, "Assessing the Effects of Information Disclosure Requirements," *Journal of Marketing*, 1976, p. 42, and David Aaker and George Day, eds., *Consumerism: Search For the Consumer Interest*, 2d ed. (New York: Free Press, 1974).

40. Jane Stein, "Warning about Salt—Will Voluntary Labelling Do the Job without a New Law?" *National Journal*, October 17, 1981, p. 1864.

41. Eugene Bardach and Robert A. Kogan. *Going by the Book: The Problem of Regulatory Unreasonableness* (Philadelphia: Temple University Press, 1982), p. 272.

42. Ibid., p. 273.

43. Ibid., p. 283.

44. Bruce C. N. Greenwald and Marnie Mueller, "Medical Malpractice and Medical Costs," in Simon Rottenberg, ed., *The Economics of Medical Malpractice (Washington, D.C.: American Enterprise Institute, 1978)*, p. 83.

45. See, for example, Stephen Sable, "A Proposal for the Administrative Compensation of Victims of Toxic Substance Pollution," *Harvard Journal of Legislation*, 14 (1977), 694–96.

46. Michael S. Baram et al., *Alternatives To Regulation* (Lexington, Mass.: Lexington Books, 1982), p. 23.

47. Harrison Donelly, "Reagan Changes Focus with Federalism Plan," *Congressional Quarterly*, January 30, 1982, pp. 147–54.

48. George E. Hale and Marian Lief Palley, *The Politics of Federal Grants* (Washington, D.C.: Congressional Quarterly Press, 1981), p. 167.

49. See Advisory Commission on Intergovernmental Relations, *The Federal Role in the Federal System: The Dynamics of Growth* (Washington, D.C.: ACIR, 1981).

50. Elizabeth Wehr, "Medicare, Medicaid Riddled by Fraud, Abuse, FBI Says," *Congressional Quarterly*, June 21, 1980, p. 1727.

51. Elizabeth Wehr, "House Approves Farm Bill," *Congressional Quarterly*, October 23, 1981, p. 2053.

52. U.S. Congress, Senate, Committee on Government Affairs, *Regulatory Reform Legislation: Hearings, Part 2* (Washington, D.C.: Government Printing Office, 1979), p. 132.

53. *Federal Regulatory Directory, 1981–82* (Washington, D.C.: Congressional Quarterly Press, 1981), p. 33.

54. See *The Status of Sunset in the States: A Common Cause Report* (Washington, D.C.: Common Cause, 1982).

55. Ibid.

56. Alan Stone, *Regulation and Its Alternatives* (Washington, D.C.: Congressional Quarterly Press, 1982), p. 273.

57. "Survey Shows Sunset Legislation Benefits," *Public Administration Times*, April 1, 1982, p. 8.

58. Diane Granati, "Scope of Regulatory Reform Bills Differ," *Congressional Quarterly*, April 3, 1982, p. 740.

59. 634 F2d 408; see also U.S. House vs INS; U.S. Senate vs INS, cert. granted, 454 U.S. 812 (1981).

60. —— F2d —— (D.C. Cir. 1982).

61. American Bar Association, Commission on Law and the Economy, *Federal Regulation: Roads to Reform* (Washington, D.C.: A.B.A., 1979), p. 548.

62. Lester M. Salamon, "Federal Regulation: A New Arena for Presidential Power," in Hugh Heclo and Lester Salamon, eds., *The Illusion of Presidential Government* (Boulder, Colo.: Westview Press, 1981), p. 160.

63. White, *Reforming Regulation*, p. 21.

64. Larry Weiss, "Reagan, Congress, Planning Regulatory Machinery Repair," *Congressional Quarterly*, March 7, 1981, p. 409.

65. Benveniste, *Regulation and Planning*, pp. 133–34.

66. *Inside OMB*, November 19, 1981, p. 8.

67. Weiss, "Reagan, Congress, Planning Regulatory Machinery Repair," p. 409.

68. Paul Verkuil, "The Emerging Concept of Administrative Procedure," 77 *Columbia Law Review* (1978), 321.

69. U.S. Congress, House, Committee on Interstate and Foreign Commerce, *Federal Regulation and Regulatory Reform* (Washington, D.C.: Government Printing Office, 1976), p. 554. See also Leonard Janofsky, "On the Roads to Regulatory Reforms," 66A—BA Journal (March 1980), 300.

70. *Inside OMB*, November 19, 1981, pp. 3–4.

71. U.S. Congress, Senate, Committee on Government Operations/Governmental Affairs, *Public Participation in Regulatory Agency Proceedings*, vol. 3 (Washington, D.C.: GPO, 1977).

72. *Federal Regulatory Directory*, p. 40.

73. Granati, "Scope of Regulatory Reform Bills Differ," p. 741.

74. Weidenbaum, *The Future of Business Regulation*, pp. 8, 140, 149.

75. Verkuil, *"The Emerging Concept of Administrative Procedure," p. 258; Fred Friendly, "Some Kind of Hearing," 123 University of Pennsylvania Law Review* (1975), 1267.

76. Kenneth Davis, *Administrative Law: Cases–Texts–Problems* (St. Paul, Minn.: West Publishing Co., 1977), p. 514.

77. U.S. Congress, Senate, Commerce Committee, J. Grahan and V. Kramer, *Appointments to the Regulatory Agencies: The FCC and the FTC (1949–74)* (Washington, D.C.: GPO, 1976).

78. For the former view see Janofsky, "On the Roads to Regulatory Reform," and for the latter, *Federal Regulation and Regulatory Reform*, chapter 12.

79. Paul Quirk, *Industry Influence in Federal Regulatory Agencies* (Princeton, N.J.: Princeton University Press, 1981), p. 18.

80. Ernest Gellhorn and Robert Frier, "Assuring Competence in Federal Agency Appointments," 65 *ABA Journal* (February 1979), 218.

81. Larry Light, "Congress Clears Bill To Soften Restrictions on Post-Government Jobs," *Congressional Quarterly*, June 23, 1979, p. 1246.

APPENDIX I

Administrative Procedure Act

P.L. 404, 60 Stat. 237 (1946), as amended through
96th Congress, First Session (1979).
5 U.S.C.A. §§551–559, 701–706, 1305, 3105, 3344, 5372, 7521.

Table of Sections

Sec.

551. Definitions.
552. Public Information; Agency Rules, Opinions, Orders, Records, and Proceedings.
552a. Records Maintained on Individuals.
552b. Open Meetings.
553. Rule Making.
554. Adjudications.
555. Ancillary Matters.
556. Hearings; Presiding Employees; Powers and Duties; Burden of Proof; Evidence; Record as Basis of Decision.
557. Initial Decisions; Conclusiveness; Review by Agency; Submissions by Parties; Contents of Decisions; Record.
558. Imposition of Sanctions; Determination of Applications for Licenses; Suspension, Revocation, and Expiration of Licenses.
559. Effect on Other Laws; Effect of Subsequent Statute.

§551. Definitions

For the purpose of this subchapter—

(1) "agency" means each authority of the Government of the United States, whether or not it is within or subject to review by another agency, but does not include—

(A) the Congress;

(B) the courts of the United States;

(C) the governments of the territories or possessions of the United States;

(D) the government of the District of Columbia;

or except as to the requirements of section 552 of this title—

(E) agencies composed of representatives of the parties or of representatives of organizations of the parties to the disputes determined by them;

(F) courts martial and military commissions;

(G) military authority exercised in the field in time of war or in occupied territory; or

(H) functions conferred by sections 1738, 1739, 1743, and 1744 of title 12; chapter 2 of title 41; or sections 1622, 1884, 1891–1902, and former section 1641(b)(2), of title 50, appendix;

(2) "person" includes an individual, partnership, corporation, association, or public or private organization other than an agency;

(3) "party" includes a person or agency named or admitted as a party, or properly seeking and entitled as of right to be admitted as a party, in an agency proceeding, and a person or agency admitted by an agency as a party for limited purposes;

(4) "rule" means the whole or a part of an agency statement of general or particular applicability and future effect designed to implement, interpret, or prescribe law or policy or describing the organization, procedure, or practice requirements of an agency and includes the approval or prescription for the future of rates, wages, corporate or financial structures or reorganizations thereof, prices, facilities, appliances, services or allowances therefor or of valuations, costs, or accounting, or practices bearing on any of the foregoing;

(5) "rule making" means agency process for formulating, amending, or repealing a rule;

(6) "order" means the whole or a part of a final dispostion, whether affirmative, negative, injunctive, or declaratory in form, of an agency in a matter other than rule making but including licensing;

(7) "adjudication" means agency process for the formulation of an order;

(8) "license" includes the whole or a part of an agency permit, certificate, approval, registration, charter, membership, statutory exemption or other form of permission;

(9) "licensing" includes agency process respecting the grant, renewal, denial, revocation, suspension, annulment, withdrawal, limitation, amendment, modification, or conditioning of a license;

(10) "sanction" includes the whole or a part of an agency—

(A) prohibition, requirement, limitation, or other condition affecting the freedom of a person;

(B) withholding of relief;

(C) imposition of penalty or fine;

(D) destruction, taking, seizure, or withholding of property;

(E) assessment of damages, reimbursement, restitution, compensation, costs, charges, or fees;

(F) requirement, revocation, or suspension of a license; or

(G) taking other compulsory or restrictive action;

(11) "relief" includes the whole or a part of an agency—

(A) grant of money, assistance, license, authority, exemption, exception, privilege, or remedy;

(B) recognition of a claim, right, immunity, privilege, exemption, or exception; or

(C) taking of other action on the application or petition of, and beneficial to, a person;

(12) "agency proceeding" means an agency process as defined by paragraphs (5), (7), and (9) of this section;

(13) "agency action" includes the whole or a part of an agency rule, order, license, sanction, relief, or the equivalent or denial thereof, or failure to act; and

(14) "ex parte communication" means an oral or written communication not on the public record with respect to which reasonable prior notice to all parties is not given, but it shall not include requests for status reports on any matter or proceeding covered by this subchapter.

§552. Public Information; Agency Rules, Opinions, Orders, Records, and Proceedings

(a) Each agency shall make available to the public information as follows:

(1) Each agency shall separately state and currently publish in the Federal Register for the

guidance of the public—

(A) descriptions of its central and field organization and the established places at which, the employees (and in the case of a uniformed service, the members) from whom, and the methods whereby, the public may obtain information, make submittals or requests, or obtain decisions;

(B) statements of the general course and method by which its functions are channeled and determined, including the nature and requirements of all formal and informal procedures available;

(C) rules of procedure, descriptions of forms available or the places at which forms may be obtained, and instructions as to the scope and contents of all papers, reports, or examinations;

(D) substantive rules of general applicability adopted as authorized by law, and statements of general policy or interpretations of general applicability formulated and adopted by the agency; and

(E) each amendment, revision, or repeal of the foregoing.

Except to the extent that a person has actual and timely notice of the terms thereof, a person may not in any manner be required to resort to, or be adversely affected by, a matter required to be published in the Federal Register and not so published. For the purpose of this paragraph, matter reasonably available to the class of persons affected thereby is deemed published in the Federal Register when incorporated by reference therein with the approval of the Director of the Federal Register.

(2) Each agency, in accordance with published rules, shall make available for public inspection and copying—

(A) final opinions, including concurring and dissenting opinions, as well as orders, made in the adjudication of cases;

(B) those statements of policy and interpretations which have been adopted by the agency and are not published in the Federal Register; and

(C) administrative staff manuals and instructions to staff that affect a member of the public; unless the materials are promptly published and copies offered for sale. To the extent required to prevent a clearly unwarranted invasion of personal privacy, an agency may delete identifying details when it makes available or publishes an opinion, statement of policy, interpretation, or staff manual or instruction. However, in each case the justification for the deletion shall be explained fully in writing. Each agency shall also maintain and make available for public inspection and copying current indexes providing identifying information for the public as to any matter issued, adopted, or promulgated after July 4, 1967, and required by this paragraph to be made available or published. Each agency shall promptly publish, quarterly or more frequently, and distribute (by sale or otherwise) copies of each index or supplements thereto unless it determines by order published in the Federal Register that the publication would be unnecessary and impracticable, in which case the agency shall nonetheless provide copies of such index on request at a cost not to exceed the direct cost of duplication. A final order, opinion, statement of policy, interpretation, or staff manual or instruction that affects a member of the public may be relied on, used, or cited as precedent by an agency against a party other than an agency only if—

(i) it has been indexed and either made available or published as provided by this paragraph; or (ii) the party has actual and timely notice of the terms thereof.

(3) Except with respect to the records made available under paragraphs (1) and (2) of this subsection, each agency, upon any request for records which (A) reasonably describes such records and (B) is made in accordance with published rules stating the time, place, fees (if any), and procedures to be followed, shall make the records promptly available to any person.

(4)(A) In order to carry out the provisions of this section, each agency shall promulgate regulations, pursuant to notice and receipt of public comment, specifying a uniform schedule of fees applicable to all constituent units of such agency. Such fees shall be limited to reasonable standard charges for document search and duplication and provide for recovery of only the direct costs of such search and duplication. Documents shall be furnished without charge or at a reduced charge where the agency determines that waiver or reduction of the fee is in the public interest because furnishing the information can be considered as primarily benefiting the general public.

(B) On complaint, the district court of the United States in the district in which the complainant resides, or has his principal place of business, or in which the agency records are situated, or in the District of Columbia, has jurisdiction to enjoin the agency from withholding agency records and to order the production of any agency records improperly withheld from the complainant. In such a case the court shall determine the matter de novo, and may examine the contents of such agency records in camera to determine whether such records or any part thereof shall be withheld under any of the exemptions set forth in subsection (b) of this section, and the burden is on the agency to sustain its action.

(C) Notwithstanding any other provision of law, the defendant shall serve an answer or otherwise plead to any complaint made under this subsection within thirty days after service upon the defendant of the pleading in which such complaint is made, unless the court otherwise directs for good cause shown.

(D) Except as to cases the court considers of greater importance, proceedings before the district court, as authorized by this subsection, and appeals therefrom, take precedence on the docket over all cases and shall be assigned for hearing and trial or for argument at the earliest practicable date and expedited in every way.

(E) The court may assess against the United States reasonable attorney fees and other litigation costs reasonably incurred in any case under this section in which the complainant has substantially prevailed.

(F) Whenever the court orders the production of any agency records improperly withheld from the complainant and assesses against the United States reasonable attorney fees and other litigation costs, and the court additionally issues a written finding that the circumstances surrounding the withholding raise questions whether agency personnel acted arbitrarily or capriciously with respect to the withholding, the Special Counsel shall promptly initiate a proceeding to determine whether disciplinary action is warranted against the officer or employee who was primarily responsible for the withholding. The Special Counsel, after investigation and consideration of the evidence submitted, shall submit his findings and recommendations to the administrative authority of the agency concerned and shall send copies of the findings and recommendations to the officer or employee or his representative. The administrative authority shall take the corrective action that the Special Counsel recommends.

(G) In the event of noncompliance with the order of the court, the district court may punish for contempt the responsible employee, and in the case of a uniformed service, the responsible member.

(5) Each agency having more than one member shall maintain and make available for public inspection a record of the final votes of each member in every agency proceeding.

(6)(A) Each agency, upon any request for records made under paragraph (1), (2), or (3) of this subsection, shall—

(i) determine within ten days (excepting Saturdays, Sundays, and legal public holidays) after the receipt of any such request whether to comply with such request and shall immediately notify the person making such request of such determination and the reasons therefor, and of the right of such person to appeal to the head of the agency any adverse determination; and

(ii) make a determination with respect to any appeal within twenty days (excepting Saturdays, Sundays, and legal public holidays) after the receipt of such appeal. If on appeal the denial of the request for records is in whole or in part upheld, the agency shall notify the person making such request of the provisions for judicial review of that determination under paragraph (4) of this subsection.

(B) In unusual circumstances as specified in this subparagraph, the time limits prescribed in either clause (i) or clause (ii) of subparagraph (A) may be extended by written notice to the person making such request setting forth the reasons for such extension and the date on which a determination is expected to be dispatched. No such notice shall specify a date that would result in an extension for more than ten working days. As used in this subparagraph, "unusual circumstances" means, but only to the extent reasonably necessary to the proper processing of the particular request—

(i) the need to search for and collect the requested records from field facilities or other establishments that are separate from the office processing the request;

(ii) the need to search for, collect, and appropriately examine a voluminous amount of separate and distinct records which are demanded in a single request; or

(iii) the need for consultation, which shall be conducted with all practicable speed, with another agency having a substantial interest in the determination of the request or among two or more components of the agency having substantial subject-matter interest therein.

(C) Any person making a request to any agency for records under paragraph (1), (2), or (3) of this subsection shall be deemed to have exhausted his administrative remedies with respect to such request if the agency fails to comply with the applicable time limit provisions of this paragraph. If the Government can show exceptional circumstances exist and that the agency is exercising due diligence in responding to the request, the court may retain jurisdiction and allow the agency additional time to complete its review of the records. Upon any determination by an agency to comply with a request for records, the records shall be made promptly available to such person making such request. Any notification of denial of any request for records under this subsection shall set forth the names and titles or positions of each person responsible for the denial of such request.

(b) This section does not apply to matters that are—

(1)(A) specifically authorized under criteria established by an Executive order to be kept secret in the interest of national defense or foreign policy and (B) are in fact properly classified pursuant to such Executive order;

(2) related solely to the internal personnel rules and practices of an agency;

(3) specifically exempted from disclosure by statute (other than section 552b of this title), provided that such statute (A) requires that the matters be withheld from the public in such a manner as to leave no discretion on the issue, or (B) establishes particular criteria for withholding or refers to particular types of matters to be withheld;

(4) trade secrets and commercial or financial information obtained from a person and privileged or confidential;

(5) inter-agency or intra-agency memorandums or letters which would not be available by law to a party other than an agency in litigation with the agency;

(6) personnel and medical files and similar files the disclosure of which would constitute a clearly unwarranted invasion of personal privacy;

(7) investigatory records compiled for law enforcement purposes, but only to the extent that the production of such records would (A) interfere with enforcement proceedings, (B) deprive a person of a right to a fair trial or an impartial adjudication, (C) constitute an unwarranted invasion of personal privacy, (D) disclose the identity of a confidential source and, in the case of a record compiled by a criminal law enforcement authority in the course of a criminal investigation, or by an agency conducting a lawful national security intelligence investigation, confidential information furnished only by the confidential source, (E) disclose investigative

techniques and procedures, or (F) endanger the life or physical safety of law enforcement personnel;

(8) contained in or related to examination, operating, or condition reports prepared by, on behalf of, or for the use of an agency responsible for the regulation or supervision of financial institutions; or

(9) geological and geophysical information and data, including maps, concerning wells.
Any reasonably segregable portion of a record shall be provided to any person requesting such record after deletion of the portions which are exempt under this subsection.

(c) This section does not authorize withholding of information or limit the availability of records to the public, except as specifically stated in this section. This section is not authority to withhold information from Congress.

(d) On or before March 1 of each calendar year, each agency shall submit a report covering the preceding calendar year to the Speaker of the House Representatives and President of the Senate for referral to the appropriate committees of the Congress. The report shall include—

(1) the number of determinations made by such agency not to comply with requests for records made to such agency under subsection (a) and the reasons for each such determination;

(2) the number of appeals made by persons under subsection (a)(6), the result of such appeals, and the reason for the action upon each appeal that results in a denial of information;

(3) the names and titles or positions of each person responsible for the denial of records requested under this section, and the number of instances of participation for each;

(4) the results of each proceeding conducted pursuant to subsection (a)(4)(F), including a report of the disciplinary action taken against the officer or employee who was primarily responsible for improperly withholding records or an explanation of why disciplinary action was not taken;

(5) a copy of every rule made by such agency regarding this section;

(6) a copy of the fee schedule and the total amount of fees collected by the agency for making records available under this section; and

(7) such other information as indicates efforts to administer fully this section.
The Attorney General shall submit an annual report on or before March 1 of each calendar year which shall include for the prior calendar year a listing of the number of cases arising under this section, the exemption involved in each case, the disposition of such case, and the cost, fees, and penalties assessed under subsections (a)(4)(E), (F), and (G). Such report shall also include a description of the efforts undertaken by the Department of Justice to encourage agency compliance with this section.

(e) For purposes of this section, the term "agency" as defined in section 551(1) of this title includes any executive department, military department, Government corporation, Government controlled corporation, or other establishment in the executive branch of the Government (including the Executive Office of the President), or any independent regulatory agency.

§552a. Records Maintained on Individuals

(a) **Definitions.** For purposes of this section—

(1) the term "agency" means agency as defined in section 552(e) of this title;

(2) the term "individual" means a citizen of the United States or an alien lawfully admitted for permanent residence;

(3) the term "maintain" includes maintain, collect, use, or disseminate;

(4) the term "record" means any item, collection, or grouping of information about an individual that is maintained by an agency, including, but not limited to, his education, financial transactions, medical history, and criminal or employment history and that contains his name,

or the identifying number, symbol, or other identifying particular assigned to the individual, such as a finger or voice print or a photograph;

(5) the term "system of records" means a group of any records under the control of any agency from which information is retrieved by the name of the individual or by some identifying number, symbol, or other identifying particular assigned to the individual;

(6) the term "statistical record" means a record in a system of records maintained for statistical research or reporting purposes only and not used in whole or in part in making any determination about an identifiable individual, except as provided by section 8 of title 13; and

(7) the term "routine use" means, with respect to the disclosure of a record, the use of such record for a purpose which is compatible with the purpose for which it was collected.

(b) **Conditions of disclosure.** No agency shall disclose any record which is contained in a system of records by any means of communication to any person, or to another agency, except pursuant to a written request by, or with the prior written consent of, the individual to whom the record pertains, unless disclosure of the record would be—

(1) to those officers and employees of the agency which maintains the record who have a need for the record in the performance of their duties;

(2) required under section 552 of this title;

(3) for a routine use as defined in subsection (a)(7) of this section and described under subsection (e)(4)(D) of this section;

(4) to the Bureau of the Census for purposes of planning or carrying out a census or survey or related activity pursuant to the provisions of title 13;

(5) to a recipient who has provided the agency with advance adequate written assurance that the record will be used solely as a statistical research or reporting record, and the record is to be transferred in a form that is not individually identifiable;

(6) to the National Archives of the United States as a record which has sufficient historical or other value to warrant its continued preservation by the United States Government, or for evaluation by the Administrator of General Services or his designee to determine whether the record has such value;

(7) to another agency or to an instrumentality of any governmental jurisdiction within or under the control of the United States for a civil or criminal law enforcement activity if the activity is authorized by law, and if the head of the agency or instrumentality has made a written request to the agency which maintains the record specifying the particular portion desired and the law enforcement activity for which the record is sought;

(8) to a person pursuant to a showing of compelling circumstances affecting the health or safety of an individual if upon such disclosure notification is transmitted to the last known address of such individual;

(9) to either House of Congress, or, to the extent of matter within its jurisdiction, any committee or subcommittee thereof, any joint committee of Congress or subcommittee of any such joint committee;

(10) to the Comptroller General, or any of his authorized representatives, in the course of the performance of the duties of the General Accounting Office; or

(11) pursuant to the order of a court of competent jurisdiction.

(c) **Accounting of certain disclosures.** Each agency, with respect to each system of records under its control, shall—

(1) except for disclosures made under subsections (b)(1) or (b)(2) of this section, keep an accurate accounting of—

(A) the date, nature, and purpose of each disclosure of a record to any person or to another agency made under subsection (b) of this section; and

(B) the name and address of the person or agency to whom the disclosure is made;

(2) retain the accounting made under paragraph (1) of this subsection for at least five years or the life of the record, whichever is longer, after the disclosure for which the accounting is made;

(3) except for disclosures made under subsection (b)(7) of this section, make the accounting made under paragraph (1) of this subsection available to the individual named in the record at his request; and

(4) inform any person or other agency about any correction or notation of dispute made by the agency in accordance with subsection (d) of this section of any record that has been disclosed to the person or agency if an accounting of the disclosure was made.

(d) Access to records. Each agency that maintains a system of records shall—

(1) upon request by any individual to gain access to his record or to any information pertaining to him which is contained in the system, permit him and upon his request, a person of his own choosing to accompany him, to review the record and have a copy made of all or any portion thereof in a form comprehensible to him, except that the agency may require the individual to furnish a written statement authorizing discussion of that individual's record in the accompanying person's presence;

(2) permit the individual to request amendment of a record pertaining to him and—

(A) not later than 10 days (excluding Saturdays, Sundays, and legal public holidays) after the date of receipt of such request, acknowledge in writing such receipt; and

(B) promptly, either—

(i) make any correction of any portion thereof which the individual believes is not accurate, relevant, timely, or complete; or

(ii) inform the individual of its refusal to amend the record in accordance with his request, the reason for the refusal, the procedures established by the agency for the individual to request a review of that refusal by the head of the agency or an officer designated by the head of the agency, and the name and business address of that official;

(3) permit the individual who disagrees with the refusal of the agency to amend his record to request a review of such refusal, and not later than 30 days (excluding Saturdays, Sundays, and legal public holidays) from the date on which the individual requests such review, complete such review and make a final determination unless, for good cause shown, the head of the agency extends such 30-day period; and if, after his review, the reviewing official also refuses to amend the record in accordance with the request, permit the individual to file with the agency a concise statement setting forth the reasons for his disagreement with the refusal of the agency, and notify the individual of the provisions for judicial review of the reviewing official's determination under subsection (g)(1)(A) of this section;

(4) in any disclosure, containing information about which the individual has filed a statement of disagreement, occurring after the filing of the statement under paragraph (3) of this subsection, clearly note any portion of the record which is disputed and provide copies of the statement and, if the agency deems it appropriate, copies of a concise statement of the reasons of the agency for not making the amendments requested, to persons or other agencies to whom the disputed record has been disclosed; and

(5) nothing in this section shall allow an individual access to any information compiled in reasonable anticipation of a civil action or proceeding.

(e) Agency requirements. Each agency that maintains a system of records shall—

(1) maintain in its records only such information about an individual as is relevant and necessary to accomplish a purpose of the agency required to be accomplished by statute or by executive order of the President;

(2) collect information to the greatest extent practicable directly from the subject individual when the information may result in adverse determinations about an individual's rights, benefits, and privileges under Federal programs;

(3) inform each individual whom it asks to supply information, on the form which it uses to collect the information or on a separate form that can be retained by the individual—

(A) the authority (whether granted by statute, or by executive order of the President) which authorizes the solicitation of the information and whether disclosure of such information is mandatory or voluntary;

(B) the principal purpose or purposes for which the information is intended to be used;

(C) the routine uses which may be made of the information, as published pursuant to paragraph (4)(D) of this subsection; and

(D) the effects on him, if any, of not providing all or any part of the requested information;

(4) subject to the provisions of paragraph (11) of this subsection, publish in the Federal Register at least annually a notice of the existence and character of the system of records, which notice shall include—

(A) the name and location of the system;

(B) the categories of individuals on whom records are maintained in the system;

(C) the categories of records maintained in the system;

(D) each routine use of the records contained in the system, including the categories of users and the purpose of such use;

(E) the policies and practices of the agency regarding storage, retrievability, access controls, retention, and disposal of the records;

(F) the title and business address of the agency official who is responsible for the system of records;

(G) the agency procedures whereby an individual can be notified at his request if the system of records contains a record pertaining to him;

(H) the agency procedures whereby an individual can be notified at his request how he can gain access to any record pertaining to him contained in the system of records, and how he can contest its content; and

(I) the categories of sources of records in the system;

(5) maintain all records which are used by the agency in making any determination about any individual with such accuracy, relevance, timeliness, and completeness as is reasonably necessary to assure fairness to the individual in the determination;

(6) prior to disseminating any record about an individual to any person other than an agency, unless the dissemination is made pursuant to subsection (b)(2) of this section, make reasonable efforts to assure that such records are accurate, complete, timely, and relevant for agency purposes;

(7) maintain no record describing how any individual exercises rights guaranteed by the First Amendment unless expressly authorized by statute or by the individual about whom the record is maintained or unless pertinent to and within the scope of an authorized law enforcement activity;

(8) make reasonable efforts to serve notice on an individual when any record on such individual is made available to any person under compulsory legal process when such process becomes a matter of public record;

(9) establish rules of conduct for persons involved in the design, development, operation, or maintenance of any system of records, or in maintaining any record, and instruct each such person with respect to such rules and the requirements of this section, including any other rules and procedures adopted pursuant to this section and the penalties for noncompliance;

(10) establish appropriate administrative, technical, and physical safeguards to insure the

security and confidentiality of records and to protect against any anticipated threats or hazards to their security or integrity which could result in substantial harm, embarrassment, inconvenience, or unfairness to any individual on whom information is maintained; and

(11) at least 30 days prior to publication of information under paragraph (4)(D) of this subsection, publish in the Federal Register notice of any new use or intended use of the information in the system, and provide an opportunity for interested persons to submit written data, views, or arguments to the agency.

(f) **Agency rules.** In order to carry out the provisions of this section, each agency that maintains a system of records shall promulgate rules, in accordance with the requirements (including general notice) of section 553 of this title, which shall—

(1) establish procedures whereby an individual can be notified in response to his request if any system of records named by the individual contains a record pertaining to him;

(2) define reasonable times, places, and requirements for identifying an individual who requests his record or information pertaining to him before the agency shall make the record or information available to the individual;

(3) establish procedures for the disclosure to an individual upon his request of his record or information pertaining to him, including special procedure, if deemed necessary, for the disclosure to an individual of medical records, including psychological records, pertaining to him;

(4) establish procedures for reviewing a request from an individual concerning the amendment of any record or information pertaining to the individual, for making a determination on the request, for an appeal within the agency of an initial adverse agency determination, and for whatever additional means may be necessary for each individual to be able to exercise fully his rights under this section; and

(5) establish fees to be charged, if any, to any individual for making copies of his record, excluding the cost of any search for and review of the record.

The Office of the Federal Register shall annually compile and publish the rules promulgated under this subsection and agency notices published under subsection (e)(4) of this section in a form available to the public at low cost.

(g)(1) **Civil remedies.** Whenever any agency

(A) makes a determination under subsection (d)(3) of this section not to amend an individual's record in accordance with his request, or fails to make such review in conformity with that subsection;

(B) refuses to comply with an individual request under subsection (d)(1) of this section;

(C) fails to maintain any record concerning any individual with such accuracy, relevance, timeliness, and completeness as is necessary to assure fairness in any determination relating to the qualifications, character, rights, or opportunities of, or benefits to the individual that may be made on the basis of such record, and consequently a determination is made which is adverse to the individual; or

(D) fails to comply with any other provision of this section, or any rule promulgated thereunder, in such a way as to have an adverse effect on an individual, the individual may bring a civil action against the agency, and the district courts of the United States shall have jurisdiction in the matters under the provisions of this subsection.

(2)(A) In any suit brought under the provisions of subsection (g)(1)(A) of this section, the court may order the agency to amend the individual's record in accordance with his request or in such other way as the court may direct. In such a case the court shall determine the matter de novo.

(B) The court may assess against the United States reasonable attorney fees and other litigation costs reasonably incurred in any case under this paragraph in which the complainant has substantially prevailed.

(3)(A) In any suit brought under the provisions of subsection (g)(1)(B) of this section, the court may enjoin the agency from withholding the records and order the production to the complainant of any agency records improperly withheld from him. In such a case the court shall determine the matter de novo, and may examine the contents of any agency records in camera to determine whether the records or any portion thereof may be withheld under any of the exemptions set forth in subsection (k) of this section, and the burden is on the agency to sustain its action.

(B) The court may assess against the United States reasonable attorney fees and other litigation costs reasonably incurred in any case under this paragraph in which the complainant has substantially prevailed.

(4) In any suit brought under the provisions of subsection (g)(1)(C) or (D) of this section in which the court determines·that the agency acted in a manner which was intentional or willful, the United States shall be liable to the individual in an amount equal to the sum of—

(A) actual damages sustained by the individual as a result of the refusal or failure, but in no case shall a person entitled to recovery receive less than the sum of $1,000; and

(B) the costs of the action together with reasonable attorney fees as determined by the court.

(5) An action to enforce any liability created under this section may be brought in the district court of the United States in the district in which the complainant resides, or has his principal place of business, or in which the agency records are situated, or in the District of Columbia, without regard to the amount in controversy, within two years from the date on which the cause of action arises, except that where an agency has materially and willfully misrepresented any information required under this section to be disclosed to an individual and the information so misrepresented is material to establishment of the liability of the agency to the individual under this section, the action may be brought at any time within two years after discovery by the individual of the misrepresentation. Nothing in this section shall be construed to authorize any civil action by reason of any injury sustained as the result of a disclosure of a record prior to September 27, 1975.

(h) **Rights of legal guardians.** For the purposes of this section, the parent of any minor, or the legal guardian of any individual who has been declared to be incompetent due to physical or mental incapacity or age by a court of competent jurisdiction, may act on behalf of the individual.

(i)(1) **Criminal penalties.** Any officer or employee of an agency, who by virtue of his employment or official position, has possession of, or access to, agency records which contain individually identifiable information the disclosure of which is prohibited by this section or by rules or regulations established thereunder, and who knowing that disclosure of the specific material is so prohibited, willfully discloses the material in any manner to any person or agency not entitled to receive it, shall be guilty of a misdemeanor and fined not more than $5,000.

(2) Any officer or employee of any agency who willfully maintains a system of records without meeting the notice requirements of subsection (e)(4) of this section shall be guilty of a misdemeanor and fined not more than $5,000.

(3) Any person who knowingly and willfully requests or obtains any record concerning an individual from an agency under false pretenses shall be guilty of a misdemeanor and fined not more than $5,000.

(j) **General exemptions.** The head of any agency may promulgate rules, in accordance with the requirements (including general notice) of sections 553(b)(1), (2), and (3), (c), and (e) of this title, to exempt any system of records within the agency from any part of this section except subsections (b), (c)(1) and (2), (e)(4)(A) through (F), (e)(6), (7), (9), (10), and (11), and (i) if the system of records is—

(1) maintained by the Central Intelligence Agency; or

(2) maintained by an agency or component thereof which performs as its principal function any activity pertaining to the enforcement of criminal laws, including police efforts to prevent, control, or reduce crime or to apprehend criminals, and the activities of prosecutors, courts, correctional, probation, pardon, or parole authorities, and which consists of (A) information compiled for the purpose of identifying individual criminal offenders and alleged offenders and consisting only of identifying data and notations of arrests, the nature and disposition of criminal charges, sentencing, confinement, release, and parole and probation status; (B) information compiled for the purpose of a criminal investigation, including reports of informants and investigators, and associated with an identifiable individual; or (C) reports identifiable to an individual compiled at any stage of the process of enforcement of the criminal laws from arrest or indictment through release from supervision.

At the time rules are adopted under this subsection, the agency shall include in the statement required under section 553(c) of this title, the reasons why the system of records is to be exempted from a provision of this section.

(k) **Specific exemptions.** The head of any agency may promulgate rules, in accordance with the requirements (including general notice) of sections 553(b)(1), (2), and (3), (c), and (e) of this title, to exempt any system of records within the agency from subsections (c)(3), (d), (e)(1), (e)(4)(G), (H), and (I) and (f) of this section if the system of records is—

(1) subject to the provisions of section 552(b)(1) of this title;

(2) investigatory material compiled for law enforcement purposes, other than material within the scope of subsection (j)(2) of this section: *Provided, however,* That if any individual is denied any right, privilege, or benefit that he would otherwise be entitled by Federal law, or for which he would otherwise be eligible, as a result of the maintenance of such material, such material shall be provided to such individual, except to the extent that the disclosure of such material would reveal the identity of a source who furnished information to the Government under an express promise that the identity of the source would be held in confidence, or, prior to the effective date of this section, under an implied promise that the identity of the source would be held in confidence;

(3) maintained in connection with providing protective services to the President of the United States or other individuals pursuant to section 3056 of title 18;

(4) required by statute to be maintained and used solely as statistical records;

(5) investigatory material compiled solely for the purpose of determining suitability, eligibility, or qualifications for Federal civilian employment, military service, Federal contracts, or access to classified information, but only to the extent that the disclosure of such material would reveal the identity of a source who furnished information to the Government under an express promise that the identity of the source would be held in confidence, or, prior to the effective date of this section, under an implied promise that the identity of the source would be held in confidence;

(6) testing or examination material used solely to determine individual qualifications for appointment or promotion in the Federal service the disclosure of which would compromise the objectivity or fairness of the testing or examination process; or

(7) evaluation material used to determine potential for promotion in the armed services, but only to the extent that the disclosure of such material would reveal the identity of a source who furnished information to the Government under an express promise that the identity of the source would be held in confidence, or, prior to the effective date of this section, under an implied promise that the identity of the source would be held in confidence.

At the time rules are adopted under this subsection, the agency shall include in the statement required under section 553(c) of this title, the reasons why the system of records is to be exempted from a provision of this section.

(l)(1) **Archival records.** Each agency record which is accepted by the Administrator of General Services for storage, processing, and servicing in accordance with section 3103 of title 44 shall, for the purposes of this section, be considered to be maintained by the agency which deposited the record and shall be subject to the provisions of this section. The Administrator of General Services shall not disclose the record except to the agency which maintains the record, or under rules established by that agency which are not inconsistent with the provisions of this section.

(2) Each agency record pertaining to an identifiable individual which was transferred to the National Archives of the United States as a record which has sufficient historical or other value to warrant its continued preservation by the United States Government, prior to the effective date of this section, shall, for the purposes of this section, be considered to be maintained by the National Archives and shall not be subject to the provisions of this section, except that a statement generally describing such records (modeled after the requirements relating to records subject to subsections (e)(4)(A) through (G) of this section) shall be published in the Federal Register.

(3) Each agency record pertaining to an identifiable individual which is transferred to the National Archives of the United States as a record which has sufficient historical or other value to warrant its continued preservation by the United States Government, on or after the effective date of this section, shall, for the purposes of this section, be considered to be maintained by the National Archives and shall be exempt from the requirements of this section except subsections (e)(4)(A) through (G) and (e)(9) of this section.

(m) **Government contractors.** When an agency provides by a contract for the operation by or on behalf of the agency of a system of records to accomplish an agency function, the agency shall, consistent with its authority, cause the requirements of this section to be applied to such system. For purposes of subsection (i) of this section any such contractor and any employee of such contractor, if such contract is agreed to on or after the effective date of this section, shall be considered to be an employee of an agency.

(n) **Mailing lists.** An individual's name and address may not be sold or rented by an agency unless such action is specifically authorized by law. This provision shall not be construed to require the withholding of names and addresses otherwise permitted to be made public.

(o) **Report on new systems.** Each agency shall provide adequate advance notice to Congress and the Office of Management and Budget of any proposal to establish or alter any system of records in order to permit an evaluation of the probable or potential effect of such proposal on the privacy and other personal or property rights of individuals or the disclosure of information relating to such individuals, and its effect on the preservation of the constitutional principles of federalism and separation of powers.

(p) **Annual report.** The President shall submit to the Speaker of the House and the President of the Senate, by June 30 of each calendar year, a consolidated report, separately listing for each Federal agency the number of records contained in any system of records which were exempted from the application of this section under the provisions of subsections (j) and (k) of this section during the preceding calendar year, and the reasons for the exemptions, and such other information as indicates efforts to administer fully this section.

(q) **Effect of other laws.** No agency shall rely on any exemption contained in section 552 of this title to withhold from an individual any record which is otherwise accessible to such individual under the provisions of this section.

§552b. Open Meetings

(a) For purposes of this section—

(1) the term "agency" means any agency, as defined in section 552(e) of this title, headed by a collegial body composed of two or more individual members, a majority of whom are appointed to such position by the President with the advice and consent of the Senate, and any subdivision thereof authorized to act on behalf of the agency;

(2) the term "meeting" means the deliberations of at least the number of individual agency members required to take action on behalf of the agency where such deliberations determine or result in the joint conduct or disposition of official agency business, but does not include deliberations required or permitted by subsection (d) or (e); and

(3) the term "member" means an individual who belongs to a collegial body heading an agency.

(b) Members shall not jointly conduct or dispose of agency business other than in accordance with this section. Except as provided in subsection (c), every portion of every meeting of an agency shall be open to public observation.

(c) Except in a case where the agency finds that the public interest requires otherwise, the second sentence of subsection (b) shall not apply to any portion of an agency meeting, and the requirements of subsections (d) and (e) shall not apply to any information pertaining to such meeting otherwise required by this section to be disclosed to the public, where the agency properly determines that such portion or portions of its meeting or the disclosure of such information is likely to—

(1) disclose matters that are (A) specifically authorized under criteria established by an Executive order to be kept secret in the interests of national defense or foreign policy and (B) in fact properly classified pursuant to such Executive order;

(2) relate solely to the internal personnel rules and practices of an agency;

(3) disclose matters specifically exempted from disclosure by statute (other than section 552 of this title), provided that such statute (A) requires that the matters be withheld from the public in such a manner as to leave no discretion on the issue, or (B) establishes particular criteria for withholding or refers to particular types of matters to be withheld;

(4) disclose trade secrets and commercial or financial information obtained from a person and privileged or confidential;

(5) involve accusing any person of a crime, or formally censuring any person;

(6) disclose information of a personal nature where disclosure would constitute a clearly unwarranted invasion of personal privacy;

(7) disclose investigatory records compiled for law enforcement purposes, or information which if written would be contained in such records, but only to the extent that the production of such records or information would (A) interfere with enforcement proceedings, (B) deprive a person of a right to a fair trial or an impartial adjudication, (C) constitute an unwarranted invasion of personal privacy, (D) disclose the identity of a confidential source and, in the case of a record compiled by a criminal law enforcement authority in the course of a criminal investigation, or by an agency conducting a lawful national security intelligence investigation, confidential information furnished only by the confidential source, (E) disclose investigative techniques and procedures, or (F) endanger the life or physical safety of law enforcement personnel;

(8) disclose information contained in or related to examination, operating, or condition

reports prepared by, on behalf of, or for the use of an agency responsible for the regulation or supervision of financial institutions;

(9) disclose information the premature disclosure of which would—

(A) in the case of an agency which regulates currencies, securities, commodities, or financial institutions, be likely to (i) lead to significant financial speculation in currencies, securities, or commodities, or (ii) significantly endanger the stability of any financial institution; or

(B) in the case of any agency, be likely to significantly frustrate implementation of a proposed agency action,

except that subparagraph (B) shall not apply in any instance where the agency has already disclosed to the public the content or nature of its proposed action, or where the agency is required by law to make such disclosure on its own initiative prior to taking final agency action on such proposal; or

(10) specifically concern the agency's issuance of a subpoena, or the agency's participation in a civil action or proceeding, an action in a foreign court or international tribunal, or an arbitration, or the initiation, conduct, or disposition by the agency of a particular case of formal agency adjudication pursuant to the procedures in section 554 of this title or otherwise involving a determination on the record after opportunity for a hearing.

(d)(1) Action under subsection (c) shall be taken only when a majority of the entire membership of the agency (as defined in subsection (a)(1)) votes to take such action. A separate vote of the agency members shall be taken with respect to each agency meeting, a portion or portions of which are proposed to be closed to the public pursuant to subsection (c), or with respect to any information which is proposed to be withheld under subsection (c). A single vote may be taken with respect to a series of meetings, a portion or portions of which are proposed to be closed to the public, or with respect to any information concerning such series of meetings, so long as each meeting in such series involves the same particular matters and is scheduled to be held no more than thirty days after the initial meeting in such series. The vote of each agency member participating in such vote shall be recorded and no proxies shall be allowed.

(2) Whenever any person whose interests may be directly affected by a portion of a meeting requests that the agency close such portion to the public for any of the reasons referred to in paragraph (5), (6), or (7) of subsection (c), the agency, upon request of any one of its members, shall vote by recorded vote whether to close such meeting.

(3) Within one day of any vote taken pursuant to paragraph (1) or (2), the agency shall make publicly available a written copy of such vote reflecting the vote of each member on the question. If a portion of a meeting is to be closed to the public, the agency shall, within one day of the vote taken pursuant to paragraph (1) or (2) of this subsection, make publicly available a full written explanation of its action closing the portion together with a list of all persons expected to attend the meeting and their affiliation.

(4) Any agency, a majority of whose meetings may properly be closed to the public pursuant to paragraph (4), (8), (9)(A), or (10) or subsection (c), or any combination thereof, may provide by regulation for the closing of such meetings or portions thereof in the event that a majority of the members of the agency votes by recorded vote at the beginning of such meeting, or portion thereof, to close the exempt portion or portions of the meeting, and a copy of such vote, reflecting the vote of each member on the question, is made available to the public. The provisions of paragraphs (1), (2), and (3) of this subsection and subsection (e) shall not apply to any portion of a meeting to which such regulations apply: *Provided*, That the agency shall, except to the extent that such information is exempt from disclosure under the provisions of subsection (c), provide the public with public announcement of the time, place, and subject matter of the meeting and of each portion thereof at the earliest practicable time.

(e)(1) In the case of each meeting, the agency shall make public announcement, at least one week before the meeting, of the time, place, and subject matter of the meeting, whether it is to be open or closed to the public, and the name and phone number of the official designated by the agency to respond to requests for information about the meeting. Such announcement shall be made unless a majority of the members of the agency determines by a recorded vote that agency business requires that such meeting be called at an earlier date, in which case the agency shall make public announcement of the time, place, and subject matter of such meeting, and whether open or closed to the public, at the earliest practicable time.

(2) The time or place of a meeting may be changed following the public announcement required by paragraph (1) only if the agency publicly announces such change at the earliest practicable time. The subject matter of a meeting, or the determination of the agency to open or close a meeting, or portion of a meeting, to the public, may be changed following the public announcement required by this subsection only if (A) a majority of the entire membership of the agency determines by a recorded vote that agency business so requires and that no earlier announcement of the change was possible, and (B) the agency publicly announces such change and the vote of each member upon such change at the earliest practicable time.

(3) Immediately following each public announcement required by this subsection, notice of the time, place, and subject matter of a meeting, whether the meeting is open or closed, any change in one of the preceding, and the name and phone number of the official designated by the agency to respond to requests for information about the meeting, shall also be submitted for publication in the Federal Register.

(f)(1) For every meeting closed pursuant to paragraphs (1) through (10) of subsection (c), the General Counsel or chief legal officer of the agency shall publicly certify that, in his or her opinion, the meeting may be closed to the public and shall state each relevant exemptive provision. A copy of such certification, together with a statement from the presiding officer of the meeting setting forth the time and place of the meeting, and the persons present, shall be retained by the agency. The agency shall maintain a complete transcript or electronic recording adequate to record fully the proceedings of each meeting, or portion of a meeting, closed to the public, except that in the case of a meeting, or portion of a meeting, closed to the public pursuant to paragraph (8), (9)(A), or (10) of subsection (c), the agency shall maintain either such a transcript or recording, or a set of minutes. Such minutes shall fully and clearly describe all matters discussed and shall provide a full and accurate summary of any actions taken, and the reasons therefor, including a description of each of the views expressed on any item and the record of any rollcall vote (reflecting the vote of each member on the question). All documents considered in connection with any action shall be identified in such minutes.

(2) The agency shall make promptly available to the public, in a place easily accessible to the public, the transcript, electronic recording, or minutes (as required by paragraph (1)) of the discussion of any item on the agenda, or of any item of the testimony of any witness received at the meeting, except for such item or items of such discussion or testimony as the agency determines to contain information which may be withheld under subsection (c). Copies of such transcript, or minutes, or a transcription of such recording disclosing the identity of each speaker, shall be furnished to any person at the actual cost of duplication or transcription. The agency shall maintain a complete verbatim copy of the transcript, a complete copy of the minutes, or a complete electronic recording of each meeting, or portion of a meeting, closed to the public, for a period of at least two years after such meeting, or until one year after the conclusion of any agency proceeding with respect to which the meeting or portion was held, whichever occurs later.

(g) Each agency subject to the requirements of this section shall, within 180 days after the date of enactment of this section, following consultation with the Office of the Chairman of the Administrative Conference of the United States and published notice in the Federal Register of at least thirty days and opportunity for written comment by any person, promulgate regulations to implement the requirements of subsections (b) through (f) of this section. Any person may bring a proceeding in the United States District Court for the District of Columbia to require an agency to promulgate such regulations if such agency has not promulgated such regulations within the time period specified herein. Subject to any limitations of time provided by law, any person may bring a proceeding in the United States Court of Appeals for the District of Columbia to set aside agency regulations issued pursuant to this subsection that are not in accord with the requirements of subsections (b) through (f) of this section and to require the promulgation of regulations that are in accord with such subsections.

(h)(1) The district courts of the United States shall have jurisdiction to enforce the requirements of subsections (b) through (f) of this section by declaratory judgment, injunctive relief, or other relief as may be appropriate. Such actions may be brought by any person against an agency prior to, or within sixty days after, the meeting out of which the violation of this section arises, except that if public announcement of such meeting is not initially provided by the agency in accordance with the requirements of this section, such action may be instituted pursuant to this section at any time prior to sixty days after any public announcement of such meeting. Such actions may be brought in the district court of the United States for the district in which the agency meeting is held or in which the agency in question has its headquarters, or in the District Court for the District of Columbia. In such actions a defendant shall serve his answer within thirty days after the service of the complaint. The burden is on the defendant to sustain his action. In deciding such cases the court may examine in camera any portion of the transcript, electronic recording, or minutes of a meeting closed to the public, and may take such additional evidence as it deems necessary. The court, having due regard for orderly administration and the public interest, as well as the interests of the parties, may grant such equitable relief as it deems appropriate, including granting an injunction against future violations of this section or ordering the agency to make available to the public such portion of the transcript, recording, or minutes of a meeting as is not authorized to be withheld under subsection (c) of this section.

(2) Any Federal court otherwise authorized by law to review agency action may, at the application of any person properly participating in the proceeding pursuant to other applicable law, inquire into violations by the agency of the requirements of this section and afford such relief as it deems appropriate. Nothing in this section authorizes any Federal court having jurisdiction solely on the basis of paragraph (1) to set aside, enjoin, or invalidate any agency action (other than an action to close a meeting or to withhold information under this section) taken or discussed at any agency meeting out of which the violation of this section arose.

(i) The court may assess against any party reasonable attorney fees and other litigation costs reasonably incurred by any other party who substantially prevails in any action brought in accordance with the provisions of subsection (g) or (h) of this section, except that costs may be assessed against the plaintiff only where the court finds that the suit was initiated by the plaintiff primarily for frivolous or dilatory purposes. In the case of assessment of costs against an agency, the costs may be assessed by the court against the United States.

(j) Each agency subject to the requirements of this section shall annually report to Congress regarding its compliance with such requirements, including a tabulation of the total number of agency meetings open to the public, the total number of meetings closed to the public, the reasons for closing such meetings, and a description of any litigation brought against the agency under this section, including any costs assessed against the agency in such litigation (whether or not paid by the agency).

(k) Nothing herein expands or limits the present rights of any person under section 552 of this title, except that the exemptions set forth in subsection (c) of this section shall govern in the case of any request made pursuant to section 552 to copy or inspect the transcripts, recordings, or minutes described in subsection (f) of this section. The requirements of chapter 33 of title 44, United States Code, shall not apply to the transcripts, recordings, and minutes described in subsection (f) of this section.

(l) This section does not constitute authority to withhold any information from Congress, and does not authorize the closing of any agency meeting or portion thereof required by any other provision of law to be open.

(m) Nothing in this section authorizes any agency to withhold from any individual any record, including transcripts, recordings, or minutes required by this section, which is otherwise accessible to such individual under section 552a of this title.

§553. Rule Making

(a) This section applies, according to the provisions thereof, except to the extent that there is involved—

(1) a military or foreign affairs function of the United States; or

(2) a matter relating to agency management or personnel or to public property, loans, grants, benefits, or contracts.

(b) General notice of proposed rule making shall be published in the Federal Register, unless persons subject thereto are named and either personally served or otherwise have actual notice thereof in accordance with law. The notice shall include—

(1) a statement of the time, place, and nature of public rule making proceedings;

(2) reference to the legal authority under which the rule is proposed; and

(3) either the terms or substance of the proposed rule or a description of the subjects and issues involved.

Except when notice or hearing is required by statute, this subsection does not apply—

(A) to interpretative rules, general statements of policy, or rules of agency organization, procedure, or practice; or

(B) when the agency for good cause finds (and incorporates the finding and a brief statement of reasons therefor in the rules issued) that notice and public procedure thereon are impracticable, unnecessary, or contrary to the public interest.

(c) After notice required by this section, the agency shall give interested persons an opportunity to participate in the rule making through submission of written data, views, or arguments with or without opportunity for oral presentation. After consideration of the relevant matter presented, the agency shall incorporate in the rules adopted a concise general statement of their basis and purpose. When rules are required by statute to be made on the record after opportunity for an agency hearing, sections 556 and 557 of this title apply instead of this subsection.

(d) The required publication or service of a substantive rule shall be made not less than 30 days before its effective date, except—

(1) a substantive rule which grants or recognizes an exemption or relieves a restriction;

(2) interpretative rules and statements of policy; or

(3) as otherwise provided by the agency for good cause found and published with the rule.

(e) Each agency shall give an interested person the right to petition for the issuance, amendment, or repeal of a rule.

§554. Adjudications

(a) This section applies, according to the provisions thereof, in every case of adjudication required by statute to be determined on the record after opportunity for an agency hearing, except to the extent that there is involved—

(1) a matter subject to a subsequent trial of the law and the facts de novo in a court;

(2) the selection or tenure of an employee, except an administrative law judge appointed under section 3105 of this title;

(3) proceedings in which decisions rest solely on inspections, tests, or elections;

(4) the conduct of military or foreign affairs functions;

(5) cases in which an agency is acting as an agent for a court; or

(6) the certification of worker representatives.

(b) Persons entitled to notice of an agency hearing shall be timely informed of—

(1) the time, place, and nature of the hearing;

(2) the legal authority and jurisdiction under which the hearing is to be held; and

(3) the matters of fact and law asserted.

When private persons are the moving parties, other parties to the proceeding shall give prompt notice of issues controverted in fact or law; and in other instances agencies may by rule require responsive pleading. In fixing the time and place for hearings, due regard shall be had for the convenience and necessity of the parties or their representatives.

(c) The agency shall give all interested parties opportunity for—

(1) the submission and consideration of facts, arguments, offers of settlement, or proposals of adjustment when time, the nature of the proceeding, and the public interest permit; and

(2) to the extent that the parties are unable so to determine a controversy by consent, hearing and decision on notice and in accordance with sections 556 and 557 of this title.

(d) The employee who presides at the reception of evidence pursuant to section 556 of this title shall make the recommended decision or initial decision required by section 557 of this title, unless he becomes unavailable to the agency. Except to the extent required for the disposition of ex parte matters as authorized by law, such an employee may not—

(1) consult a person or party on a fact in issue, unless on notice and opportunity for all parties to participate; or

(2) be responsible to or subject to the supervision or direction of an employee or agent engaged in the performance of investigative or prosecuting functions for an agency.

An employee or agent engaged in the performance of investigative or prosecuting functions for an agency in a case may not, in that or a factually related case, participate or advise in the decision, recommended decision, or agency review pursuant to section 557 of this title, except as witness or counsel in public proceedings. This subsection does not apply—

(A) in determining applications for initial licenses;

(B) to proceedings involving the validity or application of rates, facilities, or practices of public utilities or carriers; or

(C) to the agency or a member or members of the body comprising the agency.

(e) The agency, with like effect as in the case of other orders, and in its sound discretion, may issue a declaratory order to terminate a controversy or remove uncertainty.

§555. Ancillary Matters

(a) This section applies, according to the provisions thereof, except as otherwise provided by this subchapter.

(b) A person compelled to appear in person before an agency or representative thereof is entitled to be accompanied, represented, and advised by counsel or, if permitted by the agency, by other qualified representative. A party is entitled to appear in person or by or with counsel or other duly qualified representative in an agency proceeding. So far as the orderly conduct of public business permits, an interested person may appear before an agency or its responsible employees for the presentation, adjustment, or determination of an issue, request, or controversy in a proceeding, whether interlocutory, summary, or otherwise, or in connection with an agency function. With due regard for the convenience and necessity of the parties or their representatives and within a reasonable time, each agency shall proceed to conclude a matter presented to it. This subsection does not grant or deny a person who is not a lawyer the right to appear for or represent others before an agency or in an agency proceeding.

(c) Process, requirement of a report, inspection, or other investigative act or demand may not be issued, made, or enforced except as authorized by law. A person compelled to submit data or evidence is entitled to retain or, on payment of lawfully prescribed costs, procure a copy or transcript thereof, except that in a nonpublic investigatory proceeding the witness may for good cause be limited to inspection of the official transcript of his testimony.

(d) Agency subpoenas authorized by law shall be issued to a party on request and, when required by rules of procedure, on a statement or showing of general relevance and reasonable scope of the evidence sought. On contest, the court shall sustain the subpoena or similar process or demand to the extent that it is found to be in accordance with law. In a proceeding for enforcement, the court shall issue an order requiring the appearance of the witness or the production of the evidence or data within a reasonable time under penalty of punishment for contempt in case of contumacious failure to comply.

(e) Prompt notice shall be given of the denial in whole or in part of a written application, petition, or other request of an interested person made in connection with any agency proceeding. Except in affirming a prior denial or when the denial is self-explanatory, the notice shall be accompanied by a brief statement of the grounds for denial.

§556. Hearings; Presiding Employees; Powers and Duties; Burden of Proof; Evidence; Record as Basis of Decision

(a) This section applies, according to the provisions thereof, to hearings required by section 553 or 554 of this title to be conducted in accordance with this section.

(b) There shall preside at the taking of evidence—

(1) the agency;

(2) one or more members of the body which comprises the agency; or

(3) one or more administrative law judges appointed under section 3105 of this title.

This subchapter does not supersede the conduct of specified classes of proceedings, in whole or in part, by or before boards or other employees specially provided for by or designated under statute. The functions of presiding employees and of employees participating in decisions in accordance with section 557 of this title shall be conducted in an impartial manner. A presiding or participating employee may at any time disqualify himself. On the filing in good faith of a timely and sufficient affidavit of personal bias or other disqualification of a presiding or participating employee, the agency shall determine the matter as a part of the record and decision in the case.

(c) Subject to published rules of the agency and within its powers, employees presiding at hearings may—

(1) administer oaths and affirmations;

(2) issue subpoenas authorized by law;

(3) rule on offers of proof and receive relevant evidence;

(4) take depositions or have depositions taken when the ends of justice would be served;

(5) regulate the course of the hearing;

(6) hold conferences for the settlement or simplification of the issues by consent of the parties;

(7) dispose of procedural requests or similar matters;

(8) make or recommend decisions in accordance with section 557 of this title; and

(9) take other action authorized by agency rule consistent with this subchapter.

(d) Except as otherwise provided by statute, the proponent of a rule or order has the burden of proof. Any oral or documentary evidence may be received, but the agency as a matter of policy shall provide for the exclusion of irrelevant, immaterial, or unduly repetitious evidence. A sanction may not be imposed or rule or order issued except on consideration of the whole record or those parts thereof cited by a party and supported by and in accordance with the reliable, probative, and substantial evidence. The agency may, to the extent consistent with the interests of justice and the policy of the underlying statutes administered by the agency, consider a violation of section 557(d) of this title sufficient grounds for a decision adverse to a party who has knowingly committed such violation or knowingly caused such violation to occur. A party is entitled to present his case or defense by oral or documentary evidence, to submit rebuttal evidence, and to conduct such cross-examination as may be required for a full and true disclosure of the facts. In rule making or determining claims for money or benefits or applications for initial licenses an agency may, when a party will not be prejudiced thereby, adopt procedures for the submission of all or part of the evidence in written form.

(e) The transcript of testimony and exhibits, together with all papers and requests filed in the proceeding, constitutes the exclusive record for decision in accordance with section 557 of this title and, on payment of lawfully prescribed costs, shall be made available to the parties. When an agency decision rests on official notice of a material fact not appearing in the evidence in the record, a party is entitled, on timely request, to an opportunity to show the contrary.

§557. Initial Decisions; Conclusiveness; Review by Agency; Submissions by Parties; Contents of Decisions; Record

(a) This section applies, according to the provisions thereof, when a hearing is required to be conducted in accordance with section 556 of this title.

(b) When the agency did not preside at the reception of the evidence, the presiding employee or, in cases not subject to section 554(d) of this title, an employee qualified to preside at hearings pursuant to section 556 of this title, shall initially decide the case unless the agency requires, either in specific cases or by general rule, the entire record to be certified to it for decision. When the presiding employee makes an initial decision, that decision then becomes the decision of the agency without further proceedings unless there is an appeal to, or review on motion of, the agency within time provided by rule. On appeal from or review of the initial decision, the agency has all the powers which it would have in making the initial decision except as it may limit the issues on notice or by rule. When the agency makes the decision without having presided at the reception of the evidence, the presiding employee or an employee qualified to preside at hearings pursuant to section 556 of this title shall first recommend a decision, except that in rule making or determining applications for initial licenses—

(1) instead thereof the agency may issue a tentative decision or one of its responsible employees may recommend a decision; or

(2) this procedure may be omitted in a case in which the agency finds on the record that due and timely execution of its functions imperatively and unavoidably so requires.

(c) Before a recommended, initial, or tentative decision, or a decision on agency review of the decision of subordinate employees, the parties are entitled to a reasonable opportunity to submit for the consideration of the employees participating in the decisions—

(1) proposed findings and conclusions; or

(2) exceptions to the decisions or recommended decisions of subordinate employees or to tentative agency decisions; and

(3) supporting reasons for the exceptions or proposed findings or conclusions.

The record shall show the ruling on each finding, conclusion, or exception presented. All decisions, including initial, recommended, and tentative decisions, are a part of the record and shall include a statement of—

(A) findings and conclusions, and the reasons or basis therefor, on all the material issues of fact, law, or discretion presented on the record; and

(B) the appropriate rule, order, sanction, relief, or denial thereof.

(d)(1) In any agency proceeding which is subject to subsection (a) of this section, except to the extent required for the disposition of ex parte matters as authorized by law—

(A) no interested person outside the agency shall make or knowingly cause to be made to any member of the body comprising the agency, administrative law judge, or other employee who is or may reasonably be expected to be involved in the decisional process of the proceeding, an ex parte communication relevant to the merits of the proceeding;

(B) no member of the body comprising the agency, administrative law judge, or other employee who is or may reasonably be expected to be involved in the decisional process of the proceeding, shall make or knowingly cause to be made to any interested person outside the agency an ex parte communication relevant to the merits of the proceeding;

(C) a member of the body comprising the agency, administrative law judge, or other employee who is or may reasonably be expected to be involved in the decisional process of such proceeding who receives, or who makes or knowingly causes to be made, a communication prohibited by this subsection shall place on the public record of the proceeding:

(i) all such written communications;

(ii) memoranda stating the substance of all such oral communications; and

(iii) all written responses, and memoranda stating the substance of all oral responses, to the materials described in clauses (i) and (ii) of this subparagraph;

(D) upon receipt of a communication knowingly made or knowingly caused to be made by a party in violation of this subsection, the agency, administrative law judge, or other employee presiding at the hearing may, to the extent consistent with the interests of justice and the policy of the underlying statutes, require the party to show cause why his claim or interest in the proceeding should not be dismissed, denied, disregarded, or otherwise adversely affected on account of such violation; and

(E) the prohibitions of this subsection shall apply beginning at such time as the agency may designate, but in no case shall they begin to apply later than the time at which a proceeding is noticed for hearing unless the person responsible for the communication has knowledge that it will be noticed, in which case the prohibitions shall apply beginning at the time of his acquisition of such knowledge.

(2) This subsection does not constitute authority to withhold information from Congress.

§558. Imposition of Sanctions; Determination of Applications for Licenses; Suspension, Revocation, and Expiration of Licenses

(a) This section applies, according to the provisions thereof, to the exercise of a power or authority.

(b) A sanction may not be imposed or a substantive rule or order issued except within jurisdiction delegated to the agency and as authorized by law.

(c) When application is made for a license required by law, the agency, with due regard for the rights and privileges of all the interested parties or adversely affected persons and within a reasonable time, shall set and complete proceedings required to be conducted in accordance with sections 556 and 557 of this title or other proceedings required by law and shall make its decision. Except in cases of willfulness or those in which public health, interest, or safety requires otherwise, the withdrawal, suspension, revocation, or annulment of a license is lawful only if, before the institution of agency proceedings therefor, the licensee has been given—

(1) notice by the agency in writing of the facts or conduct which may warrant the action; and

(2) opportunity to demonstrate or achieve compliance with all lawful requirements.

When the licensee has made timely and sufficient application for a renewal or a new license in accordance with agency rules, a license with reference to an activity of a continuing nature does not expire until the application has been finally determined by the agency.

§559. Effect on Other Laws; Effect of Subsequent Statute

This subchapter, chapter 7, and sections 1305, 3105, 3344, 4301(2)(E), 5372, and 7521 of this title, and the provisions of section 5335(a)(B) of this title that relate to administrative law judges, do not limit or repeal additional requirements imposed by statute or otherwise recognized by law. Except as otherwise required by law, requirements or privileges relating to evidence or procedure apply equally to agencies and persons. Each agency is granted the authority necessary to comply with the requirements of this subchapter through the issuance of rules or otherwise. Subsequent statute may not be held to supersede or modify this subchapter, chapter 7, sections 1305, 3105, 3344, 4301(2)(E), 5372, or 7521 of this title, or the provisions of section 5335(a)(B) of this title that relate to administrative law judges, except to the extent that it does so expressly.

CHAPTER 7—JUDICIAL REVIEW

Table of Sections

Sec.

701. Application; Definitions.
702. Right of Review.
703. Form and Venue of Proceeding.
704. Actions Reviewable.
705. Relief Pending Review.
706. Scope of Review.

§701. Application; Definitions

(a) This chapter applies, according to the provisions thereof, except to the extent that—

(1) statutes preclude judicial review; or

(2) agency action is committed to agency discretion by law.

(b) For the purpose of this chapter—

(1) "agency" means each authority of the Government of the United States, whether or not it is within or subject to review by another agency, but does not include—

(A) the Congress;

(B) the courts of the United States;

(C) the governments of the territories or possessions of the United States;

(D) the government of the District of Columbia;

(E) agencies composed of representatives of the parties or of representatives of organizations of the parties to the disputes determined by them;

(F) courts martial and military commissions;

(G) military authority exercised in the field in time of war or in occupied territory; or

(H) functions conferred by sections 1738, 1739, 1743, and 1744 of title 12; chapter 2 of title 41; or sections 1622, 1884, 1891–1902, and former section 1641(b)(2), of title 50, appendix; and

(2) "person", "rule", "order", "license", "sanction", "relief", and "agency action" have the meanings given them by section 551 of this title.

§702. Right of Review

A person suffering legal wrong because of agency action, or adversely affected or aggrieved by agency action within the meaning of a relevant statute, is entitled to judicial review thereof. An action in a court of the United States seeking relief other than money damages and stating a claim that an agency or an officer or employee thereof acted or failed to act in an official capacity or under color of legal authority shall not be dismissed nor relief therein be denied on the ground that it is against the United States or that the United States is an indispensable party. The United States may be named as a defendant in any such action, and a judgment or decree may be entered against the United States: *Provided*, That any mandatory or injunctive decree shall specify the Federal officer or officers (by name or by title), and their successors in office, personally responsible for compliance. Nothing herein (1) affects other limitations on judicial review or the power or duty of the court to dismiss any action or deny relief on any other appropriate legal or equitable ground; or (2) confers authority to grant relief if any other statute that grants consent to suit expressly or impliedly forbids the relief which is sought.

§703. Form and Venue of Proceeding

The form of proceeding for judicial review is the special statutory review proceeding relevant to the subject matter in a court specified by statute or, in the absence or inadequacy thereof, any applicable form of legal action, including actions for declaratory judgments or writs of prohibitory or mandatory injunction or habeas corpus, in a court of competent jurisdiction. If no special statutory review proceeding is applicable, the action for judicial review may be brought against the United States, the agency by its official title, or the appropriate officer. Except to the extent that prior, adequate, and exclusive opportunity for judicial review is provided by law, agency action is subject to judicial review in civil or criminal proceedings for judicial enforcement.

§704. Actions Reviewable

Agency action made reviewable by statute and final agency action for which there is no other adequate remedy in a court are subject to judicial review. A preliminary, procedural, or intermediate agency action or ruling not directly reviewable is subject to review on the review of the final agency action. Except as otherwise expressly required by statute, agency action otherwise final is final for the purposes of this section whether or not there has been presented or determined an application for a declaratory order, for any form of reconsideration, or, unless the agency otherwise requires by rule and provides that the action meanwhile is inoperative, for an appeal to superior agency authority.

§705. Relief Pending Review

When an agency finds that justice so requires, it may postpone the effective date of action taken by it, pending judicial review. On such conditions as may be required and to the extent necessary to prevent irreparable injury, the reviewing court, including the court to which a case may be taken on appeal from or on application for certiorari or other writ to a reviewing court, may issue all necessary and appropriate process to postpone the effective date of an agency action or to preserve status or rights pending conclusion of the review proceedings.

§706. Scope of Review

To the extent necessary to decision and when presented, the reviewing court shall decide all relevant questions of law, interpret constitutional and statutory provisions, and determine the meaning or applicability of the terms of an agency action. The reviewing court shall—
  (1) compel agency action unlawfully withheld or unreasonably delayed; and
  (2) hold unlawful and set aside agency action, findings, and conclusions found to be—
  (A) arbitrary, capricious, an abuse of discretion, or otherwise not in accordance with law;
  (B) contrary to constitutional right, power, privilege, or immunity;
  (C) in excess of statutory jurisdiction, authority, or limitations, or short of statutory right;
  (D) without observance of procedure required by law;
  (E) unsupported by substantial evidence in a case subject to sections 556 and 557 of this title or otherwise reviewed on the record of an agency hearing provided by statute; or
  (F) unwarranted by the facts to the extent that the facts are subject to trial de novo by the reviewing court.

In making the foregoing determinations, the court shall review the whole record or those parts of it cited by a party, and due account shall be taken of the rule of prejudicial error.

PART II—THE UNITED STATES CIVIL SERVICE COMMISSION

CHAPTER 13—SPECIAL AUTHORITY

§1305. Administrative Law Judges

For the purpose of sections 3105, 3344, 4301(2)(D), and 5372 of this title and the provisions of section 5335(a)(B) of this title that relate to administrative law judges, the Office of Personnel Management may, and for the purpose of section 7521 of this title, the Merit Systems Protection Board may investigate, require reports by agencies, issue reports, including an annual report to Congress, prescribe regulations, appoint advisory committees as necessary, recommend legislation, subpoena witnesses and records, and pay witness fees as established for the courts of the United States.

PART III—EMPLOYEES

Subpart B—Employment and Retention

CHAPTER 31—AUTHORITY FOR EMPLOYMENT

§3105. Appointment of Administrative Law Judges

Each agency shall appoint as many administrative law judges as are necessary for proceedings required to be conducted in accordance with sections 556 and 557 of this title. Administrative law judges shall be assigned to cases in rotation so far as practicable, and may not perform duties inconsistent with their duties and responsibilities as administrative law judges.

CHAPTER 33—EXAMINATION, SELECTION, AND PLACEMENT

§3344.   Details; Administrative Law Judges

An agency as defined by section 551 of this title which occasionally or temporarily is insufficiently staffed with administrative law judges appointed under section 3105 of this title may use administrative law judges selected by the Office of Personnel Management from and with the consent of other agencies.

Subpart D—Pay and Allowances

CHAPTER 53—PAY RATES AND SYSTEMS

§5372.   Administrative Law Judges

Administrative law judges appointed under section 3105 of this title are entitled to pay prescribed by the Office of Personnel Management independently of agency recommendations or ratings and in accordance with subchapter III of this chapter and chapter 51 of this title.

Subpart F—Employee Relations

CHAPTER 75—ADVERSE ACTIONS

§7521.   Actions Against Administrative Law Judges

(a) An action may be taken against an administrative law judge appointed under section 3105 of this title by the agency in which the administrative law judge is employed only for good cause established and determined by the Merit Systems Protection Board on the record after opportunity for hearing before the Board.

(b) The actions covered by this section are—

(1) a removal;

(2) a suspension;

(3) a reduction in grade;

(4) a reduction in pay; and

(5) a furlough of 30 days or less;

but do not include—

(A) a suspension or removal under section 7532 of this title;

(B) a reduction-in-force action under section 3502 of this title; or

(C) any action initiated under section 1206 of this title [i.e., by the Special Counsel of the Board].

Model State Administrative Procedure Act (1981)

ARTICLE I—GENERAL PROVISIONS

§ 1-101. [Short Title]

This Act may be cited as the [state] Administrative Procedure Act.

§ 1-102. [Definitions]

As used in this Act:

(1) "Agency" means a board, commission, department, officer, or other administrative unit of this State, including the agency head, and one or more members of the agency head or agency employees or other persons directly or indirectly purporting to act on behalf or under the authority of the agency head. The term does not include the [legislature] or the courts, [, or the governor] [, or the governor in the exercise of powers derived directly and exclusively from the constitution of this State]. The term does not include a political subdivision of the state or any of the administrative units of a political subdivision, but it does include a board, commission, department, officer, or other administrative unit created or appointed by joint or concerted action of an agency and one or more political subdivisions of the state or any of their units. To the extent it purports to exercise authority subject to any provision of this Act, an administrative unit otherwise qualifying as an "agency" must be treated as a separate agency even if the unit is located within or subordinate to another agency.

(2) "Agency action" means:

(i) the whole or a part of a rule or an order;

(ii) the failure to issue a rule or an order; or

(iii) an an agency's performance of, or failure to perform, any other duty, function, or activity, discretionary or otherwise.

(3) "Agency head" means an individual or body of individuals in whom the ultimate legal authority of the agency is vested by any provision of law.

(4) "License" means a franchise, permit, certification, approval; registration, charter, or similar form of authorization required by law.

(5) "Order" means an agency action of particular applicability that determines the legal rights, duties, privileges, immunites, or other legal interests of one or more specific persons. [The term does not include an "executive order" issued by the governor pursuant to Section 1-104 or 3-202.]

(6) "Party to agency proceedings," or "party" in context so indicating, means:

(i) a person to whom the agency action is specifically directed; or

(ii) a person named as a party to an agency proceeding or allowed to intervene or participate as a party in the proceeding.

(7) "Party to judicial review or civil enforcement proceedings," or "party" in context so indicated means:

(i) a person who files a petition for judicial review or civil enforcement or

(ii) a person named as a party in a proceeding for judicial review or civil enforcement or allowed to participate as a party in the proceeding.

(8) "Person" means an individual, partnership, corporation, association, governmental subdivision or unit thereof, or public or private organization or entity of any character, and includes another agency.

(9) "Provision of law" means the whole or a part of the federal or state constitution, or of any federal or state (i) statute, (ii) rule of court, (iii) executive order, or (iv) rule of an administrative agency.

(10) "Rule" means the whole or a part of an agency statement of general applicability that implements, interprets, or prescribes (i) law or policy, or (ii) the organization, procedure, or practice requirements of an agency. The term includes the amendment, repeal, or suspension of an existing rule.

(11) "Rule making" means the process for formulation and adoption of a rule.

§ 1-103. [Applicability and Relation to Other Law]

(a) This Act applies to all agencies and all proceedings not expressly exempted.

(b) This Act creates only procedural rights and imposes only procedural duties. They are in addition to those created and imposed by other statutes. To the extent that any other statute would diminish a right created or duty imposed by this Act, the other statute is superseded by this Act, unless the other statute expressly provides otherwise.

(c) An agency may grant procedural rights to persons in addition to those conferred by this Act so long as rights conferred upon other persons by any provision of law are not substantially prejudiced.

§ 1-104. [Suspension of Act's Provisions When Necessary to Avoid Loss of Federal Funds or Services]

(a) To the extent necessary to avoid a denial of funds or services from the United States which would otherwise be available to the state, the [governor by executive order] [attorney general by rule] [may] [shall] suspend, in whole or in part, one or more provisions of this Act. The [governor by executive order] [attorney general by rule] shall declare the termination of a suspension as soon as it is no longer necessary to prevent the loss of funds or services from the United States.

[(b) An executive order issued under subsection (a) is subject to the requirements applicable to the adoption and effectiveness of a rule.]

(c) If any provision of this Act is suspended pursuant to this section, the [governor] [attorney general] shall promptly report the suspension to the [legislature]. The report must include recommendations concerning any desirable legislation that may be necessary to conform this Act to federal law.

§ 1-105. [Waiver]

Except to the extent precluded by another provision of law, a person may waive any right conferred upon that person by this Act.

§ 1-106. [Informal Settlements]

Except to the extent precluded by another provision of law, informal settlement of matters that may make unnecessary more elaborate proceedings under this Act is encouraged. Agencies shall establish by rule specific procedures to facilitate informal settlement of matters. This section does not require any party or other person to settle a matter pursuant to informal procedures.

§ 1-107. [Conversion of Proceedings]

(a) At any point in an agency proceeding the presiding officer or other agency official responsible for the proceeding:

(1) may convert the proceeding to another type of agency proceeding provided for by this Act if the conversion is appropriate, is in the public interest, and does not substantially prejudice the rights of any party; and

(2) If required by any provision of law, shall convert the proceeding to another type of agency proceeding provided for by this Act.

(b) A conversion of a proceeding of one type to a proceeding of another type may be effected only upon notice to all parties to the original proceeding.

(c) If the presiding officer or other agency official responsible for the original proceeding would not have authority over the new proceeding to which it is to be converted, that officer or official, in accordance with agency rules, shall secure the appointment of a successor to preside over or be responsible for the new proceeding.

(d) To the extent feasible and consistent with the rights of parties and the requirements of this Act pertaining to the new proceeding, the record of the original agency proceeding must be used in the new agency proceeding.

(e) After a proceeding is converted from one type to another, the presiding officer or other agency official responsible for the new proceeding shall:

(1) give such additional notice to parties or other persons as is necessary to satisfy the requirements of this Act pertaining to those proceedings;

(2) dispose of the matters involved without further proceedings if sufficient proceedings have already been held to satisfy the requirements of this Act pertaining to the new proceedings; and

(3) conduct or cause to be conducted any additional proceedings necessary to satisfy the requirements of this Act pertaining to those proceedings.

(f) Each agency shall adopt rules to govern the conversion of one type of proceeding to another. Those rules must include an enumeration of the factors to be considered in determining whether and under what circumstances one type of proceeding will be converted to another.

§ 1-108. [Effective Date]

This Act takes effect on [date] and does not govern proceedings pending on that date. This Act governs all agency proceedings, and all proceedings for judicial review or civil enforcement of agency action, commenced after that date. This Act also governs agency proceedings conducted on a remand from a court or another agency after the effective date of this Act.

§ 1-109. [Severability]

If any provision of this Act or the application thereof to any person or circumstance is held invalid, the invalidity does not affect other provisions or applications of the Act which can be given effect without the invalid provision or application, and for this purpose the provisions of this Act are severable.

ARTICLE II—PUBLIC ACCESS TO AGENCY LAW AND POLICY

§ 2-101. [Adminstrative Rules Editor; Publication, Compilation, Indexing; and Public Inspection of Rules]

(a) There is created, within the executive branch, an [administrative rules editor]. The governor shall appoint the [administrative rules editor] who shall serve at the pleasure of the governor.

(b) Subject to the provisions of this Act, the [administrative rules editor] shall prescribe a uniform numbering system, form, and style for all proposed and adopted rules caused to be published by that office, and shall have the same editing authority with respect to the publication of rules as the [reviser of statutes] has with respect to the publication of statutes].

(c) The [administrative rules editor] shall cause the [administrative bulletin] to be published in pamphlet form [once each week]. For purposes of calculating adherence to time requirements imposed by this Act, an issue of the [administrative bulletin] is deemed published on the later of the date indicated in that issue or the date of its mailing. The [administrative bulletin] must contain:

(1) notices of proposed rule adoption prepared so that the text of the proposed rule shows the text of any existing rule proposed to be changed and the change proposed;

(2) newly filed adopted rules prepared so that the text of the newly filed adopted rule shows the text of any existing rule being changed and the change being made;

(3) any other notices and materials designated by [law] [the administrative rules editor] for publication therein; and

(4) an index to its contents by subject.

(d) The [administrative rules editor] shall cause the [administrative code] to be compiled, indexed by subject, and published [in loose-leaf form]. All of the effective rules of each agency must be published and indexed in that publication. The [administrative rules editor] shall also cause [looseleaf] supplements to the [administrative code] to be published at least every [3 months]. [The loose-leaf supplements must be in a form suitable for insertion in the appropriate places in the permanent [administrative code] compilation.]

(e) The [administrative rules editor] may omit from the [administrative bulletin or code] any proposed or filed adopted rule the publication of which would be unduly cumbersome, expensive, or otherwise inexpedient, if:

(1) knowledge of the rule is likely to be important to only a small class of persons;

(2) on application to the issuing agency, the proposed or adopted rule in printed or processed form is made available at no more than its cost of reproduction; and

(3) the [administrative bulletin or code] contains a notice stating in detail the specific subject matter of the omitted proposed or adopted rule and how a copy of the omitted material may be obtained.

(f) The [administrative bulletin and administrative code] must be furnished to [designated officials] without charge and to all subscribers at a cost to be determined by the [administrative rules editor]. Each agency shall also make available for public inspection and copying those portions of the [administrative bulletin and administrative code] containing all rules adopted or used by the agency in the discharge of its functions, and the index of those rules.

(g) Except as otherwise required by a provision of law subsections (c) through (f) do not apply to rules governed by Section 3–116, and the following provisions apply instead:

(1) Each agency shall maintain an official, current, and dated compilation that is indexed by subject, containing all of its rules within the scope of Section 3–116. Each addition to, change

in, or deletion from the official compilation must also be dated, indexed, and a record thereof kept. Except for those portions containing rules governed by Section 3–116(2), the compilation must be made available for public inspection and copying. Certified copies of the full compilation must also be furnished to the [secretary of state, the administrative rules counsel, and members of the administrative rules review committee], and be kept current by the agency at least every [30] days.

(2) A rule subject to the requirements of this subsection may not be relied on by an agency to the detriment of any person who does not have actual, timely knowledge of the contents of the rule until the requirements of paragraph (1) are satisfied. The burden of proving that knowledge is on the agency. This provision is also inapplicable to the extent necessary to avoid imminent peril to the public health, safety, or welfare.

§ 2-102. [Public Inspection and Indexing of Agency Orders]

(a) In addition to other requirements imposed by any provision of law, each agency shall make all written final orders available for public inspection and copying and index them by name and subject. An agency shall delete from those orders identifying details to the extent required by any provision of law [or necessary to prevent a clearly unwarranted invasion of privacy or release of trade secrets]. In each case the justification for the deletion must be explained in writing and attached to the order.

(b) A written final order may not be relied on as precedent by an agency to the detriment of any person until it has been made available for public inspection and indexed in the manner described in subsection (a). This provision is inapplicable to any person who has actual timely knowledge of the order. The burden of proving that knowledge is on the agency.

§ 2-103. [Declaratory Orders]

(a) Any person may petition an agency for a declaratory order as to the applicability to specified circumstances of a statute, rule, or order within the primary jurisdiction of the agency. An agency shall issue a declaratory order in response to a petition for that order unless the agency determines that issuance of the order under the circumstances would be contrary to a rule adopted in accordance with subsection (b). However, an agency may not issue a declaratory order that would substantially prejudice the rights of a person who would be a necessary party and who does not consent in writing to the determination of the matter by a declaratory order proceeding.

(b) Each agency shall issue rules that provide for: (i) the form, contents, and filing of petitions for declaratory orders; (ii) the procedural rights of persons in relation to the petitions and (iii) the disposition of the petitions. Those rules must describe the classes of circumstances in which the agency will not issue a declaratory order and must be consistent with the public interest and with the general policy of this Act to facilitate and encourage agency issuance of reliable advice.

(c) Within [15] days after receipt of a petition for a declaratory order, an agency shall give notice of the petition to all persons to whom notice is required by any provision of law and may give notice to any other persons.

(d) Persons who qualify under Section 4-209(a)(2) and (3) and file timely petitions for intervention according to agency rules may intervene in proceedings for declaratory orders. Other provisions of Article IV apply to agency proceedings for declaratory orders only to the extent an agency so provides by rule or order.

(e) Within [30] days after receipt of a petition for a declaratory order an agency, in writing, shall:

(1) issue an order declaring the applicability of the statute, rule, or order in question to the specified circumstances;

(2) set the matter for specified proceedings;

(3) agree to issue a declaratory order by a specified time; or

(4) decline to issue a declaratory order, stating the reasons for its action.

(f) A copy of all orders issued in response to a petition for a declaratory order must be mailed promptly to petitioner and any other parties.

(g) A declaratory order has the same status and binding effect as any other order issued in an agency adjudicative proceeding. A declaratory order must contain the names of all parties to the proceeding on which it is based, the particular facts on which it is based, and the reasons for its conclusion.

(h) If an agency has not issued a declaratory order within [60] days after receipt of a petition therefor, the petition is deemed to have been denied.

§ 2-104. [Required Rule Making]

In addition to other rule-making requirements imposed by law, each agency shall:

(1) adopt as a rule a description of the organization of the agency which states the general course and method of its operations and where and how the public may obtain information or make submissions or requests;

(2) adopt rules of practice setting forth the nature and requirements of all formal and informal procedures available to the public, including a description of all forms and instructions that are to be used by the public in dealing with the agency; [and]

(3) as soon as feasible and to the extent practicable, adopt rules, in addition to those otherwise required by this Act, embodying appropriate standards, principles, and procedural safeguards that the agency will apply to the law it administers [; and] [.]

[(4) as soon as feasible and to the extent practicable, adopt rules to supersede principles of law or policy lawfully declared by the agency as the basis for its decisions in particular cases.]

§ 2-105. [Model Rules of Procedure]

In accordance with the rule-making requirements of this Act, the [attorney general] shall adopt model rules of procedure appropriate for use by as many agencies as possible. The model rules must deal with all general functions and duties performed in common by several agencies. Each agency shall adopt as much of the model rules as is practicable under its circumstances. To the extent an agency adopts the model rules, it shall do so in accordance with the rule-making requirements of this Act. Any agency adopting a rule of procedure that differs from the model rules shall include in the rule a finding stating the reasons why the relevant portions of the model rules were impracticable under the circumstances.

ARTICLE III—RULE MAKING

CHAPTER 1—ADOPTION AND EFFECTIVENESS OF RULES

§ 3-101. [Advice on Possible Rules before Notice of Proposed Rule Adoption]

(a) In addition to seeking information by other methods, an agency, before publication of a notice of proposed rule adoption under Section 3-103, may solicit comments from the public on a subject matter of possible rule making under active consideration within the agency by causing notice to be published in the [administrative bulletin] of the subject matter and indicating where, when, and how persons may comment.

(b) Each agency may also appoint committees to comment, before publication of a notice of proposed rule adoption under Section 3-103, on the subject matter of a possible rule making under active consideration within the agency. The membership of those committees must be published at least [annually] in the [administrative bulletin].

§ 3-102. [Public Rule-Making Docket]

(a) Each agency shall maintain a current, public rule-making docket.

(b) The rule-making docket [must] [may] contain a listing of the precise subject matter of each possible rule currently under active consideration within the agency for proposal under Section 3–103, the name and address of agency personnel with whom persons may communicate with respect to the matter, and an indication of the present status within the agency of the possible rule.

(c) The rule-making docket must list each pending rule-making proceeding. A rule-making proceeding is pending from the time it is commenced, by publication of notice of proposed rule adoption, to the time it is terminated, by publication of a notice of termination or the rule becoming effective. For each rule-making proceeding, the docket must indicate:

(1) the subject matter of the proposed rule;

(2) a citation to all published notices relating to the proceeding;

(3) where written submissions on the proposed rule may be inspected;

(4) the time during which written submissions may be made;

(5) the names of persons who have made written requests for an opportunity to make oral presentations on the proposed rule, where those requests may be inspected, and where and when oral presentations may be made;

(6) whether a written request for the issuance of a regulatory analysis of the proposed rule has been filed, whether that analysis has been issued, and where the written request and analysis may be inspected;

(7) the current status of the proposed rule and any agency determinations with respect thereto;

(8) any known timetable for agency decisions or other action in the proceeding;

(9) the date of the rule's adoption;

(10) the date of the rule's filing, indexing, and publication; and

(11) when the rule will become effective.

§ 3-103. [Notice of Proposed Rule Adoption]

(a) At least [30] days before the adoption of a rule an agency shall cause notice of its contemplated action to be published in the [administrative bulletin]. The notice of proposed rule adoption must include:

(1) a short explanation of the purpose of the proposed rule;

(2) the specific legal authority authorizing the proposed rule;

(3) subject to Section 2-101(e), the text of the proposed rule;

(4) where, when, and how persons may present their views on the proposed rule; and

(5) where, when, and how persons may demand an oral proceeding on the proposed rule if the notice does not already provide for one.

(b) Within [3] days after its publication in the [administrative bulletin], the agency shall cause a copy of the notice of proposed rule adoption to be mailed to each person who has made a timely request to the agency for a mailed copy of the notice. An agency may charge persons for the actual cost of providing them with mailed copies.

§ 3-104. [Public Participation]

(a) For at least [30] days after publication of the notice of proposed rule adoption, an agency shall afford persons the opportunity to submit in writing, argument, data, and views on the proposed rule.

(b)(1) An agency shall schedule an oral proceeding on a proposed rule if, within [20] days after the published notice of proposed rule adoption, a written request for an oral proceeding is submitted by [the administrative rules review committee,] [the administrative rules counsel,] a political subdivision, an agency, or [25] persons. At that proceeding, persons may present oral argument, data, and views on the proposed rule.

(2) An oral proceeding on a proposed rule, if required, may not be held earlier than [20] days after notice of its location and time is published in the [administrative bulletin].

(3) The agency, a member of the agency, or another presiding officer designated by the agency, shall preside at a required oral proceeding on a proposed rule. If the agency does not preside, the presiding official shall prepare a memorandum for consideration by the agency summarizing the contents of the presentations made at the oral proceeding. Oral proceedings must be open to the public and be recorded by stenographic or other means.

(4) Each agency shall issue rules for the conduct of oral rule-making proceedings. Those rules may include provisions calculated to prevent undue repetition in the oral proceedings.

§ 3-105. [Regulatory Analysis]

(a) An agency shall issue a regulatory analysis of a proposed rule if, within [20] days after the published notice of proposed rule adoption, a written request for the analysis is filed in the office of the [secretary of state] by [the administrative rules review committee, the governor, a political subdivision, an agency, or [300] persons signing the request]. The [secretary of state] shall immediately forward to the agency a certified copy of the filed request.

(b) Except to the extent that the written request expressly waives one or more of the following, the regulatory analysis must contain:

(1) a description of the classes of persons who probably will be affected by the proposed rule, including classes that will bear the costs of the proposed rule and classes that will benefit from the proposed rule;

(2) a description of the probable quantitative and qualitative impact of the proposed rule, economic or otherwise, upon affected classes of persons;

(3) the probable costs to the agency and to any other agency of the implementation and enforcement of the proposed rule and any anticipated effect on state revenues;

(4) a comparison of the probable costs and benefits of the proposed rule to the probable costs and benefits of inaction;

(5) a determination of whether there are less costly methods or less intrusive methods for achieving the purpose of the proposed rule; and

(6) a description of any alternative methods for achieving the purpose of the proposed rule that were seriously considered by the agency and the reasons why they were rejected in favor of the proposed rule.

(c) Each regulatory analysis must include quantification of the data to the extent practicable and must take account of both short-term and long-term consequences.

(d) A concise summary of the regulatory analysis must be published in the [administrative bulletin] at least [10] days before the earliest of:

(1) the end of the period during which persons may make written submissions on the proposed rule;

(2) the end of the period during which an oral proceeding may be requested; or

(3) the date of any required oral proceeding on the proposed rule.

(e) The published summary of the regulatory analysis must also indicate where persons may obtain copies of the full text of the regulatory analysis and where, when, and how persons may present their views on the proposed rule and demand an oral proceeding thereon if one is not already provided.

(f) If the agency has made a good faith effort to comply with the requirements of subsections (a) through (c), the rule may not be invalidated on the ground that the contents of the regulatory analysis are insufficient or inaccurate.

§ 3-106. [Time and Manner of Rule Adoption]

(a) An agency may not adopt a rule until the period for making written submissions and oral presentations has expired.

(b) Within [180] days after the later of (i) the publication of the notice of proposed rule adoption, or (ii) the end of oral proceedings thereon, an agency shall adopt a rule pursuant to the rule-making proceeding or terminate the proceeding by publication of a notice to that effect in the [administrative bulletin].

(c) Before the adoption of a rule, an agency shall consider the written submissions, oral submissions or any memorandum summarizing oral submissions, and any regulatory analysis, provided for by this chapter.

(d) Within the scope of its delegated authority, an agency may use its own experience, technical competence, specialized knowledge, and judgement in the adoption of a rule.

§ 3-107. [Variance between Adopted Rule and Published Notice of Proposed Rule Adoption]

(a) An agency may not adopt a rule that is substantially different from the proposed rule contained in the published notice of proposed rule adoption. However, an agency may terminate a rule-making proceeding and commence a new rule-making proceeding for the purpose of adopting a substantially different rule.

(b) In determining whether an adopted rule is substantially different from the published proposed rule upon which it is required to be based, the following must be considered:

(1) the extent to which all persons affected by the adopted rule should have understood that the published proposed rule would affect their interests;

(2) the extent to which the subject matter of the adopted rule or the issues determined by that rule are different from the subject matter or issues involved in the published proposed rule; and

(3) the extent to which the effects of the adopted rule differ from the effects of the published proposed rule had it been adopted instead.

§ 3-108. [General Exemption from Public Rule-Making Procedures]

(a) To the extent an agency for good cause finds that any requirements of Sections 3-103 through 3-107 are unnecessary, impracticable, or contrary to the public interest in the process of adopting a particular rule, those requirements do not apply. The agency shall incorporate the required finding and a brief statement of its supporting reasons in each role adopted in reliance upon this subsection.

(b) In an action contesting a rule adopted under subsection (a), the burden is upon the agency to demonstrate that any omitted requirements of Sections 3–103 through 3–107 were impracticable, unnecessary, or contrary to the public interest in the particular circumstances involved.

(c) Within [2] years after the effective date of a rule adopted under subsection (a), the [administrative rules review committee or the governor] may request the agency to hold a rule-making proceeding thereon according to the requirements of Sections 3-103 through 3-107. The request must be in writing and filed in the office of the [secretary of state]. The [secretary of state] shall immediately forward to the agency and to the [administrative rules editor] a certified copy of the request. Notice of the filing of the request must be published in the next issue of the [administrative bulletin]. The rule in question ceases to be effective [180] days after the request is filed. However, an agency, after the filing of the request, may subsequently adopt an identical rule in a rule-making proceeding conducted pursuant to the requirements of Sections 3-103 through 3-107.

§ 3-109. [Exemption for Certain Rules]

(a) An agency need not follow the provisions of Sections 3-103 through 3-108 in the adoption of a rule that only defines the meaning of a statute or other provision of law or precedent if the agency does not possess delegated authority to bind the courts to any extent with its definition. A rule adopted under this subsection must include a statement that it was adopted under this subsection when it is published in the [administrative bulletin], and there must be an indication to that effect adjacent to the rule when it is published in the [administrative code].

(b) A reviewing court shall determine wholly de novo the validity of a rule within the scope of subsection (a) that is adopted without complying with the provisions of Sections 3-103 through 3-108.

§ 3-110. [Concise Explanatory Statement]

(a) At the time it adopts a rule, an agency shall issue a concise explanatory statement containing:

(1) its reasons for adopting the rule; and

(2) an indication of any change between the text of the proposed rule contained in the published notice of proposed rule adoption and the text of the rule as finally adopted, with the reasons for any change.

(b) Only the reasons contained in the concise explanatory statement may be used by any party as justification for the adoption of the rule in any proceeding in which its validity is at issue.

§ 3-111. [Contents, Style, and, Form of Rule]

(a) Each rule adopted by an agency must contain the text of the rule and:

(1) the date the agency adopted the rule;

(2) a concise statement of the purpose of the rule;

(3) a reference to all rules repealed, amended, or suspended by the rule;

(4) a reference to the specific statutory or other authority authorizing adoption of the rule;

(5) any findings required by any provision of law as a prerequisite to adoption or effectiveness of the rule; and

(6) the effective date of the rule if other than that specified in Section 3-115(a).

[(b) To the extent feasible, each rule should be written in clear and concise language understandable to persons who may be affected by it.]

(c) An agency may incorporate, by reference in its rules and without publishing the incorporated matter in full, all or any part of a code, standard, rule, or regulation that has been adopted by an agency of the United States or of this state, another state, or by a nationally recognized organization or association, if incorporation of its text in agency rules would be unduly cumbersome, expensive, or otherwise inexpedient. The reference in the agency rules must fully identify the incorporated matter by location, date, and otherwise, [and must state that the rule does not include any later amendments or editions of the incorporated matter]. An agency may incorporate by reference such matter in its rules only if the agency, organization, or association originally issuing that matter makes copies of it readily available to the public. The rules must state where copies of the incorporated matter are available at cost from the agency issuing the rule, and where copies are available from the agency of the United States, this State, another state, or the organization or association originally issuing that matter.

(d) In preparing its rules pursuant to this Chapter, each agency shall follow the uniform numbering system, form, and style prescribed by the [administrative rules editor].

§ 3-112.   [Agency Rule-Making Record]

(a) An agency shall maintain an official rule-making record for each rule it (i) proposes by publication in the [administrative bulletin] of a notice or proposed rule adoption, or (ii) adopts. The record and materials incorporated by reference must be available for public inspection.

(b) The agency rule-making record must contain:

(1) copies of all publications in the [administrative bulletin] with respect to the rule or the proceeding upon which the rule is based;

(2) copies of any portions of the agency's public rule-making docket containing entries relating to the rule or the proceeding upon which the rule is based;

(3) all written petitions, requests, submissions, and comments received by the agency and all other written materials considered by the agency in connection with the formulation, proposal, or adoption of the rule or the proceeding upon which the rule is based;

(4) any official transcript of oral presentations made in the proceeding upon which the rule is based or, if not transcribed, a tape recording or stenographic record of those presentations, and any memorandum prepared by a presiding official summarizing the contents of those presentations;

(5) a copy of any regulatory analysis prepared for the proceeding upon which the rule is based;

(6) a copy of the rule and explanatory statement filed in the office of the [secretary of state];

(7) all petitions for exceptions to, amendments of, or repeal or suspension of, the rule;

(8) a copy of any request filed pursuant to Section 3-108(c);

[(9) a copy of any objection to the rule filed by the [administrative rules review committee] pursuant to Section 3-204(d) and the agency's response;] and

(10) a copy of any filed executive order with respect to the rule.

(c) Upon judicial review, the record required by this section constitutes the official agency rule-making record with respect to a rule. Except as provided in Section 3-110(b) or otherwise required by a provision of law, the agency rule-making record need not constitute the exclusive basis for agency action on that rule or for judicial review thereof.

§ 3-113.   [Invalidity of Rules Not Adopted According to Chapter; Time Limitation]

(a) A rule adoption after [date] is invalid unless adopted in substantial compliance with the provisions of Sections 3-102 through 3-108 and Sections 3-110 through 3-112. However, inadvertent failure to mail a notice of proposed rule adoption to any person as required by Section 3-103(b) does not invalidate a rule.

(b) An action to contest the validity of a rule on the grounds of its noncompliance with any provision of Sections 3-102 through 3-108 or Sections 3-110 through 3-112 must be commence within [2] years after the effective date of the rule.

§ 3-114. [Filing of Rules]

(a) An agency shall file in the office of the [secretary of state] each rule it adopts and all rules existing on the effective date of this Act that have not previously been filed. The filing must be done as soon after adoption of the rule as practicable. At the time of filing, each rule adopted after the effective date of this Act must have attached to it the explanatory statement required by Section 3-110. The [secretary of state] shall affix to each rule and statement a certification of the time and date of filing and keep a permanent register open to public inspection of all filed rules and attached explanatory statements. In filing a rule, each agency shall use a standard form prescribed by the [secretary of state].

(b) The [secretary of state] shall transmit to the [administrative rules editor], [administrative rules counsel], and to the members of the [administrative rules review committee] a certified copy of each filed rule as soon after its filing as is practicable.

§ 3-115. [Effective Date of Rules]

(a) Except to the extent subsection (b) or (c) provides otherwise, each rule adopted after the effective date of this Act becomes effective [30] days after the later of (i) its filing in the office of the [secretary of state] or (ii) its publication and indexing in the [administrative bulletin].

(b)(1) A rule becomes effective on a date later than that established by subsection (a) if later date is required by another statute or specified in the rule.

(2) A rule may become effective immediately upon its filing or on any subsequent date earlier than that established by subsection (a) if the agency establishes such as effective date and finds that:

(i) it is required by constitution, statute, or court order;

(ii) the rule only confers a benefit or removes a restriction on the public or some segment thereof;

(iii) the rule only delays the effective date of another rule that is not yet effective; or

(iv) the earlier effective date is necessary because of imminent peril to the public health, safety, or welfare.

(3) The finding and a brief statement of the reasons therefor required by paragraph (2) must be made a part of the rule. In any action contesting the effective date of a rule made effective under paragraph (2), the burden is on the agency to justify its finding.

(4) Each agency shall make a reasonable effort to make known to persons who may be affected by it a rule made effective before publication and indexing under this subsection.

(c) This section does not relieve an agency from compliance with any provision of law requiring that some or all of its rules be approved by other designated officials or bodies before they become effective.

§ 3-116. [Special Provision for Certain Classes of Rules]

Except to the extent otherwise provided by any provision of law, Sections 3-102 through 3–115 are inapplicable to:

(1) a rule concerning only the internal management of an agency which does not directly

and substantially affect the procedural or substantive rights or duties of any segment of the public;

(2) a rule that establishes criteria or guidelines to be used by the staff of an agency in performing audits, investigations, or inspections, settling commercial disputes, negotiating commercial arrangements, or in the defense, prosecution, or settlement of cases, if disclosure of the criteria or guidelines would:

(i) enable law violators to avoid detection;

(ii) facilitate disregard of requirements imposed by law; or

(iii) give a clearly improper advantage to persons who are in an adverse position to the state;

(3) a rule that only establishes specific prices to be charged for particular goods or services sold by an agency;

(4) a rule concerning only the physical servicing, maintenance, or care of agency owned or operated facilities or property;

(5) a rule relating only to the use of a particular facility or property owned, operated, or maintained by the state or any of its subdivisions, if the substance of the rule is adequately indicated by means of signs or signals to persons who use the facility or property;

(6) a rule concerning only inmates of a correctional or detention facility, students enrolled in an educational institution, or patients admitted to a hospital, if adopted by that facility, institution, or hospital;

(7) a form whose contents or substantive requirements are prescribed by rule or statute, and instructions for the execution or use of the form;

(8) an agency budget; [or]

(9) [an opinion of the attorney general]; or] [.]

(10) [the terms of a collective bargaining agreement.]

§ 3-117. [Petition for Adoption of Rule]

Any person may petition an agency requesting the adoption of a rule. Each agency shall prescribe by rule the form of the petition and the procedure for its submission, consideration, and disposition. Within [60] days after submission of a petition, the agency shall either (i) deny the petition in writing, stating its reasons therefor, (ii) initiate rule-making proceedings in accordance with this chapter, or (iii) if otherwise lawful, adopt a rule.

CHAPTER 2—REVIEW OF AGENCY RULES

§ 3-201 [Review by Agency]

At least [annually], each agency shall review all of its rules to determine whether any new rule should be adopted. In conducting that review, each agency shall prepare a written report summarizing its findings, its supporting reasons, and any proposed course of action. For each rule, the [annual] report must include, at least once every [7] years, a concise statement of:

(1) the rule's effectiveness in achieving its objectives, including a summary of any available data supporting the conclusions reached;

(2) criticisms of the rule received during the previous [7] years, including a summary of any petitions for waiver of the rule tendered to the agency or granted by it; and

(3) alternative solutions to the criticisms and the reasons they were rejected or the changes made in the rule in response to those criticisms and the reasons for the changes. A copy of the [annual] report must be sent to the [administrative rules review committee and the administrative rules counsel] and be available for public inspection.

§ 3-202. [Review by Governor; Administrative Rules Counsel]

(a) To the extent the agency itself would have authority, the governor may rescind or suspend all or a severable portion of a rule of an agency. In exercising this authority, the governor shall act by an executive order that is subject to the provisions of the Act applicable to the adoption and effectiveness of a rule.

(b) The governor may summarily terminate any pending rule-making proceeding by an executive order to that effect, stating therein the reasons for the action. The executive order must be filed in the office of the [secretary of state], which shall promptly forward a certified copy to the agency and the [administrative rules editor]. An executive order terminating a rule-making proceeding becomes effective on [the date it is filed] and must be published in the next issue of the [administrative bulletin].

(c) There is created, within the office of the governor, an [administrative rules counsel] to advise the governor in the execution of the authority vested under this Article. The governor shall appoint the [administrative rules counsel] who shall serve at the pleasure of the governor.

§ 3-203. [Administrative Rules Review Committee]

There is created the ["administrative rules review committee"] of the [legislature]. The committee must be [bipartisan] and composed of [3] senators appointed by the [president of the senate] and [3] representatives appointed by the [speaker of the house]. Committee members must be appointed within [30] days after the convening of a regular legislative session. The term of office is [2] years while a member of the [legislature] and begins on the date of appointment to the committee. While a member of the [legislature], a member of the committee whose term has expired shall serve until a successor is appointed. A vacancy on the committee may be filled at any time by the original appointing authority for the remainder of the term. The committee shall choose a chairman from its membership for a [2]-year term and may employ staff it considers advisable.]

§ 3-204. [Review by Administrative Rules Review Committee]

(a) The [administrative rules review committee] shall selectively review possible, proposed, or adopted rules and prescribe appropriate committee procedures for that purpose. The committee may receive and investigate complaints from members of the public with respect to possible, proposed, or adopted rules and hold public proceedings on those complaints.

(b) Committee meetings must be open to the public. Subject to procedures established by the committee, persons may present oral argument, data, or views at those meetings. The committee may require a representative of an agency whose possible, proposed, or adopted rule is under examination to attend a committee meeting and answer relevant questions. The committee may also communicate to the agency its comments on any possible, proposed, or adopted rule and require the agency to respond to them in writing. Unless impracticable, in advance of each committee meeting notice of the time and place of the meeting and the specific subject matter to be considered must be published in the [administrative bulletin].

(c) The committee may recommend enactment of a statute to improve the operation of an agency. The committee may also recommend that a particular rule be superseded in whole or in part by statute. The [speaker of the house and the president of the senate] shall refer those recommendations to the appropriate standing committees. This subsection does not preclude any committee of the legislature from reviewing a rule on its own motion or recommending that it be superseded in whole or in part by statute.

[(d)(1) If the committee objects to all or some portion of a rule because the committee considers it to be beyond the procedural or substantive authority delegated to the adopting agency, the committee may file that objection in the office of the [secretary of state]. The filed objection must contain a concise statement of the committee's reasons for its action.

(2) The [secretary of state] shall affix to each objection a certification of the date and time of its filing and as soon thereafter as practicable shall transmit a certified copy thereof to the agency issuing the rule in question, the [administrative rules editor, and the administrative rules counsel]. The [secretary of state] shall also maintain a permanent register open to public inspection of all objections by the committee.

(3) The [administrative rules editor] shall publish and index an objection filed pursuant to this subsection in the next issue of the [administrative bulletin] and indicate its existence adjacent to the rule in question when that rule is published in the [administrative code]. In case of a filed objection by the committee to a rule that is subject to the requirements of Section 2-101(g), the agency shall indicate the existence of that objection adjacent to the rule in the official compilation referred to in that subsection.

(4) Within [14] days after the filing of an objection by the committee to a rule, the issuing agency shall respond in writing to the committee. After receipt of the response, the committee may withdraw or modify its objection.

[(5) After the filing of an objection by the committee that is not subsequently withdrawn, the burden is upon the agency in any proceeding for judicial review or for enforcement of the rule to establish that the whole or portion of the rule objected to is within the procedural and substantive authority delegated to the agency.]

[(6) The failure of the [administrative rules review committee] to object to a rule is not an implied legislative authorization of its procedural or substantive validity.]

(e) The committee may recommend to an agency that it adopt a rule. [The committee may also require an agency to publish notice of the committee's recommendation as a proposed rule of the agency and to allow public participation thereon, according to the provisions of Sections 3-103 through 3-104. An agency is not required to adopt the proposed rule.]

(f) The committee shall file an annual report with the [presiding officer] of each house and the governor.

ARTICLE IV—ADJUDICATIVE PROCEEDINGS

CHAPTER 1—AVAILABILITY OF ADJUDICATIVE PROCEEDINGS; APPLICATIONS; LICENSES

§ 4-101. [Adjudicative Proceedings; When Required; Exceptions]

(a) An agency shall conduct an adjudicative proceeding as the process for formulating and issuing an order, unless the order is a decision:

(1) to issue or not to issue a complaint, summons, or similar accusation;

(2) to initiate or not to initiate an investigation, prosecution, or other proceeding before the agency, another agency, or a court; or

(3) under Section 4-103, not to conduct an adjudicative proceeding.

(b) This Article applies to rule-making proceedings only to the extent that another statute expressly so requires.

§ 4-102. [Adjudicative Proceedings; Commencement]

(a) An agency may commence an adjudicative proceeding at any time with respect to a matter within the agency's jurisdiction.

(b) An agency shall commence an adjudicative proceeding upon the application of any person, unless:

(1) the agency lacks jurisdiction of the subject matter;

(2) resolution of the matter requires the agency to exercise discretion within the scope of Section 4–101(a);

(3) a statute vests the agency with discretion to conduct or not to conduct an adjudicative proceeding before issuing an order to resolve the matter and, in the exercise of that discretion, the agency has determined not to conduct an adjudicative proceeding;

(4) resolution of the matter does not require the agency to issue an order that determines the applicant's legal rights, duties, privileges, immunities, or other legal interests;

(5) the matter was not timely submitted to the agency; or

(6) the matter was not submitted in a form substantially complying with any applicable provision of law.

(c) An application for an agency to issue an order includes an application for the agency to conduct appropriate adjudicative proceedings, whether or not the applicant expressly requests those proceedings.

(d) An adjudicative proceeding commences when the agency or a presiding officer:

(1) notifies a party that a prehearing conference, hearing, or other stage of an adjudicative proceeding will be conducted; or

(2) begins to take action on a matter that appropriately may be determined by an adjudicative proceeding unless this action is:

(i) an investigation for the purpose of determining whether an adjudicative proceeding should be conducted; or

(ii) a decision which, under Section 4-101(a), the agency may make without conducting an adjudicative proceeding.

§ 4-103. [Decision Not to Conduct Adjudicative Proceeding]

If an agency decides not to conduct an adjudicative proceeding in response to an application, the agency shall furnish the applicant a copy of its decision in writing, with a brief statement of the agency's reasons and of any administrative review available to the applicant.

§ 4-104. [Agency Action on Applications]

(a) Except to the extent that the time limits in this subsection are inconsistent with limits established by another statute for any stage of the proceedings, an agency shall process an application for an order, other than a declaratory order, as follows:

(1) Within [30] days after receipt of the application, the agency shall examine the application, notify the applicant of any apparent errors or omissions, request any additional information the agency wishes to obtain and is permitted by law to require, and notify the applicant of the name, official title, mailing address, and telephone number of an agency member or employee who may be contacted regarding the application.

(2) Except in situations governed by paragraph (3), within [90] days after receipt of the application or of the response to a timely request made by the agency pursuant to paragraph (1), the agency shall:

(i) approve or deny the application, in whole or in part, on the basis of emergency or summary adjudicative proceedings, if those proceedings are available under this Act for disposition of the matter;

(ii) commence a formal adjudicative hearing or a conference adjudicative hearing in accordance with this Act; or

(iii) dispose of the application in accordance with Section 4-103.

(3) If the application pertains to subject matter that is not available when the application is filed but may be available in the future, including an application for housing or employment at a time no vacancy exists, the agency may proceed to make a determination of eligibility within the time provided in paragraph (2). If the agency determines that the applicant is eligible, the agency shall maintain the application on the agency's list of eligible applicants as provided by law and, upon request, shall notify the applicant of the status of the application.

(b) If a timely and sufficient application has been made for renewal of a license with reference to any activity of a continuing nature, the existing license does not expire until the agency has taken final action upon the application for renewal or, if the agency's action is unfavorable, until the last day for seeking judicial review of the agency's action or a later date fixed by the reviewing court.

§ 4-105. [Agency Action against Licensees]

An agency may not revoke, suspend, modify, annul, withdraw, or amend a license unless the agency first gives notice and an opportunity for an appropriate adjudicative proceeding in accordance with this Act or other statute. This section does not preclude an agency from (i) taking immediate action to protect the public interest in accordance with Section 4-501 or (ii) adopting rules, otherwise within the scope of its authority, pertaining to a class of licensees, including rules affecting the existing licenses of a class of licensees.

CHAPTER 2—FORMAL ADJUDICATIVE HEARING

§ 4-201. [Applicability]

An adjudicative proceeding is governed by this chapter, except as otherwise provided by:

(1) a statute other than this Act;

(2) a rule that adopts the procedures for the conference adjudicative hearing or summary adjudicative proceeding in accordance with the standards provided in this Act for those proceedings;

(3) Section 4-501 pertaining to emergency adjudicative proceedings; or

(4) Section 2-103 pertaining to declaratory proceedings.

§ 4-202. [Presiding Officer, Disqualification, Substitution]

(a) The agency head, one or more members of the agency head, one or more administrative law judges assigned by the office of administrative hearings in accordance with Section 4-301 [, or, unless prohibited by law, one or more other persons designated by the agency head], in the discretion of the agency head, may be the presiding officer.

(b) Any person serving or designated to serve alone or with others as presiding officer is subject to disqualification for bias, prejudice, interest, or any other cause provided in this Act or for which a judge is or may be disqualified.

(c) Any party may petition for the disqualification of a person promptly after receipt of notice indicating that the person will preside or promptly upon discovering facts establishing grounds for disqualification, whichever is later.

(d) A person whose disqualification is requested shall determine whether to grant the petition, stating facts and reasons for the determination.

(e) If a substitute is required for a person who is disqualified or becomes unavailable for any other reason, the substitute must be appointed by:

(1) the governor, if the disqualified or unavailable person is an elected official; or

(2) the appointing authority, if the disqualified or unavailable person is an appointed official.

(f) Any action taken by duly appointed substitute for a disqualified or unavailable person is as effective as if taken by the latter.

§ 4-203. [Representation]

(a) Any party may participate in the hearing in person or, if the party is a corporation or other artificial person, by a duly authorized representative.

(b) Whether or not participating in person, any party may be advised and represented at the party's own expense by counsel or, if permitted by law, other representative.

§ 4-204. [Prehearing Conference—Availability, Notice]

The presiding officer designated to conduct the hearing may determine, subject to the agency's rules, whether a prehearing conference will be conducted. If the conference is conducted:

(1) The presiding officer shall promptly notify the agency of the determination that a prehearing conference will be conducted. The agency shall assign or request the office of administrative hearings to assign a presiding officer for the prehearing conference, exercising the same discretion as is provided by Section 4-202 concerning the selection of a presiding officer for a hearing.

(2) The presiding officer for the prehearing conference shall set the time and place of the conference and give reasonable written notice to all parties and to all persons who have filed written petitions to intervene in the matter. The agency shall give notice to other persons entitled to notice under any provision of law.

(3) The notice must include:

(i) the names and mailing addresses of all parties and other persons to whom notice is being given by the presiding officer;

(ii) the name, official title, mailing address, and telephone number of any counsel or employee who has been designated to appear for the agency;

(iii) the official file or other reference number, the name of the proceeding, and a general description of the subject matter;

(iv) a statement of the time, place, and nature of the prehearing conference;

(v) a statement of the legal authority and jurisdiction under which the prehearing conference and the hearing are to be held;

(vi) the name, official title, mailing address and telephone number of the presiding officer for the prehearing conference;

(vii) a statement that at the prehearing conference the proceeding, without further notice, may be converted into a conference adjudicative hearing or summary adjudicative proceeding for disposition of the matter as provided by this Act; and

(viii) a statement that a party who fails to attend or participate in a prehearing conference, hearing, or other stage of an adjudicative proceeding may be held in default under this Act.

(4) The notice may include any other matters that the presiding officer considers desirable to expedite the proceedings.

§ 4-205. [Prehearing Conference—Procedure and Prehearing Order]

(a) The presiding officer may conduct all or part of the prehearing conference by telephone, television, or other electronic means if each participant in the conference has an opportunity to participate in, to hear, and if technically feasible, to see the entire proceeding while it is taking place.

(b) The presiding officer shall conduct the prehearing conference, as may be appropriate, to deal with such matters as conversion of the proceeding to another type, exploration of settlement possibilities, preparation of stipulations, clarification of issues, ruling on identity and limitation of the number of witnesses, objections to proffers of evidence, determination of the extent to which direct evidence, rebuttal evidence, or cross-examination will be presented in written form, and the extent to which telephone, television, or other electronic means will be used as a substitute for proceedings in person, order of presentation of evidence and cross-examination, rulings regarding issuance of subpoenas, discovery orders and protective orders, and such other matters as will promote the orderly and prompt conduct of the hearing. The presiding officer shall issue a prehearing order incorporating the matters determined at the prehearing conference.

(c) If a prehearing conference is not held, the presiding officer for the hearing may issue a prehearing order, based on the pleadings, to regulate the conduct of the proceedings.

§ 4-206. [Notice of Hearing]

(a) The presiding officer for the hearing shall set the time and place of the hearing and give reasonable written notice to all parties and to all persons who have filed written petitions to intervene in the matter.

(b) The notice must include a copy of any prehearing order rendered in the matter.

(c) To the extent not included in a prehearing order accompanying it, the notice must include:

(1) the names and mailing addresses of all parties and other persons to whom notice is being given by the presiding officer;

(2) the name, official title, mailing address and telephone number of any counsel or employee who has been designated to appear for the agency;

(3) the official file or other reference number, the name of the proceeding, and a general description of the subject matter;

(4) a statement of the time, place, and nature of the hearing;

(5) a statement of the legal authority and jurisdiction under which the hearing is to be held;

(6) the name, official title, mailing address, and telephone number of the presiding officer;

(7) a statement of the issues involved and, to the extent known to the presiding officer, of the matters asserted by the parties; and

(8) a statement that a party who fails to attend or participate in a prehearing conference, hearing, or other stage of an adjudicative proceeding may be held in default under this Act.

(d) The notice may include any other matters the presiding officer considers desirable to expedite the proceedings.

(e) The agency shall give notice to persons entitled to notice under any provision of law who have not been given notice by the presiding officer. Notice under this subsection may include all types of information provided in subsections (a) through (d) or may consist of a brief statement indicating the subject matter, parties, time, place, and nature of the hearing, manner in which copies of the notice to the parties may be inspected and copied, and name and telephone number of the presiding officer.

§ 4-207. [Pleadings, Briefs, Motions, Service]

(a) The presiding officer, at appropriate stages of the proceedings, shall give all parties full opportunity to file pleadings, motions, objections and offers of settlement.

(b) The presiding officer, at appropriate stages of the proceedings, may give all parties full opportunity to file briefs, proposed findings of fact and conclusions of law, and proposed initial or final orders.

(c) A party shall serve copies of any filed item on all parties, by mail or any other means prescribed by agency rule.

§ 4-208. [Default]

(a) If a party fails to attend or participate in a prehearing conference, hearing, or other stage of an adjudicative proceeding, the presiding officer may serve upon all parties written notice of a proposed default order, including a statement of the grounds.

(b) Within [7] days after service of a proposed default order, the party against whom it was issued may file a written motion requesting that the proposed default order be vacated and stating the grounds relied upon. During the time within which a party may file a written motion under this subsection, the presiding officer may adjourn the proceedings or conduct them without the participation of the party against whom a proposed default order was issued, having due regard for the interests of justice and the orderly and prompt conduct of the proceedings.

(c) The presiding officer shall either issue or vacate the default order promptly after expiration of the time within which the party may file written motion under subsection (b).

(d) After issuing a default order, the presiding officer shall conduct any further proceedings necessary to complete the adjudication without the participation of the party in default and shall determine all issues in the adjudication, including those affecting the defaulting party.

§ 4-209. [Intervention]

(a) The presiding officer shall grant a petition for intervention if:

(1) the petition is submitted in writing to the presiding officer, with copies mailed to all parties named in the presiding officer's notice of the hearing, at least [3] days before the hearing;

(2) the petition states facts demonstrating that the petitioner's legal rights, duties, privileges, immunities, or other legal interests may be substantially affected by the proceeding or that the petitioner qualifies as an intervener under any provision of law; and

(3) the presiding officer determines that the interests of justice and the orderly and prompt conduct of the proceedings will not be impaired by allowing the intervention.

(b) The presiding officer may grant a petition for intervention at any time, upon determining that the intervention sought is in the interests of justice and will not impair the orderly and prompt conduct of the proceedings.

(c) If a petitioner qualifies for intervention, the presiding officer may impose conditions upon the intervener's participation in the proceedings, either at the time that intervention is granted or at any subsequent time. Conditions may include:

(1) limiting the intervener's participation to designated issues in which the intervener has a particular interest demonstrated by the petition;

(2) limiting the intervener's use of discovery, cross-examination, and other procedures so as to promote the orderly and prompt conduct of the proceedings; and

(3) requiring 2 or more interveners to combine their presentations of evidence and argument, cross-examination, discovery, and other participation in the proceedings.

(d) The presiding officer, at least [24 hours] before the hearing, shall issue an order granting or denying each pending petition for intervention, specifying any conditions, and briefly stating the reasons for the order. The presiding officer may modify the order at any time, stating the reasons for the modification. The presiding officer shall promptly give notice of an order granting, denying, or modifying intervention to the petitioner for intervention and to all parties.

§ 4-210. [Subpoenas, Discovery, and Protective Orders]

(a) The presiding officer [at the request of any party shall, and upon the presiding officer's own motion,] may issue subpoenas, discovery orders, and protective orders, in accordance with the rules of civil procedure.

(b) Subpoenas and orders issued under this section may be enforced pursuant to the provisions of this Act on civil enforcement of agency action.

§ 4-211. [Procedure at Hearing]

At a hearing:

(1) The presiding officer shall regulate the course of the proceedings in conformity with any prehearing order.

(2) To the extent necessary for full disclosure of all relevant facts and issues, the presiding officer shall afford to all parties the opportunity to respond, present evidence and argument, conduct cross-examination, and submit rebuttal evidence, except as restricted by a limited grant of intervention or by the prehearing order.

(3) The presiding officer may give nonparties an opportunity to present oral or written statements. If the presiding officer proposes to consider a statement by a nonparty, the presiding officer shall give all parties an opportunity to challenge or rebut it and, on motion of any party, the presiding officer shall require the statement to be given under oath or affirmation.

(4) The presiding officer may conduct all or part of the hearing by telephone, television, or other electronic means, if each participant in the hearing has an opportunity to participate in, to hear, and, if technically feasible, to see the entire proceeding while it is taking place.

(5) The presiding officer shall cause the hearing to be recorded at the agency's expense. The agency is not required, at its expense, to prepare a transcript, unless required to do so by a provision of law. Any party, at the party's expense, may cause a reporter approved by the agency to prepare a transcript from the agency's record, or cause additional recordings to be made during the hearing if the making of the additional recordings does not cause distraction or disruption.

(6) The hearing is open to public observation, except for the parts that the presiding officer states to be closed pursuant to a provision of law expressly authorizing closure. To the extent that a hearing is conducted by telephone, television, or other electronic means, and is not closed, the availability of public observation is satisfied by giving members of the public an opportunity, at reasonable times, to hear or inspect the agency's record, and to inspect any transcript obtained by the agency.

§ 4-212. [Evidence, Official Notice]

(a) Upon proper objection, the presiding officer shall exclude evidence that is irrelevant, immaterial, unduly repetitious, or excludable on constitutional or statutory grounds or on the basis of evidentiary privilege recognized in the courts of this state. In the absence of proper objection, the presiding officer may exclude objectionable evidence. Evidence may not be excluded solely because it is hearsay.

(b) All testimony of parties and witnesses must be made under oath or affirmation.

(c) Statements presented by nonparties in accordance with Section 4-211(3) may be received as evidence.

(d) Any part of the evidence may be received in written form if doing so will expedite the hearing without substantial prejudice to the interests of any party.

(e) Documentary evidence may be received in the form of a copy or excerpt. Upon request, parties must be given an opportunity to compare the copy with the original if available.

(f) Official notice may be taken of (i) any fact that could be judicially noticed in the courts of this State, (ii) the record of other proceedings before the agency, (iii) technical or scientific matters within the agency's specialized knowledge, and (iv) codes or standards that have been adopted by an agency of the United States, of this State or of another state, or by a nationally recognized organization or association. Parties must be notified before or during the hearing, or before the issuance of any initial or final order that is based in whole or in part on facts or material noticed, of the specific facts or material noticed and the source thereof, including any staff memoranda and data, and be afforded an opportunity to contest and rebut the facts or material so noticed.

§ 4-213. [Ex parte Communications]

(a) Except as provided in subsection (b) or unless required for the disposition of ex parte matters specifically authorized by statute, a presiding officer serving in an adjudicative proceeding may not communicate, directly or indirectly, regarding any issue in the proceeding, while the proceeding is pending, with any party, with any person who has a direct or indirect interest in the outcome of the proceeding, or with any person who presided at a previous stage of the proceeding, without notice and opportunity for all parties to participate in the communication.

(b) A member of a multimember panel of presiding officers may communicate with other members of the panel regarding a matter pending before the panel, and any presiding officer may receive aid from staff assistants if the assistants do not (i) receive ex parte communications of a type that the presiding officer would be prohibited from receiving or (ii) furnish, augment, diminish, or modify the evidence in the record.

(c) Unless required for the disposition of ex parte matters specifically authorized by statute, no party to an adjudicative proceeding, and no person who has a direct or indirect interest in the outcome of the proceeding or who presided at a previous stage of the proceeding, may communicate, directly or indirectly, in connection with any issue in that proceeding, while the proceeding is pending, with any person serving as presiding officer, without notice and opportunity for all parties to participate in the communication.

(d) If, before serving as presiding officer in an adjudicative proceeding, a person receives an ex parte communication of a type that could not properly be received while serving, the person, promptly after starting to serve, shall disclose the communication in the manner prescribed in subsection (e).

(e) A presiding officer who receives an ex parte communication in violation of this section shall place on the record of the pending matter all written communications received, all written responses to the communications, and a memorandum stating the substance of all oral communications received, all responses made, and the identity of each person from whom the presiding officer received an ex parte communication, and shall advise all parties that these matters have been placed on the record. Any party desiring to rebut the ex parte communication must be allowed to do so, upon requesting the opportunity for rebuttal within [10] days after notice of the communication.

(f) If necessary to eliminate the effect of an ex parte communication received in violation of this section, a presiding officer who receives the communication may be disqualified and the portions of the record pertaining to the communication may be sealed by protective order.

(g) The agency shall, and any party may, report any willful violation of this section to appropriate authorities for any disciplinary proceedings provided by law. In addition, each agency by rule may provide for appropriate sanctions, including default, for any violations of this section.

§ 4-214. [Separation of Functions]

(a) A person who has served as investigator, prosecutor, or advocate in an adjudicative proceeding or in its preadjudicative stage may not serve as presiding officer or assist or advise a presiding officer in the same proceeding.

(b) A person who is subject to the authority, direction, or discretion of one who has served as investigator, prosecutor, or advocate in an adjudicative proceeding or in its preadjudicative stage may not serve as presiding officer or assist or advise a presiding officer in the same proceeding.

(c) A person who has participated in a determination of probable cause or other equivalent preliminary determination in an adjudicative proceeding may serve as presiding officer or assist or advise a presiding officer in the same proceeding, unless a party demonstrates grounds for disqualification in accordance with Section 4-202,

(d) A person may serve as presiding officer at successive stages of the same adjudicative proceeding, unless a party demonstrates grounds for disqualification in accordance with Section 4-202.

§ 4-215. [Final Order, Initial Order]

(a) If the presiding officer is the agency head, the presiding officer shall render a final order.

(b) If the presiding officer is not the agency head, the presiding officer shall render an initial order which becomes a final order unless reviewed in accordance with Section 4-216.

(c) A final order or initial order must include, separately stated, findings of fact, conclusions of law, and policy reasons for the decision if it is an exercise of the agency's discretion, for all aspects of the order, including the remedy prescribed and, if applicable, the action taken on a petition for stay of effectiveness. Findings of fact, if set forth in language that is no more than mere repetition or paraphrase of the relevant provision of law, must be accompanied by a concise and explicit statement of the underlying facts of record to support the findings. If a party has submitted proposed findings of fact, the order must include a ruling on the proposed findings. The order must also include a statement of the available procedures and time limits for seeking reconsideration or other administrative relief. An initial order must include a statement of any circumstances under which the initial order, without further notice, may become a final order.

(d) Findings of fact must be based exclusively upon the evidence of record in the adjudicative proceeding and on matters officially noticed in that proceeding. Findings must be based upon the kind of evidence on which reasonably prudent persons are accustomed to rely in the conduct of their serious affairs and may be based upon such evidence even if it would be inadmissible in a civil trial. The presiding officer's experience, technical competence, and specialized knowledge may be utilized in evaluating evidence.

(e) If a person serving or designated to serve as presiding officer becomes unavailable, for any reason, before rendition of the final order or initial order, a substitute presiding officer must be appointed as provided in Section 4-202. The substitute presiding officer shall use any existing record and may conduct any further proceedings appropriate in the interests of justice.

(f) The presiding officer may allow the parties a designated amount of time after conclusion of the hearing for the submission of proposed findings.

(g) A final order or initial order pursuant to this section must be rendered in writing within [90] days after conclusion of the hearing or after submission of proposed findings in accordance with subsection (f) unless this period is waived or extended with the written consent of all parties or for good cause shown.

(h) The presiding officer shall cause copies of the final order or initial order to be delivered to each party and to the agency head.

§ 4-216. [Review of Initial Order; Exceptions to Reviewability]

(a) The agency head, upon its own motion, may, and upon appeal by any party, shall, review an initial order, except to the extent that:

(1) a provision of law precludes or limits agency review of the initial order; or

(2) the agency head, in the exercise of discretion conferred by a provision of law,

(i) determines to review some but not all issues, or not to exercise any review;

(ii) delgates its authority to review the initial order to one or more persons; or

(iii) authorizes one or more persons to review the initial order, subject to further review by the agency head.

(b) A petition for appeal from an initial order must be filed with the agency head, or with any person designated for this purpose by rule of the agency, within [10] days after rendition of the initial order. If the agency head on its own motion decides to review an initial order, the agency head shall give written notice of its intention to review the initial order within [10] days after its rendition. The [10]-day period for a party to file a petition for appeal or for the agency head to give notice of its intention to review an initial order on the agency head's own motion is tolled by the submission of a timely petition for reconsideration of the initial order pursuant to Section 4-218, and a new [10]-day period starts to run upon disposition of the petition for reconsideration. If an initial order is subject both to a timely petition for reconsideration and to a petition for appeal or to review by the agency head on its own motion, the petition for reconsideration must be disposed of first, unless the agency head determines that action on the petition for reconsideration has been unreasonably delayed.

(c) The petition for appeal must state its basis. If the agency head on its own motions gives notice of its intent to review an initial order, the agency head shall identify the issues that it intends to review.

(d) The presiding officer for the review of an initial order shall exercise all the decision-making power that the presiding officer would have had to render a final order had the presiding officer presided over the hearing, except to the extent that the issues subject to review are limited by a provision of law or by the presiding officer upon notice to all parties.

(e) The presiding officer shall afford each party an opportunity to present briefs and may afford each party an opportunity to present oral argument.

(f) Before rendering a final order, the presiding officer may cause a transcript to be prepared, at the agency's expense, of such portions of the proceeding under review as the presiding officer considers necessary.

(g) The presiding officer may render a final order disposing of the proceeding or may remand the matter for further proceedings with instructions to the person who rendered the initial order. Upon remanding a matter, the presiding officer may order such temporary relief as is authorised and appropriate.

(h) A final order or an order remanding the matter for further proceedings must be rendered in writing within [60] days after receipt of briefs and oral argument unless that period is waived or extended with the written consent of all parties or for good cause shown.

(i) A final order or an order remanding the matter for further proceedings under this section must identify any difference between this order and the initial order and must include, or incorporate by express reference to the initial order, all the matters required by Section 4-215(c).

(j) The presiding officer shall cause copies of the final order or order remanding the matter for further proceedings to be delivered to each party and to the agency head.

§ 4-217. [Stay]

A party may submit to the presiding officer a petition for stay of effectiveness of an initial or final order within [7] days after after its rendition unless otherwise provided by statute or stated in the initial or final order. The presiding officer may take action on the petition for stay, either before or after the effective date of the initial or final order.

§ 4-218. [Reconsideration]

Unless otherwise provided by statute or rule:

(1) Any party, within [10] days after rendition of an initial or final order, may file a petition for reconsideration, stating the specific grounds upon which relief is requested. The filing of the petition is not a prerequisite for seeking administrative or judicial review.

(2) The petition must be disposed of by the same person or persons who rendered the initial or final order, if available.

(3) The presiding officer shall render a written order denying the petition, granting the petition and dissolving or modifying the initial or final order, or granting the petition and setting the matter for further proceedings. The petition may be granted, in whole or in part, only if the presiding officer states, in the written order, findings of fact, conclusions of law, and policy reasons for the decision if it is an exercise of the agency's discretion, to justify the order. The petition is deemed to have been denied if the presiding officer does not dispose of it within [20] days after the filing of the petition.

§ 4-219. [Review by Superior Agency]

If, pursuant to statute, an agency may review the final order of another agency, the review is deemed to be a continuous proceeding as if before a single agency. The final order of the first agency is treated as an initial order and the second agency functions as though it were reviewing an initial order in accordance with Section 4-216.

§ 4-220. [Effectiveness of Orders]

(a) Unless a later date is stated in a final order or a stay is granted, a final order is effective [10] days after rendition, but:

(1) a party may not be required to comply with a final order unless the party has been served with or has actual knowledge of the final order;

(2) a nonparty may not be required to comply with a final order unless the agency has made the final order available for public inspection and copying or the nonparty has actual knowledge of the final order.

(b) Unless a later date is stated in an initial order or a stay is granted, the time when an initial order becomes a final order in accordance with Section 4-215 is determined as follows:

(1) when the initial order is rendered, if administrative review is unavailable;

(2) when the agency head renders an order stating, after a petition for appeal has been filed, that review will not be exercised, if discretion is available to make a determination to this effect; or

(3) [10] days after rendition of the initial order, if no party has filed a petition for appeal and the agency head has not given written notice of its intention to exercise review.

(c) Unless a later date is stated in an initial order or a stay is granted, an initial order that becomes a final order in accordance with subsection (b) and Section 4-215 is effective [10] days after becoming a final order, but:

(1) a party may not be required to comply with the final order unless the party has been served with or has actual knowledge of the initial order or of an order stating that review will not be exercised; and

(2) a nonparty may not be required to comply with the final order unless the agency has made the initial order available for public inspection and copying or the nonparty has actual knowledge of the initial order or of an order stating that review will not be exercised.

(d) This section does not preclude an agency from taking immediate action to protect the public interest in accordance with Section 4-501.

§ 4-221. [Agency Record]

(a) An agency shall maintain an official record of each adjudicative proceeding under this chapter.

(b) The agency record consists only of:

(1) notices of all proceedings;

(2) any prehearing order;

(3) any motions, pleadings, briefs, petitions, requests, and intermediate rulings;

(4) evidence received or considered;

(5) a statement of matters officially noticed;

(6) proffers of proof and objections and rulings thereon;

(7) proposed findings, requested orders, and exceptions;

(8) the record prepared for the presiding officer at the hearing, together with any transcript of all or part of the hearing considered before final disposition of the proceeding;

(9) any final order, initial order, or order on reconsideration;

(10) staff memoranda or data submitted to the presiding officer, unless prepared and submitted by personal assistants and not inconsistent with Section 4-213(b); and

(11) matters placed on the record after an ex parte communication.

(c) Except to the extent that this Act or another statute provides otherwise, the agency record constitutes the exclusive basis for agency action in adjudicative proceedings under this chapter and for judicial review thereof.

CHAPTER 3—OFFICE OF ADMINISTRATIVE HEARINGS

§ 4-301. [Office of Administrative Hearings—Creation, Powers, Duties]

(a) There is created the office of administrative hearings within the [Department of ————], to be headed by a director appointed by the governor and confirmed by the senate].

(b) The office shall employ administrative law judges as necessary to conduct proceedings required by this Act or other provision of law. [Only a person admitted to practice law in [this State] [a jurisdiction in the United States] may be employed as an administrative law judge.]

(c) If the office cannot furnish one of its administrative law judges in response to an agency request, the director shall designate in writing a full-time employee of an agency other than the requesting agency to serve as administrative law judge for the proceeding, but only with the consent of the employing agency. The designee must possess the same qualifications required of administrative law judges employed by the office.

(d) The director may furnish administrative law judges on a contract basis to any governmental entity to conduct any proceeding not subject to this Act.

(e) The office may adopt rules:

(1) to establish further qualifications for administrative law judges, procedures by which

candidates will be considered for employment, and the manner in which public notice of vacancies in the staff of the office will be given;

(2) to establish procedures for agencies to request and for the director to assign administrative law judges; however, an agency may neither select nor reject any individual administrative law judge for any proceeding except in accordance with this Act;

(3) to establish procedures and adopt forms, consistent with this Act, the model rules of procedure, and other provisions of law, to govern administrative law judges;

(4) to establish standards and procedures for the evaluation, training, promotion, and discipline of administrative law judges; and

(5) to facilitate the performance of the responsibilities conferred upon the office by this Act.

(f) The director may:

(1) Maintain staff of reporters and other personnel; and

(2) implement the provisions of this section and rules adopted under its authority.

CHAPTER 4—CONFERENCE ADJUDICATIVE HEARING

§ 4-401. [Conference Adjudicative Hearing—Applicability]

A conference adjudicative hearing may be used if its use in the circumstances does not violate any provision of law and the matter is entirely within one or more categories for which the agency by rule has adopted this chapter [; however, those categories may include only the following:

(1) a matter in which there is no disputed issue of material fact; or

(2) a matter in which there is a disputed issue of material fact, if the matter involves only:

(i) a monetary amount of not more than [$1,000];

(ii) a disciplinary sanction against a prisoner;

(iii) a disciplinary sanction against a student which does not involve expulsion from an academic institution or suspension for more than [10] days;

(iv) a disciplinary sanction against a public employee which does not involve discharge from employment or suspension for more than [10] days;

(v) a disciplinary sanction against a licensee which does not involve revocation, suspension, annulment, withdrawal, or amendment of a license; or

(vi) . . . .]

§ 4-402. [Conference Adjudicative Hearing—Procedures]

The procedures of this Act pertaining to formal adjudicative hearings apply to a conference adjudicative hearing, except to the following extent:

(1) If a matter is initiated as a conference adjudicative hearing, no prehearing conference may be held.

(2) The provisions of Section 4-210 do not apply to conference adjudicative hearings insofar as those provisions authorize the issuance and enforcement of subpoenas and discovery orders, but do apply to conference adjudicative hearings insofar as those provisions authorize the presiding officer to issue protective orders at the request of any party or upon the presiding officer's motion.

(3) Paragraphs (1), (2), and (3) of Section 4-211 do not apply; but,

(i) the presiding officer shall regulate the course of the proceedings,

(ii) only the parties may testify and present written exhibits, and

(iii) the parties may offer comments on the issues.

§ 4-403. [Conference Adjudicative Hearing—Proposed Proof]

(a) If the presiding officer has reason to believe that material facts are in dispute, the presiding officer may require any party to state the identity of the witnesses or other sources through whom the party would propose to present proof if the proceeding were converted to a formal adjudicative hearing, but if disclosure of any fact, allegation, or source is privileged or expressly prohibited by any provision of law, the presiding officer may require the party to indicate that confidential facts, allegations, or sources are involved, but not to disclose the confidential facts, allegations, or sources.

(b) If a party has reason to believe that essential facts must be obtained in order to permit an adequate presentation of the case, the party may inform the presiding officer regarding the general nature of the facts and the sources from whom the party would propose to obtain those facts if the proceeding were converted to a formal adjudicative hearing.

CHAPTER 5—EMERGENCY AND SUMMARY ADJUDICATIVE PROCEEDINGS

§ 4-501. [Emergency Adjudicative Proceedings]

(a) An agency may use emergency adjudicative proceedings in a situation involving an immediate danger to the public health, safety, or welfare requiring immediate agency action.

(b) The agency may take only such action as is necessary to prevent or avoid the immediate danger to the public health, safety, or welfare that justifies use of emergency adjudication.

(c) The agency shall render an order, including a brief statement of findings of fact, conclusions of law, and policy reasons for the decision if it is an exercise of the agency's discretion, to justify the determination of an immediate danger and the agency's decision to take the specific action.

(d) The agency shall give such notice as is practicable to persons who are required to comply with the order. The order is effective when rendered.

(e) After issuing an order pursuant to this section, the agency shall proceed as quickly as feasible to complete any proceedings that would be required if the matter did not involve an immediate danger.

(f) The agency record consists of any documents regarding the matter that were considered or prepared by the agency. The agency shall maintain these documents as its official record.

(g) Unless otherwise required by a provision of law, the agency record need not constitute the exclusive basis for agency action in emergency adjudicative proceedings or for judicial review thereof.

§ 4-502. [Summary Adjudicative Proceedings—Applicability]

An agency may use summary adjudicative proceedings if:

(1) the use of those proceedings in the circumstances does not violate any provision of law;

(2) the protection of the public interest does not require the agency to give notice and an opportunity to participate to persons other than the parties; and

(3) the matter is entirely within one or more categories for which the agency by rule has adopted this section and Section 4-503 to 4-506 [; however, those categories may include only the following:

(i) a monetary amount of not more than [$100];

(ii) a reprimand, warning, disciplinary report, or other purely verbal sanction without continuing impact against a prisoner, student, public employee, or licensee;

(iii) the denial of an application after the applicant has abandoned the application;

(iv) the denial of an application for admission to an educational institution or for employment by an agency;

(v) the denial, in whole or in part, of an application if the applicant has an opportunity for administrative review in accordance with Section 4-504;

(vi) a matter that is resolved on the sole basis of inspections, examinations, or tests;

(vii) the acquisition, leasing, or disposal of property or the procurement of goods or services by contract;

(viii) any matter having only trivial potential impact upon the affected parties; and

(ix) . . . .]

§ 4-503. [Summary Adjudicative Proceedings—Procedures]

(a) The agency head, one or more members of the agency head, one or more administrative law judges assigned by the office of administrative hearings in accordance with Section 4-301 [, or, unless prohibited by law, one or more other persons designated by the agency head], in the discretion of the agency head, may be the presiding officer. Unless prohibited by law, a person exercising authority over the matter is the presiding officer.

(b) If the proceeding involves a monetary matter or a reprimand, warning, disciplinary report, or other sanction:

(1) the presiding officer, before taking action, shall give each party an opportunity to be informed of the agency's view of the matter and to explain the party's view of the matter; and

(2) the presiding officer, at the time any unfavorable action is taken, shall give each party a brief statement of findings of fact, conclusions of law, and policy reasons for the decision if it is an exercise of the agency's discretion, to justify the action, and a notice of any available administrative review.

(c) An order rendered in a proceeding that involves a monetary matter must be in writing. An order in any other summary adjudicative proceeding may be oral or written.

(d) The agency, by reasonable means, shall furnish to each party notification of the order in a summary adjudicative proceeding. Notification must include at least a statement of the agency's action and a notice of any available administrative review.

§ 4-504. [Administrative Review of Summary Adjudicative Proceedings—Applicability]

Unless prohibited by any provision of law, an agency, on its own motion may conduct administrative review of an order resulting from summary adjudicative proceedings, and shall conduct this review upon the written or oral request of a party if the agency receives the request within [10] days after furnishing notification under Section 4-503(d).

§ 4-505. [Administrative Review of Summary Adjudicative Proceedings—Procedures]

Unless otherwise provided by statute [or rule]:

(1) An agency need not furnish notification of the pendency of administrative review to any person who did not request the review, but the agency may not take any action on review less favorable to any party than the original order without giving that party notice and an opportunity to explain that party's view of the matter.

(2) The reviewing officer, in the discretion of the agency head, may be any person who could have presided at the summary adjudicative proceeding, but the reviewing officer must be one who is authorized to grant appropriate relief upon review.

(3) The reviewing officer shall give each party an opportunity to explain the party's view

of the matter unless the party's view is apparent from the written materials in the file submitted to the reviewing officer. The reviewing officer shall make any inquiries necessary to ascertain whether the proceeding must be converted to a conference adjudicative hearing or a formal adjudicative hearing.

(4) The reviewing officer may render an order disposing of the proceeding in any manner that was available to the presiding officer at the summary adjudicative proceeding or the reviewing officer may remand the matter for further proceeding, with or without conversion to a conference adjudicative hearing or a formal adjudicative hearing.

(5) If the order under review is or should have been in writing, the order on review must be in writing, including a brief statement of findings of fact, conclusions of laws, and policy reasons for the decision if it is an exercise of the agency's discretion, to justify the order, and a notice of any further available administrative review.

(6) A request for administrative review is deemed to have been denied if the reviewing officer does not dispose of the matter or remand it for further proceedings within [20] days after the request is submitted.

§ 4-506. [Agency Record of Summary Adjudicative Proceedings and Administrative Review]

(a) The agency record consists of any documents regarding the matter that were considered or prepared by the presiding officer for the summary adjudicative proceeding or by the reviewing officer for any review. The agency shall maintain these documents as its official record.

(b) Unless otherwise required by a provision of law, the agency record need not constitute the exclusive basis for agency action in summary adjudicative proceedings or for judicial review thereof.

ARTICLE V—JUDICIAL REVIEW AND CIVIL ENFORCEMENT

CHAPTER 1—JUDICIAL REVIEW

§ 5-101. [Relationship between This Act and Other Law on Judicial Review and Other Judicial Remedies]

This Act establishes the exclusive means of judicial review of agency action, but:

(1) The provisions of this Act for judicial review do not apply to litigation in which the sole issue is a claim for money damages or compensation and the agency whose action is at issue does not have statutory authority to determine the claim.

(2) Ancillary procedural matters, including intervention, class actions, consolidation, joinder, severence, transfer, protective orders, and other relief from disclosure of privileged or confidential material, are governed, to the extent not inconsistent with this Act, by other applicable law.

(3) If the relief available under other sections of this Act is not equal or substantially equivalent to the relief otherwise available under law, the relief otherwise available and the related procedures supersede and supplement this Act to the extent necessary for their effectuation. The applicable provisions of this Act and other law must be combined to govern a single proceeding or, if the court orders, 2 or more separate proceedings with or without transfer to other courts, but no type of relief may be sought in a combined proceeding after expiration of the time limit for doing so.

§ 5-102. [Final Agency Action Reviewable]

(a) A person who qualifies under this Act regarding (i) standing (Section 5-106), (ii) exhaustion of administrative remedies (Section 5-107), and (iii) time for filing the petition for review (Section 5-108), and other applicable provisions of law regarding bond, compliance, and other preconditions is entitled to judicial review of final agency action, whether or not the person has sought judicial review of any related nonfinal agency action.

(b) For purposes of this section and Section 5-103:

(1) "Final agency action" means the whole or a part of any agency action other than non-final agency action;

(2) "Nonfinal agency action" means the whole or a part of an agency determination, investigation, proceeding, hearing, conference, or other process that the agency intends or is reasonably believed to intend to be preliminary, preparatory, procedural, or intermediate with regard to subsequent agency action of that agency or another agency.

§ 5-103. [Nonfinal Agency Action Reviewable]

A person is entitled to judicial review of nonfinal agency action only if:

(1) it appears likely that the person will qualify under Section 5-102 for judicial review of the related final agency action; and

(2) postponement of judicial review would result in an inadequate remedy or irreparable harm disproportionate to the public benefit derived from postponement.

[Alternative A.]

§ 5-104. [Jurisdiction, Venue]

(a) The [trial court of general jurisdiction] shall conduct judicial review.

(b) Venue is in the [district] [that includes the state capital] [where the petitioner resides or maintains a principal place of business] unless otherwise provided by law.

[Alternative B.]

§ 5-104. [Jurisdiction, Venue]

(a) The [appellate court] shall conduct judicial review.

(b) Venue is in the [district] [that includes the state capital] [where the petitioner resides or maintains a principal place of business] unless otherwise provided by law.

(c) If evidence is to be adduced in the reviewing court in accordance with Section 5-114(a), the court shall appoint a [referee, master, trial court judge] for this purpose, having due regard for the convenience of the parties.

§ 5-105. [Form of Action]

Judicial review is initiated by filing a petition for review in [the appropriate] court. A petition may seek any type of relief available under Sections 5-101(3) and 5-117.

§ 5-106. [Standing]

(a) The following persons have standing to obtain judicial review of final or nonfinal agency action:

(1) a person to whom the agency action is specifically directed;

(2) a person who was a party to the agency proceedings that led to the agency action;

(3) if the challenged agency action is a rule, a person subject to that rule;

(4) a person eligible for standing under another provision of law; or

(5) a person otherwise aggrieved or adversely affected by the agency action. For purposes of this paragraph, no person has standing as one otherwise aggrieved or adversely affected unless:

(i) the agency action has prejudiced or is likely to prejudice that person;

(ii) that person's asserted interests are among those that the agency was required to consider when it engaged in the agency action challenged; and

(iii) a judgment in favor of that person would substantially eliminate or redress the prejudice to that person caused or likely to be caused by the agency action.

[(b) A standing committee of the legislature which is required to exercise general and continuing oversight over administrative agencies and procedures may petition for judicial review of any rule or intervene in any litigation arising from agency action.]

§ 5-107. [Exhaustion of Administrative Remedies]

A person may file a petition for judicial review under this Act only after exhausting all administrative remedies available within the agency whose action is being challenged and within any other agency authorized to exercise administrative review, but:

(1) a petitioner for judicial review of a rule need not have participated in the rule-making proceeding upon which that rule is based, or have petitioned for its amendment or repeal;

(2) a petitioner for judicial review need not exhaust administrative remedies to the extent that this Act or any other statute states that exhaustion is not required; or

(3) the court may relieve a petitioner of the requirement to exhaust any or all administrative remedies, to the extent that the administrative remedies are inadequate, or requiring their exhaustion would result in irreparable harm disproportionate to the public benefits derived from requiring exhaustion.

§ 5-108. [Time for Filing Petition for Review]

Subject to other requirements of this Act or of another statute:

(1) A petition for judicial review of a rule may be filed at any time, except as limited by Section 3-113(b).

(2) A petition for judicial review of an order is not timely unless filed within [30] days after rendition of the order, but the time is extended during the pendency of the petitioner's timely attempts to exhaust administrative remedies, if the attempts are not clearly frivolous or repetitious.

(3) A petition for judicial review of agency action other than a rule or order is not timely unless filed within [30] days after the agency action, but the time is extended:

(i) during the pendency of the petitioner's timely attempts to exhaust administrative remedies, if the attempts are not clearly frivolous or repetitious; and

(ii) during any period that the petitioner did not know and was under no duty to discover, or did not know and was under a duty to discover but could not reasonably have discovered, that the agency had taken the action or that the agency action had a sufficient effect to confer standing upon the petitioner to obtain judicial review under this Act.

§ 5-109. [Petition for Review—Filing and Contents]

(a) A petition for review must be filed with the clerk of the court.

(b) A petition for review must set forth:

(1) the name and mailing address of the petitioner;

(2) the name and mailing address of the agency whose action is at issue;

(3) identification of the agency action at issue, together with a duplicate copy, summary, or brief description of the agency action;

(4) identification of persons who were parties in any adjudicative proceedings that led to the agency action;

(5) facts to demonstrate that the petitioner is entitled to obtain judicial review;

(6) the petitioner's reasons for believing that relief should be granted; and

(7) a request for relief, specifying the type and extent of relief requested.

§ 5-110. [Petition for Review—Service and Notification]

(a) A petitioner for judicial review shall serve a copy of the petition upon the agency in the manner provided by [statute] [the rules of civil procedure].

(b) The petitioner shall use means provided by [statute] [the rules of civil procedure] to give notice of the petition for review to all other parties in any adjudicative proceedings that led to the agency action.

§ 5-111. [Stay and Other Temporary Remedies Pending Final Disposition]

(a) Unless precluded by law, the agency may grant a stay on appropriate terms or other temporary remedies during the pendency of judicial review.

(b) A party may file a motion in the reviewing court, during the pendency of judicial review, seeking interlocutory review of the agency's action on an application for stay or other temporary remedies.

(c) If the agency has found that its action on an application for stay or other temporary remedies is justified to protect against a substantial threat to the public health, safety, or welfare, the court may not grant relief unless it finds that:

(1) the applicant is likely to prevail when the court finally disposed of the matter;

(2) without relief the applicant will suffer irreparable injury;

(3) the grant of relief to the applicant will not substantially harm other parties to the proceedings; and

(4) the threat to the public health, safety, or welfare relied on by the agency is not sufficiently serious to justify the agency's action in the circumstances.

(d) If subsection (c) does not apply, the court shall grant relief if it finds, in its independent judgment, that the agency's action on the application for stay or other temporary remedies was unreasonable in the circumstances.

(e) If the court determines that relief should be granted from the agency's action on an application for stay or other temporary remedies, the court may remand the matter to the agency with directions to deny a stay, to grant a stay on appropriate terms, or to grant other temporary remedies, or the court may issue an order denying a stay, granting a stay on appropriate terms, or granting other temporary remedies.

§ 5-112. [Limitation on New Issues]

A person may obtain judicial review of an issue that was not raised before the agency, only to the extent that:

(1) the agency did not have jurisdiction to grant an adequate remedy based on a determination of the issue.

(2) the person did not know and was under no duty to discover, or did not know and was under a duty to discover but could not reasonably have discovered, facts giving rise to the issue;

(3) the agency action subject to judicial review is a rule and the person has not been a party in adjudicative proceedings which provided an adequate opportunity to raise the issue;

(4) the agency action subject to judicial review is an order and the person was not notified of the adjudicative proceeding in substantial compliance with this Act; or

(5) the interests of justice would be served by judicial resolution of an issue arising from:

(i) a change in controlling law occurring after the agency action; or

(ii) agency action occuring after the person exhausted the last feasible opportunity for seeking relief from the agency.

§ 5-113. [Judicial Review of Facts Confined to Record for Judicial Review and Additional Evidence Taken Pursuant to Act]

Judicial review of disputed issues of fact must be confined to the agency record for judicial review as defined in this Act, supplemented by additional evidence taken pursuant to this Act.

§ 5-114. [New Evidence Taken by Court or Agency before Final Disposition]

(a) The court [(if Alternative B of Section 5-104 is adopted), assisted by a referee, master, trial court judge as provided in Section 5-104 (c),] may receive evidence, in addition to that contained in the agency record for judicial review, only if it relates to the validity of the agency action at the time it was taken and is needed to decide disputed issues regarding:

(1) improper constitution as a decision-making body, or improper motive or grounds for disqualification, of those taking the agency action;

(2) unlawfulness of procedure or of decision-making process; or

(3) any material fact that was not required by any provision of law to be determined exclusively on an agency record of a type reasonably suitable for judicial review.

(b) The court may remand a matter to the agency, before final disposition of a petition for review, with directions that the agency conduct fact-finding and other proceedings the court considers necessary and that the agency take such further action on the basis thereof as the court directs, if:

(1) the agency was required by this Act or any other provision of law to base its action exclusively on a record of a type reasonably suitable for judicial review, but the agency failed to prepare or preserve an adequate record;

(2) the court finds that (i) new evidence has become available that relates to the validity of the agency action at the time it was taken, that one or more of the parties did not know and was under no duty to discover, or did not know and was under a duty to discover but could not reasonably have discovered, until after the agency action and (ii) the interests of justice would be served by remand to the agency;

(3) the agency improperly excluded or omitted evidence from the record; or

(4) a relevant provision of law changed after the agency action and the court determines that the new provision may control the outcome.

§ 5-115. [Agency Record for Judicial Review—Contents, Preparation, Transmittal, Cost]

(a) Within [————] days after service of the petition, or within further time allowed by the court or by other provision of law, the agency shall transmit to the court the original or a certified copy of the agency record for judicial review of the agency action, consisting of any agency documents expressing the agency action, other documents identified by the agency as having been considered by it before its action and used as a basis for its action, and any other material described in this Act as the agency record for the type of agency action at issue, subject to the provisions of this section.

(b) If part of the record has been preserved without a transcript, the agency shall prepare a transcript for inclusion in the record transmitted to the court, except for portions that the parties stipulate to omit in accordance with subsection (d).

(c) The agency shall charge the petitioner with the reasonable cost of preparing any necessary copies and transcripts for transmittal to the court. [A failure by the petitioner to pay any of this cost to the agency does not relieve the agency from the responsibility for timely preparation of the record and transmittal to the court.]

(d) By stipulation of all parties to the review proceedings, the record may be shortened, summarized, or organized.

(e) The court may tax the cost of preparing transcripts and copies for the record:

(1) against a party who unreasonably refuses to stipulate to shorten, summarize, or organize the record;

(2) as provided by Section 5-117; or

(3) in accordance with any other provision of law.

(f) Additions to the record pursuant to Section 5-114 must be made as ordered by the court.

(g) The court may require or permit subsequent corrections or additions to the record.

§5-116. [Scope of Review; Grounds for Invalidity]

(a) Except to the extent that this Act or another statute provides otherwise:

(1) The burden of demonstrating the invalidity of agency action is on the party asserting invalidity; and

(2) The validity of agency action must be determined in accordance with the standards of review provided in this section, as applied to the agency action at the time it was taken.

(b) The court shall make a separate and distinct ruling on each material issue on which the court's decision is based.

(c) The court shall grant relief only if it determines that a person seeking judicial relief has been substantially prejudiced by any one or more of the following:

(1) The agency action, or the statute or rule on which the agency action is based, is unconstitutional on its face or as applied.

(2) The agency has acted beyond the jurisdiction conferred by any provision of law.

(3) The agency has not decided all issues requiring resolution.

(4) The agency has erroneously interpreted or applied the law.

(5) The agency has engaged in an unlawful procedure or decision-making process, or has failed to follow prescribed procedure.

(6) The persons taking the agency action were improperly constituted as a decision-making body, motivated by an improper purpose, or subject to disqualification.

(7) The agency action is based on a determination of fact, made or implied by the agency, that is not supported by evidence that is substantial when viewed in light of the whole record before the court, which includes the agency record for judicial review, supplemented by any additional evidence received by the court under this Act.

(8) The agency action is:

(i) outside the range of discretion delegated to the agency by any provision of law;

(ii) agency action, other than a rule, that is inconsistent with a rule of the agency; [or]

(iii) agency action, other than a rule, that is inconsistent with the agency's prior practice unless the agency justifies the inconsistency by stating facts and reasons to demonstrate a fair and rational basis for the inconsistency [; or] [.]

(iv) [otherwise unreasonable, arbitrary or capricious.]

§ 5-117. [Type of Relief]

(a) The court may award damages or compensation only to the extent expressly authorized by another provision of law.

(b) The court may grant other appropriate relief, whether mandatory, injunctive, or declaratory; preliminary or final; temporary or permanent; equitable or legal. In granting relief, the court may order agency action required by law, order agency exercise of discretion required by law, set aside or modify agency action, enjoin to stay the effectiveness of agency action, remand the matter for further proceedings, render a declaratory judgment, or take any other action that is authorized and appropriate.

(c) The court may also grant necessary ancillary relief to redress the effects of official action wrongfully taken or withheld, but the court may award attorney's fees or witness fees only to the extent expressly authorized by other law.

(d) If the court sets aside or modifies agency action or remands the matter to the agency for further proceedings, the court may make any interlocutory order it finds necessary to preserve the interests of the parties and the public pending further proceedings or agency action.

[§ 5-118. [Review by Higher Court]

Decisions on petitions for review of agency action are reviewable by the [appellate court] as in other civil cases.]

CHAPTER 2—CIVIL ENFORCEMENT

§ 5-201. [Petition by Agency for Civil Enforcement of Rule or Order]

(a) In addition to other remedies provided by law, an agency may seek enforcement of its rule or order by filing a petition for civil enforcement in the [trial court of general jurisdiction.]

(b) The petition must name, as defendants, each alleged violator against whom the agency seeks to obtain civil enforcement.

(c) Venue is determined as in other civil cases.

(d) A petition for civil enforcement filed by an agency may request, and the court may grant, declaratory relief, temporary or permanent injunctive relief, any other civil remedy provided by law, or any combination of the foregoing.

§ 5-202. [Petition by Qualified Person for Civil Enforcement of Agency's Order]

(a) Any person who would qualify under this Act as having standing to obtain judicial review of an agency's failure to enforce its order may file a petition for civil enforcement of that order, but the action may not be commenced:

(1) until at least [60] days after the petitioner has given notice of the alleged violation and of the petitioner's intent to seek civil enforcement to the head of the agency concerned, to the attorney general, and to each alleged violator against whom the petitioner seeks civil enforcement;

(2) if the agency has filed and is diligently prosecuting a petition for civil enforcement of the same order against the same defendant; or

(3) if a petition for review of the same order has been filed and is pending in court.

(b) The petition must name, as defendants, each alleged violator against whom the agency and each alleged violator against whom the petitioner seeks civil enforcement.

(c) The agency whose order is sought to be enforced may move to dismiss on the grounds that the petition fails to qualify under this section or that enforcement would be contrary to the policy of the agency. The court shall grant the motion to dismiss unless the petitioner demonstrates that (i) the petition qualifies under this section and (ii) the agency's failure to enforce its order is based on an exercise of discretion that is improper on one or more of the grounds provided in Section 5-116(c)(8).

(d) Except to the extent expressly authorized by law, a petition for civil enforcement filed under this section may not request, and the court may not grant any monetary payment apart from taxable costs.

§ 5-203. [Defenses; Limitation on New Issues and New Evidence]

A defendant may assert, in a proceeding for civil enforcement:

(1) that the rule or order sought to be enforced is invalid on any of the grounds stated in Section 5-116. If that defense is raised, the court may consider issues and receive evidence only within the limitations provided by Section 5-112, 5-113, and 5-114; and

(2) any of the following defenses on which the court, to the extent necessary for the determination of the matter, may consider new issues or take new evidence:

(i) the rule or order does not apply to the party;

(ii) the party has not violated the rule or order;

(iii) the party has violated the rule or order but has subsequently complied, but a party who establishes this defense is not necessarily relieved from any sanction provided by law for past violations; or

(iv) any other defense allowed by law.

§ 5-204. [Incorporation of Certain Provisions on Judicial Review]

Proceedings for civil enforcement are governed by the following provisions of this Act on judicial review, as modified where necessary to adapt them to those proceedings:

(1) Section 5-101(2) (ancillary procedural matters); and

(2) Section 5-115 (agency record for judicial review—contents, preparation, transmittal, cost.)

§ 5-205. [Review by Higher Court]

Decisions on petitions for civil enforcement are reviewable by the [appellate court] as in other civil cases.

List of Acronyms

ABA	American Bar Association	EPA	Environmental Protection Agency
ACLU	American Civil Liberties Union	FBI	Federal Bureau of Investigation
ACT	Action for Children's Television	FCC	Federal Communications Commission
ACUS	Administrative Conference of the United States	FCIC	Federal Crop Insurance Corporation
AFDC	Aid to Families with Dependent Children	FDA	Food and Drug Administration
		FEA	Federal Energy Administration
AFL–CIO	American Federation of Labor—Congress of Industrial Organizations	FEC	Federal Election Commission
		FERC	Federal Energy Regulatory Commission
ALJ	Administrative Law Judge	FIFRA	Federal Insecticide, Fungicide, Rodenticide Act
APA	Administrative Procedure Act		
BIA	Bureau of Indian Affairs	FMC	Federal Maritime Commission
BLS	Bureau of Labor Statistics	FM & CS	Federal Mediation and Conciliation Service
CAB	Civil Aeronautics Board		
C/BA	Cost-Benefit Analysis	FOIA	Freedom of Information Act
CCC	Calorie Control Council	FPC	Federal Power Commission
CDC	Center for Disease Control	FRB	Federal Reserve Board (Also Fed)
CEA	Council of Economic Advisors		
CETA	Comprehensive Employment and Training Act	FTC	Federal Trade Commission
		GAO	General Accounting Office
CIA	Central Intelligence Agency	GRAS	Generally Recognized As Safe
COG	Councils of Government	ICC	Interstate Commerce Commission
CPSC	Consumer Product Safety Commission		
		IND	Notice of Claimed Investigational Exemption for a New Drug
(D)HEW	Department of Health, Education and Welfare		
(D)HUD	Department of Housing and Urban Development	INS	Immigration and Naturalization Service
DHHS	Departmet of Health and Human Services	IRC	Independent Regulatory Commission
DMSO	Di-methyl Sulphur Oxide	IRS	Internal Revenue Service
DOD	Department of Defense	ITT	International Telephone and Telegraph
DOE	Department of Energy		
EEOC	Equal Employment Opportunity Commission	MBO	Management by Objectives
		MHDC	Metropolitan Housing Development Corporation
EO	Executive Order		
EOP	Executive Office of the President	MSPB	Merit System Protection Board

464

NAACP	National Association for the Advancement of Colored People		Budget
		OSHA	Occupational Safety and Health Administration
NAB	National Association of Broadcasters	OSTP	Office of Science and Technology Policy
NACO	National Association of Counties	OTA	Office of Technology Assessment
NAS	National Academy of Science	OTS	Orthotoluene Sulfonamide
NAS	National Accounting Systems	PICCO	Pennsylvania Industrial
NCAA	National Collegiate Athletic Association		Chemical Corporation
		PPBS	Planning-Programming-Budgeting System
NDA	New Drug Application		
NEA	National Education Association	RARG	Regulatory Analysis Review Group
NHTSA	National Highway Traffic Safety Administration	SCRAP	Students Challenging Regulatory Agency Procedures
NIRA	National Industrial Recovery Act		
		SEC	Securities and Exchange Commission
NLRB	National Labor Relations Board		
		SSA	Social Security Administration
NRA	National Recovery Administration	TSS	Toxic Shock Syndrome
		TVA	Tennessee Valley Authority
NRC	Nuclear Regulatory Commission	USDA	United States Department of Agriculture
OCR	Office of Civil Rights	USOE	United States Office of Education
OFCCP	Office of Federal Contract Compliance Programs		
		VA	Veterans' Administration
OMB	Office of Management and	ZBB	Zero Base Budgeting

Table of Cases

Abbott Laboratories v. Gardner, 307, 315n

ACT v. FCC, 242

Adderly v. Florida, 82n

Aetna Life Insurance Co. v. Haworth, 307

Airline Pilots Association v. Quesada, 265–266

Allegheny-Ludlum Steel Corp., United States v., 245, 254n

Alyeska Pipeline Service Co. v. The Wilderness Society, 303

American Airlines v. Civil Aeronautics Board, 287n

American Farm Lines v. Black Ball Freight Service, 253n

American Tobacco Co., United States v., 159

American Trucking Association v. United States, 49n

Amoco Oil v. EPA, 254n, 311

Andreson v. State of Maryland, 198n

Aptheker v. Secretary of State, 74

Argersinger v. Hamlin, 83n

Arizona v. California, 35

Arnett v. Kennedy, 114n, 223n, 287n

Ashbacker Radio Corp. v. FCC, 270

Association of Data Processing Service Organizations v. Camp, 301

Association of National Advertisers, Inc. v. FTC, 243, 248

Atlanta v. Ickes, 315n

Atlantic Refining Co. v. Public Service Commission of New York, 130

Atlas Roofing Co., Inc. v. Occupational Safety and Health Review Committee, 50n, 283

Automobile Club of Michigan v. Commissioner, 225n

Baker v. Carr, 297

Barlow v. Collins, 301

Barr v. Matteo, 326

Barron v. Baltimore, 82n

Bell v. Burson, 287n

Bethlehem Steel Corporation v. EPA, 316n

Bi-Metallic Investment Co. v. Colorado State Board of Equalization, 287n

Bishop v. Wood, 106, 115n, 260

Biswell v. United States, 189

Bivens v. Six Unknown, Named Agents of the Federal Bureau of Narcotics, 324, 327

Blount v. Rizzi, 82n

Board of Curators of the University of Missouri v. Horowitz, 263, 287n

Board of Regents of State Colleges v. Roth, 114n, 258, 262

Bolling v. Sharpe, 55

Bowles v. Willingham, 203

Bradley v. Fisher, 336

Brig Aurora, The, v. United States, 32, 51n

Broadrick v. Oklahoma, 82n
Brown v. Board of Education, 55
Buckley v. Valeo, 59, 81n
Burns v. Fortson, 59
Butler, United States v., 29n
Butterfield v. Stranahan, 33
Butterworth v. Hoe, 51n

CAB v. Hermann, 198n
Cabell v. Chavez-Salido, 84n
Califano v. Sanders, 315n
Camara v. Municipal Court, 82n, 189
Camp v. Pitts, 312, 313
Cantwell v. Connecticut, 82
Carlson v. Green, 330
Carolene Products Co., United States v.,
    81n
Carroll v. Knickerbocker Ice Co., 289n
Chadha v. Immigration and
    Naturalization Service, 390
Chrysler Corporation v. Brown, 95, 234
Citizens Committee to Save WEFM v.
    FCC, 224n
Citizens to Preserve Overton Park Inc. v.
    Volpe, 244, 295–296, 313, 316n
Civil Service Commission v. National
    Association of Letter Carriers, 82n
Coleman v. Miller, 315n
Colonnade Catering Corporation v.
    United States, 189
Consolidated Edison Co. v. National
    Labor Relations Board, 288n, 316n
Consumer Energy Council v. Federal
    Energy Regulatory Commission, 390
Couch v. United States, 198n
Craig v. Boren, 81n
Crandall v. Nevada, 74, 83n
Crozier v. Fried Krupp
    Aktiengesellschaft, 82n
Cudahy Packing Co. v. Holland, 52n

Dalehite v. United States, 322
Dandridge v. Williams, 81n, 115n
Darby, United States v., 29n
De Angelo, United States v., 193

Decatur v. Paulding, 315n
Dixon v. Alabama State Board of Higher
    Education, 287n
Dixon v. Love, 279, 287n
Doe v. Bolton, 75, 83n
Doe v. Commonwealth's Attorney, 83n
Doe v. McMillan, 329
Donovan v. Dewey, 192
Dow Chemical v. Blum, 223n
Dowling v. Lancashire, 50n
Duke Power Co. v. North Carolina
    Environmental Group, Inc., 304
Dunlop v. Bachowski, 45, 296, 317n
Dunn v. Blumstein, 83n

Eastern Kentucky Welfare Rights
    Organization v. Simon, 253n
Economou v. Butz, 328, 337
Edelman v. Jordon, 343n
Edwards v. California, 83n
Edwards, United States v., 83n, 193
Eisen v. Carlisle and Jacquelen, 302
Eisenstadt v. Baird, 83n
Elrod v. Burns, 82n
Endicott Johnson Corporation v.
    Perkins, 185
Environmental Defense Fund Inc. v.
    Hardin, 287n
Environmental Defense Fund Inc. v.
    Ruckelshaus, 51n
Estelle v. Gamble, 83n
Ewing v. Mytinger and Casselberry, Inc.,
    223n
Examining Board v. de Ortero, 84n
Ex parte (see name of party)

Fahey v. Mallonee, 35
FCC v. Allentown Broadcasting Corp.,
    289n
FCC v. Pacifica Foundation, 82n
FCC v. RCA Communications Inc., 50n
FCC v. Sanders Brothers Radio Station,
    300
FCC v. WNCN Listeners' Guild, 224n
FCC v. Writers Guild, 224n

FEA v. Algonquin Sng. Inc., 34
Federal Crop Insurance Corp. v. Merrill, 219
Field v. Clark, 49n
Fitzpatrick v. Bitzer, 338
Flaherty, In re, 51n
Flast v. Cohen, 300–301, 303, 305
Florida East Coast Railway Co., United States v., 236, 245, 254n, 268
Foley v. Connelie, 84n
FPC v. Texaco, 265
Frank v. Maryland, 188, 189
Freedman v. Maryland, 82n
Friends of the Earth v. FCC, 224n
Frothingham v. Mellon, 300
FTC v. American Tobacco, 160
FTC v. Cement Institute, 288n
FTC v. Cinderella Career and Finishing Schools, Inc., 223n
FTC v. Gratz, 160
FTC v. Ruberoid Co., 51n
Fullilove v. Klutznick, 63

Gagnon v. Scarpelli, 270, 287n
Gardner v. Toilet Goods Association, 308
Gendron v. Levi, 288n
General Electric Co. v. Gilbert, 253n
General Telephone Co. v. United States, 254n
Georgia Pacific Co., United States v., 225n
Gibbons v. Ogden, 26, 27
Gibson v. Berryhill, 275
Gideon v. Wainwright, 83n
Gilligan v. Morgan, 315n
Gitlow v. New York, 82n
Gnotta v. United States, 315n
Goldberg v. Kelly, 105–106, 107, 198n, 266–267, 269, 279, 286n, 314
Goldberg v. Weinberger, 225n
Goldwater v. Carter, 315n
Gomez v. Toledo, 342n
Gonzalez v. Freeman, 287n
Goss v. Lopez, 81n, 115n, 261, 270, 271, 279

Greenholtz v. Inmates of the Nebraska Penal and Correctional Complex, 264
Gregoire v. Biddle, 326
Griffeth v. Detrich, 286n
Griffiths, In re, 84n
Griggs v. Allegheny County, 82n
Grimaud, United States v., 33
Griswold v. Connecticut, 71, 72, 83n
Grosso v. United States, 198n
Guest, United States v., 83n

Hampton v. Mow Sun Wong, 76, 79, 84n
Hampton, J. W. Jr. and Co. v. United States, 33, 50n
Hans v. Louisiana, 343n
Harlow and Butterfield v. Fitzgerald, 329
Harmon v. Bruckner, 315n
Harriman v. ICC, 184
Haynes v. United States, 198n
Holton v. Benford, 329
Home Box Office, Inc. v. FCC, 114n, 241, 242, 254n
Humphrey's Executor v. United States, 41, 145n, 160
Hutchinson v. Proxmire, 342n
Hutto v. Finney, 338

Imbler v. Pachtman, 336
Indian Towing Co. v. United States, 323, 332, 341n
Industrial Union Department, AFL-CIO v. American Petroleum Institute (and) Marshall v. American Petroleum Institute, 37, 381
Ingraham v. Wright, 81n, 83n, 287n
In re (see name of party)

Jacob Siegel Co. v. FTC, 289n
Jacobson v. Massachusetts, 82n
James v. Wallace, 83n
Johnson, People ex rel. Isaacs v., 51n
Johnson v. Robinson, 295

Kastigar v. United States, 198n
Kelley v. Johnson, 83n

Kennecott Copper Corp. v. EPA, 254n
Kent v. Dulles, 50, 83n
Kilbourn v. Thompson, 183
Kissinger v. Halperin, 328
Knauff v. Shaughnessy, 264
Knight, E. C., United States v., 49n
Korematsu v. United States, 59

Lamont v. Postmaster General, 82n
Lansden v. Hart, 254n
Larsen, In re, 288n
Lazy FC Ranch, United States v., 225n
Lee, United States v., 315n
Leefe, In re, 288n
Lemon v. Kurtzman, 82n
Lichter v. United States, 34
Londoner v. Denver, 258, 265, 279
Luther v. Borden, 315n

Maher v. Gagne, 339
Maher v. Roe, 83n
Marcello v. Bonds, 276
Marchetti v. United States, 193
Marshall v. American Petroleum
  Institute, 314
Marshall v. Barlow's Inc., 82n, 191
Marston v. Lewis, 83n
Martinez v. California, 343n
Martinez-Fuerte, United States v., 198n
Mathews v. Diaz, 79, 84n
Mathews v. Eldridge, 267, 286n
Mathis v. United States, 198n
McCarthy v. Philadelphia Civil Service
  Commission, 84n
McCartney v. Austin, 82n
McDonald v. Santa Fe Trail
  Transportation Co., 62
McElrath v. United States, 341n
McLaughlin v. Florida, 81n
Meachum v. Fano, 287n
Mead Data Control, Inc. v. United States
  Department of Air Force, 225n
Medical Committee for Human Rights v.
  SEC, 224n
Meek v. Pittinger, 82n

Memorial Hospital v. Maricopa
  County, 75
Meyer v. Nebraska, 83n
Miami Herald Publishing Co. v.
  Tornillo, 82n
Misurelli v. Racine, 115n
Mizolami v. United States, 341n
Monell v. New York City Department of
  Social Services, 337
Monroe v. Pape, 333
Moore v. East Cleveland, 83n
Moos v. United States, 341n
Mora v. McNamara, 315n
Morgan v. United States (1936), Morgan
  v. United States (1938), Morgan,
  United States v., 281–282
Morrissey v. Brewer, 263
Morton v. Ruiz, 253n
Morton Salt Co., United States v., 186,
  198n
Moser v. United States, 225n
Munn v. Illinois, 29n
Muskopf v. Corning Hospital, 332
Myers v. Bethlehem Shipbuilding Corp.,
  316n

Nader v. Allegheny Airlines, 309
Nader v. Bork, 253n
National Broadcasting Co. v. United
  States, 34
National Cable Television Assn. v.
  United States, 36
National Petroleum Refiners Association
  v. FTC, 253n
National Welfare Rights Organization v.
  Mathews, 245, 311–312
Newman v. United States, 51n
New York Central Securities
  Corporation v. United States, 34
New York Times Company v. United
  States, 82n
Nixon v. Administrator of General
  Services, 51n
Nixon v. Fitzgerald, 329
Nixon, United States v., 232, 253n

NLRB v. Bell Aerospace Co., 253n
NLRB v. Express Publishing Co., 289n
NLRB v. J. H. Rutter Rex Mfg. Co., 287n
NLRB v. Phelps, 288n
NLRB v. Sears, Roebuck Co., 225
NLRB v. Wyman Gordon Co., 253n
Nuller, United States v., 198n

O'Bannion v. Town Court Nursing Center, 259
O'Brien v. Brown, 315n
O'Conner v. Donaldson, 84n, 334
Office of Communications, United Church of Christ v. FCC, 224n, 288n, 316n
Oklahoma Press Publishing Co. v. Walling, 185
Ostereich v. Selective Service System Local Board No. 11, 315n
Owen v. City of Independence, 338
Oyler v. Boles, 51n

Pacific Coast European Conference v. United States, 239
Palko v. Connecticut, 82n
Panama Refining Co. v. Ryan, 35
Parrish v. Civil Service Commission,198n
Paul v. Davis, 263
Payner, United States v., 194, 198n
Pell v. Procunier, 82n
Pendarvis v. United States, 341n
Pennsylvania Chemical Corporation, United States v., 225n
Perkins v. Lukens Steel Co., 261, 300
Perry v. Sinderman, 84n, 286n
Phillips v. Commissioner of Internal Revenue Service, 223n
Phillips Petroleum v. Wisconsin, 129
Pierce v. Society of Sisters, 83n
Pierson v. Ray, 335
Planned Parenthood v. Danforth, 83n
Polk County v. Dodson, 336
Portland Cement Association v. Ruckelshaus, 254n

Procunier v. Navarette, 334
Public Utilities Commission of Ohio v. United Fuel Gas Co., 316n

Quern v. Jordon, 338

Ramanou v. Dental Commission, 51n
Randolph v. United States, 288n
Rayonier, Inc. v. United States, 323
Red Lion Broadcasting Co. v. FCC, 82n
Regents of the University of California v. Alan Bakke, 60
Reid v. Smith, 50n
RFC v. Bankers Trust Co., 50n
Richardson v. Perales, 277
Richardson, United States v., 303
Robel, United States v., 82n
Robinson, Ex parte, 287n
Roe v. Wade, 59, 83n
Rosado v. Wyman, 339
Runyon v. McCrary, 83n

San Antonio Independent School District v. Rodriguez, 115n, 287n
Sangammon Valley Television Corp. v. United States, 242
Santa Clara County v. Southern Pacific Railroad, 81n
Saunders v. Piggly Wiggly Corp., 288n
Saxbe v. Washington Post Co., 82n
Scanwell Laboratories v. Shaffer, 287n
Schechter, A. L. A. Poultry Co. v. United States, 30
Scheuer v. Rhodes, 333, 343n
Schlesinger v. Reservists' Committee to Stop the War, 303
Schware v. Board of Bar Examiners, 115n
Scott v. Negro Ben, 50n, 51n
SCRAP, United States v., 316n
Scripps-Howard Radio, Inc. v. FCC, 300
Securities and Exchange Commission v. Chenery Corp., 289n
Securities and Exchange Commission v. Sloan, 223n
See v. City of Seattle, 82n, 189

Semler v. Dental Examiners, 81n
Service v. Dulles, 253n
Shankland v. Washington, 49n
Shapiro v. Thompson, 74, 75
Shapiro v. United States, 49n, 193
Shaughnessy v. Pedreiro, 295
Shaughnessy v. United States, ex rel
  Mezei, 84n, 287n
Sherbert v. Verner, 82n, 286n
Shuttlesworth v. Birmingham, 50, 82n
Sierra Club v. Morton, 316n
Simon v. Eastern Kentucky Welfare
  Rights Organization, 304
Skidmore v. Swiff and Co., 253n
Skinner v. Oklahoma, 72
Slaughter-House Cases, The, 74, 83n
Slochower v. Board of Education, 286n
Sosna v. Lowa, 84n
Spalding v. Vilas, 325
Stark v. Wickard, 315n
Steward Machine Co. v. Davis, 29n
Storer Broadcasting Co., United States
  v., 265
Stump v. Sparkman, 335–336
Sugarman v. Dougall, 84n
Sumpter v. White Plains Housing
  Authority, 286n
Sunshine Anthracite Coal Co. v. Adkins,
  50n

Tagg Brothers and Moorhead v. United
  States, 34
Tax Analysts and Advocates v. IRS, 224n
Templeton v. Dixie Color Printing Co.,
  287n
Tennessee Electric Power Co. v. TVA,
  301, 315n
Tenney v. Brandhove, 342n
Testan, United States v., 320
Texaco Inc. v. FTC, 274
Texas Pacific Railway Co. v. Abilene
  Cotton Oil Co., 308
Thiboutot, State of Maine v., 339, 369
Thirty-Seven Photographs, United States
  v., 82n

Thomas v. Collins, 66
Thomas v. Review Board of the Indiana
  Employment Security Division, 66
Times Film Corp. v. Chicago, 82n
Toilet Goods Association v. Gardner,
  308
Traux v. Raich, 84n
Tumey v. Ohio, 288n

United Airlines v. Wiener, 341n
United Public Workers of America v.
  Mitchell, 307
United Steelworkers of America v. Brian
  F. Weber, 61
Universal Camera Corp. v. NLRB, 289n,
  310
Utah Power and Light Co. v. United
  States, 225n

Vail, United States v., 254n
Valley Forge Christian College v.
  Americans United for Separation of
  Church and State, 305
Vermont Yankee Nuclear Power Corp.
  v. Natural Resource Defense Council,
  Inc., 129, 145n, 245–247, 312
Village of Arlington Heights v.
  Metropolitan Housing Development
  Corp., 316n
Virginia Petroleum Jobbers Association
  v. FTC, 289n
Vitarelli v. Seaton, 253n
Vitek v. Jones, 287n, 288n

Walz v. Tax Commission, 82n
Ward v. Village of Monroeville, 288n
Warner-Lambert v. FTC, 289n
Warth v. Seldin, 303, 304
Wayman v. Southard, 49n
Western Pacific Railroad, United States
  v., 316n
Whalen v. Roe, 82n
Whitten v. California State Board of
  Optometry, 50n
Wickard v. Filburn, 27

Widmar v. Vincent, 65
Wiener v. United States, 145n
Williamson v. Lee Optical, 81n
Wisconsin v. Constantineau, 263
Wisconsin v. Yoder, 82n
Withrow v. Larkin, 275
WNCN Listeners' Guild v. FCC, 224n
Wolff v. McDonnell, 269, 270, 287n, 289n
Wong Yang Sung v. McGrath, 84n, 245
Wood v. Strickland, 334
Wright v. DeWill School District, 82n

Writers Guild of America, West, Inc. v. FCC, 224n
Wyatt v. Stickney, 84n
Wyman v. James, 115n, 189–190, 198n

Yakus v. United States, 49n
Young, Edward T., Ex parte, 315, 343n
Youngstown Sheet and Tube Co. v. Sawyer, 51n

Zahn v. International Paper Co., 302
Zemel v. Rusk, 74
Zicarelli v. New Jersey State Commission of Investigation, 198n

Index

Adjudicatory procedures
  agency appeals procedures, 280–281
  evidence, 277–278
  notice, 269–270
  prehearing conference, 272
  presiding officer, 272–277
  public intervenors, 271
  right to counsel, 270–271
  versus rule making, 227–230, 265–266
  separation of functions, 276–277
Administrative Conference of the United
  States, 11, 272
Administrative Law Judges, 272–274
Administrative Procedure Act (federal),
  45, 67, 70, 85–96, 196
  adjudicatory hearings, 268–274,
    276–278
  applications, 212
  due process, 53–54
  exhaustion, 307
  informal actions, 201, 215, 216
  interpretive rules, 232–233
  judicial review provisions, 293–295,
    297, 309–310
  negotiated settlements, 209
  presiding officers, 277
  procedural rules, 231
  rule making, 227, 231, 232, 235–239,
    241, 245–246
  sanctions, 282
  sovereign immunity, 298
  standing, 299
  subpoenas, 180–181
Administrative Procedure Acts (state),
  96–99, 112, 277–278
Advisory opinions, 206–207, 222
Aid to Families with Dependent Children
  program (AFDC), 105–106, 110,
  175, 178, 189–190, 259, 285, 340,
  358, 385
Aliens, 38, 76–80, 264
  See also Immigration and
    Naturalization Service
Applications, 211–213
Appropriations statutes, 85, 108–110
Authorizing statutes, 85, 99–104

Bias
  in adjudicatory proceedings, 274–276
  in rule making proceedings, 243–244
Bivens Tort, 327–328

Central Intelligence Agency, 90
Civil Aeronautics Board, 100, 116–117,
  150
Civil Rights Act of 1871, section 1983,
  108, 328, 333–339
Civil Rights Act of 1964, 4, 60, 61–62,
  128, 130, 132–133
Coal Mine Health and Safety Regulation,
  100, 102, 175, 192, 247
Commerce power, 26–27
Commission on Federal Paperwork, 174
Common law, 25, 298, 318

Congress, 14, 15, 26, 27, 86, 91–94, 102,
    104, 143, 155, 163, 195
    delegation of power, 30–39
    formal controls over regulation,
       118–120
    impact of regulatory expansion on, 366
    informal actions, 217
    informal powers over regulation,
       121–124
    regulatory reforms, 388–391
Consumer Product Safety Commission,
    103, 173, 247, 249, 325
Cost-benefit analysis, 349, 354–356,
    356–357, 377–380
Court of Claims, 319–321, 392
Courts
    controls over regulation, 129–130
    impact of regulatory expansion on,
       367–368

Delegation of power, 1, 30–39
    state level, 39
Deregulation, 373–375, 376–377
Discretion, 43–46
    state level, 46
Discretionary actions
    judicial review of, 295–297
    tort liability for, 322–323
Due process, 52–55, 73, 77, 106,
    257–259, 260, 262, 264, 333

Economic regulation. See Regulation I
Eleventh Amendment, 338
Environmental Protection Agency, 4, 11,
    103, 120, 124, 126, 134, 142, 173,
    202
Equal Employment Opportunity
    Commission, 61, 173, 210–211, 219,
    234
Equal protection, 55–63, 79, 80
Estoppel, 219, 220–222
Exhaustion, 306

Federal Aviation Administration, 175, 265

aircraft accident investigations,
    181–182
airport screenings, 180
DC-10, 138, 176–177
Federal Communications Commission,
    35, 66, 123–124, 129, 150, 300, 350
    family hour, 213–214
    policy statements, 208
Federal Tort Claims Act, 45, 221,
    321–324
Federal Trade Commission, 3, 44,
    99–100, 101, 103, 122, 132, 133,
    150, 181, 205, 247, 283–284, 294,
    351, 383
    antitrust investigations, 182, 184, 352
    negotiated settlements, 209
    political environment of, 159–164
    rule making power, 233
    rule making procedures, 243–244,
       247–249
FIFRA, 133–134
Fifth Amendment, 53, 55, 68, 72, 76–77,
    110, 185–188, 195, 257
First Amendment, 64–66
Food and Drug Administration, 9, 100,
    103, 109, 121, 357
    new drug applications, 131–132, 139,
       174, 175, 212
    publicity, 204–205
    saccharin ban, 12–16, 117
    toxic shock syndrome, 199–201, 226
Fourteenth Amendment, 53, 55, 76, 77,
    107, 257–258, 260, 263
Fourth Amendment, 68, 72, 110,
    184–185, 188–195
Freedom of Information Act, 69, 87,
    88–92, 94–95, 144, 218, 234

Government in the Sunshine Act, 87,
    95–96, 241, 246

Hearings. See Adjudicatory procedures,
    Opportunity to be heard
Hearings, rule making, 179, 239–240